I
SHALL
IMPERSONATE
A
MAN

AN AUTOBIOGRAPHY

James W. Morris, Jr.

Rocinante Press—Marietta, GA
ISBN: 979-8-9915964-1-1
Library of Congress Control Number: 2024922253
Title: *I Shall Impersonate a Man: An Autobiography*
Author: James W. Morris Jr.
Digital distribution | 2024
Paperback | 2024

Published in the United States by New Book Authors Publishing

Dedication

This book is dedicated to my wife
Carolyn

Table of Contents

Introduction

"I shall impersonate a man. His name is Alonso Quijana, a country squire no longer young. Being retired, he has much time for books [and the internet]. He studies them from morn till night and often through the night and morn again, and all he reads oppresses him; fills him with indignation at man's murderous ways toward man. He ponders the problem of how to make better a world where evil brings profit and virtue none at all; where fraud and deceit are mingled with truth and sincerity. He broods and broods and broods and broods and finally his brains dry up. He lays down the melancholy burden of sanity …" Alonso Quijana's Monologue, *Man of La Mancha*, Miguel de Cervantes

"Just an ordinary sinner …" Mother Abigail Freemantle, *The Stand*, Stephen King

"You don't know about me, without you have read a book by the name of *The Adventures of Tom Sawyer*, but that ain't no matter. The book was made by Mr. Mark Twain, and he told the truth, *mainly*. There was things he stretched, but mainly he told the truth." Huckleberry Finn, Chapter 1, *The Adventures of Huckleberry Finn*, Mark Twain

"What he tells himself … is that he's stuck with himself and must make the best of it." Billy Summers, *Billy Summers*, Stephen King

"And whether or not it is clear to you, no doubt the universe is unfolding as it should." *Desiderata*

"When it comes to the past, *everyone* writes fiction." Devin Jones, *Joyland*, Stephen King

"Don't believe anything you [read] and only half of what you see." Paraphrased E.A. Poe

"Been plannin' it for years." Michael "Squints" Palledorous, *The Sand Lot*

"No person deserves to be marginalized, degraded, laughed at, or humiliated. All any human being deserves and wants is dignity and respect." James W. Morris, Jr.

Prologue

Past history, particularly autobiographical past histories, can be dangerous and subject to much personal interpretation and unintentional altering of events due to the author's perspective and selective memory. And people love to take issue with this detail or that detail and argue "from their recollection" about any number of minor incidents, and this same person will be glad to tell you about those events as they remember them with crystal clear clarity … whether they happened or not. So, I am writing from my perspective, and no doubt, some of the events you will read about really did take place as I detail them, and some are simply altered by the soft embellishments of memory. But that is okay, because I am going to tell the truth, "*mainly.*"

So, why? Well, right this minute in 2020 the world is suffering through a Covid 19 pandemic. As of today, 500,000 Americans have died. Over 1,000,000 have died worldwide. Carolyn and I are staying inside quarantined, going nowhere. We cannot even see our children or grandchildren. I have read that during the Bubonic Plague of the 16th century when Shakespeare was quarantined, he wrote the play *King Lear*. And while this will in no way rival that work of genius, I guess everyone wants to leave a story to be told later to help others understand one's life and perhaps even help in the reader's own life and help them understand where they came from and where they fit.

By writing this, even though I am going to use only first names generally, I hope I will gain some understanding of myself and my life, and maybe if you read this someday you will gain an understanding of me, my life and my world and maybe your world. There is no doubt that certain honest event recollections will cause those close to me to feel disquiet. And the same descriptions will cause feelings of discomfort to my grandchildren as I shatter some preconceived notions about me as their "Pa." And should my great grandchildren or even great-great grandchildren happen to find and read these recollections, those same events may be the cause of great amusement as time relentlessly pushes toward the 22nd century and my stories become nothing more than humorous, non-threatening family lore.

So, in advance … thank you for reading me,

J. W. Morris, Jr.

Part I

I am a Boy

Chapter One
Ping Pong Ball

1.

It was the 29th of January, 1950. The Colonel (James Wingfield Morris 1924-2020), who was not a Colonel at the time, perhaps a Captain, but for this book, he will be referred to as The Colonel, and his wife (Mary Corinne Wofford Morris 1926-2013), who shall be referred to as Mom or The Colonel's Lady, just came home to their apartment in Fort Meyer, Virginia. They had been to an exceptionally dull party at the Officer's Club with far too many low ranking officers and their wives trying to look good in front of The General and The General's Lady who were hosting this particular soiree for some reason or another. But none of that matters. It was late January in northern Virginia, and it was cold, dark and snowing, and The Colonel had perhaps had one too many drinks, "Just two fingers of scotch over a little ice," and Mom had to drive him home. Mom always hated these mandatory affairs. In fact, in my entire life I can only remember The Colonel and her hosting two of these social kowtow gatherings and both when I was very young. But she disliked it even more when The Colonel drank, and she hated having to drive home. As I look back, I cannot really remember her liking much of anything most of the time.

They arrived home safely and let the baby sitter, who was minding my eight-month old sister, go home. My older sister Mary Louise, Re-Re or Re as she will be forever known, was asleep; a happy, cuddly only-child safe in the knowledge that she was the baby-queen-of-the-world and that there were no usurpers prowling around anywhere. But that was going to change for, in spite of all that was working against me that night, I came into being that cold, late evening … not that I was aware of it. Or that I would be aware of anything for a long time. For such is the fate of a ping pong ball.

2.

During the next nine months I was a happy, unhuman, human being. I was blissfully unaware of everything. I was fed. I was warm. And I did not have to do anything. I could nap when I wanted. I could wake up and tussle around if I wanted. I could do pretty much anything I wanted within my limited confines, and I did not have to seek approval or ask permission. As far as I was concerned, it was absolutely perfect. But little did I know that events were conspiring against me. Not just the typical gestation events, but world events were conspiring against me, too.

It seems that North Korea decided to invade South Korea on June 25th, 1950, for some reason. Something about world domination or what-not. And it seems, at the behest of President Truman, that The Colonel, being a lower ranking officer in the Army, still somewhere below a Major at that point - I did not really know - needed to go to Korea to help straighten the mess out. And so he did. And while he did, Mom returned home

1941 Dr. William Earl Wofford 52 y/o and wife Mrs. Mary Louise Meroney Wofford 50 y/o

to her small hometown in Cartersville, Georgia, to live in the family home with her father, Dr. William Earl Wofford the town doctor, or Pa as he would forever be known to me.

As I found out years later when I started to care a little bit about these things, Mom's mother Mary Louise (Meroney) Wofford had passed away from cancer on December 30th of the year before, so it was good for Mom to come home. It helped her, as she was five months pregnant and had my now thirteen-month old sister in tow, and her husband was going to be gone for who knew how long and maybe would not come home at all. And it helped her father, who was undoubtedly lonely knocking around in the big old house on Main Street, just him and his African-American housekeeper/maid, Middy, who made the BEST fried chicken ever.

Mom coming home was what people will call a win-win. And as for me, it became a win-win-win.

3.

I have intentionally not introduced myself until now. For in this saga it is Sunday, October 29th, 1950 at 3:50 PM, and I was not, until now, a human being. The birth certificate read James Wingfield Morris, Jr. I believe if my older sister had been a boy I would have been spared this moniker, but she was not, and I was, so, I have gotten to wag that name around all my life. And if you never have had to do it, the Jr is a royal pain to deal with, too. On all the forms, are you Morris, Jr., James W. or Morris, James W. Jr or is there even a place for the Jr.? That is why my son is not a III, but a blend of my wife's maiden name and my name. He is his own man, not a mimic of me. But I digress.

I have gone by many names and settled with that problem, but the first real name I can recall is Bubba. Now if that is not a Southern appellation, I have never heard one! The story goes that my sister, who at this point is about seventeen months old, could not say "brother" and so she said, "Bubba," and I became Bubba … for way too long! Of course none of that mattered to me. I was just a ping pong ball. I went wherever anyone wanted me to go, and I went however anyone wanted me to go. And at this point in my life, I was a "good ping pong ball." All that would change as I became "a boy," but I am getting ahead of myself.

I was born at the Wofford-Stanford Hospital, 114 West Cherokee Avenue, in that small southern town. The building was the five room clinic building of the town doctor, and not

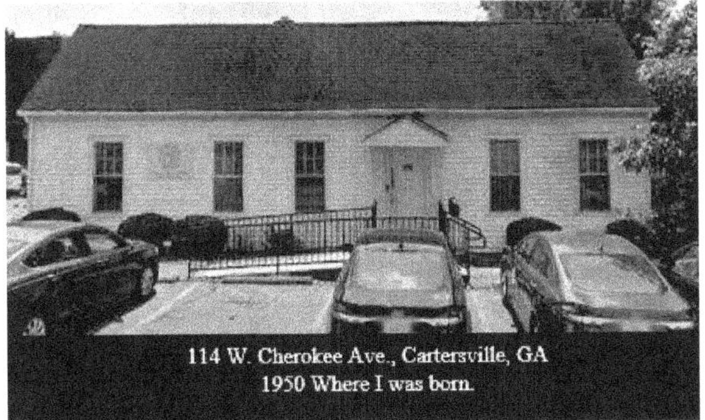

a hospital by anyone's present day standards. I was delivered by my mom's dad, my maternal grandfather, William Earl Wofford. And he was known to me as Pa all my life. I admired that man. I admired that man so much that today, at seventy my grandchildren call me Pa ... at my request and to honor that man.

114 W. Cherokee Ave., Cartersville, GA
1950 Where I was born.

When I left the hospital, Mom and Re and I lived with Pa in Pa's huge house on the corner of West Main Street and South Bartow Street diagonally across from the Presbyterian Church. The house is no longer at this location. In the early 60's it was relocated down past the bend in the road to 23 Etowah Drive. If you go to look at it, only the center portion was Pa's house. Anyway, this house would remain "huge" to me until I was much, much older and saw it in its reality for the first time. But back then, and for almost the next ten years, it was a home of endless rooms and massive grounds that were covered in Magnolias and Pecan trees, a huge gold fish pond, a big stone grill, a three car garage with tools and lawn mowers and the rich, earthy smell of gravel and gasoline. But my memories of coming home to this house and much of the next several years are subject to approximation. You see, ping pong balls do not know much, and they remember even less, but there are stories, family fables and myths handed down that have been told to me so many times I cannot actually tell you if they are real memories or not.
4.

My favorite family folk tale took place in early January of 1952. It was cold in that southern town, and I was a still wobbly, but confident, fourteen-month old tumbling around that massive house, my house. It was just my family, my mom, Re-Re as I was calling her now, Middy and Pa. Then the world changed when a large stranger arrived. It was in the middle of the afternoon because I had just waked up from my nap. The back door opened. With the afternoon sun behind him, the shadow he cast was long and almost reached where I was standing in the hallway. He was wearing big black lace up boots almost as tall as me. They were polished to a high shine. He had on a kaki uniform with shiny medals and ribbons and a kaki hat on his head that looked like a poorly designed sail boat. My mother ran to this person immediately. Re did nothing. I stood, unsteady in both mind and stature and looked. It was fine. He was a long way away from me. And I was closer to Pa than to this man, so I was good. He approached my sister. Re-Re is strong, always has been. She did not run or even whimper. My mom leaned over and took her hand and said, "Mary Louise, this is your father." Re-Re was cool. She just looked at him. I do not think she remembered him as he left when she was just a little over a year old, but as I said, she was cool. Mom then shocked me as she actually handed Re-Re to this man! After the man talked to Re-Re for a few minutes, he put her down. He then looked at me and my heart was filled with dread. He started pounding his way toward me. I could feel the floor shake with each step. Mom approached me too when I started to whine, and I could see where this was going, and I wanted no part of it. I turned on my little white-booted, high top shoed feet and ran as fast as I could for my Pa! I got to him in the nick of time and he picked me up. Up into his high arms and safety. Then, he stabbed me in the back! He handed me to my mother, and she then handed me to the stranger! Oh, he was all soft spoken and gentle, but I looked at him. Then looked at my Pa. Then I looked back again. I asked myself who was this man and why did my Pa and my mother just give me to him? And I believe that is where the rift was formed between The Colonel and me. Now some would say it was a first born male thing, but I know better. Ping pong balls may not be very smart, but they never forget how they feel.

5.

Another family yarn handed down is the legendary clogged lawn mower incident of which to this day, I plead emphatically not guilty. The story goes that in the big garage that had the earthy smell of gravel and gasoline Pa had a gas lawn mower. Pa's yard man, Casey, would use it to cut the what seemed to be the acres and acres of grass around Pa's house. Well, one day Casey came and pulled the lawnmower out ready to cut grass in the steamy Georgia summer. He checked the gas and oil, pulled the choke out and hauled on the cord. The mower caught and then died almost as quickly. He pulled again, and it sputtered but just would not catch. So, in frustration he came up to the back door of the house and knocked. Pa came to the door, and he explained rather sheepishly that he was sorry and, "Doctor Wofford, that old mower just ain't gonna start."

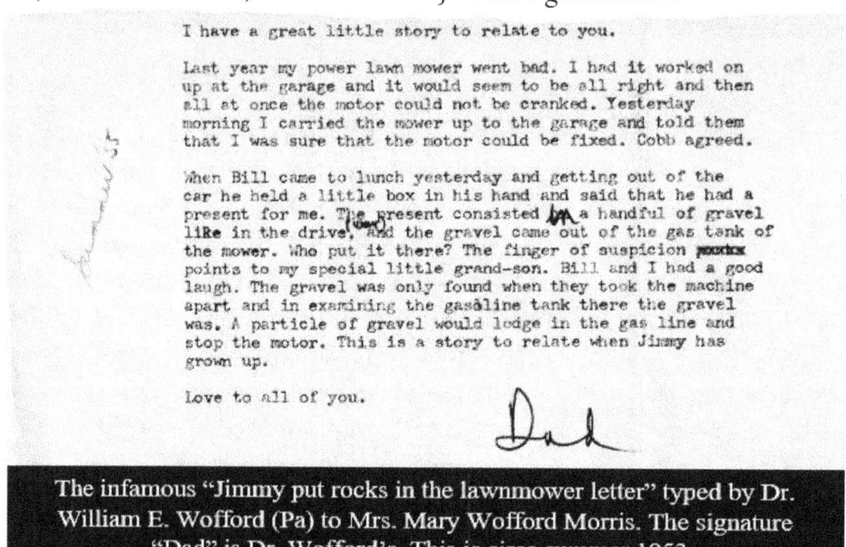

I have a great little story to relate to you.

Last year my power lawn mower went bad. I had it worked on up at the garage and it would seem to be all right and then all at once the motor could not be cranked. Yesterday morning I carried the mower up to the garage and told them that I was sure that the motor could be fixed. Cobb agreed.

When Bill came to lunch yesterday and getting out of the car he held a little box in his hand and said that he had a present for me. The present consisted of a handful of gravel like in the drive, and the gravel came out of the gas tank of the mower. Who put it there? The finger of suspicion points to my special little grand-son. Bill and I had a good laugh. The gravel was only found when they took the machine apart and in examining the gasoline tank there the gravel was. A particle of gravel would lodge in the gas line and stop the motor. This is a story to relate when Jimmy has grown up.

Love to all of you.

The infamous "Jimmy put rocks in the lawnmower letter" typed by Dr. William E. Wofford (Pa) to Mrs. Mary Wofford Morris. The signature "Dad" is Dr. Wofford's. This is circa summer 1953.

Pa said okay and said that he would have it looked at. Pa called his son Bill, my mother's older brother and my uncle and explained the problem. Now Unca' Bill had been a B-17 pilot in World War II and had come home and was running a car dealership so this was a man who knew his way around motors. He said he would be over in a little while to look it over. And he did, and what did he find? He found that someone had sabotaged the mower! Yep, some evil doer had snuck in the garage on tippy toes in the dark of night and put gravel in that darned mower's gas tank. Not much gravel mind you, but just enough to clog up the fuel supply. Unca' Bill told Pa he had cleaned it out and flushed the line and she was a perfect mower again. And this is where the story takes a wild turn. You see they never caught that villainous scoundrel, that trouble-making juvenile delinquent or delinquents who had perpetrated this dastardly deed, so they decided in a quantum leap of logic that I had done it. Me, Ping Pong Ball Bubba, a barely able to walk and talk toddler. They decided I had gone out there, all the way to this huge scary garage which to my little legs had to be about twenty miles away and found the mower, opened the gas tank and put the gravel in it, then put the little cap back on the mower and stole my way back to the big house all without anyone seeing me or being concerned that I was missing. Sounds circumstantial and highly unlikely and that is all I have to say about that.

Chapter Two
How They Made You Feel

During the next four years, I started to emerge from my ping pong ball stage and became more or less self-aware, actually I guess, more less than more, now that I reflect from 70 years old. I think when it came to losing my ping pong ball mentality, I developed slowly, very slowly. I admit I was a pretty lazy specimen of boy. Consequently, the next few years are a jumble of mixed up memories and the time order is difficult to unravel, but are still worth recounting. I'll relate my first real distinct memories as best I can. After the reunion in Pa's hallway, my trauma, and subsequent abduction the family of four moved to Fort Benning, Georgia. This was a good move as far as the family was concerned as it was still close to the home

town but far enough away to be separated. The Colonel began jump training, and we lived in a little block house at 166-B Custer Terrace. There is a picture of Re-Re and me standing outside the front door on what must have been Easter. In the picture you can see the casual, Devil-may-care attitude I was to become famous for all over me at being dressed in Easter clothes and my general thrill at the whole event. In that picture you can see Re-Re being the perfect first child daughter and cutting the wide wake that my little boat struggled in for many years. I cannot tell you the number of times I heard the phrase, "So, you are Mary Louise's brother." Now even though I did it here, this phrase was rarely followed by a period. More commonly it was followed by a question mark or in some cases even an exclamation mark! If you knew me before my goatee and looked closely at my face and looked just below my bottom lip and just above my chin you would see a little, fine scar that almost looks like someone stapled me there. They did not. At three or four, I was famous for my "long cord." Yes, it was a different time. I was allowed to wag a long electrical cord around. To my knowledge I never tried

A man and his long cord in 1952 at Ft. Benning

to plug it into anything. I just carried it around. And one summer afternoon I was carrying it around on the little concrete patio on the back of our house and my feet got tangled up in it. I was still pretty young and the whole walking thing was still experimental to me. At any rate I tripped and fell. Well, just adjacent to the patio was a gas meter. It was on the side of the patio kind of diagonal from the swing set and close to the house. It was a gawky silver thing with pipes and dials and valves, it was sticking up out of the ground almost as tall as I was, and I fell right into it. As a consequence, I lost my two, lower baby front teeth early and got my cute little staple scar just above my chin. I believe it was the first scar on my otherwise perfect little body. There would be more … some would be physical … some other.

While at Fort Benning the family had gotten our first television. It was a little black and white television in a gigantic cabinet and the highlight of the day was *The Mickey Mouse Club*. Let me mention as a sidebar here that even as a little boy I was strangely drawn to Annette Funicello. At any rate, *The Club* had a reoccurring drama segment that would alternate with *The Hardy Boys* adventures one week and *Davy Crockett, King of the Wild Frontier* with Fess Parker the next week or as soon as one serial series finished. The Davy Crockett shows would always begin with Buddy Ebsen singing the theme song: *"Borned on a mountain top in Tennessee, greenest state in the land of the free …"* Now at this time in the "19 glorious 50's" <u>every</u> little boy worth his salt had a coon skin hat with a tail hanging down in back … and

Davy Crockett Coonskin Cap

so did I. And in the back of our duplex house was a little swing set. It was a classic, gaudily painted swing set of the period with two swings, a little metal slide that would leave burn marks on your legs if you dared use it in the Georgia summer sun and a back and forth glider arrangement so a child sat on a seat at each end and pushed/pulled the glider into a back and forth motion. You do not see them so much anymore due to the dangers they pose for the current crop of bicycle-helmeted, coddled, helicopter-mom crop of children. Apparently we were either smarter in 1956 and could avoid the dangers or we were more easily replaceable. At any rate, my sister Re-Re and I would swing for hours and sing the Davy Crockett song which would spawn a fight every time we came to the part of the song that went, "He kilt him a bar [bear] when he was only three!" I would sing it with the "bar" in it and Re-Re would correct me every time, after all she was much older and wiser – seventeen months older, saying that it was "bear." This would erupt into a tussle in the grass, then crying and Mom had to be called.

At Fort Benning, there were several more events of which I have dim, fleeting memories. I recall a late afternoon in the Georgia August summer heat, and the family of three was out in the yard, and a thunderstorm was brewing. It was one of those heavy, dark boomers that comes rolling in from Alabama to the west over the Chattahoochee, and you can see it and feel it coming for hours before it gets to you. Those afternoons have humidity so water-laden it is more like air you wear than breathe. I dimly recall Re-Re and I were playing in the yard, Mom was on the little concrete patio watching us. She was sitting in one of those aluminum lawn chairs with the uncomfortable, green and white, plastic webbing and The Colonel was somewhere else. It began with a distant cloud to cloud rip of light. The bolt, the thunder and the flash were muffled by the black clouds. I looked and my mother was on the move out of her chair. Then suddenly, it was upon us. There was a jagged flash of electricity across the sky followed by a crack of thunder so quickly on its heels that they were almost simultaneous … but no rain. Then another flash across the sky and a pealing crash. I remember feeling the thunder in my chest and the look of panic on my mother's face as she gathered her two little chickens and herded us into the little concrete block house. But still there was no rain, just the smell of ozone. This went on for what to little me seemed like hours, the flashes and booms. In reality it had to have been maybe fifteen or twenty minutes. I was terrified. And when it had all passed, Mom calmly said to no one in particular, "Ha, just summer heat lightning." I have remembered that phrase all my life and listened and looked for it with every approaching storm, and each storm carries me back to that little house and our little family, safe.

Once, as a whole family, we went on an adventure that would take us across the Chattahoochee River. It had to be all of us, and it had to be the Chattahoochee as I do not remember any other river near us that could act the way this one did. We were in an old black Buick The Colonel owned, and we were on a road approaching a large steel bridge. I must admit that at this time in my life all bridges were large, but that is neither here nor there. We approached the bridge, and there was a backed-up line of cars parked with people milling around. There was a sawhorse arrangement across the road blocking the bridge along with a man in a uniform and his car with a red flashing bubble on the top. The Colonel got out to talk to the man. After a few minutes, The Colonel came to get us, and we all piled out of the car and walked with him toward the bridge where all the people were standing. We walked up to a guardrail. The Colonel picked me up, and we looked over the edge into the most horrific scene I had ever seen. Down in this deep, deep ravine there was a lower bridge. You must have been able to get to it another way. And this lower bridge was covered in rushing water! There were trees smashed up against the steel structure and water pouring over it. There was a crashing roar coming up from the gorge and to this child, it was a scene straight out of *Dante's Inferno*. The unrelenting power and overpowering noise were mind boggling and marked me for life. To this day I can still see the water and the little bridge being swallowed and my little mind wondering, what if we had been on that bridge?

2.

During these years up to about 1954, we would visit the home town often, and I would get to hang with my good friend Pa. He was the best. I do have a few memories of those days and they stand out vividly against the gray of my ping pong balledness. One memory was our early morning shaving ritual. I would be in the bathroom with Pa. He would be standing there, tall in front of the mirror in his sleeveless tee shirt, and I would be standing on a little stool just able to hold onto the sink edge with one hand and my stuffed dog animal named "Doggie" in the other. Doggie is still in a trunk downstairs. You will know him because there is no stuffing in his neck where a little guy used to carry him around. Anyway, I would look up at Pa, watching him shave in the morning. I recall a small bare bulb in a socket just above the mirror and him standing, looking intently into the mirror. Now with him, shaving was no small deal. He was not a man who would use one of those new-fangled safety razors or an electric razor, no sir. He was a straight razor man! He would mix his shaving soap up in a white mug with a brush that looked like the stumpy tail of a horse and when he had a good later going, he would later up his face. If I was lucky he would give me a little, and I would put it on my face just like my hero. Then he would strop that razor back and forth on a big brown belt making a whoop, whoop, whoop sound and get it good and sharp and then, with the steady hand of a doctor, he would raise it to his throat. I would be standing there wide-eyed, and he would deftly swipe up and down and across, rinsing the gleaming blade every so often. And when all the soap was off his face, he would take a warm towel and wipe first my face and then his face. When we were done with that he would get out a special white bottle of "good smellem" with a little stopper in the top (which I would determine later was Old Spice Cologne) and we two men would put on our "good smellem." We would then go get finished dressing and go out and see "the ladies" and let them oooooh and aaaaah over how good we two men smelled. You know, to this day, I still marvel at the little, light blue plug stopper that white bottle has and how little it has changed in almost seventy years. And I would literally kill to have that straight razor, his straight razor. Something he held in his hand. I do have parts of his stethoscope. The rubber tubing has rotted away, but I have the rest. I have a part of him.

3.

I recall that once Pa and I got up real early and the house was very cold. He told me we had to go and "stoke the furnace." I had absolutely no idea what that meant, but if my Pa was going to do it, then I was going to do it too! Now I have to explain a few things to those of you who are too young to know what I am talking about. Back in the day, a house of a well to do town doctor had central heat. And this central heat came from a furnace in the cellar. But this furnace was a coal fired furnace. And if you did not have an automatic screw-fed furnace, you had to go downstairs and shovel the coal into the furnace! And that was what Pa and I were up to that chilly morning. I had never been downstairs to Pa's cellar before, and it was a cellar, not a basement, do not be confused. A basement is usually a concrete affair with real concrete walls. And this was a cellar. I did not even know it existed. We made our way down what seemed like very rickety, scary stairs. Actually, I'm sure they were fine, it is just that when you are little, everything is a little rickety and kind of scary. Once in the cellar, I recall that even though the single overhead exposed light bulb that hung down on its wires with a string pull to turn it on, was illuminated, it was still a dark, close and very Stephen King-like place. The floor was mostly hard packed earth except where the coal was. There was a patch of concrete where the coal sat. Overhead were the floor joists and floor of the house above, no insulation.

These joists were so low that Pa had to bend over in the space, and while it was not damp, it was musty somehow. Over in one corner was the big pile of coal. It was at the bottom of a wooden chute that led up to a little door on the outside of the house. I knew as soon as I could I was going to have to investigate that door! Pa walked over to the coal and there was a big, flat-fronted coal shovel stuck in the pile. It was just standing there with its handle sticking up right at the right height for him to grab it. He took the handle, and then turned to the massive iron furnace. With an experienced flip of the shovel blade he loosened a catch on the big door and using the end of the shovel swung it open. The throat of the furnace, which was fully big enough for a little boy to get sucked into, opened and inside was a glowing pile of deep red embers. Pa took the shovel and scraped it on the concrete scooping up a large mound of black chunks of coal. Some of the shiny pieces were as big as my head! He turned with the shovel and threw the coal into the furnace with a great flurry of sparks. Then he did it again and then a third time and then with the last shovel full, in a practiced move he had done hundreds of times, he slammed the door of the furnace shut with one smooth movement. Through the slatted furnace door, I could see the pile glowing brighter and brighter. It never ignited into flames, but the glow simply grew brighter and brighter. The home started to warm from the little boy eating beast Pa kept tamed in the cellar. I never went down there again.

4.

On the grounds of Pa's home, near the driveway off of South Bartow Street there was a circular stone goldfish pond which had to be about six feet in diameter. It seemed closer to twenty or thirty feet back then. Down in the dark, lily pad covered water were large, fat, goldfish swimming lazily around. Every day they had to be fed and one bright summer morning Pa took me out to the edge of the pond. I was small and had been cautioned many times to stay away from it. There was no fence guarding that "attractive nuisance." It was a different time, and as startling as it may seem to you, somehow I managed to never have an issue with that particular body of water. Or at least I never had an issue that I remember, or an issue that became family lore. I do recall seeing the pond empty once. Pa's yard man Casey, the same man in the lawn mower yarn, was asked to clean out the pond. I watched him. He started by emptying the pond. He began with buckets and dipping them over the side of the pond while he laid on the ground. Then he put on the tallest boots I had ever seen and climbed down into the pond with a short ladder. I am guessing it was about five feet deep. Then he continued hauling up bucket after bucket until there was maybe two feet of water left in the bottom. He gently gathered up the goldfish, one at a time and put them in a separate group of buckets and then got most of the rest of the water out. He had what I would call an old push broom and he started scrubbing the stones on the side of the pond. He would stop periodically and hose off the residue and then scrub more. I do not know how it all ended as Middy called me inside to have lunch and take a nap. I assume he finished the task and escaped from the pond with his life … although honestly, I do not remember seeing him after that day. At any rate, Pa and I were going to feed the fish. Pa brought with him a large, cylindrical container with the picture of what looked like an old timey

Revolutionary War gentleman with long white hair and a black hat. He was supposed to be a Quaker I suppose, as the name on the container was Quaker Oats. Pa opened the container and took a handful of the oat meal and threw it into the pond. A fat, old goldfish immediately came to the surface and gobbled the oatmeal. Then it was my turn. I put my little hand in the box and gathered some of the slightly sticky little oats and then threw them into the pond with the same result. Then Pa did the strangest thing I had ever seen! He took some of the uncooked oatmeal and put it in his mouth and ate it! Uncooked! Raw! I was amazed. He then offered me some. Well, if it was good enough for Pa it was good enough for me. It was bland and slightly crunchy in a soft way. It did not really taste like much of anything. I guess you could say it tasted exactly like you would expect uncooked oatmeal to taste. But we two boys had stood there by the pond and shared raw oatmeal together in the warm Georgia morning. It was going to be a good day.

Down a few steps from the house and down behind the infamous garage, way in the way back of the "hineyard" as it was called, beyond where the big stone fire grill was located, and down in the far corner of Pa's yard was a large old pecan tree that was very fruitful. All around the base of the tree were hundreds of pecans on the ground. I recall one afternoon Pa and I were in the back yard. He had just picked some corn from a little stand of corn he had grown near the house and we walked down towards the tree. On the way down he set the corn on a grill, and we just moseyed along. I guess we were talking, he and I, about life, liberty and the pursuit of happiness, when he pulled up under the tree in the cool of the shade. He looked up. I looked up. Then he reached down and picked up two pecans in his big gnarled hand. He closed his hand, and I heard a crack. When he opened his hands, the two pecans had cracked open. He carefully picked the sweet pecan meat from the bitter internals of the shell. He then handed to me a perfect half pecan. The other piece he put in his mouth. I had never seen such a thing in my life! This man picked up a little brown thing off of the ground, cracked it open and the ATE it! He ate something off of the ground without cooking it or even washing it off! I carefully put the offered thing in my mouth. It was deliciously sweet. Who had ever heard of this? Eating things off of the dirty ground? It was amazing. This man was truly a magical man.

5.

The small town of Cartersville where I was born is the county seat of Bartow County. And the courthouse for the county seat is an imposing, gold domed affair, and to this day I have never been inside. The Courthouse sits right next to the Sam Jones Memorial United Methodist Church on Church Street. A perfect place for a church on Church Street. Such is a little town. A memory flash from my late ping pong ball period is of Pa and me in the back of that church. I did not know it was that church at the time. In fact, I did not know where I was, but I was with Pa so it was okay with me. Later in life I came to find out that we were attending a wedding. The date was June the 20th, 1953. I was two and a long half years old, and I had no idea what was going on or why Pa and I had to be interrupted from our important Two Boys work to be there. As it turns out it was The Colonel's youngest sister, and she was marrying a man who in later life would become my second, and much closer and caring, father figure. He would change my life, but that's for later. My sum total memory of that day is standing there with the back of a pew in front of me and Pa standing as tall as a California Redwood tree next to me. Again, two boys, but beyond that I have no recollection of the day. I relate that little story as a point of geographical reference for the next memory. The Wofford-Stanford Hospital is on Cherokee Avenue on the other side of the County Seat Courthouse from the Sam Jones Methodist church. The hospital was on the side of the courthouse that has the "Eternal Flame" that burns in memory of all the fine young men and women from Bartow County who have given their lives for our nation. The thing that has always fascinated me is, I have never seen the flame burning, but in spite of this anomaly my memories of the hospital do burn brightly in my mind. You see I was allowed to go with Pa to his office in the hospital. I would play on the floor while he saw patients. My pride and joy was an old ether pump that he gave me. If you put water in the two glass jars on either side of the motor and plugged it in and turned it on the water in the jars would start to bubble furiously. This was a source of endless fascination to me. Now, if you added to the jars some prescription capsules that Pa had gotten in the mail and did not want, so he gave them to you, and you opened those capsules and poured them in the jars and mixed it all up with bubbles you could get some outrageous colors! Of course today, the thought of giving a child capsules of who knows what chemicals and letting that child open them and play with them is not only unthinkable but also bordering on obscene. But Two Boys were obscene, and we did it none the less. Another fun activity was giving me old mercury filled thermometers that had broken and we poured the mercury into a small bowl, and we pushed it around with our fingers. It was a very cool liquid metal to play with. And we also know today how deadly it is, and how it, along with lead, can cause brain damage and even death in children, but I was allowed to play with it, and it was cool. Of course that may account for my mental state today or possibly my entire life.

6.

As part of growing up in this quintessential small southern town my sister and ran around constantly barefooted. In Pa's front yard was a massive Magnolia tree that had major above the ground roots extending outward from a dark trunk that had to be five or six feet in diameter. I mean this tree was huge. And it was constantly dropping leaves and seed pods all over the ground. I recall Re-Re and I playing in the cool under this tree for hours at a time. We would drag out some old beat up metal cars that Pa had in a toy box and play in the red Georgia clay dirt until we looked like "little heathens" as Middy would call us. I guess between the Georgia heat and the dust we must have been quite a sight. And that brings me to the afternoon she and I were chasing up the sidewalk on the South Bartow Street side just up from the driveway. It was inevitable in that day that if you ran barefoot on the concrete sooner or later someone would stub their toe. For years Re-Re and I argued if it was "stump" your toe or "stub" your toe. I was always a "stub" your toe ping pong ball, and so today it was inevitable if you ran barefoot on the concrete sooner or later someone would stub their toe, and I did. It was a vicious stub! I practically ripped the entire end part of my big toe off. I collapsed to the sidewalk immediately, burst out crying and proceeded to bleed like a stuck pig all over the concrete. Re-Re took off for the big house and in a few minutes a whole cadre of people came streaming to my aid led by, yep, Pa. Behind him was my mother and Middy and the Casey the yard man (I guess he did not die in the goldfish pond) and Re-Re was bringing up the rear. Pa scooped me up and carried me back to the house and into the kitchen and placed me on the big, white porcelain kitchen table. It was a classic 50's table with the chrome trim around the edge and four shiny chrome legs along with the complimentary red and white checked vinyl seated chrome chairs. I sat on the table whimpering. After you make a big deal of crying you cannot just turn it off like a faucet otherwise you look like you were faking it, so I continued to whimper and sniffle. Pa sat down in one of the chairs and Middy brought him a pan of cold water and some dish cloths. He worked diligently with his gold, rimless glasses pulled down on his nose. He cleaned the wound and got all the blood and debris off. It looked terrible! I had ripped a huge chunk of the end of my toe off, and it was just hanging there like a piece of meat. I just knew my toe could not be saved. Pa then called my attention to my sister on the other side of the room. She was enthralled with the whole bloody mess. I guess you could say I was partially responsible for her later becoming a nurse. So, he called my attention to her and when I looked around to see her, he just ripped that wad of skin off my toe! He was a crafty old Pa. Well, this started a whole new gusher of blood and tears and whatnot which he sopped up with hundreds and hundreds of Middy's dish towels. I am guessing I was also responsible for her getting a whole bunch of clean, new towels soon thereafter. Pa then had to coat the end of my whole foot with Mercurochrome. It was red and apparently was capable of killing every germ in the whole world because the base ingredient was, you guessed it, Mercury! Again, pardon my current mental state. Now you knew it was working because it stung like the Devil! Well, after a sufficient amount of this Mercury based antiseptic, about two gallons by my recollection, had been slathered all over my foot, Pa proceeded to bandage my toe. He got his very official doctor gauze and white, very sticky adhesive tape and went to work, and when he was finished I looked like I had a mummy foot. My entire foot was wrapped in so much gauze the when I stood on my foot I could not even feel the floor. It was a spectacular badge of honor. I wore that mummy's foot until it was so nasty my mom made me take it off. And by that time, my toe was healed. That was good because I really did not want to spend my life missing my big toe. Pa had saved my toe, my foot and my life.

7.

The only vacation I can remember taking when I was very little was a trip to Daytona Beach or Panama City one summer. I don't know where it was. I was a ping pong ball. I went wherever. But there is one event of that whole trip I actually remember. Oh, there is a family story of a little boy so exhausted from his day at beach and playing in the surf and sun that he fell asleep at dinner in the restaurant. The little boy just put his head down in his plate and fell asleep. But I do not actually remember that. What I do remember is the terrifying night of the monster cockroach! The Colonel had rented a motel room or a little house for us and we had brought Middy along to take care of the children. To be honest, I do not remember my mother or The Colonel even being at the beach, but I do remember Middy taking care of us. It was one evening and Mom and The Colonel were off somewhere. Re-Re,  Middy and I were in the room and Re-Re and I were getting ready for bed. The bed was by a wall and Middy was reading us a story to settle our little sun baked brains down, when out from under the bed the biggest bug I had ever seen skittered across the floor, moving fast. It was terrifying looking all black and shiny on its little bug legs. But when I say it was big, this thing was huge! It had to be a foot long (three inches) and a half foot wide (half inch). Middy jumped up on the bed and screamed. Well, an adult screaming and obviously panicking is never a good recipe around little children. It has a tendency to freak them out which is why this is the only thing I can remember about the whole vacation to Daytona/Panama Beach. So Middy turned on all the lights and got us up on the bed. She was armed with a broom. It was terrifying! After a period of time my parents came home. The Colonel scoured the room while we were huddled in the other bedroom. He could find nothing, but there was no way we were going to go back in that room and try to sleep with a monster cockroach on the loose. Somehow we got through the evening, though, and as I recall we moved to another motel the next day. I believe what attacked us was what they call a Palmetto Bug, which is scientific talk for monster cockroach. I still cannot tolerate cockroaches to this day.

8.

One of my first recollected failures was in this little southern town. I have dim recollections of the day. I have no idea how old I was, but I was small. Now, near the big 41 Highway that connected Atlanta to Chattanooga was the public pool. I have other memories of going to the country club pool later in my life, but this memory was at the public pool which is no longer there. The land was taken over by the adjacent Cartersville high school and the pool was removed, however on this hot summer day we, my mother and I, were there. My mother's sister-in-law Doris might have been there too. They were good friends as I recall. We were there at the pool for swimming lessons for me. Of the lessons I remember little and who was giving the lesson I remember not at all, but we were there to teach me to swim. I know I was very small because the lesson took place in the very shallow end of the pool near the steps, and today's lesson was retrieving a penny from the bottom of the pool. No goggles, nose plug, ear plugs or any such nonsense was allowed. Just hold your breath, duck under, open your eyes and grab the penny. I could not do it. I just plain old could not do it. I do not, to this day know why, I just could not do it and I felt a tremendous amount of shame that I could not do what the other children were doing so easily. I was embarrassed. At this young age I felt I was a failure. I do not recall what came after that failure that day. I do recall returning to the same pool perhaps a few months later or perhaps a year later and showing the person who had given the lessons before that I had, in fact, mastered that feat of underwater prowess. But it was too late for the little boy, for he had tasted defeat and failure for the first time that day. And unfortunately not for the last time, but that is life.

9.

One of my last pure recollections of the Two Boys must have taken place later when I was maybe four because I knew how to write my letters. Pa and I were sitting on the steps of his open front porch. The big Magnolia Tree Re-Re and I played under when I was much younger was to our right. We were sitting, as I recall, kind of over on the right side as you look at the steps from the yard. We were just sitting watching the traffic flow down West Main Street where people had to decide whether to turn onto Etowah Drive and head out toward the Indian Mounds or continue straight on Main Street toward the library. Pa was smoking his pipe, and I was just there as I so often was. It was a peaceful Two Boy's moment. I cannot remember us talking about anything, but we must have been. You know, now that I think about it, I cannot remember a single thing he ever said to me or me to him. I cannot remember any conversation he and I ever had. We must have. We had to have had. But I cannot remember a single word. We were just there. I remember getting up and going in the house letting the screen door bang as it closed and Middy yelling about me being born in a barn and me finding one of Pa's prescription pads. He let us play with prescription pads and syringes. We used to love to squirt water from them. The real fun was doing it with the needles still on the syringes so the water stream would go a long way! Yep, it was a different time all right. But I found the pad and a pencil and came back out letting the screen door bang and Middy yelling about me

being born in a barn and plopped down next to Pa. I asked him how do spell welcome. He told and spelled it out very slowly one letter at a time as I worked my five-year-old left hand as best I could to spell out the word on the paper. I thanked him and was off again. I went down the long hall in the center of the house. The house was arranged when you went from front to back with the living, dining and kitchen to the left and the bedrooms and bathroom to the right. The classically southern center hall provided ventilation through the house. As I came to the back of the house there was the screened in porch which looked over a patch of grass, beyond was the gravel driveway, the big garage, and to the right the stone steps down to the hineyard. I went to the garage and found one of Pa's hammers and a roofing nail. I went back through the house to the front porch. Pa had gone inside. I then proceeded to nail the little welcome sign to the column just to the right of the steps where Pa and I had been sitting. Even at four years old I knew what kind of a man Pa was and how big his heart was. I knew everyone was welcome in his house because of the way he always treated me. He loved me the most.

10.

In March of 1954 we added another member to the family. My younger brother Bill was born. We were still living at Fort Benning, and my life did not change much nor did I care that I had a baby brother. He was born in the same hospital I was born in and was delivered by my Pa, the greatest doctor ever. Bill even claims we have the same mother. I doubt that, but he seems to believe it, and I do not really care. The Colonel and my mother have never bothered to tell him any differently, so I let him live in happy ignorance. As I said my life did not change much. I was growing out of my ping pong ball stage, and I was registering more and more memories. Around this time, I recall a strange custom in my family. I do not know if it was a Morris family thing, a 50's thing, a southern thing or just weird, but my mother seemed focused on our bowel movements. Had we done our "tinky" (short of stinky I later figured out) today? If there was the slightest thing wrong, upset tummy, gas, short temper, it did not matter it had to have something to do with our bodily functions. And so we were a family that believed in enemas and the Castoria brand laxative. Now I absolutely hated having to get an enema. Why, the whole thought of it made me even more constipated and made me not tell anyone when I had not done my daily "business." However, I did love the taste of Castoria. Why? I have no idea, but I did. I really did! I can even remember that fact. Why the family folklore even tells the tale of my fourth birthday when I wanted my cake made with Castoria. When the day came, we had a beautiful, big chocolate cake with chocolate icing and my mom assured me that it was made with Castoria. Not! But I believed, and it was the best cake ever, and I have loved chocolate cake ever since. Go figure. Much, much later I found out from my sister Re that she plagued her children with this same obsession with poop. Perhaps that fixation was a genetic abnormality carried by the female side of my family … a poop chromosome or something.

11.

My last memory of the Fort Benning days was in 1955, and I was in kindergarten. I cannot tell you anything about my kindergarten year except by starting me a year early, I graduated high school at seventeen, a young seventeen. But the die was cast, and I was in in school at 4 years old. Now again, we need an appreciation of history. There was a polio epidemic in the world much like the Covid-19 pandemic we are dealing with as I write this while in quarantine, and a new vaccine has just been developed by Jonas Salk. The vaccine had taken almost fifty years to develop, and the vaccine was being administered in the schools to all the children. So, on the appointed day my teacher asked us four and five year olds who was to get a polio shot? Well again, it was a different time. How were four and five year olds supposed to know if they were to get a shot or not? So, being the good boy, I lined up for a shot. And they gave me one. Come to find out my Pa, the town doctor, had secured some vaccine through his channels and my sister and I had already been vaccinated earlier that year or maybe the summer of the year before. This could have been a problem as there were two different vaccines available. One used a live virus and one used a dead virus, and people who had the shot using the live virus sometimes contracted polio and some were paralyzed from the disease like FDR. As it turned out, I was fine, but I am sure there was a big "to do" over it, but I never heard, that I remember, any outcome. If that had happened today, I guarantee someone would have lost their job and possibly their teaching credential, and there would have been a lawsuit. But, it was a different time, and to be honest, it was not the last time I would screw up trying to do what I thought was the right thing that would please my parents. And, to my credit and my credit alone, I have never had polio.

12.

Before we move on to a new chapter, I want to make one last quick comment. When we moved from Fort Benning up to Kansas, to Fort Leavenworth, and from there to Michigan, I was not near enough to spend anymore long summers with my Pa. And I cannot remember any more special adventures with him. He died in 1959. He committed suicide. I did not find out about how he died until much, much later, in my twenties. The family story is he got hooked on his own drugs and lost everything. But the point I want to make is this: I cannot remember Pa and me ever talking. We did of course. I cannot remember a single thing he ever said. He must have said a lot. I am heartbroken to say I cannot even remember his voice, but I loved that man. I loved that man because of the way he made me feel. So Maya Angelou's words, "People will forget what you said. People will forget what you did, but they will never forget how you made them feel," are so very hauntingly true. I wish, at nine years old, there had been a way I could have saved my hero. I wish someone had really tried to save my hero. I do not believe anyone did. In my opinion they just turned their backs on him, but I really do not know the whole story. Pa's picture sits on my desk this minute, and he looks at me. Pa, I have tried to be just like you to my grandchildren and tried to make you proud of me. Pa, I love you.

Chapter Three
Move It, Move It, Move It

1.

In June of 1956 we moved to Fort Leavenworth, Kansas. I have no idea why, but it was to be my lot in life, to be an Army Brat. We moved and moved and moved and moved. My perspective was that my mother never liked the moving until we had been in a place about a year and then she liked it, about when it was time to move again. This made for my lifelong feelings that she was not a very happy person. But she dutifully followed The Colonel and raised children. She was a trained nurse having graduated from Vanderbilt University, but to my knowledge she never practiced her craft. This was either by intention or by fate. I do not know, but she followed The Colonel and fed and mostly raised us by herself. By now there were three of us, Re, she had graduated from Re-Re by now, me, still called Bubba but transitioning to my more permanent family name, Jimbo, and Bill who was still too small to matter much.

2.

At Fort Leavenworth I was enrolled in the first grade. Again I cannot tell you who my teacher was or the name of the school or anything that I learned, but I can tell you about getting to school. I walked. And it was not a short walk. It was a long walk. Of course I was five, soon to be six years old in October, so I everything seemed big and long and far away, but it really did seem to be a long way. It was a different time, and we were after all on an Army post so I guess one was safer … except for the dog. This I recall vividly. There was a dog along the route that I had to take to get to school, and he would bark wildly if I came near while walking. Of course I interpreted this as him coming after me and eating me alive. I was scared of that dog. So, I took a very long and roundabout way to get to school. Now you may ask, why did I not just tell my parents about the dog and they would have taken care of the problem, except I was The Colonel's first son and I had to be "a good little soldier." I had to be brave and fearless. I felt I could not tell them of my problems and appear weak. So, I took the long way around. This was not the last time I had to be "a good little soldier" and "appear strong" so as to live up to my perception of what The Colonel wanted. I walked the long way around a lot in my life. Perhaps talking to The Colonel would have shortened my walk. Or not.

3.

I also remember learning to tie my shoes while we lived there. I can remember it as clear as day. We lived in a two story barracks affair. Looking at the building we lived upstairs to the right. One afternoon I was sitting near the bottom of the open wooden stairs leading up to our home. I had on a tee shirt and jeans and my leather shoes needed tying. I emphasize the "leather" shoes because only "poor white trash" wore tennis shoes or sneakers as we called them back then. So, with the task before me I just sat there and the magical combination of shoe laces and fingers came together and voila! It was tied. I untied them and retied them. Then again and again! I had it! I recall running upstairs and showing my mother. I do not recall any reaction, but I was so pleased with my accomplishment that I can recall that event that day even today and relate it to you. And I recall that I liked the feeling of accomplishment even if others were unimpressed. It was a good day to be five.

Another event I clearly recall is a harrowing experience one afternoon. I was dressed in my uniform of the day, a tee shirt and jeans. I was outside playing, at what I do not recall, when something like a pin prick stuck my leg. It hurt, but nothing unreasonable so I kept on playing at whatever it was I was doing. Then it happened again, and again, and again. Well, I ran up the stairs to my mommy as fast as I could. I explained what was going on through tears streaming down what I'm sure was my grubby little face. We went to the bedroom and off came my jeans. Well, as soon as they came off, a yellow jacket flew out of the pants leg! My leg was stung about five times. Mom took off after the offending bee with a fly swatter intent on ending that bug's reign of terror. After its grisly death, she proceeded to administer emergency first aid, which consisted of a poultice of cold water and baking soda. After my wounds were sufficiently covered with this magical solution, and my tears were gone, and my face cleaned with a cool bath cloth and my jeans replaced, I was off to see what new kind of trouble I could get into on that warm, Kansas, summer afternoon.

My third distinct memory of our sojourn at beautiful Fort Leavenworth was another afternoon playing with a group of what I will call friends, although I do not recall any of them as being my distinct friend. The barracks where we lived was adjacent to a road and this road was beyond a fence. Immediately next the fence was a steep bank of about six feet down to a road. Well, the specific rules of the day laid down by The Colonel were that I was not to cross under that fence, and I was absolutely not to go down that bank. So, the gang and I were playing and one of the older rapscallions did exactly what I was not to do. Then several of the other more intrepid children followed and, of course in direct contradiction to The Colonel's explicit orders, I went "over the fence" so to speak. I had no more slithered under that fence than who was standing there on the other side looking down at me – The Colonel. I recall being pulled up by the back of my pants, dragged over to the wooden stairs up to the house and hauled into the bedroom. I do not recall any conversation, but I do recall the belt strap. Yes, I do recall the belt strap.

My fourth and final memory of the Great Plains of Kansas was The Big Race. It was some kind of a family picnic day for all the Army families. All of the families and children were gathered some place. It was wide open and flat with very few trees and there were a lot of people and about a million children. We had located a nice place to have our picnic under one of the few trees. Again I do not remember what was for lunch ... probably pimento cheese sandwiches and chips with cokes to drink. We always had that, it seems. I still love pimento cheese. Anyway, in the afternoon there was going to be The Big Race. There were prizes and everything and a big deal was made of the fact that it was The Big Race. All the children were invited to race. I cannot say if there were any age groups, but when we all lined up we stretched for a long way off into the distance across the Kansas plain. Thinking about everyone lined up that day reminds me of the day the government opened up the Oklahoma Territory. Hundreds of thousands of homesteaders lined up with every sort of conveyance lined up for miles on that March 2nd morning in 1889. To my little mind, there were thousands at that picnic. The first prize was a set of goggles, a snorkel and a set of swim fins; I really wanted those; I really wanted to win and make The Colonel proud of me. So, I lined up. A gun was fired, and we all took off across the uneven meadow. I had a good start and ran as fast as my little legs would carry me. There were some bigger boys and girls, but I could run like the wind, and I did. It was a different world in 1956 and 1957. Nobody ran for pleasure or exercise. There were no special running shoes; I was running in my Buster Browns. If you were "well to do" you had leather shoes. Again, only "poor white trash" had sneakers and they went by names like P.F. Flyers and Keds. And nobody stretched before a race. But there I was, sailing along and feeling good about myself. The Colonel would stand proud as his first born son walked up on the big stage; I guessed there would be a stage, and a microphone, and an announcer; and The Colonel would clap and my mother would be pleased for me as I accepted the big prize of the holy goggle set. Then I got a cramp in my right calf. It seized up, and down I went. I did not win the race, or the goggle set, or The Colonel's adoration. But I did experience failure, again. It tasted bitter, or maybe that was my just my tears.

In the summer of 1957 we moved to Michigan for two years.

4.

1531 Northwood Street, Ann Arbor

At this point in my life I was more than a ping pong ball, but I still was just "along for the ride." However, I was becoming more aware. I had no idea why we were moving or why my family did what it did. We just did. And the next move was to Ann Arbor, Michigan, to 1531 Northwood Street to be exact. As you can see, at least by now I knew where I lived, and I also knew how to answer a phone. We had very specific instructions. Mine were to pick up the phone and say, "Major Morris's Quarters, Jimmy speaking." As you can see, The Colonel was not yet a Colonel, but he was not a Captain any longer, and I had officially graduated from Bubba to Jimbo. But I could not say "Jimbo speaking." I had to be Jimmy. I found out years later The Colonel was in Ann Arbor to attend the University of Michigan and get a Master's Degree in Aeronautical Engineering, so. He did not get it. I also found out much later that he was not a very good student. Knowing that then would have help me cope later in life.

Before we moved into our house, we had to stay in a motel. The cool thing about this little strip of a motel which had maybe ten rooms all lined up parallel with the highway was out front on a strip of grass there was a stagecoach. A little odd for Michigan now that I reflect on it, but there it was, and Re and I played on it day after day. The house The Colonel bought was on a corner lot. It had shingles as siding and a separate little garage for the car connected by an open, breezeway. I recall the house as being green, but I also remember the

1531 Northwood Street #2

Colonel and a friend, named Lou Shelter I think, painted it a dark maroon red color. The painting of the house was a big deal. I recall the house as having a picture window on the long side and a full basement, as all houses in the north do. The corner lot, from my perspective, was huge. If you ran from one side across its sloping front tracing the sidewalk to the neighbors, you would be out of breath and have to fall down in the lush grass to catch your breath. I recall one winter, it was '57 or '58, we had an ice storm and the Colonel had to not only shovel all the snow, he had to chip ice off of the long, long sidewalk that wrapped the corner lot. I am really glad I was little!

My first real friend that I can remember lived next door. His name was Ali Burker. He was Turkish which meant nothing to me. He was just a friend. We went to school together at Eberwhite Elementary, hung out together and generally got in as much trouble as we could together. He showed me the cool things you could do with a magnifying glass like burn holes in leaves and torture ants. If the world was run by seven or eight year olds, it would be a cruel *Lord of the Flies* place. I showed him how to roller skate. These were old timey steel wheeled skates with a skate key and everything. You kept the skate key tied to an old shoelace which you wore around your neck. When you put the skates on, you had to use the key to adjust the length of the skate to fit your shoe length, and use the key to open two clamps on the front of the skate. Then you slip your shoe into the clamps and tighten the clamps onto the toe of your shoe with the key. Again, it is best to have leather

shoes with a stiff sole otherwise the skate slips off your shoe in mid-skate and take a header. You then buckled the back of the skate around your ankle and you were ready to go. One did not have to worry about helmets or pads or any of that sissy stuff. You could not even buy them if you wanted them. Then you stood up if you could, and off you went.

Those steel wheels on concrete would shake your fillings out! Ali and I must have skated a hundred miles on that sidewalk.

We would run around and fall down and generally just do what second and third grade boys do which is not much except look for trouble. I am not sure why I remember this but, one afternoon we decided we would play like we were all grown up and had gone our separate ways and then met up by accident after many years. We would practice walking toward each other and pretend it dawned on us who each other was and we would turn and say, "Excuse me, are you Ali Burker?" and he would turn and say, "Are you Jimmy Morris?" Then we would pretend to catch up. Writing about it, it seems pretty lame, but it is a warm and comfortable memory of my first friend for some reason.

He and I walked to school together. At Eberwhite Elementary we all walked to school, and then walked home to eat lunch, and then walk back and then walk home. A lot of back and forth which seems weird, but that is what we did, and when it is your life and you are doing it there is not much weird about it. It is just life. Kind of like having to spend a whole school year during Covid going to "virtual school." It seems weird to me but to the children doing it, it is just their life. But I digress … to go home for lunch my teacher would dismiss us by holding up a multiplication flash cards. The first child to call the right answer got to leave to go home for lunch. Then the second and the third and so on. I never left early, but likewise I was never last. Like in my family, I was just in the middle somewhere. I also recall that it was the third grade when I learned there was a word and a direction for "left" and for "right," and I recall thinking, "I'm going to have trouble with that." And I have, to this day. But at the same time, I devised a way to remember which was which that I still use today, and it has become automatic to think of it. The desks we sat in had a table arm that came up from the right. The only way you could get out of the desk was to exit to the left. And when we all said the Pledge of Allegiance the teacher would say, "Students, stand to the left of your desks," which was the only way we could stand so I learned left from right. But I still have trouble with it today at 70, and still think of that third grade desk. Life tools!

While we lived in Michigan we went to see a lot of places. Being near Detroit, we went to see an automobile assembly plant, and being near Battle Creek we went to a Kellogg cereal manufacturing facility. I do not recall much about those. But we also went to Niagara Falls. Now that I do remember. I remember it being overwhelming! There are two parts that I clearly recall. The first part was standing next to the American Falls behind a handrail right at the point where the falls go over the edge. As I stood there, there was a sense of vertigo and it messes with your frame of reference. The water rushing past you made you feel as if you were the one moving. Also the power and roar along with the mist were so overpowering you almost felt as if you could be sucked in and pulled over the falls at any moment. It was terrifying and exhilarating! I just wanted to stand there and drink in all that power. We also went on the Maid of the Mist observation boat. We went down to a dock and had to get little rain slickers. They were just cheap thin blue ponchos. That was my first clue this was going to be something more than just a boat ride. Then we were crowded onto this big tug boat kind of thing, and we chugged off toward the falls. Well, it you thought the falls were impressive standing next to them at the top near a guard rail, you need to see them from the bottom when 713,000 gallons pour over the falls per second! The sound is thunderous, and you are sure this time it is your boat that is going to be sucked in, and you are going to be pounded to death. Like your first real, big roller coaster ride, or your first motorcycle ride or the first time you kiss a girl; it is both exhilarating and terrifying at the same time.

I have always been a hands-on person from an early age. My guess is I became this way at about this time in my life. I am quite "handy" still today. I love working with my hands. So, to me it is no surprise of all the places we went the one I loved the most was our day at Greenfield Village. Today, it has become an 800 acre Disneyland-ish place, and I would love to have taken my grandchildren there, but those days are past. What I remember most is Edison's Laboratory. I visited there when I was seven or eight years old. My curiosity was just starting to bloom at that point,

and I was fascinated with all the smells and the equipment and the machines and the air of excitement and possibilities. "As the twig is bent, so grows the tree." It was my mantra as a teacher, and I did my best to bend twigs because I also remember that around that time, I had gotten a chemistry set for Christmas and then an Erector Set on another Christmas and a Lionel train and a Hydro-Dynamic building set also. I was all about doing things with my hands and my parents fed that ability. I would mix chemicals and play and learn. I would build and use motors and set up my trains different ways. I would build paper-mâché tunnels and add working railroad cross arms and electric track switches. I have never truly enjoyed

"reading" instructions, but if you show me a picture or demonstrate something once, I can quickly grasp the concept much more readily. I recall a present from the Easter Bunny, a small Rocks and Minerals book. It was my bible! I would scour the yard for hours seeking quartz, iron pyrite, or schist. The chemistry set would occupy me as I tried to make anything that would change color or fizz or smoke. My Lincoln Log set was interesting, but the Erector set was, hands down, the thing that consumed me. I would literally spend hours making robots, merry go rounds and Ferris Wheels. The set had a real plug-in electric motor, not some little battery powered thing so I could make a real functioning whatever I wanted. It was about this time that I became engrossed in my lifetime hobby, model building. I started with simple airplanes and graduated to more and more complex plastic models. The Colonel and I actually worked together on a display model with all of the rockets at the time from the Bullpup to Nike Hercules to the Atlas. There was no Redstone, yet. That is the only model I remember us working on together. Later I would build the Forrestal aircraft carrier, a Nautilus submarine that had one side that would open so you could see all the compartments, model cars by the dozens (as soon as I could save $1.50 – yep $1.50 – I would buy a model car), the Monitor and the Merrimack, a motorized tug boat, and many, many more. I can remember struggling with my first balsa plane, a small Spirit of St. Louis, sitting in the kitchen in a booth arrangement in the Michigan house. I also remember a model I was building back then in Michigan, Long Tom. It was an artillery piece and quite intricate. At that time my paternal grandfather, we called him Unca' Pete – why we called our grandfather "Uncle" is beyond me – was visiting along with my paternal grandmother, Momma. Well, Unca' Pete wanted

to help me, and he was getting in my way, so I yelled at him to stop. Telling an adult to stop helping me … that was another first in my life. Related to this, I recall a project I was doing for school. I believe we were studying Ketchikan,

Alaska. There may even be a handwritten report on it in a trunk somewhere. But I wanted to make a model of a fish catching structure out of Lincoln Logs to accompany my report. The teacher would be very proud of me for that. And the Colonel would … never mind. And I was struggling with the string I was using to try to make the nets for the model. It was not going well, and I was getting frustrated. I brought the whole mess to my mother. She was busy. When I was young it seemed she was always busy with a baby or cleaning or trying to feed our growing brood. So she turned it over to the Colonel. The Colonel solved the problem in minutes. Potatoes came to our house in a big ten-pound bag made of red strings all pre-tied to form a bag. The Colonel emptied out the potatoes over my mother's objections and cut a square from the bag and laid it into the Lincoln Log frame and voila! It was finished. It was perfect. I recall this event clearly not because the Colonel helped me or was even interested in me, but because it taught me a valuable lesson about sideways thinking. It taught me about repurposing something that was not made for your situation into something to solve a problem for you. Along with the gift of a deft use of my hands, spatial apperception and my natural problem solving skills, this lesson of repurposing would serve me all my life.

Michigan was an awakening from my ping pong ball period to real awareness. On the 4th of October in 1957 the Russians set the world on its collective ear by putting the first manmade satellite into orbit. Now this in itself meant nothing as I had no concept of who the Russians were or what orbit even meant, but I sensed it was a big deal. I have always been good at sensing, being empathetic to others, which has always been a blessing and a curse. I sensed it because of the excitement it inspired in The Colonel. He was literally foaming at the mouth about it, but it did not affect me directly so, in the egocentric world of an almost seven-year-old, who cares? I do remember one cool, crisp, fall late evening. I remember the whole family gathering on that huge Northwood Street corner lot lawn that Michigan evening. There was dew on the grass, and it got all over my shoes. The moon was a tiny cold sickle in the sky near the horizon. The sky was crystal clear and had about ten million stars twinkling in the black sky. The Colonel pointed skyward to a tiny pinprick of light. It looked like a little blinking star, but the difference was, this one was moving! A star was actually moving across the sky! It was Sputnik. It was interesting, but of course I did not grasp the totality of the moment, but I clearly remember that moment today.

That event spawned a whole new wave of television for me. My days of *Captain Kangaroo and Mr. Greenjeans*, *Pinky Lee*, *Soup Sales*, and *Buffalo Bob with Howdy Doody and Clarabelle the Clown* with the Peanut Gallery were drawing to a close. I was still a fan of *The Mickey Mouse Club* and especially Annette Funicello. I still did not understand why her, but I was becoming more aware. It had to do with the sweater she wore every week. I mean all the Mouseketeer girls wore sweaters, but her sweater was special. Look her up and you will understand this seven-year old's consternation. I was also interested in *The Andy Griffith Show* with Andy's little boy Opie – played by Ron Howard – and Opie's misadventures. I was especially interested in the opening whistling song which I heard from my bedroom because I always had to go to bed when Opie came on. But I could listen from my bed. I learned to whistle myself that year, and snap my fingers.

A show that I recall the most was *Men in Space*. And interestingly, I recall only one specific episode. In this episode it seems that men on some far away airless planet had become lost and had used up almost all their air, but this was not a problem because they had extra air canisters. The problem was, they had no wrench to access the air. However, this was not a problem because one of the spacemen had a wrench, but the wrench was inside his spacesuit, and to get the wrench he would have to open his spacesuit. So the conundrum was obvious. Do you all die or does one of the team die to save the others? Needless to say this was the 1950's when life was simple. Men were men, like John Wayne, and women were women who stayed at home and cooked and cleaned with their Hoover vacuums and were happy and fulfilled having babies, like my mother. So, the spaceman sacrificed himself for the "greater good." I had never thought about this before. It was eye-opening to this seven-year-old.

A last comment before literally "moving on" is that in December of 1959 I took my first airplane trip. We flew from Michigan to Georgia. I remember it was a propeller driven four engine plane, and you could look down easily and see the cars and people because planes did not fly very high back then. We flew down to Georgia to attend a funeral. Family lore tells that my Pa had visited Michigan earlier that year. I do not recall his visit. The story is he was addicted to drugs. The story is he needed my parents to get him more drugs, and they would not do this for him. I also guess they, nor his only son, would try to get him any help with his addiction. After all he had done for humanity, they, his family, did not have the humanity to try to help him. They just judged him as unworthy and weak. They wanted him to "pull himself up by his bootstraps." Try that sometime – it's impossible. I realize I am sympathetic to this man, my Pa, and probably a little naïve not having all the facts or the emotions or being there in the moment. Pa turned 70, November 6th, and killed himself a little over a month later on December 15th. While I am writing this, I turned 70, 71 and now 72. But I wish nine-year-old me had been able to help him, able to tell him to hang on, able to tell him how much I loved him, able to get him into a treatment program, but as I have said, it was a different time, and I was a ping pong ball. Bottom line, he returned to Georgia from Michigan and killed himself by putting a shotgun in his mouth and pulling the trigger. He did this almost ten years to the day after his wife died of cancer. He, the town doctor, had not been able to diagnose the cancer in his own wife in 1949. I believe two things led him to take his own life. First, the guilt he felt over his wife's death must have been crushing. The second, if I lost my wife and then my children turned their backs on me, I would be totally devastated. Given those two things alone, I believe I too could see suicide as a viable option. I understand my mother's sister-in-law, Doris, found him. My best friend was gone. I did not, to my recollection, attend the funeral. I do not recall flying home. But I did take my first airplane trip.

Then we moved to Vienna, Virginia, for three years and the greatest trauma of my young life.

5.

I was to live in Vienna, Virginia, for a total of almost six years. They were not six consecutive years. It was a three and three deal, but it was the longest I recall living in any town until after I was married. The first time I lived there we lived at 804 Meadow Lane. I was nine, ten and almost eleven and a half, almost

three years before we thankfully moved again. The house was a little, un-air-conditioned, three-bedroom house. My younger brother Bill (William Cranston Morris) and I shared a room. I remember there was a big deal made by the adults that there was a bay window. There was a lumpy, un-grassed back yard with a forest of sorts behind that. Across the street was an older, much taller, mentally challenged boy with a back deformity named Dicky Bosquin. He was my good best friend. He and I would play with model cars together and generally just hang out. Sometimes we would watch television and eat Triscuit wafers together.

I went to Flint Hill Elementary for fourth and fifth grade. I do not remember my fourth grade teacher or anything I was supposed to learn, but I do remember two things. I had my first girlfriend in fourth grade. I do not remember her name either, but she had red hair she wore in a long braid down her back, and she would bring two Hostess Snowballs for snack each day, and she would give one to me. That is how I knew we were boyfriend and girlfriend. The second thing I remember is studying Indians. For a Christmas present for our parents we made Indian mats from rolled up magazine pages stuck together with paper maché glue and string. Using paper maché is a skill that would come in handy later. We also made Native American pots from a glass jar wrapped with string, slobbered all over with paper maché and painted with Native American designs. Other than that, fourth grade is a blank. I do recall that our principal was Miss Burke. I recall she was a severe woman with a jutting jaw causing a pronounced under bite. My only oblique encounter with her was in the cafeteria at lunch. The room was full with what must have been a million talking children, and Miss Burke came in to make an announcement about something. The room got quiet, she started to speak, and then from somewhere there was a bang. Then another bang. She stopped talking and looked around the crowd. What disrespectful, moronic, misbehaving, malcontent child dared to interrupt? Bang! Then she located the perpetrator and was ready to rain hell down on them. It was a third grader who could not get his thermos open. His mommy had told him to just bang the side of the lid on the table, and it would loosen. He was summarily removed with great prejudice from the cafeteria. I never saw him again. I'm guessing Miss Burke had him shot.

Our fifth grade teacher was a gorgeous old woman. As I recall she was the first attractive teacher I had ever had. She was very old though, probably twenty-two or so. She had shoulder length dark hair and all the boys were in love with her. At the beginning of the year she was named Miss Dick and then, mercifully, during the year she got married and became Mrs. Hood. Funny, she must be about eighty-two or eighty-three now. Time is an interesting thing. Anyway, in the fifth grade we were tasked to study Virginia history, and there were three events that stand out about my fifth grade year.

The first was it was 1961 and the Civil War Centennial was a big deal especially in Virginia. We must have studied it because all of us fifth grade boys got gray Confederate "slouch hats" and ran around at recess playing Civil War. No one wanted to be a "Yankee" but I guess someone was because we ran around the playground yelling "bang-bang" until almost all of us were dead.

The second memory was a production we put on for a PTA meeting where all the fifth graders danced *The Virginia Reel*. We had to dance it and dance it with the girls and touch their hands and hook arms and bow, and they had to curtsey and it was terrible. On the night of the performance, we had to wear breaches that came to our knees and stocking socks and shiny black shoes with fake buckles and poofy white shirts with string ties. The girls had to wear long dresses that had petty coats under them making them look like hoop skirts. We danced and sweated and performed our little hearts out that night and then closed our gala performance by the off-key singing of that old Virginia standard *Carry Me Back to Old 'Virginny.'* That evening with great gusto we belted out: *"Carry me back to ole' Virginny. There's where the cotton and the taters grow. There's where the birds warble sweet in the spring time. There's where this ole' darkey's heart is long to go."* Yep, it was a different time. In 1997 the Virginia legislature retired this song as the State Song … can't imagine why.

Third was an awesome experience and my first really major getting into trouble at school experience. Oh I had had minor scrapes – getting caught cheating on a spelling test, bringing a tiny toy camera to school that squirted water … minor scrapes, no federal offenses, all misdemeanors. But this was to be my crowning achievement. We all came into school one Monday and shuffled to our classrooms. When my buddies and I arrived at our class there was no Mrs. Hood. Now to arrive at your classroom and find no teacher what-so-ever is unheard of today, but as I have said several times before, these were different times. Apparently over the weekend the custodians had evidently waxed the floors because they shined like mirrors. Well, as I have noted, if you were from a well-to-do family you wore leather soled shoes. If you were not, as I have said before, you wore "sneakers." And sneakers could get a really good grip on those old waxed floors and leather souled shoes were very slippery. And if you had on leather souled shoes and you held onto the backs of the belts of two sneaker wearing boys, why they could haul you around that classroom just like Charlton Heston in *Ben Hur*! The movie had come out in 1959 and we were all familiar with famous chariot scene. So, around we did go … until Mrs. Hood walked in the room. We were busted big time. After much discussion and talks with our Principal Burke … scary … it was determined that we three miscreants should sit in the classroom, with no teacher present – it was a different time – while everyone else was out at recess and on a sheet of paper we were to take 2000, subtract 2, and add 1 until we reached 0. Of course we were to total everything and show all our work. So, with our legs chained to the desk legs and handcuffs hanging from our little wrists we three labored, day, after day, after day. Now along about the third day, when we realized we would all be in seventh grade before we finished, we decided a little inventive math was needed. So, we decided at random points we would make minor math errors like $682 - 2 = 610$. And then a little further along so it was not too obvious $475 - 2 = 423$. Using our method, we were finished in one more recess period. We even all finished about the same time to make it look good. Then we gathered our sheaf of wide ruled notebook papers with five neat columns on each page front and back and carried them outside to the beautiful Mrs. Hood. She gave them a cursory glance. Smiled at each of us making us feel very curious and told us to go play and to not do that again. We all solemnly agreed, looked down, shuffled our scuffed shoes, said we would all be good boys forever, and dashed off to play. To my knowledge Mrs. Hood was none-the-wiser. I think she knew exactly what we had done. As a former fifth grade teacher, I KNOW she knew exactly what we had done.

In the summer time when we got out of school, we had summer vacations that spread out in front us like a long, warm carpet lasting forever. My family belonged to a Vienna Woods Swim and Tennis Club, and I was allowed to ride my bike there. It was more than several blocks away, and I cannot believe I was allowed to go, but it was a different time. And if you proved yourself at the pool by taking a rigorous test, you did not even have to have a parent with you! Well, by this time after my false swimming start in my little Georgia home town, I was quite the fish. In order to qualify for your badge, you had to take the club's swim lessons which meant you had to arrive early in the morning, take the classes and the test.

I recall getting up early in the Virginia summer mornings, trundling into the kitchen and getting my bowl of *Frosted Flakes* and then heading out on my bike. I had to ride down Meadow Lane past Tapawingo Road to Kingsley Road and turn left. Then up Kingsley for about 600 miles to turn left on Cottage and a right on Harmony and I was there. I remember being there so early that the sun was just a watery ball in the early summer ground mist. Then we had to get in the freezing cold pool complete with goose bumps and blue lips. Then we had to learn all the strokes and water safety tips. There was no reading or written tests. It was all "hands on" doing, and I sailed through all the swim classes and proudly wore my shark badge on my little Speedo swim trunks. With that badge, I could breast stroke, crawl, side stroke, tread water and float on my back for hours. I could even retrieve a penny from the bottom of the ten-foot-deep end! So there you go, early-in-my-life Cartersville swim teacher. Next I had demonstrated I could swim the length of the Olympic pool, tread water for five minutes and float on my back for five minutes to earn my special additional tag for my suit that would allow me my first real freedom. I would spend endless hours at that pool getting sunburned and then turn "as brown as a little nut." My friends and I played *Sea Hunt* for hours with our goggles and fins, which I bought with my allowance of 25 cents per week after scrimping, saving and denying myself any models for weeks and weeks. This time I did not even have to win a race to get my goggles and fins … I just bought them. This pool had three diving boards, a low board, a spring board and a ten meter, sky high, high board! The only thing I ever did from that monster bad boy board was jump for dear life. It was a good time to be alive. Think the movie *Stand by Me* based on the Stephen King novella *The Body*.

In January of 1961 my second brother, Brian Meroney Morris, was born. Today I understand where all these weird middle names come from … Cranston … Meroney. I do not have many recollections of this event other than my mom had a hard time with this pregnancy and was confined to bed rest for the last part, and Aunt Doris (Doris Virginia Whitfield Wofford) came up from Cartersville to help take care of us rowdy, three children. My world was at maximum ego-centric at this point. There is fine line between ping pong ball and ego-centric. During one, you have no control over the events surrounding you so you just bounce along. When the ego-centric phase arrives, you are still bouncing along with little control, but you do not do it with the ease and willingness you used to. Now you have a little freedom, and everything that happens is about you and you are vocal about whether you like it or not. You start to "buck the system" as The Colonel used to say to me constantly. Also, your recollections are also sharper and more vivid but only as the events apply to you.

6.

That summer of 1961 we went back to my Georgia home town to visit. I recall it clearly because we had a July 4th cookout at The Colonel's parent's house. The house up on "The Hill" where Unca' Pete Marion Wingfield Morris) and Momma (Marie Louise Williams Morris) lived. Unca' Pete was a fascinating outdoor cook. He had a big concrete and rock grill in the "hine yard." In a small ramshackle shed that looked like an old dog house with a chicken wire door on it, he kept his secret grill lighter … kerosene! The little house shed looked like something from *Dog Patch*, the mythical home of *Lil' Abner* in the funny papers. Unca' Pete would haul his "fixins" out of the little house which was scary because there was always at least one massive wasp nest in there. A wasp nest seemed never to be a concern to Unca' Pete. Unca' Pete was the wasp nest finder champion. It did not matter if it was up at the eave of the garage, in the little, nasty Dog Patch hutch, or on the eave of the house he had one solution – burn them out! He would get a long pole, wrap one of Momma's old reject dish towels around it, soak it in kerosene, light her up and stick it right up on the nest! Wasps would burn, crackle and some would escape, but they got what they deserved. They were scary and nasty. But again, I digress. So the grill, Unca' Pete would start with a whole bag of charcoal. Who puts a whole bag of charcoal in a grill? He would just rip it open and pour it in his monster grill and then douse it with kerosene from a gallon glass white lightening jug. With a warning to everyone to, "Stand Back!" he would strike a wooden Diamond kitchen match on the side of the grill, casually light up the half of an old chewed on cigar that always hung from his mouth (nasty) and then toss the match into the grill. WHOOSH! The grill would erupt like a rocket sending a gush of flame fifteen feet up the chimney and into the evening sky making the overhanging leafy tree branches sway with the super-heated air blast. Now, boys this age already have a supernatural love of fire, so to this young, ten-year-old boy, this was almost a spiritual experience. All hail the God of Fire! This event was accompanied by the ceremonial drinking of much beer and guffawing by the adult males. Then his wife, Momma, would send down the T-bone steaks. There were hamburgers for the children. Unca' Pete would then toss the steaks on the grill grate which looked like a reinforced piece of plaster lath – now I know it WAS a reinforced piece of plaster lath. After the steaks started cooking and dripping grease onto the white coals there would be periodic explosive flair-ups which were dealt with an old, plastic squirt catsup bottle filled with water. Then it was time for what you would call today the steak marinade, *Lee and Perrins Worcestershire Sauce* and melted butter in a little beat-up sauce pan. Nothing else would do. I keep a bottle in my fridge even today just for religious uses. To top everything off, Unca Pete would fill the *Lee and Perrins Worcestershire Sauce* bottle cap with the fiery liquid and toss back a "shot" of the sauce. He would offer it to me, and I would always decline. Today after a shot, I offer it to my grandchildren. They decline, also. Now all of that is nice, but none of that speaks to the infamous July 4th story. After dinner when all the adults and old folks, of which I am now one of those gentrified humans – how Carolyn and I got here I do not know – would sit around and drink something from small glasses and watch the fireflies wink in the evening's fading light. Everyone was there: The Colonel's mom, Momma, and dad, Unca' Pete, The Colonel's youngest sister Toochie (Marian Louise Morris Rogers) … she was Toochie because when she was little Unca' Pete, her father, started calling her "his little Toochman" for some reason … and her awesome husband the former Navy Captain and Annapolis graduate, Georgia Tech professor and my savior, Unca' Nelson (Nelson Kimball Rogers), the Colonel's next younger sister and Carolyn's savior, Marybelle (Marybelle Morris Swift), and her very humorous husband the insurance salesman, Don Swift (Donald Charles Swift), Mom's brother, Unca' Bill (William Earl Wofford, Jr.) the bomber pilot, and his strikingly lovely wife, Doris (Doris Virginia Whitfield Wofford), and various sundry offspring cousins and brothers and sisters. The children were running around with sparklers. That was all that

were allowed under Georgia's fireworks law. Then, there was that outlaw package of explosive Black Cats. I am not sure which adult had brought them. I suspect it was my mother's brother, Unca' Bill. He was always the bad boy, and a real, genuine hero. He had had been the pilot of a B-17 named *Slick Chick* in World War II, completed over 50 bombing missions over Germany and

returned home safely. Unca' Bill had wanted to fly for a fledgling airline named Eastern, but his mother, Pa's wife, had said no. So he became a car salesman. I cannot help but wonder how his life would have turned out if he had been allowed to pursue his dream. As it was he was severely injured in a car wreck around 1965 and died years later at 76 years old. But again, I digress. So, the children and I had the Black Cats and some matches! A plan was devised to run into the back yard, stand in the middle of all the adults and throw a Black Cat. I was elected to do the dastardly deed as I was a show-off, idiot boy. I carefully took one of the firecrackers off the common fuse they were tied to. As I was performing this delicate operation, you would have thought I was in the movie *The Hurt Locker*. Finally, I had one free. I took a match and the Black Cat and off I went with others trailing behind. I saw the gathering. Old people sitting in folding aluminum chairs and white wooden Adirondack chairs. I lit the match. I lit the fuse and ran to the center of the crowd. As I got ready to throw the firecracker, it went off in my hand! I was horrified. Here I was, a child of ten, and I had blown my hand off up to my elbow at least! I looked down in horror as tears poured from my eyes. All my fingers were still there! I was overjoyed! My mother was already on her feet, and I was being consoled and fussed at all at the same time. I believe my uncles and Unca' Pete were laughing their heads off. So much for July 4th, 1961.

While we were visiting Unca' Pete, in a rare moment of grand-paternal exhibitionism, he alone took us to the Etowah Indian Mounds. I have been there since several times taking my children and grandchildren, but this visit was marked to me by one particular event I recall. One must appreciate the segregation system in the 1960's in Georgia to appreciate this story. I am not going to regale you with the horrors of the times except to say The Strand Theater on the Square in Marietta had a separate entrance on the side, on Cherokee Street, that black people could use because they had to sit in the balcony. They could not sit with the "white folks." You can still see where that entrance was today if you know what you are

July 15, 1959 – The Big Three at "Momma and Pete's" and I have my totem pole art set from the Etowah Indian Mounds

looking for. And you can read about Emmett Louis Till in 1955, the Montgomery Bus Boycott of 1955, "Bombingham" and the 16th Street Baptist Street Church bombing of 1963 to get a deeper flavor of the times. Or you can visit the Center for Human and Civil Rights in Atlanta to realize that blacks were "girls" or "women" but never "ladies," and all black men were "boys" … or worse. At any rate, at the Indian Mounds it was blazing hot. There is no heat like mid-July Georgia heat, 97° with 90% humidity. It is weather you wear, and along with the gnats – more about them later – it can be a force to contend with especially if you are older … but not when you are eleven. So, after climbing the mounds and running around like little Indians whooping and yelling even I needed a drink. I headed for the outdoor drinking fountain. I was in luck; there were two fountains and both were empty. I waked up to one and pushed the button. I could feel the water was very warm as I leaned over to drink. Then Unca' Pete yelled at me to stop! "Don't drink from that! Drink from the other one." I was glad he told me that because when I pushed the little white porcelain knob on the second fountain, cool water came out. I was refreshed. As I walked away and looked back at the cool water fountain a sign above it read, Whites Only. The warm water fountain had a sign too, Colored Only. It was a different time. I recall Unca' Pete letting us buy a souvenir that day. I bought a set of two, styrofoam totem poles you could paint. It was something like a model I could paint and use my hands to do. Interestingly, the Etowah Indians never had totem poles.

As I mentioned, those Georgia summers could be brutal weather-wise. There was the oppressive heat and humidity and the gnats. It seems today that the gnats have retreated further south to down around Statesboro, but in the early 60's we were dead in the middle of the gnat zone. And those things would get in your eyes and nose, but the worst was when they got in your ears. They would get in there and get way down in your ear canal where nobody could get them out, and they would buzz and buzz until you went crazy. Then Mom or Doris would bring you into the air-conditioning, lay you on the sofa with the offending ear up and put a few drops of alcohol in it. After a second the buzzing stopped and you could turn over and put a Kleenex to your ear

Unca Bill and Doris's home at 47 Arrowhead Drive, Cartersville

and the offending monster would pour out with the alcohol. Then you were ready to go again and you were out in the heat and sun in a second to see what mischief the others had been up to while you took a pit stop. We often visited up at "Dar and Unca' Bill's" house on Arrowhead Drive. Their yard was immense, and I mean huge. For an eleven-year-old it was more like a couple of football fields big. Three years later I would get to cut this yard, but that is another story I will tell you about when I am fourteen years old. Re and I would go up there, I guess Bill would go too, but he was more of a nuisance than a real person. We would go to their house and run around with a "bad boy" named Jer-Boy. Jer-Boy's daddy was Jerry White and a Cartersville lawyer and they lived two houses beyond Dar and Unca' Bill on Arrowhead Drive. Jer-Boy also had a sister, Laura, but that is also another story. Last year, I found out Jer-Boy had also become a lawyer and his daddy had become a judge and that Jerry and Jer-boy had passed away, within a week of each other.

Dar and Unca' Bill belonged to the Cartersville Country Club because Unca' Bill was a golf freak like Unca' Pete. I remember getting to caddy for The Colonel and Unca' Pete and Unca' Bill once and I remember one of them was getting ready to swing and I wanted to impress the older guys with my golf knowledge so I yelled, "Fore!" because that is what you did. Everyone knew that. They always did that in cartoons. Well, I caught the devil for that, and somehow I was never asked to go along again. Anyway, we loved to go to the country club and swim in their pool. It had a spring board and high board and everything. It was not as big as the Vienna Woods pool, but it would certainly do in the Georgia heat. But for some reason, we could never go there until after lunch. And we could not go there until at least an hour after we ate lunch for some

Summer 1960 the Big Three - Mary Louise Morris Bramble 11y/o, James Wingfield Morris Jr 9 y/o, William Cranston Morris 6 y/o on swings at Momma and Unca Pete's house at 6 Jones St.

stupid reason. But we loved going and we would spend our mornings on Arrowhead running around the yard yelling at the puffy summer cumulus clouds not to bunch up together and make thunderheads and bring rain and spoil our country club swim time.

Re and I would often spend time up on "the Hill" with Momma and Unca' Pete. I recall being on the little back porch of their house in the early morning, Georgia humid, cool sitting at my little white table, and I would have my *Frosted Flakes*. If I was lucky, I would even have fresh peaches on my cereal. I would be sitting there looking out over the red painted brick stoop, past the swing set that Re and I would swing on and swing so high the legs of the swing set would pull off the ground, to the "hine" yard watching Unca' Pete's mostly orange yard cat named Kalinsky roam the yard looking for who knew what. Then Unca' Pete would come down the hallway fresh from a shower in the tiny one person shower he had installed in a closet turned bathroom next to the family room smelling of after shave. He would be wearing a "wife beater" tee shirt with suspenders holding up his pants and when he saw me he would immediately start wailing, "Momma! Who is this eating all my Sugar Post Frosties? And my peaches!" To this I would laugh and Momma would reassure him that there were plenty of peaches and cereal. He would then sit in the kitchen and have his coffee and breakfast. Every morning it was the same thing, day after day. And it made me laugh, every morning, day after day.

After Unca' Pete went off to his job, he was an accountant for E Z Mills for years and then opened his own accounting shop on Main street across from the Presbyterian

Church, my morning was often spent sitting on the front porch on the "glider" or out front of the porch on the "stoop" and playing on the walkway leading from the street to the house. Across the street was an old woman who we called the witch. I do not know why. It was probably because she and Momma had had a tiff once upon a time. At the end of the walk to the porch there was a sidewalk which ran along the street. From the sidewalk at the street, you would walk up three concrete steps and there was a twenty-five-foot walkway up to the four brick steps to the stoop and the front porch. Momma would sit on the brick porch steps and Re and I would go down to the street sidewalk. Then we would play *Red Light/Green Light* until someone would reach Momma and squeal with delight! Re and I also spent countless hours playing Solitaire or building card structures on that porch. Another exciting adventure was to go out to the back of the garage where there was a storage room, the "hine room." There was a lot of "hine" stuff in old Georgia. The room was up about four rickety wood steps past the gigantic fig bush on your right that yielded the most delicious figs and the room had a lock on the door that had an "old timey" key. You can barely see the entrance to the "hine room" in the far right of the earlier picture of the totem poles trio. When you opened the door and blast of overheated summer air would roll out in your face. First you would look up to see if there were any wasp nests, then inside, in addition to the chifferobe which I now have in our home, was a treasure trove of board games and old toys that we reveled in hauling into the house to play with. Those antique games and toys would be worth a literal fortune today!

About 12:00, Momma would start getting us excited because Unca' Pete would come home for lunch every day. As soon as we heard the crunching sound as his old Plymouth's tires hit the gravel of the driveway, we would start running around like maniacs trying to find a place to hide from him. Then he would come in the back door with a bang of the screen door. Hopefully we had found a place to hide by then. And we usually did. And each time it was in the same place, Unca' Pete's little closet bathroom and his little two-foot by two-foot shower stall. The two of us would crowd in his little shower and pull the curtain closed. The space was all white porcelain coated metal and smelled of Ivory soap and after shave. Now Unca' Pete could not have been a very smart man because we always hid in the same place, but we would hear him trooping all over the house looking for us. Our excitement level increased as we heard him getting closer and closer. We worked hard to stifle our nervous giggles and laughter. Then suddenly, he would be upon us and sweep the shower curtain back with a single fast swipe and yell, "BOO!" We would scream and almost wet ourselves. It was thrillingly terrifying each and every time we played that game.

7.

This brings me to fall of 1961 and first half of 1962. I was eleven and went into the sixth grade that fall of 1961. Some of the popular music of the period was *Big Bad John*, about a guy who worked in a mine and was sung by Jimmy Dean. Actually it was not so much sung as talked. I guess it was sort of like todays hip hop music, without all the foul language. Jimmy Dean more like just read poetry. Another 1961/62 Jimmy Dean song was *PT 109*. It was about John Kennedy and his exploits in World War II. Kennedy had just been elected in January 1961 and everything was about this new and youthful president. His reinvigoration of the space program by challenging NASA to reach the moon before 1970 had the country breathless. I recall the whole school gathering in the cafeteria on May 5th, 1961, to watch the school's one black and white television as Alan

Shepard launched from Cape Canaveral, soon to be Cape Kennedy and then changed names again back to Cape Canaveral as it is today, rocketed up and was the first American in space. A Russian, Yuri Gagarin, had beaten us into space weeks before, but everyone in the school gathered in the cafeteria and watched the whole thing, liftoff, orbits and reentry. It all lasted about fifteen minutes, and I witnessed a real piece of history.

I guess my life was pretty typical of all white, middle class, preteens in the early 60's. I had chores to do like cut the grass, which would not have been such a horrible job except we had a crappy, vintage 1932, six-ton push mower. None of that fancy motorized stuff for The Colonel as long as he had cheap eleven-year-old labor. Every Saturday it was up at the crack of dawn, quickly eat some breakfast and then outside for yardwork. First up was cut the grass and the rows better be straight or you would do it again. You also had a bag arrangement on the back to catch the clippings. Of course we were always up so early that the grass was still heavy with dew, and it would clump up and jamb the crap mower and get all stuck in everything. Then we had to edge the yard. Again, none of this electrical stuff for The Colonel. It was long stick with a circular blade on the end. You rammed it along the edge of the concrete driveway or curb and then you had to sweep up the remains. This upbringing instilled my love of yardwork which still exists today.

For this and trash removal, and kitchen setting and cleanup duties, which I will detail later, I was paid twenty-five cents a week. So saving up for my hobby of model building when a model cost $1.50 was a laborious and time consuming affair. But I persevered. I recall building a model of the Monitor and the Merrimack. They were motorized, and I would go down to a drainage ditch at the end of Kingsley Street which had not yet joined Nutley Street and float my models in the stagnant water that gathered there. I also got a really cool frogman for Christmas one year. I guess he was my parents nod to my swimming and love of the show *Sea Hunt* with Lloyd Bridges. The frogman was motorized, but I had no place to play with him. He was about eighteen inches long and too big for a tub, too nice for my drainage ditch and too little for the pool. During this period, I continued being into trains, and by that time and had a good collection of Lionel H scale trains. My son James Lyon has them now if he has not sold them. I had a cool train setup in the basement on two saw horses and a four by eight piece of plywood. I had a little pocket-sized book about trains and how to use my paper maché skills to make tunnels. I loved that book. I think I may still have a copy on my basement shelf. I could spend hours in the basement playing with that set up. I had little fake trees and plastic bushes to go along with the electric switches and things I mentioned earlier.

I was also getting into .049 gas powered cars and planes. I had a small, toy go cart and I loved that thing too. It was a control line car. So you would set the fuel supply to about three turns of the fuel supply governor, hook up the big dry cell battery with a clip to the glow plug on the motor. The motor kind of worked like a diesel engine today in that once it is started the glow plug keeps igniting the fuel without having a spark plug like wire or anything. You would then prime the motor by squirting a little fuel into the exhaust port of the motor and then turn the motor over until it caught. As soon as it was running you would pull the battery leads off and thin the fuel mixture to the engine with the governor until the motor hit a clean, high pitched whine. As I write this I can almost smell the delicious odor from the engine's exhaust. You would then hurry to the control line about 50 feet away and release the car. For the next five minutes you would walk in circles as the car zoomed around you. After about six runs you were falling down dizzy.

For fun we whiled away our days playing a mixture of cowboys and World War II with lots of shooting noises and climactic overly dramatic deaths. If we weren't playing with our model cars, my friend Dickey would often play with me along with my little brother Bill (William Cranston Morris) who was seven and a pain. I recall one game of cowboys where we were playing that our guns had been stolen, and we had discovered their hiding place. I grabbed my gun and said, "This is my gun! I know it because it has J.M. on it!" Then Dickey picked up his gun and said a similar thing with his initials D.B. on it. Then Bill picked up his gun and said, "This is my gun! I know it because it has B.M. on it!" Well, this was met with howls of laughter and much rolling around in the grass laughing! Bill didn't get it. We ended up in a tussle and Mom probably had to intervene. Bill and I would tussle constantly, and it was made worse because we had to share a very small front bedroom. If you look at a picture of the 804 Meadow Lane house, our bedroom was the first two windows to the right of the front door. I would also play football with the neighborhood guys. I had several friends. There was Mark and his older brother John. John had failed a grade, so he was in the same grade as Mark and me. There was a guy named Jimmy from the next block down from us. The four of us would also ride our bikes far and wide around Vienna. We would be gone for hours and our parents never seemed to care. "Just be home for dinner." The world was different then.

For our mandatory religious training we went to church at Vienna First Presbyterian Church. The pastor was Reverend Horace Lukens, and there are two things that stand out in my mind. The first was there was no air conditioning in the church, and in the summer it could get miserable. And the second was Reverend Lukens preached the longest sermons of any person ever. They seemed to go on for hours and hours, and when you combined this with youthful energy and no air conditioning, it made you want to stand up and scream. I will talk more about church when we return to Vienna in 1964.

And while we are screaming, I recall our dentist, Dr. Tessatory I believe, who discovered my dental hygiene left a little to be desired as he informed the Colonel and me that I had five cavities. That was painful. Not as painful as sermons with an un-air conditioned Reverend Lukens, but pretty bad none-the-less.

I left Flint Hill Elementary and went to a new school that was just built within walking distance of our house that fall of 1961. It was Marshall Road Elementary. My teacher was one Miss Grove. I was never clear if it was Mrs. Grove or Miss Grove, but she was very mean, so I guess I figured she was not married … or maybe she was married and that made her mean! I remember her as being very fat and having gray hair. Her classroom discipline technique was to grab the offending male student by the hair and shake their head violently. As I have said, it was a different time. I remember the sixth grade having to take a standardized test series. It took about a week or so to get through all the tests and by day four or so I was fed up. So, I just started filling in A, B, C, D, E, then E, D, C, B, A until I had bubbled all the answers. Well, I guess the results came back that I was a moron because this spawned a parent-teacher conference. I never heard any repercussions from this meeting. I guess they all decided I was a moron and just decided to let it go.

I also remember at lunch everyone was served the same thing, and you had to eat everything on your plate before you could get ice cream. This policy was very strictly enforced. You had to bring your tray and plate up to the window, get approval, then go get your ice cream. So on this one day I was served creamed spinach along with other delectable goodies. Well, serving any child creamed spinach that looks like vomit and expecting them to eat is cruel and unusual punishment. And so we all did what all red blooded American boys would do. We found a child who did not want any ice cream. Stupid. Piled all our creamed spinach on his plate. Then we all went to get our ice cream. It must have worked because, again, there were no repercussions that I know of. Of course when that child took his plate to the window there had to be some consternation when they saw this gigantic pile of creamed spinach. To this day I will not eat creamed spinach, but I can choke down some spinach with enough lemon and garlic and butter on it. But speaking of choking stuff down there is one all American drink I have never been able to abide … white milk. The story is that when I came off the bottle, I quit white milk. Chocolate milk is fine. Even strawberry milk is fine. Vanilla milkshakes are fine, but plain white milk … along with its nasty cousin Cottage Cheese … to this day makes me gag.

At recess we would all go out back and play baseball or football or whatever was in season. During baseball season there were always heated discussions about who was better – Mickey Mantle or Roger Maris as they were in a batting contest. I recall one strange day we started to go out to play. Again, it was just us and no teachers when we were suddenly stopped. The playground was closed and all the sixth grade boys were called to the cafeteria. Our principal, a man, addressed us. On the playground someone had found a "rubber." Then he kept talking and said something about a "condom." I did not know if these two things were the same thing or two different things. Well, I do not know about the others, but this made no sense to me. I had no clue what he was even talking about. In my house we had no magazines that even hinted of things sexual. Even that lurid *Life Magazine* was banned, and that titillating *National Geographic* was banned. I had not had "the talk" with The Colonel about "the birds and the bees" so I was totally in the dark. I remember during a gathering of football boys the term "boner" came up. I played along like I knew what was going on, but again I was clueless. Ultimately the Colonel relented and threw a book at me that was supposed to explain everything. It explained nothing. And that book was not tossed at me again until I was in the eighth grade, and by then it was too late. But all the sixth grade boys got a "stern talking to" and then we were dismissed. I never heard any more about that event. I guess it solved itself without my help or input. But then again, who needs the help of a moron?

8.

Okay, I have stalled around long enough. It is time to deal with the most life altering and life shaping event of my life to that point. An event that has colored every relationship I have had since and has had more to do with my overall life philosophy than any event since. In my sixth grade class was a boy, Mike Baber. He had failed a couple of grades, so he was significantly larger than most of us, and he was angry. In my class were my other friends, Mark and Jimmy and John. We also had a Black boy in the room whose name I do not recall, and I would not even recall him at all except Mike picked on him constantly. At recess they would get into vicious fights. Miss Grove would haul them inside than shake their heads. Then they would fight again. This was okay to the rest of us because as long as Mike Baber was beating up on this boy, he was not beating up on any of us, or me in particular. This worked fine until one day, walking home from school, I came into his sights for some reason. It was probably because I was five and a half feet of string bean. I could not have weighed 70 pounds wringing wet. Anyway, he threatened to beat me up. When this happened, all my "friends" fled. Not a single one stood with me. Again in my short life, I was terrified. I managed to get home that day, but I was scared. I waked to school the next day as I always did. Mornings were no problem as we all walked at random times. But in the afternoon we were all released at the same time, so I was an easy target. Well, again, he followed me calling be names like "sissy" and another term I did not understand, "pussy," and my friends fled. I was a pariah. No one wanted to be around me for fear of becoming a target. I stood alone. I wish I could tell you I was brave and fought the bully, but I was not brave. On some mornings I would feign a stomach ache to stay home from school. I could not tell The Colonel. He was an Army man who had fought in Korea, and he was all brave and stuff, and he would not want a crybaby weakling coward for a son. I could not tell my teacher because this happened after school on the way home. She would just shake Mike Baber's head, and then I would get pounded after school. I could not tell my mother. She was pregnant with my third brother and was in danger of losing him and was confined to bed rest and "light duty" as The Colonel would call it. As I saw it, I was alone. One day after school I even tried to become Mike Baber's friend. We went to his house and played some records, and I checked out all his stuff. I recall being late for dinner because I did not want to leave too early and piss him off. I caught the devil for being late, but I did not care because I was trying to survive. And somehow between stomach aches and dodging my way home and trying friendship, I was never beaten up by him. Still, to this day, I have never been in a real fight. I'm not sure if that is a good thing or a bad thing, but I vote for good thing. Fortunately for me, The Colonel was reassigned that summer of 1962. I was able to move away from the problem, but the wounds were deep and lasting.

I believe that one, sixth grade experience has colored my entire life and shaped my personality. Honestly, I think it changed me for the better. So much so that I am considering dedicating this missive to Mr. Mike Baber wherever you are. On the plus side of the damage to my psyche, I tend to fight for the underdog, will not tolerate bullies in any way shape or form including the internet or in a marriage as well as not tolerating bullying either physically or psychologically. I am a champion for any child or person or animal that is downtrodden. I believe this event led me to teaching in elementary school and being a "gentle man." I try to be empathetic and walk in other's shoes when I talk, write or act. I loathe confrontation, although I will engage, especially if I perceive there is an injustice or inequality of power involved. I try to see humor in all events, good or bad. This has made me "Professor Funny Brother" to my siblings as I tried to calm the family waters with humor when a storm blew up. This soft, taking a humorous approach to confrontation, gentlemanly quality makes some people think I am soft or a coward. Nothing is further from the truth. The dark side of the bully event damage to my psyche is my tendency to never forget an intentional or unintentional hurt from another. The result is I can and will seek my revenge if warranted. I have a basic lack of faith in people, but in all honesty a faith in humanity as a whole. I have very, very few real friends and the ones I have, other than my wife and immediate family and one or two others, I hold at arm's length emotionally and mentally. I perceive myself as a good-humored optimist with a touch of realist thrown in for balance. I love to fight for what is good and right and have tendency to tilt at windmills. As I said, I do have faith in humanity, and its inherent goodness. I do believe in Karma. I do believe in God. I am a solitary man, comfortable in my own skin and comfortable being alone with me. To many people I meet, this makes me seem aloof and unapproachable. And that is okay with me as my walls are up all the time and very few are allowed inside … unlike you, who may read this. Honestly, I do not like being emotionally and psychologically naked. I believe inside I am a vulnerable, warm and loving person. So, if you are reading this, "Welcome inside."

9.

We left Vienna and moved to Blue Ridge Summit, Pennsylvania, late in that summer of 1962. By this time my third and last brother, Peter Charles Morris, had been born in June of that year. As The Colonel said, "Pete is the tail gunner." Blue Ridge Summit is so close to the Maryland - Pennsylvania state line I would walk across it to see my only friend, Jessie. We went there so The Colonel could work in the "top secret facility" everyone knew about under a mountain known as *The Rock* near Fort Richie. We lived in an old house on Summit Street. I think the house was an unoccupied manse for the Lutheran Church right next door. It was sort of a Craftsman style house with a lot of stone like the church. It had two stories and a very spooky dug out cellar. My room was a second floor room on the front of the house with two windows. The houses in this town were left over houses from when people would escape the summer heat of Washington for the cool air of the mountains, and it was up … in … the … mountains. Close to nowhere. I guess it was so the "top secret base" would remain a "top secret base."

The nearest town of consequence was the sprawling, wild and wooly town of Waynesboro, and my sister and I were enrolled in Waynesboro Jr. High School. We went there one day to enroll in the school. We parked in front and walked in the main doors with Mom. The school was big and old with high ceilings and transoms over the doors and huge windows. The desks had flip up lids with inkwells! Yes, a hole for the ink bottle to sit in. I did not see the school again until the morning we arrived for

1962 13636 Summit Ave, Blue Ridge Summit, Pennsylvania

the first day of school. The buses let us off at the side of the building. I had no idea where I was. So, I remember running around to the front of the building, lost. My wet eyes had dried by the time me and my little sack lunch arrived at the front of the building, and the only door I knew. Not my best moment or memory. I also recall getting my first F, it was in social studies no less, at this school. I also remember venturing into the sports world at this school, playing intermural basketball before school. I recall a shot I made at the basket and it bouncing off the top of the backboard. All the boys on both teams laughed. I felt humiliated. I have never really participated heavily in any team sport since, and while watching my grandsons play basketball, or anyone play, to this day and if they make an awkward shot my mind goes back, and my heart goes out, and I yell, Good try!" or something to uplift them. Today I realize people make good shots and poor shots everyday … it's called life, and you can probably learn more from the poor shots than the good shots. Another sports memory of that school is learning to climb a rope all the way to the top of the gym some 5,000 feet above the floor. There were no mats below you and if you flagged half way up or fell from half way up, you just died I guess. It was a different time. I did finally make it to the rarified, hot, boy-sweat, filled air at the top of the gym … it smelled like … success. We also had to learn to wrestle. God I hated that. Getting down on the slippery mat and embracing a sweaty guy. God, I really hated that! And when you were done with PE another humiliation awaited you, gang showers. I guess it was a holdover from World War II or something but we HAD to take a communal gang shower after PE. It was horrible, especially when you are twelve. I recall the PE coach admonishing us not to share towels, "Do not share towels!" he would yell. "What is the last thing the guy before you will dry? His ass! What is the first thing you will dry? Your face! So do not share towels." I can hear it in my mind today as clearly as that day. What can I say? A different time?

I also discovered a talent I had. We had shop classes that year. We had wood shop where we all made the requisite bird house taught by the shop teacher who, I'm sure, was missing a few fingers. I think the position of wood shop teacher in all schools has a requirement that you are missing at least one digit. The shop class would rotate from wood shop to electrical shop to mechanical drawing and then, and I am not sure why, music class where I discovered that I could not carry a tune in a bucket; a fact my wife will attest to this day. I also discovered, as I always suspected from model building, that I was one very "handy" guy. I could make my hands do whatever I wanted them to do, and if you showed me something once, I could duplicate it quickly and accurately. If you made me read about it, I would struggle, but eventually I could get it, but tell me or show me a diagram, and I got it immediately. In electrical shop I learned to solder and join wires correctly and make simple repairs. I even made a transistor radio from a kit I bought and would lay in my bed turning the dial and listening for anything and everything. Because we were high up on a mountain I could even pick up WLS in Chicago on that little crystal set. I would lay there and listen to Casey Kasem count down the top ten rock and roll hits of the day. But it was the mechanical drawing shop class that set me on a course to ultimately become an architect. I found I could see things in my brain in three dimensions as clearly as if I was looking at a picture. I could manipulate this object and rotate it and see it in my head from all sides. That year, I began drawing and designing, as well as building, my own balsa boats and airplanes. I actually had a Talent! I *had* been given a Gift, and it would serve me all my life! I was more than just a ping pong ball! I also discovered, and understood, that it was important for a teacher to help a child discover their talents, rather than just humiliate them by finding out how few of the students could actually spell Pennsylvania (I still cannot do it). I discovered that you never knew where, when or how that talent would be discovered. And when a student felt that joy of a "found talent" they would remember you forever and how you made them FEEL, and they would want to discover more about themselves, and they would want to learn more. These revelations also served me later in life when I actually became a fifth grade teacher.

The music at the time was transitioning from Elvis Presley to Chubby Checker and the dance rage was *The Twist*. There was a "sock hop" one night at the school in the gym and I went. I recall this because it was the first time I actually danced with a real girl. I have no idea who she was, but we danced and when we danced I tried to impress her by not doing *The Twist* but more of the classic rock-and-roll jitter bug kind of dance. I do not know if I impressed her or not, but I felt pretty cool so who cares. My favorite singer was Elvis Presley. I have a 45 rpm record of his that I played until the grooves were almost worn off. It has *Hound Dog* on one side and *Don't Be Cruel* on the flip side. It is somewhere in my stuff. I had it framed and hanging in my fifth grade classroom for twenty-five years. It is the real thing. Re's favorite person was Pat Boone, and I would have to let her use the record player so she could listen to that fop sing *Love Letters in The Sand*. Gag. And my younger brother, Bill, who was becoming less and less of a ping pong ball of course needed a singing idol like Re and me. The Colonel gave him Tennessee Ernie Ford. Ha!

10.

October 1962, Blue Ridge Summit, PA – William Cranston Morris in center. From lower left and clockwise: Mary Corinne Wofford Morris (Mom) with Brian Meroney Morris in her lap, Col James Wingfield Morris, his mother – Marie Louise Williams Morris, James Wingfield Morris Jr (me), Nelson Kimball Rogers (Unca' Nelson), Marian Louise Morris Rogers (Aunt Toochie)

I was becoming a rebel and a real, honest to goodness, bad boy. I smoked my first cigarette that year. I was tasked with taking the trash out, so I pilfered one of the Colonel's Salem cigarettes and a match and lit up out by the trash cans. I think Re saw me but I do not think she ratted me out. I also recall being hungry all the time. I could never get enough to eat. This probably had to do with puberty, but we did not eat until the Colonel got home and that was about 7:00. Now in this little town there was no mail delivery to your house. You had a post office box in the post office/drug store/lunch counter/sundry grocery store building across the street from the house. And I would often go over there and buy a whole bag of Cheetos or something and sneak them into the cellar and hide them, so I could eat them whenever I wanted. I also would go over there to the lunch counter and order a bowl of chili that I would eat with lots of crackers. The crackers were free if you got the chili. To fund this, I recall pilfering $20.00 from my mom's wallet once. To this day I am ashamed of doing this, but I did it. And a few years ago I actually paid that $20.00 back to The Colonel although I do not think he understood why. There is a limit to my honesty I guess. In the general store there was a rack with magazines on it and some of the magazines were *True Detective* and *Real Men* type magazines with scantily-clad buxom women in compromising situations on the covers. These women were often wearing stockings and garter belts and high heels, and I recall looking at these covers and feeling strange stirrings I did not understand. But the images of these women in stockings still haunt me. I could go into more detail about these covers, but I think you have gotten the drift. I guess "As the twig is bent, so grows the tree." Also, during this time I was given a BB gun. It gave me a feeling of great power and brought me great misery. I killed a bird. I did not accidently shoot a bird. I purposely shot that bird, and I was a dead aim. It almost killed me. I also recall The Colonel being confronted by the church that someone was shooting BB holes in their windows. When The Colonel confronted me, I said I did not do it. And I did not do it on purpose, but I suspect that I was the only one for miles around that had a BB gun and that some of my errant shooting probably did that damage. I put The Colonel through hell being his son. I recall The Colonel's younger sister, Toochie, and her husband Unca' Nelson and their Momma coming to visit for the fourth of July, and I made fireworks from saltpeter, charcoal and sugar. Nobody lost fingers or a hand that day. I recall being a bad boy in school also. We were to write a story for English class. I guess it could be about anything because I chose to take one of my comics about war and copy the story from the comic to be my story. It was plagiarism in its finest form. I copied all the quotes and everything. It was quite challenging actually as I had to write the story without any of the pictures. It was sort of like trying to make a screenplay for a novel. I think that paper is in my trunk somewhere. Yes, I was not a ping pong ball any longer, I was a full-fledged bad boy.

Numbers are interesting to me and particularly averaging and its parallel to life. When you add several smaller numbers together, say 4, 5 and 6, and divide by the total number of numbers, 3, it results in an average of 5 … no big deal. But if you take these same 4, 5 and 6, and you throw in one number, a little larger, not huge but larger, like 20, the average radically changes to 8.75. It almost doubles the average. But when you have say 10 numbers and you total them and they total say 100 and then divide by this larger number of numbers the average is 10. But if you then add 25 into the total of 100 and divide by 11, the average changes to 11.36. Not a big change from 10 at all. All of this math is to awkwardly say, when you are young you are more radically shaped by events than when you are older. In your youth, smaller events seem to hold more consequence, and while we were in Blue Ridge Summit, BRS, I had several unique and life altering events.

BRS was a small burg and there were not many boys my age, but I mentioned there was one boy named Jessie. He apparently did not have a last name, poor child, but he and I would pal around the town on our bikes and sniff out ways to get in trouble. A unique part of this little town was that a full-fledged railroad went right through town maybe 100 yards from our house. And it is weirdly true, after a while you do not even hear the train or its whistle. Well Jessie, who lived on the Maryland side of the tracks, and I, on the Pennsylvania side – we must not have even gone to the same school – would get together and go over by the little library which was a converted train station and put pennies on the tracks for trains to smash. I know this does not sound like a big deal, but when you think about two twelve year olds hanging around train tracks where fully loaded massive multiple locomotive driven trains would plow through dragging thousands of tons of freight cars at unreasonable speeds, there is a possibility of a mishap. But I digress. Our favorite sport was putting those pennies on the tracks and letting the trains smash them flat. One early fall afternoon Jessie and I decided we needed a fix, so we headed for the library. The leaves had just started to change, and I recall I had on a light jacket. We walked around the large veranda covered porch on the library to the train track side our pockets jingling with pennies and a quarter or two. We looked both ways like we were crossing the street and then jumped down to the granite rocks on the track bed and inched over to the rails. I recall our biggest concern was what if our coins somehow derailed the train? Of course even this biggest concern could not dissuade two preteen boys from their appointed duty. We inched up to the rail and laid a have dozen pennies and a quarter on the track. The train only got one quarter as that was the price of a comic book, and so it was very valuable. After placing our bootie, we climbed back up onto the porch and waited. The air was cool with the promise of an even cooler evening to come. A breeze rustled the crisping autumn leaves and then, as if carried with the air, came a train whistle, deep and mournful. Soon, lumbering up the tracks with three diesel electric locomotives pulling her was our prize. The train whistle blasted again as it approached the road crossing, and we stood on the edge of the platform as people had done in this little town for a hundred years. As the big square fronted behemoth evened itself with us, the engineer saw us pumping our scrawny arms in the air and laid down on the horn again. The locomotive's scream shattered us. All we could do is hold our hands over our ears and cringe and yell as we felt the air being pushed in front of the engine hit us, and then the overwhelmingly delicious smell of diesel exhaust enveloping us in it delightful cloud. The locomotives pounded past and the comparative quiet of the box cars and gravel cars and tanker cars with their myriad of painted scrawls on them rolled past us two prepubescent wanna-be bad boys. We had succeeded and had not caused a horrible wreck that afternoon, a double win. As the red caboose signaled the end, we jumped off the landing to recover our bootie. The vacuum wind of the train had not even subsided, and we were already scrabbling around in the rocks looking for the coins. The air blast of the engines and subsequent cars always blew the coins all over the place, so we had to be treasure hunters and look carefully to locate all our ill-gotten gains. Those flattened coins we worked so hard for were just the same as the coins my grandchildren want to make when we visit museums in Birmingham and up at Allatoona Lake overlook by just inserting the coins and cranking a handle. My old way was much better. So, if you have boys who are barely able to think two cohesive thoughts, pennies, and put all that in proximity to lumbering, several ton locomotives that could not stop if they wanted to, you have not only a recipe for disaster but great boy fun too! What could go wrong? We spent hours and wasted thousands of dollars of our meager money on those tracks. Yes, it was Great Boy Fun.

I also recall that Jessie had a go cart, and we would drive that thing all over the place. We did this without helmets or any protective gear of course. Heck, this was before there were even seat belts in cars, and both sets of parental units would admonish us to "not drive in the street!" But of course, we did … there were no sidewalks in BRS. One afternoon after driving it especially hard we needed to turn it around, so I grabbed the back bumper to pick it up. As I did, my left forearm touched the exhaust pipe. The exhaust pipe was about two inches in diameter with small 1/8th inch diameter holes in it and it was red hot. As I lifted the cart, my left forearm touched the pipe, and I got my first real scar. I was neatly branded by the pipe, and to this day if you know what you are looking for, you can still see my go cart brand.

Earlier I mentioned a boy's predilection for fire, and I was no different from all other boys until one night coming home from the movies with Jessie. he and I were coming home from the movies over at Fort Richie one night. Because The Colonel was The Colonel, I could take my friends on to the sacred grounds of "The Base." It was too far to walk to the Base from our houses, so someone had to have driven us. But we were coming home from watching one of the greatest movies ever. This time, 1962/63 was a golden age in Hollywood for boys. We would watch such greats as *633 Squadron*, *Dam Busters*, *Sink the Bismarck* (which I would use in my classroom as a teacher a hundred years later) and *Reptilicus*. But this particular evening we were returning home from the screening of that screenland epic, *The Day of the Triffids*. Now if you have not seen this particular sci-fi epic, you need to indulge yourself. It was particularly horrifying to two twelve year olds. And on the way home, as we neared our houses there was a faint glow in the distance. The closer we got, the larger the glow became until we passed one of the grand old wooden homes this area was known for, and it was on fire. We drove past. The volunteer firemen were not even here yet. When we got home we begged Jessie's parent to let us walk back up as see the fire. Jessie's dad agreed and came with us. His mother begged off. I guess true pyromania only flows in the veins of males. When we got up the road again closer to the house, we could feel the heat in the cool evening air radiating off the structure. A crowd was gathering now. I could hear the wale of sirens in the distance. Even to my young eyes I could see a fire truck was going to be useless. The three story house was now fully involved and a monster was eating it alive. There was a seething noise coming from the fire. It sounded like that train engine, lumbering and powerful sucking air and pluming exhaust. The fire was so huge it was causing its own wind as it breathed in from all around it. Trees swayed and sparks flew upward in a blast of smoke. I stood transfixed. I stood marked. When the firemen finally got setup all they could do is try not to let the fire spread to what nearby trees had not already been consumed and any nearby buildings. The stately home fell into itself in a shower of sparks. As the fire started to subside, and we turned to leave, I was a changed boy. The fire had seared my soul. I hoped no one died. There would be no more playing with matches in basement of Momma's house in the Georgia hometown. There would be no more fascination with

Unca' Pete lighting the grill. My pyromaniac tendencies had been scorched out of me that night in that flaming pyre. It truly is an ill wind that does not blow some good.

11.

I did visit that library every once and a while when I absolutely had too. Sometimes my schoolwork actually required I do some real work. My passion became centered around one book in particular, *The American Heritage Picture history of the Civil War*, copyright 1960. I have a copy of it on my bookshelf right behind me as I write this. I think I was the only person to check this massive book out. I would trundle into the library, locate my book, take it up to the librarian, and present my library card. She would take the book and my card. Opening the book to the back, she would take the identifying card from the book. She would then take a blank 3x5 card and stamp it with the return date and place it in the little card holder slot in the back of the book. Then she would hand me the book and my library card. Very old school, I know. The thing I loved about this book were the maps of the battles. They were more than just dry little maps. They were artist's color drawings of the battles with little men and cannons and explosions and horses and made the battle come alive in my brain. Given my talent with my hands and my rapidly developing visualization skills, I loved to create three dimensional dioramas of the scenes. Pair this book with a Christmas present of a Civil War Set complete with little blue and gray soldiers, cannon and caissons, horses and mortars and I would play for hours setting up mock battles. Then I would retire to a distance away and pick off soldiers from each side with my BB gun. I would shoot blue or gray soldiers. I was an equal opportunity havoc wreaker. But as I said I actually used the library for real school work when forced. I recall an assignment to draw a paramecium for biology. I had to go and actually do some real work in the library as the only book that had a drawing of this microscopic animal was in such high demand, they would not check it out to anyone, even their most devoted Civil War buff. So, I sat there and labored under the high fluorescent fixtures with trains shaking my desk as they went by, to copy this thing on my wide lined, three-hole notebook paper. I guess I did a credible job. I do not recall even getting a grade, but I do remember one particular Friday afternoon though.

The Biology classroom we were in had lab tables, and I sat at a table with three others. I was a middle sitter. The class was unusually unruly that afternoon, but it did not bother me. Suddenly in the middle of class a gigantic tired came over me. Such a gigantic tired that I put my head down on my folded arms on the lab table and went to sleep, complete with drool on the table and everything. I was awakened by the teacher announcing that the whole class except Jimmy Morris had extra homework because of all the bad behavior. That was okay with me, but I really could have cared less. Somehow, and I honestly do not remember how, I made it home. I went up to my room and fell into my wonderful bed and dropped immediately into a deep, exhausted sleep. I have no idea how long I slept. I recall Mom checking on me. I recall a doctor coming to my room. I recall being very hot and then almost immediately being very cold. When I awoke, some three days later as I came to find out, I had contracted Scarlett Fever from somewhere. Many of my classmates caught it too. I was quarantined for a week before I could return to school. That was the scariest disease I have had in my life, but I did get some good rest.

Around my birthday in 1962, the world decided to have an adventure. It seems the ultimate Halloween scare was taking place in the Caribbean. We were all going to die, and I was only turning twelve. It seems that Premier Khrushchev of what was then the USSR, the Union of Soviet Socialist Republics, now Russia, decided that putting medium range missiles in Cuba was a good idea. After all the United States had the same kind of missiles in Turkey and Europe all aimed at him. So, working with Fidel Castro who had taken over the island in the 50's from a man named Batista, Khrushchev started shipping the missiles into the communist controlled island. Our government got wind of this by flying U2 aircraft over Cuba and taking pictures of what was going on. When confronted, Khrushchev was silent and so The Cuban Missile Crisis was underway. I actually have very little direct memory of it personally affecting me other than we had to do a lot of duck and cover drills at school so we would be protected from a nuclear blast. Ha! After all it was my birthday and still, as a pending twelve years old, the world was still pretty much all about me, but I do recall that The Colonel was not around much. He was spending all his time inside The Rock, because if we were all going to be incinerated in nuclear war we wanted our nation to be able to retaliate and vaporize the other guys, too. I know my

mother was not a happy lady during this. She was alone at home with a studious 13-year-old girl, a 12-year-old bad boy wanna-be, an 8-year-old dufus, an 18-month old ping pong ball and a 4-month old blob, our brood … or were we a small third world nation? I was never sure. I recall there was a lot of news broadcast television interruptions as I was trying to watch my favorite show *Bonanza*. It was very aggravating. I would like to tell you that I was hanging on every broadcast to see if I was going to live or die, but I was not paying any attention, and I am not going to recount for you the blow by blow history of that very tense week on the world stage. You can look it up. It was about to be my twelfth birthday, and all I cared about was what was I going get. Interesting, to this day I do not recall what I got, but I do vividly recall the tension I felt in our little house on the mountain in Pennsylvania (which I still cannot spell).

Fort Richie did have one thing going for it besides the only movie theater this side of Waynesboro, a lake. There was an officer's club overlooking the lake and we used to get a really great ribeye sandwich there on the rare occasion that Mom revolted and got fed up cooking for her swarm. The lake was a medium size affair, not huge. I mean you could not throw a rock across it, but you could easily ice skate across it. And that brings up the fact that I was the world's worst ice skater. I used to ice skate there, mostly on my ankles.

I just could not keep my ankles standing up straight. My sister Re did not seem to have any problem gliding along in her white skates, but me my manly brown skates was a different story. When I was done skating the ankle part of my skate's boot was all scraped and the leather all torn and scuffed. There was no danger of my skate's blades wearing out in this millennium. The boot part? Another story. But the lake was not always frozen and I remember making a model of a motorized tug boat and taking it to the lake to run it. It would have been a good lake for a frogman, but he was long gone. I recall it was a warm day, but I was still wearing a wind breaker, and I had my boat carefully cradled in my arms. It was maybe eight inches long. She was a beaut! Normally, I would slap my models together as quickly as I could. Slap some paint on them and some decals and call it done. Can you say ADHD? But it seems I took my time with this boat. I guess I knew she was really going to sail, so I wanted her sea worthy. She was a fine craft, the day was bright and as the writers say, "full of promise." I edged down past the dock to the water's edge. I leaned over and tested the motor. She revved up fine. I set the rudder at an angle so my tug would not just run away. I was very smart. Then I gently laid her into the lake. She took off in fine style. I watched her bobbing in the ripples of the lake, and she even cut a little wake as she hummed along. My mind's eye saw a powerful tug boat puffing out diesel smoke as it headed out to shepherd a wayward bulk carrier to her berth after a long transatlantic voyage. My tug hummed a perfect circle and came right back to me. I did have a little concern that the tug's freeboard was awfully small, but she was a sturdy craft and made with care. She had new batteries, a fair weather day and a fine skipper. I adjusted her rudder for a slightly larger circle, fired up her motor and set her on her way. She steamed proudly out into the lake in a much larger arc. Was the rudder set for too wide a circle? Was she too far out in these hostile waters? As it turned out she was set perfectly and sailed in a wide circle and almost returned to the exact spot on the lake where I had set her. I gathered her up. Turned off her motor, took her home and relegated her to the trash heap of discarded toys that every middle class, first-world boy of twelve had at that time.

12.

In 1963 we moved to Carlisle Barracks, Pennsylvania, so the Colonel could attend the Army War College. For me this year was twelve years old to thirteen years old, and if I were title this section I would title it "The Awakening." We lived in a little house on a corner. I have no address, the Colonel could not shed any light and Google Earth did not help me find the house by simply looking. I also cannot tell you the name of my school. I do recall it was a two to three story older brick building in the town of Carlisle. None of the current Junior High Schools in the area are old enough to be the school, so my guess is the city built new schools and decommissioned my older school. I do recall being made to take a religion class by my parents. No doubt they could see trouble looming so pushing me toward the priesthood seemed a good idea. I am just kidding, but I remember I did not want to take the class which was off campus in a church nearby. I walked there. I do remember at least one other poor wayward bad boy who was made to take the class. We walked together in glum silence in the sun, the rain and the snow to the class so our souls would be saved. It did not work, but you are shaped by all your experiences.

13.

This Carlisle period in my life marks the closest The Colonel and I ever came in our relationship, and there were a couple of events that brought us together. The most exciting adventure was the Carlisle Junior League Gun Club. The Colonel and I, and my little brother Bill I think, would go to the shooting range, and we young men were instructed in the art of firing a rifle. In our case it was a 22 rifle. We were taught in the prone position, the sitting position and standing. We fired at targets that were fifty feet away. We were taught how to shoot, and then we would compete with other gun clubs and earn certificates and medals. As it turns out, I was pretty good at shooting. I even won some matches, got some medals and actually felt again that there was something I was good at. I even think The Colonel was a little proud, but he would never say it. Also, he and I took a couple of trips together. A trip we took as just the two of us was to Antietam battlefield. I do not remember anything about the trip other than the fact that we went. And, as part of big group from the Colonel's War College we went on a big bus to Gettysburg battlefield. It is interesting, again, that I do not remember anything about the trip other than the big bus and the fact that the Colonel would not buy me a $10.00 Confederate Stars and Bars flag as a souvenir. Today I understand that event better. He was in the U.S. Army. The Confederate flag stood for people who fought against the United States. The flag represented traitors to him. To me, it was just cool. I wish he had seen the event as a teachable moment. He did not. So again, my recollection of the day centers around: "It's not what you say; it is how you make someone feel."

14.

I titled this section "The Awakening." The awakening is my sexual awakening. This awakening, when I was twelve/thirteen, would alternately haunt and fascinate me and follow me for the rest of my life. In retrospect I can say I am and always have been a very sexual being. From the first moment that I discovered there was a difference in male and female, I have been entranced by women. I believe now, and was totally ignorant then, that females are smarter, stronger, more empathetic, can endure more pain and are generally just better than males. I often joke that it is obvious that God made men first, worked out the bugs, and then created women. Women are Human Beings 2.0. This was also when the Colonel again threw a book at me about "The Birds and the Bees" and basically said, "Good Luck." Such was the sex education in my house. As I mentioned those two racy magazines *National Geographic* and *Life* were taboo in my house. Frankly, I am absolutely amazed I have any brothers and sisters. Heck, I am amazed I am even here such was the nature of sex talk in my household. I got my entire education on the street so to speak, not that I am complaining. I am a little amazed, and thankful, that there were no accidental pregnancies given the lack of information I received.

So, now the door is opened, and I will speak to my sexuality through this narrative. I have wrestled with how to handle this aspect of my biography, and I have decided that gentlemen are discrete about their encounters, and I will do my best to help you understand how I was shaped by my sexuality without being too embarrassing to myself or the ladies I was lucky enough to be allowed to share a learning experience. Launching into this period I want to tell you about my first "girlfriend," Dawn. I recall that The Four Seasons had a song that came out that year named *Dawn* and it was "our song." Dawn lived across the street from me. I do not recall anything about her as far as looks. I do recall that we went to the post theater to see a movie once. I cannot tell you the name of the movie, but I do distinctly recall being terrified to take her hand. I literally could not bring myself to take such an overt sexual act. So, I promised myself the next time one of the actors said the word "the," I would take her hand. And by all the saints in the next line one of them said "the," and I grabbed her hand. I probably terrified her the way I jerked for her hand, but I had it! Mission accomplished!

Now in the world of "Bases," holding a girl's hand does not even count as a base. So to my recollection, Dawn and I never even played baseball. However, there was a young lady who lived up the street. I do not even recall her name or age … I believe she was older … but I do recall she was well endowed. She expanded my mind and helped me along to second base. I was now officially hooked on women, or at least girls at this point in my life. Now, if you combine this ravenous need for knowledge with a livestock yard not far from our house and several adventurous friends in the same predicament education wise as me, you have an interesting combination.

My three friends and I headed out on our bikes on a chilly Saturday morning just being boys when we discovered the Carlisle Livestock Yards. It was an eye-opening and enlightening experience. There were cows and chickens and goats and all manner of livestock being herded into an arena, and people were bidding and buying them. There was no one at the gate or any reason to stop us, so we sauntered in and found a bench to sit on out of the way. It was a small arena with the animals being brought in on one side and led out the other. There were all of these farmer types, mostly men, and an auctioneer would babble his auctioneer babble, and men occasionally would raise their hands and then a gavel would bang and that cow or whatever would be removed and another animal brought in. Now we had no idea what the auctioneer's string of words meant so we agreed the best course of action was to keep our hands down and mouths shut, but we found this dusty, earthy, smoke-filled showcase to be fascinating. We were brought up about as far away from this atmosphere as a boy could be, so, all these men, smoking and cursing and some taking drinks from brown paper sacks was a new world and better than any movie we had ever seen. We sat there for hours as animals of all ilk's were brought in and out. We whispered our speculations about where they were going and what would happen to them. Then the biggest bull we had ever seen was led into the arena. A man with a rope and another man with a long pole attached to a collar around his huge neck lead him in. He was the biggest and most fearsome brute of a cow we had ever seen and his privates were humongous which elicited much excited comment from us. After several hours the overall general novelty wore off, and we tired of the smell and the smoke and headed out to our bikes. On the way loud squealing caught our attention, and we sidled over to a pen to take a look at what all the commotion was about. Well, all the commotion was the most vivid sex-ed lesson of our young lives. There in the pen were boy hogs and girl pigs and the boy hogs were bound and determined to have their way with the girl pigs. And several did. And the four of us were educated. The light bulb went off. Now, we all looked at each other like this was totally expected and that this was nothing new to us, but nothing could have been further from the truth for this thirteen-year-old. Perhaps the other guys had had those torrid *Life* magazines and *National Geographic* magazines lying willy-nilly around their houses where they could get a liberal dose of sex education, or perhaps their fathers had taken some time and really discussed the facts of life instead of just throwing some lame book in the room and then running for the hills, but not this city boy. And what I saw explained 95% of what I needed to know. Oh, there were finer points yet to be understood, but I had the basics. And it was terrifyingly enlightening.

On another warm spring morning, the four of us set out on a bicycle expedition to a nearby town. We were headed about eight miles to the east northeast to a town one of the other boys had discovered on a map. The name of the town was Middlesex, and you can guess why the four amigos were going there. We were going there to see why anyone would name their town Middlesex. We did not get started until around 10:00. The plan was to leave earlier when it was still cool, but one of the guys had a flat tire, so we had to wait around while his older brother patched the tire and got it pumped up again. But with cards clipped to our fender struts with clothespins so they would click against the spokes, we headed out; a vicious motorcycle gang on the hunt for people who were of the middle sex variety … whatever that was. It was about five miles as I recollect, and we made good time traveling up Route 11. We stuck to the gravelly shoulder of the road and rolled into town about 11:00. What we found was very deflating. It looked like any other small burg just off the interstate. We stopped at a 7-11 and fueled up on chips and jerky and soft drinks. I think I had a Nehi Orange soda in a tall glass bottle pulled from a big metal cooler with an ice bath in it and a sign on the side the outside touting Coca-Cola. You had to put your quarter in a slot inside the cooler and then travel your bottle by holding the neck of it down a slot in a rail to the end where you could release it by pulling up. Then you used the bottle opener on the side of the machine to pop the metal cap off which dropped into a container on the side of the cooler. It was all very slick and unheard of today. But perhaps one of the coolest parts of the day was when we finished our drinks and wholesome lunch, we took the bottles to the man inside the store, and he gave each of us 2 cents back, a deposit on the bottles. Can you say "recycle." All and all it was shaping up to be a good day, but we had seen what we came here to see, and it was pushing 12:30. We had already been here through lunch. I do not remember informing my parents we were going, and I do not remember them being upset because I missed lunch. But, as I have said, it was a different time. I do not recall the rest of the day. I assume we got home because I am writing this today. The whole day was very anticlimactic, except for the Nehi Orange soda machine.

I have a scar on my left shin. Hardly noticeable today at 70+, but it is still there. I'll show you if you want. Carlisle Barracks had a huge parade field. It was a famous field because when the Carlisle Indian School had been there a very famous Olympic athlete, Jim Thorpe, had played ball there. Overlooking the parade field were grandstands and they were a perfect place for boys to run and play. These were substantial affairs, huge and concrete and unforgiving if you fell. And I did. One hot July afternoon I was running up those grandstands with friends of mine, and I missed a step and went down on my shin. There was a piece of gravel. It was maybe the size of a pea right on the edge of the step and my shin met that pea gravel, and it was lodged in my leg. Your shin does not have a lot of padding. It is pretty much just skin covering and bone, but that darn piece of gravel jammed itself in there and stuck. I sat down on that step and just picked it out and then the blood started. I bled like a stuck pig … all down my shin, into my sock and shoe. It must have hurt, but I do not recall that. I made my way home and my mother got me cleaned up, mercurochrome was applied … brain damage again. Again, I guess between all the mercurochrome I was subjected to and playing with broken thermometers in Pa's office I have good excuse to be the way I am. A Band-Aid was applied to my leg, and I was sent back out into the world to play until dinner time. Things were different then.

During this time my brother Bill and I shared a bedroom upstairs in the highest part of the house. Our bedroom was up in the rafters and our room had knee walls with storage in the wings. One afternoon I went into the storage area to get my baseball glove from a box of sports junk. While the door was open, our pet cat, Candy, got in the attic, and I had to get her out. I had adopted the title of unofficial caretaker of Candy … even her litter box was in my room. I guess my parents felt the room could not really smell any worse what with two boys in there already. I had been feeding and generally taking care of her since we got her in Vienna a few years before. For all intents and purposes, Candy was "my" cat. While getting the cat out of the attic, I stumbled on an Army trunk filled with girl's and women's winter clothes in it. Now, reflecting back, at this point I would call myself in either an almost full blown puberty phase or a full blown puberty phase of "The Awakening." At any rate, standing there in the too warm uninsulated wing of the house, beads of sweat popping out on my forehead, looking into that trunk I had opened full of girl's and women's clothes caused a stirring I had not felt since the second base experience. I reached into this conglomeration of silks and satins and crinolines and nylons and moved my hand across them. I was immediately entranced. At least I was entranced until I heard The Colonel call me from the yard down below. I distinctly remember immediately feeling embarrassed, like I had committed some terrible wrong. I had trespassed into a world of girl's and women's undergarments and clothes where I had no business … and I would never be the same.

Outside the house was the same old thing. Cut the grass with that same old, difficult, heavy @#%#@& push mower and wash and wax cars. Now it was not just cutting the grass with this stupid push mower that was a pain, but we still had to collect the clippings in this basket affair that was on the back of the mower. And as I mentioned the cut lines had better be straight, and do not miss any grass or you could bet you would be doing it over. And we lived on a corner lot! Now I was the oldest son. Bill and the others were too young at this point to cut grass or do much of anything so I got all The Colonel's jobs: grass cutting, raking, edging, cars, KP duty. It was great fun. All this still for 25 cents a week, but I do recall having an epiphany one afternoon. I discovered that if you did your absolute best at whatever job The Colonel tasked you with, it would mean several things. First, you would not have to redo the task which would have taken even more of your valuable time away from playing football or baseball or war or whatever with your friends. Second, it would confound and confuse The Colonel who would not know what to say if he could not criticize you and that was mystifyingly satisfying in itself. And third, you found you actually felt good about yourself. So I guess this revelation combined with my Presbyterian upbringing and all those religious classes I had to take was having some effect on me. I guess I was what you could call "learning."

15.

Carlisle also had one of those moments in time that is seared into my memory. One of those moments that is so profound and overwhelming that you can literally see the moment in your mind even to this day. Such was this moment. I was in English class. My desk was against the wall on my left side. The classroom had very high ceilings as the building was quite old. From my desk I could look across the five rows of desks to the tall casement windows. I recall leaves of various reds and yellows, some falling in a gentle late autumn breeze that promised winter. They almost looked like huge snowflakes that would soon take their place in this middle Pennsylvania town. I cannot really recall what inane topic the teacher was droning on about, maybe sentence diagramming, because whatever the subject was, it was swallowed up by the announcement on the school intercom speaker located high on the wall above me. In the morning when the announcements came on, there was a crackle of static that always preceded the principal and his Pledge of Allegiance followed by the Lord's Prayer (it was a different time) followed by the National Anthem. The teacher stopped teaching at the first burst of static. We all turned our attention to the box, thankful for whatever interruption to the lesson at hand was about to be shared. "Teachers and students, I am sorry for the interruption, but I wanted to inform you that President John F. Kennedy was shot this afternoon in Dallas Texas. He is dead. He died of his wounds at about 1:00 Central Standard Time. We will have standard school dismissal this afternoon, and I will be back at 3:00 with any updates and the afternoon announcements. I am sorry. Thank you." It was Friday, November 22nd, 1963. It was about 2:20. That is where my vivid memory stops. I do not recall my last period class or going home or anything much beyond shock. This event was bigger than Mike Baber, bigger than the house fire, bigger than the Cuban Missile Crisis. This was the first event in my young life big enough to shake the foundations of my world and make me question the sanity of man, although it was not to be the last. As the weather promised, we had our first dusting of snow the next day, Saturday, and the nation and the world went about business in a daze. I recall that my sister Re was struck hard by the tragedy, but we did not talk about it. Re's and my relationship was not at that point yet, nor would it be for about six or seven more years, but I do recall she was shaken. The news coverage of the event was pretty much the only thing on the television on the three channels. The assassin, one Lee Harvey Oswald, had been apprehended and was being held in jail in Dallas. Under a sun drenched Dallas sky, there were pictures of the casket being loaded on Air Force One and a picture inside the plane of Lyndon B. Johnson being sworn in as president with the late president's wife Jackie Kennedy at his side, her pink outfit still having blood spatters on it. Pictures that are now iconic and burned into the public memory.

Sunday morning came. The snow had stopped. The dusting melted under the late, fickle November sun. All of us "troops" were up early as per standard Sunday protocol. The Colonel was the cook on Sunday mornings, and he prepared his usual Sunday morning breakfast of bacon, cold toast and too dry scrambled eggs. We choked it down, and Re and I cleaned up the kitchen. I had already dressed for Sunday School and church, so I settled down in front of the television to wait on the others. I was sitting on an overstuffed ottoman we had. It had a heavy paisley brocade design that matched the two equally overstuffed rocking chairs adjacent to it. The news coverage was of Lee Harvey Oswald being transferred from one jail to another jail. It was live coverage as the two overweight Dallas policemen, both in suits and one on each side of Oswald, brought him out in front of the cameras into what seemed to me to be a too crowded area of the police station basement. As Oswald came into full view, and I was looking for the first time at the real, live man who had shot Kennedy, a man stepped forward, his back to the camera, and fired two or three shots into Oswald. Oswald crumpled down in the arms of the police. Others grabbed the man who had shot Oswald, Jack Ruby. I sat there slack-jawed. Stunned. But interestingly this event was not nearly so shattering to me as the original assassination news. I guess my psyche had already been desensitized by Friday's terrifying event, but I jumped up none-the-less and ran sounding the alarm to the rest of the house. I have no strong recollections of the next few days. We had school on Monday and Tuesday and then we were out for Thanksgiving. It was a somber Thanksgiving. There was a funeral procession somewhere in there. A caisson and a horse with a backward boot as JFK was taken to Arlington Cemetery. John-John saluted. I was very sad for him and his sister. Some of my youthful joy and faith in the world was stripped away that week. But I bounced back quickly because my place in the family was to be the one who lightened all situations, the jokester, the nothing-really-matters child, in other words – the classic I don't give a shit, spendthrift second child.

16.

Let me add in closing our year in Carlisle that my only other recollection of this time is my brother Brian, who we called Rusty because of his red hair. There were swings outside our house in the back yard. There were Army post installed big swings, not some little piddling swing set. These were real honkers, and you could really catch some serious air on them. Under the swings was just barren packed earth with small exposed dirt clods and gravel. Rusty wanted to swing and he wanted me to push him. At this time, I am thirteen and he is maybe three, so he is this little guy and way too small for these swings. These swings did not have any little kid safety swing seats like they would today. All they had was just plain old wooden, splintery seats. I got him up on the swing and started swinging him gently. I was not a complete idiot. "Higher, Jimbo!" So, I pushed him higher. "Higher, Jimbo!" as he giggled a three-year old's laugh. And so I pushed him what turned out to be one last time that afternoon. As he came back down from the push, back toward me he slipped out of the swing and went face first onto the hard packed ground. He busted his mouth something fierce and it was a bloody mess. Well, I scooped him up and hauled him to the house where my mother screamed at me, "What happened?" as Rusty bled all over the kitchen. As he was healing he looked like a little Quasimodo without the hump, but I felt terrible none-the-less. My brother was hurt on my watch and under my care. That would never happen again.

17.

In the summer of '64 we moved back to Cartersville, Georgia, my small southern hometown. This period of my life was from summer 1964 to October of 1965. I was thirteen years old and turned fourteen that October of 1964. We moved into a little house at 401 West Avenue. We came back because the Colonel had pulled what the Army called a "hardship tour" to Korea. That meant no family allowed to go. And so we headed home to the small southern hometown where I was born and some family still lived. We moved into a rented

house at 401 West Avenue, and Re and I enrolled at Cartersville High School. It was my freshman year of high school.

While I had spent several summers in this town, you never really know a town until you live there. Again, my Aunt Doris and Uncle Bill lived in town as well as Aunt Toochie and Uncle Nelson and my paternal grandmother, Momma and her husband Unca' Pete. We settled in during that summer, and we headed off to school in the fall. I got to know several guys and a couple of girls: Tommy, Button, Gary, Rhett, Margaret Rose, Laura, Lamar, Bill, Judy including some junior class ladies: Linda, Susan, Janet. Some of those names will come up in the following stories.

I recall that on October 17th of 1964 the Colonel's father, Unca' Pete, passed away from heart failure. This was not a huge surprise as one thing he was noted for was his smoking cigars. He always was smoking a cigar, and if he was not smoking it, he was chewing on the nasty end of it. At any rate, he died. The Colonel came home from Korea, and there was a funeral. Again for some reason, I do not recall much about that. I do know I was a totally self-involved teenager because the only two things I remember about that October/November are the Sadie Hawkins Dance and getting a .049 gas powered, U-control line airplane for my birthday.

18.

The Sadie Hawkins Dance was a dance named after the *Lil' Abner* cartoon strip character Sadie Hawkins. She must have been very forward because the premise of the dance is that the ladies invite the gentlemen. And Margaret Rose asked me. The way it took place is I got a call one evening at Momma's house on her new phone. It was her new phone because up until about 1955, she did not have one in the house. So, ever since 1955 the house phone was referred to as "the new phone." At any rate, Margaret Rose called me there and asked me to the dance. We must have talked for a long time, with a lot of silences, because neither of us knew how to get off the phone, and when I did get off, Momma was upset with me for being on the phone so long. Anyway, I remember my mother insisted I get her a corsage; I had no idea you did that, and we went to the dance, about which I remember only one thing. As we were leaving a big Senior, football guy was leaving with his girlfriend. He had hoisted her up upon his shoulder and was carrying her like a sack of potatoes. I do recall she was wearing a pair of very short cutoffs. She was squealing and occasionally he would reach up and slap her on the butt. As he did this she would squeal even louder. Then he said something like, "I'm gonna take you out in the woods and spank you good." This made her laugh and giggle even more. This seemed strange to me, and I pondered this event and I finally figured it out when I was about twenty-five. I also had some inkling as to where they were going and what they were going to do. I guess I was what they call "maturing."

The most important thing that fall was my birthday as I turned fourteen. Every day I would walk home from school. My mother would take us to school in the morning, and then I would walk home. I guess Re took the bus home because she never walked with me. It was always Button and Gary and me or Lamar and Bill and me or Lamar, Tommy and me, but we would walk home from the high school all the way across town to our homes. It was a different time. As we walked we could stop in a little soda shop down around East Church Street and Douglas Street. It was a little hole in the wall joint and long since gone. We would get a cherry coke for a quarter and play a tune on the juke box for a nickel. My favorite song was *The Wanderer* by Dion.

I had no idea why I like it. I guess "*it had a good beat and was easy to dance to.*" This is a reference to a popular television show at the time, *American Bandstand* with its long enduring and perpetually young host, Dick Clark. You could tune in to this show every afternoon after school and catch up on the songs, groups and latest dance moves. Anyway we would continue our walk through town by The Grand movie theater where they would play such movie greats as *Robinson Crusoe on Mars*. Then work our way down to East Main Street where there was a department store, and in that store window was the be all to end all boy dream possession – an .049 gas powered model of a Dauntless Dive Bomber. It was so cool! And so I started a never ending campaign to relentlessly tell my mother I wanted that for my birthday. And guess what? I got it! It was one of the coolest toys I ever had. Now the trouble with a U-control gas powered plane is you need someone to hold the plane after you get the motor running until you can get out to the U control line handle. Well, I ingeniously (if I do say so myself) solved that problem. I rigged up a nail in the ground with a loop tied to it. On the back wheel of the plane I tied another loop. I then held the two loops together with a pin that had a string that led out to where my control handle was. As have told you before, I would start the plane using a big battery to heat the glow plug, open the fuel tank three turns of the needle, then prime the motor with a little squirt of glow plug fuel and flip the propeller being careful not to let your fingers get in the way. Once the motor caught you would turn the fuel back with the needle valve until the motor smoothed out to a steady hum. Next I would run out to the control handle, then pull the pin and two loops would come apart and the plane would start its take off roll. I was a genius. I loved that plane, and it started me on the road to many other gas powered planes and cars.

Continuing the walk home, after that department store window we would cross the railroad tracks and stop at Young Brothers Pharmacy. They are still there, right next to the railroad tracks on Main Street with their Coca-Cola sign on the side of their building.

Dr. "Choke's" Office

A stop there would be mandatory to pick up a ten cent bag of pork rinds to help you along your long trek home. Then a walk up the Main Street hill and at the intersection with South Bartow Street was the first Presbyterian Church where we went to church EVERY Sunday. This is where my friend Bill would drop off as his father was the minister, and he lived right next to the church. This intersection and diagonal from the church is where my Pa's house was years before. By this time, Pa had been dead for five years, and his house had been moved down on Etowah Drive as I mentioned earlier. At the intersection, I would turn to the left, to the east, on South Bartow and walk over to Leake Street, turn right, south, walk past where "Dr. Choke's" office was on the left, then turn left on Luckie Street. Our house was down on the right at the intersection with West Avenue.

19.

Another of my memories was when Momma, The Colonel's mother, my paternal grandmother, would have us "young'uns" up to spend the night occasionally. When we came up we were treated like kings and queens. It was during one of these stays that Margaret Rose had called me about the *Sadie Hawkins* dance. Anyway, we would watch television on her *color* television! This was a huge deal in a world where most television was still black and white and stations went off the air at 11:30 or 12:00 with a picture of a kind of target with an Indian head in the center. We would sleep in the big bed in the back room. Then in the morning we would get our favorite breakfast. Mine was always Momma's buttermilk waffles with real melted butter on them. I still love making them to this day in my trusty, old, takes forever waffle maker. The recipe is in with all my recipes if you want to have a taste of my childhood. The key is the melted butter, use salted, unclarified butter, that is poured over the waffle at the last minute. I remember that Momma used the same little beat up pan that Unca' Pete used for his steaks to melt the butter. This ritual continued even up through my college years.

After Sadie Hawkins, Margaret Rose and I continued as girlfriend and boyfriend. I was also interested in Margaret Rose's cousin, Laura, Jer-Boy's sister. She lived up on Arrowhead Drive near my Uncle Bill and Aunt Doris. I was kind of interested in Laura, but as I recall, Laura was never that interested in me. On the other hand, Margaret Rose was interested in me which made like her more. I do not recall ever taking Margaret Rose to the movies or anything. Mostly I would walk down West Avenue to her house at 103 South Avenue, and we would sit on the porch swing and eat Ruffles with Bacon Horseradish dip and drink Cokes and kiss. I was still very young in the boy-girl department. I still love Ruffles and Bacon Horseradish dip.

I do recall an opportunity, or what I now, in retrospect, perceive as an opportunity, missed. It was a weekend and I was out roaming around C'ville with one of my upper-class ladies, I believe it was Linda. She had her license and we were just out driving around. After a while we ended up at the Dairy Queen, which was located on Tennessee Street right behind the football stadium bleachers. It is no longer there, but if you look across Tennessee Street from Scott's Walk-Up Bar-B-Q place toward the high school bleachers that are still there, the Dairy Queen used to stand near there on Tennessee Street. Anyway, for some reason Linda had decided to park behind the Dairy Queen. I recall I bought us an ice cream in a cup and we were sharing it with one spoon. We were just sitting in the car, behind the place, in the dark car, sitting near each other sharing spoons of vanilla ice cream, she was behind the wheel and she asked me to scoot over by her in the middle next to her so we would not spill any ice cream. When we finished the ice cream, I was surprised we did not leave. We just sat there next to each other. She put her arm around me. I think I asked where we were going next. She said something about waiting for someone, maybe Susan. I said okay. A few minutes later after nothing happened, we left and I do not recall the rest of the evening. It was probably that unremarkable. I do not actually remember. But now I think I do know why we were there in that dark parking lot, and it had nothing to do with ice cream. I think I missed an opportunity with a junior class girl. C'est la vie.

20.

Sometime during that fall, it was after a football game, Gary, Button, Lamar, and I concocted a plan along with some other friends to have a spend the night party at Button's home's barn out on Mission Road just on the town side of Burnt Hickory. The plan was we would all bring our sleeping bags and stow them before the Cartersville Purple Hurricanes had their football game. Then, after the game, we would retrieve the sleeping bags and head out for the barn. So, everything must have worked well because I remember being there in the barn around 11:00 with all the guys. What made the night so memorable was the cow chip battle. You see this was the barn where Button's parents kept their cows. And cows do five things: they eat, they sleep, make baby cows, make milk and poop. Well, this barn was loaded with small, dried up, hard cow dung chips; just right for throwing, and before you know it we had divvied up sides and the battle was on! Some of us, including me, were up in the loft and some were down on the floor. The loft people were at the disadvantage because, logically, there were no cows in the loft. Duh! So, the only chips we had were the ones we carried up or the ones thrown up at us. That cow chip battle is all I definitively recall. We must have thrown chips for hours. Then we must have slept some and then gone to Button's house across the road to have some breakfast, and then straggled home in the early morning. I vaguely remember walking home in the cool dragging my sleeping bag. The Georgia morning sun was a pallid disc just creeping up into the sky through an early morning mist. Everything smelled of morning dew, chopped cotton and faint wood smoke. A smell that I would forever associate with that epic battle. As I write this, the barn is still there. It is on the right, about 480 Mission Road, as you leave town.

Another school chums related memory is witnessed by the scar on my left thumb just above my knuckle. Again I remember being with Button and Gary. We had been at the football game, and we were headed out after the game. For where I have no recollection, but we were headed out. We were not leaving from any of the approved exits. We were headed out over a chain link fence at the side of the bleachers. Button went first and Gary went next. I was the last man, and as I went over the top I caught my hand on a ragged edge of the chain link at the top of the fence. It must have torn me pretty badly because the scar is still very visible today. I do not remember getting any special first aid, which also probably contributes to the scar's prominence. In my opinion, I was just a teenage boy being a teenage boy. I will share more about Gary and Button and our really BIG adventure later, but I want to touch on some more family memories from that year.

21.

The Colonel was gone to Korea, except for the short return for his father's funeral, and Mom must have asked Uncle Bill, her brother, to try to be a buddy. And I think he tried his best. I recall him taking me up in his small two seat plane once. It was awesome! He was a really gifted pilot in my opinion. We flew over Cartersville and buzzed Momma's house. Momma and my mother were outside waving towels. He also stalled the plane which was cool. He put the little plane in a steep climb and kept pulling the nose up until the plane's engine could not pull the plane up any longer. That is a stall. Then, as the plane starts to slip backward, you throw the rudder over causing the plane to turn to the side and start to nose down. There is a moment in the stall when you are weightless. It was so cool.

He also took me shooting one afternoon. We went out near the Etowah Indian Mounds to a bridge over the Etowah River. The bridge is still there although it is rusting and crumbling. If you go out Douthit Ferry Road to where it crosses the Etowah River and look to your left you will see the bridge. When Uncle Bill and I went it was still an operating bridge. I recall a warm day when we headed out. Uncle Bill brought a bunch of cans and two twenty-two rifles. We clobbered those cans as they floated down the river. It must have been not long after that that Uncle Bill was in a serious car crash. I do not know the details, but his lower legs were damaged to the point that he basically never walked again without the aid of a walker. I recall him being laid up in bed for a long time. Uncle Bill was always nice to me. We were never that close, but he was always nice to me.

Another cool event I remember is the Cartersville High School Science Fair. We would get extra points in our science class if we entered. Our Algebra teacher, Ms. DeLay even gave us extra points if we submitted a math project. I did both because I was such an overachiever and needed the extra points! I'll reverse the order as I explain the projects. The math project was kind of cool. It showed that no matter what kind of triangle you had, the sum of the three angles was always 180 degrees. There were three different triangles, an obtuse, a right and an acute. They were made up of puzzle pieces you could take out and lay on a straight shelf proving my point. That project, which I thought was excellent, got me nowhere. The science project though, was a winner. The project was a series of overlays over a map of the Pacific Ocean that showed that the fault lines of the Pacific Crust paralleled the volcanoes forming the Ring of Fire. It was pretty simple, but it got me an Honorable Mention at the high school fair. That allowed me to go to the Regional Science Fair over in Rome, Georgia, at Berry College. I thought was a long way away. At Region I won Second Place I think. The competition must not have been too stiff. And that win got me a trip to the State Science Fair all the way off about a thousand miles away in Athens, Georgia, at the huge University of Georgia, and that was an overnight trip! It was heady stuff for a fourteen-year-old. I do not remember much about the fair other than it was held in a gigantic hall, probably the gymnasium, but I could be wrong. I do not remember if I won anything, nor do I remember where I stayed for the night, but I do recall breakfast the next morning. It was buffet line deal, and as I walked down the line a serving lady barked at me, "How do you want your eggs?" I was startled and could not think of anything except *sunny side up*. So, I said, "Sunny side up." And that is what I got, two, almost raw eggs jiggling on my plate and staring up at me. I did not eat them. They were gross. But I still think of them now every time I order eggs anywhere, usually *over light*. My awards from that high point are somewhere in a trunk in the house. In fact, I think I even have a checkered napkin that I stole from the Athens's breakfast place, or maybe it was from the dinner place from the night before. I was a rascal.

22.

As a lead in to the greatest adventure of my fourteen-year-old life let me say that learning French in my Freshman year of high school from a good old southern boy named Mr. Keith who had a BS from West Georgia College was a complete waste of time. I thought maybe I had a mental block to learning a foreign language, which I may, but this guy was no help at all. I must have passed French I, but I learned nothing for my time. I know this for a fact because the summer after my Freshman year I would go to the public swimming pool with Tommy and Gary and the others. This was the same pool that was right next to the high school that I had initially failed my swim instructions years before. Our favorite pastime while swimming was eating frozen Reese's peanut butter cups, diving off the spring board and singing along to Sam Cooke as he crooned *What a Wonderful World*. The particular verse that would have us yelling at the top of our lungs was

> *"Don't know much about history,*
> *Don't know much about biology,*
> *Don't know much about a science book,*
> *Don't know much about the French I took!"*

When we hit that last line we would scream it at the top of our lungs. And then fall all over the pool laughing, Reese's chocolate all over our faces without a care in the world. It was a great summer. That is when my mother came to me with a proposal. There was a man in town named Gilbert Martin, and every summer he would get an old school bus and head down to Mexico City and harvest orchids for his flower business on the way. He would also fill the school bus with a couple of college guys, Rodney and Jim in our case, and a wad of high school boys looking for adventure. She said I could go but I would have to earn the fifty dollars spending money myself in order to go. Well, as it turned out, Button, Gary, Neil, Charles, Hugh and Craig along with others were going so I was all in! Now I just had to earn fifty dollars and get all kinds of shots. So, I began a campaign of grass cutting. To be honest, I was either not a very good business man, which I was/am not, or I was too sensitive to taking advantage of my grandmother and aunts and uncles whose grass I was going to cut. But the deal was five bucks to cut the lawn. Not five bucks an hour or five bucks for a small lawn and more for a bigger lawn, the deal was five bucks. Years later, my Uncle Nelson, Nelson Kimball Rogers, said he would have paid me twice or three times that much if I had asked. But, I had no father to ask, and so I worked my fanny off sweating in the Georgia sun cutting yards for five bucks each. It seemed like it took me forever, but it was only ten yard cuttings, and at three yards a week it could not have taken a month, but when you are fourteen, a month in the summer can equal several years. Well, finally I earned my money, got my Yellow Fever and Malaria shots and the finally the day arrived to leave on *one of the greatest adventures of all time.*

23.

It was an early, warm July morning in 1965 after my freshman year. I recall the morning humidity still evaporating from the bushes and the aroma of freshly mowed lawns in our noses as Craig, Neal, Cliff, Gary, Hugh, Steve, Button Lewis, Jimmy, Charles and me along with our college age chaperones Rodney, Mr. Nix, Barney and the head guy, Gilbert Martin gathered at Gilbert's home at 203 McCanless Street in Cartersville to leave on our trip to Mexico City.

The basic route, as I have tried to trace it, was west from Cartersville to Montgomery, Alabama, then down to Mobile and west through Baton Rouge toward Texas. We may have stopped on the way, but I don't recall that. What I do recall is all of us getting a bath in the Sabine River at the Louisiana Texas border. I recall a stop in Corpus Christie because the old school bus we were traveling in needed a new generator. I recall us camping out at a rest stop near there. It was late when we camped out and I found a soft, vine covered area to put out my sleeping bag. In the morning I discovered the soft vines were laced with Poison Ivy. I am very allergic to Poison Ivy, but that morning it was too early to tell.

But by later that day, as we pulled into Brownsville, Texas, my allergy was in full bloom all over my legs. I was itching like crazy! The plan was to camp in Brownsville at an RV/bus park. We arrived, the old bus disgorged us, and Gilbert treated me with the only thing he had on hand, Clorox Bleach. It was grow up time. He dabbed it on my legs with cotton balls from the first aid kit, and it burned like the old mercurochrome had burned because I had been scratching. I took off running down the road yelling like a banshee. But I have to add that it must have worked, because I do not remember any more problems with it after that. I think we spent two nights in Brownsville. We bathed at the RV communal bathroom/shower and relaxed.

Across the street from the RV park was a drive in theater and Button and Gary and I decided we would take in a show. Little did I know a lifelong obsession was about to form – an obsession that would color my young pubescent brain forever. An obsession that would impact all my female relationships until I married and then into my married life. It only cost us about 25 cents each to get in because we did not have a car, and the guy at the ticket booth did not really know what to do, but after a little discussion we walked in, bought some popcorn and a coke and plopped ourselves down on a dirt mound, pulled a speaker off its pole and set it on the ground and then my life changed.

It was a warm Texas night and as darkness and the 16 mm projector started to flicker in the low projector building I was introduced to Sean Connery and his James Bond as we watched a double feature, *From Russia with Love* and *Dr. No!* I was spellbound. Remember, I was 14 years old. I was in the throes of full puberty and the impact of this suave, British, womanizing, brilliant secret agent was almost incalculable on my psyche. I wanted to be him. I wanted to travel the world and have a woman in every port and be rich and cool and say the hell with everything! I do not know that if the movie had been *The Sound of Music* that I would have wanted to join a choir or if it had been *Mary Poppins* that I would have wanted to be a chimney sweep, but I knew that night as I climbed into my sleeping bag that I wanted to be "Bond, James Bond." Now, as I reflect from my current vantage point, I can say that evening did not have an overall positive effect on my life. But, it happened and it could not be unseen, and I was affected. I guess I should be thankful the movie was not *The Texas Chainsaw Massacre*!

The next morning several of us rebellious teenagers decided we wanted to go swim in the Gulf of Mexico. Gilbert advised against it and said he would not take us, but we decided to go anyway. So, we struck off to the beach along a road that had a sign pointing to the Gulf. Now being immature, stupid teenage boys we did not stop to consider how far it might be, or consider anything to do with water or food, or consider anyone else, or Gilbert Martin's plans; we just struck out. We left midmorning and by 2:00 we were regretting our decision. We had been walking for hours. No cars had come along the road and there was no sign of water or how far it might be. But of course that is not going to detour a bunch of hormone driven adolescents from continuing forward. We had shed our shirts, and all of us were getting sunburned as the Texas July sun cooked us. And we continued on. By 3:30 or so we were beginning to doubt ourselves, but we continued on. It was around 4:00 that a big lumbering school bus came up the road. It was full of hooting and hollering boys and driven by a not very happy Gilbert Martin. We were lucky though. He stopped, and after a suitable and well-deserved dressing down we boarded the bus. Surprisingly, he continued on toward the beach. I now think he wanted to impress upon us the ridiculousness of our plan. The water was at least ten more miles. We had only walked maybe half way there. For our trouble, we were hungry, thirsty and sunburned. I think you call that "just deserts." When we got to the beach Gilbert "let" us go swim, and then we got to ride back to Brownsville in our wet clothes with sand in all our … parts. "Yep, just deserts."

From Brownsville we crossed into Matamoros. Getting out of the United states is no big deal. We were to find out that getting back in was a bigger deal. But we traveled on into the great country of Mexico. It was the first time I had really left the United States. Oh, I had been to Canada at Niagara Falls when we lived in Michigan when I was little, but this was a whole different deal. People did not even speak English! On the way, we stopped in several towns and stayed at a hotel somewhere on the way. I would like to tell you I was more than just a passenger, more than a random, clueless teenager, and tell you that I had done homework and knew where we were going and what to see, but I did not.

I was just one of several ping pong ball adolescents bouncing wherever Gilbert Martin chose. But there were two stops on the way down that left an impression.

We stopped at a town named El Naranjo in the Mexican state named San Luis Potosi and camped near a beautiful waterfall called El Salto Falls. We spent several days there. We were able to wash our clothes and ourselves in the river and we ate very well at a restaurant in town where one ordered one thing – beef steak and potatoes and Cokes. You did not drink the water in Mexico and this was long before bottled water was a thing. So, it was Cokes. Of course for a bunch of teen aged boys this was fine. We did not care about dental hygiene, nutrition or weight. We were all in our prime and burned anything we ate so fast we were all skinny rails. I recall it rained one night. It was torrential rain, and it started when we were in town at dinner. Our campsite was soaked. Everything not in the bus, including our sleeping bags and clothes, was soaked. We arrived back at camp in the pouring rain and had to spend the night on the bus. Somehow I had a towel with me on the bus, and it would have made a great blanket, but Button Lewis had to get out of the bus for something, and he was soaking wet and cold. So I gave him my towel to cover himself as he slept. I recall I was cold that night, but it helped Button. The afternoon of the next day, after drying all our belongings on clothes lines strung between trees, we moved on to the next adventure.

My next memory was stopping at the great Teotihuacán Pyramid of the Sun and Moon in Tula near Teotihuacán de Arista about 25 miles northeast of Mexico City. Of course I had not done any studying of the Aztec Empire or their timeline or the effect the Spanish had on destroying their civilization. It was pitiful. This was before there were large museums or informational kiosks on the site, so Gary and Button and I just wandered around climbing the pyramids, acting like we were diving off, sitting on the sacrificial alters and generally being Ugly Americans. Our ignorance is astounding to me as I write this. What is also astounding to me is I have no recollection of eating. I know we ate breakfast, lunch and dinner, but I have no clear recollection of eating anything (other than beef steak and potatoes) the entire trip.

After what I am sure was an afternoon at the pyramids, we headed off to Mexico City. We stayed downtown at what is now the Virreyes Hotel on José Maria Izazaga. It was a four story brick structure with small balconies. Again, I do not remember much about the stay. Where we ate, what we ate and where we slept are a blank. I remember a bunch of us locking poor Cliff out on a balcony. I remember inhaling helium and making our voices sound like chipmunks. I remember visiting a church, or perhaps it was a cathedral, and paying a guide. I think I was with Rodney. At any rate, it meant nothing to me. What did register was a trip to the bull fights at the Plaza de Toros and watching several bull fights, or rather several bull killings. It was pretty gruesome which for a 14-year-old meant it was pretty cool in the warped way a teenager sees things. And that sums up the visit to Mexico City. Pretty poor if you ask me.

We headed out and headed for home. I recall singing to *Down in the Boondocks* by Billy Joe Royal and making fun of Little Stevie Wonder (he wonders when he's gonna get slapped!) and the hilarity of the phrase "shoot wad" which we came up with in the hotel parking lot in Mexico City while we were pitching pennies. We all had an idea there was a more sexual overtone to the phrase although none of us knew exactly what to do with the idea. On the way through Mexico I have flashes of small towns on mesas and buying a pineapple and hacking it open with my new machete. They were so cheap I had bought two for a ridiculous price. Pesos were about 40 to the dollar I think, so we were rich men. Something that costs 120 pesos was about 3 bucks. At any rate the two machetes are now in the hands of my grandsons, Bryce and Bodie. I also bought a beautiful chess set that is now with my granddaughter, Caitlin. But the real adventure began when all of us teamed up and bought real switchblade knives. Oh they were beauties all flashing steel and clicking noise as the blade locked into place with the press of a button. We were a mean bunch of hoodlums and ready for whatever the world could throw at us. We all carried them like badges of honor. We were real, swaggering, hormone fueled men in our white tee shirts, plaid shorts, white socks, skinny legs and high topped tennis shoes.

Switchblades were/are outlawed at this time in the United States which brings us to reentry into the great USA. We arrived at the entry point, and we presented our credentials. I have no idea what those credentials were. I know it was not a passport or a driver's license, but we had something. Perhaps a note from our mommy was all we needed. But before we were allowed back into the country a very, very large border patrol officer sat us all down on the curb. He had a black shirt on with all kinds of patches and badges. His forearms were the size of our thighs and his upper arms that strained against his short shirt sleeves were bigger around than anything we possessed. All of us tough hoodlums had made a pact that no one would "squeal" that we had bought vicious killing machines in Mexico. We sat there defiant even though we were all lined up like criminals. The officer asked us if any of us had switchblade knives. How did he even suspect that? Did he line up every teenager, boy or girl, coming across the border with a note from their mommy and ask them if they were carrying switchblade knives? I think not. I believe one of the adults had ratted us out! He explained they were illegal and we could kiss the rest of our life away if we even attempted to bring them across the border. We would be in jail for years with who knows what kind of lowlife criminals wanting to do all kinds of things to "fresh fish." The jig was up. We all looked at each other. I do not know who was first, but quickly we all confessed. Then we went into our stuff and hauled out our beautiful chrome and steel beauties. The officer had us open them. They flashed open one last time in the Brownsville. The sun glinted off of the deadly, polished blades. He had us lay them diagonally against the curb with the blade up. Then we each stomped on them and they snapped at the junction of the handle and blade. We were then allowed to pick them up and keep them if we wanted. We all threw them in the trash so as not to remind ourselves of our brief, glowing James Dean moment and our utter failure at being rebels. I guess if we had just been carrying weed, we would have been okay.

Once back in the country, I do not remember anything until we got home. All the parents were lined up at Gilbert's house. You would have thought we had been gone for months. It had been ten days, two weeks at most. We piled off the bus all stinky with filthy laundry that was really only suitable for the trash, not the washing machine. Yes, we were home, and still had over month before school! Six weeks was an eternity in a

14-year-old world, so we were back to the pool, singing and being carefree hoodlums running amuck in Cartersville until school started just after Labor Day.

24.

My sophomore year started like any other school year at least until The Colonel got home from Korea. We had been in school about six weeks when he blew into town and announced we were moving back to Vienna, Virginia. He said this like it was a good thing. For me, as you can imagine, it conjured up all kinds of horrible memories not to mention having to move in the middle of the school year just when I had made some REAL friends and was accepted as "one of the guys." I mean, I had this place scoped out. I had a girlfriend. I was accepted. I had won a science fair so I was not a complete academic looser … even though compared to my sister I was on par with Quasimodo. And Re was in a similar boat. So she and I started a campaign to stay in Cartersville and live with Momma. Ah! There was rebellion in the ranks, a real mutiny. But not for long of course. Near my birthday we left 401 West Avenue, Cartersville, Georgia, and headed for 8708 Westwood Drive, Vienna, Virginia.

25.

The house we moved into was near Tyson's Corner at the intersection of 123 and Route 7 in a subdivision named Tyson's Green. My room was the upstairs center window. I recall when we got there and I was told that was my room, I looked out the window and thought to myself that it was a good room. I could see up and down the street if any bullies were coming to beat me up.

The Colonel was to be stationed at the Pentagon again, and I was to enrolled in a new school again. As I turned 15 that October, 1965, Re and I headed to George C. Marshall High School in Falls Church. The only recollection I have of my first day as a sophomore enrolling was walking into the first classroom. I stood at the door holding all my books which were issued at the office. Needless to say, I felt like the consummate New Kid. Never felt this? Well, you feel kind of stupid, kind of sweaty, kind of like you wish you had picked out different clothes, any different clothes would do. You feel all their eyes on you sizing you up. Is this guy a Nerd, a Greaser, a Jock, a Loser or is he just a Goof-Ball. Of course the teacher announces your name to the class trying to be all cheery but underlying in her voice is the exasperation of knowing he or she is going to have to alter all kinds of records to include you in the already overcrowded classroom and his/her roll. The teacher is sizing you up, too. Is this kid going to be smart and helpful or a troublemaker? Well, given he is a boy, the vote is troublemaker until proven otherwise. "Take a seat in back, James."

As I scanned the room all I could see was about 30 faces looking at me. I was so tired of being "The New Kid." As I looked toward the back of the room where the only seat was I saw them … Mark and his grade failing brother John from the sixth grade! GREAT! *This was shaping up to be exactly as bad as I knew it would be.* Of all the classes in all the schools in all the worlds I had to walk into this one. What were the chances? Astronomical! But I have no more recollections of the day other than I had to carry my books back and forth to school for a couple of weeks because there were no lockers to be had. GREAT! As it turned out, I never really had contact with Mark or John during high school which was fine with me. And no bullies ever came up my street.

Yep, being the New Kid sucks, but like so many things it is a double edged sword. On the suck side: you never form any lasting relationships which stunts your emotional growth. It becomes hard for you to form serious and lasting relationships later in life. You become introverted and tend to learn not to rely on anyone but yourself because no one is around long enough to show their "count-on-ability" and you are never around long enough to be "count-on-able" for them. You do not make friends. I tended to see people I do not know as a threat. I still do to this day. On the unsuck side you become very self-reliant, and you are very content keeping your own counsel. To this day I do not have many close friends. I have my wife and my children and grandchildren.

The other thing that is a result of moving around and never being near the family roots, Cartersville, is that the family tends to turn inward. Our family celebrated birthdays, Christmas, Easter, and all family events as a small nuclear group. In other words, we did not include my parent's brothers and sisters or mothers or fathers in our plans. To this day, because of this upbringing, I feel I am somewhat estranged from my brothers and sister. Being around them is awkward for me. I am most comfortable being with my own little nuclear family. To sum-up … I am introverted, independent, and seem cold and aloof upon first meeting. I am not gregarious or whimsical except with my most trusted, close family, but humor is my armor. When situations get tense, I tend to crack a joke even using black humor if necessary. I mean, "What are you going to do?" My wit is sharp and caustic at times and do not ask for my opinion unless you want my honest, unvarnished answer unless you are emotionally very close to me. But I digress.

26.

Soon, I settled into school. I did eventually get a locker and had to buy a combination lock (14-16-10) which I still have. It is very easy to open now! Classes fell into rhythm and I started to meet people. Bill, Lynn (a boy) and Scott and I became The Four Musketeers. We were all sort of loners and did not really fit the Greaser/Jock/Nerd classification. Down the street were Ray and Pratt on Burning Tree Drive. They were a year ahead of me. Across the street was John and next door, 8710, was Vicki. She was kind of a "fast" girl, and we never really got to know each other for some reason. On the other side of the house (8706) was a guy from California whose name I cannot remember, but he introduced me to The Doors and *Light My Fire* and that was cool! On the cul-de-sac extension of Burning Tree Drive running almost parallel to my street was Carol and her friend Cathy from another neighborhood and then there was Pratt's sister Terri and her friend Cathy from down the street from her house. From Michigan there was Jean who was Cathy from down the street's friend, and it was Jean who warped me forever and made bangs on a woman a fetish of mine. All these names will come up as I share some of the best times of my life.

As a result of me being an October birthday and my parents enrolling me in kindergarten when I was 4 and about to be 5 that October, I was a young Sophomore. I was actually 14 and turned 15 that October 29th, 1965. The consequence of this was that all my peers were getting their learner's permits for driver's licenses when I was still a year away. It was my Junior year before I got my learner's permit and a Senior before I got my license. This meant I rode around with a lot of my friends in high school. It also meant if I wanted to go on a date, the Colonel had to drive me. I recall an early date with Terri. Terri as I mentioned was Pratt's sister. Her father was in the Navy and they lived down the street on Burning Tree Drive. I guess if I was going to say I had a steady girl in high school, Terri was who I dated the most. Terri was a year behind me in school. The things I recall about her were that she had a beautiful face mainly because of her nose. She probably hated her nose. I thought it was beautiful. She was very athletic. She ran track which is where I met her. Being an athlete, she had small breasts and her standout feature was that she had legs that would not quit – yep, she had the legs of a thoroughbred!

I remember us going on one of our first dates. At this time all the rage was boys wearing long hair with bangs swept across their foreheads like The Beatles. So I tried. Of course being the army brat son of The Colonel my hair was kept fairly short for the times, so getting any bangs was tough. But I tried for my date, and the Colonel decided since he had to drive me that he would ridicule my efforts. He combed his thinning hair forward and drew a thin pencil moustache across his lip and proceeded to me my driver that night looking like that. Well, he ended up having to meet Terri's dad which was all very awkward, so I guess it all worked the way it was supposed to. Lesson: do not make fun of other's looks. I do not remember anything about the date, but I remember how the Colonel made me feel.

As I said, Terri became more or less my steady girl, and I did not treat her well. I wish to this day I could find her and apologize for being an ass. We dated. We "parked." She taught me to French kiss. She learned from my friend Bill who she dated when I was dating someone else. We went to my Junior Prom together. We went to The Subway which was a rock and roll hangout for high schoolers with loud music and crazy dancing. She came to church with me a few times, but I would not wish that on anyone. When we returned to Vienna, we returned to the First Presbyterian Church and Reverend Horace Lukens was still there in the same un-air conditioned church preaching the same unbelievably long sermons. The only difference was that I was now fully grown, not fully in control, but fully grown, with all the hormones that come with that and sitting there on a Sunday morning in the heat with hormones raging and Lukens droning on and on. It is a very lucky thing that nobody was shot.

When Terri and I were not dating, I dated Carol. My life seems to revolve around the name Carol or Carolyn. Carol was a beautiful girl. I'm sure she thought she was too heavy, but I thought she was beautiful. She was so lovely and sweet, she was untouchable. We experimented with kissing and that is about it. Carol is another person I wish I could find and apologize to. I took a girl named Ann to the Senior Prom. I took Ann because she was a cheerleader and popular. I should have taken Carol. I have always wanted to apologize for that. I don't think she went to her Senior Prom because I did not ask her. I was an ASS. In retrospect my Senior Prom situation was a lot like that of Napoleon Dynamite. So, go find the movie *Napoleon Dynamite* and watch it. Watch the prom part. I was Napoleon and my date was the girl he took. And if you find my prom picture you will see the resemblance between me and Napoleon is striking.

I could move on, but I want to write about Terri's 16ᵗʰ birthday party and its ramifications. I was to be Terri's date and Terri's friend Cathy from down the street brought her friend from Michigan, Jean. This is the Jean who turned bangs on a woman's face a style fetish of mine. And again, I was a complete ASS. I fell head over heels in love with Jean. Let me add at this point – *It may be puppy love, but it's love to the puppy*. So, Terri's birthday party was terrible for Terri, because I was unabashedly stalking Jean, and she was all about me. Jean and I were an item, and she invited me to come to her house for Thanksgiving. She lived in Warren Michigan. The plan was for me to fly up on Wednesday evening after school and fly back on Sunday. I used my money to buy tickets, The Colonel got me to National Airport in the rain, and away I went.

It is always interesting to me what I recall and what I do not recall. I do not remember getting there or anyone picking me up or going to her house or meeting her parents or any of Thanksgiving. Only two things stand out in my memory. One was Saturday evening and the other was Sunday morning. Saturday evening Jean and I went out on a double date with her friend and her friend's boyfriend. We may have gone to a movie or something, but all I remember is making out with Jean in the backseat as we drove around in the dark and cold wet of late November in Michigan. There was "our" song, *Never My Love* by The Association, playing and it was very warm and comfortable in that back seat as we cruised along. Then the song *Judy in Disguise* by John Red and his Playboy Band came on the radio. In the refrain, "Come to me tonight, come to me tonight. Taking everything in sight …." As we cuddled, I whispered that in her ear. And she heard me. And later that night as I was asleep in her college age brother's room, she came to me. She was wearing a pink bathrobe. I stood up and we kissed. She suggested we get in the bed. She let the robe go. She was wearing a black baby-doll nightie. And I was terrified. I was terrified of many things that night, but one thing in particular: getting her pregnant. So, we made out some more. I kept a sheet between us. So, depending on how you look at it; it was either an opportunity missed or a bullet dodged. But again, as the twig is bent, so grows the tree, to this day.

The next morning with all our propriety back in place and no real worries, we went to my first Catholic church service. And I laid pretty low until we came to the Lord's Prayer. I did not want her parents to think I was a complete heathen so I enthusiastically joined in. Well, the Catholics say the Lord's Prayer a little differently than Protestants. It seems the Protestants were not happy with the prayer as it is in the Bible, so they added a little extra to the end. The part about "For thine is the kingdom and the power …" was not being used that morning in Jean's church, but I did a little two microsecond soliloquy for the congregation to make sure they knew they were not up with the liturgical times like I was. Jean grabbed my arm quickly. So, those are my two recollections. I still have a thing for women with bangs. I never saw Jean again. But I saw Terri again.

As a final recollection of that Thanksgiving weekend, when I arrived home I found out my parents had put my cat Candy to sleep while I was gone. She had become my cat over the 10 or so years we had her. I believe we got her when I was in the second grade. They explained how it "had to happen." And now that I am grown, and having "had" to put three sweet cats to sleep, I guess I understand … but them putting Candy to sleep while I was gone is still a painful memory.

27.

I was a working dog in high school. "Idle hands are a Devil's workshop" … especially when it comes to boys. The original deal with my parents was I could get a motorcycle as soon as I got the money to buy one, but that all went "up the spout" so to speak as soon as I got a job. I worked for a man named Roger at the local Vienna 7-11. I did it all – stocked shelves, ran the register, bagged ice from the ice machine in the back, kept the freezer and cooler stocked from back behind the shelves behind those big glass doors, loaded and then bagged and then cleaned the chicken rotisserie machine, got to drive Roger's 3 speed on the column old, beat-up truck sometimes, swept the parking lot, did inventory, worked at his remote store run by his overly made up, bee hive hairdo wife whose name I think was Ruby, worked the early shift, the late shift, sold myself beer and condoms and *Playboy* magazines and generally had a ball! Roger was my first employer and the best boss ever.

My friend John from across the street worked next door at the Burger Chief. Yep, Chief, not Chef. He was an assistant manager, and he would work the late shift too sometimes. When I got off at 11:30 after cleaning up and mopping, he was usually cleaning up at his place. I would go over next door and we would chow-down on leftovers, and we accidentally invented something that could have saved the whole Burger Chief franchise if we had only realized it. It could have made John and me rich! One night we were goofing around as only high schoolers do, and we piled two burgers and some cheese on a bun, and it was great! We had accidently invented the double cheese burger, and we did not even know it. Then we did a triple. It was even more delicious! This was long before McDonalds ever thought of a double cheeseburger. I mean this was 1966. John and I could have made a fortune, but instead we just sat out in the warm Virginia night on the curb of the Burger Chief with the bugs flying around the fluorescent lights, swapped stories and ate our inventions. It was the best of times

One summer, probably 1967, Bill, Scott, Lynn and I got a plan together to head to Ocean City, Maryland. We got Lynn's mom to agree to chaperone us "wild and crazy guys." Lynn's dad owned a Buick dealership, and we got to drive one of his new Buick Skylark convertibles! We took off. I do not remember how long we were there or much about it except we buried Scott up to his neck on the beach, and he could not get out until we let him, and that we decided to go to the movies one day because it was raining. The only movie playing on the boardwalk at 11:00 in the morning was a western with Clint Eastwood. None of us had never heard of him, but the price was right, the poster looked good (in high school you do a lot of judging books by their covers) so we piled into the dark coolness. We stoked up on refillable tubs of popcorn and pure Coke. We were young and heart problems and weight watching was NOT something these four, 6-foot-tall, 115 pound skinny guys were worried about. The movie we ended up watching was *The Good, The Bad and The Ugly*, and it was fantastic! None of us had ever seen anything like it. It was realistic, loud and almost three hours long! We sat there in the theater and watched it THREE times! It was full dark when we came out and Lynn's mom was pissed when we got home. I guess she thought was had been abducted or something, but we were fine if maybe a little hyped up on Coke caffeine.

Sometime in that summer of 1967, soon after school was out, another bullet was dodged. It was an exceptionally hot June in Virginia, and I convinced The Colonel and his wife to let me sleep in the basement where it was cool. It was a perfect, dark cavern, and I loved it. The only light crept in from the door to the outside in the back corner. Other than that, it was dark solitude. During the day I would work for Roger, and in the evenings I would date whoever and then sleep in the basement at night. One person I was dating is Cathy from down the street. She was a year behind me in school. And this is the same Cathy who had introduced me to Jean of the Thanksgiving bullet dodge. We would go driving and go to movies, and we were more friends than serious boyfriend and girlfriend. We would just goof around at Rock Creek Park and hang out.

I need to digress a moment about "hanging out." One Sunday we went out in The Colonel's VW. I was driving so I was at least 16 and had my license so this was summer of '67 I guess. Cathy and I pulled into the neighborhood. I was going slow. I got ready to shift, and hit the brake instead of the clutch. Now in 1967 we were still a long way from seat belts, so when I hit the brake, even at 20 miles per hour, Cathy hit the windshield with her forehead. The windshield spidered, and she got a doozy of a bump. Well, The Colonel was in the yard when we pulled up and there was no way to hide the damage to the car or to Cathy. As it all turned out she was fine, and The Colonel got his car fixed. Funny the things you recall.

So, back to my story. Cathy found out I was sleeping in my basement and said she could do the same thing, and we should do that and then go out in the middle of the night and walk around the neighborhood and hangout. This sounded pretty exciting and cool to me so we made a plan. She showed me where the door to her basement was, and we set a time for our big adventure. The evening came, and I went down to my hole to sleep. Needless to say, sleep was the last thing on my mind. I tossed and turned and then around 1:30 I quietly snuck out. You know, it is the only time I can remember sneaking out, but I did. I made my way down Westwood Drive to Burning Tree Lane, past Terri's house to Higdon Drive. Cathy's house was like 8724 or something. I made my way around back and tapped lightly on the door. The door opened and Cathy snuck out. She had on a short tank top with her tummy exposed and short-shorts and flip flops. Her top barely covered her. We bummed around the neighborhood talking and I recall, in a bold move, she took my hand. Now this was a bold move because we had not even kissed or anything. We walked up Higdon Drive to Pine Valley Drive around the block and then back down Westwood Drive. Cathy then suggested we go to my basement. That sounded good me, so we snuck around the back of the house and into my dark, cool cavern. We made our way over to my cot/bed/sleeping bag and sat down. We chatted nervously and then kissed for the first time. She could kiss like no tomorrow. Someone had taught her well. It was dark. It was cool. For two teenagers experimenting, it was perfect. Needless to bore you with what our kissing led to that evening in the basement, but let me say that I recall a lot of quiet groping before I chickened out. Another bullet dodged. If I can add a little footnote here … I recall I heard that she got pregnant a year or so later during her senior year in school. I was off at college. I do not know anything of that outcome, except to say, if she had the child, that child would now be about 52 years old and all the tears and recriminations that probably went on about her being pregnant would be so much water under a long ago bridge. Perhaps that child is a famous heart surgeon or saved another person from drowning or something. Lessons, lessons, lessons.

Northern Virginia had some wicked winters with piles of snow. Snow days were worshiped and prayed for from December to March. Our house sat in such a way that when the wind came from a certain direction, it would sweep all the snow off the neighbor's driveways and pile it four and six feet deep on ours. So, you guessed it, being the eldest male and the first born male there were certain duties I was expected to undertake with no whining. They were grass cutting, car washing, raking, edging of lawns and snow shoveling. So, out I would go, bundled up and still freezing because I had no body fat at all and start shoveling. You know that story about Tom Sawyer and the whole fence whitewashing episode? Well, it is bull. I tried everything I could to get my younger brother Bill, who was a strapping young man of about eleven at this time to help me … or do it for me … but it was a lost cause. So, I shoveled. But the night time was a different matter. There were two things to do at night: sled and play Hearts.

The sledding was particularly good as the neighborhood had some decent hills and all the Dads would go to work and then come home with their cars all hot and their tires with chains and that would melt and pack the snow that would then turn to ice at night. You could kill yourself if you were not careful. There was a street up from ours named Pine Valley Drive (the same one famous for the Cathy middle of the night walk around) that had a hill that was long and steep and not straight. Now our Radio Flyers did pretty well on the straightaway but on ice, in a curve, whooooo Lordy Momma – you could die. But you learned to steer with your feet and bail out before you crashed. There was nothing quite like sledding until 11:00 at night under the street lamps on Pine Valley Drive. The other great thing about the heavy snows were snow days. This was long before computers and virtual school and all that crap so a snow day as a pure goof off day. Pratt and I would go to Ray's house, turn on the Mommas and the Pappas singing *California Dreamin'* and play "hunt for the Bitch." We could play Hearts all night long if we were left to our own devices, but we were "good boys" so we'd knock it off about 1:30 or 2 and trudge home in the freezing cold. But Hearts we did play. As I recall we played a particularly cut throat game, and no one came out of the evening unscathed, and someone always had to be declared the Champion of the World until the next marathon session was played.

Around this time, I joined an Explorer Scout troop. The troop was based in the Vienna First Presbyterian Church and our focus was spelunking. I loved it with the helmets with carbide lamps, bedding rolls, camping in caves and eating over a camp stove. I remember Mom used to always include little precooked sausages in my meal packets. I would warm them up over a stove in a little fry pan and they were fabulous! And cave camping wasn't like camping outside. It was like camping in a really, really cheap motel – no bugs, no animals, constant temperature … I would call it almost "gentlemanly" camping … if there is such a thing … today, I have to agree with Carolyn. Gentlemanly camping is any motel where the doors open to the outside and not onto a hallway! One time our troop actually got to meet a real astronaut who came talk to our troop. The astronaut was the first American to walk in space, Lieutenant Colonel Ed White. He had walked in space on June 3rd, 1965, and he came and told us all about it. Tragically he, along with Gus Grissom, the second American to travel into space, and Roger Chaffee perished on January 27th, 1967, in the Apollo I capsule fire.

Anyway, I remember one time my troop of Explorers were tasked with traffic control at a Boy Scout outing somewhere around Northern Virginia. One interesting aspect was that my younger brother Bill's Boy Scout troop was one of the troops that were going to participate in the jamboree. So we arrived Friday night so we could be on duty early Saturday morning. The next morning early my troop was out in a field directing traffic and handing out maps to where each troop's campsite was to be. Being older and being Explorers and being part of the team that were directing people and not really participating in the events, we had a campsite near the parking lot on what I will call the high ground. Also being there early, we were able to pitch our tents and get our gear stowed before everyone arrived. As Saturday progressed, the weather started to cloud over a little, and when Bill's troop arrived, I showed them to their campsite. It was down a hill and kind of in a ravine as I recall. It was not a great site, but it was where their troop was assigned. More campers arrived and the field was getting muddy and the day was getting more overcast. Finally, everyone was there and my troop was off duty and I guess the other troops were doing games and whatnot. That evening about 11:00 was Tattoo and lights out. The camp settled, and I snuggled into my bedroll with the other three guys in my tent. After the requisite period of playing grab ass, telling stories about our experiences with girls which were all lies, farting and trying to gross each other out … again, think *Stand by Me* … we drifted off to sleep. Sometime in the night I was awakened by rain drumming on the tent. And I mean it was coming down in buckets. I knew where Bill's troop was camped and knew this rain and his site were a bad combination. I got up and put on my poncho and grabbed my flashlight. It was a miserable night. The rain was pouring down and the temperature was dropping. I thought about my brother Bill and his troop's campsite. I got up, put on my poncho, and after some slipping and sliding and getting lost and actually cursing using the few words I knew, I finally located Bill. Today I am a veteran swearer and can keep up with any sailor in the world. But that rainy, cold night needed some of my personal, limited repertoire. Bill's sleeping bag was soaked, and he was frozen. I checked with his tent mates and his scout leader and took him up to my camp site. I wish I could tell you I had taken all his tent mates with me, but I do not remember doing that … I just took Bill. After some climbing and falling and more swearing we got back to my tent. We got Bill in some dry clothes and into my sleeping bag. It was close, but I had a big bed roll not a sleeping bag. He was warm and dry and everyone got off to sleep finally. The next morning, we awoke to mud and snow! The jamboree was cancelled, and my troop had to try to get everyone out of the field through all the mud. It was the crappiest camping trip ever, and I vowed to only camp in caves from then on, which I did do with my youngest brother Pete years later.

I was also the designated car washer. As I mentioned in the 8th grade or so I had learned to just go ahead and do the best job I could the first time so The Colonel would not bitch and moan. By this time, I was interested in driving, so I did not want the big, green, family truckster station wagon or the little VW Beetle to look like trash, so I really did not mind my weekly duty as car wash man. In fact, I made a startling discovery I clearly recall, and employ, to this day. The Colonel always wanted the water to be cleared from the hose after every use. I do not know what he thought was going to happen. Perhaps in the middle of July we would suddenly have a cold snap and water in the hose would freeze and expand and split his precious $2.50 hose, but we had to disconnect it from the house, put our mouth on the filthy end of the hose and blow until our eyes popped out of our heads and all the water was cleared from the hose. One day I had to wash the VW. The VW sat down the gentle slope of the yard at the street. So, I hooked the hose to the house spigot and dragged the hose down the yard to wash the car. When I was done and it was time to blow the hose out and roll it up so it passed inspection, I walked up the yard and disconnected it from the house. Well, the strangest thing happened. All the water flowed down the hose and out the open end! It was a miracle! That damned gravity had done its thing again. Then I learned you did not have to have a hill to make this happen, if you just picked up one end and walked along raising the hose a couple feet off the ground it would empty itself. My eyeballs were saved. No more worrying that I might blind myself by blasting my eyeballs out when I was still a young lad by having to blow out the garden hose. Course I still had to roll it to pass inspection, and I have not found a way to make that any easier.

The other chore that my sister and I had to do was to set the table, clear the table and clean the kitchen. We would alternate the chores. The easiest was setting the table and clearing it. The worst was cleaning up the kitchen. Somehow I constantly got stuck with KP duty. Setting the table for seven — yes, there were seven of us at our peak … a small third world nation – was no biggie. Forks and napkins on the left, knife and spoon on the right. The knife was closest to the plate and the edge was facing the plate. The last thing was always butter and lemons and condiments. The lemons were cut into triangular eighths so as to maximize the number. There were seven of us after all. One upside to the chores was I learned how to juggle when I was tasked with lemon duty. Still can juggle as a matter of fact. Clearing the table was the same process in reverse. Still no big deal. You could be done clearing the table in five minutes flat. Now, cleaning the kitchen was a different matter. Everything had to be washed before it was put in the dishwasher. And if you were lucky you had a disposal. Otherwise everything was scraped into a garbage holder in the sink which was nasty. But still the whole operation would take about twenty minutes. No big deal unless you are a teenager and want to be anywhere but in the stupid kitchen especially when it is summer and beautiful.

The worst of the worst was Sunday duty. First of all, The Colonel would cook breakfast to give my mother a "break" … one meal out of twenty-one meals … wow! I have to tell you, cooking was not The Colonel's forté. He made the worst scrambled eggs ever. They were overcooked and dry as sand. But we all choked them down anyway lest we incur his wrath. But later in the day came the coup-de-grâce, kitchen clean up duty. After having to go to Sunday School and then sit still in church with Reverend *Drone on Forever* Lukens, we came home and endured my mother being mad because she had to cook. Finally, we would eat Sunday lunch about 2:00, and then we had to clean up. Invariably it seemed, we always had overcooked pot roast (because it cooked all morning while we were sitting in the 110° heat of First Presbyterian Church of Vienna) and rice and boiled Brussel sprouts (nasty). Then it was kitchen clean up time. Now rice that has been, for some reason, put through a colander in the cooking process and with some of the rice remaining being left in said colander while you ate and tried to keep smiles on your faces and not to say anything that will upset either your mother or The Colonel is a real trial to get through. Anyway, at the end of the interminable family Sunday lunch – it has to be about 9:30 at night by now – there were two jobs to be done, either clean the table or clean the kitchen. Re and I rotated that job. On my KP days, Re would pile all the table clearing stuff in the kitchen. Then wipe off the table and sweep the floor, all in the time it took me to just ready to attack the kitchen. Of course usually this meant I was goofing off and cutting jokes and making her laugh as I mixed all the garbage from lunch together, squished it into a glass or something and called it a "Food Ethical." I know that name makes no sense, but that is beside the point. Then we get to the rice colander. This rice is now chemically bonded to the steel. A covalent bond has formed making it almost physically impossible to remove it. Now I would like to tell you I came up with some innovative way to overcome this problem like soaking the colander for 72 hours in gasoline or something, but I was a guy in a hurry. So, leaving logic and science, along with the flame thrower, behind, I went straight for muscle and Brillow pads. I used as many of those pads as I needed to and the colander be damned. Somewhere in the world are colanders that have been scrubbed until the metal is so thin you can see through it! And so finally, about time to start preparing dinner, I was done. My whole day shot. God I hated Sundays.

I have to admit Sunday evening dinner was the only upside of the day. In a tradition that reached back eons in Wofford history, we did "grab it and growl." You see, the way I figure, it started in my Pa's house because Middy, the old black maid that cooked and kept house for Pa, was off Sunday evenings (mind you she had already cooked breakfast and a huge lunch for us – not her family) so we all had to fend for ourselves. Now in Pa's house this meant left over fried chicken and homemade potato salad. But in our house it meant cold pot roast and what little old pieces of rice not still stuck to the colander. But it was food of my choice, and I did not have to set a table or clear a table or clean a kitchen, so it was all good. After all, I had just gotten out of the kitchen from my colander battles anyway.

28.

We all had our favorite teachers in High School. One of mine was an English teacher my senior year, Mr. Vergason. This was opposed to my senior year Algebra II/Trig teacher Captain Gallagher who had body odor bad (just ask Re) or Ms. Kronyak who tried her hardest to teach me even more French, or Ms. Case who all of us guys had the hots for. I do not even remember what she tried to teach me, but she was a babe … I guess Ms. Case must be about 80 to 85 by now … Hmmm. Anyway, Mr. Vergason lived out in one of the world's first Live/Work/Play communities named Reston. I know he *lived* there. I know he *did not work* there, and I am guessing he must have *played* there a little. So, two out of three ain't bad. Well, the four Musketeers decided one night we would TP his yard. I realize some of you may not know what TP'ing is. It is going to someone's house in the night and throwing rolls of toilet paper around the yard and up in the trees and all over the place. It is generally a sign of affection, but it is a pain to be on the receiving end of a TP party. We took two cars that night so we could make a fast get away. I was riding with Lynn. Scott and Bill were in another car. We parked a block away and were being very stealthy. We papered his yard in spectacular fashion and just as we were finishing the lights came on! Mr. V. charged out of the house and we hauled ass toward the cars! At this point we could hear sirens, and we knew we were dead meat! Lynn and I jumped in his car, and he started the engine. I reached over and said, "No. Turn off the engine and hide!" We ducked down and the police went right past us. We waited until the commotion died down and then drove away leisurely like the two fine, law-abiding, church-going, young men that we were. I do not recall about Bill and Scott. I think they escaped also, or maybe they are still in jail. It was a dog eat dog world!

My really most favorite teacher by far and the one that influenced my life more than he ever knew or realized was Mr. Stewart, my Industrial Arts – Mechanical Drawing teacher. In his class I found real success and motivation. I was a natural draftsman. As I have said, I could easily visualize objects in three-dimensions and had a real talent for drawing with a T-square and angles and compasses and all the equipment I was to eventually earn my living with. If he is still alive, he would be 85 or 90 now. I know he would be proud to know I went on to become an architect and then a teacher. So, thank you, Mr. Stewart. You were a fine teacher and showed this lost high schooler a way in life. If you, gentle reader, look through all my "stuff" you may find a draftsman's brush with 1968 inscribed on the handle. This was used to brush eraser dust off of drawings. I used it in high school, all through college and through my entire career as an architect. It is a real heirloom.

Between my junior year and senior year, I took driver's education. I want to say Mr. Smith taught the class, and I know Lynn's daddy, who was the owner of Peacock Buick in Falls Church, donated the cars for us to use. We had new 1967 Buick Skylarks to learn to drive with. Again, I discovered something I had a natural knack for. The classroom portion was a breeze, but the hands-on portion was a challenge. We had to learn how to slalom the car between cones, drive with one set of our wheels between little cones with Ping-Pong balls on top of them and then drive backwards through the same cones without knocking any of the balls off, stop with our bumper right on a line, parallel park in a tiny little space without touching the cones and do all this with the convertible tops down and the Rolling Stones screaming *Satisfaction* and *Paint It Black* over the radio! It was AWESOME! I made an A in the course. On the driving portion I lost 3 points by going over the stop line with my front bumper by 3 inches. I still think about that moment every time I pull up to a stop light with a line on the pavement and think to myself, *"I can't get nooooo, satisfaction. I can't get nooooo, girly action …"* Yep. It was the best of times. It was the worst of times. Mostly … the best of times.

Martin Luther King was assassinated on April 4th, 1968. I wish I could tell you that it had a profound effect on my life, but I was so self-centered and self-consumed that it hardly registered on my memory that it even took place. I am ashamed to admit that … but it was true.

Here, I must pay homage to my high school graduation. Momma, Marie Louise Williams Morris, my paternal grandmother, came up all the way from Cartersville to Vienna for the occasion. And being the self-centered and self-consumed child that I was, I could not have cared less. I was a bad boy. This period in my life was the end of everything I had ever known, and I was scared to death. I was a self-consumed little ass. I was graduating high school with a 2.3 GPA (unremarkable number to say the least), I was accepted to Clemson University (although I have no idea how … strong SAT scores I suspect … and I had never even visited the campus), I had screwed up my Senior Prom, Terri would not even talk to me, nor would Carol or Kathy. But I did have a job, and I spent that summer mostly working for Roger and hanging with John. As a backdrop to all of this turmoil was the raging War in Vietnam. It was summer 1968. If you are not sure what that has to do with anything, Google 1968, and look at the glory and tragedy that was that remarkable year. As I said, I was scared to death. I wish I had a father … or grandfather. As it eventually turned out, I did have a surrogate father, my Unca' Nelson Kimball Rogers, The Colonel's younger sister's husband.

Right after graduation, The Colonel was transferred to Ft. Campbell, Kentucky, to be one of two brigade commanders. This was the home of the 101st Airborne Screaming Eagles. They were polishing young men, and then sending them off to the slaughter that was Vietnam. Vietnam was a death sentence in 1968, but I had a "college deferment." That meant I did not have to go be killed as long as I kept a 2.5 GPA. I was going to screw that up royally soon enough, but I am getting ahead of myself. The family moved to Ft. Campbell. It is north of Nashville, right above Clarksville, Tennessee, and below Hopkinsville, Kentucky. It is just over the Tennessee line in Kentucky. It was a hole. But fortunately, I was to be escorted to Clemson University in late July so I did not have to put up with my mother's moody bi-polar hatred of the place.

Chapter Four
"Freedom Is Just Another Word …"

1.

And late July, 1968, a naïve, lazy 17 year old boy was taken to Clemson University by The Colonel. Late in his life The Colonel revealed to me how much he cared for me at the time as he related the only reason he "let" me go to Clemson was that he thought it was a military school. He did not ever understand or care enough to even find out where I was going to college. My declared major at Clemson was to be Mechanical Engineering … I had no idea what that was, but someone had told me that was what I needed to major in, and I did. And so, one very hot July day The Colonel and I were sitting uncomfortably next to each other in a large un-air conditioned hall with about 600 guys (and maybe fifteen girls) and their parents being "oriented." When that was done, The Colonel left. And so began my life on my own … sort of … and finally.

"Look to your left. One of you will be gone next semester. Look to your right. One of you will be gone next year." It was a different kind of college experience in 1968. There was no remedial help. There was no competition among colleges for money, and so they did not care if 2/3rds of their freshman class flunked out. It seemed as if it were almost a point of pride among colleges. And besides there was always a good job awaiting us draft age males if we left college. We could join Uncle Sam and save the world from the domino effect of communism by going to fight in beautiful, sunny Vietnam.

Aug. 1968, Col. James Wingfield Morris 43y/o with James Wingfield Morris, Jr. 17 y/o at Clemson

August 1968 – A Clemson "Rat" – James Wingfield Morris Jr.

But I was there. I was in a dormitory with football players. It was a nice dorm. There were other dorms that were not so nice – The Tin Cans, so named because they were totally made of metal. They were built during WWII very economically. They were not air-conditioned, six stories tall and if one banged on a wall, of which there were many, it could be heard all over … campus! But The Colonel made sure his boy was in the "nice" brick dorm. His job was finished. My mother had made me matching bed spreads in orange with purple pillow cases for my roommate and me.

It was a very gay and a typically Mother thing to do. I know my roommate, Mike, must have thought I was "queer as a three-dollar bill."

Generally, on college campuses today hazing is either banned or severely frowned upon, but not in 1968! It was a TRADITION! And stupid. At Clemson, the first thing freshmen were to do was to get all our hair shaved off, get a rat cap and a rat bell and generally look like an idiot. And as soon as The Colonel left, I did just that. And looked like an idiot. And my rat cap and bell are in a footlocker in the basement. Generally, rats had to do anything an upperclassman told them to do which usually involved pushups … idiotic. But I did them. It was my first, and in retrospect, last time I would be degraded and humiliated and take it like a laughing, well, idiot. The only rat related rule was you could not be hazed while in class or in your dorm studying. I have a strong recollection of those early rat days of going to a pep rally before a big football game. All us rats filed in and sat in the rat section together. Then the girl rats arrived and there was no place for them to sit and so one upperclassman yelled, "Rats! There is no place for the lady rats to sit!" Thinking that this would make us "southern gentleman rats" make room for them, but that is not what happened. A rat yelled back, "They can sit on my face!" Now, I thought this was a most unusual thing to say. It made no sense to me, and I "pondered it in my heart" for several years before I fully grasped what that young man meant … interesting. That young rat-man was light years ahead of naïve me. After all, and as I have noted, in my house we were not allowed to have *National Geographic* or *Life Magazine* as they were considered lewd publications as they may have a glimpse of cleavage or, God forbid, a topless native woman. But let me add, we did have the Sears Catalog! And many a young man in my day got most of his education from that venerated publication. Many of us Boomer Boys still have fetishes to this day due to those advertisements of stockings, garter belts and girdles. But, I digress.

Clemson was a military school but only on Thursdays. And I scored high enough on my SAT's that I was in Air Force ROTC, rather than Army like most of the other guys. But ROTC was a course you took like any other. Many boys did not take the ROTC course and consequently were not put on the Vietnam fodder treadmill. But we all had to keep a 2.5 so we would not become 1-A on our Draft Status, and be shipped out to Nam. We were issued little blue uniforms with little blue hats and they tried to teach us to march. Generally, we were a pretty rag-tag group, but I found class to be very interesting. In a class I remember particularly clearly, we were given an aerial photograph of an installation we were to bomb. Then we were shown photographs as if we were a pilot coming toward the site, and we had to identify the target. I was exceptionally good at it. I now understand it had to do with a brain trait called spatial apperception, which is a trait I was blessed with.

But before I get into classes I want to make it clear I was a terrible student. I was a visual and auditory learner. If you could show me, just once, the how and the why of a concept, I had it … cold. But if I had to read and figure out the concept myself, I was lost. I had no real idea how to study. Now, I was a good reader when motivated and interested, but a poor reader when it came to interpreting the text, determining what was important and what was not and gleaning a concept.

Several of the other classes I recall that I took that year were Mechanical Drawing, Psychology and Calculus I. The mechanical drawing was a breeze, and I literally blew that class away. I definitely had and developed a real talent for drafting and all things Mechanical Drawing, visualizing objects and interpreting them, and yet I had no guidance how to utilize that talent. Psychology was taught by a man who was about 150 years old. He was definitely a proponent of the "2/3rds of you will be gone concept" and made it his mission to breathe real life into said concept. He also told all of us 17-year-old boys (yes I was only 17 until October of 1968 – I was still a real child) that sex was over-rated. Well, that idea went over like a lead balloon to all of us over-sexed, female starved young men. Also, he was an asshole. And then there was Calculus I ... what can I say. I did not understand it. I do not understand it. I have NEVER had an occasion to use it. I have never had a need to use it. It is useless math for the sake of math as far as I am concerned, and I to this day I have very little use for something that only exists for itself and serves no purpose. My Calculus I class was in an auditorium with 300 other students and taught by a graduate student. This single class destroyed my GPA. It was a 5 credit hour class and wreaked havoc with every other grade.

As I said I was naïve and did not understand anything about dropping classes before a Drop Date, and I got hammered by this class. During my fall semester, I failed this class spectacularly. And my winter semester I failed this class again, spectacularly. And in the spring I failed this class again, spectacularly. However, I do wish to give a weak defense for my first college showing. Studies about learning and learning styles later in my life as I studied to become a teacher, revealed to me that the brain does not develop the ability to grasp extremely abstract concepts until later in life and mine was a very young, very weak 17-year-old brain. Calculus was just plain beyond my ability to make heads or tails of it. Now, when I was 45, and I went back to school for my teaching degree, I had to take a course in Calculus and Analytic Geometry ... and made I made an A. It, at least, made some sense to me at 45. Now, I still have never used it or even felt I had an occasion to need it. The bottom line, academically at Clemson, I left school after summer school in 1969 with a 1.3 overall GPA. I was rapidly losing my "college deferment" from the draft.

2.

That year at Clemson did hold some interesting "becoming" adventures for me. There was a bar in downtown Clemson called the "Study Hall." You know, your mom calls the dorm and asks to speak to their child and the guy who answers the phone says, "He's at the study hall and I'll leave a message on his door." And all is good. Whenever I hear the song *Eleanor Rigby* by the Beatles I recall sitting at the bar in the Study Hall eating a pickle and drinking a beer. You could drink beer at 18 in South Carolina. I guess they figured if you were old enough to vote and old enough to go a die for your country you were old enough to buy a beer ... very progressive for the south in 1968. Downtown Clemson also had the only movie theater for thirty miles in in any direction, and it was in that theater that about a thousand Clemson idiots went to see the film *Barbarella* with Jane Fonda. The film promised to be loaded with sex and naked women. It was not. We were very disappointed. Another case of reality intruding on fantasy.

It was at Clemson University that freshman year that I first inhaled a cigarette. My roommate Mike smoked. He also taught me how to light my farts but there is not much of a story there. It is exactly what it sounds like … methane gas is flammable. He also taught me to eat fish I had caught. We went fishing and caught a fish called Crappy. We cleaned them and his mother fried them, and we ate them. That was the first time I had eaten any fish other than a "fish stick." But again, I digress. I fancied myself quite the man when it came to smoking. If you recall, when I was in the seventh grade I had stolen one of my mom's and The Colonel's Salem cigarettes and smoked them out by the trash cans in Blue Ridge Summit so I had been puffing for a while, but I had never really *smoked*. I had never inhaled. So, a bunch of guys and I were at a basketball game, and we were smoking and cheering, and I accidently inhaled the smoke. The whole world grayed out, and I got so dizzy I had to sit down. It was awesome! And I was hooked! The combination of being cool, nicotine and smoke was now to become a habit that I would have for the next twenty-seven years. Reflecting now, for each worldly step forward, I lost a bit of myself. I traded being cool smoking for my health the next thirty years.

Along this same time a bunch of guys decided to head over to Lake Hartwell to go skinny dipping. Again, my life experience was broadening like crazy. We all piled in upper classmen's cars and headed out one evening. Of course all of us anticipated that we would be joined by girls, but again reality intruded and there were none. The evening ended up being just a bunch of naked boys splashing around in the dark and goofing off. It was stupid. And while I was swimming in the cold lake water my finger shrunk, and as I shook some water off my hand my high school class ring slipped off and was lost to the dark and watery depths of Lake Hartwell. For the life altering experience of skinny dipping, I paid with my high school class ring.

When Thanksgiving came around it did not make sense for me to go all the way home to Fort Campbell, so I went to Cartersville to have Thanksgiving there. But somehow I had to get there. There was a bus line from Clemson but the only way to get to Cartersville was to take the bus to Columbia, South Carolina, then catch a bus to Atlanta then catch a bus to Cartersville which was a stop on the way to Chattanooga. So, I searched the bulletin board and found a ride to Atlanta if I shared the gas tab. I left on Wednesday in a VW, and this guy took me to Atlanta. I arrived in Atlanta late on Wednesday just in time to find out the next bus north was not until 11:00 at night and would put me in Cartersville at 1:30 AM. No good. So I decided to hitchhike for the first time in my life. Somehow I caught a ride with a man traveling north. All I remember is he pointed out to me the big old knife he that hung in his car near his leg. I guess he was as afraid of me as I was leery of him. But he took me all the way to Cartersville and dropped me in town about 7:00 PM. I guess I had Thanksgiving with Momma. I do not really remember. What I do remember is what Uncle Nelson and Aunt Toochie did for me. To recap: Aunt Toochie was The Colonel's younger sister. The children in Momma and Unca' Pete's family were: The Colonel, Marybelle (Swift) and Marion – *Toochie* – (Rogers). Unca' Nelson (Toochie's husband) took me under his wing. Unca' Nelson became my surrogate father, and I will forever love him for that. At that Thanksgiving, Nelson and Toochie put me on their car insurance so I could drive one of their cars when I was in town. They (he) did not have to do that, but they (he) did. When Thanksgiving was over, Nelson took me to Marietta to catch the bus. The bus was to go to Atlanta, then I would have a layover and catch a bus going to Greenville late in the evening getting to Clemson at 2:00 in the morning or so. Well, that was not acceptable so I convinced the bus driver to let me out at 75 and 285, and I started hitchhiking. I do not remember it as being noteworthy, so it must have worked. I do remember standing by the road, it was raining with cars blasting past me in a cloud of spray. But, I made it to Clemson and survived.

And when Christmas break came I was to head home to Fort Campbell. The only way to get home was again to take a bus. I as becoming a bus veteran, and the only bus available left Clemson at about 8:00 at night. Its route was through the mountains toward Knoxville and then across the state to Nashville. It was to be an all-night affair. So with no other choice available, I clambered aboard in downtown Clemson, and we were off. I recall it was cold and rainy. I also recall that somewhere along the way I met a girl, and we chatted briefly, then she got off in Knoxville, and I rode on. I got to Nashville about 9:00 in the morning. There was no bus north toward Fort Campbell, which seems odd to me now, but the plan was I was to call Mom, and she would come all the way down and pick me up. And she did. Interestingly, I do not remember anything about that 1968 Christmas, nor do I recall how I got back to Clemson. But I did … probably on a bus.

During that winter semester I again tried to conquer Calculus, and as I noted failed miserably again, but I did meet a girl. She was a senior at Walhalla High School, and she came to a basketball game at Clemson where we met. I had to move quickly in those days as I did not have a car, so I chatted her up pretty heavily that night, and she gave me her number and agreed to a date. Now I was in a real pickle. I had a date but no car. Fortunately, I had met an upper classman in Air Force ROTC who lived in my dorm, and we had become friends. He had a little red Karman Ghia, and he agreed to let me use it. And on a Friday night in the early spring I actually had a date. I found her house. As I recall her house was a kind of ramshackle affair back in the mountains near Walhalla. The impression I got was that her family was poor, but she was a very sweet girl. I met her parents who were very kind to me also. So, my family education and upbringing of "looking down on people" who were not "of the proper station in life" was somewhat upended. I grew up with the whole concept of African American females were "women" and never "ladies." As I reflect on it today, this "superiority complex" was something The Colonel and The Colonel's Lady taught us not so much through direct words, but it was taught through attitude and comments. I have also come to understand that you cannot see something in someone else that you do not see in yourself. So, I wonder if this "superiority complex" came from an "inferiority complex" that my parents felt, and they tried to overcompensate by looking down on others. At any rate, this young lady was very sweet, and her parents were very kind, and we had a wonderful evening. Without detail, I will say we ended up parking in a mountain glen that evening. For a senior in high school she was quiet knowledgeable and experienced and adept but another bullet was dodged. We dated uneventfully for a few months and then drifted apart.

Later that spring I was invited by an upper classman to go up to Clemson's sister school Winthrop College in Rock Hill, South Carolina, with four other guys to a dance. We four were to be blind dates for some girls at this all-girls school. The upper classman had a girlfriend at Winthrop, and she had convinced him to bring a bunch of us up there to the dance. We were the way the upper classman was going to pay for his gas. We must have spent the night there, or we drove back really late at night, I do not really remember. But there are two things I do remember. One was how to steer a car with your knees while you are lighting a cigarette, and the other was *Uncle Charlie*. Apparently this upper classman and his girlfriend were "having relations," and at the designated time every month he and his girlfriend anticipated her period arriving meaning they were not pregnant. Now calling someone in a dormitory at college in 1968/69 was much different than it is today as cell phones were still forty years in the future. You would call the dorm phone, usually a pay phone arrangement hanging on a wall, and whoever picked it up would go and try to find whoever you wanted to talk to … or just walk away and leave the phone off the cradle if they were too lazy or not inclined to help, or perhaps they were in a hurry to get to class. At any rate, when that blessed event, her period, occurred each month, the girlfriend would call him on the land line, and let him know with much gushing and lovey-dovey talk, or if she had to leave a message with whomever answered the phone, the coded message she left was that *"Uncle Charlie had arrived safely."* And he would know they had "dodged the bullet" again.

I recall two friends from my Clemson days. One was Ron and one was Jay. I'll talk about Jay later. Ron was from Charleston. He roomed in the same Jock dorm as I did and we were both trapped there on weekends. Neither of us could go home so "Birds of a feather" and all that. I recall us buying some really nasty wine and sitting in the dorm room playing Hearts with a couple of other guys we scrounged up. Ron introduced me to boiled peanuts, which I thought were nasty in the beginning but have grown to love over the years. To this day I don't squeeze one of those little goobers out of the salty, soft, wet shell and pop it into my mouth that those days at Clemson don't come rushing back as we "hunted for the bitch" late into the evening and smoked Tennessee River Crooks and drank cheap wine.

Later when I was at Southern Tech and The Colonel et al were stationed in the Canal Zone, Panama, Ron met me in Charleston because I was to board a MAC (Military Airlift Command) flight from Charleston AFB to the Canal Zone, and Ron and I went out drinking. As I recall the flight was to leave about 3 in the morning and we staggered into the terminal drunk as skunks, and he waved me off in the middle of the night. I flew on a windowless C-141 Starlifter. It was one of the longest, most miserable flights I ever took. Not the worst, but right up there. And then, arriving with a throbbing hangover at 11:00 in the morning and stepping off the plane into the blazing sunlight, 100 degrees, 89% humidity of Panama and into the loving arms of my mother and sister and then having to go out to lunch. All I wanted to do was puke and sleep. Neither was in the cards.

I met Jay at Clemson when I returned in the summer of 1969 to try to pass Calculus. I did not pass Calculus, but I met and roomed with Jay. I have four strong recollections of Jay. The first is he showed me how to use a hair dryer and back brush my hair to get the curls out of it. My "beautiful" hair had all this natural curl that all the old people in my family said "made me so pretty I should have been a girl." And this hair had been the bane of my existence since the Beatles came on the scene with their long hair and every boy wanted their hair like theirs. If you can locate my prom pictures from 1967 and 1968 and the picture of me in my 1968 annual, you will see my pitiful attempts to be cool. But Jay changed that and now I was "cool."

Jay and I also headed up to his home in Charlotte, North Carolina, one weekend, and I went to the UNC campus and I saw "Carol of Vienna, Virginia, I should have taken her to the prom fame." I do not remember much about that except I saw her, and it was awkward.

The other two Jay events were us being boys. Jay brought a paper back porno book back to school with him after one weekend away. Well, I was totally enthralled with this book and read it cover to cover several times. No doubt I should have been studying, but this book was of real interest to me. As I have said, I could read and digest information when interested and motivated … and I was both interested and motivated. So, after we had read the book to tatters, we decided it was such a fine piece of literature that we should donate it to the Clemson University library. So, we assigned it a Dewey Decimal Number (you may have to look that one up boys and girls) and made a Dewey Decimal Card to go in the card racks which were kept in little drawers in a huge cabinet where you looked up books. And one night we snuck into the library and put the book in its proper area: nonfiction, sociology, reference. And installed the card properly in the card catalog area. And that was my donation to Clemson University. I did not claim a tax deduction. Jay might have. The second event was a weekend opportunity to do anything but study – work. Some contractors came to the dining hall one Friday night and asked to no one in particular, "Who would like to earn some cash tomorrow?" Well, Jay and I were always penniless so we signed up. We had no idea what we were to do, but we signed up. We did not even know how much we were going to be paid. Kind of like *Napoleon Dynamite* and the chickens … such was our brilliance. Saturday morning, we were out front of the dorm at 6:00 AM as the summer South Carolina sun was just breaking above the pine trees. A truck rolled up and Jay and I climbed aboard with about ten other fools. It felt like *Cool Hand Luke* without the striped pants. We rode perhaps five miles out on the road that led to Clemson from the interstate. The same road I had hitched rides on before in the cold dark. The only difference was the sun was up and the temperature was pushing up above 85 degrees and it was only 7:00 in the morning. At about 7:30 we arrived at two, single story office buildings. There were ladders up to the roof. Half of us we were instructed to grab shovels and the other half wheel barrows. Jay and I grabbed shovels. We were told to climb up and the Superintendent would tell us what to do. Well, the contractor had been sand blasting the inside of a large machinery penthouse on the roof, and there were little mountains of sand everywhere inside this penthouse. Need I say the penthouse was not air conditioned, and there was very little air circulating. But, like *Cool Hand Luke* and the road paving adventure, we dug in. We would fill little wheel barrows with big rubber wheels that would not damage the black tar roof as they rolled, roll them to the edge of the roof and dump them down a chute that led to boys with wheel barrows on the ground who would wheel it over to a truck and shovel it into the truck. By 10 in the morning the temperature in the roof top area we were working in had to be 110. We were pouring sweat. At 12 we were allowed to stop and were given a sandwich and water … almost like *Napoleon Dynamite*. And finally about 4 we were done. Literally and figuratively we were done. We were baked and sunburned and sore and dehydrated and done. All the sand was moved. We were taken back to campus and each given $20.00. Now $20.00 back then went a whole lot further. When I was dating Carolyn later in 1972 we could go to a movie and get pizza after for $20.00 so the day's labor had not been for naught. As I recall, Jay and I blew it on a steak dinner and beer that night.

That same summer I witnessed a historic event. Who knew where that inauspicious little jaunt of Alan Shepard back when I was in the sixth grade would take America, but there I was, 4:17 p.m., July 20th, 1969, at Clemson University in a high rise dorm common room with Jay and a bunch of other college hopefuls glued to the one television in the building trying to make out from the grainy, black and white images what in the world, or what *not* in the world, was going on. If you look at the original broadcast, you will see that it is difficult to understand exactly what is happening, but we did understand Commander Neil Armstrong's words, "That's one small step for man, one giant leap for mankind." Man was on the moon. I do not have any recollections of what we did after that. I recall a whoop when it actually happened, but other than that, nothing … probably studying.

I ended that summer semester passing Calculus with a D. Vietnam was raging. The Tet Offensive had proved we could not win there, but President Johnson's actions had left us mired between death and hopelessness. I had no student draft deferment. I had a 1.3 GPA. I was, again, a failure. There was but one option.

3.

I returned home to Fort Campbell, Kentucky. That remaining summer of 1969 was probably one of the two lowest points in my life. To me, there was only direction left, to join the army. There are four things that stand out in my recollections about that brief time I had at home that summer: taking a test for OCS, Uncle Nelson, a trip to Marietta and Nancy.

As I said, Vietnam seemed to be my only option. I was going to follow in The Colonel's footsteps and join the army. He would certainly be proud of me then! So, one afternoon, I went to a barracks and took a test to see if I could go to Officer Candidate School, OCS. The test was basically a comprehensive I.Q. test. I recall I scored a 130 and was a prime candidate for OCS. Vietnam was chewing up young lieutenants and sending them home in body bags faster than Uncle Sam could manufacture them, so the army and marines were starving for young fodder. It seemed I was destined for "Nam," but unbeknownst to me a savior was working behind the scenes, Uncle Nelson, The Colonel's younger sister's husband, the Annapolis graduate, Navy Captain and professor at Georgia Tech. He told my parents about small college called the Southern Institute of Technology, Southern Tech, STI, located in Marietta, Georgia. I believe he had made some calls and had arranged for me to get an interview with professor Chester A. Orvold, AIA, the head of the Architectural Engineering Technology Department. My mother was totally against the idea. "No son of hers was going to attend a 'trade school.'" I guess she would rather have seen me die in a rice patty rather than attend a "trade school," but that is just me thinking out loud. Apparently, The Colonel prevailed and Re and I chugged down to Cartersville in a little white VW, so I could interview at STI. We stayed at Momma's house up on The Hill and were treated like royalty. Momma did not care about failures. She loved me unconditionally. But, I recall I was less than enthusiastic about the whole go back to school idea. I was at a very, very low place.

Professor Orvold met me in his office in the old architecture building. I recall him as being a very, very old man with so many wrinkles he was more prune than man. But he was a salesman! He and I talked, and then he introduced me to Mr. Muller. Mr. Muller was professor there and had written a book on drafting which the college used. I still have the book if you search my shelves. It is a light blue color and packed with last century's standards and advice about drafting and architecture. That book is beautifully "old school." I love that book. And miracle of miracles, when I left Professor Orvold and Mr. Muller that day I was convinced that not only I would be admitted STI, but that I could possibly be successful there. When you are at the bottom the only way to go is up. To this day, I still believe that Uncle Nelson had pulled some stings for me. No college would have taken me with a 1.3 and a record of failures like I had amassed. Little did I realize how STI would change my life forever. But for now, I returned to Fort Campbell to wait for school to start.

4.

Back at Fort Campbell, The Colonel actually seemed relieved that I was not going to die in Vietnam although he never said anything to me. I went to work bagging groceries for tips at the fort commissary and painting the wooden noise screen fence behind our house. I recall bringing my record player out back of the house and playing The Rascals songs as loud as I could while I painted in the blasting Kentucky heat. I also made a homemade movie with our 8mm hand held camera titled *Jimbo's X Rated Movie*. The last time I saw it, it was in the possession of my brother Brian Meroney Morris. It was a simple little thing. A mishmash of special effects: my brother Pete speeding at double speed down a road on his bike, The Colonel in full fatigues and helmet jumping up in the air and disappearing (something psychological there) and other short clips. Pretty stupid overall but a hit with the siblings. Another thing that needed to be taken care of that summer was my impacted wisdom teeth. You have not lived until you have had all four of your impacted wisdom teeth cut out with Novocain being the only anesthetic used by an Army dentist. It was a brutal and bloody affair. I'm sure it cost The Colonel nothing.

The one upside to that brief confused summer was a girl across the street named Nancy. Things I can say about Nancy: she was attractive, she was blond, she smoked, she was more sexually experienced than I was, and she filled out a swimsuit in spectacular fashion. I recall one of The Colonel's contemporaries commenting to him, and him relaying to me, "Sir, are you okay with your son playing with those dangerous things?" Yes, Nancy was a brief but exciting affair. I am not going to comment on bases as I honestly do not recall — we were brief as I said — but we packed a lot into our several weeks. The Nancy Affair was something else. We saw *Lawrence of Arabia* together, went parking, went to the swimming pool, hung out with a local garage band learning to play *Magic Carpet Ride* by Steppenwolf and doing a credible job, especially on the drum solo, and took her to a dance with that band playing, and we went water skiing. I guess my time at Fort Campbell was not horrible, but I was on auto pilot. Whatever problem came into my path, I learned to deal with.

5.

In September of 1969 I was dropped off at Southern Technical Institute, STI. There was no sitting through orientations, no haircuts, no Rat Caps, no handmade blankets or big deal with The Colonel. I was just dropped off by my mother with all my stuff, and she left. At this point, I was much wiser about college and how it worked, but I was at the bottom of a gigantic GPA hole. I figured about the only way I could go was either up the college ladder or to Vietnam, so I started climbing hoping I could climb faster than Uncle Sam. In the end, it was fate that determined that race.

After some consideration, I think the best way to talk about my three and one quarter years at STI is to talk in terms of themes rather than trying to keep a timeline narrative. So, I will relate STI under the headings of Academics and '69 – '72 Events, College Jobs and Travel, and finally Friends, Family & Personal Relationships.

Academics / '69 –'72 Events

As I said I was a much savvier college student when I arrived in September. I knew what courses I needed to graduate, what a prerequisite was, what a drop/add date was and meant. I was ready to play the game. The first course to give me trouble was a Structural Analysis class. I could not get the idea of "Moment" in my brain so I dropped the class and audited it for the rest of the quarter. By the end, I got it and took the class the next quarter and got an A. I continued plowing through course after course and was slowly pulling my GPA up. I did have to take Calculus again, and it still gave me trouble, but I hung in there and escaped with a C. Then I had to take Calculus II. I struggled and struggled with that class. I had learned to play the game, so I met with the professor. I met with the professor so many times he probably thought he was tutoring me. Coming into the final he told me, "Mr. Morris, you make any kind of a showing on the final, and I will pass you under one condition. You promise me you will never teach math." I did make a "showing," and I did promise him.

Although as it turned out I lied about teaching math. You know, it just occurred to me that even though I had to learn Calculus, I never once needed it at Southern Tech … or during my professional career … or as a teacher … or ever. Interesting. I'll wait. Perhaps someday a person will run up to me in the Walmart and want me to integrate a function … whatever that means.

My drafting courses were a breeze. I loved drawing and was quite accomplished at it. It's funny, another architecture student, whom I was to marry in the future, when asked why she was in studying to become an architect said, "It was because she wanted to save the world through the built environment." When people ask me that question I would tell them I wanted to become an architect "because I like to draw. And that I'm good at it." I know, lame … but it's a true story. I loved Surveying. Getting out on the campus with a transit and tripod and stadia rod and chain was heaven to me. The whole STI curriculum was very hands-on, and I thrived! I learned contour mapping, cut and fill calculations, closing boundaries, roadway super-elevation and subdivision layout. One of my favorite teachers was Dub Newman. Mr. Newman taught the classroom portion of surveying, and he was an excellent teacher. Later in my life, when I was a teacher, I would employ one of his tactics. He would walk up behind you during a quiz, look over your shoulder and say, "For five points I'll tell you if your answer to question three is correct." Well, if you were unsure and the question was worth ten or fifteen points, you would take him up on the offer. If you did take him up on the offer of help, he would mark next to the question, -5, then say, "It's correct." Man, you felt stupid! But then, if it was wrong! He would tell you. Then he would offer that for five more points I'll tell you where you went wrong. I never took him up one that. I had already lost five. I would find my mistake by myself. He was cool.

Another interesting prof was Mr. Melvin. Mr. Melvin taught HVAC and the cool thing about him was he always late to class. Now back then, I'm not sure what it is like today, but back then if the professor was ten minutes late, you could leave. No harm, no foul, but he would invariably walk in at the nine-minute mark almost every time. The other thing was he always had his coffee cup with him. In the early mornings he had his cup and looked bleary-eyed and had the shakes. If you went up to ask him a question you could smell the whiskey. Usually by the end of class the shakes were gone. Ah, the world of architecture. In the Structure Engineering Department, we all had to take two classes of Structural Analysis. This was usually taught by Mr. Myatt. Well, Structure Analysis I was a sophomore class and when I started that class the only calculator one had was a slide rule. Many of you reading this will have to look that up. I have mine in the drawer next to me. It is a beautiful precision instrument by the German company Dietzgen. It was a Decimal Trig Type Log-Log and very cool. I challenge you to learn to use it … both sides including the Log functions. But, when I took Structural Analysis II in 1972, my senior year, technology had taken leaps and bounds! We actually signed up to reserve a time to go to the Calculator Lab. This was a room in the architecture building that was kept locked at all times due to the very valuable contents in the lab. Mr. Myatt had to unlock the lab to let you in and then his office was right across the hall so he could keep a watch on the lab and its expensive contents. In the lab and literally chained to the wall were electronic calculators. They were about a foot square, plugged into the wall and they could add, subtract, multiply and divide. That's all, just four functions.

They had no memory, no other abilities, but four functions. They had cost about $500.00 each. It was much faster and easier to make your calculations and much more accurate, but I really missed swinging that slide rule around and around in its case by the loop. And if you need a slide rule, there is one in the bottom drawer of the cabinet to my left of my computer. Oh, in case you ever decide to carry a slide rule in its case, never use the loop to hang it from your belt. Only nerds do that.

STI was an Architecture and Engineering *Technology* School. We were a division of Georgia Tech, which we referred to as North Avenue Trade School. We at STI were the hands-on doers. Supposedly, Georgia Tech grads were the thinkers. But all of us had to take Liberal Arts courses to round us out as human beings and several professors come to mind that were excellent. There was Mr. Blair who had a little pot belly, wore his pants way to high and had a weedy little moustache, but the man taught a mean Technical Writing course. There was Mr. Secrist the American History professor who gave me a lifelong love of history. Mr. Secrist was actually quite respected in the Civil War Historical community. He has written several books, and I got to hear him at an event at UGA some many years later. After his speech I came up to him and introduced myself. I was a fifth grade teacher at this point, so it was easily thirty-five years after I had left STI. He greeted me warmly and insisted he remembered me – there was no-way. He was an excellent professor. There were Mr. Hayes, Mr. Tumlin and Mr. Bates, English teachers all, but my favorite was Ms. Roberta Gates. She taught World literature I and II. I still have a couple of papers I wrote for her. One about Dante's Inferno is around somewhere. But when I think of Ms. Gates, I think of *Romeo and Juliette*. Ms. Gates was teaching a class on Shakespeare and that particular play to her class, and in that class was a lady whom unbeknownst to me I would marry in only three short years. Next door to Ms. Gates's classroom in another classroom, I was trying to figure out the best way to technically explain some inane point to Mr. Blair's satisfaction. Ms. Gates stopped her class and came to my classroom and asked Mr. Blair if she could borrow me for a few minutes. She brought me to her classroom so that Miss Carolyn Ethel Lyon and I could read Romeo and Juliette's famous balcony scene for the class … very cool for me. Must have been embarrassing to Miss Lyon.

Another interesting professor was Mr. Black … although Carolyn insists it was Mr. Wemberly … who taught Business Economics. It was generally known all over the campus that Mr. Black fancied himself quite the "lady's man" and was not above hitting on coeds. At any rate, it was my last quarter of school which meant it was fall of 1972. Miss Carolyn Lyon and I were engaged by then and quite the item on campus, and we were in Mr. Black's class together. Miss Lyon was taking a fairly heavy load as I recall including Astronomy and I was struggling to fill my quarter with classes because I had basically completed all my course requirements. One of the final assignments in the class was to complete a paper on a case study. We were all assigned different cases. Understanding Carolyn was under a time crunch, and wanting her to have more time to go out with me on dates, I offered to do her case study for her. She agreed and I completed both hers and mine. I believe I did mine first to warm up and then did hers. Anyway when the grades came back, her paper was an A and mine was a B. She got an A in the course and I got a B. So, do not tell me a great set of legs and sitting in the front of the class in a skirt did not make a difference in 1972!

Two particular recollections I will classify just as *Events* that were integral to my education took place while I was at Southern Tech. One was a massive, well perpetrated joke on me and the other was deadly serious. One weekend morning about 1:00 I came back to the dorm after a date and most of the hall was empty. At this point I was a Dorm Counselor and Hall Supervisor so I knew all of the guys on the hall and many in the dorm. But the place being quiet at 1:00 AM on the weekend is not totally unusual as STI was a suitcase college, so it emptied out on the weekends, but this particular night it was eerily quiet. I finally found a buddy, Larry, who told me everyone was down in the lounge listening to something this guy's shortwave radio. So, I tumbled downstairs and found many of my friends gathered closely around a radio that this one guy had tuned to somewhere. There was a lot of static and through the static you could hear an announcer with a heavily accented voice talking quickly and in a high pitched, tense voice. He was describing a nuclear blast that had taken place. He was frantic and his words were getting tangled in the static as he reported bombers being heard overhead as rockets being fired. You have to appreciate that this time period was full of fighting and dying in Vietnam every day and it was all over the evening news. Anything seemed possible. All the guys crowded around seemed aghast and terrified. And I bought it … hook, line and sinker! I listened and talked to them and they got me more and more revved up. This was very well rehearsed. I was frantic! I raced upstairs grabbing some change on the way to the only phone on our hall. Each floor had one pay phone in the center of the building. I started pounding quarters into the phone to call my parents in Panama. After much messing with the overseas operator I managed to get the call to go through and wake The Colonel up. I told him what I had heard, and what should I do? At this point all the guys from downstairs spilled out of the stairway laughing their heads off. They had made a tape and were playing the tape on the radio like it was a real broadcast. I told The Colonel, and he hung up. Well, they got the best of me that night. I am sure The Colonel thought I was a fool, but I have come to appreciate that night. It was a magnificent piece of theater, and I was suckered good!

On December 1st, 1969, the federal Government held a draft lottery. It was the first time this had been done since 1942 when World War II was ramping up and the volunteer pool had depleted. This 1969 lottery was for people born between 1/1/1944 and 12/31/1950 and would determine a pool of young men that would be immediately called up for military service in order to fill the rapidly declining ranks of young men needed to be sent into the meat grinder that was the Vietnam War. I say meat grinder because in 1968, 16,900 U.S. soldiers were killed and in 1969 - 11,800 had died. Combined those two figures they would equal the entire population of Marietta, Georgia, in 1970, and the 1969 death figure alone exceeds the entire population of Cartersville in 1970. The lottery was meant to induct into the armed forces all young men whose draft status was 1-A … like me. The event was televised. The first birthdate called was September 14th. It was number one. The second was April 24th. It was number two. And so the evening went. As the numbers rolled out, several of my friends in the dorm had very low numbers. Starting the next day, the government called up all men with lottery numbers one through I'm not sure what number. As 1969 rolled into 1970 more and more groups of numbers were called. In order to speed the induction process along when "your number was up," all 1-A classifications were notified to report for their physicals. The physical was to make sure there was not some physical reason you should not be 1-A. I got my notice and was told to report to the draft board in Cartersville to take a bus down to Atlanta to Fort McPherson for my physical. The morning I was to leave it I recall it was pouring buckets of rain. I had to get a buddy of mine to drive me to Cartersville because I did not have a car. The Colonel did not feel me having a car was needed, but that is a whole other subject. My friend took me to Cartersville from Marietta and we got to the address on the notice with about a half hour to spare. It was still dark and the rain was still pouring, and the building at the address was closed up tight and dark. Panic! I'm not sure how, but I was able to find someone who told me the draft board office had recently moved to the other side of town and they gave me an address and directions. God bless that person. And I arrived at the bus with five minutes to spare. Thus a long day of standing around in my underwear being poked and prodded and being pronounced "fit as a fiddle" or rather "fit enough to die" took place. On the bus ride back to Cartersville late that day, I convinced the bus driver to let me out at the intersection of US 41 Highway and Clay Street, now called the South Marietta Loop, just a stone's throw to the campus. To answer your question, my number was 229. The draft in 1970 cut off at 195. Fate had stepped in.

Let me close my Academics portion with a little note. If you recall, I transferred to Southern Tech from Clemson with a 1.3 GPA. Not long after arriving at STI, I realized I had better "buckle down*" and "get with the program*" or I was going to end up "living in a cardboard box*." *Note: all motivational quotes courtesy of The Colonel. So, I ended up graduating STI with a 3.35 GPA. Not nearly the GPA my soon to be wife, Carolyn, had accumulated, but I feel it was respectable none the less especially after my high school showing of 2.3. I consider that STI GPA as a small success in my life.

[It is now July 12th, 2021. At this point, I want to give you, gentle reader, an update. As I started writing almost year ago the pandemic was in full swing. It is tapering down now with the introduction at the beginning of the year of a vaccine. Unfortunately, there are many ignorant people in the world. I guess there are and always have been the ignorant. The USA is hovering at 69% vaccinated with the Stupids holding out for various reason from "I don't trust the government" to "They are injecting tracking chips into us" to "this is the first step, next they will take our guns." Lord have mercy. Deaths in the USA are now 606 thousand (more than the Civil War) and 4.03 million worldwide. Carolyn and I and the immediate family are well. We have all been vaccinated and are not traveling and are avoiding large gatherings. As an interesting outcome of the pandemic, Miss Caitlin spent the majority of her 5th grade year right here in Carolyn's and my house as she went to school virtually. I tried to provide backup and support for her studies given my 25 years as a 5th grade teacher. We had a good time and interspersed her world with 13 school related and exercise related field trips.

On September 30th of last year, The Colonel passed away just after his 96th birthday. As executor, clearing up his estate is occupying quite a bit of time. Being named executor is a classic double edged sword. There is an honor in being asked, and then the pain in executing your responsibilities. Due to the pandemic we have not had the burial yet. His ashes along with Mom's remaining ashes are to be interred on October 8th of this year.

I do want to add one more comment. I believe, today July 2021, we as a nation are in the midst of a bloodless Civil War and no one is aware of it yet. The war is between, for a better term, our Better Angels and a dark force that has been unleashed by the former "president" (and I use the term

College Jobs and Travel

During my Southern Tech years, I held many interesting jobs. As I mentioned, while on campus I was a Dorm Counselor and Hall Supervisor and during the summers I went home to The Canal Zone in Panama where The Colonel and family were stationed and worked for the PanCanal Company. The house they lived in was left over from when the canal was built. It was in Quarry Heights and the upper level had been air conditioned so sleep was possible.

As Dorm Counselor and Hall Supervisor I was primarily tasked with maintaining calm on the hall and working every other weekend as supervisor for my half of the Howell Dormitory. I was paid $35.00 a month for this job. Now that does not seem like a princely sum but remember "back in the day" I could go out on a date, take her to the movies, buy popcorn and drinks and then go out for pizza and drinks for under

$20.00! Yep, different time. When I had Dorm Duty on the weekends it was mostly just hanging around, patrolling the halls a couple of times, telling people that drinking in the dorms was *verboten* and then not doing anything about it as long as they kept it down to a dull roar, and catching up on classwork.

There was one weekend in 1970 which will live forever in my memory. As part of my job as a dorm super I was on the dorm entertainment committee. We would rent movies for all the dorm guys who didn't have wheels and couldn't take off for the weekend. So, when it was my weekend this one weekend to have "duty," we rented the movie *The Flight of the Phoenix*. Now this was the *back in the day* when you rented a movie we are talking about a 16mm movie on a big spool you placed on a movie projector and showed on a screen. So, we got this terrific 1965 movie with Jimmy Stewart as Frank Towns, Sir Richard Attenborough as Lew Moran and Hardy Krüger as the antagonist Heinrich. Along with Ernest Borgnine and George Kennedy it had a compelling cast. So, all us dorm rats sat in the common area near the cafeteria and ate popcorn and watched the movie. When the movie was done someone said they had some beers upstairs and even though it was highly illegal we all tumbled upstairs to his room and started to party. When the beer stash got low we all chipped in and got Eli to go get more. Now Eli was from Panama also and he and I became quite good friends. You will hear more about him later. We sent Eli because he was Panamanian, tall, and dark and had a heavy beard so he was the only one of us that looked 21. Eli came back with more than enough beer and we made quite the night of it. Finally, about 3:00 in the morning we were down to the last beer. There were only a few of us left at this point. All the rest had long since headed to their racks to crash. And we were left with a dilemma. Who was going to get the last beer? We decided to have a push-up contest. I started and did as many pushups as I could. Then the next guy had to do that many and as many more as he could. Then the third guy had to top all that and do more. Then it was back to me. I had to match all the extra ones done beyond mine

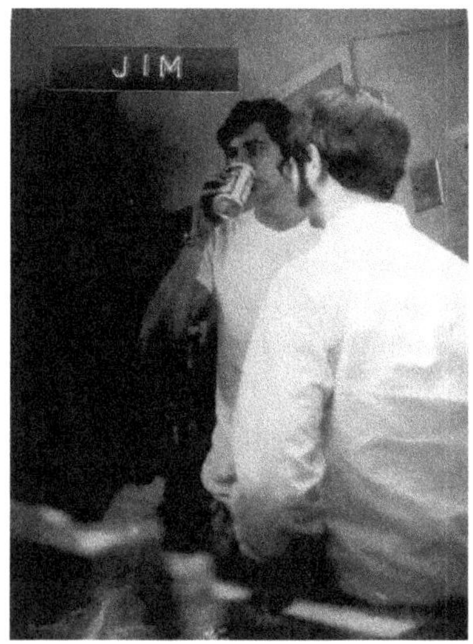

and as many more as I could do. This went on for over an hour. I do not have any idea how many pushups we did that night, but I do remember that finally we all just split the beer and staggered off to our racks. While I do not remember how many we did, I do remember quite vividly the next morning. When I say next morning I mean like 1:00 in the afternoon when I finally rolled out of bed. Of course my mouth was all cottony, and I was dying of thirst. I grabbed my tooth brush, some tooth paste, opened my door and dressed in my skivvies headed for the drinking fountain located near the bathrooms. Got there after struggling down the hall and proceeded to drink like a man just out of Death Valley. Finally slaked, I staggered into the restroom/shower area to "freshen up" and two things surprised me. First of all, let's talk about the bathroom. The restroom/shower area had a bank of sinks with mirrors to the left and to the right were the stalls. Around the corner were the urinals and gang shower area. Yes, gang showers … how disgusting. But this was a different time right after WWII and "men were men" and we all showered in a common shower room. It had been this way since I was in seventh grade, and I hated every minute of it. Showering with other guys while comparing your privates and the way you were built and the amount of hair you had or did not have was … yep, disgusting. Anyway, I took care of my toilet needs, and then walked to the sinks to brush my teeth and splash a little water on my face, and this is when the two things happened. First of all, I had half inch, black, magic marker dots all over my face and second, I could not lift my arms. The black dots were revenge for a prank some of us played on a dorm friend named Digger. While Digger was out on a date, we took everything out of his room and moved it onto the lawn out on the common area between the dorms. It was a nice neat pile, and when he got home about 1:00 there it all was, and we were all watching from our rooms and burst out laughing. I guess if you are going to prank someone you should not be hanging out of a dorm window laughing like a hyena and basically saying, "Hey Digger, I did it!" So, he got his revenge that night. He and another friend had snuck into my room through my window. The dormitory was designed so that two adjacent rooms had a concrete ledge outside connecting their windows. It might have been a fire thing. At any rate, all

95

you need to do is get a coconspirator who lives next door to your target and you can pretty much get into anyone's room … as long as their windows are unlocked … which mine were … foolish kid. And the dots came off with a lot of soap and hard scrubbing with a wash cloth. My face was raw for a week, and I looked like I had a bad sunburn, but it was good revenge. And the whole arm thing? That was the result of too many pushups! Slowly over the next week the arm thing passed too, but I have never gotten in any pushup contests since, or done that many pushups … even in the Navy! And I think there was another lesson I learned that night. That I did not have to subject myself to getting blind drunk and feeling like crap the next day if I did not want to. Call it a maturity thing. Getting old and gaining wisdom is a long road and can be very tiresome. But, as "They" say, "Think how far civilization could advance if every generation did not have to stick their fingers in the fan."

The job on campus was good during the school year, but in the summers of 1970 and 1971 I was employed in two of the best jobs I ever had to that point. The Colonel had moved his tribe of Bill, Russ and Pete (Re and I were off at school) to the Panama Canal Zone for his last tour of duty. We lived in Quarry Heights on Ancon Hill overlooking the Thatcher-Ferry Bridge, The Bridge of the Americas now, and the Pacific entrance to the Canal. As I recall the house we lived in originally housed engineers working on the canal, and the house was relocated from somewhere near the Culebra Cut to the Quarry Heights location. This place was literally paradise on earth. The family had a maid named Mira and a gardener whose name I do not recall. Panama is maybe 9 degrees above the equator. This place has two seasons, wet and dry. The wet season is from April to September and the dry season is from October to February. The difference is that during the wet season it rains twice or three times a day and in the dry season it only rains once or twice a day and the Trade Winds moderate the usually oppressive heat and humidity. The temperature is always lows of 75 and highs of 95 with a humidity level of at least 85% all year round. Through the year, the days vary in length by only about hour or less due to the proximity to the Equator. Another interesting facts is it is the only place in the world you can watch the sun rise in the Pacific Ocean and set in the Atlantic, and you can do it all in one day. That's pretty cool. I actually did it a once. And it was a good time to be in the Canal Zone. The United States basically owned a swath of land five kilometers each side of the canal with our own laws, schools, speed limits and police. It was a sovereign nation in the middle of a sovereign nation. The land grant to the United States for the canal land was granted "in perpetuity" – in other words … forever. The Zonians were good with it. The Panamanians were not so good with it. They equated it to the scenario of France owning a piece of land a several miles wide on each side of the Mississippi River right through the heart of the United States. Of course how it came to be and the history of the canal is a tale full of twists and turns and intrigue. The book *The Path Between the Seas* by David McCullough is an excellent recounting of the history. Ultimately, under President Jimmy Carter, the Zone was deeded back to Panama and they took over control of the canal on December 31st, 1999. It was a *Paradise Lost* (thank you Milton). But all of that is neither here nor there. I was there in the Canal's heyday. During my wonderful summers there, I worked for "The Man," the only Man in the Zone other than the military, The PanCanal Company.

The first summer, 1970, I got a job in the Maintenance Division. My job was in the office, thank goodness. My friend Eli had gotten a job also only his job was cleaning scale off the inside of a huge floating temporary dock leaf that were used to block canal water if they needed to work on the actual leaves of the locks. His was brutally hot and dirty work. Mine was not … fate. The men at the Maintenance Division did not really know what to do with me so they put me to work making signage. They asked me if I knew how to do Leroy Lettering, of course I said yes. I had no clue what to do. So, they presented me with a set of the equipment needed, and I figured it out from there. Leroy Lettering is too complicated for me to try to explain without a picture. The ink was put into the pin barrel (A) with an eye dropper. The scribe (C) traced the letter in a set of grooved standard letter strips

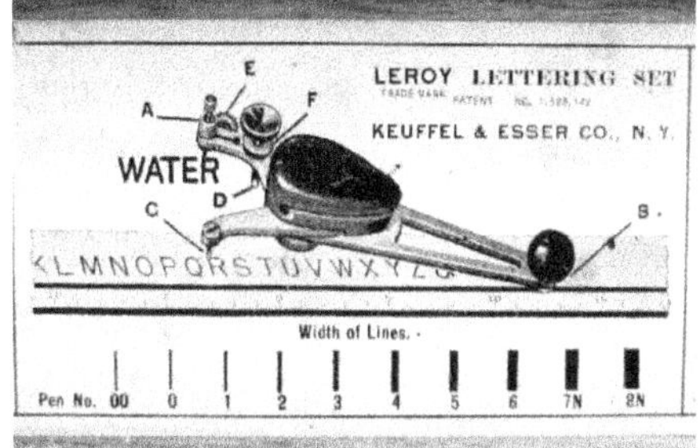

while (B) followed a slot in the strip to keep everything straight. The pin barrel (A) could be replaced with various sizes from 00 to 8N to vary the width of the line it produced. If you look around in one of the trunks in the basement you may find a desk nameplate that says *James W. Morris Jr, Left-Handed Architect*. That desk plate was made by me at the Maintenance Division and sat on my desk for years. But my strongest recollection of making signage was the number of times I misspelled the word "maintenance"! There was no "delete" or "go back" key or any way to erase. You simply started over. It is interesting to note that this system of lettering was used for several years after Carolyn and I had started working in architecture and continued using it until about 1975 when press-on letters became a God-send solution.

Another recollection while working there is a research project I was assigned. Apparently there was a building in the Zone that was subsiding and the Maintenance Division was tasked with sifting through thousands of photographs made during the building of the canal to see if we could determine what was underneath the foundations of the subsiding building. I was allowed to spend hours in the vault in the dome of the main administration building sifting through wonderful black and white pictures from the early 1910's to try to find that one "Ah-Ha" picture … which I did! But in the process I uncovered beautiful photographs of black workers in their tattered clothes and white supervisors in their bow ties and straw hats, stopping and posing as the shutter was clicked. It was fascinating. All of those people, with their hopes and dreams and fears and joys are dead now. All their hopes and dreams and fears and joys forgotten. Dust to dust. I would love to return and catalog the pictures and publish a book of those pictures so they may live again. And perhaps that is what this writing is about; the desire to live on in some small way.

The second summer, the summer of 1971, I worked for the Engineering Division in the big Panama Canal Company Administration Building. This was a job that you wore a tie and nice clothes to go to everyday. I was an Engineering Assistant. A lofty title for a know-nothing college kid, but I worked as hard as I knew how, which was not very hard. I was still a baby worker and watched the clock every day. I especially recall two things I did during that summer of work: the drain and the energy dissipater.

The first was locating a drain that needed to be cleared. There was an area of land between two roadways in the Zone and it was an eternal swamp. And if there is one thing that is taboo in the Zone it is any swampy area. During the construction of the canal, Col. Gorgas worked very hard to rid the Zone of mosquitos that carried dreaded Yellow Fever and this swampy area was exactly the kind of breeding ground they loved. So, my engineer boss and I set about locating drainage drawings of the area. We found one and it did in fact show a large drain in the center of the bog. Next we had to confirm if it really did, in fact, exist. We planned our expedition for an early morning. We did this for two reasons. One was to get in there before the sun was too high and the second was to beat the inevitable afternoon monsoon rain. You see when it rained in Panama it was not a polite mist or a steady drizzle or even a sprinkling rain. It was not even a steady rain. When it rained it rained in drops as big a quarters and absolutely drenched you to the skin in ten seconds. It could knock you off a motorcycle if it really got to rolling, so we definitely did not want to be out there in the swamp if the rain started and the area started filling with water. We got there about 8:00. We were in hip waders with big suspenders over our shoulders. We had on long sleeved shirts and heavy gloves and boots. Then he handed me a long pole. He said it was to probe around for the drain but then he mentioned fending off snakes. Now, I was okay with this until he brought up snakes. You know, Panama snakes, the kind that eat large dogs and small horses. At least that is what my brain conjured up. Anyway, down we went off the road and into the weeds. When we were fully in the stalks of the reeds towered two and three feet above us. There was not a breath of wind to be felt. The temperature was hovering around 90 with the humidity above 80%. I remember being so amazingly hot I could hardly think. We probed around and walked in the muck for what seemed like hours. It was actually only about 45 minutes when we located the drain. It was about five feet by five feet and was choked with weeds and dead plants. We planted my pole in the ground so the guys from my last year's Maintenance Division job, I guess, could come and clear the grate. Then we slogged our way out of the pit. I was never so glad to be out of a place in my life. It also convinced me that an education and an indoor job was the best plan for my life.

The energy dissipater was my first real design and drawing task and it was very, very cool. One of the biggest problems the Zone has is dealing with water runoff near the Culebra Cut. The Cut is where the canal penetrates through the Continental Divide, the string of mountains forming a spine down Panama's center. The dirt on each side of the Cut keeps sloughing off and sliding down into the canal so managing the water at the top of the hills on each side is paramount. My boss's job was to analyze the problem and design a way to cause the water to stop cutting into the side of the hill that fell away to the canal below. He came up with a big concrete box with a bunch of holes on one side of the box and an inlet hole on the other. The water would pour into the box and then be let out on the other side through a bunch of smaller holes, its energy thereby dissipated. He worked up the design and handed it off to me to develop the drawing. It was my first real drafting project! I drew it describing the thicknesses, the resteel to be used, the size and placement of the openings and all the criteria. After he reviewed it and made corrections we printed it, and he sealed it and sent it off. I had no idea where he sent it until one afternoon he said we were taking a trip. We climbed into a PanCanal Company Car with a driver (!) and we went, of all places, to my old Maintenance division offices! We walked in and all my friends from the year before were there, and I took a lot of good natured ribbing about having a tie on, and about having learned everything from them the summer before, and didn't I want to come on back down to the docks with them instead of being up on the hill in a "big house." Then they took us out back and unveiled the dissipater! It was HUGE! I could not believe how big it was. We then got an invitation to come out to the Cut and see it installed the next week. Unfortunately, I was returning to school that next week and would not be there to watch its installation. My boss sent me pictures, but they have been lost to time.

At this point I cannot help but talk about getting back and forth to the Canal Zone. Re and I always traveled "Space A." This meant we would go to the Air Force base in Charleston and wait for "space to be available" on a flight going to the Canal Zone. Coming back from The Zone we would do the same thing in reverse. I cannot remember a single flight that was not memorable. I have previously mentioned Ron from Charleston and flying in a windowless C-141 Starlifter drunk as a skunk and arriving in Panama's oppressive sun and heat. These stories are of that same ilk.

Let me start with the worst one (even worse than the Starlifter flight). This was a Space A flight on a C-5A Galaxy. It was then end of a Christmas vacation in the Zone and Re and I were traveling back to college. I want to say it was 1971, but I am not sure. Anyway we had waited and waited and all the flights were full, and we were getting short on time when a C-5A Galaxy arrived. It was heading to Charleston which was perfect. It had plenty of room for us, which was perfect. It was coming from Vietnam, and the rear cargo area was loaded with shiny, aluminum coffins with remains of soldiers who had died in Vietnam … not so perfect. But we were out of time so we climbed aboard. It was perhaps 1:00 in the afternoon. The plane sat on the tarmac and by the time we were aboard it was a hot, dank tomb, literally. Now flying on an Air Force cargo jet is not ANYTHING like flying on a passenger plane. There are no windows. There are no seats. You sit along the outer wall of the plane in little sling seats that are impossible to get comfortable in. One does not realize when one is flying how much you rely on outside visual references to tell if you are moving. So, in an aircraft with no windows, once you are moving at speed, you have no sense of movement at all unless the plane dips or lurches or slows. It is very eerie. And that was the five-hour flight: no sense of movement, no food, sitting in the dark, sitting in uncomfortable seats facing caskets of remains of brave soldiers who had paid the ultimate price so I could fly back to college and enjoy my life. It was sobering.

Eventually it was over. We landed in Charleston. In Charleston, the Air Force base shares the runway with the commercial terminal so getting to that terminal was no big trick. Once there we had to try to get a flight to Atlanta. We had to fly stand-by and at Christmas all the flights are usually full. But flying from Charleston must not have been all that popular because by 8:00 that night we were on a flight. By 9:30 we were in

Atlanta. When we landed, we were to call Uncle Nelson then take a cab to the Biltmore where he would drive all the way down to Atlanta from Cartersville and pick us up. The man was/is a Saint. So we proceeded to call and then make our way to the cab stand. By 10:30 we were at the Biltmore and by 12:00 midnight we were safely ensconced at Momma's house on "The Hill." Of how Re got back to school and how I made my way down to Marietta to STI. I have no recollections, but flying with the dead still haunts me.

My other vivid memory of making my way home was also a Christmas experience and centered on Re getting married. She was marrying a man named Jerry and the wedding was to be in Charlottesville, Virginia, where she went to school at UVA. I drove up from Marietta in the VW I had brought back from The Zone which I will talk about in a minute. The rest of the family flew in from The Zone. Nelson, Toochie, Bill, Doris and Momma were to take a train up from Cartersville and Marybelle and Don were to fly in from Dallas. I was tasked to meet the train and get the Cartersville crew to their hotel. I do not know what time I left to meet the train, but it was late. Reminds me of a train Carolyn and I waited for in Civitavecchia, Italy.☺ So, around 4:30 AM I woke up in the car. It was snowing. No train. Finally, about 5:45 the train pulled into the station and I greeted everyone, piled them into the big car I had borrowed and off we went. Uncle Nelson was surprised and glad to see me. I recall that. He was a good friend. I should have gone to see him in his last days as he was dying of cancer. I failed him.

Of the wedding itself, I cannot remember anything. From the stories I heard, I do not think my mother did anything. Story of her life. My mother was a registered nurse who never, to my knowledge, worked a day in her life outside the home. I think that is why she never took to Carolyn. Carolyn was and always has been a professional: a professional wife, a professional mother, a professional architect, a marketing professional. Always striving to take care of her husband, family and work outside the home, often sacrificing her advancement to stay home and take care of Jenna and James and allow me to bask in the perceived false light disguised as "success." But when the wedding that I do not recall was done the family, minus Re, traveled to Washington, D.C., to catch a flight back to the Zone. The Colonel had made reservations for himself, Mom, Bill, Russ and Pete to get home. Me, he booked a flight to Charleston to fly Space A and a gave me a hearty "good luck Jimbo." Which now that I think of it, was amazingly cool with me. I was glad to be shut of them after days and days of being with the fam. So, in the middle of Washington National Airport (It would become Reagan National Airport years later) The Colonel went one way and I went another way … literally. We had been doing it figuratively for years.

I boarded a plane and flew off to Charleston. They boarded a non-stop flight to Tocumen International Airport. I was a veteran of making my way all alone by now and had no real hiccups getting to the Charleston Air Force Base. There I queued up to wait standby for Space A to Albrook Air Force Base in Panama. I called Ron, and we got together for a couple of beers and some shag dancing out at a hole in the wall at Folly Beach. We got back to the base at 9:00 in the morning for a 10:00 flight. That is when the fun started. I walked out onto the tarmac and there sat an old tri-tail Constellation with four prop engines. The plane that was developed by Howard Hughes and was the work horse of his airline back in the day. Today this plane belonged to the Ohio Air National Guard. It was very cool. This plane was equipped with real seats, but no stewardesses and we did have brown bag lunches. I sat next to some cute girl but talking was useless. The roar of the engines drowned out anything said. So about 10:30 in the morning we rolled out. We flew and flew and flew and flew. The plane was crazy slow compared to today's jets and finally about 6:00 we started to descend. But it was not Albrook Air Force Base. I had no idea where we were. I thought I had screwed up royally, and we had gone to Tahiti or something (which would have been awesome). I asked one of the Air Force guys, and he said we were at Ramey Air Force Base in Aguadilla, Puerto Rico, and tomorrow we would fly on to Panama. Tonight we would all be fed and put up in the BOQ (Bachelor's Officers Quarters). So, off I wandered.

I was upset. The Parental Units had no idea where I was, and I had no way to let them know. This was eons before cell phone technology. And then suddenly, I remember I was very calm. No one in the whole world knew where I was. I was free … totally free, total freedom. And it felt GREAT! So, I had dinner in the Officer's Mess then went to the barracks. I remember *Gunsmoke* with James Arness was on the black and white television. I settled in … totally relaxed.

The next day we boarded the "Old Connie" and headed for The Zone. I do not recall how long the flight was or anything, but when we landed I found a phone and called home. My mother answered the phone. She was beside herself with panic. Her baby boy had flown off into oblivion and no one knew to where or if I was okay or even alive. I smiled. I was fine. I was more than fine, I had tasted real freedom.

Friends, Family & Personal Relationships

And since I am talking about the two Canal Zone years, I will share some friendships I made and some adventures while there first.

When I think of the Canal Zone almost the first person who comes to mind is Eli. I actually met Eli at Southern Tech if you can believe that. He was from the Zone originally and my parents had moved there and somehow we met at STI. Pretty weird. I mentioned him earlier talking about my 1970 summer job at the Maintenance Division and a party at STI. Eli and I had quite a few adventures together, but one that really sticks was when I was tasked with bringing the white Volkswagen back from the Zone to the United States. It seems my sister was going to need a car soon at UVA where she was studying to be a nurse. So, The Colonel bought a white, 1968 VW, and I was tasked to bring it back to the states when I returned to STI after the summer of '70. The plan was I could use the car fall of 1970 and then give it to Re at the wedding gathering to use in January of '71.

It was a late summer morning when Eli and I piled into the VW to take it across the Zone to Colon, the Atlantic port and canal entrance where it would be processed to be put on the SS Christobal. We then took the train back across the Zone to the Pacific side to await our departure in two days. So I packed up and got ready to leave and return to college. As I recall Mom and The Colonel took me to leave. I met Eli at the dock and we found the cabin we would share. Now, the SS Christobal had had a long and storied career. She had been in service since 1939 and served in WWII as cargo ship with some areas for passengers. She had ferried Zonians back and forth to the States for years. There was a law that all American citizens who

worked in the Zone had to return to the States every few years. I think this was so people who lived and worked in the Zone were reminded that the Zone was not a state of the United States and could be turned back over to the Panamanians at any time. Anyway, Eli and I found our cabin and then went back out onto the ship to explore. I vividly recall we were standing on an open deck above the flying bridge wings waving to people on the dock when an officer on the bridge looked up at us and indicated to cover our ears. Apparently I did not understand the message he was miming because right after that the ship's horn blew, and it was so loud all I could do was cower, doubled over and try to get my hands up to cover my ears. I had never heard anything so loud in my life! It was terrifying. So, if you talk to me today I am hard of hearing, you can attribute it to 60's Rock and Roll and *Adventures on the SS Christobal*.

I am reminded that Eli and I had drunk a lot of beer that summer and aboard ship the bar was open so we proceeded to drink … beer. We left port and the old Christobal started plying the seas northward. She would head up past the western coast of Cuba so close we actually saw that imprisoned nation and then to New Orleans where she would offload us. The ship was not one of today's luxury liners. She was a working ship, and Eli and I soon discovered that drinking beer on a small cargo vessel in the open seas did not mix. Yep, vomit. Being the resourceful college men that we were, we shifted from beer to gin and tonic. That is where I developed a taste for that legendary drink. Still to this day when I enjoy a G&T, I am carried back to that carefree time in college when I taste that ice cold slightly bitter, slightly sweet, limey concoction.

The evening of the first night we met our table mates at dinner. They were two girls whose names also have been lost to history, but Eli and I made a bet to see who could bed one first. I know – totally inappropriate and juvenile – but that was me in the fall of 1970 … a soon-to-be 20-year-old, randy college boy. That occupied our time for most of the four-day cruise. I also recall on that too short voyage the ship had movie night one evening. Eli and I went and snuggled with our table mates and watched *Krakatoa, East of Java*. It was a totally inappropriate movie for a ship voyage as it involved volcanoes and tsunamis and ships sinking! My other recollection was our approach to New Orleans. Below N.O. is a huge delta formed by the Mississippi River. And we traveled in that delta for half a day and what was our last night. I recall sitting on the upper deck and just watching all the swamp go by for what seemed like forever. The beauty of the setting sun just below some low hanging clouds to my left and approaching dark on my right as night crept over the delta and all the alligators and snakes and glorious beauty of that wilderness still stirs me. My son James and I cruised out of N.O. once, and I wanted to relive that experience, but the Royal Caribbean ship left late in the day and came back in the night, so I never got to see my delta that way again. I recall Eli and I docked in New Orleans and got the car and all we wanted was to get on the road to Marietta and a real McDonald's hamburger. I do not know if we were up against a college deadline for registration or what, but here the two of us were in one of the biggest party towns in the United States and all we wanted was to get on the road … and eat a hamburger from McDonald's. You know, I am struck as I write this is how much I got to do as a young man, but also how many experiences I wasted. "Too late smart," The Colonel would say. Eli and I made it back to Marietta. And neither of us won the boat bed bet.

I am not sure if it was the first or second summer I was down there, I believe it was the first summer, the summer of '70, I met a girl named Audrey. How we met I am not sure. I think my brother Bill (William Cranston Morris) who was living with The Colonel and Mom and going to high school, may have introduced us. She may have been a friend of Bill's future wife, Janie. I do not know, but I have several wonderful recollections of Audrey. She was a sweet young lady, attractive and very giving. I can clearly recall three specific events with Audrey: an evening with her when her parents were out of town, an interesting afternoon when she went out deep sea fishing with my family and me on the CINC's (Commander in Chief – pronounced "Sink") boat and a visit she paid me at STI the next year.

I am not going to dwell on the evening her parents were away. Suffice to say we had her house to ourselves, and we had a wonderful time. The CINC's boat is more interesting. We went out on the boat which was about a thirty or forty-foot power yacht several times deep sea fishing for Bonita and Dolphin. Let me clarify that the Dolphin we caught are not the Dolphin you are thinking of. These are smaller fish with mild meat and a good eating fish. The boat was crewed with several men who would take care of menial tasks like baiting hooks and cleaning fish. The Colonel and his royal family were much too important for tasks like that. So the day was pretty much a pleasure cruise. Beer was consumed. Fish were caught and fun was had. On this particular fishing trip Re was engaged to the man named Jerry who came down and joined us on one fishing expedition. Re married him that December when I had the middle of the night meeting people at a train station adventure. We may talk more about him later.

During this particular trip out on the boat it was a spectacularly, brilliantly blue day in paradise. It was hot, as it always is in Panama, and cruising away from Amador on the CINC's boat that morning being waited on hand and foot made one feel like royalty. Everyone wore swim trunks or bathing suits and hats and tons of sunscreen. We motored out through light chop and were soon out past the San Blas Islands where the San Blas Indians live. The San Blas are famous for their molas, a cloth art work used to decorate clothing or to be framed. There are several in the family. I think James and Angela have some framed molas in their home. Anyway, the sea calmed, and the crew baited and put out the poles, and we started to troll. We cruised for an hour or so and then there was a hit and the excitement began. You would pull the pole out of the hole where it was standing upright and get in the "fighting chair." This was a chair in the center of the back of the boat that had a little metal cup between your legs where you would place the butt of the pole. Then you would lean forward and pull back. As you leaned forward again, you would reel some line in. This was the process until the fish was landed. It was pretty cool. Sometimes you would go for a long time with no strikes … like over an hour. It was during one of these lulls that Audrey and I went down into the air conditioned cabin to get some relief from the heat and to see if between the two of us we could find something more exciting than fishing to do. After we had been down there for fifteen or twenty minutes, The Colonel embarrassed, degraded and humiliated us both by sticking his head down and telling us to get up on deck. I am going to leave a discussion of the rest of the day as the day, and the relationship, were ruined, but it led to the next event I recall.

The Colonel and his wife had to go to a party. My mother absolutely hated any kind of social event. Mom was an interesting person and had been raised in a very protected atmosphere. I perceive it was an upbringing of entitlement as she was the town doctor's only daughter, and she pretty much did not have to do anything she did not want. I perceive this continued into her marriage and Mom could act like a petulant, spoiled child when something did not go her way. I recall her throwing a shoe once although I do not recall the circumstances. Often at family gatherings such as Christmas she would go to her room crying and be inconsolable if something or someone made her angry. Also it did not matter where we moved Mom would not like it for at least a year. Then she would love it and not want to move. Then we would move again, and the whole cycle would start again. It is with this in mind that I share the evening The Colonel and his wife came home from a party. Mom was, needless to say, angry and stormed upstairs and told me to "take care of your father." The Colonel was drunk. The first and only time I can recall him drunk. I got him into the downstairs bathroom where he proceeded to "worship at the porcelain altar." I do not recall much beyond that about that evening except Mom's attitude really made me angry. And she continued her "mad" for several days. Finally, I could not take it any longer, and I confronted them both. As I recall they were standing in the door to the house, and I was down the several steps. I basically told them that Mom acted like a spoiled child and that The Colonel not only allowed it, he enabled her to act that way, and that there was no way I would tolerate that in my marriage. I also told The Colonel he had embarrassed me the other day on the boat, and that he and they should be ashamed. It was quite an event. A week later summer was over, and I left for college. That particular event was never discussed or brought up again. I was not murdered in my sleep by army hit men, and as far as I can recollect it made no difference in their relationship or the way my mother acted. In retrospect at 70 years old and having been married almost 50 years to the most tolerant woman in the whole world, I want to add this comment. In every marriage we "enable" the other person to some extent. It is called "love" and "being a spouse." But what I had a problem with back then, and now I see more clearly, is that the way my mother acted was childish, yes, spoiled, yes, but the problem was when her actions spilled over and hurt her family and children – THAT was the problem. I guess The Colonel was too busy "chasing the brass ring" and "climbing the ladder" to bother with trying to change her or help us. I do know for a fact, now, that the way they acted damaged me and also my sister Re.

But I digress. Somehow that next summer of 1971 in the Canal Zone I met the second of the three most physically beautiful women I ever knew. The first was Jean of the Thanksgiving Michigan visit. And this was the second, Leslie. Leslie was of the Jesus Christ Church of Latter Day Saints persuasion, and she was one gorgeous young lady. I have a couple of memories of us, but one of my most outstanding memories of her was when my brother Bill and I double dated with Leslie and her sister to the Atlantic side to swim at a beach just below Fort San Lorenzo where the Chagres River dumps into the Atlantic. Why we went all the way over there just for that I do not recall. There were beautiful beaches on the Pacific side. There was one Pacific side beach out the causeway at Fort Amador with a shark net and everything, but for some reason we went to the Atlantic side that day. I recall Leslie and her sister brought lunch including carrot sticks, "Natures natural toothbrushes," Leslie would say. And the waves that day were stupendous! They had to be ten or twelve feet. Bill and I rode waves all morning, got pounded several times, and then went diving in the Chagres River after lunch. The current was very strong, but the coolest thing was that we found cannon balls from Fort San Lorenzo, some at least twenty inches in diameter, laying on the river bottom. There was absolutely no way to move them. They had to weigh at least several hundred pounds and there is probably some law against disturbing them anyway. But they were really neat to see and touch. Touching 200-year-old history, or a 1,000-year-old cathedral, is always thrilling to me. And let me add the barracuda were thrilling also! It only took one to swim up to me and look me square in the faceplate of my dive mask for me to decide that discretion IS the better part of valor and scramble to the shore and the safety of dry land. But it was a beautiful day in paradise.

My other significant memory of Leslie was when she invited me over for dinner with her family. Now this may seem like the most mundane thing to include but the evening is worth hearing about. Mind you this was the first time I had really had an opportunity to meet Leslie's extended family, other than picking her up for a date and getting the whole glaring father eye deal. So, this was a big deal. And not only was it going to be Leslie's parents and her siblings, of which there were two sisters and three brothers (Yes, I know, I have a ton of siblings too, but this many was a little much even for me), her grandparents were visiting from the States. I do not know which side of the family they were from. That kind of thing was immaterial to me then. Anyway, I was invited for dinner. I do not know if I was being sized up for marriage material or what, but I'm pretty sure I failed the course that night. You see Leslie was fascinated that I was left-handed. Why? I don't know. Maybe it is a Mormon thing. So, she was fascinated with this so she put me at the end of the table with her on my right so I could eat with my left hand. And she made a big deal about it with everyone, explaining why I had to sit there and everything. I just smiled. I did not want to embarrass her and then not get any make-out time later. But, the only problem is that the only thing I do with my left hand is write. I do everything else with my right hand like a "normal" person. So, here I am forced to eat with my left hand … and we had spaghetti! Do you know how hard it is to eat spaghetti with your non-dominant hand? It is difficult, and look cool, and make small talk with granny across the table, and … well, you understand. I do not recall spilling any spaghetti or sauce in my lap or on my shirt so I guess it was a good night. I actually believe there are pictures of us that night in one of my albums in the basement. We are standing in front of a staircase as I recall. I have on a tie and look uncomfortable. Strange evening.

When I was in high school, The Colonel and my mother said I could get a motorcycle if I paid for it. That whole arrangement went up in smoke as soon as I got a job. Well, in the Canal Zone my brother Bill got to get a motorcycle. Pisser. I mean it was barely a motorcycle. It was a Honda 50. With two people on it, it could barely make it over the Thatcher Ferry Bridge. But he had a motorcycle. When I came down to the Zone the first time I saw it. The Colonel decided I did not need to know until I had to know, so they kept it a secret. Anyway, that's cool. I didn't really give a crap. So, I got down there and Bill showed me the bike. Now mind you I was quite familiar with bikes by then. A friend at STI named Dwayne had one, and I used it sometimes, so I was familiar with shifting with my left foot and accelerating with my right hand and operating the clutch with my left hand and all that. So, Bill takes me to a parking lot to show me the bike and let me ride it. Well, the only thing he neglected to tell me was that the accelerator on this bike tended to stick – OPEN! So, I got on and accelerated and tried to let off the gas to pull in the clutch to shift and the bike just kept winding up and up! And when I let the clutch out in second the bike tried to jump. Long story short, I dumped the bike, got a severe case of road rash, screwed up the foot peg and was embarrassed. That day was not one of my best. Everyone was cool, and I think Bill felt he should have warned me, but the bike got fixed and life went on. The point of my story is that riding that bike was a supreme escape for me. When I rode it I felt free. All my worries and cares would melt away. And later in my life, back at school, when things would worry me I would recall riding that little bike in the country side of Panama with no helmet and the wind in my hair, and I would be able to relax. Still to this day, riding my motorcycle takes me to another place, one of calm and freedom.

I do have two other recollections about that bike – one scary and one ethereal. The scary one has to do with taking the bike down to the city of Panama to get the bike serviced. We would take the bike to a place down in the middle of the city. And riding or driving in the city of Panama is nothing like up here in the States. People drive with their accelerator, their brake and their horn. The lines on the road a just a suggestion. A single lane street in the city of Panama could have two or even three lanes of traffic and old jalopies, cheeva-buses with lights and motorcycles all vying for a lane while pedestrians had no problem stepping out into traffic anywhere and anytime. It was pandemonium mixed with a cacophony of horns and Spanish and general bedlam. It was cool. Anyway, the helmet Bill and I used had an American flag sticker on the back of it. It kind of broadcast to everyone the we were not Panamanian … and when riding in Panama, that was not the best thing. The Panamanians were getting quite vocal about not liking having Gringos owning a strip of land down the middle of their country. There had been riots and a U.S. soldier had been killed right around the time I was down there. So, here I am riding down the street in Panama City in the not best part of town with a big old American flag sticker on my helmet – kind of like having a big old target on my back I guess. So, I was done with the service on the bike and was headed back toward the Zone down this two lane street, with three lanes of traffic clogging it up, when a car pulls up next to me, and a guy turns and looks at me. I look over, and he is pointing a 45 caliber pistol at me. The hole in the barrel looks like a cannon, and I totally freak out! We were coming up on a side street to my right and I blasted around that turn as hard as I could and accelerated down the street away for the cannon! I bobbed and weaved around to make sure they were not following me and made it back to the Zone a long way from the house. But I was back in Zone and not dead. And that was good. I did not take the bike back downtown again for a long while.

A recollection of an adventure on the bike led to one of those serendipitous occurrences that becomes life altering. The evenings in Panama were a magical time. The rains would slack off due to the cooling of the evening when temperature eased as the sun fell low in the sky. Breezes would pick up as the jungle cooled and the ocean held onto its heat. If you were still you could hear all of the animals stirring in the depths of the wild world always just feet from you. Everything from cutter ants that could strip a plant or carcass to bare bones in hours to parrots and Macaws to monkeys hooting and hollering. It was a surreal paradise. And when you were out on your bike at this witching hour, your senses became alive with the sounds and aromas of a world going to sleep and awaking all at the same time. I was on a road paralleling the canal just north of the twin Miraflores Locks on my left headed toward the single Pedro Miguel Lock when I noticed a road heading off to my right into the jungle. I decided to take this "road less traveled by" and it "made all the difference." (Apologies to Robert Frost) It started out as a single lane, unpaved road but as it began to climb it became more of a path and the jungle began to close in on both sides. At this point one must appreciate jungle. There is a difference to the uninitiated in jungle and rain forest. In a rain forest the forest floor is open. You can walk pretty much unencumbered, and you can see all around easily. However, jungle is totally different environment all together. A jungle is dense and suffocating. In a jungle if you can see four feet you are in a clearing. If you are claustrophobic, the jungle is your nightmare world. Vietnam and Panama have jungles. The path inclined upward and became more rutted and the jungle pressed in so tightly I was forced to abandon the bike, but I did not quit. Why? I am not to this day sure, but I climbed on. The jungle was so close and like the search for the elusive drain in the reeds, there was not a breath of wind. Sweat was pouring off of me. Then, suddenly, the vegetation eased and opened up, and I found myself alone, all alone, on a small hill. The first thing I recall was the night sky. By now the relentless Panamanian sun had been reduced to nothing but a thin purple line along the western horizon, and the sky was ablaze with thousands of stars. The moon had not yet made its debut. I am sure there are places in North America where you can still see the sky in all its majesty, possibly Canada, but Georgia is not one of those places. There were billions of winking stars. It was breathtaking. Then I noticed the vegetation cooled breeze wafting up from the jungle I had emerged from and the night animal sounds. Then I looked around. Far to my front right at about 1:00 was the Thatcher Ferry Bridge and beyond that hundreds of vessels waiting to traverse the canal and beyond them the jet black ocean blended into the inky night sky. To my right at 4:00 and below me were Miraflores Locks and a little to my back right was the Pedro Miguel Lock. In between them was the small Miraflores Lake and traversing that lake was a huge orange and black freighter making its way toward its final two step lock journey to the Pacific Ocean. In the blaze of the flood lights, the canal workers below looked like industrious ants handling lines and driving the mules that guided the behemoths through the locks safely. Yet, I could not hear a single sound from all that commotion below me. I was the king of all I surveyed. I was "king of the world" for that instant in my life. That place in time and in my life truly was paradise on earth. And I never shared that spot with anyone. It was my special place … a lost world … lost in time … a moment captured but never to be repeated.

As a family we had several adventures while in Panama. One adventure was to visit a beach house down the coast from the Canal Zone headed southwest. I have a couple of short recollections about this day. The first was Re and I yelling at the buzzards that seemed to be everywhere and throwing, and not hitting any of them, small green apples at them and yelling "El Condor Passa." I know, stupid and inconsequential but a memory none-the-less. My second memory of the day is more vivid. The beach was very interesting in its geologic make-up. I recall a beautiful white sand area near the jungle about twenty feet wide extending toward the ocean, then there was a black volcanic sand area about forty feet wide and then the sandy area nearest the ocean was tan and very grainy and uncomfortable to walk across. So, the challenge was to get to the water from the white sand area where the bohío was to the water. In the heat of the day the black sand barrier was formidable to cross. You could seriously burn the bottoms of your feet trying to cross it. So, rather than taking the logical course to wear your sandals and cross it like a sane person, Bill and I would back up in the soft white sand, get a running start and try to cross it in three or four large bounding steps. Stupid. But that is what we did and it hurt! Anyway, along the beach there were rivulets that flowed from the jungle into the ocean all along the beach and some could be difficult to cross due to the speed of the water and the steep banks they cut through the sand. Late in the day after being at the beach the family was carrying all our gear back to the house. Everyone had a load including the youngest and smallest, Pete (Peter Charles Morris). At this point I was about twenty so Pete must have been about nine. At any rate, I had crossed a particular gushing rivulet. It was about three feet deep and running rapidly. I was heading along the beach when I heard a short yelp. Pete had gotten down the four-foot bank on the far side of that little river, and I do not know if he was carrying too much or simply lost his footing, but he was down. He was in the river being swept along, and as I saw it, needing help. I dropped what I was carrying and rushed back, jumping into the stream and grabbing him up all sputtering and gagging. Then he was okay. We gathered up his cargo that was now making its way down toward the ocean and trudged up the beach together. I am guessing Pete has no recollection of this. And he may have been okay and could have probably struggled through the water without my help, but I felt the need to intervene and to me it was one small moment that made me feel worthwhile.

That beach event brings to mind another interaction that Pete and I had in Quarry Heights where we lived in Panama. The house we lived in was up on stilts to provide ventilation under the house and prevent rot. It was high enough that nine-year-old boys could walk and play under the house without bending over. And Pete and Rusty often did. The house was interesting also in that it had wide verandas on all sides, screens and no glass in any windows. This is because the house was designed in 1910, long before air conditioning was invented and the only air cooling you got was an errant breeze during the dry season. But the upstairs of the house had been outfitted with plastic sheeting on all the screens and had window air conditioners to make the sleeping area habitable. Needless to say, mold was a constant battle and if you did not set your sugar bowl in a saucer of water ants would come in the night. If you did not combine rice in your salt shaker to absorb the humidity, the salt would turn into a solid block in a matter of hours. But, back to Pete. I was in the driveway, under the carport tasked with replacing the lower coolant water hose on the Colonel's "Family Truckster" station wagon and having a terrible time in the heat and humidity of "paradise." I did finally get the hose on the engine after having another of my garden hose draining inspirations. The hose simply would not slip over the water outlet on the bottom of the engine. Struggle as I might I just could not get it to slip on. The hose was the right size, but it was made to fit very snugly. I could get the hose started on the engine but the friction of slipping it completely over the outlet pipe was just too much. So, after over an hour of fruitless effort it occurred to me to try to overcome the friction. I went in the house and got a jar of Vaseline Jelly. I smeared it on the inside of the hose and on the pipe from the engine. When I next engaged the pipe the hose slipped on as smooth as silk. Ta Daaaaaa, I am a genius! But, again I digress. So, I was working on the coolant hose, and Pete was playing near me, kind of under the house with his G.I. Joe doll. He used to get endless grief from me about playing with dolls. And, unbeknownst to me, he was enjoying a peppermint lozenge. The kind of peppermint that was the little hard disc of candy, not the kind that is more of a little ball that dissolves quickly. As I work I hear Rusty yelling that something is wrong with Pete. I scoot out from under the car and Pete is doubled over and holding his throat. Somehow I knew he was choking. Quickly I grabbed him from behind and attempted a Heimlich maneuver as best I knew how. I pulled my fist up and into his solar plexus twice. No result. Then I bent him way over and slammed my hand onto his back and the offending peppermint came flying out and across the driveway. Pete was a little shook-up as was I, but everyone was okay. Pete went inside crying, and I went back to work on the reluctant hose.

[Again, I am paused in writing. This is becoming quite a feat of writing, but I am enjoying it immensely. Today is September 5th, 2021, and I am in the midst of rebuilding the deck at 1920 Falcon Wood Drive, NE. It will be beautiful when I am done, but for now the old autobio is on hold while I rip, replace, screw, and stain. Covid 19's Delta Variant is still ravaging the world although we have several vaccines if the Stupids will only take it … as Agent K said in <u>Men in Black</u>, "Humans are dumb, panicky dangerous animals and you know it." My beautiful, brilliant Caitlin (Caitlin Rose Morris) is 11 and "over a half" as she will tell you. She has started Palmer Middle School. She is into Warrior Cats, percussion and is making A's in all subjects which are all advanced classes by the way. Bodie (Bodie Lang Blackwell) is a newly minted freshman at UGA and dating a young lady named Margot. Bryce (Bryce Harper Blackwell) is in his junior year at UGA and still focused on being a doctor and still very much in love with his lovely young lady, Anna. Jenna (Jenna Morris Blackwell) and Adam (Timothy Adam Blackwell) are building a house on Lake Lanier. James (James Lyon Morris) and Angela (Angela Dawn Swope Morris) are remodeling their house and property and are as happy as ever. Last night we all went to see <u>Hamilton</u> at the Fox Theater. It was a wonderful performance on a spectacular late summer evening in Georgia.]

My last "Zone" story under this banner is the New Year's Eve party at the Tivoli Hotel. You know, the Zone has taken on an almost mythic quality … almost like *The Twilight Zone*. I am thinking it was 1971. I met and took a lovely young lady to the party. There is a picture of her in one of my albums. I do not recall a lot about that night except the waiter coming up to us and

asking for our drink order. I should not say he came up to us. It was more like Lurch creeping up behind us and suddenly asking in a low deep voice, "Drink order, Sir?"

I actually jumped when he said it! Well, I was a real newbie in the drink ordering department so this must have been before Eli's and my trip on the good ship Christobal otherwise I would have ordered a gin and tonic. But he caught me unawares and I blurted out "Scotch on the rocks." You know, Scotch, like Butterscotch … only NOT! My date asked for a coke. I felt foolish and then felt very much more foolish when my drink arrived. It was like drinking gasoline! Horrible! But I nursed it along through the night and finally enough ice melted that it only tasted like kerosene, and I was able to drink it. Almost. And we welcomed the new year in that venerable old hotel … a few days later I went back to STI.

Southern Tech proved to be a wonderful place for me. Not only did it allow me to recover my grades and some sense of being able to achieve something in this world and not be an abject failure and end up "living in a cardboard box," but it also gave me many friends and renewed an old flame. Ken, Larry, Richard, Ronnie, Tom, John (known as Digger) and Digger's sister, another Ken, Ruben, Eli, Chris, Bonnie, Mike, Bob, Terri from high school days and most especially my future wife Carolyn. About some of them, I will say a lot, about others only a line or two, not because they were not good friends, but because I do not want to make this into a 500-page novella.

Ken was my first roommate when I came to STI. He was from Ball Ground, Georgia. We got along well and then drifted apart the second year. I was a Senior in early 1972 when Dean Van Gorder called me to his office to say Ken had been killed in a car wreck and asked if I would go to Ball Ground First Baptist Church and represent the college. Several others and I went. I have since tried to locate his grave with no luck. Where we went for the funeral has been lost to me as was my first friend at STI.

Larry was an older student. He had been to Vietnam and survived physically and mentally and became a mentor to me when I became a Dorm Super. He was a really nice guy, one of the "good guys" and a hard working student. He never partied with us; he was much too serious and mature far beyond any of us draft dodgers – although he never treated us like that or called us that. I called us that.

Richard was the only one of us in the architecture program, except Carolyn, who had any real talent in my opinion. In fact, if you are reading this and ask Carolyn about him, she knew him longer than I did actually. In my collection of pictures, you will see a picture of a model house a team of us built as a project in one of our classes. STI was a very hands-on school. You did not just learn the theory of shooting a line of levels and 'throwing a chain," you got out and did it. Well, the school could not have us out building houses, but they could have us build a to scale home with all the sill plates, top plates, studs, double studs, lintels, joists, rafters, beams, columns, siding, windows and every other part of a home and Richard was the one who's plan was selected to be the one we built. He was a very talented architect.

Ronnie was a backbone of our cadre. He was the only one who was actually married! To a real girl! A real *experienced* man! And he lived off campus in a real house. He was exceptionally cool! Ronnie was also in the architecture program and was pretty good at it as I recollect. He would always joke about his "studio" out back of his house was several old refrigerator containers hooked together. Being as the only one of us who had a house, our parties were usually at his place.

You know it is strange. Tom was a groomsman at my wedding, but I do not remember that much about his exploits with us. I know he was good friend and was at several of Ronnie's blowout parties, but I cannot recall anything specific.

John who was known as Digger was the quietist of the group. He drove a red '69 Chevelle with mag wheels and a Hurst shifter and was quite the hit with the ladies to hear him tell it. I recall many a late Saturday night in my dorm room drinking and smoking and listening to Digger regale us with his macho exploits. I'm guessing most of it was bravado and made up stuff, but he was fun to be around, and if you needed a ride somewhere he was the first to offer. Digger had a sister. A 19-year-old hippy girl who I dated once. We went to a movie and then got pizza. We headed back to the dorm and found some beer on the way. I never saw her again.

Another Ken was a really good friend. He drove a Mustang and we would often bum around together. We even favored each other when it came to looks. So much so that – and I have never told anyone this – when I needed to take a test on the United States Government and U.S. History he took my I.D. and took the test for me. The two of us had several adventures together. I recall one which was a double date we went on down near Macon at Tift College … which, like STI, is now not there anymore. We went down to date Lynn and Margot, identical twins … and I mean identical! They were so identical, it was eerie. On another adventure we went for a long weekend to his hometown of Sylvania, Georgia. We left campus after classes on Friday and drove deep into the night to get there. It was about 5 hours away and we got there about midnight. Ah, the life of a college student. We went dove hunting and generally were just boys looking for ways to get in trouble. He was a good buddy.

Ruben was another good friend from the architecture program. He was in the Student Chapter of the AIA with me when we formed it. I became the president. A young lady named Chris was also in it as was Carolyn, which made meetings a little tricky. Ruben was also one of my groomsmen. Ruben and I kept up contact after college and Carolyn and I attended his wedding to a local hometown girl in Fort Valley, Georgia. I remember we all went water skiing while we were there, and I discovered that Carolyn was quite the skier. Ruben was a good friend.

Eliezer David Lugo … Eli … my high pitched voice Panamanian good, good friend. Of all the people I met at STI, I would have to put this guy as one of the best. We were dorm rats together, traveled back and forth to Panama together as I have said, and because he was tall and had the ability to grow a beard and looked 21, he was the designated liquor buyer for the squad. He and I even went on a double date with him with my sister Re and me with Audrey to the Panama Hilton one evening. My sister was not impressed. Eli had a kind of high pitched voice and was a riot when he had a few drinks under his belt. I could go on and on, but you will see his name over and over as I talk about The Zone, our exploits and my time there.

Chris was a girl and one of the few besides Carolyn on the campus of STI. She was an architecture student and worked for the campus radio station. We dated pretty heavily until I met Carolyn. I remember she was into smoking pot, and I came to pick her up for a date once, and she invited me into her apartment. It reeked of pot! She asked if I wanted some, and I left to wait for her in the car. You see, a conviction for possession of, or using pot, was a federal offense back then, and that would have ruined my chances of getting a license to practice architecture, so I did not imbibe. I also knew with my addictive personality – by now I was a pack a day smoker – I knew if I tried marijuana I would be mainlining heroin before the week was out. So I just steered clear of it … until I was 67 years old! Chris was a sweetie, and I learned a lot from her.

Bonnie, a lovely young lady I met at the Ridgeway store on 41 Highway down near and across from the Clock Tower Business Park where I was to join Carlson Associates some fifteen years later. She was working in the fish and aquariums pet department. She was a very attractive just graduated senior in high school about to go to Georgia Southern University … how prophetic. There is a picture of her in one of my albums downstairs. It is a professional modeling picture. She is sitting on a stool. Go find it. I would sneak her into my dorm room … had to sneak her in as it would not do for the hall supervisor to be caught with a girl in his room. I remember asking her to a dance once at STI after she had gone off to Georgia Southern. When asked if she could go, she had said sure, but I would have to come get her so I drove down to Georgia Southern, picked her up on Sweetheart Circle and drove all the way back in one day just to take her to the dance Then I drove her back the next day. I think we had a good time together. I was very narcissistic back then. I hurt feelings and was generally an asshole of a person when it came to girls if you want my honest opinion of me in my early twenties. To be honest, I would have hated for my daughter or for my granddaughter to run into me.

Mike. What can I say about this guy? He was from Barnesville, Georgia. He was my first encounter with a homosexual, but let me clarify quickly – I never had any physical homosexual encounter with him. It took me a long time to understand what his motives were because Mike and his sexual bent was so foreign to me. Literally, I was a "babe in the woods." I had just never met a homosexual before. What can I say? Well, I am not sure how we met, but we hit it off and we actually ended up rooming together one quarter. To me, it was all innocent enough. We would play tennis on the weekends and play chess in the library sometimes. Mike even came down to The Zone one summer I recall, and it was during that visit that I first started to think something was squirrely about him. I remember waking up one morning. He was in a bed parallel to mine, and he was just lying there staring at me. I thought that was kind of creepy. Also, he also always seemed to have too much money. He found out about my relationship with Audrey and paid to fly her up from The Zone one weekend. He found out about my old relationship with Terri from high school and communicated with her, and then he arranged for me to fly out to Tulsa to see her at the University of Tulsa and attend the KΔ Man dance with her. There is a picture of Terri and me at that dance somewhere. But the problem is that he paid for those flights, and it never occurred to me that anything was weird about that. If you look in the STI yearbooks you will see the two of us on the Dorm Counsel together and the Judicial Counsel together. But after the Canal Zone visit and rooming with him one quarter, I knew something was wrong with this guy. I got Dean Van Gorder to move me to another floor and room to be the supervisor. By now I was dating Carolyn and Mike tried to get in the middle of that by calling her and telling her lies. He called her once and told her I had gotten a girl pregnant. I think he was jealous. But the coup-de-grace came when I went out to my car to leave on a date with Carolyn and found someone had put, or tried to put sugar in my VW's gas tank. I actually drove the car maybe 500 feet across from campus to the gas station to fill up the afternoon of the date, and when I put the nozzle in the tank I discovered the sugar. Fortunately, I had caught it in time. Sugar can really gum up an engine. I got it all cleaned out and it ended up fine, but I was now pissed. I had fully deduced who it was and what was going on, so I went to see the Dean of Students, Dean Van Gorder. I explained the whole situation. He said there was not enough evidence to do anything on his end, but if it were him he would take matters in his own hands and deal with the problem. "Don't hurt him or lay a hand on him, but deal with him before there is a bigger problem," were his words. So, I did, the very day after the meeting with the Dean. I recall it was rainy and dark after dinner that evening. I got Digger and Ken who had been aware of my problem and the three of us went to visit Mike at his room. He was a hall supervisor and was rooming alone … shock and surprise. I knocked on the door. No one answered. I pounded on the door and told him who it was. When he opened the door, I got in his face. Digger and Ken stood back. I was furious. I was almost yelling. I did not care if the dorm hall heard me or not. In fact, I hoped they did. They needed to be aware what kind of a person was on their hall. I told him what I knew was going on. Told him about his calls to Carolyn and that I knew he was the one who had f_cked with my car. Of course he denied it. I wasn't having it! I told him he was f_cking liar. I told him he was very sick person and that if anything else, anything at all, even a little bit remotely strange happened to me in the future, I was going to come back here and beat the shit out of him. It was the first (and only) time I have ever threatened anyone in my life. All my fears of being in a fight and getting hurt, like I was with another Mike in the sixth grade, had vanished. I was in a rage. I was another person. And you know what? Strangely enough, that was the end of the Mike story. He had nothing to do with me after that. That closed the darkest chapter of my STI years. Looking back now, I hope he made his way in the world and got some help down in Barnesville because he really was one sick puppy.

Bob. It's funny, the old adage "to never burn your bridges" was never truer than my friendship with Bob. We roomed on the same floor in the Howell dorm when I was a supervisor. Bob was down the hall, and we struck up a friendship of sorts. To be perfectly honest, I found him to be a loud-mouthed, rather boring gun-nut. But we hung out together sometimes and got along. I recall he took me out one day to a place off the Old 41 highway to fire his pistol. I do not remember much about that event other than the pistol was chrome, it was a revolver and it was loud as all get out. It scared the pee-turkey out of me when he let me fire it once. You will read more about Bob later and how never burning bridges is a good thing.

burning bridges is a good thing.

Terri… while not a person directly at Southern Tech, somehow I was in touch with Terri from high school back in Vienna, Virginia, and she invited me out to the University of Tulsa to attend a Kappa Delta, KΔ, dance. It was the KΔ Man Dance. This was May of 1971 although I do not remember the exact date. Somehow I conjured up the money to fly out there and Terri met me at the airport. I do not remember much about the weekend. This is a picture of the two of us taken at the dance. We are a far cry from the two children who went to the

113

Jr/Sr. Prom in 1967. It is amazing what four years and a little college will do to you. I recall staying at a house somewhere. I do not recall much about the dance except I got a big glass thing that said KΔ Man on it. The day after the dance we went out to a lake somewhere. There are pictures of Terri in a yellow swimsuit. I never saw Terri again after that weekend. Sad. I wish I could see her again to apologize for all the undeserved hurt I gave her. She deserved better. I hope she found it.

6.

On to a lighter subject! I have mentioned the name Carolyn before. Her full name was Carolyn Ethel Lyon. I am using her full name when I have only used first names to this point because this was the woman who changed my life. I have mentioned three most physically beautiful women before. One was Jean of Michigan fame. Number two was Leslie of Canal Zone fame and three was/is Carolyn. As I have come to know her over the last fifty years, I know she was/is not only one of three of the most physically beautiful women I had ever met, but she is the most beautiful inner person I ever met. Yes, this was She. But by way of a full introduction, I want to include a piece I wrote to her back in 2017, over five years ago now, to help her understand the morning when I first saw her. The title of the piece was *Three Seconds*. And if you read it through, you will see why

"It held the promise of fall, that morning. The sun was creeping through the Georgia pines, and there was a misty, feathery early morning fog lifting through their skinny tops. All of this gave the light a weak appearance, but we all knew it would warm in the afternoon. September in Georgia could still trick you, but none of that mattered to the small gaggle of musketeers tumbling down the hill from the dorms. We were fearless and the masters of all we surveyed. Having been away and working for the summer, we were all flush with cash and wild stories of our adventures. We had had dorm breakfast that did not settle well because we had been at Ronnie's house partying the night before celebrating our return to school. Ronnie was the only real man among us because he was married and rented a house off campus. He was in the architecture program like Ruben and Richard and me and was always telling us about having a drafting table set up in a box outside the back of his house. But the night before, when we all went to look at his box, like so many things when you are twenty, was more fantasy than reality, but it had made a good story and always got laughs when we gathered in my dorm room between classes to smoke and brag about grades, future plans and our women … not especially in that order.

Getting liquor for the party was still a challenge because of our ages. Yes, it was a time when we carried draft cards, and we could fight and die in Vietnam, but we could not drink in the great state of Georgia. We could vote in Georgia but not drink. Why, we could even drink in the progressive state of South Carolina … now there is an oxymoron … "progressive state of South Carolina" … but not in Georgia. So, the only one of us that even looked legal due to his Hispanic facial hair was Eli, a tall Panamanian dorm rat with a high voice, whom I had met on travels back and forth to The Zone. He and I had just come up from Panama several days before on the Christobal, and he and I had made the run down to the liquor store near the McDonalds at I-75 and West Paces Ferry in my Volkswagen and brought back more liquor than any of us needed for the party. Ronnie's parties were "epic."

So, even though it was morning and John, who we called Digger for what reason I have no idea, Ronnie, Eli, Ruben, Richard … the only architecture student among us with any talent … and I had eaten our unsettling breakfast and our class registration time was nearing, and we all had our classes planned out, and we were all still a little hung over, we made our way down the hill. That pitiful sun was probably a blessing, and it was promising to be a goof off kind of day that only happens when you are in college, and you have no real responsibility, yet you perceive yourself an adult. Maybe we would buy some books later and then find our classes and then eat lunch and then goof off and shoot the shit and hang out and then go over to Krystal and eat ten or twelve "gut bombs," and then head out for a promised county fair that was supposed to be down at the Target way down on 41. Maybe I would ask Chris to go. She and I dated. Or maybe Bonnie if she was she was still at home and had not left for Georgia Southern yet, and see if anyone wanted to go with me. Maybe

The gaggle of amigos shuffled down the hill from Norton Hall toward our futures that were still as hazy as that early morning fog. Three-quarters of the way down the hill you could hear the commotion and see the lines that were registration. The class registration system consisted of seeing your counselor and getting approval for your eighteen, wimpy load, to twenty-one, massive load, hours of classes you wanted to take, figuring out a schedule and then going to the individual class tables and hopefully getting a computer card for that class, then turning the bundle in and you were done! Of course if the class you wanted happened to be full, then you were back to square one and had to figure it out all over again and would probably end up with an afternoon lab on Friday or 8:00 classes every day of the week. These were always dreaded, although being a morning person anyway, I loved 8:00 classes. Hopefully I could get all my academics done by 11:00 and then have a lab on Monday and Wednesday and that would rock. But we were veterans of this class registration system, and so we all knew there could be one more card for a full class if you knew which Dean to talk to or Chester Orvold or Jim Faucett or even Dean Van Gorder would help out a poor dorm counselor if push came to shove. Yes, there were no cares that morning … 'God was in his heaven and all was right with the world.'

At the curve at the bottom of the hill, we were all looking for the end of the snakey line of students when it happened. There She was. Oh, there had been many, many "shes" but this was the She. It was like there was no one else there that morning. One minute you are with your friends and the next it is just the two of you. There was no gym building. There were no other fifteen hundred people. There were no friends. There was just two people. Me and … She. She was in line just outside the gym door. She must have gotten there much earlier. She was in brown suede boots, tights, a plaid kilt skirt and a sweater top. The sun filtered through her long, dark blond hair almost making a halo around her face much as it does still today, forty-six years later, when she is singing or on the beach or on the ships when we cruise. She was the most beautiful thing I had ever seen … a little turned up nose, gorgeous legs, perfect breasts and immaculate make-up. I stopped and stared. I felt like I stood there for an hour just looking. It must have really been about three seconds, then the guys pushed and shoved me forward. They probably thought I was just a little hung-over still. "Come on Morris. Let's get this over with."

No, the last thing I wanted was to "get this over with." I had seen the future. I had literally, in three seconds, seen the future. Oh, it would be a long road to the altar and to our children and to our forty-fourth anniversary, and there would be great adventures, and great escapes and great

115

excitement and great heights and great lows, but I had seen the future … and She was oblivious. She probably thought that She was just registering at Southern Tech because She had transferred from Georgia Tech, and that She had to do something with her life. And She did not see her future husband that morning. She did not see the wooing, the love, the roses, the marriage, the children, the work, the travel, and the life we would build together in spite of everything and everyone. No, She was oblivious. She was just registering for classes. But I watched her that morning later from the balcony in the gym, and I knew. Oh, I would deny it. She would deny it. I would fight it. I would ignore it, but the future for Carolyn and me, like in the past, was written. And it was impossible for us, The Lovers, who had spent so many lives together in the past centuries, not to find each other and continue our journey through the ages.

Carolyn had been a basketball player at her high school, Wheeler. She had played the French Horn in the band and been on the homecoming court and had been in the National Honor Society. She had transferred over to STI from Georgia Tech's architecture program because the same demon Calculus had gotten her as had gotten me at Clemson. There was/is a quiet magic to Carolyn. There always was/is. There is a brilliance behind those green eyes. I believe that is what captured my heart. She was my equal. That is what I had been searching for in a mate … my equal … or my superior. The first time we actually talked, and she will back me up on this story, she was standing next to the architecture building near the roadway on its lower end. She was just standing there holding her books. I was walking down from the post office and came down street and turned to go up the building to go to class. I was going to pass right by her! What could I say? I was one of 2,000 boys on campus. What could I say to make her remember me? I had to say something. I HAD to! "The elevator doesn't stop here anymore." That was it. As I walked by her, THAT was what I said. That was all Mr. James-too-suave-and-too-cool-Bond-Morris could think of to say. Ta-Daaaaa! What a dufus thing to say. But, there it was. I said it. I smiled. She smiled, and I walked on up to class. And from those very, very meager and humble beginnings, our life together began. Oh, that building had no elevator. No building on campus did.

Chapter Five
To Dream the Impossible Dream

1.

From the beginning, there was a problem. I did not know there was a problem, but there was. Carolyn was already engaged. She was engaged to a guy named Rick. Rick attended college in Florida. Where they met, and how they met, to this day I do not know, but Carolyn was already engaged. But I was smitten. Too be honest, I did not know we would be married when I first met her, but I was to find this out soon enough. Carolyn very reluctantly agreed to go out with me. I think our first date was to a drinking and dancing place down near Peachtree Battle called Uncle Sams. I believe I can honestly say that the ship the SS Christobal and Uncle Sams are why I suffer from hearing loss today. It was unbelievably loud and for some reason, even though we were not 21, we were able to drink. Ah! Now I remember! The United States dropped the drinking age to 18 in 1970. It must have had to do with Vietnam and midterm elections, but anyway the drinking age was lowered. So, Carolyn and I went to Uncle Sams on our first date. There are two things I remember distinctly about that date. One – Carolyn ordered Scotch to drink. If you recall, I had made that mistake back in the Zone at a New Year's Eve celebration, and I was not going to do that again. But Carolyn did! I was IMPRESSED! And she drank it. I was doubly impressed! I ordered a gin and tonic, my go to drink since the SS Christobal. We had a good time as I recall. You know first date – everyone is on their best behavior and I recollect it was a good evening from my standpoint. After Uncle Sams, we headed home and got her home around midnight. As I said, I was on my best behavior. We parked in the driveway of 111 Sewell Lane. A single level, neatly kept, brick home. I got out and walked around the car and opened her door like a gentleman should (and still should and do to this day). We walked up the short walk and up the three steps to the porch and the front door. I think we kissed. It was a modest and chaste kiss … best behavior. Then I opened the screen and then the door. Two – and to my surprise and Carolyn's chagrin, her daddy had left the door unlocked but had put the chain lock on the door! We have laughed about that chain lock for years. Her daddy, Robert, must have really wanted to get rid of her! But not to be deterred, I got a screwdriver out of my car's tool kit and basically broke into her house by unscrewing the chain lock off the wall. You *know* what I was going for: *impress Carolyn*. That and I thought the first date was way, way too early for her to spend the night with me! ☺ So summing up, I broke her into her house, kissed her politely, got her into her house safely and headed for my dorm.

[This latest pause in writing comes as we laid my father (yes, The Colonel) to rest at Georgia National Cemetery yesterday, October 8th, 2021. After an unusually rainy week the sky cleared yesterday morning and the sun came out. Skies were blue with puffy clouds and my father had a well-attended funeral with 21-gun salute, taps, speeches by a "Sky Pilot" – listen to The Animals song by the same name if you do not understand the reference – and bagpiper playing Amazing Grace. This was followed by a reception for the family at the famous First Presbyterian Church of Cartersville. I pray, with him laid to rest, I can move on and let go of some of the resentment in my heart you have felt in reading this work of … what is the word … atonement … revelation … self-examination … reflection … or is it as the singer Sean Rowe intones, "I'm just trying to leave something behind."]

So, back to my story. The next weeks and months are a tangle of classes, travel to Panama, Bonnie, Chris, Leslie, Terri and Audrey but overshadowing all of this was Carolyn. I recall going to the movies and then going to a pizza restaurant where the Marietta Diner sits near what was the Southern Tech campus – STI is now a branch of Kennesaw State University – and the whole evening costing less than $20.00. I also recall following Carolyn one day on campus. We were changing classes and I saw her and was trying to catch up. That whole moment was immortalized in a single photograph in the

1973 STI Annual, The Log. But there are some specific memories and more interesting stories worth telling.

We went on a date to Stone Mountain on beautiful fall afternoon. It must have been fall as there were leaves on the trees but the weather was cool. I recall a crisp, blue sky with cotton ball clouds. Of course I was being my perception of Mr. Cool, "suavay-loco," James Bond boy and working my tail off to impress Carolyn. We were headed toward the mountain through some trees. The mountain loomed up above us as we approached. I was doing my best Nathaniel "Hawkeye" Poe imitation and breaking trail for my Cora Munro when I reached up to move a branch out of Carolyn's way. As I did, I put my hand in a big old gob of bird poop! Well, this was hilariously funny to Carolyn and of course it spoiled the whole persona I was developing. And then I too burst out laughing. Well, with no tissue or paper towel I had to use some leaves to clean my hand, and of course, there would be no hand holding for the rest of that date. What we did after that and where we ate and how we got home are all lost to history as they say. Of them I have no recollection. In fact, that single bird poop incident is all I recall from that whole day with any clarity. And you know, Life is funny; little did I even dare to imagine that at a hotel in that very park some decade or so later our son would be conceived.

At STI we were both in the Architectural Engineering Technology course of study. That course was never supposed to generate architects but supporters to architects, draftsmen as they were known back "in the day." Draftspersons in today's parlance. But Carolyn and I both fought through to get our licenses … but I digress. At STI we in the AET program, with the help of Professor Jim Fausett, started a chapter of the American Institute of Architects. The first year I was the president. Both Carolyn and Chris were in the chapter along with Richard who, as I have said, was the best architectural student I

FROM LEFT TO RIGHT: MR. FASSETT (FACULTY ADVISOR), JOHN AXLEY, CHRIS DODD, CAROL LYON, G.A. ADDINGTON, JIM WIGGINS, S.W. FOLSOM, RONNIE PATRICK. ROW 2: RICHARD TODD (TREASURER), JIM MORRIS (PRESIDENT), D.J. DONAR, RODNEY HARRISON, ROBERT SCHREPFER, J.D. BAILEY, DARRELL PHILLIPS, RUSSELL BEACH, DAVID DANGAR (SECRETARY), R.S. ENGLISH, STEVE HENDERSON.

knew. We got a charter from the AIA and met sporadically with no particular agenda. I was the first chapter President. I have no idea if it is still active today or not. But it was a way to be close to Carolyn and to try to impress her. In the picture, Chris is seated next to Carolyn.

[Again ... a pause and I apologize. It is now December 4, 2021. As I mentioned earlier, I paused to rebuild the deck at 1920 Falcon Wood Drive to have it ready for Thanksgiving and then to finally inter my father's ashes and now to lay Cary Jack Snelgrove, Carolyn's older sister Kathy's husband, to rest. May you rest in peace my good friend Jack.]

Back to my story of wooing Carolyn. As things developed at school Carolyn and I were asked by Mr. Baker if we would participate in STI recruitment visits throughout Georgia. I was all for it and Carolyn agreed too. YES! And the two of us took off in my little white Volkswagen headed to Macon and a convention there. I recall that for some reason we stayed overnight in a motel in Perry, Georgia. And outside that motel, on the lawn, was a large child's playscape featuring giant turtles that children could climb on, and we did. I recall the sun setting and Carolyn and me sitting on a turtle "talking philosophy." In other words, me wooing her. Other than sitting with her and talking, I do not recall anything about why we were even there. I know we traveled as far as Valdosta, but I do not remember anything about giving a talk about STI or setting up a booth or handing out flyers or anything. I think we also attended a college fair in Macon at the Civic Center. Again, I recall nothing except being with Carolyn. One event does stand out though. I vividly recall driving along and Carolyn falling asleep with her head against her door window glass and me thinking, "This is working because she trusts me enough to fall asleep while I drive." Either that or she was just exhausted from being around me. We Morris men can have that effect on women.

Soon after this period Carolyn told me she wanted to talk. So, we met on some steps/planters on the Norton Dorm side of the library there on the campus. And I can clearly recall that day. The sun was shining although it was cool. We sat on the steps and Carolyn looked directly into my eyes and said, "Jim, I just want to be friends. You see, I am already engaged." I was crushed. I was devastated, but I was also man enough to honor her wishes ... for a couple of weeks. I dated Chris and Bonnie, but my future with Carolyn was set. There was a point at this time, and I did not know this until much later that Chris and Carolyn had a conversation and Chris told Carolyn that she (Chris) had my body, but Carolyn had my heart.

And so slowly and relentlessly I began the pursuit again. She tentatively agreed to go to a concert at STI with me to see The Doobie Brothers. There is a picture in one of the annuals of us at the concert. Me, with cigarette in hand and chukka boots and Carolyn with her arm on my shoulder laughing at something. Our relationship must have been fairly developed at this point as she is leaning on me. *In the last several months, we brought the name of the band The Doobie Brothers up at a gathering with our children and they looked at us like we just came in from the moon. "Who were The Doobie Brothers?" they asked.*

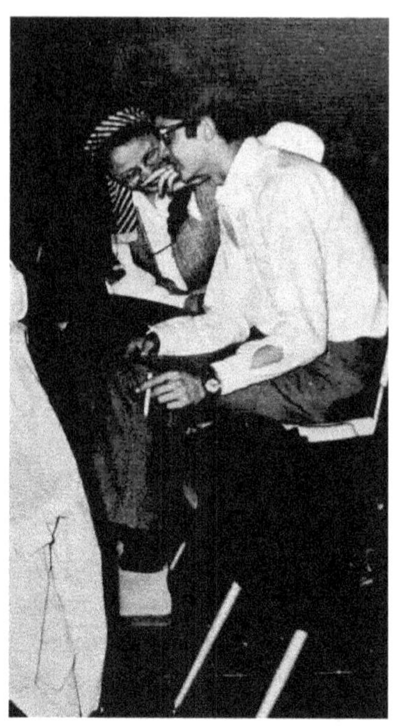

The relationship grew, and I had made a decision that this was the woman I was going to try to marry and spend my life with. Our dating became more frequent and exclusive. I made the decision that if I was going to ask Carolyn to give up Rick I had to be prepared to offer her at least as much as she was prepared to give up for me. All of this came to a climax when Carolyn was asked by a good friend from Georgia Tech, Jayne, to be in her wedding to Robert in Miami. Carolyn flew down and the wedding took place. Jayne and Robert had no clue about me, so Rick was Carolyn's escort for the wedding. As I recall the wedding took place in the midst of a hurricane, but that could just be in my mind as a metaphor for the turmoil Carolyn must have been going through. At any rate, on Sunday Carolyn flew back from Miami, and it just so happened that she flew back on the same flight that Jayne and Robert were on. They all deplaned together. Now this was "back in the day" before the new Atlanta airport had been built. It was the old Atlanta Hartsfield when just anyone could walk out to the gate and meet, or see off, a plane. So when Jayne and Robert and Carolyn walked off the jet way, I was waiting for Carolyn with a dozen red roses. Needless to say Jayne and Robert were stunned, and Carolyn was taken aback a little too. I think that day I made my

statement to Carolyn. And she did not reject me outright, so that was a good thing. Come to find out, Carolyn had left the engagement ring on the dresser in Miami.

I decided it was time to show Carolyn all the skeletons in my closet and so we went up to Cartersville to visit Momma. My opinion was that Momma "took a shine" to Carolyn as soon as she met her. There is a picture of our visit. You can see the "hine stoop behind us and to the right you can just make out the swing set The Big Three were photographed on. My only question is, who in the world took the picture? Momma sure looks proud of us. She was the BEST!

2.

As it worked out I was to graduate one semester before Carolyn. I would graduate in December of 1972. Carolyn would graduate in June of 1973. So, I had been struggling with the question of what I was going to do once I graduated for quite a while. During the preceding summer (of 1972) I did not return to the Canal Zone. I had gotten a job and been employed with American Engineers and Surveyors. Working for them turned out to be a very fateful thing. My advice, NEVER burn your bridges. I still lived in the dorm and was a summer semester Supervisor, but I was working off campus. At American Engineers we mostly did loan surveys. The boss was one Charlie Dean. He was a loud mouthed, womanizing divorcee who loved to party. The office was located in Sandy Springs just north of the perimeter on Roswell Road. Dean's second in command was David Burre. David was the one who did all the work in the firm. He would manage the survey crews, a rough bunch of hard drinking and raucous men, as well as doing most of the real design work. I worked with a young man, whose name I do not recall I am sorry to say, and we mostly did small loan survey plots. He was nice to me. He had been in Alto prison, but was working hard on turning himself around. I do recall that I caught crabs that summer. Undoubtedly they came from one of the survey crew who had infested a bathroom near the office with them. I did not pass them on and was cured of them in no time.

I believe it was during that summer of 1972 that Dad came up to visit to buy a house as he was retiring as I mentioned. He needed to use the little white VW to get around so I, of course, let him have it. After all, it was his car. Everything was going well except for one tiny flaw. After the sugar in the gas tank event, I had purchased a locking gas cap for the car. Yep, you guessed it. I failed to give Dad the key to the cap. So, he ventured off one day in the car with no way to fill the tank. It all worked out okay. He made it back to my dorm where he was sleeping in my room on what he called a "wing and a prayer." I felt foolish of course, but it all turned out alright in the long run.

Near the end of that summer of 1972 with one more semester before I graduated, I decided when I graduated I wanted to become a Navy pilot. Why? Why not go into architecture? I had beaten the draft. Why ask for trouble and Vietnam? I do not have any good answers for any of those questions. I guess I sort of felt a need to follow the military tradition of my family. My brother Bill had entered the Air Force Academy sometime around this time. Going in the Navy seemed a way to have a job once I graduated and please my father. As it all ended up, nothing could have been further from the truth, but it seemed logical to me at the time. A way to prove my manhood and as I said, to please The Colonel.

During this final semester with my illustrious Navy career looming and flush with summer cash from my working at American Engineers and Surveyors, I asked Carolyn Ethel Lyon to marry me. Apparently, she said yes. So next I went and talked to Mr. Robert (Bob) Frederick Lyon. I asked him if I could marry his daughter. Apparently, he said yes. Carolyn and I then went down to Atlanta to Baily, Banks and Biddle and picked out her engagement ring. It was 1/3 carat and cost about $350.00 as I recall. I put it on layaway and began making payments.

Secretly I paid the ring off more quickly than Carolyn and I planned. Then, innocently, I asked her if she would go to dinner with me. We got all gussied up as I told her we were going to Herren's for my birthday. I picked her up that evening in late October of 1972, and we headed down to Atlanta. Herren's was established in 1934 by the prizefighter Charlie "Red" Herren. The original Atlanta restaurant was near where the Rialto Theater stood on Luckie Street between Farlie and Forsyth Street. Neither landmark is still there, but Herren's was known for being the first Atlanta restaurant to integrate in 1962 and for their fresh, in-the-tank, you-select-it lobster. It was an elegant place. As I think back, I picture the *Dr. Zhivago* restaurant when Zhivago patched up Victor Komarov after Laura

Mr. and Mrs. Robert F. Lyon of Marietta announce the engagement of their daughter, Carolyn Ethel, to James Wingfield Morris Jr., son of Col. and Mrs. James Wingfield Morris of Chamblee.

Miss Lyon is the granddaughter of Mrs. John Snowden Hacklett and the late Mr. Hacklett of Nashville, Tenn., and Mr. and Mrs. John Koch of Jackson Heights, L. I., N. Y.

Mr. Morris is the grandson of the late Dr. and Mrs. William Carl Wofford of Cartersville, and Mrs. Marion Wingfield Morris and the late Mr. Morris, also of Cartersville.

Miss Lyon will receive a bachelor of engineering technology degree in architecture from Southern Technical Institute in June.

Mr. Morris received a bachelor of engineering technology degree in architecture from Southern Technical Institute. He will enter Naval Flight Officer Candidate School in Pensacola in late January.

Plans for the wedding, which will take place at Powers Ferry United Methodist Church, will be announced later.

CAROLYN ETHEL LYON, JAMES MORRIS JR.
Engagement Announced   Marietta Wedding Planned

Antipova shot Victor. Very rich and well appointed. Kind of an old Atlanta Bones restaurant. Anyway, we arrived, and she had a gift for me for my birthday, and little did she know, I had the ring. We picked out our lobsters from the live tank and were escorted to our seats. Carolyn wanted me to open my gift, so before we ate I opened it. It was a beautiful sculpture of Don Quixote de la Mancha. Carolyn gave me this because we had been to see the movie with Peter O'Toole playing the part of Alonso Quixano and Sophia Loren as his Dulcinea. We had also been to a dinner theater and seen the play presented live. She knew he was one of my heroes and had gotten me this very thoughtful gift. When we had opened her gift and were settling down to our salads, I pulled out the ring box and … I don't think I went down on my knee by the table … ask Carolyn, she would recall … I opened the ring box and formally asked her if she would marry me! Apparently she said yes! An older couple at an adjacent table saw what was going on and sent a bottle of champagne to our table. I have always wanted to pay that gesture back to a young couple and will someday in the right place. It was a perfect evening and the smartest thing I ever did, was done.

3.

"The Civil War began on April 12, 1861. All commercial traffic on the Mississippi stopped. Sam (Clemens – Mark Twain) was aboard one of the last steamboats to make it from New Orleans to St. Louis … hoping only that it (the war) would be over soon so he could return to the river. Eventually, he went back to Hannibal, where some of the young men with whom he'd once played Robin Hood had formed a small Confederate militia unit called the Marion Rangers. Sam signed on, too, mostly just for something to do. His friends elected him second lieutenant, he remembered; there was no first lieutenant. He was not with them long. Factual details of his time as a rebel soldier are few, but the Marion Rangers seem to have spent most of their time hiding in the woods and fleeing from the rumor of advancing Union troops. Within two weeks the homegrown unit disbanded. Most of Sam's friends went on enlist in the regular Confederate Army. Sam did not. He 'skedaddled.'" Quote from *Mark Twain, An Illustrated Biography*, by Geoffrey C. Ward, Dayton Duncan, Ken Burns, pp 26-27, IBSN 0-375-40561-5

I finished my studies in December of 1972, and I was signed up to become a Naval Aviator. I was to enter Naval Flight Officer Training at Pensacola, Florida, Naval Air Station in January of 1973. What follows is a true accounting of that experience. No matter what tales you have heard about the Vietnam War ending and the Navy not needing pilots … this is the truth of the story.

The week after New Year's 1973 had been unusually cold for a long stretch, and on Friday, January 5th, a low came up from the Gulf of Mexico across Alabama. We knew we were in for trouble when it crossed over Birmingham headed northwest and coated that city in ice and snow. The front arrived in Atlanta early in the morning of Saturday the 6th and began covering us in ice. By noon the city was paralyzed. Thousands were without power and the roads were a disaster. I had left school having ended my studies and come home to Commodore Drive in Chamblee, Georgia, where my parents lived to stay until I left for the Navy. By Sunday January 7th the front had passed but as they say, the pain lingered. But I was due to report on the 8th so my trusty little white Volkswagen and I ventured off into the glistening morning. I headed out around a very dicey I-285 to the west and then down I-85 toward Montgomery, Alabama. When I reached Montgomery the ice and snow had lessened it grip and it was clear driving. In Montgomery I turned onto I-65 and then 113 and 31 down into Pensacola.

I do not recall where I spent the night, but I was a free man, on my own, "pulling my own little red wagon." This was a colloquialism I had heard all my life from The Colonel. He would say to me, "You can decide when you are 'pulling your own little red wagon.' But today you are under MY roof and I will decide." I got up early the next morning anxious to begin my new adventure. I found what I recall was a Waffle House and got some breakfast. Then I was off to join the Navy and fly and see the world! As I was backing up my Volkswagen, I backed right into a short, maybe 14-inch-tall, unseen concrete filled steel post. It went right, exactly between my two tailpipes and bent a perfect half circle indention in my car's back skirt. Had I known at the time, this was an omen of things to come.

The next events are a blur. Events stand out in my memory, but I cannot separate them or put them in any kind of time order or sequence. If you want an idea of my ordeal, watch the movie *An Officer and a Gentleman* with Richard Gere. It will give you some feeling of my experience.

I do recall parking my car that morning early on January 8th, 1973, in a parking lot on the Navy base. I did not take anything with me. I had gotten no instructions what to bring, so I did not bring even a tooth brush or razor. "The Navy will issue everything you need, including a brain." This was mistake Number 1. Somehow, I found where I was to report and then the "blur" begins. There was much yelling at me for no apparent reason. I did pushups and ran around. I was put with several other inductees. We were haphazardly marched to get all our hair shaved off all the while being yelled at. Our heads were shaved (like Clemson … so my head was shaved … again). We were then marched to get our one piece coveralls called Poopies. And we were called Poopies. We were then issued our uniforms and marched back to the barracks. We were assigned our bunks and told to "get then squared away" amid much yelling and screaming by other flight officer candidates who were much further along in the process. The older flight officer candidates were our tormentors and mentors. Of course none of us put our "gear" away correctly or made our bunks correctly – of course no one showed us how – so upper classmen came in and tore our bunks apart and dumped all our stuff on the floor while yelling, "What is the 3rd general order of a soldier?", "What is the 5th general order of a soldier?" Apparently there are eleven of them, and no one had bothered to tell me what they were so I had no idea. So I was constantly doing pushups for not knowing what I did not know, and no one would tell me what they were.

Meals were a similar fiasco. As we Poopies shuffled along with our metal trays and sailors plopped whatever was for that meal on our trays upperclassmen were yelling about General Orders and berating us for not knowing them. When we finally sat down to eat we were told we had five minutes and we were expected outside for P.T. (physical training). So, we woofed what we could and spilled outside to endure more yelling and running around. Finally, the day ended and we returned to our barracks. We bathed. Me with no soap or razor or toothbrush and me too terrified to ask where to get some. Another Poopie loaned me a razor. My finger was my tooth brush and I bummed some soap. Hair shampoo was not needed as we were all bald. Once in the rack (bed) we fell asleep instantly, exhausted from our first thrilling day. Lights out was at 10:00. At 12:00 an upper classman came down the hall screaming and banging on all our doors, "Mattress inspection! Get your asses out in the hall with your mattress!" We all climbed out and we in the brilliant lights of the hall holding our mattresses as we were screamed at about … yep, General Orders. After much yelling and Yes Siring and Yes Sargenting and many push-ups we were allowed back in our racks which we had to make back up. Then about 3:00 it happened again! Same thing all over again. Then reveille was at 5:00. Back in our Poopie suits and outside in the dark for an hour of P.T. before breakfast.

I recall a picture taken of our class. It is somewhere in a foot locker. I'll try to find it and include it. We were a sorry looking lot of bald, scared little boys. We also had to have full physicals including an electroencephalogram (EEG). Part of the test was to lie still and awake in a dark room quietly. Well, we were all so exhausted we all fell asleep. The person administering the test then banged something on a desk to wake us up. I remember one guy failed it. He was immediately "washed out." Apparently, I passed. Another test was to measure us specifically to see if we would fit in the Navy jets. All this time I had focused on being a RIO (Radar Intercept Officer – think Goose in *Top Gun*) in an F-4 Phantom. A jet so powerful that it was said, "This jet is proof that with enough power even a brick can fly." And a RIO, not a pilot, because my eye sight would not let me be a pilot. During these measurements I was informed my arms were too short to fly in a Phantom. What the what?

Another memory was our first barracks inspection. We all had to have our shoes spit shined and our brass polished and all our insignia properly attached and all our "cables" (errant strings) removed. I got my shoes spit shined because that was one thing I had been taught by The Colonel. I got my brass polished. My insignia was another matter. There were two collar insignias that had a rope on them, and the rope was supposed to be pointing toward the inside (I think, maybe it was to the outside, I don't know). At-any-rate, I had it backwards. Pushups and screaming from a Navy officer. I think I also had a "cable." More screaming. But the coup-de-grace was the Navy way of tucking in your shirt tail. You know … "There's the right way, the wrong way and the Navy way." Anyway, I had been taught by The Colonel from when I was very small to fold the shirt at the waist with the tuck to the back. Well, the Navy way was exactly opposite. Still to this day whenever I tuck in my shirt I think about that. I was starting to see the ludicrousness of what was going on around me.

One morning we were issued rifles, and we were to run for five miles with the rifle.

At times holding it over our heads. At times on the beach through the sand. It was tremendously hard. I recall being able to do it. I recall several others not being able to do it and "DORing" on the spot. To DOR is to Drop On Request. It was the ultimate humiliation at The Naval Air Station at Pensacola. Basically you quit. You were immediately removed from the squadron and you disappeared. One guy was overweight and had suffered immensely because of it. Constant humiliation. He was crying one night because he had graduated from college with a degree in history and could not find a job anywhere so he had joined the Navy. Now he was about to DOR and had no idea what he would do. He sounded close to suicide. I do not know what happened to him.

My final straw was the night I was the OOD (Officer of the Deck) I went on duty at 2:00AM and was to be on duty until 6:00. I should be able to tell you what "bells" those were, but I can't now. After an exhausting day and no sleep, I was to be the OOD for four hours in the middle of the night and then take a math test the next morning. The OOD basically patrols the barracks and makes sure there are no fires, and everyone is safe. I guess you could call it sentry duty. Now through all of the fun and games there was a Marine Drill Sargent overseeing all of us. His name was Sargent Delaney ... Sargent *Mad Dog* Delaney as he was known. When you addressed him you addressed him as Sargent, not Sir. "I am not some ___, _____, ___ officer!" he would scream at us. Yes, watch R. Lee Ermey in the movie *Full Metal Jacket* to get the drift. Well, as OOD I was on duty when this man came on duty at 5:00. I remember he yelled at me to get him some coffee. I did and it was either too hot or not hot enough or something, but he threw it at me and cursed me, and I gave him 50 push-ups. That man was terrifying ... and insane. After that event, I decided I was on my way out of this psycho ward.

When I took the math test the next morning I was exhausted. I failed it, and then decided right then and there and informed my immediate CO I wanted to DOR. Much screaming and name calling ensued, but the die was cast. I did not give a damn about The Colonel, The Navy or anything. I did not have to put up with this stupidity any longer. I was not going to be degraded or humiliated any longer. I think a couple of other guys followed my lead that morning, but I am not sure. Fortunately, the contract I had signed did not make me stay in the Navy. Some contracts made you stay in for two years as a seaman. I was able to get out. I was immediately moved to the DOR barracks to await my processing out papers. They came late the next day. I had been in the Navy two weeks. My honorable discharge is dated January 23, 1973. That afternoon, I put my civilian clothes back on, walked to my car, got a peaceful meal somewhere outside Pensacola, drove to a motel for the night and called Carolyn. She was the only person glad to hear my voice, and the only person happy I was coming home. Oh, I also think that I heard that Ho Chi Min was tremendously relieved. He knew now for sure that the United States would not win the War in Vietnam. I had "skedaddled."

4.

I returned home in disgrace ... degraded and humiliated ... in my opinion. The Colonel never said anything except, "It's time for you to get a job." There was to be no decompression time, no let's talk about it time, no helping me understand time, nothing. So, I contacted American Engineers and Surveyors, good old Charlie Dean. And, presto, I had a job. In reflection, I thank God for that man. He may not see himself like that, but he saved me.

I had returned in late January and the next few months flew by. My hair grew back. I would never have it shaved off again. My self-esteem began to grow back also. Life would test me again. There would be two more strenuous attempts to degrade and humiliate me, but the attempts would be met with different results by a different man.

I have no particular or specific recollections of this January to June, 1973, time period other than Carolyn and I taking Russ and Pete (now 12 and 11 respectively) down to a wildlife preserve near Callaway Gardens. I believe it is still there though maybe the name has changed. I believe it was called *Lion Country Safari* when we went. I do not remember anything about the day that was special, but I do remember that Rusty made a pronouncement when we returned home. Rusty declared that, "Carolyn is the cleanest girlfriend that Jimbo has ever had." Carolyn and I were seeing each other every chance we got. She was trying to finish at STI, and I was working and saving as much as I could. Carolyn was driving a little, red, poorly maintained VW, and I was driving my white, 68 VW, which had a new rear skirt and new muffler and tail pipes. Dad and I actually worked together in the carport of his Chamblee home at 4148 Commodore Lane to replace the parts I had damaged down in Pensacola … almost like a Father and Son would do.

 Carolyn and I had decided the best thing was for her to finish school. Actually, I think she would have married me the moment I returned from my brief but eventful Naval career, even though I was still bald as a que ball, but I felt it was more important for her to get her degree. I guess I knew if we got married, there would be very little studying being done. And, as things worked out, my feelings were quite unknowingly prophetic. We located some apartments on the east side of US 41 Highway down in the valley just south of Windy Hill Road. The apartments were named Bordeaux West. I guess Carolyn and I knew someday we would travel to Paris! Coincidentally, the apartments were right next door to (just to the south of) the Richway Store where I had met Bonnie years before. We rented a one bedroom, 800 square foot apartment for me to live in until we got married. I could not wait to move out of The Colonel's house. And I have never spent the night, even once, under his roof since I left. In our apartment, Carolyn and I had a stupid four-foot-tall wooden barrel I brought from Panama, some cinder block and wood shelves I made which held my statue of Don Quixote, a little black and white television I had from college, and my stereo from college, a yellow blow up chair, a red bean bag chair, a two chair dinette we got from somewhere and after we were married, Carolyn's double bed and chest of drawers. I guess I slept on the floor until we got married. That, and Carolyn's broken down VW and my white VW, was the sum total of our belongings when we got married. As Carolyn and I had gotten more and more serious in college, I had started attending church with her at Powers Ferry Methodist Church. The church was located at the Northwest corner of the 120 Loop and Powers Ferry Road in Marietta. It is not there anymore, at least not as a Methodist church. As a church, it folded around 2020. But in the 1970's it was a great church. I would show up at Carolyn's house and Carolyn's mother, Nanny as she was called, Virginia as she was called and Mildred Virginia Shacklett Lyon as she was named, would make Carolyn cook for me. Now, I have to be honest and Carolyn will bare me out on this, she has never loved the kitchen, but Nanny was determined Carolyn was going to "catch this man" and "the fastest way to a man's heart is through his stomach" so the old sayings go. So, Carolyn would cook bacon and drop biscuits, and then we would head off to church. During this time, I left Presbyterianism and became a Methodist, a much warmer and more loving religion. This change to Methodism and the Methodist Church was to affect the rest of my life and to be a catalyst for many wonderful things that were to happen.

5.

Carolyn and I finally set a date for our wedding. It was to be June the 9th at 8:00 in the evening. The wedding was to be the evening of the morning we both officially graduated from Southern Technical Institute. Even though I had technically graduated in December of 1972, STI only held its formal graduation ceremony once a year in June. And then we were going to be married in the sanctuary of Powers Ferry Methodist Church by Reverend Rudy Baker that evening.

I do not believe my parents ever liked Carolyn or Carolyn's parents, Bob and Virginia. I think The Colonel, now retired and trying to sell insurance for Acacia … he was a miserable insurance salesman … and his Lady felt they were too good for this middle class family from Marietta. This feeling continues in Carolyn's and my memories to this day. I do not understand why The Colonel and his Lady felt this way and acted in this hurtful way. Carolyn's dad was an Engineer with Lockheed and flew all over the world selling Jetstar Aircraft to Saudi princes and such and Virginia was a nurse just like my mother except Virginia was a real practicing nurse. Virginia actually worked for a living. But Carolyn was taking their first born son whom they *loved and cherished* (he wrote dripping with sarcasm) away. I do not understand and, as my parents are both dead now, will never understand.

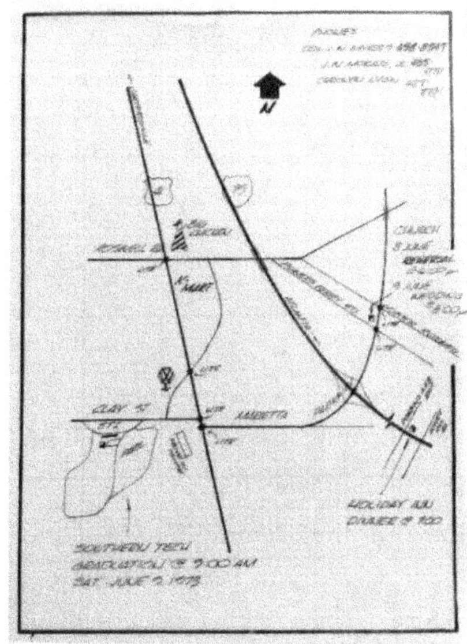

Be that as it may, Carolyn and I were going to get married the world be damned. Again, the smartest thing I have EVER done. The afternoon before the wedding we had our wedding rehearsal and our first hiccup. Reverend Rudy Baker was very sick. He had laryngitis and could not do the wedding. So, The Colonel pressed his preacher, Reverend Moss Robertson, into service. We rehearsed and then we all went to the rehearsal dinner which was paid for by The Colonel. We all met at what was then the Holiday Inn on I-75 at its southeast intersection corner with Terrell Mill Road (South Cobb Drive). It is a Motel 6 now I believe. The picture is of a map I made at work for all of our guests. It is all hand lettering by me using my ink pens. The original was on vellum.

The next morning, June 9th, 1973, dawned with all the heat and humidity only a Georgia summer can produce. But the temperature was lost on me, and at least it was not raining. I was graduating; I was getting married; and I was leaving with my *wife* for a week at the beach. My recollections of the graduation were that the entire family was present with the exception of Re. I do not recall that Re, who had married Jerry Spicher back a few years ago, was present as she and Jerry were living in Oregon. But I vividly recall Nelson and Toochie and Marybelle and Don, my grandmother Momma, and Doris and Unca' Bill being there. I know Carolyn's grandmother Granny Shacklett was there, and I'm sure there was a contingent of Carolyn's other Nashville relatives, the Shackletts. I know that Bob Lyon's mother and stepfather, known to me only as "Granny and Grandpa Kotch" were down from New York. The college graduation that morning was held in the gym. The same very same gym from the "Three Seconds" narrative where I had first seen Carolyn. Beyond that, I cannot tell you a single thing about that graduation. There are about six pictures in an album Carolyn put together labeled '73 -'77.

6.

Morris-Lyon Vows Repeated In June

Carolyn Ethel Lyon of Marietta became the bride of James Wingfield Morris Jr of Cartersville on June 9 at 8 p.m. in Powers Ferry United Methodist Church, Marietta. The double ring ceremony was performed by Rev. E. Moss Robertson.

The bride is the daughter of Mr. and Mrs. Robert F. Lyon of Marietta, and the groom is the son of Col. (ret.) and Mrs. James W. Morris of Chamblee.

The bride, given in marriage by her father, wore a gown of organza trimmed with alencon lace and seed pearls. The bishop sleeves were appliqued with lace. The full, bias-cut skirt formed the chapel-length train. Her fingertip mantilla, which was attached to a Juliet cap, was edged in lace. Pink and yellow roses surrounding an orchid were carried on a white satin bible.

She was attended by her sister, Kathy Bilyeu of Marietta as matron of honor. Bridesmaids were Bobbi Lyon and Ginny Lyon of Marietta, sisters of the bride. Flower girl was Melissa Bilyeu, the bride's niece.

Best man was Col. Morris, the groom's father. Ushers were Bill Morris, brother of the groom, Tommy Curles of Albany, and Ruben English of Powersville. Pete Morris and Rusty Morris, brothers of the groom, were acolytes.

A reception was given in the church fellowship hall by the bride's parents. Mrs. Robert Smith of Atlanta kept the bride's book. Assisting in serving were Linda Morgan, Betty Jo Post, and Donna Ralston.

After a wedding trip to Florida, the couple is at home in Smyrna. The groom is associated with American Engineers and Surveyors, Atlanta, and the bride is associated with C. P. Roberts, Engineers and Architects, Inc., Atlanta.

MR. AND MRS. JAMES WINGFIELD MORRIS JR.
Bride Is Former Carolyn Ethel Lyon

Later that day, Secretariat won the Triple Crown. My Best Man was The Colonel ... naturally ... "If I do this, he will love me." My groomsmen were my brother Bill, Ruben from STI and another friend from STI named Tom. You have not heard of Tom up to this point. We went to STI together, but beyond that I have no real particular recollections of him. Which to me is interesting because I thought enough of him to ask him to be one of my groomsmen.

Anyway, the afternoon of the wedding was spent hanging out at Bordeaux West with Dad and Bill and watching Secretariat win the Triple Crown. I'm sure I ate some dinner although what and when and where are lost. We made our way to the church in the evening. I guess it was around 7:00 when we arrived. There is a picture of Bill and Dad and me out back of the Powers Ferry UMC sanctuary in the wedding pictures. The ceremony had been planned by Carolyn, and it was beautiful. My wonderful

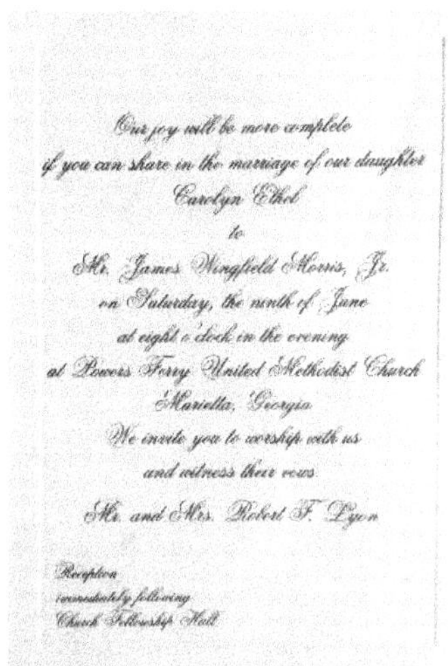

Aunt Marybelle Morris Swift stepped up to coordinate everything in the back of the church for Carolyn and cemented a lifelong friendship with Carolyn. The only two hiccups I was aware of was that Rudy Baker, our Powers Ferry Methodist Church minister who was to officiate at the wedding caught the flu or something, and Moss Robertson, my parents minister, was called in to pinch hit. The second hiccup was that someone forgot to turn on the air conditioning in the sanctuary. Carolyn says she recalls us reciting our vows and looking into my eyes as a bead of sweat trickled down my nose. One of the songs sung was "The Impossible Dream" from *Man of La Mancha*. My parents said later (hatefully) that they thought it was "inappropriate." "Why would you sing about an impossible dream at your wedding?" But they were ignorant, the solo was done beautifully, it was special to my Dulcinea and me, and WE loved it. Lesson: do not hate what you do not understand.

Following the ceremony, we all retreated to the cool of the basement fellowship hall of the church, and as was the custom of the day, we had melon balls and other finger food. Carolyn's friend Jayne, who had married Robert in Florida and met me for the first time at the airport when I was meeting Carolyn who was coming in from their wedding, helped with the guest register. There is a picture of her in the wedding book. I cannot really tell you what was there to eat other than cake, because I have no idea. I do not recall eating anything except a piece of cake shared with Carolyn. And there was none of that stuffing cake in each other's faces. We both agreed that was just not a very nice way to start a marriage. There are pictures in our wedding book of the ceremony and the reception and me in awful check pants and Carolyn looking beautiful in a short dress and my '68 VW which my brothers filled with balloons and paper and had written all over. Little did they know Carolyn and I were going one exit down I-75 where Dad had left his car for us to take to Florida. My brothers ended up having to clean up my car. So, Carolyn and I were off to Perry, Georgia, for the first night of our honeymoon. From there we were headed to the Holiday Inn in Panama City, Florida, The Redneck Rivera! The *only* destination where all self-respecting 22-year-old newlyweds in 1973 went to honeymoon. Carolyn must have been terrified. I guess I would have been if I'd had any sense. But I was not; I had my little red wagon firmly in tow.

Part II

Pulling *Our* Own "Little Red Wagon"

At this point in the narrative I have talked about the first twenty-two years of my life. Part II is going to look at the next fifty plus through my eyes. It's funny, just writing the word "fifty" is a little scary to me which is revealing in itself. And I have been thinking about how to cover this time of my life. Should I try to break it into distinct pieces of marriage, children, jobs and friends? Or simply take it all on a timeline and discuss all the pieces together and intertwined which is what they were — each piece influencing and shaping the next piece? I believe the best way is the intertwined approach. It may get a little confusing to you, gentle reader, but living fifty years of marriage can be confusing.

Chapter One
The Early Days

1.

Carolyn and I had a wonderful honeymoon. I recall when we arrived at the Holiday Inn in Panama City the first thing we noticed was that the pool area had been partially washed into the Gulf of Mexico! Now remember, this was before the days of the internet and free long distance calls. Everything was "snail mail" and long distance phone rates. Today, I would have changed hotels immediately. Then, one

had no way to communicate rapidly, and I had already paid for the week by check months earlier. It was a different, stupid, simpler and slower world. But, as I said we had a wonderful honeymoon.

One of the first things we did, ignoring the obvious, was to hit the beach and get burned to a crisp. But this was the way it was done in 1973. You burned, then pealed then tanned. You did not worry about sunscreen or skin cancer. So, we did. Carolyn especially got fried to a crisp. There is a picture of her, red as a beet and smiling ear to ear. Of course, the one thing we did not do is swim in the pool! I remember us getting all dressed up one evening and going to the requisite dining spot, Captain Andersons, where we waited in a line for a table as they did not take reservations. I assume we had dinner, which was probably a "Captain's Platter" of fried food. Who worries about cholesterol when you are 22? Carolyn and I went back in 2020 over Thanksgiving to Panama City with James and Angela and Cait and we found Captain Andersons. It was closed that day due to Covid. It looked a little sad. I guess it was still a "place to go" so to speak but it just looked a little tired. I also remember us going to a local landmark which was a tall tower you could go up on and look up and down the beach. There are several pictures of us on the tower. One of the pictures is of our hands, one over the other, showing off our new wedding bands. We recreated this picture a year or so later with the small hand of our daughter Jenna (then Mary Virginia) over our hands. We then recreated this picture again in 2017 with our hands on a column of the Coliseum in Rome. I am such a sucker for sappy stuff like that. Anyway, those are my major recollections. Carolyn probably has a million more, but those are my major memories of a honeymoon week on "The Redneck Riviera."

2.

After Panama City, we drove home to our little Bordeaux West apartment and began our lives together. I remember one of the first things we had to do when we got home was to go shopping for "household supplies." You know, things like brooms and dish rags and food and stuff like that. So, we drove (I think) next door to Richway … yep, the same one where I met Bonnie. I recall a hot June day in 1973. We bought what we needed. I do not recall what all we needed, but I do remember the sticker shock! We spent 70+ dollars! Yes, over $70 on brooms, food and what-not. I was blown away. Of course writing about it today in 2022, I have to chuckle to myself. We were so young, and I was so ignorant … Lordy, so, so very ignorant! But what I do recall is that we were happy … we did not know what we did not know and that was okay with us. Now Carolyn may have a different perspective on how happy we were given that our little marriage was going to be tested, and *she* was going to be one taking the test. I was going to be taking a pop quiz compared to her taking an exam.

Sometime around the time we returned home we unknowingly started one of the most wonderful and blessed events in our lives. At about nine days into our married life, we conceived our daughter, Mary Virginia Morris, now Jenna Morris Blackwell. Of course, we did not know it at the time. To us, we were just two newly married children getting our feet on the ground and trying to learn about each other and trying to figure out the whole being married thing. We were soon to find out, though, that we were pregnant.

When Carolyn and I found out we were pregnant it was a kind of a shock but then again it wasn't. We informed the family to mixed reviews. The only person I recall that was genuinely happy for us was The Colonel's mother, Momma. Momma (Marie Louise Williams Morris) was Carolyn's role model of how to be a grandparent. We both loved her deeply and she loved us right back. The thing that endeared her the most to me was that she truly loved Carolyn. Other reviews from the family were statements from my mother such as "Well, you know Carolyn could talk to Re (my sister who was an OBGYN nurse now) about birth control." How insulting. Anyway we were pregnant and Carolyn was dealing with all the joys of pregnancy like morning sickness. What we did not know was that there was an underlying condition.

One of our first significant purchases was a car. Again, I look back and chuckle. We had my VW. Carolyn's VW was running on three cylinders and we sold it to a person I worked with at American Engineers. Our first new car was a 1973 MG Midget. We bought it from Baker Motors who were located at the corner of Piedmont and Peachtree Street downtown. It was British Racing Green with tan interior. I do not recall its original price, but as close as I can research, it was about $2,000. We took out a loan just like "big girls and boys." I still have the car manual I bought to go with the car. It is downstairs on the shelf. Why we bought such a ridiculous car I do not recall, but we did! I remember we took the car up to Cartersville to show Momma (The Colonel's mother) and Uncle Nelson and Toochie and Aunt Dar and Uncle Bill, and on the way home it started to rain. At the top of the windshield where you attach the convertible roof were two latch points. The metal latch points were riveted to the metal windshield surround. In fact, they were through-riveted and no one had sealed the rivets, so as soon as the rain hit the windshield it started streaming through the rivet holes! Carolyn and were laughing and holding tissues up to catch the rain. That little adventure should tell you the level of craftsmanship used on these cars. That MG and the second one I bought later (because I am a glutton for punishment) were to be the biggest royal pain-in-the-ass cars I have ever owned. Let me go ahead and get some quick MG car tales into this legend while they are on my mind. Like the time the brake master cylinder leaked. The brake master cylinder was located on the firewall of the car above the brake pedal so when it leaks it drips in your brand new Big Boy brown buckle shoes! And then the accelerator pedal is connected to the carburetors, of which there are two and they have to be "balanced," with a thin cable and if this cable should break … say when you are halfway to work … you better hope you have the knowledge and tools with you to fix it because this was way before cell phones and if you break down near the Chattahoochee River on Riverside Drive you are pretty much screwed. Fortunately, I did have the tools and the knowledge. I was missing an umbrella though. It was a great morning! Enough about cars.

Carolyn and I both worked. Carolyn had gotten a job at C.P. Roberts Engineers and I was still working at American Engineers and Surveyors. As I have shared, I worked in Sandy Springs and Carolyn's office was in a small office park in Dunwoody just north of 285 on Chamblee-Dunwoody Road. C. P. Roberts Engineers was to figure prominently in our lives as you will see. Now late in 1973 the middle eastern oil producing nations, OPEC, became unhappy with America's stance on helping Israel during the war Israel was in with its neighbors so OPEC decided to embargo the United States as far as oil exports. At this time the USA got most of its oil from the Middle East so gas prices spiked and oil became scarce. Prices went from 35 cents a gallon – yep 35¢ – to $1.40 a gallon. There were gas lines, rationing and odd-even days you could buy gas. Fortunately, Carolyn and I had two very fuel efficient cars, the MG and the little white 68 VW, a practice we have always maintained to this day. But we still car pooled. I would drive us to Sandy Springs. We would stop at Dunkin Donuts and get a donut if Carolyn felt like it. As I said, Carolyn was dealing with morning sickness and the only thing she could tolerate was radishes. Go figure. But she would drop me off and then head over to her office.

Carolyn's pregnancy was difficult, and we were not sure why. Please remember this was 1973. In the world of medicine, it was little better than the Middle Ages as compared to today which has now progressed to the late 1700's. Her doctor suspected a number of things but could not pin down anything. She would get violent pains that would send her to bed. She would vomit after eating a somewhat bland meal. Her system, already totally messed up by being pregnant, was a disaster, and there was nothing I could do about it. But Carolyn "soldiered on" (to borrow a phrase from The Colonel). She went to work, cleaned the little 800 square foot apartment, washed clothes in the apartment washer/dryer area, cooked our food, grocery shopped, took care of me and generally was Wonder Woman. At this moment I am asking myself, "What the hell did you do during all this?"

We must have had a six-month lease at Bordeaux West, because sometime around February of 1974 we moved to Chimney Hills apartments. It was right before Jenna was born. Chimney Hills was known for each apartment having a fireplace, hence the "Chimney" part of Chimney Hills. It was also on a sort of hill. These apartments were somewhere between I-75 and Powers Ferry Road on Windy Hill Road. As you are traveling from I-75 toward Powers Ferry the apartments were on the left. Anyway, we rented a two-bedroom apartment. We were moving up in the world! The apartment had an area for a washer-dryer so we got our trusty Sears credit card and bought a pair. They were a very trendy, cutting edge for the early 70's "Harvest Gold" color – none of that plain old Mom and Pop White for us! Now Carolyn could do laundry right there in the apartment. This was critical because our new arrival was due soon. As was the custom of the time, though times were slowly changing, Carolyn quit her job at C.P. Roberts in order to have Jenna. There was no six weeks or nine weeks' maternity leave. Carolyn quit her job and this is how I came to work at C.P. Roberts Engineers, Inc.

Carolyn and I took a trip one weekend to Nashville as I recall. It was my first experience with the whole Nashville clan. There was Granny Shacklett (look at our wedding pictures), Nanny, Aunt Dot (who wasn't really an Aunt) and her husband Bob, and another Dot (the daughter of Mamie) and her husband James, Aunt Mamie, Aunt Christine, Aunt Louise, Uncle John, Uncle Jessie and his wife Frankie, Uncle Earl, and then to quote Carolyn, "They all had children,": Ronnie Shacklett was married to Brenda Lee (the country singer), "two other cousins who Carolyn cannot remember their names," Buddy who was Uncle Earl's son and who was a state senator, Dale who died in a car wreck, Gary and Lorraine, and Danny and Donna. To quote Carolyn, "There were a lot of them." I assume Bob Lyon, Carolyn's daddy was there, but curiously I do not recall him being there. Anyway, we went up for some kind of a gathering at a farm outside Nashville in the middle of the summer Tennessee heat. We were supposed to be there for lunch so Carolyn and I arrived after a drive from Atlanta that morning about 11:00. Now I had been through Nashville before as I traveled from Cartersville to Fort Campbell, but I had NEVER really *been to Nashville* until that day! So we arrive and remember Carolyn is pregnant and what she ate and did not eat and when she ate made a big difference as we were soon to find out. Well, we could not eat at 12 because we were waiting on someone. I do not know who, but the Nashville Shacklett women were bound and determined that we were not eating until one of these myriad of brother, cousins and random people arrived. 1:00, no lunch. 2:00, no lunch. Well, the longer we waited the sicker Carolyn got, and finally I put my foot down, albeit gently, to Nanny and got Carolyn some food, and she was better. There was nothing I could do about the unbearable heat and needless to say the barn where we were on this farm had no air-conditioning. Yep, misery … and I wasn't even pregnant! Well, the afternoon proceeded I assume because Carolyn and I are here today … something I cannot say for all the rest of the "Nashville Clan." The second thing I remember about that trip was after we spent the night somewhere we went to one of the aunt's houses for breakfast. And I had NEVER seen a breakfast like this before! For breakfast there was grits, fried potatoes, fried eggs, fried bacon, fried country ham, fried pork chops, white bread, biscuits, a white gravy mad from left over fried fat from the meats mixed with flour and gallons of coffee. Think your worst Cracker Barrel nightmare breakfast, and you will have an idea what it was like. This was apparently a normal Nashville breakfast, hence the rest of the Nashville Clan not being with us today.

As Carolyn became more and more pregnant she became more and more uncomfortable and the doctors still did not know exactly what was wrong. We knew the baby was healthy, but my fear was that Carolyn had something wrong and only one of them were going to survive. It was a terrifying time … not only for Carolyn but for me also. I had done this (pregnancy) to her and now there was nothing I could do except to stand by and support. There were light times though. I recall, and Carolyn and I still joke about this today, I came home from work one day and Carolyn greeted me at the door. We kissed and my only comment was, "You smell great! You smell like ham!" How romantic I was. A regular Rhett Butler. Anyway, we were on a very tight budget and Carolyn had found a way to buy us a luxury, a ham. She had cooked it for us, and it and she really did smell delicious. Another time, right before Jenna was born, four days to be exact although we did not know that then, on March 14th it was Carolyn's birthday. She was turning 23, and I baked her a cake. As I recall it was a white or yellow cake with white icing and it was *as dry as the Sahara Desert*. I mean barely able to choke it down dry. My first foray into baking was a dismal failure, but a good learning experience, and Carolyn smiled and ate it and loved me.

And on March 18th, 1974, nine months and nine days after we were married, Miss Mary Virginia Morris, nickname Jenna, presented herself at Kennestone Hospital in Marietta at 5:23 PM. She was 6 pounds 1¾ ounces and about 19½ inches long. She was beautiful. This was the time when men were not allowed in the delivery room. We were shuttled off to the father's waiting room where we waited patiently and readied ourselves to buy our mandatory box of cigars that had a little band that said either "It's a Boy" or "It's a Girl." How quaint all that seems today. The nine months and NINE days after we were married is critical because the *nine days'* part meant we did not have sex *before* we were married, and believe me everyone on both sides of the family was counting and watching and secretly wondering. I guess I am glad she did not deliver early. But, today, I ask the question, "What if she had delivered early? Who today would give a damn? No one. And our Jenna would still be our beautiful Jenna and doing wonderful things." We Americans spend too much time minding other people's business and not enough time minding our own. And besides, the nine months and nine days left everyone guessing. Did they or didn't they? And I will leave you guessing too. Wink. Wink. I recall the nurses handing Jenna to me. She was so tiny and I was smitten! Her whole hand was not the length of my index finger. I recall that she did have a Carolyn trait, her little fingers had a slight crook in them. She was tiny, bald and beautiful! I was in love.

So, after a week (yes, you read it right) in the hospital Carolyn and Miss Jenna came home. And you never know how woefully underprepared you are until you bring your first baby home! But, with the courage and pluck that comes with youth, ignorance and enthusiasm we "endeavored to persevere" (Chief Dan George in the movie *The Outlaw Josey Wales*), and then about five weeks later Carolyn had her most severe gall bladder attack yet. It was a Sunday evening, and there was absolutely no choice except to rush her to the hospital. Her pain was excruciating.

I called Carolyn's mom, Virginia "Nanny" Shacklett Lyon. I was in a panic. A five-week old baby and a wife I thought was going to die. Fortunately, Nanny was home and came immediately. I guess I gave her some rudimentary instructions about Baby Jenna – like I knew anything really – and packed Carolyn in the car and off to the hospital. Honestly, I do not remember anything about the next several days. I remember Carolyn was in surgery, and they cut her from her abdomen to her sternum. Today they do the same surgery laparoscopically and the incision is a quarter of an inch. Carolyn's scar was five or six inches long. After surgery there was only one thing I could think you do and that was to try to let her know that everything would be alright, that we would make it through this, that even after all the trauma I had caused – a baby and the resulting inflamed gall bladder – we were sound. I wanted to reassure her somehow. And as of this writing, this does sound stupid, but I bought her what to me was a beautiful one-piece, blue bathing suit. She had only worn two-piece suits up to this point. I felt a one-piece would cover what she perceived was a horrible, ugly scar and reassure her the future would hold more trips to the beach and "fun in the sun." I think she wore it. I honestly do not remember. I am going to chalk that bathing suit up to "it's the thought that counts."

4.

We settled into being "an old married couple" even though neither of us had any idea what that really meant. I think that each newly married couple has to discover what that means for themselves. For us it meant I went to work in my little MG to C.P. Roberts Engineers. The firm had broken off from a venerable old Atlanta firm Robert and Company. Robert and company dated back to the 1920's with a strong textile background. And C.P. and several others broke off in the early 70's to form their own firm with a heavy marketing emphasis on the dying American segment of industry – textiles. The firm was led by old C.P. and his most senior man was Colin S. Monteith. Mr. Monteith was a proud graduate of the Citadel, and he was one of the finest men I have ever known. He was very generous to Carolyn and me and sort of took me under his wing. I think he was one of the first men in addition to Unca' Nelson I could look up to and emulate. The structural engineering area was led by Dick Holly. Mr. Holley was a short man who was very intelligent. He loved to garden and took great delight in showing off his tan arms as he strutted around in his short sleeved white shirt, tie and pocket protector with multiple pens. I remember him for a joke he used to repeat to us younger men, "It takes me all night to do what I used to do all night." Then he would roar with laughter. Of course we were all young studs and newly married and did not really get it. Today … I get it. The HVAC area was handled by a rotating series of old men none of whom I really recall. The electrical area was led by the youngest of the "old men," Mr. Al Sharp. Mr. Sharp had a draftsman who was a good draftsman but was not the brightest bulb. No matter the conversation, his favorite line was, "Well, I don't know about that, but I'll tell you what …" at which point he would launch into a long rambling discussion about whatever he wanted to talk about. He was an interesting man. And there was an architect in the office. There had to be. There had to be someone to seal drawings. I am not sure who was the architect when I joined the firm, but they hired a new one not long after I arrived. His name was E.F. Rutemeyer and he was a dick. I vividly recall him being brought around the office and being introduced for the first time. My good friend and fellow MG owner, Bill Malpass, and I were drafting on some working drawings. Rutemeyer stopped at my table and looked down at my stair detail drawings. "You know rounding the handrail like that costs money. It would be more economical to just weld them at sharp angles." He walked on no doubt thinking he had just impressed Mr. Monteith. Well, he did impress me. He impressed me that he was a DICK!

One of my favorite early learning experiences at C.P. Roberts Engineers, Inc. was mastering the blueprint machine. The blueprint machine was really a blueline machine. You would place your drawing over a matching piece of light sensitive yellow paper. You would then feed the two sheets through the upper portion of the machine. A bright light would "burn" away all yellow from the light sensitive paper except where your lines were. This light sensitive paper would then be fed into the lower half of the machine which exposed it to ammonia vapors. These vapors reacted with the yellow lines and turn them blue, and voila a blueline print. In my time at C.P. Roberts I must have spent hours and hours printing drawings.

As a sidebar note that has nothing to do with anything, on August 8th in 1974 President Richard M. Nixon resigned. This was a result of what was known as The Watergate Affair. And a man, Gerald R. Ford, became president. The interesting part of this story is that 1. Nixon was the only president to that date to ever resign the presidency and 2. Gerald R. Ford was the first president that no one had elected to that office. You see in 1973 the elected Vice-President Spiro T. Agnew had been forced to resign due to pleading no contest to tax evasion when he was a governor of Maryland. Vice-President Agnew was replaced by the still in office at that time President Nixon with Gerald Ford, so when Nixon resigned, we had President Gerald Ford, the president no one elected. It was an interesting quirk of history.

5.

Somewhere along in late 1974 or early 1975 Carolyn went to see her doctor with a lump in her breast. Given our track record so far in our marriage, she and I both feared the worst. I recall being in the hospital as she went in for a breast biopsy. They excised the tissue and sent it down to the lab. The doctors waited for the results. If it was a malignant tumor they want to either remove it or remove her breast while she was there, in surgery, under the anesthetic. The result came back to the doctors waiting in the operating room – malignant. But before her doctor would proceed to remove her breast, he sent word back down to the lab to take another look. This was a young, healthy, twenty-three-year-old woman. Were they certain? And the second opinion came back that it was not cancer.

It was a form of fibro-cystic disease. So, she did not have her breast removed. Thank God for the intelligent surgeon who asked the hard question that day. Never be afraid of a second opinion or second guessing yourself before making a life altering decision.

Carolyn and I decided that continuing to pay the high rent at Chimney Hills was just not working for our budget. I would get paid every two weeks and when all bills were paid and groceries bought we had maybe twenty dollars left to live on for two weeks. We were truly one paycheck away from being homeless. Interestingly though, I do not think that ever even occurred to us. We just kept on doing the best we could every day. So, one day Carolyn came across a little house at 1986 Sherwood Drive in Marietta. Throughout our marriage Carolyn has always been pulling rabbits out of her hat, so to speak, and each time she did she always make our life better. The rent was $135 per

1981 Sherwood Drive. Marietta

month, less than half of the Chimney Hills rent, but still I resisted. It was a dumpy little house across from Powers Ferry School. It needed everything. But again, Carolyn saw the potential and I was eventually persuaded. Looking back, I believe that little house saved us and allowed us to save a little money that eventually led us to buying our first house, then second, then third, then … well, you get it. But first, the house needed to be painted on the inside. So off we went to good old Mr. Sears and Roebuck (this was years before Home Depot and Lowes) and bought several gallons of paint colored *Misty Stone* and rollers and pans and brushes. I even remember the Sears salesman giving us the hard sell on the most expensive paint. Carolyn and I then painted the whole inside of that little house in one weekend! And soon thereafter we bade Chimney Hills good-bye and we moved our little family into Sherwood Drive.

In 1975 Carolyn's older sister, Kathy Bilyeu, who had gotten divorced from her first husband Chuck Bilyeu (who was such a creep that his only picture has been removed from our wedding album) sometime between our marriage and Sherwood Drive, remarried. She married a wonderful man, Cary Jack Snelgrove, a former sailor and submariner, a car salesman from Anderson Chevrolet on Roswell Road just up from The Big Chicken, and a soon to be postal employee. After their marriage, she and Jack moved in right next door to us on Sherwood Drive. Their house was on the Powers Ferry Road side of our house, and Jack and I were to have many adventures together.

I have two distinct and vivid recollections of our Sherwood Drive time. One took place in December of 1975. Jenna was 9 months old. It was nearing Christmas, and we had put up a small tree on the barrel I had rescued down in Panama. My mother had insisted they bring it to the states when they moved up to Chamblee in 1971. I was on the floor playing with Jenna and she was standing by the couch holding on to it. She had learned to pull up and stand weeks before. Carolyn was across our little living room and happened to have our 8mm movie camera out and was videoing Jenna and me. And then it happened! Jenna just launched off from the couch and walked unsteadily toward Carolyn. She had just walked for the very first time, and we caught it on tape! Of course there were cries of glee and hugs all around and coos of approval. Our baby would not stop making her mark in this world from that moment on. So proud! The tape has been transferred to a CD and is "findable" somewhere in all our stuff.

The second event was thrilling although Carolyn probably would disagree with that description. I was at work at C.P., and Carolyn called me. She was at home taking care of Jenna as all dutiful wives should be (sarcasm). I picked up the phone which was a wall phone in the drafting area. Again, this was looooong before cell phones and long before I had a phone at my desk. Carolyn was absolutely frantic! "Jim, you have to come home! I went in the kitchen and there was this huge rat standing there! Please come home!" Well, needless to say, I was on the road in a flash! I went from Chamblee to Sherwood Drive in record time! As I was driving the rat got bigger and bigger and by the time I got home that rat was a R.O.U.S.! (Check out the movie *Princess Bride*). Anyway, I came charging into the house with a broom, and an attitude. My wife and child were in danger! They were being attacked by this R.O.U.S., and I had to rescue them. This was a chance to be a hero! However, one problem … no R.O.U.S.! Gone! Poof! So, here is Carolyn insisting she was practically attacked by this monster rat and there is no rat to be found … anywhere! Now there were two things I immediately knew about out little Sherwood house. One was that it sat on a crawl space as was the custom for little houses built in the heyday of the Bell Bomber Plant, and two, our days in this house were numbered. Because Carolyn had seen this monster in the kitchen, that was where I started looking when I was trying to find where it possibly could have come from. And there, right where the dryer vented into the crawl space, which was a no-no, but in this little house it did not really matter, was an opening just big enough for a monster rat to creep in to terrorize my wife. Reluctantly I had to investigate this creepy nether land … the crawl space. The access to the space was on the right side of the house as you face it from the street. Armed with a big stick I gingerly opened the small door. There were no lights. Only the dim sunlight from the foundation vents and there against the front wall was a nest of rats! OMG! How gross! Now to be honest, I have no recollection of how I got the R.O.U.S.'s out. I know it involved traps and such, but I sealed up all access to the crawl space, and we were probably looking for another house that afternoon.

I remember two events that included just Bob Lyon and me. They are both sort of like very old grainy photographs. I recall the events, but all of the details around the edges are very faint. When Carolyn and I moved into Sherwood, we needed so much in terms of furniture and appliances. Coming from apartments, things like refrigerators and stoves were provided for us. Of course we had our washer-dryer combo in the *color du jour* – Harvest Gold, but that was about it. Somehow Bob Lyon got a line on a refrigerator. It cost Carolyn and me nothing; probably because Bob and Virginia paid for it. At any rate he and I went to pick it up. I cannot tell you where, but I can tell you we rented a small open U-Haul trailer, hooked it to his car and brought the refrigerator home. I vaguely recall riding in the open trailer to stabilize the refrigerator, but that may just be my imagination and fanciful recollection. Anyway, Carolyn and I had a refrigerator. The second Bob Lyon adventure was that a Nashville relative had a dining set they were giving away as they had gotten a new set, I guess. They were more than willing to donate it to the poor Marietta relatives as long as we came and picked it up. So, you guessed it, Bob Lyon was tagged again to drive me to Nashville, which was a fateful town for him as it you will find out, to pick up said table and chairs. As I recall it we did the whole drive up, pick-up and drive back in one day. And so we headed out. Now Nashville is four hours away, so if you drive up, again rent a U-Haul trailer – this one enclosed as I recall – load up, be pleasant, then drive back with food stops, bathroom breaks and whatnot, you are looking at a twelve-hour day easy, probably more like fourteen hours. But Bob and I did that … mostly Bob Lyon. And it was all at no cost to Carolyn and me. I do not recall what Bob Lyon and I may have talked about or any of the particulars, but I do know he did that for Carolyn and me. It may have been at Virginia Lyon's insistence, but he did it for us. I think about that today when my children/grandchildren need something, and I understand why he did it. There is not much you won't do for your daughter or son or granddaughter or grandsons.

As I mentioned, while we were living at Sherwood Drive, Kathy and her new husband Jack moved in next door. Now Jack was a builder. He would build anything and undertake any project, and he usually did it with no plans on paper. This drove Carolyn and me crazy what with our being architects in training and what not. So, Jack was going to build a covered, shed roof porch on the back of his house. I mozied over one afternoon to see if I could help him. And he did let me help! He let me pull old nails from boards! This nail pulling incident has become a family joke for about 50 years now, so if you hear anything about it from Carolyn's older sister Kathleen Marie Lyon Snelgrove, it is a true tale.

Around the time we were in the Sherwood house we were able to take a couple of short trips. Jenna stayed at Carolyn's mother's house as my parents were still raising my brothers Peter Charles Morris and Brian Meroney Morris, so they made us feel that Jenna was not really welcome there. One trip was to down near Macon to see Ruben who was in my wedding. I recall two things about that trip. One was that the motel room we stayed in smelled like someone had cleaned it with a very perfumed antiseptic. It was gross. Again, remember this was before the internet and Yelp and all those helpful warnings people now post on the web. I assume we stayed there anyway because you had to pay upfront to secure your reservation. Kinda like staying in a Holiday Inn at the beach where the pool had been washed into the ocean. Anyway, the second thing was we went water skiing with Ruben on Lake Tobesofkee, and I have to say Carolyn was a water skiing crazy woman! I can still see her on that lake coursing along confidently over the wake, a smile from ear to ear. I was astounded. I had learned to ski back in college when I was home at Fort Campbell one summer, but I had no idea Carolyn could ski. I still smile to this day thinking about it.

A second short trip was our first adventure to Chattanooga. Again, I (we) had driven through before, but we had never stayed there or really even seen the city, so we made it a destination. I wanted to make it super special, so I talked to an architectural rep I knew who sold roof curbs and was based in Chattanooga thinking he would know great places to stay. I tried to describe to him a place I had seen from afar looking up toward Lookout Mountain. He said he knew just the place and put me in touch with them. Again, this was looooong before the internet so I made a reservation for Friday and Saturday night. So the big day comes and Jenna goes to stay next door with Aunt Kathy this time, and off we go. I had bought Carolyn a surprise, a nightgown (Guys, a suggestion … do NOT ever do this – it's like buying your wife any present with a cord on it. Just say NO. A nightgown is a very personal selection, and when a guy buys one, it is never for your wife. Be real, it is for you). Anyway we get to Chattanooga and the motel is not on Lookout Mountain. It is on the side of a hill to your left as you come sweeping down the Missionary Ridge into the city on I-24. The place was called The Knights Inn, and it was a dump! Believe me, these days of having the internet to be able to look places up are so much better. But again, I had paid for the first night to secure the reservation, so I was stuck. We decided to make the best of it and go eat dinner. The closest restaurant was a dive now called Sugar's Ribs. If you look up Sugar's Ribs, the motel is just behind it. Anyway, we were walking into the restaurant and there, posted above the entrance was a sign saying "It is unlawful to bring your knives or guns into this establishment." We did not eat there, but it has become a humorous standard by which we still today judge restaurants. If there is no sign, it's probably okay to eat there. We left and got in the car and headed into Chattanooga to find dinner. Our drive took us into one of the seedier parts of the city. We made sure the doors were locked. It would have been really nice to just whip out our phones and Google restaurants … but alas. So we rode down into the dark. Laughing, I shared that, "I have been lost in better cities than this." Which has now become our mantra in cities from Los Angeles to Barcelona to Rome. So we rolled into the city, and lo and behold we ended up on the doorstep of The Chattanooga Choo-Choo Hilton! We parked and walked around, starving. That evening we ended up having a sumptuous meal in a dining car with drinks and steaks and laughing the whole time. When we left dinner I checked and they had a room available for Saturday night, which we booked immediately. And late in the evening we trudged back to The Knights Inn, where I presented my dud of a present and laughed some more. We slept with a chair jammed under the door knob! But we had a great Saturday and loved the room Saturday night and the complimentary breakfast buffet Sunday morning. And I was learning another valuable lesson … *Spend The Money Necessary*. Oh, the place up on Lookout Mountain I had seen from a distance, wasn't a hotel. It turned out to be Covenant College. Lord, I wish we had internet back then!

6.

1976, the bicentennial of our country! And it was an election year. As it unfolded, Gerald ford would be out and our illustrious governor Jimmy Carter would win the election for his one term as President. It was the year Apple and Microsoft were incorporated also. But I get ahead of myself.

The R.O.U.S. did have a lasting effect and it was a good one. Carolyn and I bought our first house. It was at the corner of Hazelwood Drive and Scott Drive in Marietta. Now please do not get all excited and drive off all wild-eyed to find it, because it is no longer there. It was torn down and a prefab metal building built on the land that is now a garage or car shop or something. But for Carolyn and I it was a 'perfect' starter home. We paid about $27,000 for it (less than the cost of our 2021 CR-V). It was a little house on a crawl space, had a tiny living room, and even tinier dining room, a kitchen that opened to a den with a fireplace and sliding glass doors to a patio, two bedrooms, one bathroom, a floor furnace, no air-conditioning and

a screened in porch with a storage room below that. I think our house payment, all in with taxes and insurance, was about $450 per month. I recall Granny and Grandpa Koch visiting once and he asked me, "So Jim, what'd you pay for this dump?" So, there you go Grandpa Koch.

Now you know what "we" paid.

As I look back, it was a crappy little house, but we knew nothing about buying houses, and we got no help from my parents. Carolyn and I paid for the whole thing by ourselves. It was *our little red wagon*, and we were going to pull that son-of-a-gun all by ourselves! In this picture

you can see Jenna (Mary Virginia "Jenna" Morris Blackwell in the "hine" yard, as well as the porch. I recall several things about that first little house: the storage area under the porch flooded every time we had a good rain, I installed a 220-volt outlet for our dryer, the house sewer line clogged, the washer drain line broke, the corner lot was huge, and we apparently pissed off the neighbors when we fenced our own back yard,

termites and rot ate away the supports for the sliding glass door, a car crashed into the house, Jenna had her second birthday party, and Carolyn and I literally loving the den with the fireplace.

Lesson – Always, always, always get a home inspection … even if you think you are two hot-shot architects. The first excitement I recall is the storage area under the concrete porch flooding. The porch was an add on to this 1940's bungalow. It had steps down to an area under the porch. The area was about 10 by 10 and not quite tall enough to stand up in – almost, but not quite. The floor sloped to a square hole in the floor. There were work benches on one side and a little slit window looking out on the back yard. Light was a single exposed bulb on the ceiling with a pull cord. I remember there was a rainy period for several days, and when it stopped raining, I headed down to the storage area for something and to my shock there was about a foot of water standing in the room! Now I understood what the hole in the floor was for. It was not a drain. It was for a sump pump! So, we bought one and dealt with the flooding storage area from then on.

This little house had no dishwasher or outlet for our dryer. For the dishwasher, we just washed dishes by hand. I do recall a little dishwasher contraption that looked like a big popcorn popper with a clear top, and it sat on a counter, and you hooked a hose up to the sink faucet and the water pressure drove a washer arm. It was the best we could do. But we really needed an outlet for our dryer. Jenna was still a little one and we used cloth diapers (the way God meant it to be), and we had to dry them somewhere. So, I mentioned this at work and I will never forget this, Mr. Colin Monteith, the V.P. of my workplace, volunteered to help me. He told me what I needed to buy and then, one Saturday, he came over all the way from DeKalb County and helped me install a line. I will never forget that act of kindness. He passed away in 2019. Another father figure I will never forget.

The night the sewer line clogged was a Sunday night, and it was raining. I called Rotor-Rooter, and a hippy-dippy looking young man came and after much ado cleared the line. It was the first time I had really been into the bowels of the crawl space – and not the last – and it was nasty … but not as nasty as it was going to get. As I said "George Carlin" cleared the line, but in the process I am convinced he broke the washer drain line which fed into the main line. Only he did not tell anyone. One afternoon, not long after the clearing of the sewer line, we were doing laundry and the washer went to drain cycle, and I heard something under the house. So, with trusty flashlight in hand I went exploring in the bowls of Hazelwood again. It was a muddy mess filled with lint and dirty water that had gathered in all the low spots of the dirt crawl space. I quickly saw where the washer line joined the sewer line and saw that it was broken off. The person who had owned the house before us had cut a hole in the sewer line and inserted the washer line into the pipe with generous amounts of pitch and duct tape. I believe this is why the sewer line had clogged originally. Well, I did some research, bought what I needed (this was before Home Depot mind you), cut the sewer line (stink-o-rama), installed the Y connector, reconnected the washer line and took a victory lap around the manhood track as thousands of males cheered. Actually it was only Carolyn who looked at me with admiration, and that was all I needed.

The Hazelwood house as I said was a corner lot. It was a huge corner lot and I spend hours and hours cutting grass and raking leaves. We have not owned a corner lot since I might add. The lot was so big all the neighborhood children used it as a baseball field and as a cut through. Apparently it was just a neighborhood understanding that this was the way it was. So, having a two-year-old who loved to run and play in the yard and swing on the swing set I designed and built, and not wanting her to be exposed to neighborhood dogs and wanting her to be safe, we had a chain link fence installed around our property. Well, this mightily pissed off the neighbors who let me know about it … morons. I tried to explain our reasons, but we had committed some gruesome sacrilege, and Carolyn and I were doomed to never be forgiven … idiots.

Another adventure involving my dearly beloved crawl space was when the sliding glass door to the back patio stopped sliding in its track. Something was obviously amiss with the track support, and the only way to check it out was to go underneath and look at it. @#%*&#. So I did. Now the door was naturally almost as far away from the crawl space access as you could get. Fortunately, it had been long enough for all the water that had come from the washer to soak into the ground but it was still a muddy slog on my belly. Once under there, it was obvious that the den also had been added to the house. I slowly made my way to the eighteen-inch clear space under the door. I could see what the problem was. Long dead termites and water from a poor door installation had rotted away the sill under the door. *I was quickly making up my mind that if I ever did work on a house I was going to do it right or have it done right. I guess this was an extension of my epiphany relative to doing chores for The Colonel in the eighth grade – do it right the first time.* And after several trips to the hardware store and several hours under the house in my new favorite place in the house … the crawl space, I had replaced the sill and shorn up the beams so the door would operate properly.

The next Hazelwood adventure took place late one evening, after Jenna had gone to bed and Carolyn and I were watching television. There was a thunderous boom and the house shook. "What-the?" C and I jumped up and ran out the back sliding glass door (which now ran smoothly on its tracks). A car had slammed into our carport! As I said, the house was at the intersection of Scott and Hazelwood. A car of teenagers had come down the Hazelwood hill and tried to turn left onto Scott and had not made the turn. They had come across the yard and slammed into the corner of the carport. Fortunately for us, the carport had a brick base about four feet tall. They did some damage but they damaged their car a whole lot more. The police came and the car was hauled off. We got the damage repaired, and I do not remember a great deal more about that event.

1976 was the year my brother Bill and Janie got married. They got married in Maryville, Tennessee, which is just outside Knoxville. To be honest, I do not recall much about the wedding. We drove up, stopped in Chattanooga to visit Rock City, spent the night in Maryville, attended the wedding and came home. The same can be said for Ruben's wedding in Macon that year. In fact, I recall even less about that wedding!

An event I remember better was taking Jenna to Stone Mountain for the first time. There are family pictures of the day. There is one picture I vividly recall of Jenna sitting on a rock about half way up the mountain. I seem to recall a yellow flower but that may be a trick of memory. I carried Jenna most of the way up the mountain and once at the top, we were terrified she would fall off somehow. Actually, I think new parents are perpetually terrified.

Our Hazelwood house was within walking distance of the church where we got married, Powers Ferry UMC. It was C's home church and where her parents and sisters went to church. While attending there I got involved teaching the high school Sunday School class. Teaching high schoolers in Sunday School was to end up being a fateful decision as you will see. I do not recall many of the children, but I do recall one named Angie. Why? I am not sure, but I do recall her. Lord, she must be almost 60 now! Anyway, I taught the class and it grew to be very large. This was my first chance to be a teacher and I loved it. As the class grew I met Gene

McRee and his wife Julie. Gene was important in the MYF evening program and he got me involved in that part of Powers Ferry's program. My strongest recollection, other than chili dogs in the church basement where Carolyn's and my wedding reception was, were the retreats Gene and I went on to Camp Glisson outside Dahlonega. There were other counselors that went along also. One was Bob Sapp who taught me not to tell long winded old guy stories to teen agers who could not relate. He also taught me to quit teaching at the right time. Anyway, another counselor was Clay Price. He was the fourth in the group of counselors. I tell you all this to talk about the most impressive thing Gene did and I will never forget it. The last evening of the retreat, we would have a worship service, there would be scripture and short sermons, and Gene would play the guitar and sing children's favorite songs (♫ *Thy word is a lamp unto my feet and a light unto my path …*) and then, when we were done we would have the Hour of Silence. The Hour of Silence was exactly what it sounds like … everyone was challenged to spend an hour not talking. Just an hour with your own thoughts in the quiet of the woods. You could walk off or sit in the chapel or just find a quiet place, but you could not talk for an hour. At the end of this time, we would ring the big bell and everyone would return to the chapel and Gene would close the evening with a song and a prayer. We would then scramble to the dining hall for hot chocolate and pastries. This small event impressed me so much that I would replicate it in every retreat I led from then on.

7.

The next year, 1977, was earth shattering for out little family. There was one event that forced me to grow up, take the mantle of responsibility and pull on the little red wagon as hard as I could. Carolyn's daddy, Robert Frederick (Bob) Lyon, a good, good man died. It happened on October 23rd, and the rest of the year pales beside the memories and Carolyn's heartbreak at the loss of her father. Her heartbreak was my heartbreak. Bob had gone up to Nashville with his next to the youngest daughter, Ginny – Virginia Anne Lyon – to attend a school function of some kind. And while there, one evening, he had a massive heart attack. He was taken to the hospital. His wife, Virginia (Nanny) was called. Carolyn was called. Carolyn packed and flew up to Nashville taking her mother (and maybe her sisters Kathy and Bobbi – Roberta Orlena Lyon – also, I do not recall). Jenna and I stood by. Late that evening I got the call that he had passed away. I called my parents and made arrangements for the next day for Jenna to stay with my sister Re. I also got Dad's car (thank you Dad) as my little VW and MG were too small to be ferrying people around and left for Nashville. I remember the drive up was all Elvis Presley music as he had just passed away in August. Once I got there it was chaos. Emotions were all over the place. Granny and Grandpa Koch were coming down from New York. Bob's brother, a heart surgeon, was also coming down, Carolyn was destroyed, Nanny was a wreck, as I said, chaos. I remember calling my father looking for some guidance … he was worthless. Bob's brother, Alan the heart surgeon, was worthless. Alan came, assessed the situation and left to return back to New York, and left everything in my woefully young and inexperienced hands. I never really forgave him that. But, I stepped up as best I could. Got money from a bank on our credit card because C and I had no real savings. Took care of my wife and mother-in-law. Got Carolyn and Carolyn's paternal grandparents Granny and Grandpa Koch back to

Atlanta, after pausing in Chattanooga to fix a flat, and tried as best I could to handle as many of the details as I was even remotely capable of handling. Now, do not get me wrong. I was nothing close to a savior. Carolyn handled more than her share of decision making and responsibility shouldering. Carolyn is and always has been an amazing and powerful woman. I cherish her. But, long painful story short, we got everyone back here including Bob's remains. Had a funeral and buried him on a hillside overlooking a pond in the Kennesaw Memorial Park at 1306 Whitlock Ave., Marietta.

As I said Bob's death made the rest of the year pale in comparison. Yet I'm sure Carolyn and I went to work, Jenna grew and bills got paid … to borrow and bastardize a 1957 quote by Allen Saunders often attributed to John Lennon of Beatles fame: "*Life is what happens [while you are paying bills].*"

But there was one other tall tale of '77 worth recounting, and that was the Cary Jack Snelgrove Fishing Expedition. Jack and I had started fishing together up at Lake Allatoona. Now let me be the first to say that my fishing skills are legendary … they are legendarily BAD. I couldn't catch a fish if it jumped in the boat. I do remember once back in high school when I went on a church retreat, and we were near a pretty fast moving river. A girl and I went down there with nothing more than fishing poles and bread, and we caught fish hand over fist! She even taught me how to clean and fillet a fish. But I must have used up all my fishing luck that day because since then I have been a terrible fisherman. Why, I even caught a rock once! Fought that little son-of-a-gun rock all the way to the pier. Again, there is a picture of me and my rock somewhere. It is infamous. So, anyway, Jack and I were fishermen on Allatoona. Well, Jack was the fisherman, and I was again the nail puller and fisherman's assistant. We tied up one night under a bridge near the town of Acworth, hung out a light and Jack proceeded to catch Crappy after Crappy. I think I caught one that whole evening and that is probably because Jack handed me his pole with one already on it. But none of that has anything to do with my story. As I recall it was a Sunday night about 9:00 and it was pouring rain and thundering and lightning. The phone rang. It was Jack and he said he needed help. Well, I would do anything for Jack. He was my good friend, and he had my back, too. He had gone fishing with his son from his first marriage up at Allatoona, and he needed me to come up and get them and bring them home. It must have been some kind of truck breakdown problem I guessed. So, I got the directions and hopped in my car and was off to the lake. To this day I do not remember exactly where they were or how I found them on "that dark and rainy night," but I did. I recall pulling into the parking lot and pulling around to where you put boats in the water. I aimed my car at the boat ramp and there were Jack and his son standing in the rain looking like two soaked puppies. Then I looked at the boat ramp closer. Tied to one of the piers was the boat. And then I saw the problem. From under the lake at the foot of the boat ramp were two headlights faintly shining up at me through the silty green water. Somehow, and I never really got the full story, as the pick-up truck was backing the boat trailer back down the ramp it just kept on rolling … right under the water, stopping at the bottom of the ramp … err, lake. I guess I never got the full story because it was no time to start asking foolish and embarrassing questions. I got the boys home, and I am sure Jack got the boat and the truck and the trailer home somehow, but it was another interesting family story … that was never discussed again.

I believe it was in 1977 that we took Jenna, age three and a half or almost four out to dinner at a "fancy" restaurant. We just wanted her to experience it, so we all got all dressed up and went to dinner in downtown Atlanta at Coach and Six on Peachtree. The dinner was perfect and Jenna was a perfect dinner companion. She was poised and delicate and a perfect angel. As we were leaving the head Maître D pulled up next to me and told me how concerned they were when Carolyn and I came it with such a young child, and then proceeded to compliment me (us) on her behavior. I guess to this day I do not know how I feel about that rather back-handed compliment. But it is a little bit late to take issue with it I guess. Suffice to say Jenna has been a perfect daughter her entire life. I know this is an observation through a proud Father's eyes, but I hope I have been half as good a Father to her as she has been a Daughter to me.

8.

As a reference, when it comes to 1978, Jenna turned four, Carolyn turned twenty-seven, and I turned twenty-eight, and there are several recollections I have. On the job front, I am still with C.P. Roberts, and I have my first real opportunity on a project, Darworth. The Darworth facility was for a company that made caulk as I recall. It is/was located in LaGrange, Georgia. I have no idea if it still exists. But it was to be a classic piece of architecture clad in requisite double tees (a double tee is a precast concrete unit when looked at from the end looks like two T's next to each other – like this TT. It is used horizontally in bridge construction a lot, but C.P. like to use them as wall units and stand them on end with the legs of the T's sticking out. Look around, you'll see them.) Anyway Paul Grupe, who had joined C. P. as a structural engineer and I led the Darworth effort. And as far as I recall we only screwed up once when a structural brace crossed in front of a four-foot by four-foot louver opening. I have pictures of the facility downstairs somewhere. From a working standpoint that is about all I recall for that year.

The bigger event, and I think my timing is right, my sister Mary Louise Morris Spicher (Mary Louise Morris Bramble) got divorced from her first husband, Jerry Spicher. There was talk of drugs he was involved with, but I am not really clear on that. The divorce was a sidebar to a much bigger event that I recall much more clearly and further widened the rift between The Colonel and me. The family was gathered at The Colonel's Chamblee home, and he was burning up hamburgers and making us all eat them, and it came time for Carolyn and Jenna and me to leave late in the afternoon. It must have been summer because it was hot. Anyway as we were leaving, and I was walking up the hill that was the drive way toward the car, I made a comment that the way Jerry Spicher treated my sister "really pissed me off." Now I do not know if The Colonel had had too much to drink – which is what I suspect today – or what, but he rounded on me and in front of my wife and child (mind you I am almost 30 years old at this point) says, "Young man, do you even know what that means? I will not have you using that language around my wife or in my presence." Or something to that effect. I was humiliated! I was totally embarrassed in front of my wife and my four-year-old daughter, although Jenna probably does not recall this event at all. I was speechless. How dare him, the drunken old fool. I calculate he was only fifty-four years old, but he was an old man to me.

This bit of tête-à-tête caused a major rift for years. I believe Carolyn still has letters my parents wrote to me about this event. My parents were big on writing letters, not talking, but writing letters. And many of them were very painful letters. There was a lot of … what is the right word … not hate, not frustration, perhaps envy … I do not know … maybe a combination of all of those words in the relationship between my parents and Carolyn and me … mostly me I'm afraid. And Carolyn was an innocent bystander who became "collateral damage" of their and my toxic relationship.

I wanted to close 1978 with an upbeat tale. My brother Pete, who at this point was about sixteen, was a boy scout, and their troop took a trip up to McMinnville, Tennessee, to Cumberland Caverns. Somehow Pete asked me if I wanted to go along knowing that years ago, as I mentioned earlier, during my brief sojourn with the Explorer Scouts when I was in high school, our troop was into spelunking. I jumped at the opportunity, and so we were off one early Saturday morning in a caravan of cars headed up I-75. We got there late in the afternoon and were taken into the caverns with all our sleeping bags and gear — yes we were going to spend the night in the caverns. After we all got situated, and had a bite to eat, we headed out into the cave with a guide. We were not going to go on the usual route that the public took. We were going on some real spelunking! The most excellent caving with helmets and carbide lamps … actually at this point I think they were battery powered … and knee and elbow protectors and eye protection … whole nine yards. Thus began a six or seven hour physically demanding crawling, squeezing, snaking adventure into one of the coolest caves I have ever been in. There were crevasses so narrow that there were questions if some of us would fit through that then opened into vast chambers tinkling with droplets of crystal-like water forming huge stalactites and stalagmites, some joined into columns and some in their infancy. It was a fairy world of lace fans and translucent rock, of clear flat pools of blue-black water and small creatures who had never seen light in their lives. It was a fascinating experience, and one I will treasure. I wonder if Pete even recalls that weekend. When we finally got back to the area where we would sleep around midnight. I was filthy, hungry, soaked with sweat and cave drippings, exhausted and thoroughly whipped! It was awesome. After some food and a warm cup of something – the cave was a perpetual 50 something degrees – we bedded down and the lights went out and so did we. There is no darkness like the dark of a cave. It is total. I mean you cannot see your hand one inch from your face it is so dark. Still to this day, when I see a Sci-fi movie about being lost in a cave, I get really creeped out. Awesome!

9.

The next year was a big year for the little Morris family. In 1979 Jenna started kindergarten, and we finally were able to move out of the Hazelwood Drive house. 1979 was the year Carolyn and I designed and had built 318 Indian Trail. But the design and building were not without adventures. Nanny, Carolyn's mom Mildred Virginia Shacklett Lyon, was instrumental in helping to make this happen. Carolyn's mom lived on Sewell Lane. It was named this because all the land around the area belonged to the Sewell Family farm. Carolyn grew up playing on what was left of the farm at the end of the street she lived on. And Nanny had a good friend, Ruby Sewell Wright — one of the last of the Sewells — and she owned a half acre property on Indian Trail down near the cul-de-sac, and being quite old, she agreed to sell us the land for $5,000. So, Carolyn and I needed to come up with the cash and the only way to do that was to sell Hazelwood. We put it on the market and ended up selling it for just a little more than we bought it for. As I recall we had two bidders. One was a young newlywed couple and the other was … I do not even remember. Anyway being the astute business people that we were, we sold it to the young couple even though their bid was less than the other person. And we took the money from the sale, and bought the land. We had to live somewhere while the house was being built, so we moved into some apartments down Franklin Road for the six months it would take our builder, Jim Sharnak, to complete our little bungalow.

In the middle of the property was a big, ancient oak tree we wanted to save, but there was just no way and it had to come down. But it was forever memorialized in that the mantle in the house is cut from that mighty oak. There are pictures of the progression of the construction including a little Jenna running around the construction site. I recall one picture in particular of the foundation and flooring of the main floor in place and little Miss Jenna standing there proudly … no walls, just floor. I recall a dust-up over whether Jenna could continue to go to kindergarten at Powers Ferry Elementary because the apartments were actually inside the City of Marietta limits, but we were able to overcome this and life went on. I recall one building *Catch-22* our builder helped us overcome. In order to get the Certificate of Occupancy for the house, we had to get the gas furnace permitted which could not be permitted until the gas was turned on which could not be turned on until the furnace was permitted! Interesting. But eventually, the house was finished for a total of $40,000 which

seems like a ridiculously low amount today for a new house, and we moved in. Laughingly, I recall that one of our cost cutting moves was to not install air conditioning during the initial build. We had the furnace prepped and everything was ready, we just saved that cost … that will give you an idea how broke we were. But it was a solid little house, well insulated with aluminum, double pane windows when insulated windows in residential construction were something very new … and then the seals failed, and I was in a constant fight with the manufacturer to replace the failed glass, but Carolyn and I were out there being architects and moving up in the home ownership world. It ended up being our home for about nine years. Jenna found a close friend in the next door neighbor just down from us, Patti Gernatt. It was a good home for us, and coincidentally as of this writing I believe the house was lived in at one time by Patti Gernatt and her young family.

On the job front I worked on Bigelow Sanford in Lyerly, Georgia. It was a nasty little addition to an existing facility, and I do not recall much about it other than C. P. Roberts was scraping the bottom of the project barrel. The economy was tightening, and for a period of six months I quit C. P. and went to work for Lockwood Greene Engineers downtown. Other than being close to Carolyn who was working just down the street at Cooper Carry, it was the worst six months of my career. Lockwood Greene was under contract to deliver a helicopter plant for Bell Helicopter to the Iranians to be built outside Tehran, and the schedule was tight. Everyone at LGE was on forced overtime which was good for Carolyn's and my pocketbook but was difficult. A forced 60-hour work week is four extra hours a day, so you get there at 6 and leave at 7 at night with an hour for lunch. It was a beast. And after six months, which was the minimum I had to work at a place to get credit to be able to take my architectural license exam, I begged Colin Monteith to take me back. And they did. When I returned there was a new young engineer trainee working there, Paul Grupe. But, the lack of work at C. P. still meant that I was "farmed out" to work downtown at another firm and was sent by Eugene F. Rutemeyer to make note cards of every county in Georgia listing the City Manager, Mayor, and phone numbers of anyone Rutemeyer could contact to see about work. I did this by physically going downtown to the Atlanta library and sitting there researching and physically writing on little index cards this information! Ahhh, the days before the internet were amazing! But eventually Carolyn and I got through 1979.

10.

Probably the high point of the next year was that Paul Grupe met Carolyn's younger sister Ginny, who we had gotten a job at C. P. Roberts as a secretary. And sometime in 1980 they were married. I do not recall anything about the wedding. I cannot say where it was, although I suspect it was at Powers Ferry UMC, or what time of the year or anything. I do recall that one of the Lyon Nashville relatives gave her away. Carolyn could probably tell you. But, they got married, and that was good … for a while.

I mentioned that Carolyn and I elected to not install A/C in the house, and of course, the next summer was a record setter! Weeks on end of heat! We got a big old window unit from somewhere, probably the Lyons, and put it in the window to the left of the fireplace and the Family of Three camped out on the floor in the living room of 318. Needless to say, Mr. Sears and Roebuck did some business late that summer. I poured a pad for the compressor under the deck and if you go you to 318 you can find Jenna's handprints and a date in the corner of the pad, got the compressor there, installed the coil in the furnace, hooked up the power and the lines and we were in business. It was an exciting time to be a Family of Three!

That year Carolyn took Jenna and went to Nashville for several days. While they were gone I took myself to the movies one night. I wanted to go see the new movie *Jaws,* but the lines were too long, so I went the dollar theater to see a movie that had recently come out called *The Exorcist.* It terrified me! It scared me so badly I had to leave in the middle of the movie! It terrified me so badly that I left the little theater in what was the Town and Country Shopping Center on Roswell Road and went over to the K-Mart at the corner of Roswell Road and the 41 Highway, across from the Big Chicken, just to walk around and make sure the world was okay. I recall it was raining and there was no way I could go home. There was nobody there! And it was dark, and it was spooky!

Job-wise C. P. made a big change. They moved their office from Chamblee to over at the intersection of I-285 and I-85. I want to say it was called Century Plaza or something, but it added another twenty minutes on 285 to my commute and it sucked. But, for what reason I do not know, cash I guess, they did it, and I went too. We did get a big commission that year, a new spinning facility for Bigelow Sanford in Marion, North Carolina. It was to be state of the art. The basic design involved five-foot diameter pipes being installed under the floor and running the length of the spinning room back to huge fans and filters to sweep the lint from the air in the spinning room down and away from the workers. It was the biggest project I had ever worked on. I recall Colin Monteith going up for an inspection once. We had to fly into Ashville and then drive to Marion. I recall spending the night in some cheap motel and a cricket keeping me up half the night until I final found it and killed it with my shoe. I also recall that there was one major mistake we had to overcome due to my stupidity. There were several large power operated fire doors needed to separate the spaces and their motors were mounted up at the top of the doors. Also, uncoordinated by Paul Grupe and me, were large tracks for overhead loom cleaners. Well, you guessed it. As the loom cleaner rolled down its track it wanted to crush the door operators right off the walls! We solved the problem by lowering the operators for the doors as I recall, but I learned another valuable lesson about knowing ALL facets of the building design and making sure everyone was talking and looking at each other's work.

I had also gained enough working credit that I was going to be allowed to sit for the Architectural Registration Exam the next summer. So, the winter of 1980 was spent studying all the NCARB materials I could get my hands on to prepare for the test. I recall a Sunday afternoon sitting in a white fabric recliner chair we used to have, in the living room of 318 with my back to the window to the right of the fireplace and the weak winter sunlight coming in over my shoulder studying. 1981 was promising to be interesting.

11.

As I write this, I sense that I am leaving out so much about Carolyn and her work and Jenna and her birthday parties and having little girls, including Patti and the little girl from across the street, spend the night and going out to dinner and paying bills and going to church and MYF and cooking dinner every night and getting cars taken care of and Jenna learning to ride a bike and going to work each day and taking care of our little family and loving Carolyn and our adventures taking my other love Jenna to Rock City and Ruby Falls and all the minutia that weaves together to make a life. But all of those wonderfully beautiful moments, unfortunately, tend to fade into the background of one's life. They become the canvas that bigger, more traumatic and joyous events are painted on and that is a shame. As I write, I smile recalling sneaking up on Jenna's birthday gathering of a group of her friends who were in the garage of 318. They were all acting like singers as *Footloose* played on her record player and I snuck up to the sliding glass door of the basement with a Halloween mask on and scared them, sending them shrieking up the stairs to the safety of Carolyn … and another stroke of the brush on the canvas … I smile again.

Again as a reference point, in 1981, Jenna was 7 and Carolyn and I were the ripe old ages of 30 and 31. That year, my parents were 57 and 55. However … as I write this on the 18ᵗʰ of December, 2022, Caitlin will be 13 on January 1ˢᵗ, James is will be turning 40 on January 11ᵗʰ of next year. Jenna will be 49 in March of 2023, and Carolyn and I will turn 72 and 73 in 2023.

With all that said … I did not pass the Architectural Examination that year. But the story of the exam is a tale unto itself. The examination to be an architect in the State of Georgia is five days long. My test was held at Georgia Tech. The first four days are written tests usually two a day. One in the morning for four hours and then the afternoon session for four more hours. These exams covered structural design, plumbing, heating air-conditioning and ventilation, site planning, architectural history and electrical design. You could bring any reference materials you wanted, but the exam was designed that you did not have time to look anything up. You either knew it, or you were a good guesser. The architect was expected to be the original Master Builder – the overseer of all other trades and expected to have a working knowledge, if not a mastery, of all the disciplines. These portions during the first four days were a situation where if you passed one section and failed another, you could keep your passed portions and the next year you only had to take the portions you failed. They were also a warm up for the fifth and final day. The final fifth day is a twelve-hour long exam, twelve *continuous* hours … 8:00 AM to 8:00 PM. In other words, you stop to go to the bathroom; it is your time. You stop to eat; it is your time. You stop to drink some water; it is your time. This is the Design Exam, and it is Pass/Fail. You either pass it or you fail it and retake the whole Design Exam again the next year. You walk into the test that day, and no one knows what you are going to be required to design. Up to this point you have studied what students were asked to design in the past. You know what a winning design looks like and what failures look like, but you have no idea what you will be tasked with. You have come armed with a thermos of water and some kind of energy fuel. My fuel of choice was Star Crunch Bars. I have no idea why. I also carried all my drafting equipment including a drafting board with a parallel bar mounted on it. It is in Carolyn's stained glass Hobbit Hole on her shelves. You will see a handle mounted to the top of it. This is how I carried it. For this exam you were not allowed any reference material at all. Just your wits. You had to produce a floor plan or plans, and elevation or elevations and a site plan. You had to pace yourself through the day, and if you found yourself at 12:00 with a design that did not meet the criteria or violated some aspect of the code or was just a crap design there was no time to start over. I recall going to the bathroom about 4:00 and there was guy in there crying. He had not budgeted his time and there was no way he would finish by 8:00. He was screwed. My design problem was an urban site in Hartford, Connecticut. I had to design a multistory library. I worked through the day and felt pretty good when I finished at 7:45, and as I found out a couple of months later, I failed the design portion. I passed all the "academic" parts, but I had to retake the Design part the next summer … great. I got my scores on all the academic parts, and I did a respectable job. Seems to me I recall that the electrical part was my lowest score. But on the Design, all I got was a "Fail." I got no critique of where I went wrong or any "helpful hints for hopeful heroes." Just "Fail." Excellent. So, one would then sign up for the next year, and I did.

At work, Burlington, Marion, North Carolina, continued and I was now making site visits all by myself. It was a huge vote of confidence from Colin Monteith and C.P. Roberts.

One cool thing that happened that year was the very first Indiana Jones movie, *Raiders of the Lost Ark*, came out. There had not been any movie like that ever! And it was awesome. I will be honest with you when I tell you I have seen that movie at least thirty times, and I would watch it again right now if I could. One weekend even Jack and I went to see it at the dollar theater. Yep, totally a coolest ever movie.

12.

1982 started out crazy! In January Atlanta was hit with a snow storm the likes of which the city had not seen since that fateful 1973 ice storm. In the picture of 318 Indian Trail you might had noticed the date of January 12th, 1982, on it. It started snowing about 10:00 that morning. No big deal, just some snow. Well, by 1:30 or 2:00 it was obvious this not your ordinary January snow dusting. It was coming down blizzard style and would snow for two more days … but nobody knew that on the 12th at 12:00. And, too late, offices started closing. Carolyn was still working downtown at Cooper Cary, and she had our stick shift Honda Civic. I was working over at I-85 and 285, and I had our rear wheel drive metallic blue Monte Carlo that Jenna had spilled fingernail polish remover on the hood of (but that is another story). Little, eight almost nine-year-old Jenna was staying with her Aunt Kathy. Kathy and Jack had bought 73 Indian Trail and Carolyn's older sister Cathy was keeping children to earn some extra money. The schools had closed and Jenna was safe and sound. Now at this time, I-75 was only two lanes in each direction and so was 285. There were, of course, no cell phones and everyone was sort of out there on their own. I smile, it was a different time all together. I tried to call Carolyn before I left the office, but her office was already closed. I assumed she was making her way home. It was treacherous! You could not see the lines on the roads and 285 and 75 had three and sometimes four lanes of traffic. There were cars sliding into other cars. There were trucks stalled at the foot of seemingly gentle rises because they could not get traction. Any super-elevation in the highway was a danger as you could lose traction and slide to the left or right into another car. I adopted a stay to the right policy where I could keep my wheels on the right rough side of the highway. I would also shift in and out of drive to go forward being careful to stay off the accelerator and the brakes. The drive home that evening took my over four hours. The worst part was trying to exit 75 at the South Marietta Loop. It was a sweeping up to the right exit ramp, and it was slick as glass! Fortunately for me there were six or eight high school boy good Samaritans who were there pushing cars up the ramp. They would manhandle one car and then come down to the bottom and get the next car. They helped me up the ramp. Finally, I pulled into our driveway. I was immediately relieved to see Carolyn had beaten me home by about a half hour. It had taken her almost four and a half hours. I was never so glad to see anyone in my life. I recall Carolyn had already stopped at Kathy's and picked up Jenna, so my little family was safe. We go dried off and warmed up and put on our winter clothes and went out that evening into the dead quiet of our winter wonderland. It was beautiful. Look up the 1982 Atlanta Snow Jam for some very cool pictures … no pun intended. (See earlier picture of 318 Indian Trail)

Just a quick note about this. On February 14th, Valentine's Day, Carolyn and I gave each other our grandfather clock. It stands in the living room of Falcon Wood Drive today and has become the "clock of lore." You will read about it later, undoubtedly! The small brass plaque inside gives the date and the inscription that Carolyn gave the clock to me … but we really gave it to each other. It has traveled extensively since then and had its guts replaced once since 1982. I have wound it countless times and watched my children and grandchildren wind with great reverence knowing they were being trusted with a great responsibility. And while you can certainly buy more expensive clocks, and you can buy bigger clocks, and you can buy older clocks, this beauty still keeps good time and has been a stalwart friend watching over us as our lives pass by its face and has faithfully counted the minutes slowly, meticulously and certainly through the ages of my family and my adult life … Tempus Fugit. Thanks clock.

Carolyn and I also made a momentous decision in April of that year. We decided that we wanted to have a second child. It always tickles me when I hear about couples who try for years to get pregnant. Carolyn and I have never had that problem. We decided we wanted a second child, so we got Kathy to keep Jenna one weekend, and we off to our favorite Stone Mountain. Yes, the Stone Mountain of when we were dating, and I put my hand in the bird poop Stone Mountain. We got a little "room at the Inn" so to speak. We ordered pizza that evening and got some beer, and I recall the movie *Same Time Next Year* with Alan Alda was on the television. We ate pizza and drank some beer and son of a gun, the next morning, and Carolyn will bear me out on this, she said, "Jim, I'm pregnant." And she was! So, this may have ruined all your future visits to Stone Mountain Park, but history is history and … well, there you go.

On the work front C. P. got a new award, a new Burlington Loom Facility in Erwin, North Carolina. And I gutted up for my second attempt at the Design portion of the Architectural Exam. Again, I hauled my board and drafting supplies down to Georgia Tech and set myself up in one of the architecture drafting labs where the exam was to be. I brought my same Star Crunch Bars … and to this day I have not eaten another one … and my water. This year's test was an Airport! It was an Airport in California just outside L.A. I had never designed an airport. I was your basic industrial architect. Had they given me a textile loom plant or a carpet plant I could have finished the entire exam in about an hour. Now fortunately one of the guesses someone at the exam preparation group had proposed was a small regional airport, so I had studied somewhat where things went and how to configure an airport. And twelve hours later I had a design to turn in. I have to tell you I had very little faith in my design, but I did know that my G's which now had become stylized to look like 6's and my handwritten font had really developed into a personalized font of a veteran architect. So, who knows. And a few months later a letter came and informed me I had Passed, and I was an official Registered Architect in the State of Georgia! The date on my license is September 17th, 1982. Registered architects comprise just 2% of the United States population, so I felt pretty good about myself. And Carolyn and I wanted to celebrate and announce it to the family, so we invited The Colonel and his Lady to come to dinner at one of our favorite restaurants, *The Boston Sea Party*, to surprise them with the big news. They were too busy to come … so Carolyn and I went out to celebrate … just us. It was enough. Their loss.

Unlike our first pregnancy, this pregnancy proceeded relatively smoothly for Carolyn. And that was the greatest blessing of 1982 for our little family. Jenna was very excited waiting for our addition. Carolyn and I did not do an amniocentesis to find out if it was going to be a boy or girl. Instead we enjoyed working on names for each. If it was a boy, that was an easy decision for us; he would be James Lyon Morris. We changed the middle name for several personal reasons not the least of which was I did not want him to have to carry a III around with all of the weight and responsibility I felt that involved. Plus, adding the Lyon carried on Carolyn's family name which was very important to us given Robert Lyon's untimely death. I recall we struggled with a girl's name and ultimately decided on Adrienne Leigh Morris.

Chapter Two
The Middle Days

1.

983 started with a wonderful event! James Lyon Morris, 6 pounds - 11 ounces, 20 inches, was born on January 11th at 1:57 PM. Once again, my second child was considerate in his birth timing had Daddy home for dinner! There were many memorable things about that day that I recall. One was how the expectations of the father had changed. When Jenna was born, the father was relegated to the father's waiting room. In that room we all sat around in our suits and ties with our fedoras on reading the *Wall Street Journal* while we smoked and drank coffee waiting for "the little woman" to produce our progeny. And when the blessed event was announced by a nurse rushing into the room we were expected to be ready to hand out stale cigars wrapped in "It's a Girl" or "It's a Boy" cellophane like we had some instrumental part to play in the whole delivery process. Now not all of that is true but it was much more *Mad Men-like* than my 1983 experience. In 1983 the nurses were almost incensed that I did not want to be in the delivery room. Let me add that Carolyn and I had discussed this and she was in total agreement with this decision. The nurses disdainfully showed me to a small, sterile, almost an alcove-like room with one or two old *Time* magazines. I was the only guy in there, and there I sat until Carolyn had delivered. Carolyn was very efficient and I do not recall it was very long that I had to sit there and endure the looks of the nurses as they passed by. I do recall Carolyn's first words, "How about a son!" And James Lyon Morris was handed to me in a swaddling blanket. He was not even all cleaned up yet, but he was beautiful. I carried him off to the side of the room while they attended to Carolyn, and he and I had our first "Two Boys Time." We talked about a wide range of things as he looked up at me. Carolyn had helped me make my best friend. And after only about twenty-four hours I brought Carolyn and "Jamie" (a nickname he would quickly discard for the more formal James) home to Indian Trail and our little family was now four. Carolyn and I had replaced ourselves in the world and that would be the extent of our procreation.

In August of that year, my brother Brian (Rusty) graduated from North Georgia College, assumed the rank of second lieutenant in the US Army and married Jill King of Cartersville. Again I do not recall much about the wedding but I do recall it was whole military thing with Rusty and Jill walking out of the chapel and walking under arched swords, and the last swordsman in line touching Jill's bottom with his sword … a very sexist military thing I guess … still kinda cool … it was a different time.

On the job front there were major changes. My friend Paul Grupe (Ginny's husband) had left C.P. Roberts and joined a design build firm name Carlson Associates. He was actually employed by the A&E arm of Carlson named Aldrich Associates. And through Paul I got an introduction to Russ Cudmore, the VP in charge of Architecture and Engineering. And in mid-1983 I made the jump from C.P. to Carlson. This was a huge change for me as Carlson was not only into industrial but they were also into corporate buildings and a whole new world opened for me. When I joined Carlson, I was hired as a draftsman until I proved my worth. Carlson was to change my life in the next nine years.

Carlson's offices were just off US 41 just below Windy Hill Road at the clock tower. Interestingly their offices were just across 41 from Bordeaux West, Carolyn's and my first address after we were married, and it was across the street from what was the Richway store where I had met Bonnie some twelve or so years earlier.

Besides working with Paul Grupe, I met Jim Robinson, a true design architect. If you looked up the word "architect" in the dictionary there would be a picture of Jim Robinson. His most distinguishing feature was his, what I would call, a Fu-Man-Chu moustache of sorts. You know from the upper lip it curled down each side of his mouth ending at his chin. But, to this day, even though he and I butted heads more than once, I respect him, and we still stay in touch at Christmas. The other person I met and worked closely with was Russ Cudmore. He was the Vice President in charge of Architecture and Engineering. Russ actually hired me. Another man I was going to become very familiar with was Dan Hunter. Dan was a manipulator, and he was good at it. I did not understand this until it was waaaaay too late as you will see. Jim Wakefield out of the Boston office – a mentor and friend. The head honcho over Russ Cudmore, who ruled the whole organization in Atlanta, was Robert Moultrie. He was way above me, and I did not have a lot of contact with him. Other players I recall working with were David Hildreth, another draftsman, Mike Davies, a project manager on the construction side, Ben Stone, a character who not only was about 80 years old and ran the print room with an iron fist, and was a Colonel in the Civil Air Patrol, Bill Fraser and Larry Aronson, other PM's on the construction side, Bob Thorn, a landscape architect of some ability and various other actors in the play that was Carlson. I will introduce more of the performers as the play develops.

My first project and the one that promoted me to Architectural Project Manager was Airport Executive Center in Tampa, Florida. It is a square, thirteen story office building with a parking deck attached. You can still visit today. It was no big deal to the world, but it was my first foray into office buildings, curtain design, traction elevators, site planning with a methane mitigation system, caisson foundations and big time meetings with Jamie Jurado, the owner in Tampa, and regular site visits on my own flying to Tampa to review construction and solve site issues. It's funny, it was a Design-Build job, but for the life of me I cannot recall the PM's name. I do remember him fondly though. I would fly down to Tampa on an early bird – as you will see I became the king of the Early Bird – and he and I would review the project until maybe 2:00. Then we would go to "lunch." He introduced me to the very first Hooters restaurant in the nation. It was there in Tampa in an old burger King or something. It was very much as Hooters are today. Why mess with a good idea is what I always say! Then one day for "lunch" Jamie Jurado wanted to meet. So the PM and I met him at a "club." And this "club" was special. As you were eating your lunch, lobster and what-not, young ladies in lingerie would walk around modeling lingerie you could purchase. I assume you could also purchase the young ladies, but I never purchased either. Another recollection was a problem we ran into. In the parking deck the owner wanted to use cabling for the guardrail system. This is used everywhere today, in fact the back deck and the handrails at the front steps of 1920 Falcon Wood Drive have it, but in 1983 it was unused and untested. As the architect of record of the project, my first project I sealed since being approved by NCARB (National Council of Architectural Registration Boards – it is how architects get approved to practice in other states. As I looked back, it made E.F. Rutemeyer's "I am registered in all fifty states" look pretty lame), I would not seal that portion of the design. It was built that way anyway with my objection being filed in Hillsborough County.

Let me add a little note here if I may … of course I may … I'm writing this! Today is a very, very cold - 17° Christmas morning in 2022. Carolyn and I just went up to Jenna's home on the lake and shared their first Christmas Eve lunch in their new house. Jenna and Adam were their gracious selves. Bryce was there with his lovely Anna and Bodie was there with his vivacious Margot. James, Angie and a soon-to-be thirteen-year-old Caitlin are off in the Caribbean on a Holland America cruise with Angie's family, Mana and James Swope, their son John and April and their daughter Claire. On the home front, Carolyn and I have just recovered from our very first bout with Covid. Carolyn inadvertently brought it home from her Kennesaw State University Community Choir rehearsal. Fortunately, we were "vaxed-to-the-max," and it was more like a flu than the debilitating death sentence that has to date killed nearly a million in the USA alone. I sold my motorcycle and bought a little red Mazda MX-5 that is cute as a button. We call her "Zoomer." It will be a quiet Christmas morning around here with small gifts, and I will make a coffee cake for us to share. It has been a wonderful year with a Thanksgiving trip to Savannah with James, Angie and Cait in a little house on 37th street that came with a 6:15 AM train! Carolyn and I started the year in the Caribbean, we got new insulated windows this year for the house, made a second cruise with James, Angie and Cait to the Caribbean and Coco Cay, enjoyed Cait playing tennis in the state finals in a sweltering Macon and are planning our Paris trip in April of 2023 for our 50th Anniversary.

2.

1984 was a blur. I was the hottest, newest thing at Carlson and getting noticed by a Dan Hunter in Texas. On the family front we made our first trip to Disney World. Jenna would have been ten that year and we went in August. Jamie was about 20 months and content to be pushed around in the Florida heat in a stroller. Carolyn and I were thirty-three and thirty-four respectively. I recall that we stayed in the hotel that was an A-frame affair with the monorail coming right into the hotel. There is video of all of this on our CD's in Carolyn's office. One thing you will see is the children and Carolyn complaining because it's "too hot!" And it was fiendishly hot that August in central Florida. More about the visit? I wish I could share more, but it is all a blank … or rather a blur.

The major note I have for Carlson this year is Intermedics just south of Houston in Angleton, Texas. Houston, Texas, was the location of the Houston office of Carlson, and it was run by Dan Hunter, architect. Hunter had corralled an office building design-build contract for a company called Intermedics who made heart pacemakers. For some reason, that would not be clear to me until years later, Hunter plucked me from all the underlings to be his "boy." On the Intermedics project I truly became the project manager under his design decision making project architect status. I thought it was because of my talent.

I recall one particular meeting with the owner's rep, whose name I cannot recall now, in Houston. Russ Cudmore and I left on an early bird from Hartsfield-Jackson one morning – early birds were to become my life – and flew into Houston Intercontinental Airport. We flew in there as we were meeting in Hunter's Houston office on the north side of the city. If it were to be a site visit, we always flew into Houston's smaller Hobbie Airport on the south side of the city. This particular morning weather-wise things were quiet in Atlanta but in Houston, unbeknownst to me, we were flying into a vicious weather event. A cold front low had swept in off the plains and collided with a warm, very moist high pressure system just over Houston resulting in tornadoes and wicked thunderstorms. In fact, I believe it was just earlier that morning an arriving plane had hit a down burst and crashed. Cudmore and I flew in oblivious to this turmoil. We got our rental car and drove to the office. Sure, it was pouring rain, but welcome to Houston! We went into the office, and we were meeting in an interior conference room with no windows so, as I said, we were oblivious to the carnage and destruction taking place outside. That is until we broke for lunch and went out. The rain was coming down in buckets and the downspouts off the office buildings were funneling so much water into the storm water system that the manhole covers were being blown off under the pressure of the geyser of water! It was a site to behold. Tornadoes had peppered the city, and destruction was everywhere. Now again, this was before the days of cell phones, so I was in a bubble of ignorance. Meanwhile back in Atlanta, all Carolyn was seeing was death and disaster on the news all around Houston, and she was frantic. She had no way to check on me and all she heard from me was silence. I had no idea what the news media was saying. After lunch we returned to the office, and I thought to give Carolyn a call to let her know all was well, and we'd be returning that evening. And it is a good thing I did call! I believe if I hadn't Carolyn might have put Jenna and James in a car and headed out to Houston! Needless to say she was both relieved to hear all was well and also giving me an earful for not calling. Of course I was totally unaware but I took the emotion she was expressing as just that, Love. Well, we got home safely that evening and the project continued.

The PM on the construction side was a man named Bill Fraser. He was new to the company but was a "good guy." He and I would get much closer on another project. The design proceeded, and we moved into early site work and foundations. Hunter had two hot buttons on this project: curved steel in the atrium and scissor stairs in the atrium that had no vertical supports at the landings. And he got them both with much grumbling from the structural engineers and the construction guys who had set the price for construction before these design features were set. I remember Hunter coming into Atlanta and wanting to go see the steel after work. Being his dutiful underling, I took him to the yard were the steel was being fabricated, but we arrived too late to go inside. But Hunter, being Hunter, found a hole in the fence and the two of us climbed in and looked around the yard until we found it. We could have gotten in a lot of trouble for this, but Hunter was Hunter. And his steel was curved. As the projected developed I made many site visits, flying into Hobbie and driving past the Flaming Armadillo Club, why I remember that I do not know, I never went inside … it looked like a pretty rough place. I guess the name just fascinated me. At any rate, Intermedics got built.

While Intermedics was getting built, Hunter secured a contract for a small building in Sugarland, Texas, for Schlumberger. I do not recall much about this little project. There were other architects and draftsmen on the project. I was sort of the "Assistant to the Project Architect," Dan Hunter … playing with the title from the television show *The Office*, like Dwight Schrute I was not the Assistant Project Architect … I was the Assistant *to the* Project Architect … the gopher. I remember being summoned to Houston one time in the evening for a meeting the next morning. I landed at Intercontinental and went to pick up my car. Well, Hunter had already rented it for me, and it was waiting. The only problem was the idiot had taken the keys! I cannot really recall how I untangled that mess but it had to do with myriad phone calls and waiting. Eventually, late, I got the car, and now Hunter wanted dinner. By now it was maybe 10:00 at least. I was way beyond hungry. But we went to dinner … me, Hunter, and the design architect – some guy Hunter had found in Houston that he could bully and boss around. At dinner we ate crawdads, and some of them, drank Tequila. I stuck to Lone Star. The reason all this sticks in my mind is two things (again): one was Hunter getting the design architect guy to eat the worm at the bottom of the Tequila bottle and the second was Hunter and this guy sucking the heads of the crawdads. Neither of which I participated in. Why we met the next day? Don't remember. Don't care. Schlumberger got designed and built.

It was that summer that Carolyn was invited by her friend Jayne Smith (from the Miami wedding Jayne and Robert Smith) to bring Jenna and James and go down to Florida with Jayne and her young ones to Jayne's family's condo and spend a week. Carolyn took her up on the offer. I'm not sure if Carolyn wanted to do that, but she did and she NEVER did it again. I recall that week because of one thing. One thing was that I repainted the vaulted ceiling in the living room of 318 which involved long ladders and heights and was not great fun.

3.

1985 is a very full year! Since I filled 1984 with work, let's look to family in this new year. James is now two and Jenna is eleven and very active. For several years now she has been dancing with The Lynette Grubb School of Dance. Later to be The Dance Stop. She was really good at shuffle-step and shuffle-step-step. We did not know it then of course, but she will continue dancing through high school and then, at Georgia Southern, she would actually take over from a teacher in a class on dancing and taught the class! But that is all in the murky future, and today was today and Jenna had a dance recital. They were usually at the auditorium at the Cobb Civic Center at the corner of Fairground and Clay Street. They were a big deal! Carolyn had to get tickets for the whole family. Jenna's cousin, Melissa Snelgrove, was also in the same dance studio, so it was very much a family affair. As an aside, you know, I think my parents came to one of Jenna's dance recitals … I could be wrong … but I do not think so. Anyway, there were practices the day before and the morning of and Carolyn was deeply involved in all of it. There were snacks to be brought, and little girls to be corralled and controlled as they waited for their dance numbers. Then there were costume changes as the recital shifted from jazz to tap to ballet. It must have been a maelstrom backstage. Jenna's dance recitals were a yearly affair and both enjoyed and endured. After the recital and requisite roses had been given and pictures taken, we would go out for a fancy desert. The place I recall the most was named Winfield's at the Galleria. Jenna would get whatever she wanted and Carolyn and I the same. I would have to be the hotshot executive in his suit and order expresso and smoke cigarettes. Again, being very much in the mold of a character on *Mad Men* before the show was even thought of. Looking back, I see myself as a ridiculous caricature.

The other art my sweet Jenna was into was piano. I do not recall her piano teacher's name, but we also had piano recitals. They were much more art and sophistication as opposed to the dance recital circus atmosphere. I do not recall how long Jenna took piano, but it was several years. She was very good at it in my humble and uneducated opinion.

Again we added another member to the family, the world famous Kitter-Bee. Kitter-Bee was a dark calico and would be with us for many, many years. Around eighteen years I believe. But she was a good cat. She was a cat's cat. She would give you as much love as she wanted to give you and no more. In the evenings, she would come up for her requisite ten minutes of socializing, and then she was done with you, and she would leave. Again, I jump ahead a little and I note that no matter how long Timothy "Adam" Blackwell hung around, all he would get from Kitter-Bee was a hiss and a growl. Smart cat!

There were three family marriages in 1985. My sister Mary Louise who had gotten a divorce from Jerry Spicher due to, my understanding, his use of drugs. More than that I really cannot comment. But, Re got married to Tim Bramble. I do not remember anything about their wedding because Carolyn just reminded me that I was not there! Carolyn was and took Jenna and Jamie. Another wedding was my brother, Peter Charles (Pete) Morris who had graduated from West Point making The Colonel immensely happy. Pete married Elizabeth Allen of the Buford Georgia Allens. It was quite an affair and according to everyone around me, I was in the wedding. But alas, again, I have no recollection of that wedding either. This non-recollection of weddings seems to be a problem I have for that year. My only explanation is that I was so involved with Carlson and my projects that ALL else just evaporated from my memory. Now with Pete and Liz's marriage I do have one recollection. There was a party at someone's house before their marriage and Carolyn and I were there. And some wine was spilled on a very light colored carpet. I believe the wine was a white wine and the carpet may have been white in fact. And me, always being ready to help, knelt down and started to blot it up. The only problem was that the napkin I was using was red! And I ended up leaving a red smear on the white carpet. It obviously embarrassed stupid me because I recall it to this day. So, there are going to be stupid things you do in your life and … well, there you go. The third marriage I do recall a little about because I was asked to give away the bride! It was

Carolyn's youngest sister Roberts "Bobbi" Orlena Lyon who got married to Greg Miller. Because Carolyn and Bobbi's father, Robert Lyon, had passed away, Bobbi honored me by asking me to give her away. The ceremony was held at Power's Ferry UMC with Reverend Lumpkin presiding. Again I have to be honest, other than giving Bobbi away, I do not have any distinct recollections of the wedding.

On the family still, I do recall Carolyn and my trip to The Grove Park Inn that year. Carolyn had found it in *Southern Living* magazine, and we took a weekend jaunt to Ashville. It was to be the first of many trips we would take to that enchanted city. I recall us arriving and finding our way to Macon Avenue and driving up the hill to the Inn. I believe it even started to snow. And as you top the drive at the lodge there is a sweeping gentle downhill grade to your left and you can see the massive port-cochère and all the valets helping with luggage. The Grove Park is an impressive building on an impressive site. We slowly drove down and parked and the valets sprang into action helping to unload bags and assisting us through the immense doors into the Great Hall and to the registration desk. It was early winter, and there were fires blazing in both of the giant fireplaces at each of the ends of the hall. We registered and were taken to a small elevator behind the fireplace to the right as you faced the registration desk. When we stepped in, there was an elevator operator as this elevator was of the very old style that relied on a brake to stop at or very nearly at the floor. You see this is old time movies all the time and here we were two architects stepping back in time. Now our first visit to the Grove Park was enchanting and the GP was nothing like it is today. When Carolyn and I first went there were no wings of guest rooms sticking off perpendicular to the main lodge. There was no spa down the sloping hill from the lodge, and the dining room was the same dining room that hundreds of patrons had eaten in for almost a hundred years. It was very much the hotel from Stephen King's book *The Shining,* and that similarity was not lost on the two King fanatics as we took in this magnificent grand old hotel. A sad casualty to the march of time we noticed in later visits was the decorum in the Great Hall. There are signs that indicate one is to speak in "hushed tones only" and be respectful of other guests. This quiet respect has gone by the wayside in these "modern it-is-all-about-me-and-the-louder-talk-the-more-important-I-am times." I also recall that we had requested a room on the very top floor of the lodge and were treated to sloping ceilings and small dormer windows that looked out toward the valley below and the smokey Blue Ridge Mountains beyond. That first night there we had an adventure. We were tucked warmly in our Mission design (Frank Lloyd Wright would be proud) queen bed when about 3:00 in the morning a banging started! "I sprang from [our] bed to see what was the matter." I finally located the noise. It was coming from the steam radiator in the room. Now, in my entire life I had never been exposed to a radiator type heating system, and I was totally confused. My sleep muddled brain thought maybe some children were down below us banging on their radiator! Then it occurred to me that it was simply the "modern" wonder of steam heat! The pipes were expanding as the heat was turned on in the building. Dinner the next evening was a charming event. The dining room, as I mentioned, was the same one that had been serving guests since GP opened in 1913. We arrived; me in a suit and tie and Carolyn looking exquisite in a black ensemble. We were greeted at the door by a tuxedoed gentleman who escorted us to our table. Our waiters were charming and polished, and they took all the time in the world taking our order and serving and generally pampering us. Just being in that historic room with the pictures on the walls of all the long dead "important" people whose names are lost to time was both heartwarming, and yet Stephen "Kingishly" chilling at the same time. One almost felt them looking over your shoulder saying, "Enjoy, as we are now, you will soon be." Try as we have on our many subsequent visits, we could never quite capture the quaint and thrilling charm of that first experience of the ambiance and thrill of the regal old girl known as The Grove Park Inn. She has grown and changed over the almost forty years we have known her, and I am sorry, she has not changed for the better. Too many rooms in new wings, dining is hurried and perfunctory, everything is money, money, money. Gone is her quiet dignity.

On the Carlson front, I was a full blown project manager and rising up the corporate ladder quickly. Intermedics and Schlumberger got built and our next big project was taking shape … American Express in Greensboro, North Carolina. If you want to find the building, it was ultimately built out near the airport on Airport Center Drive at Regional Road. It is the building with the sweeping, curved parking areas. The story of American Express Greensboro begins with meetings in New York with AMEX in their headquarters downtown in Manhattan. Dan Hunter, Nick Cawood (an office manager on the construction side out of the Charlotte office), and I went on an afternoon flight to LaGuardia. It was late in the year and the weather threatening, but we made it. We booked into a hotel downtown somewhere and the three of us headed to Times Square. We found dinner at a minor restaurant and a strip show at a sleazy gross theater with live sex acts. It was pretty nasty, but I was being a "Big Boy" so I had to say it was cool. It wasn't. Anyway the next day we met with AMEX big wigs at their building with a view of the Statue of Liberty and the harbor and Ellis Island. I have to admit it was impressive. We spent the day talking and bullshitting each other and I guess it was productive because we got a contract to start the site search. This was to be very hush, hush to keep land prices low. Anyway Hunter and Cawood left early, and I was left to finish up. When I finally got away it was sleeting and beginning to snow. Standing on the street hailing a cab in that weather stinks … but I did it, and after running to my gate as they were getting ready to close the door – there was no TSA to deal with back then – I got the last flight out to Atlanta that night before they closed the airport. Great fun! It was to be the first of many "great fun" experiences with AMEX. (And Carolyn to this day knows why I was not in a hurry to revisit The Big Apple … but I did in 2023 as you will see.)

I do recall AMEX visiting Atlanta several times. Three times stick in my memory. One was in the office, and we were meeting in the big conference room with a ridiculously big round table. I am in mind of the Knights of the Round Table big. And all of were sitting around late in the day after what must have been a productive day because Hunter and the AMEX boys all fired up big nasty cigars. I mean there was so much smoke it hung like a pall from the ceiling. And I was right there with the best of them smoking my Salem 100's like a chimney. It was a different time. A second time was after another particularly good day we took them to Bones restaurant down in Buckhead. I got stuck with the bill

… on my AMEX card of course. The bill was $1700 plus. There were about nine of us as I recall. I had trouble figuring out the tip! Anyway that was the most expensive dinner I have ever paid for. And the third was when my second in command, Larry Johnson, (a really, really good man … he died of pancreatic cancer around 1990) took the AMEX crew to The Gold Club in Atlanta. I was meeting with Disney or Citicorp or someone and could not go. Anyway, The Gold Club as you can guess was a strip club somewhere along Piedmont Road in Atlanta. I think it is on Cheshire Bridge Road now. But this was the night that Channel 5 decided to interview people coming out of the club, and there was Larry on the 11:00 news big as life and totally drunk! I was kinda glad I was not there that night. I think I recall that Larry got a DUI that night too. It was great fun all around.

The first stage for the AMEX Data Center project was to look at several properties and select one. This was mostly handled by others in the office, and I was merely an interested bystander for this part except for one critical time. Searching for properties was a clandestine affair. We did not want to tip off land owners who we were representing because they would jack their prices up yet we needed to find a several acre tract with certain requirements like access to two power grids, near an airport and a city of reasonable size. As we flew around, we looked at maybe six different sites in the southeast. We had selected areas where the weather was stable and there was an educated population to draw employees from. We focused on the site in Greensboro, North Carolina, but there was one problem. We could purchase a perfect block of land in the office park, but the problem was that right in the middle of this block was a section owned by a man who wanted to build a scissor factory. I know, but anyway negotiations went on for a couple of weeks before we agreed on an amount of money and to swap another tract of land in the same park for his "factory." I have no idea if he ever built his scissor factory. Now, while doing this I got registered in North Carolina through NCARB. I was to be the Architect of Record on this project. And in the process of doing this I made a mistake on my application. I put down that I worked for Carlson Corporation and not Aldrich Associates which was the A/E arm of Carlson. Competition for this contract with AMEX was keen, and once it became public where the project was to be built and by whom, big firms came out of the woodwork trying to unseat us, and one almost did. Heery and Heery, an Atlanta based D/B firm and our regular competition, attacked. They riffled through all the paperwork with the state and discovered my error. They made a huge deal about me not even knowing who I worked for and so I should not be allowed to practice in North Carolina. It went to court. And I flew to North Carolina and met with our lead attorney, King somebody, Nick Cawood and some others, and we went to court. It was explained that I was just an idiot and the paperwork was cleared up. No big deal, but it was pretty scary to this little boy wandering around wearing his big boy shoes. I do recall that after court we had a nice lunch that day. Heery and Heery would get theirs later.

As all that was taking place, the firm was getting involved in a new data center for Citicorp. I was to be involved in that too. It was to be constructed in Tampa. The same town where Airport Executive Center was built. Somehow Nick Cawood was involved in this project too, and of course this meant more trips to NYC. Fortunately, Citicorp knew exactly where they wanted to put their center so the project moved much more quickly.

At this point in my life, I was flying somewhere almost weekly. Usually it was an early bird out and a late bird home. It got to the point I could actually get up about 4:00, dress, drive to the airport for a 6:15 flight, get on the plane and then fall back asleep leaving a note on my lap to wake me up for breakfast. I actually would buckle myself in and then sleep through take-off. The late bird back put me in the house usually about 10:00 at night. The next morning, I was back at the office. I do not have to tell you who carried the "Lyon's" share (pun intended) of the family raising, household work, shopping and everything that goes with having a family including keeping me happy during this period of years … Carolyn.

The last thing I want to tell you about in 1985 was when I ruined all my luck for the rest of my life. I actually won a car! Yep. The legend is true. Not far from our house at the corner of Lower Roswell Road and the 120 Marietta Loop was a Shell station. Today it is a Quick Trip I think and much more modern. I would buy gas at this station all the time. This was the old-timey day when you would put the gas in your car and then go inside to pay. You would hand them cash or your credit card and they had a little machine they would put your card in and physically push a roller over the card and the card would imprint your information on a two layer carboned paper. You would take the top copy. They would keep the bottom copy. Well, this particular day the person taking the credit card was having trouble with his little machine. They would jam all the time, so it was taking a longer than usual time. I looked around and saw a sign that read "Win a New Thunderbird!" As I was standing there with nothing to do, I filled out the little paper and dropped it in the box and immediately forgot about it. The person finished the gas charge ticket, and I drove off. A couple of weeks later I was standing in a cubicle reviewing someone's drawing when I was paged to a call on line one. I picked it up and the person verified who I was, then said, "You are the apparent winner of new Thunderbird!" Well, the first thing I did was pop my head up and look around to see who was on a phone and watching me. I just knew it was a prank. Paul Grupe or someone was pulling my leg. But no! It was legit! And after gathering some more information, I made an appointment to go to some Ford dealership on I-85 up around Jimmy Carter Avenue and receive my prize. So, in a few days, Carolyn and I took James and headed over to the dealership. After some photographs and handshaking and paperwork, I drove home a new, white, turbocharged, 1985, Ford Thunderbird Coupe. That Thunderbird was the absolute WORST car I ever owned. You know what Ford stands for … <u>F</u>ix <u>O</u>r <u>R</u>epair <u>D</u>aily! And that was this car! The car's electrical system was so bad the car would run one minute and then not run when you got back in it. It left the family of four stranded at the Cracker Barrel on South Cobb Drive one night. It left James and me stranded on Lower Roswell Road. It left Carolyn and me stranded in Charleston. The turbocharger was also messed up, and it took the Ford people four weeks in their shop to figure out what the problem was. Plus, I did not know this, but when you win a major prize like that, it is considered income when it comes to your taxes. So, try adding about $27,000 to your income at the end of the year and see if it doesn't blow your tax plans to smithereens! Fortunately, we sold the little Honda we owned to Jack and Kathy for their daughter Melissa who was in high school. She promptly wrecked it a few weeks later. And selling the little Honda gave us the cash we needed to feed the tax man that next year. The car was good looking on the outside and when it was running it was awesome … when it was running. And as Forest Gump said, "That's all I have to say about that."

4.

1986 was the year of the airplane for me. It seems every recollection of that year has to do with flying somehow or someway. For our family we took our first family trip to California. For the "work me," Carlson had me flying everywhere. There was Amex in Greensboro, North Carolina, there was Citicorp who wanted a data center like the one we were working on for Amex so that meant more NYC and Tampa, Florida, where the facility would be built, and a new client, Disney which meant California and Disney World in Orlando, Florida. For all of this crap, as well as covering for Hunter as he got married to the second of three times and took several weeks for an African safari, I was "given" the title of Vice President of Architecture.

One of my strongest recollection of 1986 took place early in that year. It was January 28th. I was in Greensboro inspecting the AMEX construction site and dealing with screw-ups and foul-ups on the drawings. It was cold, I remember that. I had flown in the night before and was planning to stay that night. And work for two days with AMEX people and Bill Fraser our construction PM. We were in the construction trailer looking at some drawings. The television was on. It was mounted up near the ceiling and was just background noise. The plans were spread in front of us. Bill Fraser, the construction superintendent and I were looking down at them when whatever program on the television was interrupted. The space shuttle Challenger had just exploded killing everyone on board including the first teacher to ever try to go into space. It was one of those JFK moments. One of those moments that you can recall everything thing in that moment. It is frozen in your memory. You cannot remember what was before or what was after, but you remember THAT moment. I do recall we went to lunch later that day, and every television was turned on, and the news was all bad. It was our first space disaster with the shuttle although there would be another. And unlike the Apollo I disaster in 1967 that killed Gus Grissom, Edward White and Roger Chaffee, this was televised for all the world to see in glorious living color splashed all over your television set. It was a somber day. I flew home later that day. I needed to be with my family.

That summer we took our first family trip to California because I was working with Disney. I had been flying to California almost weekly, and I took the opportunity and some of my hundreds of frequent flyer miles to bring Carolyn, Jenna and James with me to sunny California. Again, to be honest, my recollections of their adventures are limited as I was in meeting with Disney daily, but, as usual and God bless her, Carolyn took the children all over the place. They went to Disneyland in Anaheim and Universal Studios amusement park in LA. One story I recall is when Carolyn took the children to Universal. They wanted to go on a particular ride that was apparently a little scary in parts. And to make sure there were no child meltdowns during the ride, the ride workers had scary costumed workers who would pop up by the open cars and try to frighten the guests. Well, James was all of three and a half years old on this trip and when the character popped up by him, he was scared to death and immediately started crying and melted down. Needless to say, that was the end of that ride! We stayed at the Safari Inn in Pasadena. It is a classic motel, and if you know what you are looking for, it has been used as a set piece in several movies. In the evenings the fam would pick me up, and we would do all the tourist things: Grauman's Chinese Theater, the Hollywood walk of fame where the stars are on Hollywood Boulevard, the Hollywood sign, Highway 1 and Malibu and the Pacific Ocean where we ate at a little roadside Lobster shack right where Topanga Canyon Road joins the Pacific Coast Highway named *Peace, Love, Lobster*. You ordered your ridiculously cheap lobster, and it was served on a paper plate with a bib and butter. During this time while we were out there, I was usually meeting with the Disney "Imagineers" and the project people. I recall one afternoon we were taking a break and I got to meet Mark Hamell. *Star Wars* movies had first come out in '77 and the newest one, *Return of the Jedi* had come out in '83. Disney was doing something with him and new ride, and I got to meet him. He was short. But the real highlight of the trip was on that same day, late in day, Carolyn and the children came to pick me up. I was done and we were going to head for the airport. The fam was waiting in the lobby, and Carolyn looked up and there was Michael Jackson and this entourage heading through the lobby to leave. Apparently Michael was there filming a segment for Captain Io, a soon-to-be new Disney ride. As the tale is told by Carolyn, she turned to Jenna and said, "That's Michael Jackson." Jenna, a confident twelve-year-old, said it was definitely not. So, Carolyn politely asked, "Would you please tell my daughter that you are Michael Jackson?" And he did in his little high falsetto voice! A little later I came out to leave but had missed all the excitement. Jenna was absolutely bubbling. Carolyn looked proud.

The whole Disney contract, which ultimately turned into a nightmare as Mickey Mouse turned into The Black Rat — more on this later, started with the idea of a Design-Build contract, Carlson's bread and butter, to build two new Disneyworld venues in Orlando. The piece I was the most heavily involved in was called Pleasure Island, a derivative of the Pinocchio story. The other was a new set piece in Epcot, the Norway Pavilion. Pleasure Island was to be my baby. The Disney people came to Atlanta and part of my V.P. job was to sit in meetings and then wine and dine them. This was a challenge as I was trying to impress these L.A. folks who lived in the fantasy world of Disney. One particular lunch I recall was when I took the whole crew to Aunt Fanny's Cabin. It is a long defunct restaurant that was in the old South style with fried chicken and cornbread and black-eyed peas and black cooks and waiters and a bunch of racist "shuckin' and jivin'" and "Yes Siring" and "Yes Ma'aming" going on. None of that would be tolerated today, hence the restaurant's "defunctness" but as I have said, "It was a different time" even though it was only forty years ago. Through all of this we got the contracts, and we were on our way to be Walt Disney's next A&E / Construction victim.

5.

I continued the blur of flying and being *so* very important (if you know me, you know that was sarcasm) in 1987. The year was full of piano recitals, dance recitals, MYF Retreats and a very exciting vacation at Edgewater Beach Resort. Work, as I said, was flying everywhere, Citicorp Tampa, AMEX's new Fort Lauderdale facility, an interesting meeting with an old college acquaintance, and Carlson being bought by SAE Paris.

When I think of this year, I see my beautiful daughter who turned thirteen sitting at a piano, the lights in the auditorium are low and there is a single spotlight on her. For some reason I see her in a red velvet dress and she is playing a lovely musical piece. It may be Mozart, it may be Bach, it may be Beethoven, it does not matter. She is the most talented and lovely creature, and she is my only daughter. Little did I know at that time, sitting in the dark theater overwhelmed with love what a beautiful, caring, talented person she would grow up to be. After the recital Carolyn and I gave her roses. At thirteen, I'm sure the impact of that expression was lost on her. With that vision I also see her on stage at a dance recital. By this time, she is way beyond the simple shuffle-step or shuffle-hop-step that Ms. Lynette started all her pupils with. She is into Jazz as well as tap, and when the seeming hours long recital is done, there are more flowers and a trip to Jenna's favorite restaurant, Winfield's, in the Galleria across from Cumberland Mall where all kinds of deserts and praise and accolades were to be bestowed.

I continued my work with Gene McRee and his wife Julie with the Powers Ferry MYF Sunday nights as well as teaching Sunday School. Our retreats to Camp Glisson were a highlight especially the Hour of Silence that ended with a bell being rung and everyone gathering in the little chapel as Gene played his guitar and sang, "Thy Word is light is a lamp unto my feet and a light unto my path …" can hear him now even as I sit here in 2023. He was, still is, a special man.

Carolyn arranged our vacation that year and in June we headed for the Redneck Riviera again. Why did we keep going to Panama City I do not know, but this year was to be special; like her work to find the Grove Park which she says she found in *Southern Living* magazine, Carolyn booked us a week at the Edgewater Beach Resort. It was, far and away without a doubt the absolute nicest place we had ever stayed. Jenna and Jamie (he had not declared himself to be "James" yet) **loved** it! But they loved it for an interesting reason. You see, at home old squeaky money saving Jimbo had an antenna on the house. And I quote "I cannot see paying for programs that come free over the air!" So, Jenna and Jamie were excited, and we even had trouble getting them to go to the beach, because it had cable television and they could watch MTV and the one – yes one – HBO channel!

And Carolyn and I thought it was special because it had a pool that had not been washed into the ocean. We did the standard stuff we always did when we went there: Captain Anderson's Restaurant (which by now was looking a little shabby – and we have never eaten there again) and we tried to find the big tower where we had taken the wedding ring picture and the second wedding ring picture with Jenna's little hand picture … but it had been torn down! There are some pictures of our visit to PC and Edgewater that year. One particular picture I recall is Jenna and Jamie sitting on the balcony watching the ocean and eating their breakfast. Edgewater was a far cry from the Holiday Inn and the Mark II motel … a far, far cry! We visited there at least one more time. And then again in 2021, but I get ahead of myself.

At Carlson, I have mentioned Larry Johnson and Tim Bramble, but I have not brought up that around this time I got Tim Bramble a job in the accounting department at Carlson. No big deal, just history. I also got Julie McRee a job at Carlson after she got a divorce from Gene McRee. She and Gene had divorced as I understand it, after Gene wanted to marry Michelle who was in his MYF program at the time … that tells you something about her age too … very scandalous at the time … thirty-five or so years ago. Time, like water running over a rock, smooths and softens all things. Michelle is an exceptionally lovely person and they, Gene and Michelle, are still married as of this writing. Another person at Carlson who was a friend and important was Jim Stamper. He was the lead structural engineer after Paul Grupe left. He was a good guy. And one more person at Carlson who was important in my life was an exceptional Construction Project Manager named Drusilla (Dru) Saddler. She was always very nice to me and helped me, and I helped her, on several projects. We worked together on several construction issues. It is funny what one remembers. I remember Dru's birthday was the same day as the Revolutionary General Count Casmir Pulaski of Poland. He has his very own honorary square in my favorite city of Savannah.

Anyway, Citicorp Tampa was nearing completion and almost ready to be turned over to the client. I had been down many times over the course of its construction and the PM Nick Cawood and I had eaten in the Little Havana area of Tampa several times. I mention this because if you ever get a chance to visit there, be sure to go and get some authentic Cuban food there. It is awesome. So, Citicorp's building was almost ready and the "Boys form NYC" wanted to see a full blown test of the emergency generators. Both AMEX's and Citicorp's facilities were data centers. This meant when you had a problem with your credit card or any other problem with the company, you would call their 1-800 number and a person the data center would answer your question. This was before all calls went to India and wherever. So, the criteria for data centers was that they could never go off line … 24 hours a day, 7 days a week … period. They were designed so that they had power feeds from two different grids, and if for some reason both grids went down, there was full emergency power generation to back up the center. Additionally: a center would typically have fuel for these generators to last five days, water and food to supply their staff for seven days, EMP protection, entrance protection and typically be built on an artificial berm to prevent a truck bomb from even being able to approach, and an underground personnel detection system like PantherNet in the ground surrounding the facility. Data centers were quite a big deal. Anyway, on this particular day all Carlson's disciplines were represented for this big test. The test would be conducted at high noon (a bit dramatic for my taste but it was Citicorp after all – they were the AMEX wanna-bees of the day). The test would be conducted by pulling the main breaker and disconnecting the facility from the main power supplies and then the battery back-up would kick in until the generators were up to speed and could take the load. As it happened I was standing by the generators about 11:30 that morning waiting for the gathering that was expected at about 11:45. And as I stood there, all of a sudden, the generators kicked in and fired up with a huge whine and bellow of exhaust. It was so unexpected and sudden it scared me and I recall I jumped. This was immediately followed by everyone talking on the walkie-talkies at once. This was before cell phones. People were screaming, "Who started the test early!" and "What the hell is going on!" Well, as it turned out the generators had done exactly what they were supposed to do. We determined in our forensic report that where the two power feeds came into the main switch box in the building, that the electrical subcontractor had not sufficiently tightened a lug bolt on one of the feed wires down and a resistance had built up and at that moment, that morning, the feed had arced, blown the panel to pieces and cut the outside feeds to the facility thus signaling the batteries to take over and triggering the generators to kick in. Everything worked exactly as it was supposed to. It was quite a day, that day.

Based on Greensboro which was up and running, AMEX contracted with us to build a new data center in Ft. Lauderdale, Florida. So, I was back in the air to NYC some more. And while this was going on an old STI buddy, Bob Shelor came back into my life. I mentioned Bob at STI before under the "never burn your bridges" adage. Bob was the guy with the gun. Bob and I had not had any contact at all after Southern Tech so what followed was a very surprising incident. It was a normal hectic day for me when one of our sales people came into my little office. I had graduated to my own little office with a window by now. I was no longer in a cubicle out on the floor – so very important was I! But the sales guy came into my office, and asked if I could sit in on a sales meeting with a crew from the Bosch Corporation. Sure, I had nothing else to do that morning (Ha!) … so I went to the conference room with the way too big circular table. From the construction side, Mike Davies came in. The sales guy handed me a tentative agenda he had thrown together. The agenda listed the attendees. From the Bosch side, the head guy was one Robert Shelor. I wondered, but did not say anything. They arrived and walked into the conference room, and there he was, Bob Shelor. I walked around the table and pulled Bob into a bear hug and said something like, "Bob, you son of a gun, where have you been?" He was as startled to see me as I was him.

"Jim! It is so good to see you!" or words to that effect. You could see the salesman visibly exhale a breath of relief because he then knew, we had the contract … no matter what. And we did! And it turned out to be a very painful project, but we had the contract. I ended up, at Bob's insistence, flying with him to Charleston, Bosch's home office, that evening. So, I came home, grabbed a few things, dumped on Carolyn again, and flew to Charleston for a couple of days.

I believe knowing Bob and securing Bosh was the contract that made me a Senior Vice President of Architecture and Engineering. This was Russ Cudmore's position. Russ Cudmore, the man who had hired me at Carlson four years before. Russ had been my mentor for four years, and he was Dan Hunter major corporate competitor and nemeses. The only way I could the Sr. V.P. of A and E was if Russ was fired. And he was. The way I see it today, this promotion was all so that I, Dan's personal gofer, could take his position. I should have known, if they would do it to Russ Cudmore, they could (and would) do the same thing to me, but I was too caught up "drinking the Kool-Aid." I was important. I wore suspenders and a suit and tie and white starched shirts. I flew everywhere. I even wore cowboy boots when I went to Texas! Lord have mercy on me.

The last 1987 event I want to remark on is Carlson being bought by SAE Paris. It was early in 87 I believe that the whole Carlson organization was bought by a French firm, SAE. SAE was buying a stake in USA. They wanted a design-build arm and an A&E arm to go with their Texas construction company. They had also bought an electrical contractor from California named Heller. I think they planned on all of us working together to corner the United States construction market. I guess it was a good plan, and I am sure someone made a lot of money.

SAE was known in Europe as a large construction firm that built or was part of mega projects. They were the primary contractor in building the tallest high rise building at the time in Beijing, and SAE was a major player in the building of the Channel Tunnel, the Chunnel, between Calais, France, and Folkston, England, which Carolyn and I are going to experience personally in a couple of months when we travel in April of 2024 to France and England.

At the beginning, there were no noticeable or immediate effects of the take over other than Dan now had a big boss from SAE whose name I cannot recall, but he was an American … a liaison of sorts between Paris and us Colonials. But as I reflect, I see small incremental changes that were made that ultimately led to my leaving … or being asked to leave.

6.

For perspective, James turned five, Jenna turned fourteen, Carolyn turned thirty-seven and I turned thirty-eight as the year 1988 rolled through its circle around the sun. Probably the biggest event of the year was Carolyn becoming an Architect!

As I have written about before, becoming an architect is an arduous process and the registration exam is equal to any medical or legal examination. Because Carolyn and I graduated from Southern Tech and not the five-year program at Georgia Tech, we had to apprentice under a licensed architect for ten years. It harkens back to the age-old process that silversmiths like Paul Revere had to undertake. Back then you were almost an indentured servant to the master craftsman. Even today, one has to "practice under" that architect for at least six months for that six months to even count. I bring all this up because Carolyn not only had the tenacity to get all her "indentured servant" time by working at Cooper Carry Architects – Cooper Carry are the architects who designed the big box abomination of a hotel on the riverfront in Savannah – and then at Smallwood, Reynolds, Stewart, Stewart (SRSS), she then sat for the grueling exam and passed it while raising two children and keeping her husband happy. This was no small feat. And today she is part of an elite group of women, women who are architects, which are less than eight percent of the <u>world's</u> population. Carolyn is an impressive woman by any measurement and has achieved a distinction not only as an artist and architect but as a wife and mother beyond most women in the world. I do truly admire her, but she, still to this day, remains humble and self-effacing when talking about her accomplishments.

James, Jamie back then, has been a car guy since forever. Some of my earliest recollections are of him in church at Powers Ferry UMC kneeling on the floor in the sanctuary with his back to the pew in front of us playing with his matchbox cars on the velour cushions. They were his "tars." And I recall taking Jamie and a group of his friends from preschool along with Uncle Jack, Cary Jack Snelgrove, and his stepson, Robbie (Robert Snowden Snelgrove, Cathy's son by her first husband Chuck Bilyeu) down to Atlanta to the tractor pulls. We would drive down and eat at The Varsity at I-75 and North Avenue and then go down to the, I believe it was called, Phillips Arena back then. Today Mercedes-Benz stadium or State Farm arena has taken its place. The tractor pulls were preceded by Monster Trucks like Grave Digger jumping around and crushing other cars as they wreaked mayhem all over the dirt filled stadium floor. It was a carbon-monoxide, exhaust pipe roaring, little boy's dream. And Jack and I got a kick out of it too! This tradition lasted for several years around James's birthday, and still to this day in early January and February they still have these events and my memory still casts "back to the day."

Another exciting family event that year was the sale of 318 Indian Trail and the purchase of 385 Millbrook Trace. Carolyn and I were "moving on up." We were hot stuff. A Sr. V.P. and his smoking hot, registered architect wife with their two perfect children. Yep, we were living the yuppie, socially climbing, upwardly mobile 80's dream. It must have been late that year when we moved in because I vaguely remember moving a decorated Christmas tree ... but I may be wrong. 385 was big old  barn of a house in the Gant Quarters – Millbrook Farm subdivision off Lower Roswell Road in "prestigious" East Cobb. All the finest schools, Wheeler High School where Carolyn was in the first full four-year class to graduate in 1969 – her team's basketball trophies are still in the trophy case – or were the last time I was there – and East Cobb Middle School. The East Cobb Middle School on Holt Road across from Wheeler was torn down around 2021 and replaced with a modern elementary school.

But the first real recollection of 385 Millbrook was when we had our first substantial rainstorm. You see being the hot-shot architect I did not bother to have the house inspected by a professional. I did it myself. And so when we had the first real rain, both skylights in the "sunroom" poured water! I guess it was more of a "rain room." And I was really embarrassed ... some architect! And of course, as was the way we did it, my friend Jack came to my rescue with a big blue tarp and helped me stop the flood. Oh, the fancy and erotic fireplace in the master bedroom, it also leaked ... just not as badly. But you know what? I do not know that even a trained and licensed home inspector could have picked those things up. The previous owner had masked the defects well. Anyway, I have made sure to have a home inspection done on both houses since then. Lesson learned. I never really liked that house. Carolyn loved it and still talks about it with reverence; "It's where I raised my children," she will tell you. And yes, upon reflection, there were birthday parties, and graduation parties, and family gatherings and Christmas mornings and Easter mornings and the grandfather clock striking 11:00 (the hour all dating was to be over), and the brick floor whose joints were constantly crumbling and the remodel of the kitchen, and the meals eaten at the table in the breakfast alcove between the kitchen and the "rainroom," and the rabbits we inherited who were supposed to be both female but were not, and the hurricane snowstorm that if Jenna's car had been parked where it usually sat would have been crushed, and homecoming parades with floats built in our driveway, and … well a lot did happen in that house … home.

It was along about this time a new actor arrived on the scene. Jenna was going to East Cobb Middle School and was playing basketball one evening. Carolyn and James and I were there, sitting in the overly hot gymnasium as rain poured down outside watching our lovely daughter play with her friends when a boy came and sat next to me. Timothy Adam Blackwell had entered our lives. And little did I know, or could I have ever imagined, the effect this brave young man would have on not only Jenna's life, but our lives. And, to Adam's everlasting credit, he sat there through the whole basketball game, the WHOLE game, trying his best to make small talk with this old man. I had just met Jenna's future husband and the father of Carolyn's and my future grandsons, and I did not even know it.

Another memory I have of this time is the day I went out to lunch at either Taco Bell or Dell Taco. I think it was Del Taco. I ate there and drove the T-bird back and went to my office to do what I am sure was very important earth saving work. After a little while I began to feel strange. I was a little dizzy and felt upset to my stomach. Finally, it was bad enough that I had to call it a day and head for home. As I was making my way to the front office along the hall to tell the receptionist I was leaving, I was so dizzy I had to slide along the wall to not fall. I let her know, made my way back to my office for my coat and briefcase (all us important Mad Men carried brief cases – mine are still around somewhere), and weaved my way out to the car. I left and drove all the way across the street to where the Richway was, or used to be at the time, can't remember when it closed, pulled into a parking spot and then threw up my whole lunch all over the dashboard. Feeling a little better I made my way home which is a lesson to never trust another driver. You never know what condition they may be in even in the middle of the day! I pulled into the garage, got out and managed to slide/pull myself up from the basement to the kitchen where upon Carolyn was shocked to see me all covered in vomit and looking, I'm sure, like death warmed over. I recall standing over the kitchen sink, still puking and holding a wet dish rag of my eyes which was the only way the room would not go spinning out of control. Carolyn got me into the other car and we went over to our doctor's office where we were met with a wheel chair. After a shot to settle my stomach, and me, it was decided it was not a heart attack. Carolyn took me home and poured me into bed. I was sick and exhausted. When I awoke the next day feeling better I found Carolyn had cleaned the Thunderbird completely, including using toothpicks and Q-tips on the dash to get all of my … "lunch" out of all the crevices in the instrument panel and off of all the interior. The T-bird was again spotless. Carolyn is amazing. It was food poisoning, and I have never been to Del Taco again. It was several years before I ate Mexican food again.

On the job front, it was another year of projects, most of which I was working on were finishing. The AMEX Ft. Lauderdale led to one of the most interesting days I had ever experienced. It started with a flight into Ft. Lauderdale in a rain and windstorm. As the day progressed the weather cleared, and the sun came out and the temp shot up into the 90's. Late that day I got on a plane to fly to Boston to meet with Jim Wakefield. Jim Wakefield was the equivalent in the Boston office to Hunter in Atlanta. Wakefield had sort of taken me under his wing and helped me with the whole financial aspects of a large firm. I was to meet with him to review all the Atlanta project's financials. I left Lauderdale that hot and sultry evening flying to Boston. When I arrived it was again pouring rain when I checked into my room in Cochituate, a western Boston suburb and home to Carlson's home and Boston office. That night a front rolled through, and I awoke to snow coming down with six to eight inches already on the ground. In about 24 hours I had experienced every kind of weather there was to experience. And late that evening I flew home to Atlanta to "normal" weather. Kind of a cool little story.

That summer Carlson held an office picnic party at Sun Valley Beach out near Powder Springs. It's permanently closed now, but it was off Holloman Road off Hiram Lithia Springs Road out in west Cobb. I do not remember much about the day other than it was a baking hot Georgia summer day, and Jenna and James got to swim their hearts out. That summer Carlson moved its offices from the location at the clock tower on US 41 to a low rise, two story office park building on Powers Ferry Road near Northside Drive just up from Ray's On the River. The office park we were in is gone now, but Ray's is still there. Carolyn and I just had dinner there a few months ago on our anniversary. It brought back less than savory memories of Hunter conducting annual reviews while eating lunch there. Jim Robinson designed the insides of the new office. There were a bunch of fixed low partitions and small offices all around the outside so us big shots could have windows and the poor underlings had to toil away in their cubbies. It was "TPS Land" (watch the movie *Office Space*). There was even an area as you step off the elevators for the big, round, stupid conference table. I call it stupid because it was actually so large that if you tried to pass a paper across it to the other side and you did not give it a good enough push, it could actually settle in the center of the table where no one could reach it. Then you either climbed up on the table looking like an idiot or got a big stick we kept in the corner and reached out over the table, again looking like an idiot, and scooted the paper so someone could reach it.

It was this year that SAE decided it was time for all the VP's and Sr. VP's to come to Paris to their office. So, Carolyn and I packed our stuff and climbed on the now defunct Eastern Airlines and flew to Washington, DC, landing at Washington's National Airport which is now Reagan National Airport. And in true Eastern Airlines form, the first thing they do is lose our luggage. A great start. We were in Washington for 36 hours of meetings with the SAE liaison guy, and I do not remember ANYTHING about the meetings other than there were people from all the other companies there, too. The first evening Carolyn and I rented a car and drove out to Vienna and found 8708 Westwood Drive in Tysons Corner and George C. Marshall High School. We spent the night without our bags, and then I was in more meetings. We were to leave that evening on Air France.

Around lunch I had a break, and I told Carolyn I did not think we should go as we had no clothes. Well, Carolyn let me know quickly that she was going to Paris with or without me! She said that we could buy new clothes and everything we needed in Paris. Now this really did make sense, and I changed my tune. Why I had thought about not going was simple. I did not want to appear out of control especially in front of my wife, and we were poor. We could not afford to buy new clothes in Paris. I know, I know … stupid. But I was in way over my head, and I was no Sr. VP much less someone who was important enough to go to Paris. I was just a draftsman who for whatever reason ended up here. But Carolyn was right. And soon after lunch I got a call from Reagan Airport. Our bags were there. I took the car and grabbed them in plenty of time to get us to Dulles Airport and our flight. I had learned a valuable lesson. Trust your wife, and try to trust yourself. Try.

The Air France flight was wonderful I assume as I do not recall anything about it, and we landed at Charles de Gaulle the next morning *with our luggage*. We landed about 7:00AM and of course were tired as it was about 1:00 in the morning to us. Ahh, the wonderfulness of international travel! We were whisked to our little apartment room down in the 16th Arrondissement. It was a darling little room on the third floor overlooking a little courtyard where there was a school playground … how prophetic. The room was so small two people could not pass side by side between the wall and the foot of the bed. It was European and perfect. We slept for about two hours and then "sallied forth" into Paris. I had said if I do nothing else while I am in Paris, I want to put my hand on the Cathedral of Notre Dame. Our first adventure came in the fabled Metro station. We had a map of the city (which I have mounted on foam core and is at my feet as I write) and the desire to get to the Île de la Cité. So, we are standing in the Metro station near our hotel and looking at the Metro map and looking lost when a Parisian gentleman (I think I am recalling it was a man) came up to us and in his best broken English said … basically … "It's obvious you ain't from around here." He then went on to explain how to navigate the Paris Metro. Carolyn and I cannot wait to get back soon! After his tutorial we very smoothly and expertly zipped to the literal heart of Paris and popped up from the station. It took us a minute to get our bearings and then, there she was … one of the most sought after and beautiful gothic cathedrals in all of Europe. We touched her. Later in our visit we returned and went inside and viewed her magnificent Rose stained glass window and stood where thousands have stood for centuries. The love and care and sacrifice to build her was evident in every window, statue, stone on the floor and pew. She is as glorious as you can imagine. One cannot visit Notre-Dame de Paris as she had an accidental fire in 2019 and will not reopen until late in 2024. We finished the day with dinner where I demonstrated my fluency in French. Carol will confirm this story. I thought I was ordering a hamburger and potato soup, but we ended up with a burger, okay, with a fried egg on it and instead of potato soup we got raw fish soup! (potato = pomme, fish = poisson).

The next morning, we had croissants and meats and coffee at the hotel. Then I was off to meetings with SAE and Carolyn had the whole day and a whole city to explore. The meetings started with breakfast again where we Colonials were presented with what looked like an oversize coffee cup. We did not know if it was for cereal or coffee. It ended up being for coffee, and we ate breakfast. Then there were meetings about profit and loss and projects and blah, blah, blah. That evening Carolyn and I explored the City of Light some more. We found the Louvre and it being late in the day, made our way expressly to see da Vinci's Mona Lisa. The takeaway … it is very small! Dinner was at somewhere, and we ended up that evening back near Notre Dame where Carolyn wanted to find small tapestries of the famous sites in Paris. Carolyn always has a plan (like her 50-year plan … inside joke, sorry). And in the shadow of the cathedral, we found a little shop with exactly what she had in mind. You can see these very tapestries framed and hanging on the walls as you go up the stairs at Falcon Wood Drive. This purchase was to become a tradition in our lives.

The next day I was off early in the morning to the coast at Pas-de-Calais to view work on the Channel Tunnel, the Chunnel, to which our new parent company was a prime contributor and contractor. The day was long and fascinating. The Chunnel was a joint venture amongst contractors for Europe and the United Kingdom. The contractors were using tunnel boring machines, TBM's, to dig through the earth under the English Channel. The material they were digging through was known as Marl. The machine was a huge cylindrical shaped digger with teeth on the front that rotated in a circle. As they rotated the machine advanced and the marl was then mixed with pumped in sea water and then pumped out. The slurry was then deposited on the beach as waste. I was watching this happen, and I saw them squirting this slurry all over a German bunker left from Rommel's famed Atlantic Wall construction. Someone asked one of the engineers about this destruction of history and he told us that there was nothing about those bunkers or the German occupation of France that the French peoples had any desire to remember. That made total sense.

I asked one man sitting next to me how the French felt about Americans? I said I had heard that the French did not care for us, but all my experiences in his country so far showed me a kind and generous, helpful people. The gentleman said that the French people will always remember the Americans, what the Americans did to help the French people during World War II, and that they will always have affection for us. I countered with our country appreciating France's help when we were trying to win our independence from the British in the 1700's. We shook hands.

Later at lunch one of the engineers was asked how did they know, if the English were boring from one side and the French from the other, that they would meet? He calmly gave a long technical explanation about satellites and geosynchronous orbits and lasers. He said that when they were about 300 meters from each other they would drill a pilot hole and again, using a laser, aim it through the hole at a target, adjust anything that was needed and then proceed. So, one of our construction guys in a southern accent said, "So you guys are basically gonna get close, dig a little hole and take a look?" The French engineer reluctantly and with a very superior look said, "Oui." We all laughed. And one reason we all laughed was the French representatives had had their own little joke on us Colonials. When we had arrived at this beautiful little restaurant overlooking the coast for lunch, we all were seated at tables outside and on the tables were pitchers of what looked like grape juice and tasted like grape juice. All of us helped ourselves. The sun was warm, the air was cool and the company convivial. We were enjoying the breezes off the channel and seated under a lovely arbor, and lunch was about to be served. We had gotten up early and it was now midafternoon. The typical French lunchtime. As it turned out the pitchers were filled with Kir. Kir is a French aperitif concoction. They take a not so great white or rosé wine and cut it with a blackberry liqueur like Crème de Cassis at a ratio of about eight or nine parts wine to one-part liqueur. It is a delicious before or after dinner drink, sweet and soft on the tongue. And it will creep up on you, and bang you in the head later! As it did to all of us on the very, very long bus ride home!

The Chunnel visit was the Friday culmination of my work that week. I think we were leaving to go home on Sunday, and so I had a little sight-seeing time with Carolyn. The last places I recall us visiting was a Metro ride to the base of a hill in northeast Paris know as Montmartre. Up on this hill is where all the artists hang out. It is where Van Gogh painted and Le Moulin Rouge is located. But the hill is topped with a beautiful, pink and white marble Catholic church known as the Sacré-Coeur Basilica, Sacred Heart Basilica. Carolyn and I climbed the hill to the top and saw the church. They were having mass, so we did not enter and interrupt. Sacré-Coeur is another of our future destinations. The next day we flew home to Atlanta through JFK via Air France and Delta. The flight was interminably long, but we made it without me having to eat any foie gras.

The other event late that year was a meeting in Houston of all the Sr. VP's and above. Again, another waste of time as there were only two things I remember from that weekend. One, I had forgotten my hair dryer. Now this was before hotels provided anything like that, so in a pouring Houston rain I had to grab a taxi at 10:00 at night and find a drug store that was open to buy a stupid hair dryer. The second thing I remember was that I made the mistake of making the totally brown-nosing comment on how great the meeting was, and that it should be a yearly gathering. Well, you guessed it. At the very end of the meeting the SAE liaison guy stood up, said thanks to all of us for our hard work this year, and that we would all gather next year in Atlanta and that Jim Morris of Carlson Group would arrange and host the event. Great …

I was also in charge of our Christmas party that year. The venerable, old, annual forced time of cheer. Almost as much fun as a deathly hot afternoon at Sun Valley Beach. It was held at a restaurant on a hill overlooking and just north of I-285 between Powers Ferry Road and New Northside Drive along Riveredge Parkway. It's gone now, but it was the "Something, Something Mining Company," and all decked out to look like an old mining company … hence the name – duh. Dan came up with the idea of giving medals for Project Manager of the Year and Electrical Engineer of the Year and crap like that. I have, or had, one somewhere. I might have tossed it. The one other thing I will always remember was a dress Carolyn wore to one of those Christmas parties. It was black velvet and it was cut so low in the back it went almost down to her … well, it was cut very low in the back, and it had three bows holding the two sides in back together. She … was … stunning! After all, she was the wife of a Sr. VP (Ha). The thing that she and I still laugh about was that Dan Hunter could not keep his hands off her. He was constantly touching her back. It would have been laughable had it not been so obvious. Anyway, the liquor was free, the food was average at best, I planned a Christmas party, and the boss got handsey with my wife … typical 1980's stuff.

This year was also the official collapse of Carlson's adventures with Disney. I was trying desperately to hold the project together as it spiraled out of control. I was easily working twelve and fourteen hour days and flying to California twice and sometimes three times a month. Dan Hunter and I had our first serious falling out when I got an ear infection and the doctor said no more flying for several weeks. Hence Hunter had to shoulder some of the Disney burden and he did not like it. I had "failed" him as he said to me. It was the beginning of my end. Little did I know in four years I would be gone. The whole Pleasure Island and Norway Pavilion projects had gone seriously awry because Disney's "Imagineers" could not stop *imagining*. Design/Build works when a client is able to establish with architects his design criteria and agree on a design early and stick with that design. The process breaks down when the client's people cannot settle down and keep changing the design, which is exactly what happened to both Disney projects. This is where Mickey Mouse becomes the Black Rat. Driving A&E and construction firms into bankruptcy is what Disney is famous for doing. And 1988 was the culmination of our contracts with them. It ended favorably for us. We got paid. But we never worked with them again. And I believe, even though I helped salvage the legal effort – there is a binder downstairs called Disney legal with all my work that the lawyers used in it – my days at SAE Carlson were now numbered. The big wigs would not forget the fiasco that was Disney. Our old nemesis, Heery and Heery, took over these projects from us with Disney. They ended up crashing and burning and suing Disney too. They were also involved with another project, Thunder River. That project crashed and burned too, as I recall. I guess my point is that Disney is/was a notorious client to be involved with. The projects of Pleasure Island and The Norway Pavilion were eventually completed. Pleasure Island was named something else, and it was not anything like the original design inception.

7.

1989 was the year Carolyn started to get seriously sick. I thought for the first time that I may lose her. We left a slowly dying Powers Ferry UMC and joined a church that would eventually open a door for us and then close our door on organized religion. We saw the "Stones" and Carlson continued to be a madhouse.

My love had started taking an over the counter drug in 1987 named Tryptophan. It was to help with anxiety and depression and general overall mental health. I am going to make just a quick comment here and am not going to belabor this point. Carolyn had a difficult childhood. She was abused by a relative in Nashville at a young age, and she was mentally abused as she grew up. In my opinion, Carolyn was lucky to be alive when I fell in love with her at Southern Tech. And all of this came together around 1987 when she tried to self-medicate after doing exhaustive research. Unfortunately, and unknown to her the Chinese company that was the major supplier of Tryptophan was selling a tainted product. It first exhibited itself benignly and hidden under the guise of Carpel-tunnel Syndrome. That was in 1987 and Carolyn had surgery on both wrists to relieve the pressure and numbness. She and I and the doctors all thought that the Carpel-tunnel was because of the years and years of strenuous hand work required of an architect. Both of us now know our arthritis in our hands is the result of our profession as architects. In '88 the slow poisoning was resulting in numbness in her feet and legs and cramping in both at night. Again, we blamed it on work and shoes and "just getting older." In 1989 it started to become obvious that something else was going on. There were patches of skin on her legs that were starting to harden. It was around this time that Carolyn started doing research into the company supplying the drug to the world. The next few years were scary for us. The question that rapidly became the center point of my existence was would Carolyn survive?

Carolyn and I finally decided to leave Powers Ferry United Methodist Church. It was obvious to us that it did not provide the kind of youth oriented program the children needed, and it was not satisfying our spiritual needs either. After all, we were hot-shot East Cobb Yuppies on the way up. We *deserved* a progressive church with a young and talented minister. We moved from old P.F.U.M.C. to Mt. Bethel UMC! The yellow church on Lower Roswell Road and Reverend Randy Mickler. We visited the church for several weeks and were taken with this young minister and his congregation. One thing that impressed us was his children's sermon. Each week a child selected the week before would bring a favorite object to church and during the children's sermon, present it to Randy. Then, Reverend Mickler would have to come up with a children's sermon centered on that precious object on the spot; which he did consistently week after week. The congregation at this church were predominately young and *upwardly mobile*; just like we were. We were hooked. And this church would serve us well for seven years.

The Rolling Stones were performing in Atlanta! Today I cannot believe they would play a venue as small as Grant Field at Georgia Tech but in 1989 they did. Carolyn and I got tickets and headed down to Tech. We were very familiar with the layout and where to park as Unca' Nelson, God bless him, who was a professor in the Industrial Management College had asked us to come down to several Tech games during this time, so we knew the best places to park and everything. Carolyn had gone to Tech for two years in 1969-71, was an AΞΔ sorority girl before coming out to meet me at Southern Tech. Anyway, we had tickets to one of the hottest bands in the world, and they were good seats. We were off to the right of the stage but close enough to really see the band. Mick Jagger was … well, Mick Jagger jumping and strutting. Charlie Watts, who passed away in 2021, banged out *Satisfaction* while the entire stadium sang along. Ronnie Wood and Keith Richards, all in their prime 40's, left all the other Rhythm and Blues bands in their dirt as they sang songs by Muddy Waters and B.B. King. They played songs they shared with The Animals and The Kinks. I remember the pot was plentiful that night, and the air was thick with it. Smells and music are strong recollection triggers. You know, it's funny, I can see that stage and hear the Stones and smell the marijuana and see my beautiful thirty-seven-year-old Carolyn sitting next to me, but I cannot recall what we ate for dinner or who was taking care of the children or even what happened after the concert. Memory is an elusive thing. And old memories are even more elusive things. I guess that's why I'm writing all this while I still can, but I have the feeling I'm leaving so much out. Oh well, if you can, talk to Carolyn, she can fill in the miles and miles of gaps.

In the world of work, we got two new major commissions that year. Both were buildings for AMEX, and they were in Phoenix, Arizona. Now at this time I was involved in many different projects at a "global" level. I was always involved in the upfront calculations of fees, the A/E schedule and overall strategy. I was in contract negotiations and signing, and I was the Architect of Record sealing documents all over the country. In hindsight, which is always 20/20, if I'd had any sense I would have followed Carolyn's approach, let someone else take the responsibility, but I was a hot dog big shot, so I sealed projects and filed the documents. There is a small blue box with the word Acacia on it. The box was given to me by The Colonel when he tried to sell life insurance for Acacia — he was terrible at it. The box code is 6-9-3. But in this box are business cards of "all the people I have been" as well as my registration stamps from various states. I guess they should be destroyed. I digress, AMEX Phoenix was to be twin data centers. They were side by side in downtown Phoenix and extremely unremarkable architecturally speaking.

1989 was the year I pulled off the SAE Regional Meeting I had been tagged for in Dallas the year before. Hunter was not pleased that I had to do this. Mainly because my time and the time of people who worked on getting this all arranged were pure overhead dollars. Anyway, working with my secretary, yes Mad Men have to have secretaries to type all their notes and memos and letters, we worked on the regional gathering. I even had a little tape recorder I carried around so I could dictate stuff – mostly brilliant flashes of business wisdom – for her to type … Carolyn always snickered when I would whip it out and tell myself something amazing. And speaking of business brilliance, it was around now that I learned a valuable lesson.

I know as I write this, I am all over the place this morning. Apologies.

Being the Sr. VP I had meetings with the heads of the various departments under me: architecture, electrical, HVAC, plumbing, structural and project management. One morning I called a meeting of the team. Only one department showed up, plumbing. Everyone else was busy on projects or out of town at building sites. And I realized a lesson that would serve me the rest of my life. The only reason I could do what I was to do was if the others followed me. I had to lead, not manage. And the only thing a position of responsibility afforded you, was to allow you to serve others, to clear obstructions from their path, to work longer and harder than any of them so they could do their job. To this day, I try to remember that lesson.

But … the Regional Meeting. With the help of my secretary we found a venue. We planned to use the Atlanta Marriott Northwest nestled between I-75 and I-285. Little did I know that Carolyn and I would use that same Marriott for James and Angela's rehearsal dinner in eighteen years. Anyway, we booked rooms for all the company people who we coming into town. We arranged speakers. We bought gift baskets that were to contain a SAE coffee mug, wine from Chateau Elan, Moon Pies and other "Southern" stuff. I got an architect in the office, Gary Summerlin, a fellow Southern Tech grad I had hired, to work on a big eight-foot by ten-foot collage of all Carlson Associates work (We were no longer Aldrich, we were now Carlson Associates … would have made my old registration adventures in North Carolina easier) and planned an agenda. Today, January 23, 2023, at 6:10 AM, as I sit in my robe and write about it, the whole event does not seem like such a big deal. But back then, it was huge … to me. There are even pictures of it around here somewhere. We did a whole after the event assessment, and it was a success as I recall.

The weather cooperated, and everyone sat in conferences and listened like drones and drank and ate and listened like they were interested and ate and drank and stood around, and then it was over, and the only recollections that the meeting ever took place are right here. In fact, it was such a success I do not think there was ever another regional meeting after Atlanta. I guess they just did not feel like they could compete with Atlanta's efforts … or that the regional meetings just weren't worth it … or that meetings in general aren't worth it. I go with the first thought.

8.

A new decade roared to life. Carolyn got sicker. Prophetically, I started teaching Sunday school at Mt. Bethel UMC. I turned 40, and Carlson was Carlson.

Carolyn stopped taking Tryptophan. Everything she read convinced us the drug she was taking was tainted, and she was now exhibiting serious symptoms. Her skin was hardening and developing patches. Her hair was falling out. Her joints were becoming inflexible. She started consulting a local doctor, and he confirmed and officially diagnosed her condition as eosinophilia myalgia. I do not recall that there were any drugs to combat her condition. Basically she had to stop taking the drug and hopefully her body would eventually cleanse itself and be able to repair itself.

Carolyn was devastated. She had tried to improve herself and treat herself holistically and had, thanks to a Chinese firm, poisoned herself. It was in 1990 that we consulted a local lawyer, Alan Manheim, and began the long journey to sue the company. In the meantime, Carolyn needed some spiritual uplifting and she got this from two sources. One was the choir at Mt. Bethel Church. She had begun singing with them, and her association with the choir was good. They were a loving family who embraced her, and the choir gave her a focus outside herself. The choir director, Debbie Pierce (*who just passed away in 2024 after a long battle with Alzheimer*), was a personality unto herself and was able to extract the best from each member. If I may say, at times the choir bordered on being a cult, albeit from its effects on Carolyn, a positive one. There were bar-b-ques where whole pigs were roasted in someone's backyard, Christmas parties, weekly practices and always Debbie to fawn over.

The second source of almost spiritual uplifting was from my Aunt Marybelle Morris Swift, the Colonel's younger sister. There were three children in The Colonel's family, The Colonel, Marybelle and Toochie – Marion Louise Morris Rogers. Marybelle had always been the wild child. There is a picture of The Colonel, his soon to be wife (left), Marybelle and a very young Toochie (right) in the Stork Club in New York City in the early 1940's, and you can see by the look on Marybelle's face she is up for action. Marybelle married Don Swift, an insurance salesman who had made good in Dallas and then moved to a little planned community south of Los

Angeles named Laguna Hills when he retired. Their daughter and my contemporary Mary Lou Swift (now Beckmann) still live a little distance north of there in Fountain Valley. Carolyn and Marybelle had been soulmates ever since Marybelle took over organizing the back of the church at our wedding. Marybelle was a licensed counselor who helped people and Carolyn needed her. While Aunt Marybelle was not a licensed psychiatrist she was everything Carolyn needed. So, Carolyn packed her bag and travelled out to California and spent some time with Marybelle forming a bond that would last the rest of their lives. I do not know exactly what happened out in California that year. All I do know is that Marybelle saved Carolyn's life.

I started teaching Sunday School at Mt. Bethel. At first it was just ninth grade but it quickly morphed into the whole Senior High Sunday School as word spread, and tenth, eleventh and twelfth graders started sneaking into my class. It ballooned and there were, at times, as many as fifty children in my class. I loved it and spent hours working on lessons. I became quite the self-taught bible scholar. One of my favorite personalities of the Bible was poor old Peter, and my lessons frequently focused on him and his problems. I did not know it at the time, but over my several years of teaching those beautiful children, my faith was strengthened and girded for challenges that were to come. Those children sustained me as Carolyn's sickness continued and gave me faith in God's overarching love, and the knowledge that he is able to work any adversity to his good even in this crazy, present day world.

One of my favorite Sunday School stories was one year when Christmas day fell on a Sunday. I always struggled on Easter and Christmas to come up with a lesson that would be impactful and meaningful on two of the most overworked holidays in America. I hit upon a scheme to become the persona of "Lo, the angel of the Lord." I took this from The King James Version of the *Bible* in Luke 2, verses 8 and 9:

8 And there were in the same country shepherds abiding in the field, keeping watch over their flock by night.

9 And, lo, the angel of the Lord came upon them, and the glory of the Lord shone round about them: and they were sore afraid.

I had a friend named Jeff who helped me teach Sunday School. He taught the children when I was out of town or needed a break. We were both on the job that morning and double teaming the class. Then, I had someone come down to the classroom and tell me I had to leave for a few minutes. I ducked out and left Jeff to hand "the multitudes." I scooted to another room and changed into tennis shoes that were spray painted gold, a sheet that was cut to look like a robe and tied with a gold spray painted rope, some gold tensile forming a halo roughly put on my head, picked up an old two-inch-thick phone book with a cover on it stating it was *Operation Savior I* and my little styrofoam harp and dashed back to the class.

Now before that morning I had contacted several of the parents of teenagers who I thought were going to be there that morning. I told them what I had planned and asked them to tell me some facts about their children that were not common knowledge outside the family, and they did.

And so I came crashing back into the classroom in the guise of Lo, The Angel of the Lord, and proceeded to tell them of my plight. But to gain their confidence that I was in fact and Angel of the Lord I shared a few little known facts about some of the children present. One that sticks in my mind was a fact about a young man who was born prematurely and that it was a difficult birth, and that he had spent his first few weeks in the hospital teetering between life and death. That little baby's name was Jim Elgar. He had a sister named Kathy and I ended up with her child in my fifth grade class at Mt. Bethel … but I get ahead of myself. Anyway I went on and told them about my plan, *Operation Savior I*, holding up the thick phone book as proof, that I had presented to God about how Jesus would come into the world. My plan included flaming chariots and thunder and lightning and hell fire and earthquakes, and that when I got done there would be no doubt about who Jesus was and that everyone had better shape up. I ended telling them that God had rejected my plan out right. He had other plans. And so, over my objection, God followed his plan and here we are today still arguing about "Was he the Son of God?" or "Was he not the Son of God?" It was a cool lesson. Then I told them I had many stops to make and had to leave. Sadly, there are no pictures of Lo.

Now no Christmas Sunday School class would be complete with a Christmas party and when I got back, we had one. I swept back into the classroom all apologetic and said I was sorry for missing this important morning, but Jeff and I did have a party planned. Our classroom had a sound curtain that was movable between us and another empty classroom next to us. Usually we used the whole space, but this morning I had divided it so their party was in the next room. And what a party it was! I had contacted CARE and found out what was the meal looking soup that was being ladled into cups to children overseas in Africa and war torn countries, and found out it was basically a cornmeal mixture with added vitamins. So, there on a table were cups, a large pot of tap water and a large pot of a cornmeal and water mixture with a little salt put in it so it tasted like something … and that was all. There were no cookies or punch or gifts or anything. I hope it made an impression. As you can tell, it made an impression on me.

For my 40th birthday that year Carolyn had the Bible I used for years as a Sunday School teacher rebound with a leather cover. It is in my bedside table. Inside there are many interesting notes and things I use/used to keep going. Okay, let's go there. Let's spend a moment on my belief structure. The very, very bottom line, yes, I am a religious man. I do believe in God and that Jesus was his son. I also believe that Mohammed was divinely inspired and possibly another son. The Quran and the Bible are related and parallel documents. I find it hard to believe that Christianity is the only one true religion and that those who do not believe in Him (Jesus) are condemned to hell. I do not believe one has to be baptized or you will go to hell. Newborns die every day; these innocents cannot be condemned to "hell." Look into the eyes of *your* newborn child as I have with Jenna and James and then your grandchildren Bryce and Bodie and Caitlin, and you will agree. Watch them grow, and you will understand. Relative to heaven and hell, I believe that this life is hell. And one is condemned to repeat living lives in various ways over and over until one gets it "right" and is then allowed to not have to repeat "life" again. You will meet people in your life who have lived more lives than you. Those people are "further down the road" than you and have an understanding of what is important. They do good for others. They sacrifice themselves for others. They think of others first and themselves last. Many times they are people who see serving others as being more important than the old adage "Whoever dies with the most toys wins." I do not believe you have to sit in church every week to go to heaven. Many times, I find those sanctimonious fools, including quite a few preachers I have met, are the ones that need to take several more runs through lives before they can call it quits. Am I a sinner? Yes! I say that with a resounding exclamation point. Let's just say (to borrow from one of my favorite poems *Stopping by Woods on a Snowy Evening* by Robert Frost) I have "… miles to go before I sleep," but I am trying. Failing a lot, but trying. For comparison, Carolyn is many lives further down the path than I am. And I praise her often for "… helping me to make of the lumber of my life not a tavern, but a temple." A partial quote from another beautiful poem, *Love*, by Roy Croft. I try to leave all things better after I leave than when I arrived even down to buggies in the Walmart parking lot. Stupid, I know. Read *Desiderata* by Max Ehrman in 1927 and you will start to understand my philosophy of life.

Enough! Let us turn to something much more important, Carlson (sarcasm). In retrospect, I believe this was the year that Carlson started to struggle. Was it the economy? Was it the leadership, of which I was a part? I cannot say. I just feel this was the beginning of the end (as opposed to the "end of the beginning" – thank you Winston Churchill). In 1990 we scored two more Data centers for AMEX. One in Phoenix, which I was involved in, and one in San Francisco, which I was only marginally involved in. The Phoenix project was interesting because we were trying to build it in the middle of brutal Phoenix summers. The temperatures rising to 110 degrees easily. And one cannot pour concrete in those temperatures. Pouring concrete on a metal deck that is 150 or 160 degrees boils the water out of the concrete too quickly and the concrete never cures. You are left with a concrete slab with powder on the bottom and no structural integrity. However, in downtown Phoenix there were laws about construction noises between 6:00PM and 7:00AM. And the only way we could pour in the summer heat was between 2:00 and 5:00 AM when the air and the deck were cool enough. So, I met with the city, and we talked, and we were able to secure a permit to allow us to pour in the middle of the night, but we had to accomplish all the pours in one month. Ah, the exciting life of a Sr. VP.

It was on one of these trips that I had another unusual and fascinating event. It was Thursday, August 2nd, 1990, and I finished another great day at the office and caught a late afternoon flight to Phoenix to inspect the site and then fly back the next evening. I drove to the airport and parked and caught my plane. A couple of hours later I landed in a strange land. We landed in Phoenix, and I noticed that something was different as soon as I got off the plane. The terminal was almost empty. Now it was about 10:00 at night so I thought it unusual but not weird. But the National Guard troops with guns was definitely not usual. When I got to the car rental desk I asked what was going on and the man said that because Iraq had invaded Kuwait the United States was on alert and had initiated Operation Desert Shield. Desert Shield was the buildup to Operation Desert Storm which started on January 17th, 1991, and lasted about six months. Anyway, landing in Phoenix that night was spooky as hell!

But the memory that stands out in my mind the most from 1990 and still gives me nightmares, was a trip I was asked to make to the Boston office. Little did I understand that it painted the first glossy stroke of the end of Carlson. My mission, which I chose to accept (thank you IMF), was to go to the Boston office, fire everyone, and bring the work back to Atlanta to be completed. At the time, I was a very young, 40 years old, Sr. VP and wanted desperately to please upper management. I was so naïve and was so starry-eyed-edly stupid. SO STUPID. But, armed with a roster of projects and the green audit sheets that went with them and the people in charge and working on the projects, I left for Boston. While there over the next several days I did let a number of people go and that memory pains my soul to this day. I should not have been asked to do that. Someone from Boston should have been tasked to do that. Or Dan Hunter should have done that. But NO! They looked for the stupidest guy they could find and tasked him with it. And I went, but I turned the tables on them. Once there, I determined that bringing the work back to Atlanta was not the right thing to do. Trimming the staff and matching the number of people to the number of projects was the correct thing to do. And I informed Dan Hunter of this and proceeded to do just that. Little did I realize that in just two years, they would ultimately close Atlanta and have it be absorbed into Boston! I will always have to live with what I did over that week in Boston. I wrecked people's lives and did it viciously in some cases because I was hiding behind, "I was just following orders." How many military debacles and misadventures including the Holocaust and Mỹ Lai Massacre have the participants hidden behind "I was just following orders"? My answer: too many. You may say, "Jim you are being too hard on yourself." And I say "thanks" but I have literally cried myself to sleep over some of the things I did at Carlson when I was a hot-shot, big-deal, know-it-all, bone head Sr. VP. In actuality, I was nothing but a coward. I was afraid to appear to "lose face," to not have courage to be a ruthless businessman. I was afraid to lose my salary and "perks." I was afraid I would appear weak and a loser in The Colonel's eyes. And all the while, those above me at Carlson must have laughed their heads off at me. So please do not make the same mistakes I made. Do not let anyone or anything make you do things that you know hurt others and are wrong. If you try to live a good life, things <u>will</u> work out for you. Be brave. Have faith. Have courage. And ever since my Boston lesson, I have tried.

9.

We continued to live in 1991. This may seem like a strange statement, but our little family just enjoyed being a family even though Carolyn continued to fight through her condition. She never once gave up or let our family down. She went to work and prepared meals and grocery shopped and took care of all of us even though she was dealing with pain almost daily. On the recommendation of her doctor and the agreement of our lawyer, we started going to the Medical College of Charleston and seeing specialists. They prescribed various medications, and slowly Carolyn started on her road to recovery. We tried to enjoy our trips to Charleston and it rapidly became one of our favorite cities. On one of our visits we stayed at a wonderful old B&B on King Street near Wentworth named something like King's Courtyard … that may not be it, but it was something like that. I cannot find it today. It was probably bought out and renamed, but the place was old and rickety but so very cool. We even stayed there twice. We would get up and have breakfast and then I would take Carolyn to the medical college and she would go through batteries of tests while I would hang around. Then we would go adventuring and exploring on Market Street and finding cool places to eat like Hyman's Seafood at 215 Meeting Street. We have been back there several times with the whole family. I recall being there with Jenna and Adam much later when we found out there was to be a grandchild named Bryce … but I get waaaaay ahead of myself. As I was saying, Carolyn was undergoing tests, and we were in Charleston.

Carolyn also continued singing in the choir at Mt. Bethel, and we were rapidly becoming known around the church. And Carolyn was being noticed by one "Reverend" Randy Mickler. I continued teaching Sunday School and began working with Sam Halverson and the MYF.

Another family highlight of the year was one Timothy Adam Blackwell, the young man who had faithfully pursued my one and only daughter relentlessly (today we'd use the word stalking) since middle school, graduated from high school. And besides graduating, he was off to college. I seem to recall he spent a quarter or two at a community college before heading off to Georgia Southern in Statesboro. I could be wrong on that …but he ultimately did go to Southern.

James was growing up, and we became involved with East Marietta National Little League. Back then they were a powerhouse and had even sent a couple of teams to the Little League World Series. In fact, I think they won the championship one year around this time. James was a solid player. He was not very fast on the bases, but he played catcher and was fearless kneeling back there under the swinging bat and handling the wild throws that come from a young pitcher. Carolyn and I did our part in the concession stand where, after three hours in the little hut, you came out stinking of popcorn grease. The smell was in your hair and in your clothes and you felt like you had a thin film of grease all over. It was wonderful! I even tried my hand at being a home plate umpire once … once. No matter what you did it was wrong, and the parents would let you know about it. As I said, once. I was much better at slinging hot dogs and shoveling popcorn and smelling like grease. James's baseball career did not last long. We got a coach one year who thought this was his path to the Major Leagues, I guess. If the team did not win, he made them run the bases, until he was satisfied. James had had enough baseball after the coach started pulling that stuff. We moved on.

In the world of Carlson, I was still too important. We got a new client that year, MCI. This firm was the forerunner of firms like Verizon and Comcast and T-Mobile. They were a cell carrier and were building what I would call substations all over the place. MCI had a set plan and the way they wanted all the systems of be built. What they needed us for was to basically site adapt their designs and then build them. There are a couple of events

I recall. One was the introduction to a new technology called "email." We had a dedicated printer set up just for MCI, and all communications with them went back and forth through this thing called "email." And when one came in we had a spool of tractor paper hooked up, and they email would print out with the message. It was very cutting edge for the time. We were still producing drawings by hand although several people were looking onto computer programs like AutoCAD, and we were playing with a failed experiment called Overlay Drafting. This was an approach where one would produce a single floor plan. Then instead of other disciplines redrawing this floor plan they would take the original, register it with a sheet on top of the original with a pin bar arrangement and run it through a blueline machine producing a fresh original. The concept was fraught with problems and never really worked, but Carlson was starting to "grasp at straws" as the Data Center market where Carlson had focused on for too long dried up, and the economy slowed.

A second event with MCI I recall is when the MCI reps would come to review progress on the projects. They were Laurel and Hardy pair of guys. They were Laurel and Hardy not so much from their physical appearance, but more so from demeanor. One was a loud mouth with a short temper and the other was quiet and reserved. The quiet one would leave our offices in the evenings and go walk in the malls to get his exercise. I also found out later in our talks and my visits to their headquarters outside Dallas that he was pastor of a very small church. Interesting little man, and they were quite a humorous pair until one meeting where our HVAC guys decided to re-engineer the MCI HVAC system. I cannot say if our design was better or not. All I can say is it was different and NOT what MCI wanted or paid for, and "Hardy" went ballistic. And I really cannot blame him. I was totally embarrassed, although today I do not see why I felt that way. The HVAC guys should not have done that. They redesigned it to MCI specifications. This redesign dominoed through electrical and structural and plumbing and architectural disciplines as we adjusted to the way it should have been designed originally. So, we spent A&E money I had not budgeted for, and we did not have. This trashed our profitability on that project, and I was blamed for not keeping my eyes on the HVAC department.

We also picked up another client, Heraeus Amercil (now known as Heraeus Quartz North), a German fiber optic company who wanted to build a facility near Buford. Their facility we designed and built is just north of Georgia 20 off Buford Highway in Buford, Georgia. It's a big gray building with a blue band on it. Again they had a basic design like MCI and Bosch and again, we had a difficult time performing as a Design/Build firm. In retrospect I do not know if it was the level of talent in the A/E side, or the level of project management on the construction side or the project's expectations set the beginning by our salesforce, or the fact that Carlson was trying to be all things to all people and were really out of our depth in areas that needed specialized construction firms. Some firms specialize in hospitals, some in office buildings some in government work. Carlson was trying to make money anywhere it could to satisfy SAE and had ventured into areas we were not qualified to be in. That is my perspective today looking back thirty-plus years.

In 1991 Carlson hired a new man, Jim Mountz. Technically he was hired on the construction side as some kind of a super project manager, but he also had Dan Hunter's ear, and they met in his office often.

10.

"It was the best of times, it was the worst of times." [Charles Dickens, 1859, *A Tale of Two Cities*] That just about sums it up. The incredible highs and lows of 1992 were, to use an overworked current hyperbolic term, "Epic." Jenna graduated high school, Carolyn started working at Mt. Bethel Church, I led a retreat at Crescent Beach, lost my job, and tried to work with DIC.

So let's start where I always like to start, with our beautiful family. This year was dominated by Miss Jenna graduating from Wheeler High School. An event that I remember around her graduation time was that we had a graduation party at Millbrook and invited all Adam and Jenna's friends and all the family that could make it. In the middle of the party, I noticed two young men whom I did not recognize. I asked Jenna quietly who they were. She and Adam had no idea. We had a pair of party crashers! I moved over near them and quietly asked them to leave and they did. Really, in retrospect, it was pretty ballsy, and I have to admire them … a little. Anyway, Jenna was graduating from the very same high school her mother graduated from almost a quarter of a century before – 23 years to be exact. Jenna had distinguished herself in high school playing volleyball, dancing with Lynette Grubb, being inducted into the National Honor Society and graduating high in her class all the while being chased by one T. Adam Blackwell. By Jenna's graduation I joked that Adam had eaten more dinners in our house than I had. The boy was nothing if not relentless. I had to appreciate that perseverance as it reminded me of a young man who, just a scant twenty years earlier, had stalked one Carolyn Ethel Lyon until she could not stand it any longer, felt sorry for the poor wayward lad, broke off her engagement to a promising young medical student and married me. It came as no surprise at all that Jenna elected to go to Georgia Southern. We had visited several schools but for some reason Southern had stolen her heart. Oh yeah, Adam was already enrolled there. Not that that had any bearing on the decision because she had decided to study in the Business College, and we all know that Georgia Southern had a powerhouse business school … not. She ultimately decided to change curriculum and study education which Southern was really known for today. Originally Georgia Southern was named the First District Agricultural and Mechanical School in 1906 and only had four faculty and fifteen students. It grew. We had visited there a couple of times, and I had actually been there some twenty plus years before as you may recall when I drove down to pick up an old flame, Bonnie, on Sweetheart Circle for a dance at STI. I often joke that the best thing about Georgia Southern is that it is four hours from Mom and Dad in Atlanta and one hour from the beach! But really, it was and is a beautiful school, and we were very proud that Jenna selected it. I can still see the sun beating down and feel the heat of that sweltering Georgia August day when we dropped our only daughter off to start her life as a college student. I can see her now turning and walking into Oliff Hall dormitory.

Oliff was demolished in 2008. To be perfectly honest, I do not recall being that upset or tearing up as we drove off. I knew Jenna was well prepared and besides, we still had James who was now nine years old and full of adventure.

My beautiful wife was still sick and dealing with her illness. The doctors were now identifying the poisons she had ingested and were prescribing various drugs to counteract the effects. The lawsuit was progressing, but I remember that money was very tight as we now started to struggle to pay for college as well as the doctors and drugs and trips to the doctors in Charleston. To help Carolyn started to work at Mt. Bethel Church. First she was working with Debbie Pierce in the choir room, and eventually she was tapped to be Rev. Mickler's secretary. I do not want to get all philosophical and religious as I find it difficult to believe that God personally intervenes in lives, but there is really no other explanation for the sequence of events relative to Mt. Bethel in Carolyn's and my life. As you read I will let you be the judge. At this moment in our lives we needed Carolyn to have a job, and there was no way with her illness that she could tolerate the rigors of twelve to fourteen hour days and the grind of an architectural office. Her job at Mt. Bethel was perfect and ultimately terrible at the same time. She was working closely with the preacher and singing in choir with Debbie Pierce, and I was heavily involved in the Sunday School and MYF. It seemed we were up at the yellow church on Lower Roswell Road almost daily.

That August I had a high point in my life. As I said, 1992 was that kind of year. Sam Halverson asked me if I would consider helping him put together a Senior High MYF Retreat to Crescent Beach, Florida. Somewhere in all my stuff downstairs you may come across my plans for that weekend. I remember Carolyn and James came along and we had our own room. I played music, Michael Jackson's *Black and White* comes to mind. And we talked and had my world famous *Hour of Silence* followed by Sam doing his Communion thing. It was a beautiful and fulfilling weekend with most of my Sunday School class and their friends. I smile right now to think that those children must be between 45 and 49 by now with their own high schoolers, and at this moment, I cannot recall a single name, well one … Teddy Crum … although I can see faces and hear their laughter.

Carlson's fortunes were fading along with the faltering 1992 economy. In my position I was called on to trim our staff that year. Foolishly, I was still drinking the Kool-Aid, although its taste had begun to sour in my mouth. Boston still haunted me as I was called on to let a Southern Tech friend go from the firm. Gary Summerlin, who had worked tirelessly in the architecture department to support Carlson, and had personally helped me when he created the Carlson collage mural for the big deal Regional Meeting I talked about earlier. Gary was a good man. No, he was one of the best, and I had told him, as he was working on the mural, that I would protect him and his job. Yet, I fired him. Stephen King would have described me as a Low Man. And I was.

The jobs were drying up, and I was driving and flying around with salesman to different places making presentations. We went to Dallas to present to some airline to build some facility we had no business trying to build. We went to Kentucky to try to get in on building a hot dog factory which we knew nothing about. We went to Columbus,

Georgia, to talk to Nabisco to build a facility for making cookies which we had no experience at building. We went to Toronto to talk to Dare Breton about building a facility in Canada even though we had never done any work in making crackers or had ever done any work outside the United States. We even went to Albertville, Alabama, to try to get a project to build a facility to make prefabricated homes. All of these sales calls went nowhere.

What I am about to write about is difficult, but I will tell the truth and be as honest as I can. There are different tales I have told about how all this evolved, but this is, again, the unvarnished truth. This part about being demoted, Carolyn did not know until several years ago as I was too ashamed to tell her. In September of 1992 came one of the biggest disappointments in my life … one of my lowest lows. Dan Hunter called me into his office. He had been transferred to the Charlotte, North Carolina, office to work with Nick Cawood, and he came down to Atlanta to talk with me. He told me Jim Mountz was now going to take his place in the Atlanta office, and that I was to be demoted to architectural draftsman. I was floored. I was stunned. I was crushed. I was speechless. I did not know what to say. I had no words. And after everything I had done for him and Carlson. Today I would have calmly asked why. Then I would have laid into him about all the things I had sacrificed for the company. It would not have helped, but at least I would have felt better. And at least I was not being fired. So next, and I cannot believe I did this, but I actually pleaded with him to at least let me at least be a project architect. He agreed. That day I was moved out of my little office. My first bigger office on the other end of the building had been taken away and made into a conference room a while back. I moved into a cubicle with a drafting table even though there were almost no projects to work on in the office. My star was fading fast, and I knew it … was a little stunned … but I knew it. And on the 18th of December, 1992, the other shoe dropped. I was fired. The word was "company downsizing." I got a month's salary for each year I had worked there, but there was no "golden parachute." Carlson had no money. They were on the ropes. SAE was closing unprofitable companies they had bought. So, less than a week before Christmas 1992 I was out of a job. The ironic upshot to this was that over the next few months the Atlanta work was transferred to the Boston office. The very office I was sent to close just two years before, and didn't, had just absorbed Atlanta!

It was a classic scenario, daughter in college, young son, wife, mortgage and out of a job in a down market. But there was an upside, and there is always an upside. Carolyn was employed at the church, and when the COBRA benefits ran out our church stepped in and extended health insurance to Carolyn and our family. 1992 was not the most joyous Christmas we had ever had, but Carolyn sang in a Christmas Program, we had a tree and gifts, we had food and shelter. We used my severance pay and then took money from our 401K even though it came with a healthy penalty. But we scraped by. "It was the best of times, it was the worst of times." From all of that in 1992 I learned, and I quote Groucho Marx, but it sounds more like Mark Twain, "I don't want to belong to any club that would have me as a member." And I never forgot that the rest of my working career … and beyond.

Needless to say, I immediately started looking for a job. But alas, no one was hiring. I contacted all my old Carlson contacts and people who had been clients. And when I touched base with the old college buddy, Bob Shelor, I found that he had left Bosch – let go I suspect – and was now starting his own firm, Diversified Industrial Consultants – DIC … pronounced "Dick." Carolyn laughed so hard she almost hurt herself – DIC. Really? But it was the only opportunity I had at that moment, so I carefully started working with him. The firm basically was in to help other firms maximize their floor space. This was done with a computer program based in DOS. I know, you have no idea what that is. DOS is Digital Operating System, and it is what all computers are really doing behind the icons you click on. Back in '92, '93 Apple was just playing with icons on a screen so the operator, you, did not have to enter a bunch of inane computer commands to get the computer to do anything. There was a book called *Easy DOS It,* basically DOS for Dummies, that was supposed to help you learn how to operate in this alien environment. Find an old copy if you are interested. DOS was weird, and I never got the hang of it. I did recruit another ex-Carlson employee, Mel Kitchens, to help Bob and me, but Mel saw the handwriting on the wall much more quickly than I did and soon tired of being a DIC employee with no pay and quit. I hung with Bob through the new year making several trips to his home north of Charleston and made several presentations with him to prospective clients – none of whom bought our services, but the whole no pay thing was untenable and wearing thin, and it became obvious to me that being a DIC employee was not my future. And after twenty-five years of working and all the blood, sweat, tears and treasure I had nothing. I started to question even being an architect. It was then that my Dulcinea, Carolyn, showed me my future.

11.

This year has to begin its story with Jenna and Adam getting engaged. To be honest I do not recall anything about the event, but it happened in 1993. In a couple of weeks will be Adam's fiftieth birthday, and I wanted to lead this year with their engagement. My calculations say he was twenty that year, and that would make Jenna nineteen. They had dated exclusively since she captured his heart in 1988, and he had sat next to me in the East Cobb Middle School gym. There are many pictures of this fresh faced pair at family gatherings and all dressed and smiling ready to leave for the prom. Jenna was in her sophomore year at Southern, and they seemed awfully young, but no one objected at all to their getting engaged, and as of last December (2023) they have been married twenty-eight years. Just as with Jenna being born to us so early in our marriage, Adam and Jenna were meant to be.

In the middle of all of this engagement hubbub, Jen got her wisdom teeth taken out. So as to not repeat my agony with wisdom teeth, we went to a real dentist, and she was put to sleep, and it was all as painless as possible. Let me interject here that Carolyn and I have tried all our married lives to correct and not repeat the parenting failures we were subjected to growing up. I want to think we succeeded more than we messed up with our children. I believe we both had parents who were flawed just as we, Carolyn and I, are flawed, but we tried to improve and not to damage our children as we were. The damage parents unknowingly, and sometimes knowingly, do to their children is horrendous. I just want you, my gentle reader to know that Carolyn and I were cognizant that poor parental scars "last a lifetime and a lifetime is a long time."

One way I tried to correct my childhood errors was to begin what are now legendary "Two Boys Trips." James would be ten years old and in the fifth/sixth grade that year. I recall I got the idea for our trips when I chaperoned on James's fifth grade class trip to Rock Eagle. James was in Ms. Scheer's class for fifth grade. I interject that because, totally unknown to me, I would be teaching with her on a fifth grade team just a few years in the future. At Rock Eagle another man and I were assigned to a cabin full of rowdy fifth grade boys. We were woefully underprepared for the task, but we tried our best. During one of the outings where our group of heathens were trying to solve a climbing obstacle I decided to start taking James on trips, just the two of us. The rules of the trip were simple: 1. Just James and I would go. 2. We had to drive there. He and I, in a car in close proximity. 3. Anything goes! And over the years he and I have traveled together many, many times and places and there are many kneeling pictures of me at the oddest of places. We started small and then grew the experience. We went to Charleston to go to Fort Sumter and the tour the Yorktown. The carrier Yorktown would loom large in my future. We went to the Outer Banks to see where Wilber and Orville did their thing. We went to Daytona and Cape Canaveral. We went to Washington and the Holocaust Museum which is always sobering. In Savannah at a little seafood place on the way out to Tybee, I was with James when he saw his first seriously drunk person who was making his way to the parking lot to drive off. This gave James great concern, and we talked about it. Two Boys took off to Jamestown and Williamsburg and the Yorktown battlefield. All three would loom large in my future as a research grant destination for me. There is one of my favorite pictures in the basement of me walking along at the Yorktown battlefield. While there we went to an amusement park, a Busch Gardens park I think … yep, Bush Gardens it was, and there is a picture of Two Boys screaming on the downhill run of the monster roller coaster. Our culminating and grandest Two Boys Trip was just before his wedding when we went to New Orleans again and went on a Caribbean cruise together for seven days. During these trips we talked about everything and I believe I forged an important bond that has helped James (and me) through his/my life. I'll mention some of these trips and their particulars as this story unfolds.

Carolyn and James and I periodically would head down to Georgia Southern for Parents Weekends. There were not nearly as many choices of places to stay as there are now, and we always stayed in a little motel with whirlpool tubs. I guess it was to be a romantic, college student hotspot, but to a ten-year-old James it is a perfect place for a gigantic bubble bath and a chance to watch the steam fogged television hanging over the tub and play with boats. Along in this second year I believe it was that Jenna joined the ZTA Sorority. The sorority house had the smallest rooms I have ever seen. The rooms were about 1/4 the size of a ship's cabin, but it was what Jenna wanted, and she got it. While down there we would often eat at a kind of helter-skelter restaurant in a parking lot near campus. It was a kind of plywood and mobile home mishmash, but their fried chicken was AWESOME! You may recognize the name as they sold out and franchised some years later. It was named Zaxby's. Today's chicken is nowhere near like it was back then in "the olden days." Back then the chicken pieces were huge, and they took written checks, which was unusual even for back then.

Jenna made many sorority friends, and I remember one of Jenna's "sisters" was from the little Georgia town of Fitzgerald. She was the sweetest thing, but as I stood next to her at a buffet line at an event, and we came to the bread basket she whispered, "I don't like brownie bread." It's another favorite phrase of Carolyn and mine.

Early in 1993 the lawsuit concerning Carolyn's Eosinophilia Myalgia settled. Carolyn and I needed to be done with the lawsuit for many reasons. She was on the mend, or at least as *on the mend* as she would be at this time. Her illness was a near death experience. We settled the case for a little over $250,000. The lawyer took 25%, and we took the rest, and it was in the nick of time. Me being out of work had put a lot of monetary pressure on us, and the money was a gift from God that Carolyn had paid dearly for. Suddenly we could pay for a daughter's college. We could pay for a young James's college. We made contributions back into our 401K's and could breathe again.

Around 1992 I recall we had bought Jenna a little red Hyundai to get back and forth to college. I bought it from a guy at work. It was nothing special, but it was transportation … until I got a call one evening from somewhere half way up I-16. Somehow … no oil had been put in the engine, and the car had done what all cars do when there is no oil in the engine. It had seized. I think you can imagine my concern and my consternation surrounding this, so I will not go into it. After all, I felt it was my failing in not instructing/monitoring the owner/car better. But somehow we got Jenna from there back to college or home. I imagine Adam had something to do with that. I honestly do not recall. I do recall that I did get the garage where they took it to buy the car for $800.00. And since the lawsuit had settled, we were able to buy Jen a new 1994 Honda Civic. A car that would become legendary. And we did the new car ceremony up right. I convinced her we were getting another used Hyundai, but when we got to Hennessey Honda on Highway 92 at 575, there on the showroom floor was a new Civic with a big red bow on it. It was kind of a cool thing you see in the movies, and a thing all parents would love to do for their children.

Professionally, I was still a lost puppy. I was still with DIC, and it was horrible. It was this moment when Carolyn showed me my future. At dinner one evening after James had gone off to play she said, "Jim, you love teaching. You love teaching Sunday School and the children do not think you are a goof-ball. Why don't you go over to Kennesaw State and see what it would take to turn your degree in architecture into a degree in teaching?" Funny, as I look back I do not remember being the least bit skeptical. I thought it was a brilliant suggestion … absolutely brilliant. And within a week I headed over to KSU and sat down with an admissions counselor. It would take about two years depending on courses and dedication. I could enroll in the '93 Summer Quarter. We looked at elementary education which, interestingly, I rejected out of hand. I was a not going to teach babies! It was to be middle school at least or possibly high school. As we compared my transcript from STI it looked like I would be able to finish most quickly if I pursued

Middle Grades Math/Science, so that was the direction I chose. You know us Morrises … if nothing else, we are expedient.

I was going to radically change the direction of my life. Everything I had worked for up to this point was going to be cast aside … all of my work at Southern Tech, two decades of clawing my way to get an architectural license and joining AIA and NCARB, two decades of "climbing the corporate ladder" and then falling off and hitting the ground in spectacular fashion. But what I realized at this moment of crossroads was that I had NOTHING professionally to show for twenty years of work and clawing and climbing. I say professionally because personally I had reaped rewards. I had a beautiful wife, two great children, we had had shelter and cars and food and clothes. All of this is a lot more than most people have in this world. So, for that I was thankful, but professionally I had nothing to show for those years. So I began my new direction and have never, not once, looked back. Carolyn's advice was the best advice I had ever gotten in my life.

My first stop was a dinner over near Northside Hospital with Robert Shelor. He was disappointed and pleaded a little but knew it was futile and that I was undeterred. I knew, just knew in my heart somehow, this was the way to go. I immediately applied to Cobb County Schools to be a substitute teacher and went on the hunt for subbing jobs. Again fate intervened. It so happens that a high school friend of my brother Bill and his wife Janie (Beverly Jane Tipton) from way down in Canal Zone, Dotti Whitlow, was the Assistant Principal at Daniel Middle School. I contacted Ms. Whitlow, and I was quickly in a classroom teaching mostly middle school math, but there were some social studies classes too. Meager though it was, some living money was coming in. My subbing ended one day when I was assigned to a BD (Behavior Disordered) class at East Cobb Middle. A child, who was as big as me, walked in, saw me and not his usual teacher, and threw a desk across the room! I suddenly understood how woefully underprepared I was and ended my subbing career before someone got hurt. And then God stepped in … yes, I believe that … and lent us another hand. For some reason, Mt. Bethel church was not pleased with their Associate Minister and his relationship with the lady who was leading the Sunday School program. They had to let her go. There was an education opening, and they offered me the position of Director of Children and Youth Education. I jumped at the opportunity, and on June 30th I was hired at Mt. Bethel. "And that began my Preacher phase." (To paraphrase a quote by Dustin Hoffman in *Little Big Man*)

I jumped right into the job even though I had absolutely no idea what the job was. It was truly a learn as you go deal. I met Steve Sheffield who led the athletic programs at the church. I worked closely with Reverend Sam Halverson and his sidekick Cathy Elgar. It was Cathy's brother that was one of the Sunday Schoolers that Lo, the Angel of the Lord, had found out information about. Also, and much later, I would teach Cathy's son in the Fifth Grade. Working with the youth also was one Scott Cleaveland, but I am not sure if he was part of the staff or not. I do know he was one of the nicest guys there. I met the ever present man who ran the kitchen, Downey Walker. A person who was going to be a great help and inspiration was a Diaconal Minister, Jan Durham. And the gruff but kindly man in charge of the church finances, Jim Beddow. The church staff was one of the most interesting and eclectic collection of characters I have ever met.

As the job unfolded I made a few boo-boos. One was to throw out what looked to me like trash downstairs in one classroom. As it turned out it was some kind of tree made of refuse that the teacher was using to teach children. She came to my office and gave me an earful. She was a large lady with a fiery temper. I apologized and tried to make amends, but there was really nothing I could do. I was also in charge of ordering Sunday School materials for the various classes. I messed that up once and had to return and reorder their booklets, but I generally did not screw up too badly. My twenty years in business served me well in navigating the hidden pitfalls of a new, sort of undefined and amorphous job. Steve and I climbed all over the church from the steeple to the mechanical room. I saw that the elevator had not been serviced or inspected in years and got that done. The first crazy thing I can remember doing was that fall at preschool carpool. It was near Halloween, and I dressed up as a pirate and was out helping and greeting children as they arrived. Another fun and humbling morning was when I was invited to come to a preschool classroom full of four year olds and talk about Noah. I carefully crafted my talk so it would be funny and engaging and informative. The big Sunday time came, and I sat in a too small chair and arrayed in front of me were about ten shiny and scrubbed faces looking up expectantly. I launched into my talk … not too long … not too short. And if you are a teacher or you have ever talked to children, you can tell when you have grabbed them. And this morning there was one little guy sitting up close to the front and just a little to my left, and I *had* this young man! He was engaged and fascinated and watching my every movement and was totally getting me. I was awesome! At the end, I asked if there were any questions or things they wanted to say, and his little hand shot up. Yes! This was going to be the best question and answer session ever! I called on him and he asked, "Mister, what are those silver balls in your mouth?" He was referring to my two silver crowns I had gotten a couple of years before, and they were what had engaged him … not my talk or my great delivery or the humor I had thrown in. All he saw were my two crowns. Humbled again … by a four-year-old. Another lesson learned.

After a couple of months, it was obvious I needed help. I could not single handedly cover all the bases especially on Sunday morning. I got approval to hire an assistant. The church advertised, and I met several applicants, mostly older ladies except for one. A lady came in and seemed perfect for the job. She was high energy and very engaging. I got permission to hire her. Her name was Carol Sumrell, and she was the slimmed down version of the lady whose trash tree I had thrown out. I did not know this until months later when she shared this tidbit with me. I was embarrassed of course, and she reminded me of that every time I got "the big head." But, we worked together well and did some really good things for the church and for the children.

At Mt. Bethel I was able to stretch my creative talents, and Rev. Jan Durham opened the first opportunity for me to really employ my architectural background, my visual and spatial abilities and wrap it all up in the Christmas Story. Somehow Jan had gotten a video tape a church had made in which they recreated the town of Bethlehem the night of Jesus's birth. I saw the video, and I immediately envisioned our *Mt. Bethel Journey to Bethlehem.* I will describe it to you as if you are walking through the journey. It began in the church gym/auditorium. This was where the crowd would que up. They would walk through the gym doors near the elevator. This was the outskirts of Bethlehem. Here they could contribute if the wished, and it was here the money changers would give them a few silver (plastic) coins to use in the market. They would then step into the elevator for the one floor trip down to "the city." When the door opened all their senses were assaulted. The light was dim. There was incense burning, and there were two of my big senior high boys in Roman military garb yelling to "move along ... move along." The travelers would then move down the sloping hallway and be forced by the scenery to turn left into the market. The market was my Sunday School room. It was a large space and we used 1x2 wood pieces and duct tape to form partitions which were then either covered with sheets or roll paper and painted and made to form little open shops. It was somewhat of a maze, and the traveler could not see all the way through the market. The various stalls were occupied by volunteers from adult Sunday School classes who filled their spaces with rugs, or pottery, or cloth, or food. The lights were low and back lights and small lamps were used to make a very close feeling. As you came out of the market into the hall again you came upon a prophet (Rev. Sam Halverson) speaking to children about the coming of Christ. You turned to the left and in the classrooms on the hall you found the inn. Inside you could see revelers drinking and laughing. There was a person at the door who would not let you in the room as the Inn was "full." The inn keeper ushered you along the hall. Down the hall in the last classroom on the left was the stable where you would encounter Mary, Joseph and the baby Jesus. For the three nights we did this, we tried to have a real

Mom and Dad and a real baby playing Jesus. I recall one night the baby was upset and crying, just as Jesus must have done. Then the traveler would turn to the right and there was an exit door to the parking lot, but just before leaving the person would encounter the Wise Men who would ask where they could find the baby. Upon exiting there was a star. It was a Christmas light star hanging on a light pole and shining down. It was one of the coolest things I have ever master-minded in my life. Carolyn and Jenna played parts. I was there in my guise as *Ishmael the camel dung salesman* with a sack full of what looked like dung. My face was smeared with brown makeup. James was my apprentice, *Hairball*. Yes, there are pictures. For the most part everyone played their parts ... that was the golden rule ... do not break character and almost everyone stayed in character perfectly.

At KSU I started my first education courses and was hooked from the very beginning. My first quarter I took Math 502, Mathematics for Elementary School teachers, under Dr. Marion Fox (and she was). The book by the same name as the course is on the shelf of the credenza behind me. It was not only an awesome course, it was fascinating to me and I got a 4.0 in the class! As the small dedication in the front of the book written on January 17th, 1994, says, "I got a 4.0 and loved learning." As I worked through courses I needed to take, Calculus II and Analytic Geometry were on the list. Both at Clemson and STI as you will recall, I had been miserable at Calculus, and here I had to take it again. I was terrified and did everything I could to avoid the class, but an interesting thing happened. Maybe it was my maturity and my older brain, maybe it was my sheer dedication and love of finally being able to pursue what I felt I was destined to do since I had been at Clemson almost a quarter of a century before, but I took the course and passed it with an A! And it made sense! Still to this day, I credit the professor, and I still at the ripe old age of 73 have not had anyone jump out at me from a dark alley and tell me to "integrate this Calculus problem or I'm going to shoot you!" They still yet may, but I strongly doubt it. I stand by my belief that Calculus is a waste of good numbers and oxygen. I did have another math class that was very cool. It was a night class from 8 until 10:30 which unto itself made the class memorable, but in order for us to feel the pain of being a ten-year-old trying to learn multiplication and division, we had to perform all our calculations in Base 4 or Base 6. Try to divide in Base 7 some time. You will feel like you are in third grade again! Now that was informative and an innovative professor, and while I cannot recall his name, I always strove to emulate his ability as a <u>real</u> teacher.

12.

In 1994 James was eleven. This year he graduated from East Valley Elementary and was now attending East Cobb Middle School. I recall this distinctly because in Band he elected to play the bass fiddle. Again, pictures abound of him and his instrument. There is one where he looks every bit the jazz musician in black with sunglasses and his fiddle. It was around now that he informed us that he was no longer "Jamie," he wanted to be known as "James." And so he is to this day.

This was also the year he and I took our spring break overnight Two Boys Trip to Huntsville, Alabama, to see the space exhibits there. While there we found out about Space Camp. James decided he wanted to go the Space Camp over the summer. I do not know if he was that serious when he made the comment, but later, in the summer, he went. We all trekked over to Huntsville that summer and left him. I have to be honest. That was tough. It dredged up all kinds of memories of being left at Clemson and memories of being in Pensacola in the Navy and feelings of abandonment. But, he said he wanted this and … well, there you go. A couple of nights later we got a phone call from a very homesick little boy wanting to come home. And rightly or wrongly, we did not let him. I am not sure how he feels about that today, but we made him stay in Huntsville. And he did. And he toughed it out. And James has a picture of his Space Camp class with him in the front, and he is smiling. Being a parent is fraught with decisions like that, but in those situations you can only make the best decision you can, given the light you have. Hopefully you land more in the plus column than in the minus column. And when you land one in the minus column, you try to learn from it.

I need to forgive The Colonel and his Lady. They did the best they could with their limitations and life experience. What seems so clear to me as far as how to treat your child, must not have been clear to them. They are both dead now. Mom in 2013 and Dad in 2020 and I need to let them rest in peace. And I have to request of you Gentle Reader, do not judge me too harshly. I made the best decisions for my family I could by the light I was given and with my limitations which are myriad.

Another adventure James and I had that year was Choir Tour. This was "Debbie the choir lady's" senior high choir, and the choir tour was a choir tour and mission trip. I finagled somehow to let James come along. The leaders were Debbie Pierce, Scott Cleaveland and me. The tour was basically to travel by bus all the way up to Minneapolis St. Paul in Minnesota and then come back. We (not me … the choir) sang in old folks homes and churches along the way and we handed out little cards with *The Rules for Being Human* on them. I still carry one of those cards in my wallet today. Each card had a little tiny angel pin attached to it. There is one in my cuff link case in my dresser I think … maybe not. Basically we left Marietta and headed up toward Nashville and then up toward St. Louis. I recall we all went up in The Gateway Arch in St. Louis. It was kind of interesting but really exactly what one would expect. And the view is of mostly flat land and the Mississippi. Now that I think of it, that day we ate in some kind of a big building with a bunch of different restaurants in it. It was about three stories and other than eating, I have no idea why we even stopped there. We detoured over to Chicago and then over to Minneapolis.

On the trip, I recall we stopped at a church one night to sleep. That is where we spent most nights … just bunking at any church that would have us. But this particular church was different. I remember Scott Cleaveland as being quite the rabble-rouser, and on this particular night he roused the rabble! He got a bunch of the boys, yes me and James included, to go exploring. It was late at night, the church was dark, and we headed off to all the parts of the church that no one gets to see. We found a ladder in the narthex that led upward. So, being boys … on this particular night there were no men or counselors involved … we were all just "boys" looking for trouble. And so we climbed the ladder to the first level. It was a room off the balcony and it was full of old hymnals, chairs and dust, but there was another ladder that led even more upward. So, we climbed it. At the ceiling was a trap door of sorts. Picture all of us climbing this rickety ladder and the first guy, probably Scott, reaching the three foot by three foot, white, painted plywood door. Ooooooooh … spooky! So we nudge the piece of plywood aside and shine our flashlights into the creepy, forbidden chamber. It was a belfry only there were no bells! There were loudspeakers and wires leading down to, I am sure, a control panel somewhere. And there was bat guano everywhere! It was so nasty! We ended up getting it on our hands and feet and clothes … I guess you could say, we got everything we deserved! And again humbled, we climbed down and cleaned up and were very tired the next morning.

The trip continued up to Minneapolis and we visited the Mall of America. Which was a very big deal in 1994. Probably not so much today. But they had a carousel and an ice skating rink (cute, Minneapolis, Minnesota, one of the coldest places on earth in the winter – which lasts from August to June up there – and the mall needed an ice skating rink … like they had no place to ice skate the other ten months of the year! I did visit one of America's largest video tape stores and bought the video *Captain Blood* with Errol Flynn. It is around here somewhere I think. I cannot imagine I got rid of it.

When we left Minneapolis/St. Paul we headed down the Mississippi River. I recall this because we ended up in one of my favorite towns, Hannibal, Missouri. It was one of my favorites because of one man, Mark Twain. Mark Twain, Samuel Clemens, was in my opinion one of the truest geniuses ever born. His ability to see a human foible, distill it down to its essence and the present it with a humorous barb that made it stick in your mind was nothing short of, as I said, genius. I often find comfort in his over a century old observations on everything from the church to government to education to growing up. I say with pride that I have read either all of or at least parts of everything he has written or has been attributed to him. I must admit *his* autobiography is some tough reading, and I have yet to make a real dent in it. There are two volumes of his complete work given to me by my son James in 1997 for my 47th birthday along with other tomes and collections of his witticisms. I cherish him and them. There is a picture of James and me in Hannibal somewhere.

We made trips to Georgia Southern to see Jenna and her sorority women. It was usually more so Jenna and Adam than Jenna and sorority women. We had developed a routine by now. We would go down on Friday and arrive in time to take them to dinner. We would feed everyone who wanted to eat with us steak and whatever. We would spend the night sometimes. In the morning we would slip Jenna twenty bucks and go on down to Savannah for the day and Saturday night. And then come back on Sunday.

I do recall one trip down where we actually met Jenna and Adam on Saturday and took them with James and Carolyn and me to Savannah. When we arrived it was threatening big rain. We ended up eating dinner at the Marriott … I think it was the Marriott … all the way down at the end of River Street. Anyway, we drank and Carolyn got a little tipsy which everyone enjoyed immensely. Everyone always enjoys when Carolyn gets a little loose! I recall she was making fun of the new mascot for the summer Olympics that were to be held in Atlanta. She called it Squid and was making hand chopping waves in the air. Everyone was in stitches. After we got done with dinner (and more drinks … Carolyn was rolling by now!) we headed out to find a place to stay for the night. The whole trip was kind of spur of the moment, and I had made no reservations. So, out we headed into a pouring rain to find a place to stay. We finally did find a place … I think it was the River Street Inn … anyway all they had was a single two story room with the second story overlooking the first, but we could all squeeze in, and it was very cool because … it had a ghost! Yes, a real, bona fide ghost and his name was Hank. So all the rest of the evening with rain pouring down and lightening flashing and thunder crashing we hunted Hank. Of course it was great fun to scare each other, and the girls would squeal with delight with each fright. And there was book on the coffee table where you would write about your stay in the room, and of course everyone had written about Hank, or the lack thereof. So, I settled down and put all my creative juices to work and I wrote a fanciful tale of Hank and our exploits!

Carolyn and I took a breath and escaped to Highlands, North Carolina, for a long weekend that year. We had heard of a hotel "designed in the Frank Lloyd Wright style" (it was not) and we decided to check it out. Carolyn and I still laugh at that weekend. It was so nice and cool up there we slept with the windows open. Our bed was situated with the headboard right below the windows, and it was some of the best sleep I had ever had. We awoke that first Saturday morning feeling the cool of the North Carolina mountains flowing into the room along with the beep-beep-beep of a garbage truck backing up right under our window! Then the wonderful sound of the inn's trash dumping into the maw of the truck along with the delicious smells of the inn's garbage. Ahh yes, Highlands, North Carolina. But we did not let that deter us. Ever the adventurers we forged ahead to a spectacularly lack luster day. I guess we had envisioned a Mini-Ashville. Highlands was not. But we passed the day window shopping and holding hands and laughing about Frank Lloyd Wright. We found a quaint restaurant highly recommended by the inn's owners to have dinner. Again, we were surprised. While the food was okay, the county that Highlands was in was a dry county … meaning unless you brought your own bottle of wine, you got nothing. Well, we had not and so we got no wine. Ahh, but the saving grace was the dessert to come. And when they drought the dessert cart around for us to select our dessert from, we were a little surprised. Usually the dessert cart is a show piece. You look a cart over, inform the waitress of your choice, and he or she goes and gets it from the kitchen. Well, not in this Highlands restaurant. In Highlands, the one you select on the cart is the one you get! So these deserts that have been sitting out in a corner somewhere and then wheeled around and breathed on by every person in the place and pointed at and Lord knows what, is then selected by you and, Voila! It is sitting on your table! You have to admire the efficiency of the system. There was no wasted motion in that Highlands restaurant. And that was our last stay in Highlands, North Carolina.

That was also the year I dabbled in "The Ministry." Working in the church, like everything a Morris does, I went "whole hog." And that included taking a course at Emory University (located on the dark side of the moon — try going there some day and you will see what I mean). Randy Mickler would have liked nothing better than me to follow in his footsteps. So, I looked into becoming a Diaconal Minister. A diaconal Minister in the Methodist Church is kind of a "minister lite," or sort of a draftsman to be more on point. A draftsman does all the things an Architect does except he cannot officially seal a document. A Diaconal Minister can do all the things a minister can do as long as a minister is there to give it his/her blessing. I took one course. It was bullshit. You see by late in 1994 I was heavy into my course work at KSU to become a teacher, and I was loving it! I had a 4.0 GPA and was killing the curriculum. For the first time in my life I was truly succeeding academically and my enthusiasm was obvious. I was seeing myself in a new light. I was not some red-headed stepchild. I was my genuine self; doing what I was supposed to do. The whole minister thing was a sham. Again, I harken to the movie *Little Big Man* with Dustin Hoffman. In the movie he goes through many guises, one of which is a minister and that ultimately ends in his statement, "And that was the end of my preacher phase." In late 1994 I was approaching that point. I saw preachers for what they really are … hucksters, carnival barkers. P.T. Barnum would have made a great minister if he had aimed just a little lower. Rarely do you meet a real *minister*. Most are just *preachers*. I close with a criticism by Samuel Clemens, "If Christ were here, there is one thing he would not be - a Christian."

That 1994 year had a lot going on. Steve Sheffield, the man in charge of athletics and other miscellaneous Mickler gofer stuff and I rewrote Wednesday night supper offerings. Steve ran a children's movie, and I ran Study Hall helping children with their homework. We worked with Scott Cleveland and Reverend Halverson and Carol Sumrell and took a group of children to Savannah to learn about the Wesley brothers and Methodism. That included a treat of Low Country Boil on the beach. That is still my favorite thing to cook when we have guests over and whenever I make it, it carries me back to that long weekend. Among other things there was a summer choir production where all they sang was popular songs. One of the songs they came up with was *California Girls* by The Beach Boys. And Debbie's husband, who was kind of a smartass in my opinion, came to me, the man who taught the High School Sunday School class, and asked if I could have some of the girls from my class come out during the *California Girls* song and parade around. Well, I immediately thought this was just about the worst idea I have ever heard for all the reasons I know you are thinking right now, but I immediately hit upon a parallel idea and agreed to supply the girls … pimp that I am. So the night came and the choir is belting out the song, and it comes to the part where they sing, "I wish they all could be California … girls" and out from backstage comes me and a bunch of my High School <u>boys</u> all dressed in wigs and lipstick, in drag and we started sashaying all over the stage! Well, we were a huge hit as I recall. The good Reverend was in the front row, and he got special attention. The house came down! And, for me, a tradition was born that I was to repeat later in talent shows at Mountain View Elementary and Mt. Bethel Elementary. But I get ahead of myself, and I hasten to add, again, it was a different time … a less critical time.

This year was our second Journey to Bethlehem, and I thought it was a stunning success. We had a great turnout from the local community. In fact, I remember Ms. Dru Sadler came with her family. She touched my heart by coming. Carolyn and Jenna took up parts and of course James and I were in our full regalia. The whole event was much better, and we improved tremendously over our first year. We had Reverend Sam teaching children and the Baby Jesus was crying and pooping and Mary and Joseph were doing their thing and the Wise men were there, and everyone was in character … and that is where the rub came in. You see the first year the good Reverend Doctor Randall Mickler stayed far away from the whole production. He was not one to take a risk. But when he saw how successful it was, he wanted in, so I gave him a part. He was to be one of the Wise Men. Randy Mickler was playing the part of a Wise Man the second night, and James was working by his side. After the night was over, James reported to me that Mickler was handing out Mt. Bethel Church brochures and saying things like, "Yeah, Johnson Ferry Baptist Church doesn't have anything like this." I made a tough, and probably fatal for Journey to Bethlehem decision. I went to Rev. Mickler the next day and told him that others wanted to play the part of a Wise Man and would he mind stepping aside for that coming night and let others play. He agreed. Only later that day he came to me and said, "You just fired me didn't you?" I agreed I did. We were not on such great terms after that. And Journey was ultimately doomed. I think it lasted maybe one more year after that. I had left in the fall of 1995 and Carol Sumrell tried her best to make it happen, but I had doomed it that night in December of 1994, and probably doomed myself at Mt. Bethel.

A final comment on that year. On December 26th we lost Don Swift to cancer. Don Swift was Marybelle's husband. Marybelle was my father's youngest sister and my dear, dear Aunt who hosted and counseled Carolyn through a rough time. Don was one of the kindest men I ever knew. I have mentioned him several times thus far but his remarkable sense of humor and ready laugh will always stay with me. There is a picture of him in the bookcase one day when we visited California and you can see his ready wit in him in that single picture. I miss him and Marybelle to this day. He was buried in Dallas, Texas, and Carolyn and I went out for the funeral and for our love for Marybelle. Carolyn tells me The Colonel and my mom were there too although I have no clear recollection of even making the trip much less attending the funeral … interesting.

13.

1995 … now this was quite a year! I have been making notes for each year on a pad of paper, and this year is crammed with all kinds of memories and special events. I am perceiving that my constant writing challenge is to not hurry through my memories just to be done. As I read Stephen King and David Baldacci, I am fascinated how they are able to take their time and develop a scene and a character. Being able to do that takes talent and patience … two things I lack. I have always had a problem especially with the patience thing … hurry to be done so can I do the next thing. I did it when I was in the sixth grade if you recall when I A, B, C'd, C, B, A'd the standardized test because I was bored, and did it just to be done. I also did it every time I would get a new model to build. Plane, car, boat it did not matter. I would hurry just to be finished. Then I was bored again and looking for my next challenge. Perhaps the letters ADD come into your mind. I would not be surprised, but I am trying not to do that with this piece of writing. As I write this morning, it is now March 3rd, 2023. I began writing almost three years ago in 2020 as the COVID pandemic was starting. But, enough. Let us continue our sojourn in the past.

As I said 1995 was quite a year. I guess on the home front it was special because it was the year Jenna graduated from Georgia Southern … in only three years and a quarter I might add. She is brilliant. And 1995 was the year she and Adam got married. I student taught and then graduated from KSU, quit the church and took my first job teaching. Yes, a year packed with experiences and adventures.

I realize this is all out of chronological sequence, but by now you, gentle reader, are used to my needing to move around within a year to get to some events that are way more important in my mind than others. So, apologies. Anyway, Adam had graduated from Georgia Southern in August and our darling little girl graduated in December. I recall going down and watching Jenna graduate. It was on December 10th, and it was held in the Hanner Field House. It was cold outside and very, very warm inside, but we pulled it off. I honestly do not have that many memories of that particular day/days. But we got Jenna graduated with no debt, thanks to Carolyn … and now the wedding, which was six days away.

The wedding was scheduled for the 16th of December. And it was going to be a grand affair. But, not to worry, I had taken financial precautions. Back in the spring of the year, when Jenna was home to do her student teaching at … I think Smitha Middle School … ahh well, it matters not … I called a family meeting of Carolyn and Jenna to discuss the cost of the wedding. We gathered at the kitchen table at Millbrook Trace. I was going to make it as formal as possible to reflect the gravity of the occasion. And we discussed the dress and flowers and photography and the reception and open or closed bars, the bell ringers, the music and paying of the preachers – as there were to be two of them – Randy Mickler and our real minister, Alice Rogers – and every aspect of the wedding I could think of. We had papers, and I made lists, and we discussed and put numbers to everything. The ladies listened and worked with me, and we haggled a bit, but in the end we had a budget we all could live with … meaning me. I was totally satisfied. I had done my "businessman thing" as Unca' Nelson would say. And I am proud to say that that was the last time money was mentioned relative to the wedding. And that was because the girls left the table and went off and did exactly what they wanted to do and totally ignored the meeting and my stupid lists and numbers. It's true. Ask Carolyn or Jenna.

The day of the wedding approached. Tuxes had been secured. Dresses bought. In-laws and family were safely in town. God bless Marybelle Swift. And the sanctuary of the yellow church at 4385 Lower Roswell Road was resplendently decorated for Christmas. If you go to the church today, you will see a sanctuary that has a port-cochère just to the left of what is now the huge, ghastly main sanctuary. The building with the port-cochère is where the wedding was held. I cannot really explain how very, very beautiful my daughter was that day. There is a wedding album somewhere. Jenna may have it or James, the keeper of all history, may have it or if Carolyn and I have passed, it may have been "black bagged." But Jenna, or Mary Virginia Morris as she was properly named, was an angel in white. And matching her was the weather. It was a beautiful day. I mean a stunningly beautiful December day. The sky was clear as a bell and a deep blue. It was cold, but not unreasonably so. And my daughter's beauty out shown the day. My darling wife Carolyn was absolutely glowing with pride and also a beauty that day. I was so proud to be her husband. At that moment on that day it was absolute proof that Carolyn had "turned my life from a tavern into a temple." James and I were decked out in matching black tuxes. We were quite a pair. Lord, I love that boy.

There were several moments from that day that I recall with clarity. One was a photograph I have on my desk at this moment. It was before the wedding, and Jenna was standing on some stairs. I leaned over and kissed her. The picture on my desk is one of three pictures in a single frame. The first is me holding her. She has to be maybe eighteen months. The second was taken at Wheeler High School, and we are in a hall waiting for a chorus concert she is to be in, and I leaned over and said something to her. The third is the picture taken the moment I kissed her cheek. She is looking directly into the camera and about to take the biggest leap of her life. She is beautiful … always has been … always will be.

Another moment was just the two of us. I am sure there were others around, but at this moment, there was just her and me. I leaned over and said to her that if she wanted out and did not want to get married today, I would take her, and we would leave right now with no questions asked. Of course she did not take me up on it. She knew Adam Blackwell was a good man, and all these over twenty-eight years later, he has proved himself as a good man.

I think the third moment I want to highlight was when Adam was saying his vows. The preacher, Rev. Mickler I believe … Reverend Alice Rogers gave Jenna her vows and Rev. Mickler gave Adam his vows … told Adam what to say and Adam, bless his heart, started crying. Oh, he got through his vows to Jenna, but he cried all the way through them. And I honestly believe the tears were genuine tears of joys not fear or anything else. They were tears of sheer joy. Of course at that moment he melted the hearts of every lady at the wedding. There is video of the wedding somewhere if it has not disintegrated with age. Find it and watch him giving his vows. It is precious.

Of course there was a wonderful reception at The Pavilion on Johnson Ferry Road just above the intersection with Lower Roswell Road, but don't go looking for it. It is long gone and replaced with an office building. Lord knows what the reception cost, but you know what? Today it does not matter. The memory of that reception, planned out by Carolyn and Jenna lives in pictures and memories and the cost does not. There is a lesson in there somewhere … from the balloon animal maker (my contribution to the children who were there) to Adam and Jenna's first dance song, *Chapel of Love* by the Dixie Cups, it was a celebration of new life. For Jenna's and my dance, the father/daughter dance, I chose poorly. I chose the Rolling Stones's song *Satisfaction*. It was a fun rollicking song, but if I had it to do over I would choose something by Peter, Paul and Mary or John Denver. But, I do not get a do over and there is a lesson in there also … I was too late smart as The Colonel would say. But the whole wedding was beautiful. I mean amazingly beautiful … the sanctuary decorated for Christmas … the bridesmaids … Carolyn … my baby Jenna … just beautiful!

This was also the year I student taught. Student teaching is the last step before graduation, and it was divided into two parts. The first part is an observation portion, and the second part is when you actually student teach. My vision for me being a middle grades math/science teaching student at KSU was to do my student teaching in a middle school teaching math or science … duh. But the man in charge of assignments as to who taught where, assigned me to Mountain View Elementary School in a fifth grade classroom. Writing this, it is amazing to me how that one decision by a person I did not even know could affect my life for over twenty years (and beyond). Needless to say, I visited him and voiced my objection to the assignment he had made, but he held fast and would not change his decision. Did he somehow know something? I cannot imagine how. I was simply just one of many teacher hopefuls that he had to place, and he had placed me and that was the end of that. So, one early morning in January I walked into Mountain View Elementary School. All the *real* teachers were streaming in and signing in, and I was in awe of them. Yes, I know it sounds funny, but I was honestly in <u>awe</u> of them. They were all talking and laughing and carrying their books and coffee and were getting ready after their Christmas Break to teach children. Actually, this was a teacher work day before the children arrived the next day so it was a little more relaxed, but I could not tell the difference in a "work day" and a real day yet.

I sat in the little lobby occasionally greeted by teachers coming in the door. Then the secretary – if I was good I could tell you her name but it is lost to history – who always took care of me from that moment until I eventually left in 2001. Anyway, the secretary came and got me, and I went in to meet Mr. Jim Oveby, the principal. Mr. Oveby had been a kindergarten teacher for years and was now a principal. He was very cool. His assistant principal was a woman named Hillary Straka. They were a heck of a team, and I credit a lot of my successes to the two of them. They both shepherded me and took care of me and elevated me as you will see. After some chitchat, we walked out of the office and up a ramp to a second floor. The school, which is gone now and the land now has a shopping center on it, was located on Sandy Plains Road just south of Shallowford Road. The

address of 3420 Sandy Plains Road will put you on the elevated plot of ground where the school stood. The rising entrance roadway from Sandy Plains Road with the two curving retaining walls on each side is almost the same as it was when I first arrived in 1995. Principal Oveby took me up the ramp and down the "Fifth Grade Hall," and we waited outside a classroom for the teacher who was to be my mentor teacher. We stood and two teachers came down the hall. I recall it as if it were yesterday. One of the women was older than the other. Her name was Ms. Devoe I was to learn later. She is still a good friend I see at my haircutting place sometimes. The other woman was an attractive, petite blond. I held my breath. Principal Oveby introduced me to my mentor teacher, Ms. Grace Cohn, the petite blond. I was thrilled. I knew this was going to be a good relationship.

Grace and I got along very well in my opinion and I learned a lot from her. In fact, if you had seen her room in 1995 and my room in 2016 you would immediately see the similarities: desks arranged in a U shape with five or six to a row. All the teams were color coded and you changed locations, teammates and color codes every nine weeks. She introduced me to two of my favorite elementary books: *The Kid in the Red Jacket* and *The Phantom Tollbooth*. I taught *The Phantom Tollbooth* every year I taught except one, and that was the year I dipped down to get a fourth grade class and then looped them up. (The book is actually on the shelf in the living room on the fiction side under J for Norman Juster, the author … he was an architect by profession! If you have never read it, it is great fun for adults too.) Eight years later, when I taught in Liberty County, I taught the *Tollbooth*. One of my children from that class wrote to me almost ten years after teaching him that his sophomore literature professor at Georgia Southern used that same book. It's a classic. One reason Grace and I meshed so well was that she was a very hands-on teacher. She was very much into experiential teaching, and I was that way too. I still firmly believed in the adage: "I hear and I forget. I see and I remember. I do and I understand." And true learning is only evident when experience produces an action. This is my teaching philosophy. I linked that with Howard Gardner's theory of Multiple Intelligences and taught to children's strengths. But I am getting carried away and far afield. However, you are going to see examples of this approach as I tell teaching stories. My advisor from KSU was Dr. Marj Economopolis. She was to become another mentor and friend in years to come.

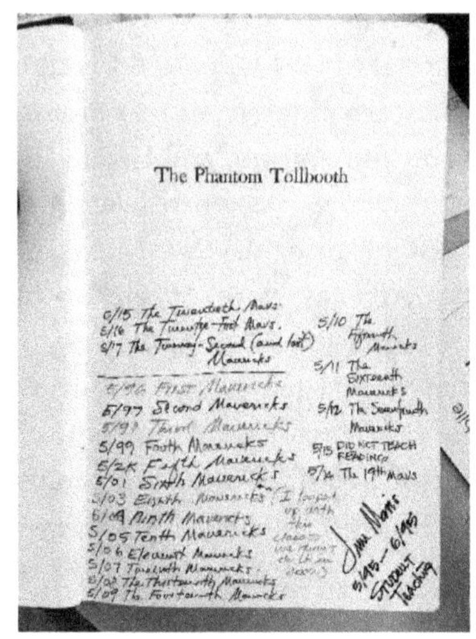

The KSU plan was a student was to do their preliminary teaching in one school and their secondary, or real student teaching, in another school, but I was fortunate and got to do both at Mountain View. I do not know if Dr. Economopolis intervened or Jim Oveby intervened or what, but I got to work under Grace Cohn for almost six months. Her influence over me was profound and as you will read, I fell in love with Mountain View and their crazy staff!

As student teaching drew to a close, I took the TCT, Teacher Certification Test. It was a walk in the park so to speak. At the same time Marj Economopolis was trying to get me to go on and get a Masters in Teaching while I was "in the groove." And so I took the GRE. That test was significantly more strenuous than the TCT, but after taking the Architectural Licensing Exam most tests like that were handled with careful preparation and a confidence that comes with age. I'll tell you now that I did enroll in the Master's program. In fact, in the coming years I enrolled in the Master's program a couple of more times. I think I was trying to repeat that initial KSU experience, that initial thrill of going back to college, those initial successes when I returned to the safety of a campus, of walking the buildings with their academic smell and learning exciting new ideas from people one respects. It was not to be. Jenna summed it up after she got her Masters some years later when she said, "A Master's Degree program is not about learning, it's about just touching the bases." And that was so true in my experience. But I was now forty-five and needed to start earning a living, so *touching bases* held no thrill for me. I wanted my very own classroom. I wanted my very own students. I wanted to teach!

I graduated in June from KSU with a perfect 4.0 GPA! I had NEVER experienced that kind of academic success EVER in my life. I was smart! STI helped me discover that I had real marketable abilities, and KSU helped me discover that I really was intelligent. And the icing on the cake was I was elected by the professors at KSU the 1995 Outstanding Kennesaw State University Middle Grades Student! As a gift KSU gave me a New York Public Library Desk Reference book. It's on a shelf downstairs. I smile at this thought because 1995 was in the very early fledgling years of the internet. People still gave people big reference books, like encyclopedias, full of information. But be that as it may, at that moment I truly felt I had, at last, found my real calling. I had felt I was meant to be a teacher as far back as 1969, but I had to take the long path to get to where I finally was. That path had made me a husband to a fantastic woman, a father to two wonderful children, registered architect, a Sr. V.P., a preacher (of sorts) and finally a teacher. Reflecting, I would not change that path that lead me there. Each event grew me into the person I was. And now I had to get a job!

Being the cutting edge new teacher freshly minted from KSU, I made a video portfolio to distribute. It still exists! In fact, I just watched it with Carolyn and it has held up pretty well I'm proud to say … meaning the philosophies of teaching I espoused in the video and the examples I gave were my guiding principles for over twenty years in the classroom, and I believe them still today. If you discover this video and are able somehow to watch it, I admit I talked too much.

I sent the video along with my résumé to several principals in Cobb and Cherokee. I even had fanciful imaginings of teaching up in the mountains at Rabun Gap Nacoochee School. They never gave/never have given me the time of day. Anyway, I did have a couple of interviews, and I had one bite. A principal named Mary Jo Moffatt at a little school in northern Cobb at 4111 Wesley Chapel Road named Garrison Mill Elementary contacted me, and after some discussion asked me if I would come in. Of course I jumped at the prospect of an interview. I saw great portent in the fact that the address was on Wesley Chapel. You see I was still employed by Mt. Bethel Church at this time and of course Methodism is steeped in the Wesley Brothers and their adventures and misadventures in Savannah, Georgia in the 1700's. I was stoked! And on a very hot and humid July 25th I pulled into the parking lot of Garrison Mill Elementary School. The sky

was a deep blue with a few puffy cumulus clouds reminding me of summer afternoons at Doris and Unca' Bill's before we would head off to the country club to swim. I parked. The waves of heated air were rippling off the parking lot pavement. I recall Principal Moffatt's car was parked under the covered play area out of the sun. I got out, swallowed and walked in to the greatest adventure of my life. As of this writing, the original school is still there.

Ms. Moffatt was very kind, and we talked for over an hour. We talked of her needs, a fifth grade teacher, my background and thoughts on teaching. We ended with her saying the requisite, "I have others to interview. I'll be in touch." But I felt good about the interview and felt good about my chances. After all, Wesley was on my side! On Friday I got the call. I was offered a position teaching fifth grade at Garrison Mill. Needless to say I again jumped at the chance. Thank you Ms. Mary Jo Moffatt wherever you are from the bottom of my heart. She asked me to come in so she could explain what needed to happen and show me what would probably be my classroom. We had another great meeting, then I was off to the sheriff's office in Marietta to be finger printed. If that came back as we expected, I then needed to go by the CCSD, Cobb County School District, office and sign a contract. If all that went smoothly, preplanning for new teachers started in mid-August. And it all did go smoothly, and I was hired by Cobb County ... for the first time. Of course I had to resign from Mt. Bethel Church which was not pretty. Reverend (and I used the term loosely) Mickler was more than a little upset. He saw me as his gofer and minion, and I saw me gone on to a dreamed-of career. There was not much he could do though. I was then free to teach. And the next twenty plus years are history as you are about to read. I did return to try to help with the last, I think it was the last, *Journey to Bethlehem* performance, but there was no heart in it. Mickler declared, "Well, that has about run its course." And it had, because it wasn't about him. By now I hope you have read enough about me to what *Journey* was really about.

In September of 1995 I walked into my very own classroom. One of my first missions was to come up with a class name, and again Carolyn came to the rescue. She suggested The Morris Mavericks, or Morris's Mavericks or just The Mavericks as the class came to be known by parents and students and the schools where I taught. We strove to be mavericks and leaders and iconoclasts while working within the system to lead and affect change. While shopping, Carolyn found a four-foot by six-foot blanket with horses on it. It looked like a tapestry. It too is in the basement, and it proudly hung on the wall in EVERY classroom I taught in. The horses denoted power, grace and beauty. Around the house you will see various statues of horses, some with colts. These were given to me by classes and students I taught over the years. They invoke a great sense of pride in me. I truly feel I made a positive difference in this world ... thanks to Carolyn.

A requirement of the Garrison Mill Administration Vice Principal Linda Bernknopf was to have teachers publish a newsletter every so often to communicate with parents. I smile again at this thought. In the true Morris approach to any assignment, I had to do it to the maximum! And so The Maverick Mailgram was born. The very first one was published on September 7th, 1995. If you look closely at this first Mailgram you will see it was printed on tractor paper which was the cutting edge of printing at the time. The font choices were also limited. Over the generations, the Mailgram was published in a paper form and distributed every other Thursday. Then in the early 2000's it also went online. The Maverick Mailgram, "All The Twice Monthly Maverick News That Is News" as the banner proclaimed starting in 1996, was a labor of love, and it was published every two weeks during every school year for every year I taught school. There are two, three-inch-thick, three-ring binders on the shelf in the basement labeled Maverick Mailgrams I and II. If you will look through them, you will see the development of a teacher, his craft, the technology of the day, and the news of our class. So, before you "black bag" my mailgrams, look through them. I guarantee you will smile and laugh and cry.

I started a couple of other traditions that year. The last eleven Mailgrams of the year were timed to share the *11 Rules for Being Human* that had been on the card we distributed while on that mega Minnesota choir tour. A second tradition I started that first year was to have the students write a letter to themselves. Each student would write a letter from their fifth grade self to their graduating from high school senior self, put it in a self-addressed, stamped envelope and give it me for safe keeping. I then held onto these letters for seven years and then put them in the mail in the late months of their last year in high school. I did this, again in the obsessive-compulsive Morris way, faithfully every year I taught. I am to mail the 2024 batch in a little over a month and the last class's letters will be mailed, and I will have completed my sacred trust begun over twenty-five years ago.

I could spin stories about that first year teaching for pages, but I will not. But I will say four things. 1. Those children are now almost forty years old, and 2. I started a second tradition that first year. I would make a picture of every class I ever taught. I would frame it and when those children came back to visit, I would show them their fifth grade selves and 3. I started a tradition of selecting a Maverick of the Year that first year. You will hear more about it later, but it was a child who had given me and the class everything. I selected the child personally. There was no voting and on the last day they were revealed with an honorary picture designating them the Maverick of the Year (MOY) along with a picture of themselves taken during the year by me. I also had a duplicate of that picture which would also hang in the class room on the Wall of Honor of MOY's. And every year children would strive to be on that wall … or at least that was the theory. It worked some years, and it did not work some years, but being a Morris I pursued it to the very last day of the very last year I taught. 4. When we had ushered those children off on buses that last afternoon of that first year, I walked back to my classroom and cried like a baby. I have not cried after a class since then. I do not know why. I just did not feel the urge after that first class. Those "firsties" were just super special for some reason. They got my tears.

The Two Boys Trip Tradition continued every year. The actual trips and destinations are vivid memories, but the specific years for some are hazy, and I cannot seem to confirm them with calendars. But I will share in correct timeframes the trips as I recall them. I believe the 1995 trip was to Wilmington, North Carolina. We chose that destination because we were on a mission to see the battleship North Carolina. If you ever try to drive from Atlanta to the Outer Banks or the Wilmington coast you will be surprised what a long haul it is. And on our way we stopped and visited a Garrison Mill teacher friend, Ms. Romaine Collin's, family. In Wilmington James and I stayed in a little B&B in town that promised breakfast, and he and I still laugh about that. What we got that second and third morning was a little basket at our door with two muffins in cellophane with two juice boxes. What a hoot! But, we two boys got to tour the battleship North Carolina, and I'm sure visited a cool museum or two.

14.

1996, our country's Bi-Centennial year was another year packed with excitement for our little family. Jenna and Adam were off being old married people, Carolyn left her job and we left Mt. Bethel … and organized religion, there was bombing at the Olympics, a major award, a trip to D.C., a cruise, a talent show and what a year it was. In 1996 my father was the same age as I am today, 72. I find that interesting.

Jenna and Adam honeymooned in the Caribbean on Royal Caribbean and that adventure of theirs in 1996 started a family tradition that continues to this day. When they returned home after Christmas they settled into an apartment Suwanee. Adam went to work for his dad, Toby Blackwell. Toby is one of the nicest men I have ever met. My understanding is that Adam had a rather rough upbringing but Toby got his life under control, remarried a wonderful woman named Paula after his divorce and has matured into, as I said, one of the nicest men I have ever met. And Paula Blackwell is just as, if not more, wonderful.

I want to step out of time at this moment and tell you about an event that just shook our family. Today is Saturday. On Wednesday, March 15th, 2023, Paula Blackwell was accidently shot in a road rage shooting gone wrong. She was an innocent bystander just driving along minding her own business and two men got into an altercation. She has been in and out of surgery for four days and as of right now, Saturday, March 18th, she is expected to recover. She was shot through the back of her car. She has lost her gall bladder and one kidney, but otherwise is expected to make a full recovery. I interject this note here because it will undoubtedly be family lore.

Jenna went to work that fall of 1996 at West Hall Middle School and began her career as a teacher which she is still pursuing today with many accolades, a Master's Degree and awards. Carolyn and I helped them where we could by buying Jenna clothes and computers and whatever else they needed.

It was also the year Carolyn had had all she could take of Randy Mickler and the hypocrisy that was Mt. Bethel Church. So, she quit. The second Morris to walk away from Randy in as many years, and he was not happy. He accused her of theft of church property because she kept copies of church bulletins she had written. Carolyn and I were incensed! We hired an attorney and laid out the facts, and the lawyer fired a letter back to the Administrative Board of Mt. Bethel that very day, and the church "folded like a cheap suit." Needless to say, she and I have been *persona non grata* ever since although we have returned twice for funerals amid whispers. And that was also the moment we both left organized religion. Oh, we tried various other churches. By now Reverend Doctor Alice Rogers, who we still consider our minister and have stayed in contact with, had left Mt. Bethel and moved to her own church in Jackson, Georgia. Scott Cleaveland moved there too. And Carolyn, James and I would travel down there and visit her church. James and Scott Cleaveland and I even did a Charleston retreat with the youth one summer. But we just could not seem to reconcile what she and I both had experienced at Mt. Bethel with organized religion. In its current form it just did not seem like what Jesus had in mind. Again, Mark Twain's famous religion quote, "…the last thing he would be is a Christian." So, we tumbled from church to church and found solace in being a family. By this time another member of Mt. Bethel, Jim Beddow who was the churches accountant, had left. Jim Beddow and Carolyn had gotten along famously as they both were no-nonsense, tell it like it is kind of people. Jim Beddow had started a firm that specialized in forensic accounting and he needed an architect to do some forensic architecture at the site of building in Texas. And so they teamed up and Carolyn began working for herself. We both learned a lot about taxes and companies and incorporation and all kinds of business stuff that year. Overall it was a very successful time for Carolyn. And even though she enjoyed the challenge, being treated as an equal and responsibility, honestly she just was not happy being a hard-charging, independent, entrepreneurial business woman.

Carolyn and James and I went on out first cruise that year. I had no idea what I was doing so we got a travel agent that Jenna and Adam had used to help us set it all up. We went on Royal Caribbean because Adam and Jenna had. That was not very original, but it was me at the time. I knew Adam and Jenna had had an excellent experience, and I did not want to risk our money, so we did the same. I learned a lot of lessons on that first cruise. The first was to research and pick my own cabin. We wanted a view of the ocean so the travel agent suggested a cabin with a window. That sounded good. It was not. It was not a window, but a single porthole about eighteen inches in diameter. Oh, one could see out if one got right up close and stood on the bed. James was in a bunk over our bed and off the wall. He thought it was cool. The second thing was to not get a cabin near an anchor. At each port we were greeted each morning with the anchor chain clanking out of the hawse hole! A third lesson was you do not have to sit at a table at dinner with other people. Our table came with a sullen, fourteen-year-old boy whom I can only guess that the parents did not want at their table. And of course, being the teacher, I tried to include him and make him feel welcome at our table. He was having none of it. So, dinner was rather painful, but lessons were being learned. I'm not sure where we went exactly on the cruise. I think we stopped at Royal Caribbean's private island Labadie in Haiti. The whole private island thing was in its infancy back then, but I believe we did stop there. We also went to Nassau because I remember going to Dunn's River Falls and losing and then finding my glasses as we climbed the falls. We chose this particular time to cruise because the Summer Olympics were being held in Atlanta that year and we decided to get out of town during all that mess. And while we were on the boat we heard about the Olympic Park Bombing on the news on the ship. Carolyn was concerned about Adam and Jenna and "what if." I reassured her there was nothing to be concerned about, and we were not going to try to call them from the Caribbean to check on them. Again, cell phones were not a thing yet, and the internet was just in its infancy. So we cruised on only to discover when we got home that Adam and Jenna were not only in the park that night, but they heard the blast and ran for their lives! So much for reassurances from Jim to Carolyn. Now, I'm sure there is a three ring binder with all this vacation information in somewhere, and I am equally sure when Carolyn and I die it will be "black bagged" with no second thought. And, so you'll know, that is cool with me.

I continued teaching at Garrison Mill for a second year, the '96-'97 school year, and it proved to be very interesting. Unbeknownst to me, Mary Jo Moffatt had sent my name in as a candidate for an award during my first year of teaching. The award was the Sallie Mae First Class Teaching Award. Only one was given out in each state, and in the fall of 1996 I found out I was the winner for the State of Georgia! By now Mary Jo had been replaced with a man whose name I do not recall, but Mary Jo had done this for me. I truly hope I thanked her somewhere along the way. This award came with a trip to Washington, D.C., for me and my family, and it was quite an honor. To me, it reinforced that I had made a good decision to follow Carolyn's advice and pursue a career in teaching. And the award was needed to bolster my confidence in the changing year to come.

I am not sure if we went to D.C. in '96 or '97, but it was a cool trip. Carolyn, James and I flew to Washington. I recall meeting with Speaker of the House Rep. Newt Gingrich, who was from Georgia and very right wing, and a person I did not care for. There is a picture of us somewhere and my distain for the man and his politics, which endures to this day, is all over me in the photograph. The other man in the picture is my "minder" from the Sallie Mae organization making sure I got where I was to go. I also had a chance to meet with Sen. Sam Nunn, but he was called to the Capitol, and I had to meet with a young, not very impressive underling. I recall a dinner where I was presented with a pyramid shaped award. The award is on a table in the living room, and there is a picture taken by Carolyn of James and me sitting at a dinner table as I open the award. There is a look of surprise on my face and a warm, look of admiration on my son's face. It is a touching photograph to me, and one I will always cherish. Other than those memories, I do not have any really keen recollections of that trip … which is interesting to me. I have no recollection of where we stayed, how we got around, how we got from the airport to wherever we stayed and how we got back home … it's interesting the things the mind throws away.

That second teaching year was a year I started to "get out there." I took on a classroom know as an Inclusion Class. Inclusion classes were to become my favorite kind of class in my career. An Inclusion Class meant that there were special needs children of varying abilities mainstreamed in to the classroom with other "normal" fifth graders (if there is really such a thing as a "normal" fifth grader). The class also requires a Special Education co-teacher be in the room to assist and make sure the special needs students are getting what their IEP,

Individual Education Plan, calls for them to have by law. My co-teacher that year was Ms. Romaine Collins. We taught well together I thought, and she taught me the intricacies of an inclusion class, special-ed IEP meetings with parents and how to serve these children. She was patient, and we developed a bond that I believe other teachers became jealous of. Our class put on a play in the cafeteria for parents and other classes who wanted to come. The play was from the book *Where the Wild Things Are*. The children made masks and became wild things as other children narrated and became the hero of the book. Two of my characters Captain Grid and Sam Scalene visited the class. I would slip out of the room on some bogus excuse, sometimes even getting the office to page me to come down to the office, while Ms. Collins watched over the class. Then I would change into my character and reappear in class. I recall on one of my visits that year, when I entered the room and introduced myself one of the children quietly said to another, "That's Mr. Morris!" with a shock. This was an Inclusion Class after all. To which the other student replied, "Just humor him … just humor him." I got a kick out of that!

There was a Garrison Mill Talent Show again that year, and Ms. Collins and I were a hit. We were the closing act, and we were The Blues Brothers. Now you may need to Google the Blues Brothers, Jake (John Belushi) and Elwood (Dan Aykoyd), to really understand me when I say Collins was Jake, and I was Elwood. We had the black suits and ties, hats and I had the briefcase Elwood carried with his harmonica inside. We had all the moves. Collins, a former cheerleader, had the Jake cartwheel down pat, and I made all the Elwood dancing moves as we lip-synced to *Everybody Needs Somebody to Love*. Look it up on YouTube, and you'll get an idea of the evening. It was cool, and it also presented a problem. Some of the fifth grade teachers started talking about how close Collins and I had become. I truly believe they were jealous of our successes. Let me just say, they made it difficult for Collins and me to do our jobs. We went to the no-name principal who was no help. And then Fate interceded once again. A teacher had joined the staff that year, and she had one more year seniority than me. We also lost a fifth grade allotment position at the end of that year. That meant I had to leave and go to another school, and my wonderful school where I had done my student teaching, Mountain View, had an opening! The lady who had been my mentor teacher, Grace Cohn, had left to go to another school. And Hillary and Jim were more than happy to have me come over to their fifth grade staff. But that was in 1997, and I get ahead of myself. I think that is going to happen more and more in this dialog as I move through my school teacher career as school years tend to span from August of one year to May of the next. It will be okay though, do not worry. I'll take care of you.

There was another 1996 event that shaped my life for years to come. Dr. Marj Economopolis, who I have mentioned earlier as a professor at KSU and my KSU faculty person who oversaw my student teaching, asked me if I would participate with her at the NCTM, National Council of Teachers of Mathematics, gathering at Rock Eagle. I said absolutely, and we presented that October. I do not recall exactly what we presented, but I talked with great pride about transitioning from being an Architect to being a school teacher. I found going back to Rock Eagle and staying in one of their cabins would bring a flood of memories back to me of when I had been a chaperone for James when he was ten. Presenting at this affair was to become an annual event for me for the next fifteen years or so.

The Two Boys Trip, TBT, that year was to Mobile, Alabama, to see the battleship Alabama. We drove down (a rule of the TBT) and stayed in Mobile. James was beginning his photography then, and we have several beautiful pictures of Mobile Bay as the sun is setting that were taken from our hotel room in Spanish Fort. The boy has talent. There are also pictures of us on the Alabama and traveling to Fort Morgan down on the tip of the eastern peninsula that juts out and protects Mobile Bay. I remember walking on the beach near Fort Morgan one beautiful afternoon. Just James and me and the Gulf stretching out for hundreds of miles to the south. We then undertook the scariest part of our journey, taking a car ferry across the inlet to Dauphin Island. I think James was convinced this was the stupidest thing we could ever do! But as you can see, we did not die. Although I still think James was more worried about the car, than he was worried about us. We then motored up 193 into Mobile for dinner.

15.

Some years, a lot happens. Some years are relatively quiet. It appears 1997 was one of the quieter years. Momma (Marie Louise Williams Morris – my paternal grandmother) passed away in the cool spring of that year. It was April 22. Almost 26 years ago to the day as I write this. I find myself with regrets this morning, but as I ponder these regrets I am questioning myself. My regret is that for Momma, Aunt Doris, Aunt Toochie, Unca' Nelson, I did not do more to see them right before they died. But as I reflect, I was there when my father died in 2020. I mean I was actually standing there over him in his bed, and it has haunted me ever since that moment. I want to remember all of my heroes and heroines the way they were. Not the way they were forced to be at the end of their life. I know that sounds selfish. It was and is. But those heroes and heroines might not have wanted me to see them as they passed away. I should let that regret go. There is nothing I can do about it anyway. I acted the way I acted. And I acted the way I want people to act as I get old and prepare to pass away. Remember me as I was and not as I will be forced to be in my last years, months and days, please. Oh well. So, Momma died in 1997 … a loss for the world. She is buried in Oak Hill Cemetery in Cartersville, Georgia. There is a Morris/Rogers marker, and she is there with her husband Unca' Pete (Marion Wingfield Morris – paternal grandfather). I do not recall much about the funeral. I'm sure it was at the Sam Jones Methodist Church in Cartersville, and I am sure it was well attended. This was the lady who taught Carolyn and me how to be grandparents. There was nothing I (we) could do that was not "the smartest," "the best," "the greatest." She never criticized only praised. She never spoke poorly of others. She followed the mantra "If you ain't got nothin' nice to say, then don't say nothin' at all." She was a marvelous woman and an awesome grandmother. Carolyn and I miss her still and talk of her often. I wish I could talk to her about … well, everything. But I cannot, and as Forrest Gump says, "That's all I have to say about that."

Carolyn spent her year doing forensic architecture with Jim Beddow. They were traveling around, mostly Houston, and working on a big warehouse fire. She was very good at what she was doing, and I know Jim Beddow appreciated her work. James learned to drive that year, and Two Boys headed to Andersonville and Cumberland Island, and I was involved with my second year at Garrison Mill and leaving and my first year back at Mountain View.

I taught James to drive that year. He learned on a stick shift Civic I had, and there has never been a quicker study. Mind you, James had been a "car guy" since before he had learned to walk. To get him to behave when Carolyn had to drag him grocery shopping, the only thing that always worked was the promise of a Hot Wheels. And his collection today is massive. But as I said, James was a quick car study. I do recall one afternoon we were out practicing. James had his learners permit, which he got the absolute day he turned fifteen, and I was in the passenger seat. We headed on the north 120 loop from the Lower Roswell Road intersection. We rounded the long curve and went through the light and down the hill toward the I-75 intersection. I told him to take the next right. He dutifully did and then realized he was on the entrance ramp to I-75 north! I recall a moment of panic, a reassurance he was in fact ready, and them him pulling out and merging into the fast moving traffic like a veteran. Soon he was zipping along at 70 with the best of them … perhaps a little terrified but handling the car as I knew he would. And still to this day he is one of the best drivers I have ever seen. He has, has always had, this innate feeling for the car and what it would and could do. Oh, he has had a few bumps along the way, but don't we all … especially driving in the Atlanta metro area!

The T B T that year was an interesting Cross-Georgia jaunt that took us to Andersonville Prison and then across the state skirting the Okefenokee Swamp and ending up at Cumberland

Island. We then headed north to Savannah and home. Being the history buffs that we were, James and I left and drove down toward Macon and then cut over to the southwest to the town of Andersonville and the infamous Confederate Civil War prisoner of war camp named Camp Sumter which was named in honor of the fort bombed at the start of the Civil War. To the North it was known simply as "Andersonville." By all accounts it was the worst POW camp in the South. I believe the North also had some pretty bad prisons, but Andersonville was particularly bad. We saw a reconstructed corner of the facility and the gate where prisoners were introduced to Hell on earth. We saw where the creek that ran through the camp was that served as both a toilet and the only source of drinking water. We saw the "dead line" and learned where that term originated. We then visited the POW Museum for a sobering glimpse of what it meant to be a Prisoner of War through the ages. Our final stop was the graveyard where 12,000 men were buried, often in mass graves. After the war Clara Barton, the founder of the Red Cross, came to Andersonville and worked to painstakingly dig up and identify as many of the men as was possible. The only person executed for the atrocities committed at Andersonville was Col. Henry Wirz. There is/was a statue erected in his honor in downtown Andersonville. We saw it that day. I have no idea if it is still there.

From Andersonville we headed across Georgia skirting just north of the Okefenokee Swamp at Waycross stopping just long enough to glimpse an alligator. Then we continued to our next destination, St. Marys, Georgia arriving in the evening. Our hotel was one of the only ones in St. Marys at the time. I am sure there are more places to stay now, but back then you took what you could get. And this was a take what you could get kind of place … it was old and interesting. The things I remember the most is we had to go searching for a phone to call home (it was BCP-Before Cell Phones) to let Carolyn know we had arrived safely, the door to the room did not quite fit closely to floor and breakfast was great! No saran-wrapped muffins in a basket with juice boxes here. It was a full egg, bacon and biscuits southern breakfast. After that we headed for the pier to catch the boat over to Cumberland Island. I hope they never change that way to get there and back. Our day on Cumberland was a dream day for James and his camera. He loved the coast and would end up photographing on Ossabaw and other barrier islands in his hey-day of picture taking, even returning to Cumberland and taking several beautiful black and white photographs of the wild horses. There are pictures in the dining and living room of his trips to the islands. Being an architect, I was most taken with the Dungeness ruins and while we walked quite a bit of the island that day we seemed to keep returning there. I could imagine seeing the building lit up in the evening as Thomas Carnegie threw another lavish soiree for rich robber barons down from Jekyll Island in another of their games of one upmanship. Men in tuxes and women in their fifth or sixth gown of the day strolling in the humidity and bugs wishing for a cool evening breeze while lanterns hung in the trees. Maybe I was born in the wrong era.

We caught the ferry back late in the afternoon as thunderstorms were threatening and continued our journey up the coast to Savannah. We stayed at a Hampton Inn in the historic district. The next day we headed out to Fort Jackson which was nothing to write about really. It was a Revolutionary War era fort, and there is just not much left to see in my opinion. On the way out to Tybee just before you leave the mainland and hit the causeways there used to be famous fish place on the left as you were headed out. It burned down years and years ago, but it was there he and I stopped for lunch and had one of those experiences that the TBT were meant for. We walked in and were ushered to a table. It had to be around 2:00 or a little later as we had already had a very full day by the time we got there. We ordered and got our drinks. I'm guessing we both had sweet tea. As we were sitting there, James picked up on the fact that a man at a table near us had already, at that early hour, had a little too much to drink. James noted that he was a bit too loud and was obviously not making much sense. Our lunch arrived. We probably got the fisherman's platter or some such nominal fish place lunch. Meanwhile the man who had had too much to drink decided it was time to leave. James watched closely as he weaved his way out of the restaurant and made it to the parking lot. James watched as the man fished out his keys and got into his car, and it was then he asked, "Dad, is that man going to try to drive after drinking?" All I could tell him was that people make bad decisions sometimes and this was one of those times. I could see he was weighing what was happening versus the consequences of the man's actions. In retrospect I guess I should have called the police or done something to show James being proactive in a situation like this was a responsible thing to do … but I did not. The drunk man drove off. Hopefully no one died as a result.

James and I continued our journey after that incident as we headed out to our next destination, Fort Pulaski, which was constructed if I recall correctly under the watchful eye of a young engineer who graduated from West Point, Robert E. Lee. It is no wonder the poor boy is interested in history. I recall the day as cool and clear and remember taking pictures of the outside of the fort where Union rifled shells spelled the doom of massed stone forts in the Civil War. We made pictures of Parrot Rifles, a particularly interesting cannon with a steel wrap around the back that made them look particularly vicious. We then headed off to Fort Screven on Tybee Island. I was hoping for another Fort Pulaski, but Fort Screven is no Fort Pulaski, but it was an interesting WWI lesson anyway. Late in the day we traveled back to Savannah, slept and headed home. Another great trip with my boy.

I have already written about leaving Garrison Mill. I have mentioned that I believe the other fifth grade teachers were jealous of both the successes and notoriety that Ms. Collins and I were getting. We were a real team, she and I. You rarely saw one of us that you did not see the other. We were in IEP meetings together and staff meetings and planning periods and lunch. And I think rumors started as can happen in a female dominated profession. Ms. Collins and I went to the new principal as Mary Jo Moffatt had retired and discussed it with him, but he did nothing. So, when I "lost" my position and the one opened at Mountain View, I jumped for it. Well, the parents of Garrison Mill were NOT happy and raised a stink. And then, as if by magic, a fifth grade position appeared at Garrison Mill! But I had committed to my Mountain View, the school I loved, so "I was history." I even had a visit from Mr. Johnny Johnson, the Cobb County School Board representative for the area asking me to stay at Garrison Mill. That was flattering but inconsequential. And he did not really try that hard. I think his effort was mostly for show (and for votes) because the school I was transferring to was also in his district, and he knew I would do well there, too. But I learned a valuable lesson about working in a female dominated environment and especially if your team teacher is even a marginally attractive female … whether you do or not, give the appearance of distance between the two of you. Do not sit together at staff meetings and do not sit near each other at lunch. Better yet, one of you eat somewhere else. This lesson would serve me well in the future.

I met a new good friend that year at Mountain View, Janie Stokes. She was tough third grade teacher who ran the Science Olympiad Team, and she got me involved in it that year. The Cobb County Science Olympiad Event was held at Southern Tech back then so I got to go back to my Alma Mater and stomp around with our team. If you count this year's involvement with Science Olympiad, that makes twenty-six years of involvement with ESO (Elementary Science Olympiad) … cool. It was also that year that I developed a strategy for teaching geometry to fifth graders that I demonstrated for years, Kinesthetic Geometry.

The basic thrust of Kinesthetic Geometry was to employ several of Howard Gardner's intelligences (musical, visual, kinesthetic …) in the introduction of the intricate language of geometry to fifth graders. For many fifth graders this is the first time they had seen this math and learning what a line IS and what line IS NOT was new to them along with all the other myriad of terms unique to geometry. I hit upon this as I thought Howard Gardner and his Intelligences were brilliant and very employable in an Inclusion Classroom setting and I always loved geometry. The coolest part of the whole thing was taking the basic hand and body motions representing the various geometric terms, learning them, and then playing a form of Simon Says with them with the class. But, as I recall, we did not call it Simon Says; we called it "Bob Says." Why "Bob Says" you ask? Funny you should ask … you see in Geometry there is a name for everything! All the shapes, the angles, lines, the circle and its parts … everything. But there is one thing that does not have a name as far as I can tell. It is the little mark you make to indicate that two perpendicular lines or line segments are indeed perpendicular. It looks like this:

So I tasked the class one day to come up with a name for this little mark. I envisioned them coming up with something like "perpendicular indicator" or "right angle notation." No, the class came up with the very mathematically precise name of "Bob." Yep. That was the best name they could come up with and so, from that day to this, that little mark was known as a "Bob." And we did not play Simon Says, we played Bob Says. The way the game was played is that I would stand in the front of the room and I would say, "Bob says, 'Line.'" And then the class would have to stand with their fingers pointing straight out to the sides which indicated a line goes on forever in each direction. Then I would say "Bob says, 'Parallel.'" And the class would have to indicated the proper gesture for parallel. And the class would get into it and as new terms came up in our math studies we would adopt new gestures. Then the game would get complicated and I would try to trick them and not say "Bob says" yet still give them a term, "Angle" and I would move to that gesture and see who followed. Of course if you followed, like in Simon Says when Simon did not say, you were out. Last person standing got the epic treat doled out for over twenty-five years as a kudo in my classroom, the world famous Jolly Rancher! I often said I could take over the world with a motivated class of fifth graders and Jolly Ranchers!

At Mountain View I was a golden child and given free rein to be creative, and I took that opportunity and ran with it. I felt it was very important to make learning as much fun as possible before the dismal, hormone swarming, competitive world of middle school was encountered. I felt that if I could get each child so enthusiastic about learning, that somehow middle school could be made more bearable, and that tide of excitement would carry them into high school excelling. So another lesson I developed and had fun with was the Sacred Glusabi Pot Ceremony. This was when fifth grade was tasked with American History from 1492 to whatever the present day was at the time. And so the whole discussion of Native Americans was mine to explore with the children. Far and away my favorite social studies book was *Our Country* by Silver Burdett Gin, copyright 1993. It is a beautiful book with just the right level of depth for fifth grade, not too many pictures and an easy readability. There is a copy on the shelf right behind my desk where I am writing right now. Anyway, I decided that I would take the class on a "virtual" field trip 1997 style. This was quite a few years before computers became a mainstay in the classroom so I went up the road and photographed an entire trip to the Etowah Indian Mounds in Cartersville. The pictures were then turned into slides and yes, they are still here in the house … and so is a slide projector I think. If not, I'm sure James has it. Anyway, I would sell the class on the idea we were going on a field trip, but I was such a great teacher that we did not need any permission slips or anything like that. All you needed to do was to bring your lunch that day, and we would just go! So, the day comes for the field trip and everyone is all scrubbed and ready for the big

trip. I am very serious about the whole thing, and we get close to time to leave, and I slip out of the class to go to the front office to make sure the bus has come. While I am out I make a quick change into one of my most favorite characters, E. T. Wah. Now E. T. would probably not be "politically correct" to portray today as he is basically a redneck, Georgia man who lives in a trailer up in Bartow County, has a

bunch of dogs, a wife named Beulah and works as a Park Ranger at the Etowah Indian Mounds … sort of. He is a man who has a heavy southern accent, gets off topic easily, does not understand how to be politically correct, says what everyone is thinking but won't say, is genuine in his love of the Native American people and what they have endured and his Indian Mounds, would give you the shirt off his back, and is kind to a fault. He also does not see anything wrong with himself or anyone around him. Basically he is a loveable goof. Anyway … E. T. comes in the room looking for me. Can't be bothered that I'm not there, makes a few honest but disparaging remarks about me, and then launches into his brown bag lunch with the children while showing them his slides, taking them on their virtual field trip and introduction to Native American Studies. When lunch is done, and E. T. is done, he slips away, and I magically reappear with apologies about the bus, and that there has been a mix-up and we cannot go to the mounds today. At which point the class explode telling me about E. T., everything he said about me, and everything they have learned while I was out!

Then, as the studies progress over several days and weeks, the class is challenged to write a small one-line text using Native American symbols I provided them. Then working in teams of three (collaborative learning) they put this symbol text on a red clay flower pot, the cheap ones you buy at any Pikes or Walmart. After we have written our text and suitably decorated the pots we put each one in a big zip-lock bag to keep it safe. On a picture perfect day, we take the pots outside to bless them using the ancient and little known Sacred Glusabi Pot Ceremony. As we get outside to a suitable place, like a concrete picnic area, we discuss how we made the pots and what they meant to the Native Americans. Then there is the inevitable call from the front office for me to come there. I leave the children, but not alone! I have arranged for an ever faithful Room Mom or Dad (God Bless Them) to be there that day while I run off leaving the children wondering. Well, who happens to come along but E. T. Wah! He is ready, willing and able to conduct the Sacred Glusabi Pot Ceremony! Why, who do you think taught Mr. Morris about it? So, he cranks up his Native American music on his boom-box he brought and tells the class, "Mr. Morris won't mind. We'll just go ahead and get started until he comes back." The children are doubtful because they have learned already that things tend to go off track when E. T. is in charge of <u>anything</u>. So, the music is playing and E. T. is chanting and the sun is shining and all is right with the world. Then he asks a team of children for their pot which is still in the baggie. He wants to hold it up to the pot gods and let them bless it. Well, as he is holding it up in the air, he fumbles it (as he is prone to do) and the pot, in the bag, falls to the concrete and shatters! The children are literally slack jawed in amazement! "Oooooh, you are going to be in so much trouble!" says one. "Wait 'till Mr. Morris sees what you have done!" exclaims another! They are incredulous. Yet, E. T. goes forward blessing, and fumbling each and every pot. Some of the teams will not even let him have their pot, but he cajoles them about how he will be soooooo careful and eventually every single pot is safely shattered in its baggie. At which point E. T. beats a hasty retreat leaving the children with their broken pots to face Mr. Morris. Who arrives soon after his departure and is rightly and visibly upset when he sees what E. T. has done.

The class then glumly returns to the classroom where I have some 12" by 18" by 5" deep plastic containers filled with sand. I give one to each team and ask them to carefully take the broken pots from the bags and bury the shards in the sacred sand, and then put the lids on the containers with their Native American team names … Cherokee, Arapaho, Niagara, Apache, Navajo etc. A few days later they trade containers. Each container has a coordinate grid marking on the edges. The teams have to dig up the shard, catalog where on the grid it was found, how deep in millimeters it was below the surface, weigh it using a triple beam balance scale, and the try to reassemble the pot and interpret what the long ago Native Americans were trying to communicate with their symbol writing. I think you can see all of the learning that took place during that part of the exercise … as well as the hands on fun. The cracked and taped up pots were then on display in the classroom for the rest of the year.

One more activity we in Maverick Classroom undertook was while we were studying Sutter's Mill and the Gold Rush of 1848/49. I told the children that this area, North Georgia, was known for gold deposits and that Mountain View once sat on one of the largest deposits, and that this morning we were going to go hunting for gold. They were of course skeptical. However, in the days before, I had bought a couple of bags of rocks from Home Depot and spray painted them gold. Then, the night before I had spread them all over the hillside at Mountain View. So, the children, always up for any adventure that would take them out of the classroom, armed with cloth bags that had dollar signs on them were unleashed. And they soon got "Gold Fever" as the first rocks were "discovered" and then more and then more! It was pandemonium with cries of "Over Here!" and "Look at this one!" The looks on their frantic, little faces were … well, "worth their weight in gold." (Sorry) Of course when we got back inside there was work to be done. I had the current price of gold per ounce posted, and we started measuring on the triple beam balance scales who actually had "discovered" the most gold. Then we converted their ounces of gold to dollars. So, there was math and science integrated into their history lessons. And of course, everyone got to keep a piece of gold and the person who amassed the largest fortune, got a Jolly Rancher. It was cool fun. And I ended the lesson with what I said almost daily to my classes … "So, tonight, at the dinner table, while you are eating your Beanie Weenie, which I have every night for dinner, and your Parental Units ask what you did today, just casually say that you discovered gold on the school grounds. Then wait for them to ask you about it."

You know what I loved the most about fifth graders, and this held true as long as I taught? That ten/eleven year olds are at an age during which they are starting to suspect that your feet are made of clay, but they are not certain! Consequently, magic and fantasy can lay around in the corners of your classroom. I loved teaching when I was allowed to teach in the way that made children WANT to learn. This meant mixing fun and challenge in their lessons. Mixing hands-on-learning in with lecture and books. Never giving away grades, but knowing when to grade this student or that student a little more leniently because they have a challenge the others do not. And teaching your lessons using <u>all</u> of Howard Gardner's Multiple Intelligences whenever you can.

16.

As I am writing this, in 2023, it will be Carolyn's and my fiftieth anniversary in a few weeks. 1998 was my parents fiftieth anniversary and 1998 was Carolyn's and my twenty-fifth anniversary. I was forty-eight in 1998 and Carolyn was forty-seven. I am calculating my dad was seventy-four and Mom was seventy-two. Right around the ages Carolyn and I are today. Interesting. But 1998 was a full year of Disney World visits, Hampton Roads and Williamsburg, Northside UMC and Mountain View adventures.

Mom and Dad's 50th Anniversary was at Re's house in Chamblee. James, the now quite accomplished photographer, immortalized the day with a photograph. He had the tripod on the stairs and the crowd was on in the living room. I can see the picture in my mind now. I have no idea where the picture may be. Possibly with Rusty who became the keeper of the photographs when Dad passed away in 2020. I will look for it and try to include it here. As I recall, there were a great collection the family there. On the following two pages, you will see an amazing collection of family. On the facing page is a guide to Who's Who in the photograph.

It was Carolyn's and my 25th Anniversary and I think we celebrated it by taking Adam and Jenna and James to the Grove Park Inn in Ashville. We all stayed in the old part of the inn up on the topmost floor. By this time the old timey elevator had been replaced and there was a new wing added so we could not eat in the old dining room. Carolyn and

I had a room overlooking the valley and James bunked in with Adam and Jenna. There was a secret code word developed that weekend. Whenever we wanted access to one another's room we used the secret code word … "Imodium." And yes, it started exactly how you think it started. It started with Adam! Anyway I do recall one evening meal we had. I was really hoping to recreate for the children the feel of the old inn, but the only dining room was on the top floor of the new wing. This new wing was, if you are looking at the Grove park from the valley, on the left. The wing on the right had been there for years. In fact, I think it was under construction when Carolyn and I first went years before. Anyway, the new dining experience was NOTHING like our previous experience, but we all made the best of it as best we could.

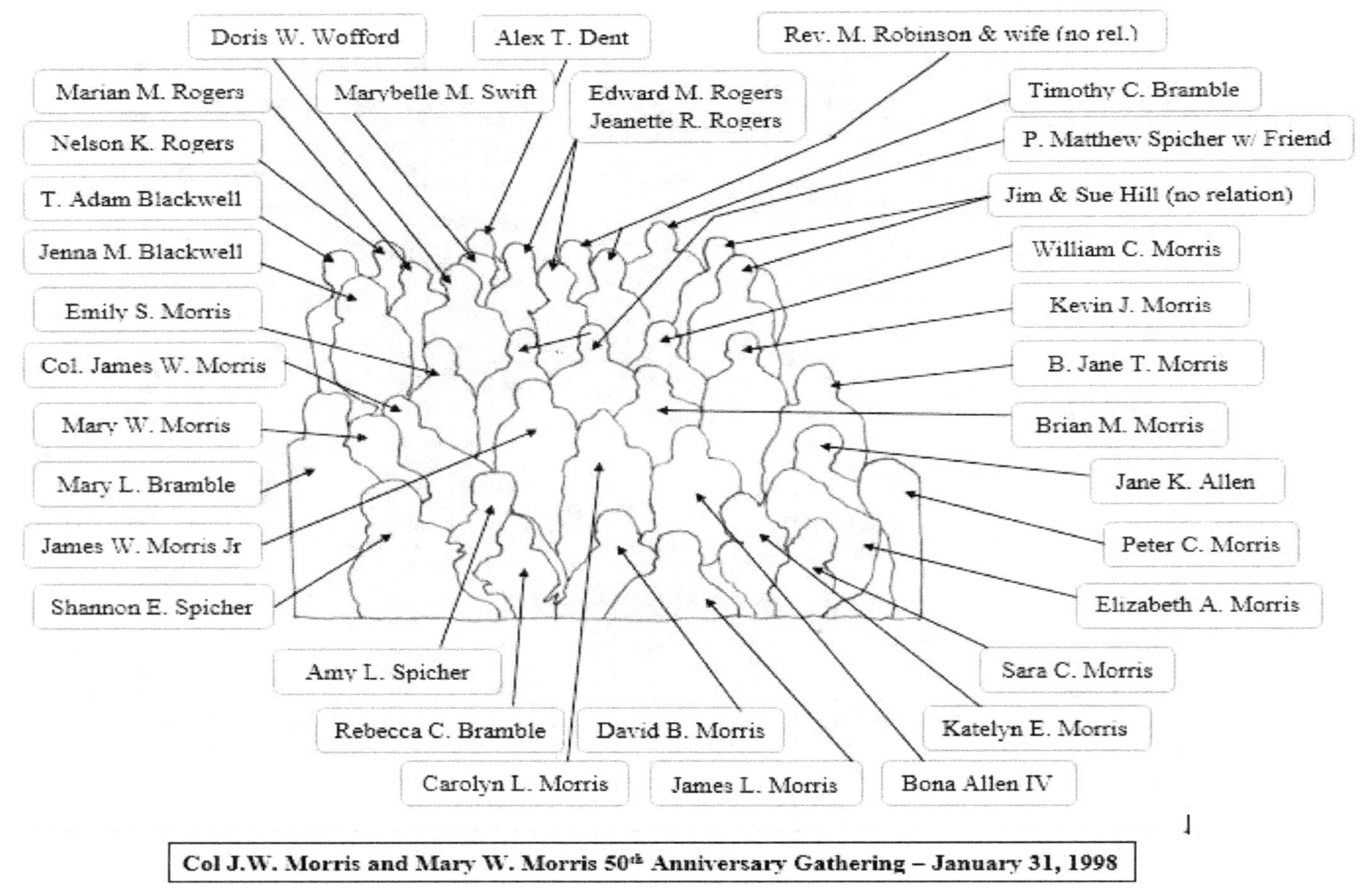

Col J.W. Morris and Mary W. Morris 50th Anniversary Gathering – January 31, 1998

Carolyn had finished her work with Jim Beddow and started work for Northside United Methodist Church. The senior pastor was one Gil Watson. My best description of Gil Watson would be a little overweight, well off, University of Georgia preppy dressing, momma's boy. But he was very nice to Carolyn and she enjoyed her tenure there, however it was a tough job. She was the newsletter and weekly program producer, and it was a very stressful job. Pulling all the information together under a weekly deadline that had to be letter-perfect as the entire congregation was there to critique every name and the accuracy of every event took its toll on Carolyn. The drive down to the church was somewhat of a killer, but we attended there as much as we could. I think Carolyn was there for about a year before burning out. I do recall a party the Rev. Watson threw at his country home out in somewhere. It was a beautiful afternoon in a beautiful place with beautiful barbeque. More than that I do not have any exceptional memories.

Two Boys were off to Williamsburg, Yorktown and Hampton Roads that year for our trip I believe. There is picture of me in Yorktown that James took. It is of me walking away. I would like that picture to be at my funeral as it would sum up the day. The memory of the trip that stands out the most is when he and I stopped at the Anheuser-Bush Brewing facility in somewhere and then were the first ones at their amusement park the next morning. There is a great picture of James and me on a coaster coming down a big slope from that day. It is on the Billy Bookshelves in the den over by where my chair is. Again, that coaster ride is my best memory of our trip. Being with James on those trips always was and always will be one of highlights of my life. I tried to forge a bond with my son that I never felt I had with my father. It was the most sacred gift I could give him. I wanted him to feel he could come to me with anything … any question … any problem and know, really know, that I would be there for him. Carolyn and I worked to give that same bond to Jenna, but I felt a real need to do it for James. I hope he will always see it that way … as that is the way I meant it to be. I hope I was/am a good father. I also recall that 1998 was the year that James went with me to the Rock Eagle Math Conference and helped me present Kinesthetic Geometry. It was nice just having him hang with "the old man" and having him there to help me.

We took a second family trip to Disneyworld that year. I could finally face the "black rat" again. It had been ten years since the whole Disney debacle, and I felt I was up to the task, after all James had been in stroller when we took Jenna back in 1984. We stayed at the Polynesian Resort on the property. We went to see whatever became of Pleasure Island, although I just could not bring myself to go into that part of the park. We visited Epcot and did the whole tour of nations although the Norway Pavilion looked nothing like our design. We went to the new Tower of Terror ride which involved an elevator drop that was pretty scary. I think that whole ride has been gotten rid of by now. One thing that does stand out in my mind was letting James head off and explore on his own. He had turned fifteen that year and this was a big deal to Carolyn and me. Letting our "little boy," who at this point was as tall as me and weighed as much as me, ride off on Monorail Pink alone was a leap of faith for us. But as you have surmised I am sure, James handled it with his usual savior faire … and probably had a ball without us. It's funny the things you recall and the things you don't.

I was into my second year at Mountain View that fall and reveling in being home there. Jim Oveby was still principal and Hillary was still the Assistant Principal and there was a wonderful collection of energetic and happy teachers there. It was a great time and a great place to be a teacher. It was a year when I got to meet and teach in the same school as a really great teacher. Jim and Hillary had hired an exceptional teacher that year. A REAL gentleman and impressive teacher named Brad Cohen. What made him both exceptional and unique at the same time was that he was handicapped. He had Tourette Syndrome. It exhibited itself daily with barks and tics, and he taught second grade and the children loved and accepted him, and he was, as I said, a great teacher. He did not let this "handicap" handicap him! He has gone on and is an administrator in Cobb County Schools, an author, motivational speaker, husband, Dad of two children and all round great guy. The book he wrote, *Front of the Class: How Tourette Syndrome Made Me The Teacher I Never Had*, was made into a movie and had Jim and Hillary played by actors in the movie. Pretty cool! I tell you all of this so you can "Google" Brad Cohen and find out all about him and his life and set the stage for another story ...

Mountain View decided they, the faculty and staff, would have an act at the children's talent night. All the children presented their various talents from piano to violin to tumbling to tap to ballet to jazz and then it was time for the faculty presentation. I had suggested we perform the same *California Girls* ensemble that I had done at Mt. Bethel Church, and the idea was accepted! So, after all the children were done, the lights came down and the song started. "Well, the East Coast girls ..." and several of the faculty ladies came out dressed in business suits. "And the Southern Girls ..." and several of the faculty ladies came out on long skirts carrying frilly umbrellas. "And the Midwest farmer's daughters ..." and several came out dressed in jeans and calico shirts. "And the Northern Girls ..." and more came out in parkas and dressed for the cold." Then after a chorus about California Girls the Beach Boys hit their stride, "The West Coast has the sunshine and girls all get so tanned ..." and that is when Brad Cohen, Jim Oveby, the custodian man and me came out on stage dressed in drag and start strutting our stuff! And yes, the house came down and no, there is no way we could get away with doing that today. Why? Well, to be honest, I'm not exactly sure why except the whole Gay, Trans, Bi thing has gotten so polarized that we cannot even laugh at ourselves anymore. Sad. But the absolute best moment of the evening came after the show. All of us transvestite performers scuttled off stage and quickly changed into normal clothes to join in the after celebration of the evening. I was standing with Brad and Oveby when one of my students came running to me and said, "Man! Mr. Morris! Did you see that last act! Those were some ugly girls up on that stage!" And he said it to me in a way that told me he had no idea it had been the three of us up on that stage. Now THAT is an awesome moment!

17.

January 11th, 1999, Monday, arrived and James turned 16! The absolute first thing he wanted was to get his license. So, we did. He was a happy boy there is no doubt about it. Somewhere along in here we bought him a car. And the story of that particular car is legend. If you recall, we had bought Jenna a new 1994 Honda Civic when her Hyundai crapped out going back and forth to Georgia Southern. Now with <u>this</u> 1994 car, I had overseen the oil changing and maintenance personally. So, Jenna and Adam were now looking to trade that 1994 Civic in order to buy a new car. Well, I knew the car had been taken care of correctly, and they were willing to sell the 1994 Civic for what Carolyn and I were willing spend sooooooo … Carolyn and Jim Morris bought the same car TWICE! Yes, the legend it true. But now you know "the rest of the story." We bought the car to help Jenna and Adam out. We could not just take the car back and leave them high and dry without a down payment or trade in. So, yes, we did buy the same car twice … and would do it again. So, James got a car, and we went to Bones restaurant to celebrate his 16th birthday complete with steaks and crumb scrapers. That 1994 Civic went on to be James's race car in college, have a cold air intake, modified brake system, carry him back and forth to Georgia Southern and serve James well into his marriage. It was a wise double purchase in my opinion!

Carolyn decided she had had enough of church work and went to work for a nonprofit organization called Lifespan. It was run by some nuns and Carolyn became good friends with Sister Kathleen Purser, the "head nun." She was a very nice lady … as you might expect. Carolyn worked with them and seemed very happy. Needless to say it did not pay very much, but Carolyn was happy doing it. One thing I was specifically involved in was their "Lunch and Learn" program. Carolyn asked me if I would be interested in doing a series of lessons on the Civil War. Of course I was enthusiastically all in! It was very cool. It was a series of about 6 lessons on the war and was pretty well attended. Of course I was competing with lessons about flower arranging and knitting so the competition was not very keen. I recall I was commenting to Carolyn about the turnout for my lessons one day, and she rightfully humbled me by saying something to the effect that most of my class were little old women who came to the class just to see a young man strut around and talk for an hour! I had not looked at it that way, but she was, most probably, entirely correct. There is a binder downstairs on the white shelves with the lessons in it. I think the culminating event was an actual field trip to Kennesaw Mountain with all the older adults. That day was kind of cool too.

A difficult part of her job was when they took care of the Alzheimer patients. They would have a day each week that the staff would take care of the family members and give caregivers a break. That was heartbreaking. I went with her one day in the summer. To see these former women who were powerful businesswomen and vibrant Mothers and daughters who shaped lives and men who were husbands and fathers and vice presidents and presidents in the business world reduced to staring off at nothing and being spoon fed was just heartbreaking. It was the circle of life and really humbled me. The reality of that day was a stark reminder of what the future could hold. Of course at that point, Carolyn and I were in our late forties, and we were still immune from anything like that. We were bulletproof! Now, almost thirty years later, it looms.

Sometime that year, around thanksgiving time I believe, Carolyn and I decided we needed get away so we cooked up a day when we would take James and head up to Rabun County to the Dillard House restaurant, meet Jenna and Adam, have lunch and then

James would go home with J & A and stay with them, and we would escape to Brasstown Valley Resort for a couple of days. We all met at the Dillard House which was a kind of family style eating place with county cooking. As we waited outside for a table James took some pictures of a clown figurine he had brought along. He later added color to the black and white picture he took and those photos are on display here at Falcon Wood. Lunch was good solid food as I recall. A lot of fried chicken and fried everything else, welcome South. After lunch Carolyn and I headed west, and James and Jenna and Adam headed south toward Gainesville. By this time, I believe, J&A were living in a house Toby and Paula had built on the lake and were getting their feet under themselves.

Carolyn and I headed out toward Brasstown Valley. Along the way, we found a beautiful forest and took a walk in the deep woods. As we were walking an interesting thing occurred. A weather front was coming through Georgia, and the front had a defined line. As we were walking the sun was falling through the canopy and it was warm enough that all one needed was light jacket, if that. Then, up ahead we saw what appeared to be a line of fog in the forest. It was a white wall, straight as an arrow through the woods in front of us about fifty feet, very "Stephen Kingy"! When we got closer we realized it was a fog bank. On our side it was warm and the sun was shining. As we passed through the fog wall, the other side was darker, drizzling rain and overcast. We stepped back out from the wall into the sun and then back again into the cloud bank … definitely very Stephen Kingy. Finally, we had to go forward and got back to our car. We were a little wet, but no monsters or bears or beasties ate us. We did not die that day!

Off we continued to the resort. I know what we were hoping for … we were hoping for another Grove Park Inn revelation or perhaps a Panama City Edgewater Beach Resort event. Neither were to be. The resort was just another hotel room hooked onto a decent (better than Highlands) restaurant. We settled in and enjoyed ourselves and our get-away time together. That evening or perhaps the evening of the next day, we headed to the dining room for dinner. We got kind of dressed up for each other and wanted to make it a special evening … and a special evening it was to be. We arrived and were seated at a very nice table for two next to a wall that extended almost to the ceiling. We ordered glasses of wine. Probably Kir for me … you cannot beat a nice aperitif before dinner. Dinner arrived, and we were enjoying eating and talking about our children and work and how good we had it when a gentleman walking up to our table. He graciously bowed slightly and said, "I think we know each other." We both gasped. It was Bona Allen! My brother Pete's father-in-law! As it turned out, just on the other side of the "wall that extended almost to the ceiling" was my brother Pete, his wife Elizabeth, their two lovely girls, Bona and his wife Jane all having a family gathering! Pete and Liz had come down from North Carolina and Bona and Jane had come from Buford. We could not believe the coincidence of the whole thing! We all hugged and reminisced and laughed and had a gay old time getting reacquainted. When we returned to our table I leaned over to Carolyn and told her how glad I was that I was here with her! Having dinner with a client or business associate would have been a more difficult situation!

On our first TBT to New Orleans in 1999, we were driving into the city and got caught up in a police chase. James was a newly minted driver and was driving the car when it happened. One minute we were cruising down the interstate and the next minute about eight or nine police cars had hemmed us in along with about twenty other cars. When we were all stopped, and all the traffic behind us, the cops jumped out, guns pulled, (at this point James is almost wetting himself wondering what he has done!) and swarmed around a car about two car lengths in front of us and just to the right one lane. A man was hauled out of the car and pushed to ground … the police were no doubt saying, "Get on the ground!" (You either understand that reference or you don't … no matter) but they then cuffed him and got him up and in a squad car and they all evaporated leaving James and I with a great story! Once in town we were starved and we went to a little café on the southwest edge of Jackson Square and probably had a po'boy of some fashion. After that we found our hotel and got our feet under us and headed out to explore the city. We ended up back at Jackson Square and perused the street vendors and the evening characters who were starting to come out. A little later as darkness fell and the gas lamps lit, we found ourselves walking along Bourbon Street when James had an *ah-ha* moment I am especially fond of. As we walked down the street there were strip clubs on each side. In the windows were pictures of these well-endowed, very attractive, scantily clad women. It was intriguing to a sixteen-year-old James and, I have to admit, to his dad. Each open door beckoned and each door likewise had a big burly bouncer sitting on a stool on guard. Except at one door. The bouncer must have had to go to the bathroom or something, but he had asked one of the performers to "hold the fort" on the stool for him. The only problem was she was, let us just say, overweight and not the least bit attractive. She had on her stripping outfit and was all rolling fat and … well, you get the picture. So we, Two Boys, observed that and kept walking. After about ten steps James said, "Dad, do you think that lady at the door was one of the strippers?" I allowed as yes I thought she was. We continued to walk, but in his face you could see a point at which Fantasy and Reality had just collided and it was a train wreck in his young, hormone washed, sixteen-year-old brain. Awesome!

We spent the next couple of days visiting the World War II Museum which, that year, was just getting started and is nothing like it is today or even when four (!) boys visited there in November of 2016, but it was okay for us on that trip. We had breakfast at Café du Monde and some beignets slathered in powdered sugar. I bought a coffee mug that morning and have it sitting right here next to me filled with my morning tea as I write. Another high point, at least for me, was visiting a cemetery up in north New Orleans. There we found a twenty-foot long by ten-foot wide by six-foot high mausoleum containing multiple crypts. This cemetery had hundreds of crypts, which in itself was not surprising as almost everyone in N.O. is buried above ground for all the obvious reasons, but the cool part of this cemetery and a testament to the spirit of the people of New Orleans was that there had been a horse racing track around it in the day. Anyway James and I made our way inside and as we walked kind of hunched over into this dank, dark semicircular cement mausoleum, near the back we found the individual crypt of General Pierre Gustave Toutant-Beauregard. Now if you do not know who this man is, you need to look him up. He was a way-cool Confederate General. I'll not fill in anymore gaps and let you look him up, but suffice to say his name was on my fifth grade Civil War spelling list. We also saw where President Jefferson Davis was buried temporarily until the Sons of the Confederacy moved his body in 1893, at the request of his widow, to be reinterred in Hollywood Cemetery in Richmond, Virginia. All in all, it was a grand day. Little did we know that our trip would be not be the last or even the next to the last to this famed city on the Mississippi.

On the school front, Mountain View again let me stretch my wings, and I owe it all to my students. A very cool thing happened because of an innocent question by one of my fifth grade ladies. I recall the class and I were coming back to the school on a bus from a small outing/field trip that day. The class size was down a few students because our Target students had gone to Jekyll Island for their annual Target class trip to the 4H Center on Jekyll when one of the young ladies asked me, "Mr. Morris, why can't we go on an overnight field trip like Target? Are we not smart enough?" Well, from that single, seemingly innocent question started ten-years of overnight field trips for all the students in my classes and eventually included taking whole fifth grades to Jekyll. Somewhere on our TBT's, James and I had been to Charleston and toured the aircraft carrier Yorktown and gone out to Fort Sumter. And I recalled that I had seen that groups of children, mostly Boy Scouts it seemed, could sleep overnight on the carrier, so another plan was hatched. We could leave early on a Saturday morning, travel to Charleston, be there in five and half hours, eat lunch, visit the Charleston History Museum, check in at Patriot's Point at the aircraft carrier CV-10 Yorktown, tour the carrier, the submarine the USS Clamagore, tour the Coast Guard cutter USS Laffey, visit the Medal of Honor Museum, sleep on the ship, visit Fort Sumter Sunday morning and be back in Marietta by Sunday evening … exhausted. And so we did! And that trip also became a staple of my class for ten-years. The whole World War II thing and the whole Fort Sumter Civil War Charleston thing fit our curriculum perfectly and Jim Oveby and Hillary Straka were more than willing to lend their support to the expedition. So, the planning began. A date was selected by the Cobb school calendar and the Yorktown's sleeping availability. I then got in touch with a group called The Travel Store and arranged a bus. Over the years, the Travel Store's managers Kathy and David Freund became good friends, and I used them exclusively for not only Charleston, but also eventually the trips to Jekyll for the whole fifth grade (not just the Target children), and it all started with a child's innocent question. I could spin story after story about the trips to the Yorktown and all the laughter and fun we had. It was teaching at its finest. Full blown hands-on experiential learning. A child had to be in pretty difficult shape not to learn something on those weekends and most came away with a lifetime of memories. (In fact, here is an email I got from one of my favorite students, Devon Murphy, some twenty years after his trip.)

The trip looked like this: we would leave the school about 6:00 AM on a coach bus. In its Hey-Day I actually had three coach buses with most of the fifth grade going. Arrival in Charleston was timed to be about 12:00, and we would stop at a mall with a giant food court on the way into the city. As the students and parent chaperones got off the bus each was given $5.00 for lunch, which back then was more than enough money. We kept them corralled in the food court so there was no danger of losing a child. Then we were off to the Charleston History Museum downtown. I have a cool picture of James, who was a senior counselor and chaperon on several trips, at the museum. This stop was eventually replaced with a stop at the museum housing the remains of the Confederate submarine the CSS Hunley. As you can guess, none of my classes just blindly went to Charleston. They had to be steeped in the lore and history of Charleston, the Hunley, Fort Sumter, and WWII and the CV-10, its battles and all the memorabilia it contained. Each student had a scavenger hunt booklet they had to fill out for a grade (ugh). After the Hunley, we headed for the carrier. I can vividly recall the first time they see the Yorktown. As you approach Patriot's Point you are shielded from the ship by trees. Then suddenly you break out and can see the ship floating there, and there was always a collective "awwwwwe" from the bus. For many this was the largest manmade object they had ever seen. Then we parked and unloaded all our "gear." Everyone was responsible for carrying their own stuff. I made a big deal of them being responsible, and for many this was their first experience of that too. From the moment they arrived at the school in the dark at 6:00 on Saturday morning and had to load their own overnight bag and sleeping bag onto the bus until we arrived back at the school at about 7:00 Sunday night, they had to keep up with their stuff. And yet I still had a collection of cameras, socks, underwear :-o, and gift shop trash displayed outside my classroom for days. So, after arriving and grabbing our "gear," we had to carry all our stuff down the 500-foot-long pier to the carrier and up myriad steps to the hanger deck where we were greeted and assigned our bunk area. The ladies usually went forward to the officer's quarters to nice two level bunks and lockers. All the guys went with me to the enlisted men's area with the classic WWII ship's bunks stacked five high with a space to sleep about eighteen inches from your bunk to the one above you. It was also the boys first experience with gang showers (which only the adult males used!). After a fire drill, the already preassigned groups were free to explore the ship from the engine room to the flying bridge including all the aircraft on the flight deck. Dinner was always exciting. There were generally two choices: spaghetti or chicken and rice. I told them when they were in the chow line when they walked up to the cooks to request steak … but no one ever did. Then when they complained about the food, I would ask if they requested the steak? When they said no, then I would tell them with a smile "Well, there you go." After dinner we explored to carrier some more as the sun set across the Cooper River and the day cooled. At 8:00 the award winning movie *The Fighting Lady* was shown in the Smoky Stover theater. That video is in my collection and worth a look see. The combination of the long day, the heat of the day, a full tummy, the cool of the theater and the movie usually prepared the children for bed. We herded all the Munchkins off to bed, there was Tattoo and then lights out. And for all the bravado of "I'm going to stay up all night" the room was dead silent in about ten minutes. Reveille sounded at 7:00 amid groans and whining. Of course James and I were already up, washed, shaved and dressed and we absolutely loved rousting everyone out! Breakfast was similar to dinner. Line up and shuffle along, get your tray and then get freeze dried scrambled eggs (which most had never experienced), grits, biscuits and a cup of juice while you grumble. Then we were back to police our area and move all our gear to the stage by the big American flag. Now there was a little time for tours or the gift shop or the submarine or the cutter or the pitiful Viet Nam fire base layout before we boarded the General Beauregard boat for a trip out to Fort Sumter. Again, the gift shop was the first stop as most students were "history-ed out" by this time and could have cared less about General Robert Anderson or his Ft. Sumter men even though we had done a whole play about them for the fifth grade earlier that year. On the boat ride back the children discovered you could buy Cheetos at the snack bar on the boat and then throw the little orange chunks off the stern to the delight of every seagull for a hundred miles around. By the time we docked it was time to hustle back to the carrier and grab our bag lunch. An apple, which absolutely no one ate, either a ham or turkey on while bread sandwich, which few ate, and a bag of chips, which everyone ate, along with a juice box rounded out lunch. Now it was load up the bus time. Everyone carrying their own pile of now totally disheveled stuff and throwing it under the bus and away we go for the six-hour trip back home. I recall one year, may have been the first year as a matter of fact, as we were rolling out the parents wanted to stop at a BP for coffee. Not being a coffee drinker, I said we needed to roll on. Well, there was a mutiny! The parents laughingly took over the bus and the driver, and they all got their coffee! It was cool.

Now you may think the fun ended there. It did not. As we headed home we made one more stop. In Augusta, on the south side, is/was a CiCi's Pizza, and we all piled in (I had called ahead to warn them) and ate pizza until we were going to burst. And now, with full tummies and another two hours to go, the bus got quiet. There were no yells for another child friendly and parent approved family DVD to be played … just silence. It was a blessing. Until the occasional, random child embarrassingly threw-up their dinner. Ah well, such is the life of a teacher. The arrival home was always a celebration. You would have thought I had abducted their children for months. And then in a flurry, the children were gone, the bus policed, hugs all around, and it was quiet. I had not lost a child. I had had no major catastrophes. And I had school in the morning. And Monday morning was a little slow getting off the ground, and each student now knew what the term "hung over" meant!

In February of that year Carolyn, James and I got the rare opportunity to see Hal Holbrook portray Mark Twain at the Fox Theater in his stage presentation of *Mark Twain Tonight*. It was so very, very cool and further endeared Samuel Clemens in my heart. I bring this up now because on Book Character Day at Mountain View I portrayed him for several years along with my children being everyone from Harry Potter to Captain Underpants (a self-assured child). Now that particular evening we saw the play happened to be Hal Holbrook's birthday, and as he came on stage for the first time, the whole Fox Theater broke out in song singing happy birthday. And this was where the man's professionalism shined. Mr. Holbrook stood there on stage, dressed fully as Mark Twain and allowed us to sing the entire song. He then cleared his throat, as Mark Twain did several times that night, never broke character and said, "How generous, and if I happen to see the gentleman, I will pass on your kindness." He then launched into a diatribe about congress, "that great gathering of the infirmed." Nothing has changed in over a hundred years.

Thinking about teaching that year, one of the science areas I was allowed to teach that year was a unit on Heat, Light and Sound, and I had great fun with this unit. As with all my teaching, I was looking at it from a standpoint of how can I get the students beyond the textbook. How can I get their hands involved and their minds really engaged? With the heat unit portions of it I combined with light unit, and we set up experiments with thermometers outside in the sun and each one covered with different color construction paper. What we discovered was the darker the paper, the higher the temperature registered. With our "book learnin'" we then struggled to say why this was true, and what were the real world applications? We looked into water in a tank. What happens when blue dyed ice water is slowly introduced into a tank of warm water? Why? How does this apply to weather? With light, I rigged up an old hand drill and a two-foot diameter wooden disc that would spin vertically. One part of the experiment was a paper disc to cover the wooden one. The paper disc was divided into pie segments with each of the ROYGBIV (colors of the rainbow – Red, Orange, Yellow, Green, Blue, Indigo, Violet) on it. As the disc would spin and a light applied all the colors would blend and guess what color was produced? Then I would take the paper disc off and there was a two-inch diameter hole in the wooden disc that, when spinning, would line up with a flood lamp bulb and we had a strobe light. The students would then dance in front of it and enjoy the stop action effect. I would also use the strobe focused on a spinning wheel and have it appear to stop spinning as I matched the two wheel's rotations. We culminated the light study by making tie-dyed tee shirts that we then used for our studies of the 1960's hippy movement. The sound studies were great fun when we made "Roarers." A "Roarer" is a six-inch long piece of inch-inch wide flat wood tied to a two-foot piece of string. When you whirl it around it makes what kind of sound? … Yep, a roar. We also made Dixie Cup and string telephones and looked at loose string versus tight string. What happens if you tie a third string onto it? What happens if you pinch the string in the middle while two people are talking? And, of course, the ever present question on "WHY?" As you can see, my teaching approach was very Socratic.

For years and years, I had a forty-gallon aquarium that Adam gave me in the classroom. It was a beautiful pain in the butt. The deal was I would supply the aquarium and the food and the maintenance (ugh), and the students would supply the fish, snails, frogs and whatever animals they wanted in the tank. We suffered through "froggy" escaping the tank over a Christmas holiday and the children finding him dead and mummified upon their return, endless bouts of ick and green tank slime, an explosion of baby snails, and the sad but every couple of months ritual of giving someone's poor fish a "burial at sea" (flush). I hauled that tank all over. From Mountain View to Mount Bethel Elementary, Frank Long Elementary in Liberty County, my Cherokee trailer classroom, and back to Mount Bethel. You can read in the Mailgrams at the beginning of each year as I explain and request fish for the tank. I finally let it rest after about fifteen years and it is in the basement waiting for a new enthusiastic owner. It was a very meaningful and beautiful pain in the butt.

Through all of this there was no mistaking my classroom. It was a museum full of posters of MLK, Gandhi, and Joshua Lawrence Chamberlain at Gettysburg. There were books and books and books everywhere for the children to peruse at their leisure. There was an old rotary dial phone and real telegraph key with a battery hook-up to a light so you could write a message, translate it to Morse Code … not Morris Code … then transmit it and see who can decipher it. There was the monkey head … yes, a monkey head. It was a coconut shell that the top came off of and was decorated to look like a monkey's face. It originally came with an alcoholic beverage inside on a cruise, and I had to buy the drink to get the Monkey Head! Inside the shell were numbers. Each child in the class had a number based on their alphabetical listing in my gradebook. If there was ever a difficult question that had to be answered like "Who gets the left over donut?" or "Who gets the last slice of cookie cake?" the illustrious Monkey Head would decide usually with the class chanting, "All Hail Monkey Head!" as I took him off the revered shelf where he kept constant watch over the class. I would then reach inside and pull out a number, and he or she would be the winner of whatever dubious gift was being decided. And when a child would be disappointed and say "I don't believe in the Monkey Head," the class would explain that that was okay because "The Monkey head believes in you." Great fun! We also had a JR Can. It was an old popcorn can full of the treat all Mavericks loved – Jolly Ranchers! I have often said that if I had a class of motivated fifth graders and enough Jolly Ranchers, I could take over the world! Or at the very least the Capitol of the United States (topical January 6th, 2021 reference)! The JR Can was used for positive motivation in the classroom. You contributed something interesting and thought provoking to our class discussion – go to the JR Can! You followed fire drill instructions perfectly – whole class gets a JR! You were the one of the three students who solved the Maverick Mailgram quiz of how many gobbles were hidden in the Thanksgiving Mailgram – you get a JR! There was also the popcorn can of random junk. I mean shower caps and lotion from Holiday Inn, a matchbox car missing a wheel, a small version of a GI Joe, more soap from Holiday Inn or Marriott. This was an award for doing something bigger than a JR worthy action. This would be helping a fellow student who fell on the playground, or keeping three-ring notebook in pristine condition during a notebook check … really important stuff! I also had four traditions that I maintained every single year I taught school. I am very proud of these four traditions, and have mentioned them before, but I wanted to expand on them a little. One was a photograph of the whole class. Each year I took a picture of the whole class and then we ritualistically hung it on the wall at the end of the school year. The students could return at any time and see themselves frozen in time in the fifth grade. The second was the reading of the book *The Phantom Tollbooth*. There is a hardback copy on my shelf chronicling each year it was taught. This was an end of year ritual and culminated with the 1960's movie of the same name and the drawing of giant posters of each chapter. The third tradition was to adopt a Maverick of the Year, a MOY. This was a decision made by me and me alone. It was a child who exemplified the characteristics of a Maverick all year long. This child showed courage, altruism, sympathy, enthusiasm, diligence and most of all love for all consistently through the school year. Some years it was a child who succeeded in the face of adversity. Some years it was a child who struggled every day, and some years it was just that child who was a joy every single day. Their pictures too hung on a wall in my classroom, and they got a copy of the same framed picture for themselves. The end of each school year was a tear-jerker! So, you are wondering about the fourth tradition. Well, on the last day of school each child wrote a letter to themselves. The letter was to their senior high selves. They had already brought in an envelope where they could receive mail in seven years. It may have been addressed where they are living now or a grandparent in Minnesota. It did not matter. The key was for them to be able to receive the letter they wrote to themselves their senior year in high school. After they wrote the letter, they would fold it and seal it in the envelope. I never read them. This was between them and themselves. I then collected all the letters and put them in a big manila envelope, put the year they would graduate on the front of the envelope and hold them for the next seven years, and then, faithfully, come April of their graduation year, I would slip them all in the mail. Sometimes I would hear back with senior pictures and graduation announcements and sometimes I would hear nothing. It did not matter. It was a tradition. As an aside, I just mailed the 2023 graduate's letters two weeks ago. I got a graduation announcement from a dear student, Emma Gott, today. She looks all grown up and beautiful. It was a good tradition, and I am sorry to see it end in 2024 as my last 2016-2017 fifth grade class graduates from high school.

In the spring of 1999 began an almost surreal journey for me, and much of what I am going to tell you about is documented in two big black portfolios. I think the best way to tell this story is to ignore the chronological breakdown and just tell the tale in one sweeping story. As I look back on this event, it was one of the truly highpoints of my life, and it began with the word "Dedication." On my desk at school and on my desk next to me are two quotes guiding my life. One is a quote from the Book of John, John 21: 15-17. It culminates with Jesus saying simply "Feed my sheep." A second meaningful statement is on a paperweight Debbie Pierce and Tom Mattocks of Mt. Bethel Church gave me, and it says "Is it good for the Children?" These were two of my cornerstones as I taught, and as I live. In my years as a Sunday school teacher I had cherished these verses in John and used them as my personal call to destiny. In the Book of John, Jesus is talking to Simon Peter and instructing him that if Simon Peter loves Jesus he is to "Feed my lambs … Take care of my sheep …[and] … Feed my sheep." I took/take this as my call to action to teach and feed and take care of all children, "Statue of Liberty Morris" as Carolyn refers to me, for children are our most precious resource. The second quote is mine, "Is it good for the Children?" I contend that if you are about to make a decision, any decision … gun control, recess now or later, to buy some Girl Scout cookies, send a birthday card, give the student and A or a B, abortion, hand out a JR, presidential election choices, give money to a person on the street, provide a compliment or motivation … any decision … weigh it against this statement: Is it good for the Children? If your answer is "yes," then by all means if you can, do it. If your answer is "no," then think again, long and hard about what you are about to do. I have found in my life that there are very, very few questions that do not fall within the realm of this question serving to help you solve your serious quandaries. I had finally found my calling in this world, a teacher. And not a middle school teacher or high school teacher or college professor. I was an elementary school teacher. I had an elementary school teacher's heart, a fifth grader's mind and had learned all my life how to have a father's compassion. The result was that in 1999 Mountain View

Elementary selected me as their school's Teacher of the Year. (From now on I will refer to this as TOTY).

At Mountain View the TOTY procedure was you were nominated by someone at the school. You then had to sign a paper that said if you were selected you would stay in the teaching profession for at least one more year and you would submit the paperwork to run for the Cobb County TOTY. Next, generally there was a runoff to narrow the field down to two teachers, and then the two were voted on and one was selected. In that spring of 1999 as I said, I was honored and selected as the TOTY for Mountain View Elementary School. They made a big deal of giving me a parking spot and … well, that is about it. And that was very kind but I rarely used the parking space as it was out of the way, and I arrived every morning at 6:45 so I generally had my choice of places to park and being a Morris, I had my favorite. The parking place did come in handy later though. My class gave me a big party and everyone had on Mr. Morris masks. The class gave me a big trophy. I have since pared it down to just the base, and it is on the shelf in the basement. The next step was to submit the paperwork for the Cobb TOTY. The Cobb 2000 TOTY application was a copy of the application for the State of Georgia 2001 TOTY application and it involved eight sections covering areas such as a biography, professional development, community involvement, one's philosophy and letters of support. I worked hard on it and submitted it on time. I was quite proud of the effort.

However, in the fall of 1999 I was called to the principal's office at Mountain View. Jim Oveby wanted to talk to me. Uh-Oh … but of course, I went. When I got there, Hillary Straka was there and a couple of other teachers from other grade levels also. We all talked about this and that, nothing in particular that I recall, then they said there was to be an assembly on Friday and that Dr. Benjamin, the Cobb Superintendent, wanted to address the school. Well, my feelings on worthless assemblies were well known. I did not like my classroom time being interrupted by anyone, but I acquiesced, but not without grumbling like an old veteran. Which in retrospect Oveby and Straka must have thought was highly amusing. And the appointed Friday arrived and all the school gathered in the gym including my class seated in the back, because Mavericks always put others first. Dr. Benjamin took the podium and began a long rambling speech about schools and this and that and blah, blah, blah … I had found a chair in the back behind my class and was sitting with my head down until I heard the words, "… Mr. Jim Morris." I was petrified! What had I done? Was I being called out for disinterest? No! I was being called out because I was selected as the 2000 Cobb County Teacher of the Year! Right now, in 2023, the county gives out three TOTY awards each year. One for high, middle and elementary school. Back then, there was only one award, and I proudly was the recipient. When it was announced, Carolyn, James, Jenna, Adam, Carolyn's sister Kathy, Carolyn's mom, Cobb School Board representative Johnny Johnson (who sadly passed away several years ago), Cobb Superintendent Dr. Richard Benjamin, Kim Bearden who was the Cobb TOTY the year before, Jim Oveby and Hillary Straka took the stage. There was a big banner and some of my children came forward to hold it. The last year's Cobb TOTY was there to congratulate me. News reporters were there also, and I was … literally … speechless. There is a picture of me walking to the stage and the look on my face says it all. I was floored. Principal Oveby and Ms. Straka were obviously pleased and would not let me forget my objections to the assembly. All I can/could do is laugh at myself for taking myself so seriously.

A sub took over my class for the rest of the day, although quite honestly, I would rather have been with them. And everyone retired to the media center for cake and congratulations. There are several touching photographs of Carolyn and me having a serious lover's conversation. It was a morning that went by much too quickly, but the die was cast as my life was forever changed … for the better, I believe. At this point I filed the paperwork to be the Georgia Teacher of the Year. I mailed it off to the Georgia TOTY Powers and tried not to think about it. In the meantime, I was honored in front of the school board. It was an interesting evening. I received a plaque with a shoe on it. It is somewhere in a box in the basement. James and Carolyn were there. And I have thought a lot about that evening since. Normally the Cobb TOTY received a car to drive for the year of their TOTY adventures as they were expected to drive around quite a bit. I did not get a car, and I believe it was because I was not the Board's unanimous choice. There must have been some conflict. Dr. Benjamin, the Superintendent, was definitely on my team, but I suspect not all were. Why? I think it had to do with the fact that I had only been teaching for five years. Oh, I made a good story, but would I stick with teaching? There was division and the Board was not in full agreement so they held the car back … and Benjamin was gone the next year. (Besides, I had already won a Thunderbird! How many cars does a boy want?) But I did not let any of that rain on my parade and you, gentle reader, should not either. I was honored. And I was honored by the Secretary of State of Georgia, I was invited to a reception at Kennesaw State University by President Dr. Betty Siegel and was asked to speak at numerous occasions around Cobb including welcoming all the teachers back to school in the fall of 2000. It was cool, and I have to admit I struggled with not getting the big head. Now one of the parts of being the Cobb TOTY was a ceremony on the Marietta Square where outlines of your hands were cut into stone and the stone with your name was laid in a special area on the west side of the square. When you may be reading this, I do not know if the stone is still there, but on October 20th, 1999, my whole class, Carolyn, my mother and Aunt Doris Wofford were there. I recall it was raining, and I gave a much too long speech, but I learned from that and tried not to repeat it.

As part of the process to become the Georgia TOTY, a committee from the Department of Education came to Mountain View to see me teach. It is a morning I will never forget. That morning the class was to learn about triangles and how, no matter the type of triangle, the interior corners always add up to $180°$, and the vehicle for this lesson was to have one of my characters, Sam Scalene – Agent 003, appear. Now in order for this lesson to come off smoothly I needed one of my old standby pieces of equipment, the venerable overhead projector! Yes, there was one in my classroom all twenty-five years of my teaching and would have one today if I were teaching. However, an overhead projector has two weaknesses. One is it needs a bulb. So, before the lesson that morning I put in a new bulb. The other think it needs is electricity. Yep, you guessed it. The class was quiet and totally engaged. The DOE folks were in their places and seemed to be interested. And Sam Scalene had made his entrance and was being all Agent 003 complete with James Bond music from his briefcase every time he opened it and his corded phone he pulled from the briefcase on which he spoke to "Control" confirming his arrival. He had warned against any of the information he was going to share falling into the hands of the sinister LPR Organization (Lines, Points and Rays) and the children had all taken the oath not to divulge what they were going to learn. The stage was set, and the room goes black. Yep, the power went out! Well, I can tell you Agent 003 started sweating at that point, but I immediately told the children that this was not unexpected. I pointed out that the dreaded LPR Organization would stop at nothing, and this was proof. We crippled along, and fortunately just when I really needed to power back, it arrived and I was saved! Of course I'm sure I got kudos from the DOE for handling the hiccup, but it did add some gray hair I'll tell you.

The next step in the GA TOTY selection process was a luncheon at the Georgia Power building downtown in March of 2000 for the twelve semifinalists. Man, you want to talk about a stilted affair. I do not remember much about it other than the chicken was rubber, the green beans were tasteless and pressure was amazing. It was the first time I met "the competition," read their résumés and they were twelve formidable teachers. They came from all teaching areas and every corner of the state and every single one of them had way more years teaching than me and every single one, I pretty sure, had more degrees and years of experience … but I had a "rags to riches" story that was interesting. I did my best to "walk the walk and talk the talk." James and I were on a TBT that summer of 2000 to Washington DC when I got the word I was one of five Finalists. The next event was the actual award night.

It was another surreal evening. Before the dinner even started we, the five finalists, quickly found out who the winner was. It was to be a twenty-eight-year veteran, a twice named school TOTY, high school math teacher from Lumpkin County named Mary Wilson Eager. She was certainly qualified to be the Georgia TOTY. And of course the Georgia TOTY would next go on to compete at a national level! And today, as I write, I will be real honest, at this point in the whole TOTY experience, I was pretty much done. The experience was distracting to say the least. Oh, do not get me wrong … I will be forever honored to have been the Cobb TOTY and it was a validation of my whole life and my work, but the TOTY race was tiring and it distracted me from my love, my classroom. The funny thing about that finalist evening is that my main recollections of the evening are Blue Bell Ice Cream, Linda Schrenko, how beautiful Carolyn was that night and my speech acknowledging her. That evening was one of those strange events when you realize it is important in your life, yet when you try to recollect … only a few snippets remain. So, I guessing Blue Bell Ice Cream was a sponsor or something and the ice cream was delicious. Still, whenever I see their product I am transported to May 5th, 2020, the evening. Jim Oveby, Jenna and Adam, James, my beautiful Carolyn and I all had a table. The evening was hosted by the State School Superintendent, Linda Schrenko, who I thought was pretty okay. As an aside, a few years later she was convicted of an embezzlement scheme as she made a bid for governor and spent eight years in federal prison. She wore too much makeup and tried desperately to look younger than she was, but she was always nice to me, and I liked her. In the big black portfolios, you will find my short speech (I tried to learn), and you will see two things – one was that when I wrote the speech I did not know which of the five of us was going to win the title that night, and the second was the inclusion of a thoughtful piece of writing by The Earl of Lytton. In it he extols the undeniable advantages of having a woman who cares about you … *"It is a wonderful advantage to a man, in every pursuit or avocation, to secure an advisor in a sensible woman. In a woman, there is at once, a subtle delicacy of tact and a plain soundness of judgement which are rarely found to an equal in a man. A woman, if she be really your friend, will have a sensible regard for your character, honor and repute. She will seldom counsel you to do a shabby thing; for a woman friend always desires to be proud of you."* That would be my wife of what is now, fifty plus years … Carolyn.

Back to 1999 … my final comment about that year is a performance my fifth graders gave at a PTA meeting on the last days before the holiday break. It was a very cool performance of a song by The Highwaymen named *The Twentieth Century is Almost Over*. Look it up on the Internet and you will see why is was particularly appropriate for that December 1999 performance.

18.

A new Millennium! There was a lot of concern about this year dawning, and it centered on the "Interweb" as James calls it. You see all during the 1900's the years were simply referred to by the last two digits … 1970 was 70 and 1922 was 22. Then computers came along, and they were set up to recognize the year by the last two digits and along comes the year 2000. What would the computers think of a year 00? Would they revert to the year 1900 and wipe everything out? Would we have a global meltdown of the Interweb? Would civilization as we know it cease to exist? Would dogs and cats start laying down together? Would nuclear holocaust take place because suddenly computers would become "self- aware" and would The Terminator would have to save us and take down Cyberdyne? Of course none of this happened, and it was all just a "tempest in a teapot." But it was fun at the time. Carolyn just continued at Lifespan; I just continued at Mountain View and just continued being a Cobb TOTY, and James just continued his studies and finished his junior year at Wheeler and cruised into his senior year. Again I reiterate, "Life is what happens while you are paying the bills."

At Lifespan Carolyn continued to make the place hum along and I was recruited to give a series of Lunch and Learn lessons on WWI. But before I did that, in the early spring I took a day trip with the older adults to Kennesaw Mountain and continued last summer's Civil War lessons with local history. Again I had a great time and was able to use many of my classroom lessons for the older adults. I had to be careful with these as some of these people were actually alive in 1914! On the bookshelf in the basement is a binder labeled WWI with my lessons in it. There is also a 2 inch square "floppy" with the lessons on it if you can find any way to download them! Ah, technology.

As I mentioned, 2000 was the year that Two Boys went to Washington, D.C. My old calendars are not really clear where we went each time we had a trip. All they say is "Two

Boys Trip" … frustrating. So, while the exact years we went here or there may be muddled, the events of the trip are correct. And I know in 2000 Two Boys went to Washington. I recall driving up and allowing James to drive a goodly part of the way. He was still thrilled to be a driver and every part of driving fascinated and excited him. As I recollect we were somewhere in North Carolina blasting along and there came up a rain storm. I mean it was raining like a cow pissing off a flat rock (don't you love my use of colorful colloquialisms ☺) and buckets of water pouring down. The heavens really opened up on James. We were driving on an expressway through a city, Charlotte I think, and traffic was heavy … real "white knuckle" driving. Sheets of rain covering us and every time a big truck went by us we would get deluged. The wipers were going as hard as they could but James never faltered or gave up. None of this pull over stuff for him! And I must admit, he handled the car well, however when we came out the other side, he happily relinquished the driving to me for a spell.

We got to Washington in the evening. It is a good solid ten or eleven-hour drive, and we were beat. We stayed in a Holiday Inn near the Air and Space Museum as I recall. Somewhere near the Mall anyway. You can see the results of our adventure on the wall in the living room of Falcon Wood Drive. James was really coming into his own with his photography and there are some beautiful shots. I just looked at the pictures again and one has the number 2K down in the corner so I do have the Washington trip pegged correctly year-wise. I remember that the father of one of my students, Eric Gordon, who was an Assistant Police Chief in Atlanta got us tickets to go inside the FBI headquarters. We got a personal tour, and James came away with a target that the FBI used to practice their marksmanship. It was a human figure with bullet holes all in it … very cool. The Dad had also helped get James and me tickets into the White House which we both found to be rather blah. I think the FBI was so cool it was kind of a high point. Another touching day was the Vietnam and Korea Memorials. James shot a ton of film that day, and our trip to the Holocaust Museum was another gut-wrenching stop. I recall we went to the Air and Space Museum and went to the 3-D movie which was very, very cool. We saw a movie narrated by Morgan Freeman about Space. It was so cool and such a teachable video, I bought it. I just looked for it and could not locate it in our collection. I probably loaned it to James at some point as he is now a teacher and a real natural at it. One of the best I may add. We visited the Holocaust Museum, the Natural History Museum, the Washington Monument and The Capitol. We got lost one morning walking from our hotel, and we had to backtrack almost the whole way because we could not get over a huge wall. We rode the subway, and generally just had a great time as we did on all our Two Boys Trips. As I mentioned in the TOTY tale, it was during this trip to Washington that I got the news on being a Finalist.

2000 was the year Carolyn and I almost moved to the mountains. She and I had harbored this dream of escaping Cobb and living somewhere up in the sky country. We toyed with Ashville because we both loved it up there and this would have been the time to make that jump, but we opted for Lumpkin County and Dahlonega. Carolyn's longtime friends Kathy and Robert Fuller had built a beautiful place up just outside Dahlonega, and we had visited them. As it turned out Kathy was on the school board, and she wrangled me an interview at the middle school. Well, they were charmed to have TOTY even consider them, and the job was mine for the taking. So, C and I started looking at homes up there and quickly determined that Atlanta had discovered Lumpkin County and there was no way we could afford anything like we had at Millbrook Trace up in the mountains. All we could find were rundown homes with mold problems and too much pine paneling! Yech. So, at the risk of hurting Carolyn's relationship with her friends, I backed out of the offer. I hated to do it, but it just was not meant to be. Our hope of sometime moving away from Cobb … and I believe subconsciously wanting to move away from my mother and father and local family and Carolyn's mother and family and finally being free of them – which as we now know never would have been able to happen had we moved or not – was put on hold for a couple of years.

Marybelle Swift's son Matthew Swift got married in 2000 to a beautiful woman named Kenya. Matt was finishing his PhD at the University of Michigan at Ann Arbor and the wedding was to be held there. We got an invitation and decided to make it a road trip up to my old stomping grounds, introduce James to Niagara Falls and generally just "open a keg of nails" as my paternal grandmother, Momma, used to say. She also had other interesting expressions like "play it by air" and no amount of discussion would convince her it was "play it by ear." Another was when she was feeling poorly she felt like a "stewed rat" which for her was as risqué as she got! And one last one, an old timey word she always used and as a child I thought was hilarious (still do) … "commode" was her word for a toilet. And to clean the commode she used Bab-o cleanser which was like Comet today. And I remember, as I write, when Jenna was young, maybe eight or nine, Carolyn and I went up to Momma's for a weekend and she asked Carolyn and me a most interesting question. She asked, "When men get together [have sex], how do they 'do it?'" I feigned ignorance and dodged the question entirely because "discretion is the better part of valor." But anyway, I totally digress, Carolyn, James and I headed up to Detroit. James and I were tag team driving, and I think we stopped somewhere in Ohio for the night. The next day we pushed onto Detroit. While there we went to Ann Arbor, and we saw my 1531 Northwood house which, as you already anticipated, looked very small and not at all as I remembered it. We also found my elementary school which again must have been totally remodeled as I barely recognized it. I do recall the hotel we were in and the fact that Kimball Rogers was there. Kimball Rogers was the very interesting daughter of Nelson K. Rogers and Marion (Toochie) Rogers. She was the second born of their three children. Edward was the first born, Kimball second and Jamie was the third. Kimball passed away in 2017 after many physical complications. The Michigan wedding was lovely, and we represented the Morris arm of the family well. After the wedding we were off to Niagara Falls and made the touristy trip around the falls on the Maid of the Mist complete with thin plastic ponchos. After a night's rest we were ready to head home, and basted off about 8:00 in the morning. We planned to just "find" a place to stay on the way home, but the Trip Gods had other plans. The drive is around twelve hours if you don't stop to eat or get gas or use the restroom. So the trip is really about fourteen or fifteen hours. As we drove, James and I tag teaming again, and got to around Cincinnati we started looking for a place to stay. As we passed Lexington, Kentucky, we watched for signs and found nothing to our liking. The next major city was Knoxville, Tennessee, and by then it was getting late, but we all just said the heck with it, we're this close, let's just go home. And we did, getting there about midnight totally exhausted and giddy. And that was the longest continuous drive I have ever been on and the last one I ever want to do … almost matched it in 2016 but that is a story for later.

On the school front I continued at Mountain View for the 2000-2001 school year. A lady, Tonya Perlot, joined the team and became a friend, and I was the team lead and had a very successful time doing that job and all the TOTY stuff. I introduced a Civil War Bowl to my repertoire of teaching that year. The Civil War Bowl was a competition that capped our studies of that conflict. The students were divided up into five teams of five or six. Each team had an expert in the field of "North" or "South" or "People and Dates" or "Who Am I" or "Battles and Places." Then each person had to be proficient in at least one other area in case on Bowl Day that team person was absent. Each expert list had twenty to twenty-five questions on it which the children had to research and know the answer to. This list was handed out before we ever started our studies and I made sure in the course of our study I would address every question so if you knew your list and were paying attention you would have all your questions answered. Finally, on Bowl day I would have five overhead projectors lined up with acetate overlays and pens available. The expert from each team in a particular field would assume the position at the projector (with the lamp off). I would ask questions, and the experts would write their responses. The experts would then sit down, and all overheads would light up and scores would be tallied for right answers. By the end there would be first place through fifth place winners. The fifth place winners would get an award of pencils or something. Then the prizes would ramp up through cheap calculators to candy bars to the ultimate first prize gift! It was a framed picture of me! Usually one of those corporate shots looking all, well, corporate. Later in the day I would personally autograph and dedicate the pictures for the first place contestants. Two things about these prizes I want to include: one was the year a first place winner wanted to trade my picture for the second place giant Snickers candy bar and two, the parent who told me that when she went into her child's bedroom there were no pictures of her parents but there was a picture of me on the child's dresser! Cool.

This year's trip to Charleston with class started with a twist that endeared The Travel Store to me forever. It was very early "o'dark:30" as my class of 30 children, about eight adults, the Travel Store Rep, Jerry Peterson and I stood waiting for our Travel Store arranged coach bus to arrive at its appointed hour of 5:45. No bus. Calmly Jerry dialed up David Freund and let them know what was happening. It wasn't twenty minutes that both Kathy and David showed up with donuts and juice boxes for the children and donuts and coffee for the adults. With much apologies they conjured up another bus from thin air and we were on our way … a little late, but the driver was able to make the time up somehow and the whole event was saved. And that was the kind of morning that contributed to my present lovely gray locks.

19.

2001 - Now THAT was a year! Our first grandchild was born, James graduated, Carolyn turned fifty, I changed schools and there was a terrorist attack on our country. What a jamb packed year. I know, I know … it is truly going to be an Odyssey.

But let's start with the first event. February 7th, 2001, at 4:03 AM Mr. Bryce Blackwell came into the world, but he was not going to make it easy on his mom Jenna. Jenna actually went into labor early in the morning of the day before, around 2:00 AM or so, as I recall. I got a call at work, but did not rush right over to Gainesville. Carolyn was on her way as soon as there were the first positive indications. Jenna spent the day (now please remember this is from my recollections and a male perspective) breathing and walking until she and Adam were sure Bryce was in fact going to come and this was not "false labor." Well, it wasn't false labor and around 2:00 PM, I think, Jenna headed to North Gwinnett Medical Center, and I was on my way over from Marietta. Then we took our places all of us sure that it would only be a matter of hours. And it was a matter of many hours. All through the long night we were there. I vividly recall sitting by Jenna's bed in the middle of the night, rubbing her back and cooing (and this is going to sound stupid) the song *Down in the Valley* softly. I don't know if it soothed her, but it certainly helped me. Carolyn and I stood by and did what we could. At about 3:00 in the morning of the 7th, after more than 24 hours in labor, both Jenna and Bryce started to have complications. I am not going to even try to outline the events leading up to the decision for Jenna to deliver by cesarean, but the decision was made that the baby was in too much distress, and it was the only option, and at 4:03 AM Mr. Bryce Harper Blackwell came into the world. What a miracle. And what a miracle he has been since the moment he arrived. I sit here and tell you as a fact … there is NOTHING like a grandchild to bring joy into your life. Interestingly Bryce will be staying with us tomorrow night here at Falcon Wood Drive because he will be taking the MCAT at KSU on Saturday (April 29th, 2023). Yep, he is all grown up with a fiancé, Anna, and I have many, many more stories to relate between 2001 and today. Bryce was born, and he did have some lingering effects of the difficult birth which, fortunately, the doctors were able to address immediately and within a few days both he and Jenna were "good to go" as they say. Carolyn stayed for several days to help and take some of the load off new mommy Jenna. I came back home that day, grabbed some shuteye, and was back at school the next day. My Room Mom that year was Ms. Rogers (McCall Rogers mommy … I recall we had McCall Rogers grandpa come in and talk to the class that year about having been an A-6 Intruder aircraft pilot in Vietnam) and she coordinated the wonderful Mountain View class to each donate a book for Bryce, and when I got to class the next day there was a big basket of books for him! They were so sweet. Just thinking that Ms. McCall Rogers must be about thirty-three now and probably has a career and children. Ah, but my mind wanders … Bryce was the most beautiful first grandson I ever had, and he has continued to make Carolyn and me proud every single day. The rest of 2001 was sprinkled with time notations in the calendar where we were able to keep Bryce and give Jenna and Adam a break. We treasured every minute with that boy, and I'm sure you are going to hear more about him (and "other one") in the following pages.

But late in the year we had an opportunity to go down to Georgia Southern with Jenna and Adam and newly minted Mr. Bryce. We went to Southern to meet up with "Uncle" Tom (as he has become known today), cook out and watch a football game. It was a glorious late Georgia summer afternoon and hotter than … yep. The first event, and Jenna and Adam can corroborate this, was right after lunch. We were all headed to the football stadium, and it became obvious that Mr. Bryce needed a diaper change in the worst way. Of course you all know by now that babies who are maybe six months old do not have very sophisticated digestive systems and Bryce was typical in that respect. Now I am not entirely sure what Jenna and Adam had fed this poor boy, but whatever it was it went through him like "poop through a goose." Adam, wanting to show what a hands-on Dad he had become took Bryce over to the van and opened the hatch in the back in order to lay Bryce down to change him. Well, upon loosening the diaper it was obvious Bryce had had, what has now in family lore become, a BLOW OUT! And the greatest part of the blow out was that old Mister Dad Adam could not handle it! I mean whatever this poor boy had been given to eat was stinking up not only the car, but everything within a ten-foot radius. And it was all over poor Bryce … his legs, up his back … everywhere! Needless to say Jenna and Carolyn jumped into the giant hole left as Adam almost passed out. Tom and I were standing by laughing our heads off at Adam. Mom and Nana got the little guy cleaned up and in a clean onesie and got all the offending clothing and whatnot secured in several airtight baggies that all moms have to carry. I think it is a law. And we were off to the game … in the heat. Now this was before Southern had very many stands for its guests, so we sat on a hillside on wooden benches nestled into the

hill. We sat under umbrellas and watched a little of the game, but the heat was stifling. Georgia Southern's field reminded me of Clemson's field … Clemson's field is nicknamed Death Valley. And this was Death Valley that afternoon. Soon it was time for Bryce's bottle, and Nanna quickly volunteered for the duty. Nanna and Bryce bailed out of the heat to try to find a little bit cooler place to feed him. After a little while I left to go find them, and what I found made an iconic photograph that is on my dresser today. Nanna found a rocking chair nestled under a shady arbor and was rocking her first grandson as she fed him his bottle. A cool breeze was stirring from somewhere rustling Carolyn's hair, and the temperature was at least ten degrees cooler where the two of them sat and rocked. Carolyn was in heaven. And in her arms Bryce was sucking on his bottle. Occasionally he would drift off to sleep, and Carolyn would gently shake him slightly, and he would again start his little mouth sucking until he would drift off again. Every time I see that picture I recall that wonderful day and a little piece of beauty in my life.

2001 was also James's high school graduation year! But I have to back up just a bit from graduation and tell you about his prom. My son James took four, or was it five, ladies to prom! Yes, you are reading this correctly. There were four girls who James knew who were graduating and had no dates to the prom, so he asked them to go with him. What a kind man. Dinner was "Dutch Treat" as I recall so they all paid for their separate dinners, but James made sure they went to the prom and got home safely. THAT is my boy. I wish I had had the selflessness and presence of mind to do something as magnanimous and kind as that when I was younger. He was, and still is, one of the finest men I have ever been acquainted with. Somewhere something went right.

James was the class of 2001 – The Space Odyssey class. You can look up the reference if you need to. During his career at Wheeler he had run the program that handled the morning announcements which were done as a video production, worked on the homecoming float committee, been a leader in the photography club and even had keys to the high school so he could work in the photography lab when he needed to. He and the photography people had taken trips to the barrier islands and we have several of his framed photographs in the dining area made on his adventures.

All of these things were done while in the summers he worked at White Water his freshman, sophomore and junior years. He would have worked his senior summer except there was a huge SNAFU. This happened the day before Memorial Day weekend of that year. James had filed his paperwork earlier that week, and he had been informed, the day before Memorial Day weekend that he had been denied a position because of his criminal record. WHAT? Yes, someone had done a background check and turned up some kind of a criminal record. Well, he and I could not let this stand. I mean he was heading to Georgia Southern in the fall and if a mistake like this took hold it could make a mess for years to come. So Two Boys headed right over to find out what was going on. The person with Whitewater said a James L Morris with James's social security number had committed some crime sometime, and they were sorry. We pursued who did this check and where could we go straighten this out? Now this must happen a lot because Whitewater was less than helpful. Come to find out there was a James L. Morris, different middle name, who had done something and the social security matched … almost! ALMOST! Yes, it was only one number off. WHAT! Again, they said they could not help, and we would have to go the police in DeKalb County to straighten this out. By now it was 3:00 in the afternoon of Friday before the holiday weekend. If we were going to fix this, we had to do it now. So, James and I hauled butt over to I-285 and Memorial Drive, over on the other side of Atlanta. Got there just in the nick of time … they were literally locking up, pleaded our case and got an officer to help us. Somehow the mistake was acknowledged and an official paper was issued to fix the problem. We sped back over to White Water. As I recall we wanted to speak to a manager. What I got was a totally disinterested young lady who offered no acknowledgement of an error on their part but did fix the record. I do not think James worked there that summer.

But the summers before he had worked there and each summer he worked himself into a position that was very irregular. For instance, he would start the summer telling children when they were spaced out enough for the slides and by the end of the summer he was walking around the park solving computer problem with a walkie-talkie on his belt. The boy was just amazing. Now during these years at WW a couple of things happened that would have a lasting effect on all our lives. Unbeknownst to Carolyn and me, he met this girl, Angela Swope, and they worked together for a summer or two and went to Wheeler High

School together. That was the first thing. The second thing, and we still laugh, sort of, about this. There was a raffle at White Water and Miss Angela won a television set. Well, the set would not fit in her car, so she enlisted James's help, which being the Don Quixote man he was, he gladly gave. Well, there was rule in our house. If you were expected home at a specific time, say 11:00 PM, you had until the final stroke of the grandfather clock's chime to be in the house or at least on the grounds, unless you had called with an extenuating circumstance. Again, I remind you, Gentle Reader, this was looooong before cell phones and finding a phone was sometimes a problem. Anyway, Mr. Don Quixote was helping her with the television and time ran out without a phone call so James was grounded for a week … or was it two … or was it six months … I forget. James can probably tell you with great embellishments and hand waving and gesticulations about the whole event and its unfairness to his life, liberty and the pursuit of happiness!

But, this whole story started with his graduation. We were planning a big to do. If you will recall Don Swift, Marybelle's husband, had passed away, and we wanted her here for the graduation of our last child, so we invited her to come from California and stay with us. And she took us up on the offer. Marybelle was quite a lady and my perception was that she liked the men. Of the three Morris children that Momma and Pete (Marie and Marion Morris) produced, and one of the two ladies they produced (Aunt Toochie was the other child) she was the one most likely to give men fits. Whenever she flew on an airplane, she always flew first class, and whoever the gentleman was sitting next to her, and it seemed to

always inevitably be a good looking gentleman, by the end of the flight she had told him her life's story and extracted from him all the details of his life. She was amazing. She always drank her coffee from a china cup with her little finger out and she was always "dressed to the nines." Yes, Marybelle Swift, later Marybelle Dent, was quite a lady. Anyway, she came to visit and stay with us for the graduation. A memory comes to me as I write this. It must have been during her stay that a comet came close to the earth and was visible from Georgia because I recall standing out on our Millbrook Trace house driveway with Carolyn and Marybelle and looking up and seeing the comet in the night sky. Interesting. I also recall that James had several cords for graduation. If you look at his picture of him actually being handed his diploma you will see his cords. I do not recall what they were all for, but he and I decided that he needed more than what Wheeler High School had authorized him to wear, so he and I went to the Joann Shop bought some cords that hold curtains back and some tassels, and we made him a few more cords. Maybe one for Photography Club and one for German Club … who knows. But look at the picture and see the joke we pulled on Wheeler High School. It was awesome. We got the boy graduated and got him headed for Georgia Southern University. There had never been a doubt where he wanted to go to school. He had remembered going down to Southern when Jenna was there and had many good memories of Two Boys being there: of scouting for railroad spikes along the tracks, of big whirlpool tubs, of a game room on campus where he could play any video game he wanted. It's funny the things that influence your college choices.

I think there was no Two Boys Trip that summer. We were getting ready for college and whatnot. And the time came for us to take our last chicken off to the big, bad world, and on August 18, 2001, we made the trip down to Southern again. James was staying in Howell Dorm. We got down there on a Saturday and as was the custom at Southern, all the professors were out to help children get unloaded and settled in their dorms. And they helped us get James in his dorm. And then I had to do the hardest thing I had ever had to do in my life … let James go. When we had dropped Jenna off back in 1992, I was very consumed in my life, and a Carlson company that was crumbling. So when we dropped Jenna off, I was not all crying and upset, because we still had another child to shepherd along. So dropping Jenna off wasn't THAT upsetting. But when I hugged James for the last time before we drove away I sensed the finality of the situation. James, my good friend who had traveled everywhere with me, was never really going to be in Carolyn and my home again … anymore. And as he turned and walked away, and I got in the car to drive off … I cried. I boo-hoo'd like a baby. I imagine we spent the night there, but we may not have, I do not actually recall. I was too upset.

Carolyn turned 50 in 2001, and I was bound and determined to do it up right! So, I secretly planned her birthday. It required Carolyn giving up control which she does not like at all. I would not call her a control freak, but let's just say she is happier knowing what the lay of the land is, but all she knew was that we were leaving on the Friday evening before her birthday at 5:00. I also told her she needed two nice outfits and a casual outfit. Reluctantly, she got home from work, and we left. I had gotten us a room at the Georgian Terrace across the street from the Fox, and we headed there. The room was perfect! It was what I will call a turret room. It was round with windows looking to the south over the green of Atlanta. We changed clothes and freshened up and went to our first stop, a restaurant called the Abbey. The Abbey was an old church that had been converted into a restaurant and was pretty cool. I do not recall much about the dinner except it was candle-lit and in a large space like a cathedral. Dinner lasted until late and we fell into bed in the hotel exhausted. The pace of our lives back then, as I reflect now in 2023, was exhausting, but we were young, and you do what you need to do. The next day, Saturday, was a relaxed trip to the High Museum and lunch and a walk around Atlanta. I do not recall where dinner was. I remember threatening to go to The Varsity just down the street but resisted the urge for two chili dogs, rings and a "big orange." If we had gone there, Carolyn would have gotten the salmon salad (joke … Carolyn would always say she would get the salmon salad if she ever ate there … which she did on occasion with grandchildren … note: The Varsity has no salmon salad). I had wanted to go to a play or something at the Fox, but there was nothing of consequence doing there. Then I thought a concert at the Woodruff, but nothing was cooking there. However, that evening we went to the Alliance theater, an intimate theater in the basement of the Woodruff Arts Center and saw a play "in the round" meaning the audience was only about six or eight people deep and we sat in a circle around the actors who were on a stage maybe twenty feet in diameter. It was very personal and kind of cool. Late in the evening we returned to The Georgian Terrace. Another restful night in our turret room and then we had to return to reality. And the reality was that Carolyn's mother would not hear of there not being a whole family party for Carolyn's fiftieth, so we returned to Millbrook to a house full of people wishing her a happy birthday. Carolyn hated that part of the weekend!

Carolyn continued at Lifespan, so James probably did not do Meals on Wheels that summer. It was maybe the summer of 2002. Carolyn was enjoying her work but the drive into and out of Atlanta was difficult, but she handled it with her usual casual focus and determination. I was enlisted to do another Lunch and Learn and so this time I focused on the end of WWI up until December 7th, 1941. And these lessons had to be "spot-on" as I was definitely getting into the time period that everyone who was in the Lifespan program lived through. It was tricky, but I used an old teacher trick of having them interject and participate in my lessons and that added excitement, interest and depth to the lessons.

In the background of that summer was my moving to Mt. Bethel Elementary. Dr. Jeanelle Brown had recruited me away from Mountain View which was not that much of a challenge. The 2000/2001 school year had been a mixed bag. On the one hand I was a TOTY and all that entailed and on the other, Jim Oveby had retired at the end of the 2000 school year and Hillary Straka had been transferred to, I believe, Post Oak Tritt Elementary. So for the 2000/2001 school year at Mountain View we had a new administration … and make no mistake, the administration makes the school (and you can quote me on that). You can have the nicest building (I'll call that foreshadowing), the nicest children and the best curriculum, but the administration can ruin all of that in a heartbeat. An example: at Mountain View under Jim and Hillary, there were birds in cages all over the school and Jim and Hillary and the PTA had hired a student's grandfather to paint little vignettes of birds on the walls all over the school. To make it even more special, this grandfather had honed his painting craft in Germany, in one of Hitler's camps for Jews and Undesirables, during World War II. His work was beautiful. So what did this new principal do as she took the reins? Yes, to show her power she had every single bird painting painted over, and the cages were removed, but do not worry Gentle Reader. Because if you went in her office, which we all had to do sooner or later, there was an open Bible on a little stand that you could kneel on and pray. I'll let you surmise what you will. When Dr. Jeanelle Brown asked me at a luncheon I was speaking at if I would be interesting in transferring to Mt. Bethel, I said I sure would. So, I applied to transfer. Now at this time the only way to get into Mt. Bethel was if someone died because no one wanted to leave … ever. This was an opportunity and the first step was to interview with the team you would be joining. Now, at this time Dr. Brown did not have a fifth grade slot available. All she had was a fourth grade position. That was okay with me if I could get into Mt. Bethel. So, I met with the fourth grade team. And on that team (foreshadow) was a lady named Jessica Appleyard. And during the meeting she reminded me we had just met several months before at a wedding. It was a wedding of one of my high school Sunday School seniors, Leslie Gordon, who I had taught years before. Carolyn and I had been friends of the Gordons at Mt. Bethel Church and had been invited to the wedding. And at the reception I had met Jessica Appleyard who was also a friend of the Gordons. She and I had been introduced and she had said, "Oh, I know who you are. You are the Cobb County Teacher of the Year and a Finalist for the Georgia Teacher of the Year." And so I walked into Jeanelle's office and there Jessica sat with the four other teachers on the team. It was a good interview to say the least. And so in the fall of 2001 I started at Mt. Bethel Elementary School at 1210 Johnson Ferry Road in Marietta, Georgia, teaching a fourth grade class. And for all intents and purposes, and for better or worse, it was to be almost my exclusive teaching home for the rest of my career.

I would be historically remiss in talking about 2001 if I did not include a commentary on this and share this event from my perspective. I had been with my new class about four weeks and they were a great bunch of children. They were not an Inclusion Class, but they were a little younger than I had been teaching. They were nine year olds mostly with a few ten year olds sprinkled in. You may recall that the email you may have read earlier in this book was from one Devon Murphy. Devon was in this fourth grade class and would become a lifelong friend. Anyway, on a typical day, the children began arriving about 7:15 and by 8:00 we were hard into our math class. I preferred math first thing when everyone was at their sharpest and that September 11th, Tuesday morning was no different than any other beautiful, cool fall morning until about 9:00. That was when we, the teachers, were informed confidentially – exactly how Dr. Brown did it I do not recall – that an airplane had hit one of the twin World Trade Towers in New York City. I remember thinking it had to be a similar occurrence to the event in July of 1945 when a bomber crashed into the Empire State Building in thick fog. That was until we were informed about fifteen minutes later that a plane had struck the South Tower. We were told that the decision had been made that we were to carry on with our normal day, and that we were NOT to let the children know. No televisions within earshot of the children were to be turned on. The administration had decided the students were to find out about this when and if the parents wanted them to know. So, I "endeavored to persevere" until the children headed off to Specials in the middle of the morning when I could get to a television in the back of the Media Center. There I found out the horror. Not only had the towers been hit, the Pentagon where The Colonel had spent many years had been hit and the towers had collapsed. I now faced the hardest part of my day. How to continue as if nothing had happened and stay alert to protect my students. I called Carolyn. We talked. She called James. He was fine. He did not want to come home. She talked to Jenna. She was upset but fine. And the children came back to the room and I taught school on a Tuesday like no other. It ranked right up there with the day Kennedy was shot, the day MLK was shot and the day Bobby Kennedy was shot … burned into my memory. On the next day, Wednesday, I was missing a few children, but for the most part almost everyone was present. We talked about the events of Tuesday but did not dwell on them. We had important stuff to do! And we moved on. I believe in my heart that the children helped me get past 9/11 more than I helped the children get past 9/11/2001.

20.

In 2002 Carolyn made some workplace changes. It was time to let Lifespan go. Her favorite nun who was a truly wonderful person moved on to other things and so did Carolyn. She was introduced to a nonprofit organization for older adults downtown that not only provided a place for them to gather but also did Meals on Wheels. The group met in the basement of a building and had a computer lab. Now to call it a computer lab was a stretch. It did have computers … of a sort. Some of them worked and some did not. They were of the earliest vintage and had probably 8mb of RAM as maybe 56mb of memory. They used 5½ inch floppy discs and had big old tube screens. There was no real internet or connection to what there was of the Web, but it was a way for the older adults to dip their fingers into the computer world. The budget was totally on donations and when (and if) Carolyn got paid was dicey at best. But Carolyn, being the soldier she was made the best of it. She cleaned the place up, we got computers running, she master-minded the Meals on Wheels and even ran the deliveries sometimes. I vaguely recall there was a dance one evening. All the adults got dressed up, and we played music and danced and ate and had a good time. There are two other vivid memories I have of her stint there besides being very nervous having her down there close to Georgia Tech late at night. One was that Panera Bread would give away to the nonprofit whatever bread they had left over at the end of the night. This is a policy they maintain to this day and is incredibly generous of them. Oh, I'm sure there are tax breaks and all kinds of other stuff but going around to several Panera stores late in the evening and collecting their donations is something I remember well. The bread always went to good use supplementing the Meals on Wheels. I never delivered any Meals on Wheels meals, but I drove Carolyn around that summer of 2002 and her stories of the conditions some of the older adults lived in were heartbreaking. The second is that James, home from Southern, helped out that summer in the kitchen actually getting the ancient stove working … how he did it I am not sure I want to know … but he did and was the King of Meals on Wheels that summer, sweating his fanny off in that kitchen. James is one amazing son and human being. But the stress of that position and total lack of adequate support took its toll on my Love and she moved on to apply for and secure a position at Cooper Middle School as a Parapro of sorts working in the office and computer lab and helping special education children. That was a tough gig, and the principal was somewhat of a prima donna and the whole place was rather dysfunctional, but she made the 02-03 school year work.

One of the absolute joys of '02 was having little Bryce come and stay with us. I smile now as I think back. He would come to us with a list of instruction a mile long from darling Jenna. What to eat and not eat, what to put on his little face for his ever present Rosacea, bed times and to-do's and to-don'ts all sent with love of a new Mommy. He was a year old that February and we would have him and Oscar the boxer dog come stay with us. One of his and my favorite things to do was to take the dog for a walk. Bryce would be in the stroller and the dog on a leash and we two men would venture out into the world of the Millbrook Trace subdivision. His first words to me were spoken as we got ready for one of our adventures. Before we left, I would always put a little baseball hat on him and then I would get mine and we would "sally forth" to do battle against all the evil dragons and "bad boys" in the neighborhood as only Don Quixote and his ever faithful companion Sancho Panza could do. One morning we got ready to leave and it was a beautiful warm spring morning, and I decided we did not need our hats. Bryce was not having it. It was something that we did, and so he spoke up. Looking earnestly up into my eyes from his stroller he patted his head and said, as clear as a bell, "Hă, hă." Meaning we could not leave without our hă [hats]. I will never forget that. In fact, as Carolyn and I gave him his college graduation gift the other day, April 28th, 2023, as he gets ready to graduate from the University of Georgia, and part of it was new hat. The hat was a "Life is Good" hat, and it had a dog emblem on the front of it. Along with his graduation present, this new hat seemed an important memory to immortalize. So we two intrepid men would head out, and inevitably as we were walking along the stroller would swerve and little Bryce would brush into a bush near the sidewalk. Then, amongst giggles and laughs, I would tell the bush to stop getting him, and we would move on until the next bush would jump out and there were more gales of little, high pitched, boy giggles. Sometimes as we were walking, and he was actually walking not in a stroller, he would stop and stick his head in the bush wanting me to tell the bush to leave him alone. Funny, other than evil boy grabbing bushes there were no other monsters on our walks. I guess Bryce, Oscar and I were just too imposing a triumvirate to mess with.

I continued into a second year at Mt. Bethel that fall. Jessica Appleyard and I did a "loop-up" thing where she came down a grade and took a fourth grade class, and I took my 01-02 class up to fifth grade. I was very pleased in that only one child out of the twenty-seven or so chose not to loop-up. My little Devon Murphy did loop up. The parents arranged a pool party at the local pool somewhere hear the school and we kicked off the school year with a raucous, wet gathering. We had a blast. I also got a new principal that year, Ms. Robin Lattazori. I was on a roll of wonderful principals. I knew crappy ones existed, but I seemed to have had many of the good ones: Ms. Moffatt, Mr. Oveby, Dr. Brown and now Ms. Lattizori. That would change later (foreshadow) but for now, I was on a streak.

Ms. Lattazori blessed the class going to Charleston and I got real bold that year. I proposed to allow all the fifth grade to go to Jekyll Island, not just the Target class. And she blessed that too. I also was involved with Science Olympiad that year. Mr. Chuck Jones, the Mt. Bethel PE teacher who would become a lifelong friend, and I worked with another lady who kind of led the effort (her name escapes me) and the three of us led the team. The Cobb gathering of teams was at Southern Tech and it was a loose affair, but it gave the children a chance to compete.

As the Cobb TOTY and a Finalist, I became part of a group that was responsible for putting on the TOTY Awards gathering where all the TOTYs of all the counties in Georgia were recognized and the new crop of finalists and winner were announced. Part of this dubious honor was getting to read not only all the TOTY application submittals for Cobb County, but also all the TOTY application submittals for the state of Georgia. Man, that was a pain! But I did it. The other semifinalists and finalists read and I ranked about hundred Cobb applications (Betsy Bunte won for Cobb the year after me) and 159 applications for Georgia! In addition to that, the State School Superintendent came to me and asked if I could help organize a huge teacher gathering at Callaway Gardens in the spring of 03. Of course I said yes. And plans were laid for a circus … yes, a real circus … complete with clowns, bands and performing acts all held in a big circus tent in the middle of summer and it was so hot everyone could hardly stand it. And they wanted me to be the ringmaster. So, being the ever present Energizer Bunny, always begging for the spotlight and attention … I agreed. We met a couple of times with the Callaway folks and several of us were given a little pin to wear. The pin meant that we could ask any employee for anything. Talk about making your head big. I never really used mine, but it was heady stuff to this little boy just wearing it. And the July weekend arrived. It had to be July because, as I said, it was hotter than hell and the humidity was exactly what you would expect of middle Georgia in July. I was given a private house to stay in (again, heady stuff) and I bought a white Mark Twain suit. It is still downstairs in one of the white closet things Carolyn and I bought. I had a cane and a straw hat and I was quite the dapper ringmaster. During the weekend I taught classes on Kinesthetic Geometry and in the evening presided over a circus. Carolyn came down one night for the circus and the Georgia School Superintendent Linda Schrenko, who by now was under investigation for funneling state education funds into her bid to become governor, was there and it was a very interesting weekend … very interesting.

In the classroom, we continued with Civil War Bowls, introduced the World War II Bowl, went to Charleston to sleep on the carrier, performed a play about *The Guns of Fort Sumter* that I wrote and the class performed (that is what Devon Murphy was referring to in his note while visiting the carrier with friends), went to Jekyll Island with the entire fifth grade, presented my Kinesthetic Geometry at GCTM (Georgia Conference of Teachers of Mathematics) … another very interesting weekend … and kept thirty fifth graders in line and on a trajectory for success as best I could. As I look back, I have no idea how I had the time, much less the energy needed to do all of those things.

21.

Now, you want to talk about a year! 2003 was one of Carolyn and my craziest years ever. I am not going to give you an introductory preview, I am just going to dive right into a year that holds all kinds of memories … some strange … some cool and some just downright unbelievable.

On February 14th, 2003, one Bodie Lang Blackwell was born. He came by C-section because no doctor wanted to risk Jenna's or Bodie's life on another regular birth. So, Carolyn and I were in Gainesville taking care of now two-year-old Bryce as we waited for the news, and at 9:15 on Valentine's Day a little 8 pound, 6 ounces, 20 ½ inch long beautifully perfect little baby boy was born. The Morris luck was continuing in that our family's babies were being born in perfect health. Carolyn and I hurried to the hospital with little Bryce and both mother and child were fine. It was the beginning of another positive event for the world. It makes me very glad that Carolyn and I conceived Jenna so early in our marriage. It was very scary for us, and as I have written, my parents frowned on us. You know what … our world and the world would be a very, very much poorer place if we had not had Jenna. I say this as we prepare today (5/12/23) to head over to Athens, Georgia again to see Bryce graduate from UGA. Day before yesterday he graduated from the Terry College of Business. Carolyn and I went over and Bryce's Anna was there and her parents and today he and several thousand others will graduate from the University. We'll be in the stadium and it promises to be a "sight to behold." But, anyway, Bodie Lang came into the world, and we have relished watching him grow. I am sure he will be mentioned again.

The year of 2003 seems to center around Carolyn's and my attempt to "break out"! We were, appreciably, kind of empty nesters in that James was safely ensconced at Georgia Southern, and we agreed now was the time if we were ever going to do it … to move away from Cobb. Why you ask? A good question. All our family was here … Carolyn's mom, Carolyn's three sisters and my mom and dad and my sister too. Jenna and Adam and little Bryce were in Gainesville. So, why move? Everything we knew and loved was here. Honestly … and I am going to be as honest as I can as I look back twenty years into the past … families <u>were</u> the main reason. We wanted to get away from our suffocating families and the looming responsibilities that were coming that Carolyn and I knew we would be the ones to shoulder. I also think we regretted not moving to Ashville years before. I think we both wanted a clean start in a new city. I think we both wanted to go down to the coast and save some children … I know that sounds foolish … but we had even looked into joining The Peace Corps that year but decided, after some investigation, that that was "a bridge too far." So, various and sundry little reasons with our families (excluding Jenna, Adam, Bryce, Bodie and James) being our major motivation.

So we started moving on our plan. Carolyn started looking into a teaching credential at the Armstrong State University, and I started looking into where to teach on the coast while continuing to teach at Mt. Bethel. I do recall going down one time to Savannah when James was younger. I do not know the year … it may have been part of a TBT as a matter of fact, but I went and interviewed at several schools. There was one middle school in downtown Savannah in a really rough part of town that we visited. I had sent an application and was greeted with an interview which went well. Then the principal gave me a tour of the school. At the end of the tour she told me that her assistant principal and she had a code word, and if the assistant principal said it and the principal said it then they had secretly agreed that this was a person to hire. And they offered me a job on the spot. Well, I had by now been in the business long enough and had subbed at schools I would NEVER work at, and I thanked them for the offer, and said I have more interviews and could I consider their offer. They said yes, and a week later I declined the offer to teach at that inner city school. I think the problem Savannah has is this … when integration became the law of the land in the 60's, the white population of this segregation minded area of the state decided they were not going to have any part of sending their white children to schools with black children, so they took them out and started private schools for all the white families with money. And I might add that black families with money did the same with their black children and they stated private black schools. That left mostly poor whites and blacks to attend the public schools with the resulting manifestations being exactly what you would expect. But, I digress from my current story. As I said, Carolyn applied to Armstrong State and was hoping for an experience like I had at KSU. She was talked into a special education degree which came with a grant covering tuition. Georgia was starting to starve for teachers, so around now they started a program that people with other degrees could take minimal courses and get into a classroom quickly while they took classes. Long story short, she enrolled to start the summer quarter of 2003, and we moved her down to Savannah, and Millbrook Trace went on the market.

My applications to schools around Savannah were largely being ignored. So, I branched out and looked to counties nearby. I sent applications to Liberty County, Bryan County and Effingham County. Liberty County was the first to respond and I visited Frank Long Elementary School in the spring of '03, and Dr. Albritton offered me a job. So, this whole adventure was taking on a life. It looked real. And Carolyn's family and my family thought we had lost our damn minds. And maybe we had, but it was our mind and Carolyn and I were going to lose it together like we had done for thirty years. We rented a second floor, two-bedroom apartment in Georgetown Woods (it may be named Waterford Plantation now) located at 100 St. George Blvd. in Savannah. As it turned out, our friend from Mt. Bethel days, Jan Durham, had a sister-in-law on the Chatham County School Board, and she helped Carolyn find a position at Gadsden Elementary. The apartment was on the south side of the city as I was traveling forty-five minutes down to Hinesville for school and Carolyn was going over to Armstrong State and then going to be traveling up into the city and teaching at Gadsden Elementary School in Savannah.

As Carolyn got started with her course work at Armstrong, I got Millbrook Trace on the market. My challenge was to not only get the house sold, but to move us to Savannah. I took it as a personal challenge … as I do with so many things. I wanted to move us myself … all by myself in U-Haul trucks. As I was getting us moved I tried to have a garage sale which was pitiful and soured me on ever doing another one. I sold nothing. The dark wood, cannon ball bedroom furniture Carolyn and I had bought when we were "rich" with a Christmas bonus from C.P. Roberts one year a long time ago went to Jenna and Adam for a spare bedroom. My office furniture went to Goodwill. And I shredded years of old taxes and papers. And there lies the one thing that I regret about moving. I have often looked back and wished I had some of the rolls of old drawings Carolyn and I drew when we were draftspersons. But, I shredded all of them. Pity. There were some really nice, all hand drawn details and thousands of architectural letters we lettered. Oh well. So the program became: I would box up rooms and move furniture down to the main level. Then I would drive over or walk over or taxi over to the U-Haul or Penske place on the 41 Highway and rent a big truck on say Monday afternoon. By Monday night at midnight, I would have it halfway loaded. After sleeping on a blow-up mattress, the next morning I would finish loading the truck … just me and a hand truck. By midafternoon I was rolling to Savannah. By 8:00 I was at the apartment and unloading. I remember rolling into Savannah one night; it was already dark, and I needed a lock for the truck. I stopped at a Walmart. My eyes were accustomed to the dark, and when I walked into the Walmart the light took me by surprise. I still sometimes to this day flash back to that memory when I walk into the Walmart. I love Walmart. Anyway, I would unload until I just couldn't any longer. Then sleep and get up the next morning, finish the unload, and hit the road back to Marietta driving directly to the truck rental place and dropping the truck off. I remember one especially lovely day I opted to walk home from the place. Now the truck place was on 41 and just north of South Cobb Drive. I do not know what possessed me try to walk home. It was probably the cheap Morris in me not wanting to spring for a taxi. So, I walked, and it was a long way over I-75 to Terrell Mill and then around to Lower Roswell Road and Millbrook Trace. And it was time to box up more stuff and wrap more furniture. Then I would rent a truck again and the whole process starts again. I recall that McDonalds was having a sale on double cheeseburgers. I ate a lot of them on the road. Meanwhile I was getting nervous about Millbrook selling in time. One of my Mt. Bethel friends told me about purchasing a Saint Joseph statue and following the instructions, and he would help us sell Millbrook. Over off Johnson Ferry Road just over the Chattahoochee is Riverside Drive and a Catholic place named Ignatius House. There I bought a St. Joseph. I followed the instructions and in three days I had an offer on Millbrook … NO LIE! Honest! Rev. Jan Durham also tried to help me again in that the Methodist Church in Savannah she was attending needed a director of youth education. She had the minister call me one evening at a very inopportune time. I listened as he described the position, and we did a phone interview right then and there. He said he had talked to Rev. Durham at length and that he had an excellent feel for people and knew I would be a perfect fit. He offered me a job right there, on the spot. But like the middle school job in Savannah and the job in Dahlonega, I just did not see the fit and had to turn him down. There was just too many moving pieces in my life at that moment and his position, and returning to a church with all its drama and self-serving preachers, was a headache I just did not need … or want.

So, the house was sold, and I had about two weeks before closing and had to start getting squared away with Liberty County and Frank Long Elementary in between all of that. Let me also add that that summer I was also heavily involved with the TOTY Organization, and we put on a TOTY celebration in Macon. I was somewhat of an emcee, and I had E.T. Wah of all people appear and congratulate all the TOTY's. The Cobb TOTY that year was from Mt. Bethel and Robin Lattazori came to Macon, and we all celebrated. I do recall one event that I still question to this day. The second evening of the event, after everything was done, and we were all retiring to our rooms, I found Ms. Lattazori in the hall crying. I walked over to her and asked her if she was alright. I remember her looking up into my eyes and pausing for what seemed to be the longest time … probably five seconds really. She looked as if she was going to say something, then she said, "Yes, Jim. I'm fine. Thank you for asking." And then she walked away. To this day I wonder what was really on her mind. I'll never know, I guess.

I got the last of our belongings moved out in time and we closed on Millbrook, the money pit, and I never looked back. On the other hand, Carolyn was upset that Millbrook was sold. She saw it as the place her children grew up. I saw it as the house with the leaking sunroom skylights, the leaking upstairs fireplace, the awful brick floor in the kitchen/breakfast area where the grout kept coming up, the crap windows, and the floors that I never had the money to refinish. Anyway enough, the orientation for Liberty County was interesting. It was much more laid back than Cobb. It seems to me now that almost everything is more laid back than Cobb County Schools! During the orientation, PAGE (the Profession Association of Georgia Educators) of which I had been a building representative for years, handed out their magazine and inside was an article that featured me and my picture making comments about mentoring new teachers. Several teachers at orientation noticed it and came over and introduced themselves to me. I was charmed of course. I then moved everything including my aquarium, almost directly from Mt. Bethel to my classroom at Frank Long Elementary, and began what was to be a very long and lesson filled year … for this teacher. I learned a valuable lesson. Do not ever judge a school by it building. Frank Long Elementary was new and beautiful. The administration was not new or beautiful. The children were not new or beautiful. I sent Robin Lattazori a note after teaching there for a month begging her to take me back to Mt. Bethel. When I went "down to the coast" as Carolyn and I called our adventure, I saw myself as some great wizard of a teacher able to change children's "hearts and minds" – to borrow a phrase from the Vietnam War time period. I found I was neither a wizard nor able to change the trajectory of a single child … well, maybe one. For instance, one of our first projects was a human body system project I had taught many times before with great hilarity. The children were to select a body system, write a short paper about it and then try to construct a model of the system "using junk laying around the house." I had to have a meeting with a parent and the principal as the parent objected to the implication that her house was filled with junk. Holy crap, I was in trouble if that was the attitude down here "on the coast." I could not get children to turn in work, do projects, read books or care about anything. It was a new world for me. I discovered something I had never realized … it is hard to care about the Gettysburg Address when you are hungry (most of my children got free breakfast and were on free or reduced lunch pricing). It is hard to care about a report when Mom or Dad are in prison. It is hard to learn your multiplication tables when Dad comes home drunk and beats your mother. It is hard to care when you are ten years old, and Mom and Dad do not care about education because they are busy with two or three jobs and just trying to survive. I was humbled. I wish I could tell you I stayed and "fought the good fight" and saved thousands of children and became a legend … but I did not. I taught them as best I could. Loved them all as best I could. That year I held back the one and only student I ever in my teaching career did not allow to pass (I do admit there was another student later in my career at Mt. Bethel that I voted "no" on passing, but he was allowed to pass only to be held back in sixth grade). I think about that child often. I colossally <u>failed</u> <u>him</u>. Did holding him back make him care more or try harder the next year or make a positive difference in his life? Or did I just cement failure in his heart. As an aside … later … much later … perhaps ten years later … at Mt. Bethel I did have the opportunity to have a child in my class who was repeating fifth grade, and this child gave my class 110% and showed me a wonderfully positive attitude. That little boy became the Maverick of the Year that year. I want to hope that little boy who I held back approached the repeat year of fifth grade like that little guy ten years later, and I want to think the little Liberty County child is now a successful twenty-something year old. I want to think that. So, I decided to run away from Liberty County and leave it to those teachers who were better suited to that environment and could do more good than me. An example of one of those teachers was the Frank Long Elementary TOTY who was elected the year I was there. I recall there was a big computer literacy push in Georgia at the time, and it centered around a computer course called InTech. Georgia Professional Standards Commission said you had to have passed the InTech course by June of 2005 or your contract would not be renewed. Now, ignoring how stupid this pronouncement was, and the fact that I had already passed InTech I and InTech II, the Frank Long Elementary's TOTY teacher's position was, "I ain't takin' no InTech and they can fire my ass if they wants." And this was from the <u>TOTY</u> for the school … and what was more troubling was that most teachers there agreed with her. While I was there, I got the feeling that they felt as if I was this white interloper (although I was not the only white teacher there) who had come down from the big city to save their poor school with his different ways of teaching and "innovative" approaches. Don Quixote had crashed squarely into the side of a windmill, and he knew it, and it hurt.

Meanwhile, up in Savannah at Gadsden Elementary, Carolyn was learning hand over fist what effect integration decisions made forty years before by Congress were having on the children of the new millennium. First, her Armstrong State course work was not going well. She was being taught things I had never even heard of in my almost ten years of teaching and being around special education most of that time. I cannot even recall what some of it was, but I know I was at a loss to even help her. And the school she was trying to teach at was horrible. First her principal was this PhD person who had no idea how to be a principal. I'll leave it there … ask Carolyn. They put Carolyn in a separate classroom with ants everywhere, and a bathroom that had not been cleaned since Roosevelt was president. Carolyn cleaned it. They gave her no teaching materials to speak of and no guidance and then gave her fifth graders who did not even know their alphabet. But the coup de grâce was after six weeks of teaching, the school had not had one fire drill or any kind of safety drill. Now this school sits almost next to the sweeping end of I-16 off of which any car or tanker truck filled with anything could come careening off of at any time and plow right into the school yard. This was alarming, very alarming to Carolyn and me. We met with Jan Durham's sister-in-law and explained our concerns. When she was not the least bit concerned and nothing happened, it was the last straw. Carolyn resigned from the school. She would not be a party to a horrible accident just waiting to happen. She then resigned from Armstrong State. And I was applying furiously back up in Cobb and Cherokee and Bartow … any place to escape our adventure "on the coast."

You know what raising a child comes down to? PARENTAL INVOLVEMENT. If a parent in not involved, the chances of that child succeeding are greatly diminished. If a parent simply says that a teacher "does not know what they [the teacher] are talking about," then there is NOTHING that teacher can say or do that is going to be good for that child. I get it. I wish more parents got it. Parents are Gods to a child. All food and safety and shelter flow from that parent. Every word uttered from a parent's mouth is gospel. Look at Maslow's Hierarchy of Needs and look at the base of the pyramid. Children cannot help it. They are just built that way by nature. It goes back eons and has to do with survival.

While I'm pontificating, let me list the things that, in my opinion, influence a child and their education starting with the most important to the least: 1. Parental attitude, involvement and love (including care and feeding and shelter) 2. The child 3. The teacher 4. The curriculum 5. The building 6. The administration 7. The school board 8. Everything else. After spending over twenty-five years in the corporate world and over twenty-five in the education world I offer the following advice: "Always be where the rubber meets the road." In other words, if you are a lawyer, be in the courtroom. If you are a doctor, be meeting with patients. If you are a teacher, be in the classroom. I offer this education scenario to consider: If the school board does not meet — will children still be educated? YES. If the administration in a school suddenly evaporated ☺ - will children still be educated? YES. If all the teachers quit - will children still be educated? NO! If all the children quit school — will the children still be educated? NO! Now you know "where the rubber meets the road." Strive always to be at that place. And you now know why I never went into administration even though Dr. Brown desperately wanted me to do that. I learned from being a Senior Vice President at Carlson how useless Senior Vice Presidents are.

So, with all that said, I do not want to leave you thinking Carolyn's and my adventure to the coast was a huge misadventure … although I have to admit, it kind of was … there were many wonderful bright spots. I recall on day there was a hurricane sweeping by the coast and Carolyn and I decided to pay it a visit. So we scrounged up a blanket from our crowded little apartment, went by a little Chinese place and got some chicken fried rice, egg rolls, Singapore noodles and some tea and headed for Tybee Island. We arrived at the time the storm was about fifty miles off the coast and the wind was howling and made our way to the beach. There, huddled in our blanket we laughed and giggled and ate our dinner. Just us and the hurricane.

Then there was the time we fifth grade teachers took the fifth grade to Jekyll Island to the 4H camp. The ride from Liberty County was fraught with danger! Actually it wasn't, but for many children this was the first time they had left the county! For many, it was the first time they had crossed a bridge! In fact, as you near the causeway out to Jekyll you see the Sidney Lanier Bridge that leads to Brunswick. It is a huge bridge reaching toward the sky. Once James, Carolyn and I were adventuring when he was younger, and James and I went over when that bridge was first being built and photographed its construction. But I digress again. As we approached the Jekyll causeway turn off and the Lanier bridge loomed ahead, one of my children almost had a conniption thinking we were going to go over THAT BRIDGE! I assured her we were not, and she calmed down. We did not spend the night on Jekyll at the 4H like I did with Mt. Bethel classes because these children had NEVER spent the night away from their homes, and they were afraid to stay there … the poor babies.

For Thanksgiving that year Carolyn and I got tickets to the feast at the famous Desoto Hilton and invited James and his best friend Ian to come down from Georgia Southern and join us. We got all gussied up in coats and ties and dresses and heels and made an afternoon of it. The weather had turned cool and blustery. Leaves were swirling through the streets and up Liberty Street as we drove into the basement parking area. We headed up in the elevator and walked into the historic lobby. We were ushered into a ballroom. A string quartet played in the corner and all the chandeliers glowed. In the center of the room was a long table full of all the Thanksgiving dishes one could want … turkey (of course), prime rib, roast beef, fried chicken, cornbread dressing, oyster dressing, cranberry sauce, green beans, every form of potatoes you can imagine, creamed corn, corn bread, biscuits, Kaiser rolls, fruit salad, Caesar salad, wedge salad, Jello salad, tossed salad, slaw, apple pie, blueberry pie, pumpkin pie, mincemeat pie, carrot cake, red velvet cake, angel food cake … if you can imagine it, it was there. And James and Ian did their best to get every dollar's worth! Carolyn and I could not even begin to keep up. I will forever recall it as one of my best Thanksgivings ever … I had my Carolyn and my boy, my tummy was full and all was right with the world.

That year I was invited to bring my Kinesthetic Geometry show to the NCTM Region Convention in Charleston. I was honored to be invited, and Carolyn and I made a weekend of it in one of our favorite old towns.

Another exciting time was when James invited us to come over to Hutcheson Island and watch him slalom his jazzed up Honda Civic. He had outfitted Jenna's old car with a cold intake pipe and to be honest, I don't know what all he had done to the car, but it was fast! Carolyn and I had tee shirts made with his car on them and wore them. He was suitably embarrassed but took it in his usual calm, encompassing stride. He was racing a specifically laid out course in his vehicle class against a clock. There was no racing car on car which made us feel better. I do not recall if he won anything but I do remember we had a great day! Our move to the coast really was a very cool adventure of a lifetime.

22.

2004 was the return to Atlanta, Cherokee County Schools, Canton, Sizemore and Nanny's Stroke. By the standards of the stories in this work, it was a pretty sleepy year, but it was not without its highs and lows. Let's start with the return to Atlanta. As you know Savannah was not to be. I do not know if Carolyn and I knew that from the start or we were just realistic, but we never bought a house down there. We just rented the apartment, so from that standpoint it was a fairly easy escape. Carolyn had righteously left the college and the school system and moved up in early 2004 to find a place for us and get a job. The house we decided on was at 520 Misty Creek in Canton, Georgia, and she landed a position at Sizemore Group Architects off Northside Drive in Atlanta.

The Misty Creek house was another learning experience. We had wanted something closer to Millbrook Trace, but the houses were rapidly becoming just too expensive so we had to look further north. In the Misty Creek house we learned that it is possible to have house that is too small … even for just the two of us. It was a cute three-bedroom house at the end of a cul-de-sac with a driveway that was too steep. So steep that when you went over the hump from the street to go down the drive, your car dragged bottom. Of course the previous owner was conveniently parked in the drive near the top every time we came to look at the house and when the inspector came to inspect the house so we did not know about this little nuisance until after we had bought the house. Live and learn is my motto. The lot the house sat on was about an acre but in the back it sloped down a very, very steep hill to, yep you guessed it, a creek! We owned half of a creek. The deck off the back of the house was a dizzying affair some three stories off the ground. It had a "master on the main" (oooooh!) And two more bedrooms upstairs. The main room was a kitchen/nook/living room. Anyway we got it for the right price, and by now I was headed to teach in Cherokee County. I wanted to go back home to Mt. Bethel, but Robin Lattazori just did not have any openings, so Cherokee it was. My discussions with Cherokee centered around Sixes Elementary and I interviewed there and everything was cool. Then, a few weeks before I was to leave Frank long Elementary Sixes lost a position, and I was out of luck going there. But there was a position teaching fifth grade math at an upper elementary school (fifth and sixth grade) adjacent to E.T. Booth Middle School at 6550 Putnam Ford Road in Woodstock, Georgia. The school is now part of Etowah High School, and everything has been incorporated into E. T. Booth. But, I was employed at least and math was a good fit, and I was Trailer Trash! My country, each pod in the school had a Caribbean country name … we were like Bahamas or something … and each pod an ELA teacher, a Science Teacher, a Social Studies Teacher and a Math teacher in two double wide trailers. We changed classes amongst the little trailer classrooms and walked up the uncovered walk to the building if we wanted to eat lunch or go to the bathroom or use the computer lab. It was an experience, but as I said, at least I had a job. And my poor Carolyn had to drive everyday all the way from Canton down to Northside drive near I-75 on 575 and 75 and then plow her way back out again in the evening. Her drive was horrendous, but one does what one has to do. My teaching team was a great group, and they accepted me graciously into the fold. I was still a little miffed at Cherokee for what I saw was leading me on about Sixes Elementary, but what could a poor refugee do except grin and bear it.

I was in no mood and much too busy (and I had learned a lot from the last time) to personally move all our crap up from Savannah, so we hired *Two Men and a Truck* to move us, and it was a good experience. So good we used them a second time. We'll talk about that later. I do recall the movers had a problem getting their truck into the subdivision. It would not pull the grade. If you go to the subdivision, Misty Creek Estates – or something like that – you will see why the only way the moving truck could get into the subdivision was to back in using reverse gear! We were up in the mountainous area of Cherokee County. The guys got in there, past the defunct and filled in pool and dilapidated club house, and got the truck situated in the driveway and unloaded our junk. I remember the house was so small we had no place for our upscale, very modern glass table with marble base and black lacquer chairs we had bought for the formal dining room at Millbrook Trace so I sold the whole mess to one of the movers. He said he would send the money as soon as he got back to Savannah. I never saw a penny. Shock! But we got moved in and had escaped the coast. Whew.

The grandsons were growing. Bryce was a rambunctious three years old and Bodie, never one to be outdone by his older brother, was walking and talking. Bodie's first words to me came when the three of us were walking up and down the hills of Misty Creek. Bryce was holding my hand, Bodie was in a stroller, we all had on our hats when Bodie excitedly pointed and said, "Tră, tră." He was pointing at a trash can. And so my second grandson's first words went down in history. We loved having The Boys come over. We worked out a deal with Jenna and Adam in that they would bring The Boys to "Motorcycle McDonalds." This was a McDonalds at the intersection of GA400 and GA306, Keith Bridge Road that had some motorcycles on display inside … for some cool reason. We would meet them there, buy The Boys something to eat and drink and then cruise back to Canton on Ga20. Their visits were a high point in our lives back then. We would take The Boys down the very steep backyard and let them throw rocks in the creek. There was a little raised platform someone had built on the hill and they would climb on it. And there was a cave down the slope near the creek that was interesting. So, I bought two little statues of gnomes and put the statues in the little cave. Then The Boys and I would go down the hill very quietly and see if we could see the gnomes. They were very crafty and sometimes we would see them and sometimes we would not, but if we did they would race back up the hill to tell Nana about their discovery! The one thing our yard was good for was a Slip and Slide! Due to the steep incline we could set up the Slip and Slide and the Bryce and Bodie could play for hours and hours and hours and hours.

Meanwhile James was knocking them dead at Georgia Southern. He was maintaining a "B" average and keeping his scholarships and doing great on his coursework. In the fall of '04 we had an opportunity to present Kinesthetic Geometry to a Georgia Southern Math Conference. Presenting with him made me so proud. And he had seen my presentation so many times he had no problem joining in and presenting himself. I do remember one downside that morning. Georgia Southern could not guarantee us a television, so in an abundance of caution, I wanted to bring James's TV. Well, everything was good until, after navigating the steps all the way down from his second story apartment carrying his television – a big sucker – I missed one last step on the sidewalk and down I went. The television went crashing onto the concrete, and I went down hard on my knee cutting it and my pants open. Talk about feeling stupid … I really did. Well, Carolyn was all over me and so was James. We got me patched up and managed to find another pair of pants (that never really fit) at a store in Statesboro and James and I successfully presented. So, if you come across pictures of us presenting and I look like I am wearing a huge pair of balloon pants … I am. And later that day we bought James and Ian an even better big old box of a television. Dads do that.

I just went back and reread my beginning of this story I began writing nearly three years ago, and something just struck me. My recollections from being younger seem more "story book fiction like," and what I am writing now seems much more clinical and historically accurate. Today's writing does not seem to have that gauzy film of long ago and far away recollection feel to it. I guess being more clinical in your memories is one of the hazards of maturity and "pulling your own little red wagon" for too long. For that I apologize. Basically, you are young for such a short time, and you are old for such a long time. I will try to write better.

A dark event of 2004 I need to relate concerned Carolyn and would consume her life for the next three years. Carolyn's mother, Virginia Shacklett Lyon (Nanny), had a stroke that year. It was a bad stroke and if some house cleaners Nanny had employed had not been scheduled to come that day, Virginia might have died on the floor of her den. No such luck for her. We cannot always choose the moment of our death and Nanny was "saved" although Nanny may not have seen it that way. It is my fervent belief that sometimes the best-lived lives are the ones that end well and by that I mean lives that, near the end, are not a burden to those who love us. Oh, the loved ones will never say that you are a burden … except in the dark of night while you are pillow talking to your closest confidant. But you are a burden. You know it. They know it. It's the circle of life. You start as a ping pong ball and end as a ping pong ball … if you are lucky. I never want to be a burden and will do everything in my power to never be one, but sometimes you have to play the cards you are dealt, and Virginia had to play her cards … like it or not. And my beautiful Carolyn had to sit at the table and play cards with her whether Carolyn wanted to or not. It was interesting to me that Virginia had always had what I will call "an acid tongue." One of her favorite phrases was, "I just say what I think." And she did, and she did not care who it hurt in the process. And she hurt many, but the one she hurt that just killed me, was when she hurt Carolyn. Many times Carolyn cried in my arms over something her mother said. Carolyn strives every day not to let this be her legacy. As I have said I am sure, you learn from your parents … what to do and more importantly sometimes – what NOT to do. So, Nanny had a stroke and was paralyzed partially on one side of her body, but what was more interesting, she could not speak. Oh, she could grunt and wail and spit and lash out with her good arm, but had great difficulty speaking intelligently. Her acid tongue was taken from her. But Virginia could still inflict pain and she did, and Carolyn's inability to make her mother happy hurt Carolyn immeasurably. Over the next several years until Virginia's death in 2007, Carolyn kept the books, paid the bills, consulted legal experts relative to Virginia's Medicaid benefits, made sure the nursing home was paid, got her to her doctor's appointments, purchased a van with a lift to transport her. Carolyn did everything a dutiful daughter, a caring human being, could do for another human being … no matter the previous pain inflicted.

That year we got two new arrivals at our little Misty Creek home. I did not go looking that day, I swear. However, as fate would have it, I ended up in a pet store on Barrett Parkway. It was in the shopping center with Best Buy and Office Depot and across the side street from the Target complex. I think the pet store is gone now, and there is an Aldi's in its place, but none of that matters. I was in there and in a cage was the most beautiful Maine Coon kitten. I fell in love immediately. And the kicker was the kitten's name was Jenna … honest! Well, to me that was almost a "sign from God." So, I called Carolyn and told her what I had found. Carolyn was hanging out with Angie that day. Why? I do not know. But the two of them were hanging out and obviously looking for trouble. They said they could come right over, and come over they did with an unforeseen outcome. They came in the store and fell in love immediately with Jenna … and her scrawny sister. Jenna and her sister were the last two kittens from a litter, and while Jenna was hale and hardy, her sister was obviously the runt of the litter. I do not recall what the sister's given name was, but we quickly renamed her "Delmar" after the lovable, third character in the movie *Oh Brother Where Art Thou*. The name seemed to fit this second little darling and yes, you guessed it. Under Angie's loving input, we left that day with not one kitten but … "Jim, we can't leave that little one, Jenna's sister alone. She'll never make it." … two kittens. And we loved those two ladies. They were the sweetest, most affectionate kittens we had ever had. I'm not going to say we "owned" them, because if you are a cat lover like I am, you never own a cat. They own you. They own your heart and soul and these two girls owned Carolyn and me. If Carolyn took a nap on the leather couch, Jenna would come and hop up on the blanket and lay down behind her legs. If there was no blanket on the couch, the girls would not get up on it. If I sat in my chair to watch television, one or both of the ladies would come and get up in my lap, do the whole push paw thing and then settle down on me. If Carolyn was in her chair, and I was not, they would sit in her lap or on the arms of the chair and watch television with us. The girls slept in the basement on the futon. Often I would go down and they were curled up together, very often with Jenna grooming her little sister. They were both beautiful and sweet kittens. Delmar passed away in 2020. She woke up one morning, and she was blind. I am choking up just writing about that morning. I took her to the vet and after an examination Dr. Barnwell said there was a lot more going on and the best thing to do was to put her to sleep. Apparently this blindness thing is something that happens to Maine Coons as they age. It has to do with heart problems and nerves. We put my sweet Delmar down, and I cried like a baby. I mean cried like a baby over that beautiful little girl. But we still had Jenna. However, the loss of Delmar also affected Jenna. You could tell. She would walk around and cry for her sister. I think her heart was broken. She did not understand where her lifelong sister went. And, a year later, Jenna developed cancer. There was a place on her back that just would not heal and near the end I could tell she was in pain. In January of 2021 I took her to Dr. Barnwell also. Again I cried and was inconsolable. Tears are running down my face at this moment as I write about these two beautiful kittens. We still refer to them as "the kittens." They lived good lives with us and gave us so much joy. It has been over three years since we lost Delmar and over two since we lost Jenna, and I still cannot bring myself to get another kitten. The pain of losing them is just too overwhelming. Maybe someday, but not today. I'm going to make a comment here and it may hurt you, my gentle reader, to read this, but I have cried more tears over those two kittens than I have cried over the loss of both of my parents. I know that is a hard thing to read about me. It is a hard thing for me to admit about myself. But, there it is. And as "they" say, "It is what it is."

23.

Absolutely the biggest event of 2005 had to be James graduating from Georgia Southern! During that eventful year I moved back to Mt. Bethel, we sold Misty Creek and moved into Falcon Wood, we kept The Boys and Jenna started teaching at Lakeview Academy. But let's jump to May 7th and jump into the most exciting part of 2005, our beautiful son's graduation. Carolyn and I traveled down on a Friday and booked into the beautiful Statesboro Inn and we were in possession of a wonderful secret. Saturday the 7th dawned clear and promised to be a very warm day for the graduation. We were all in the stadium this time. I am not sure why they did not do it in the Hanner Field House like they did Jenna's, but we were all in the stands awaiting the graduates. Carolyn and I were seated with Angie and her parents. Jenna, Adam and both boys (Bryce a rambunctious four-year-old and Bodie a full of life two-year-old) were there. Jenna was taking pictures like crazy that morning. All the graduates were in dark blue gowns, and it had to be hot, hot, hot down there on the field. As we were looking down on them, the graduates filed in from our left. They were seated and the podium with the speaker was to our right, so when they walked to get their diplomas they walked left to right up onto the closest side of the stage to us and then back down the other side and to their seats. I do not recall who the speaker was, no one ever does, but the time came and the graduates started up to the dais. James walked up and got his diploma and gave a little victory wave and headed back to his seat. He was being a good boy. I recall one of the final parts of the graduation was the Georgia Southern eagle was released, and he flew over the stadium several times and returned to his handler. I was impressed. Then we all flooded onto the field to congratulate the graduates. James was in a throng of his buddies including Ian and was very excited. I think I was the one carrying the surprise, and I think I recall handing James a small, deep blue, velvet box … the secret. Angie hurried over to James and gave him a hug. Then, as her parents, Carolyn and I and the family looked on, James – in his cap and gown – dropped to one knee, looked up at Angie, opened the small but fate filled box and asked her to marry him! Right there! On the field! In front of all his friends and God and everyone! And as you know now, she said, "Yes!" Sorry for all the exclamation points but it was a thrilling moment then and it is still a thrilling moment to write about today, some eighteen years later. (Their sixteenth anniversary is this coming Saturday!) James did it right and it was a sight to behold. I love that boy and everything he has ever done.

Carolyn was still at the Sizemore Group and had been given more and more responsibility and was still driving the long haul from Canton, and it was wearing her out. But our days in Canton were numbered. I kept bugging Robin Lattizori, and finally she was going to have a fifth grade opening in the fall of '05! Thank goodness. I came in and interviewed again and asked my friends Eileen Jedlicka, Janet Jones, Kathy Scheer (James's fifth grade teacher from years ago at Eastvalley Elementary) and Connie Perry if I could come home. Fortunately, I had not burned any bridges and the fact of being a former Cobb TOTY did not hurt. (In fact, it was to be my guardian angel in the future.) Everyone agreed, and I was able to come home to Mt. Bethel. As it turns out my move back to Cobb in 2005 was the last school move I was to make in my career. So I said adios to my Cherokee County school and my trailer and my new friends and "came home." I was touched though in that the new principal at the school I was leaving did make one last final bid to try to have me stay, but my heart was gone already. I roared back into Mt. Bethel – "God was in his heaven and all was right with the world." We, the fifth grade team, were into everything and Ms. Lattazori backed us up on everything. I took my class to Charleston. The other fifths were not into that adventure yet … they would later. We took all the fifth grade to Jekyll. We had the fifth grade softball tournament which my class won that year. In fact, in the basement is a box with all the fifth grade classes I ever taught, and that year's class picture that hung on the wall was of us the day we won the trophy.

That fall Bryce was going to start PreK and Jenna was still teaching. Adam and Jenna decided on a private school for Bryce as the schools at that time in Gainesville just did not impress them. So Bryce was enrolled in Lakeview Academy, and Jenna was fortunate enough to be offered a position on the Lakeview Academy faculty. And Carolyn and I had our first of … well maybe seven or eight Grandparents Days. Usually the first Friday in October we would begin by meeting in the cafeteria and get our picture taken with Bryce and in later years, Bryce and Bodie. Some years we would get our picture taken with Adam's dad, Toby, and his stepmom, Paula, and The Boys. Those are cherished pictures. The we would go to the gymnasium. A program featuring all the grade levels singing and performing. We would then head to, this year, Bryce's classroom to meet his teacher where a special grandparent's piece of artwork was waiting. Afterwards we would take him to the Book Fair where he could buy as many books as he wanted. Nana (Carolyn's selected grandparent name) and Pa (my selected grandparent name in honor of my Pa) were "easy touches" especially when it came to books. After the morning's events concluded, Carolyn and I usually got The Boys for lunch and to "open a keg of nails" as Momma (my paternal grandmother and role model for all grandparents everywhere) would say. It meant we would go on an adventure of some kind. As I mentioned this was the year Jenna joined the Lakeview Faculty, and it was to be her teaching home for the next fifteen years as The Boys flourished there. I know you are going to read many more Lakeview stories as I proudly chronicle our beautiful grandson's exploits.

As I mentioned, our days in Canton were numbered. 520 Misty Creek had served its purpose. It gave us a base in the Atlanta area when we came back from Savannah, but the house was just too small even for just Carolyn and me … and the kittens. So, with me being hired back in Cobb and Carolyn rapidly tiring from her "twenty minute" (sarcasm) drive to Atlanta from Canton, I started looking for a house a little closer in. I wanted to stay under $200,000 if I could. School let out and I really put the house hunt on full steam ahead. I found a home on Zillow Saturday afternoon located in Cobb just south of Woodstock at 1840 Condor Drive in Marietta. I called the listing realtor and headed out to check it out. When I got there I knew in a minute this was not going to work. First the house was "in a hole" and that is a deal killer for Carolyn and me. But I went inside anyway and the house was a mess. The basement where the cars should sit was packed with trash and junk. It was a no. But the realtor had a house just across the street at 1839 so we went and looked at it. It had the funkiest floor plan I had ever seen and knew Carolyn would reject it immediately. So, the realtor and I parted ways, and I headed out of the subdivision. I had come in from Jett Road and had seen the pool and tennis courts and really liked the neighborhood, so I thought why not look around and go out the other entrance. As I did I passed by a house that literally had just been put on the market … not three days before. It was taupe, but paint could change that, it sat on a hill – good, it had a two car garage – good, it looked like a little Millbrook Trace – good, the plumbing was copper - good. So, without a realtor I waltzed up to the door and introduced myself to Suzie and Chuck Negas. They were gracious and showed me around, and I immediately knew THIS was the house. They were asking $160K – good. The siding was the old fiberboard crap that I knew would have to go, but the dollars and repairs made sense, so I called Carolyn. She was taking a well-deserved nap, and I woke her up. Over the course of the next few days she saw the house and agreed, and we put up earnest money and got it off the market. Now, we had to sell Misty Creek. Again, the Gods were smiling. There was a young Hispanic family who really wanted the house, but getting their finances in order would be a challenge. This time period was in the middle of the real estate bubble although we did not know it was a bubble at that time and financing was wild and crazy. I did not go for that and went for my standard thirty year fixed rate deal. The little family

in Canton was having a little more of a problem. We were closing in on the end of July, and I had to start school shortly. First the Canton closing was scheduled for Wednesday the 27th. We had to cancel that because the Canton house financing was not approved. We rescheduled for July 29th. Again, a no go, and a reschedule for the next Monday, August 1st. I was getting worried about the little family's ability to finance, but they shared they really wanted the house and had wanted it a year before, but Carolyn and I had beaten them to it. Each time the closing slipped, I had to put off the movers (Two Men and a Truck again … I really liked them). Then on the 1st with my first day of preplanning on Wednesday the 3rd, we struck gold and were able to close. I hoped the little Canton family did not do something out of their reach trying to get Misty Creek. The price we put on Misty Creek was exactly what we had bought it for so I did not feel like I was ripping anyone off. The movers were sitting on ready, and we had the movers there on Tuesday and by Tuesday night at 8:00 we had all our junk in 1920 Falcon Wood Drive, NE, Marietta, Georgia. Suzie and Chuck Negas had already moved out several days before. On the next Monday, August 8th, we started stripping off the old siding and putting on Hardiplank. All in, the house would cost $188,000. As stupid as it will sound, it is currently appraised at around $450,000 just eighteen years later. We love the location. We are minutes from I-75, I-575 is even closer, and we can get to 400 in twenty minutes. Hospitals are close and Publix, Kroger and my most favorite, Walmart, are literally just around the corner … sweet! It is in a good location, and it is a good, solid house. We got lucky.

That was the year that Carolyn had to have her mother, Mildred Virginia Shacklett Lyon moved into a nursing home. After one day of research, because Virginia was in the hospital and to be released and that was all the time available, Carolyn found a home that Nanny could afford on her limited income plus Medicaid. It was off of the South 120 Loop off Wylie Road. Today it called A.G. Rhodes Rehabilitation Center. It was as good as could be gotten for Virginia. Her house was cleaned and sold "as is" to free up more cash. We bought a van with a wheelchair lift that worked 90% of the time no matter what I did to repair it, and the rest was on Carolyn and Bobbie (Roberta Orlena Lyon Miller). Virginia had gotten mad at Carolyn for moving to the coast and changed her will so the Bobbie, the youngest sister, was the Executrix and Carolyn was in charge of her care and finances. This put a huge strain on Carolyn as she could not really make any decisions without consulting Bobbie. And that was okay, Bobbie was not going to fight her on anything, but it was just another hoop for Carolyn to jump through. We had to follow the will as Virginia was incapacitated and could not make decisions for herself. So, Carolyn was "on call" 24/7 no matter if she was at work or what. If Virginia had a doctor's appointment, Carolyn had to take time to get the van, go wrestle Virginia in to the van, get to the doctors, wrestle again, listen to everything the doctor said, wrestle, drive, wrestle, get Nanny situated back in the home, then drop off the van and go back to work. Carolyn is a SAINT! I went with her several times to visit and to have meals with Virginia on special days. I was struck with the hopelessness of the place and saw a future I wanted no part of. The most heartbreaking times to me were at the meals where we would sit in the dining room, and there were these men who had once been "captains of industry" slumped over in their chairs with bibs on being fed whatever the caretakers could get them to eat. It was disheartening. And Virginia continued to be herself. One might think she might mellow given everything, but no. As I have said, she would moan and curse as best she could with the stroke taking most of her speech away. She would lash out with her good arm and hit Carolyn. It was horrible. And this was Carolyn's life for the next who knows how long. And she bore this burden as she had all her travails … with quiet dignity and beauty.

Chapter Three
The Empty Nest Days

"I wish I didn't know now, what I didn't know then."

Bob Seger, *Against the Wind.*

1.

This is a new Chapter because our last little chicken, James, was pretty much out of the nest this year. He had graduated and was working in Effingham County in middle school, and it was very, very quiet at Falcon Wood Drive. 2006 saw Carolyn still working at Sizemore Group, although she was rapidly tiring of the politics and workload and change was in the air. Here at home we had The Boys come as often as we could get Jenna to let them loose. We bought them some bunk beds and they would come for several days at a time. In the morning we would generally cook pancakes together. This was high art too as The Boys would have to decide what color they wanted their individual pancakes to be. Sometimes Bryce would choose red, which meant Bodie had to choose green. Or Bodie would choose blue, so Bryce had to choose green or red. Sometimes Bodie would mix his colors, but it seemed that Bryce was a purist. He stuck with a single primary color. And so the differences in the brothers started to show themselves even though they were only five and three. I can see them now standing on their little Ikea stools we bought them at the counter working on their pancakes like it was just yesterday. The stools are in the basement, and I'm sure they are destined for the trash someday, but not today! The stools were painted (and repainted) by The Boys in their own distinctive colors right here in the kitchen at Falcon Wood Drive. It was a great production of newspapers being laid and water color paints being selected. The Boys would then paint for, I'm sure what to them seemed like hours, maybe twenty minutes and then we had to oooooh and ahhhhhhh over their creations. But on pancake mornings the colored pancakes would come off the griddle and everyone waited for Nana (Carolyn) to exclaim over how terrible they looked as three boys giggled in the background. Then we would all eat our colored creations slathered in butter and syrup. Some mornings we would do colored waffles which elicited even worse comments from Carolyn. But the hilarity of waffles was the little, slow waffle iron Pa (Jim) used. You see at Jenna and Adam's house they had a Belgian waffle maker that would spit out big puffy waffles faster than you could eat them. While Pa's waffles came out so slowly you could color pictures or watch entire television programs while breakfast slowly emerged. First we had to wait for the waffle iron to warm up. Finally, after about an hour the little red light on the top would go out and Pa would pour some of the batter, red or green or blue never yellow

266

… I guess yellow just didn't turn the batter a crazy enough color … and carefully close the lid. Steam would stream out, the little red light would come on again and the top lid would slowly start to rise. Meanwhile The Boys are aging rapidly, and when finally, the light went out, a great production of lifting the lid and a single waffle would emerge. Would it be a *top waffle*? Top waffles stuck to the upper lid of the ancient waffle maker and were the most cherished. But usually it was just a dumb old *bottom waffle* and everyone would groan. Then the waffle hit the boy's plates, Nanna would heap on the butter, The Boys would pour syrup to their hearts content … there were few rules at Nana and Pa's house, and it was woofed down in an instant … long before the next waffle was ready to the glee and hilarity of The Boys. They would constantly remind me how fast "their mommy's" waffles were made and how far superior they were to Pa's, and why weren't we eating pancakes instead? "They cooked so much faster, Pa."

After breakfast we would watch some television. Their favorite program was *Cops*. This was probably because Uncle Chuck, Chuck Chapeau, was a Georgia State Patrol Officer. After a dose of *Cops*, The Boys would run around chasing each other, usually only in bathing suits because the pool was always in the offing, yelling "Get on the grooound!" with their little hands held up like pistols because toy guns were verboten by Mommy Jenna. After a suitable lunch of anything they wanted, we were off to the pool. The subdivision pool was just off Jett Road near the western entrance to Falcon Woods. It was and still is a very nice pool and The Boys spent many hours there. I am looking up at a picture on the shelf right this minute of Bryce doing a back dive and Bodie, mouth open (this was his trademark back in the day) with water wings on jumping into Pa's arms. Over the summers both boys became quite proficient swimmers and even though we slathered sunscreen on every five minutes, they would get "as brown as a little nut." The worst part of the pool was Adult Swim. For ten minutes (seemed like fifty minutes) every hour children had to sit out, and only adults were allowed in the pool. But The Boys accepted these arcane rules and would sit with their little feet dangling precariously in the pool waiting breathlessly for the lifeguard to finish testing the pool water, calling her boyfriend undoubtedly, then sashay back to her perch, blow the long awaited whistle and say, "All swim!" A favorite as their confidence grew was to play "Do It." This game consisted of them swimming up to Pa and yelling "Do it!" at which time I would grab the closest one and lift him from the pool and throw him as far as I could. This elicited peals of laughter and squeals of terror. This game was also especially great fun because Nana absolutely did not approve of it! "Someone is going to get hurt!" she would say often and to the boy's delight. And then you would hear, "Do it, Pa!" and another little hard body would fly through the air and come up sputtering. These wonderful, long, summer days set The Boys up to be very comfortable at the lake.

James and Ian were still fast friends and decided one year to take their cars to the NOPI Nationals at Atlanta Raceway. I am not sure what NOPI stands for but James and Ian were into it big time, so Carolyn and I headed down south of the city to see what was happening. Before we left, James called and asked if we could bring a grill. They had charcoal, lighter, condiments, dogs and burgers, drinks, but someone forget the grill. And so we conjured up a grill, probably at the Walmart, and headed down. I actually do not remember much about the day other than it was hot and there were literally hundreds of cars. We found James and Ian near the back of the crowd with their cars on proud display and their women right there putting up with them. James was still totally a car guy, and with his close buddy Ian, they made quite a pair. As I said, I do not remember much about the day. I recall James had an old license plate he had painted to match his car which was kind of cool. You see that a lot in car magazines. And … Carolyn and I had lunch and headed home.

I was reveling in being back at Mt. Bethel. I was so amazingly comfortable there and I threw myself into my class and school totally. It was so wonderful having a principal back you 110%. The principal can make or break a school, and a teacher, as we are to soon see. But at this moment in time I was King of the World, and we held the ESO, and Jekyll, and Rock Eagle and Barbie, and I met Danner.

The Science Olympiad in Cobb after two years had languished for some reason. I enjoyed being on the team back at Mountain View and during my first stint at Mt. Bethel, and we had had a Cobb County competition at Southern Tech if you will recall. But the whole competition had fallen by the wayside for some reason. That fall I had an inspiration and contacted the new science person at the County named Sally Creel and asked her if I could get it all started again here at Mount Bethel. She agreed and so we started laying plans for the next spring. We selected eighteen events to practice on and contacted several schools nearby, Eastside and Tritt I think … it may have been the current powerhouse Shallowford Falls … I forget, and I gathered a team and got Coach Chuck Jones to join me and we were off to the races! Come the spring of that school year, we gathered the three schools together at Mount Bethel. and had the first Cobb County Science Olympiad competition in years. My room mom got several of the team moms together and they sold snacks which supported our foundation and made the children very happy. The morning went well although there were a couple of hiccups. Chuck Jones was in charge of the water rocket launching and he persevered even though we had a late spring snow that morning, and it was very cold. Chuck continued launching rockets for us and with me through 2017 when he had had all the fun he could stand, and he stood down. I continued. But I know I could call on him today, and he would be right there to help. He and I are still good friends, in fact one of my few real friends. But that morning was good fun. We did have a little stumble with the tower building event. The event was supposed to be that each team was given some random materials, pencils, tape, paper towel rolls and such, and they were challenged to build the tallest tower they could that would support a baseball for ten seconds. The problem was that each team was to have the same materials, but the person running the event did not quite understand that … I know … Duh. Anyway, when my team came back from the event I asked how they thought they did and they said, "Well, we think we did good, but the other team had rulers, and we did not, so they made a taller tower than we could." I was confused so then asked if they meant that everyone did not have the same materials, and they said, "No, we all had different materials." So, minor SNAFU, and that event was not counted that year. Sally had let me get medals for first, second and third place and because we had only three teams competing, every child walked away with a medal. It was a grand and glorious morning at "Mount Special." After two more years at Mount Bethel the event had grown too large for our little cafeteria to support us, so Sally Creel and I moved it to Walton High School where we stayed until about 2017. Dr. (she had earned a Ph.D.) Sally Creel then moved it around to other high schools in the county. The one we just conducted in 2023, now known as the Cobb Regional ESO, had about 30 schools competing with over 500 Olympians. Now there are regional competitions all over Georgia, and a team has to score high enough in their region to be invited to the state competition held yearly at Kennesaw State University. The state competition we held several weeks ago on May 6th, 2023, had some 60 schools and bout 1,000 Olympians from all over Georgia competing. I like to think I had some small hand in getting that event started for children. I am still involved in the competition and James and I are the Water Rocket Event team leaders. At the event on May 6th, my granddaughter Caitlin Rose Morris helped us for the first time. You will meet *The Princess* later. I'm not saying that I was responsible for what the ESO has become in Georgia, no, far from it. But I am proud that I may have played a little part in its resurrection.

Robin Lattazori supported me and my Charleston weekend field trip again that year and all of the fifth grade joined in the Jekyll field trip once again. The Jekyll field trip was a huge undertaking, and we stretched the Jekyll 4H facility to its limits. At this time the 4H facility located on the south end of the island was an old motel that was part of a complex that had been built in 1959 called the Dolphin Motel for African Americans. The rooms were of the classic old motel room style with a 20 foot by 15-foot large room and a bathroom with a shower. It was a two story, U shaped affair with the girls bunking on one side of the U and the boys on the other. We would leave on a Wednesday morning early arriving at Jekyll at lunch. Each class supplied teams of KP duty children who would help with silverware distribution, drink pouring and clean-up duties. The children would settle into their rooms, and then spend time in classes like Beach Ecology, The Marsh, Dock Study, Maritime Forest, and the North End. The North End was always one of my favorites because the children got to be amazed by Boneyard Beach. So, you are now going to have to go to Jekyll Island and see Boneyard Beach for yourself. Trust me, it is a sight to behold. The whole time the children were there they had to keep a diary of their exploits in each of their classes, and of course in my class it was for a grade. I would tell the children that when they went to the cafeteria and walked through the line to ask the people serving the food for the "lobster" or for our second dinner to ask for the "steak." This was very much like the Yorktown Carrier prank. Of course they never did ask, and they got the standard hot dog or spaghetti or whatever was being dished out. Later, I would ask them about it and tell them my steak was perfect. They were always confused. After dinner we had a Night Walk class scheduled and hunted for ghost crabs and looked at stars they can never see in the smoggy skies of Atlanta. We would also have sand castle building activities and a wonderful class on Sea Turtles where we would learn about the TED (Turtle Escape Device). Thursday morning was a special morning, because I would wake any and all children and counselors who wanted to see the sunrise. My room of children had to participate usually amid groans and griping, but once on the beach there was a sense of wonder and awe as most of them had never done anything like this. The day was another full day of activities including The Marsh, one of my favorites. Everyone had to don marsh boots or old tennis shoes they may have brought with them. I was always an old tennis shoe man. We would hop in one of the little 4H buses and head out to the special entry point 4H used to go into the marsh. Let me just say here that I love the marsh. I love the smells, the animals, the whole thing … all of it. If I was ever able to have a house on the coast, I would want it to be overlooking the marsh rather than the beach. The beach is so sterile. The marsh is so vital and alive. Anyway we would venture into another world. A world these city children have never experienced. We would see thousands of little crabs scurrying – kind of creepy – and marsh grass, taste sea pickles, talk about the importance of the marsh as a sanctuary for migrating birds and as a sponge to soak up hurricanes that make their way inland. There is always the wonderful adventure of putting marsh mud on your face to tighten your skin. Most of us put some mud on. The Mt. Bethel children had another full day of handling snakes and learning about the animals that live at the dock. For that adventure we all walk out to the dock and the children lay down on their tummies and scoop whatever they can from the water with little nets, and then the 4H person, usually a UGA biology major working on a master's degree or something, tells them all about what they have scooped up. The only time the students are allowed in the water is when they are in Seining Class. The children wade out into the surf under the watchful eyes of a 4H person and several counselors and work a sein net to collect the wildlife that live in the shallows. Then the collection is analyzed by the 4H person to the oooo's and aaaahs of the students. It is a beautiful scene. Another of my favorites is the maritime forest. It is the lush vegetation growing far back from the beach but before the marsh really takes over. Whenever we would walk there I felt almost as if I were back in Panama. That is probably why I loved it so much. There was the requisite picture of the children climbing on the old live oak and the small board walk over the slough. We only ran into ticks once that I can recall, and they were dispatched by me quickly. By the time we had fed the children that evening, let them play on the playground and built more sand sculptures (which usually had to be along a theme selected by the counselors like Disney movies or something) that were then judged by the counselors and cleaned them all up, most were ready for bed, and most went right to sleep. Friday morning was a class, and then a boat ride from the pier at the Jekyll Island Club up and down the Intercoastal waterway. We would watch for dolphins and the children would help haul in a seining net and get a look at the animals of the Intercoastal waterway. The hauling in of the net was exciting as the students draw in the net to the chant of the first mate of "Heave, Ho, Heave, Ho." They would haul in all kinds of fish and shrimp. The shrimp were especially fascinating to these little city children because most had never seen one with its head on! Now, so you know (and not to get all dark and maudlin) this is the boat ride excursion that I would like my family to go on to disperse my ashes in that gentle waterway. Then, if you ever want to visit me after my death, you have to bring your family down to the beautiful Georgia Barrier Islands and spend a few days where Jimbo had some of the most wonder-filled days of his life with his special teacher friends and children. Be sure to drop by the 4H Center and find the big bell that the counselors use to change classes. That bell was donated by Carolyn and me to the 4H Center for all the wonderful work they did and are doing. Enough talk of all of that … after morning activities, we all reluctantly boarded our buses. "Same seats!" was the cry of the children boarding the bus. Then we pulled out waving good bye to magical Jekyll Island and headed back to Mount Special stopping on the way at a rest stop on I-16 to eat bag lunches prepared by the great Jekyll Island dining hall staff. Arriving home on that Friday evening was always heartrending. When we pulled up there were many, many parents waiting for their little cherubs, eager to hear about their Great Adventure. But there always seemed to be at least one little child whose parents had forgotten to come to get him/her. It was always heart breaking for the teachers and me but most of all the child. All the excitement of the three days ebbed away and embarrassment and self-loathing crept into the little one's heart. Parents, don't you understand?! This child will NEVER ever forget that feeling. And they will NEVER ever forgive you that oversight. It does not matter how good your reason was. You were NOT there for them when they needed you most. I have to give you a quote from that great poet Maya Angelou, "I've learned that people will forget what you said, people will forget what you did, but people will never forget how you made them feel." **It is gospel.** And as you may have noticed from reading this far that it echoes in my recollections of my own upbringing.

I again presented at Rock Eagle 4H at the NCTM convention. I loved presenting Kinesthetic Geometry to teacher groups. I had videos of children learning how to play Bob Says and pointing out the children who had Musical Intelligences and the ones who were naturally Kinesthetic and the ones who just had a good time trying to keep up with the old teacher. My class with other teachers would invariably end with the class of teachers having to play Bob Says. And of course I always had prizes to share with the winners. First prize usually involved Peanut M&M's, the Food of the Gods. I rarely stayed in the 4H facility when I went down there. I had stayed in their cabins once when I was a chaperone in James's fifth grade class (when Ms. Scheer was his teacher), and I preferred staying at motel, usually the Hampton Inn near I-20 on 441 just south of Madison. Stayed there many times and loved it.

The Mount Bethel teachers were a wild bunch and never more so than when they gathered off campus for a let your hair down Holiday party or end of year celebration. One Holiday party was especially memorable. The event staff decided to have a parade of all the Barbies (East Cobb Moms) we encounter as teachers. There was the City Barbie with her form fitting pencil skirt and white business blouse. There was the East Cobb Barbie with her form fitting jeans, pronounced breasts, sunglasses and attitude. There was the Country Barbie in her sundress and all flirty and wearing $300 cowboy boots. Then there was the Ultimate Barbie. I had gotten wind of this particular show and decided to introduce the Mt. Bethel staff to me as Barbie. This was the same basic outfit I had used in the California Girls skit at Mountain View only this one had a cigar and looked a lot rougher! Dressed in black opaque pantyhose, white strappy four-inch heels, a thigh length black skirt, large breasts under a Rolling Stones tee shirt with a big tongue on it, sunglasses, a blond wig with bangs and a cigar Barbie would waltz in to the song *Bad to the Bone* by George Thorogood & the Destroyers. She, me, was an instant hit and Barbie would appear over the years in various guises and iterations at parties to keep the staff laughing and off balance. I finally retired her after about five or six appearances when it became obvious that Barbie was playing to more the prurient interests and was no longer a novelty. I guess today with the whole Trans thing I would fit right in, or, like E.T. Wah, Barbie would be shunned in the humorless 2000's.

I met a woman in the fall of the 2006 school year who would become both a good friend and ally and ultimately an adversary. It was Melissa Danner. The fall of that year we got a new veteran teacher from the Carrolton area. Ms. Danner took the room right next to me on the fifth grade hall, and we became fast friends quickly. Even though Principal Robin Lattizori assigned another teacher to be Melissa's mentor, I decided since we were right next to each other to help her any way I could. Little things like grades and lesson plans could make a big difference. Also navigating Mt. Bethel's minutes to minute schedule was helpful. The school was full with over a thousand students so the lunch schedule was a three-minute window. You had your designated time to show up, and the cafeteria was geared for you. You had turned in your lunch count in the morning and they were expecting you relative to which choice and which milks/drinks you would be taking. Basically, we are talking the earth falling out of its orbit if you did not hit your mark. Then there were the Specials rotation. There was PE, Music, Art and Drama on a two-week cycle so you had to have your head up as you could not count on having the same Specials each day over the rotation. And teachers messed-up some days, and two classes would show up for Music, and we would have to sort out who had messed up with much hilarity amongst the students, and then you were invariably late for wherever you were supposed to be. And of course one needs to factor in picture day, and field day, and field trip days and it could be bewildering if you "did not keep your head while all about you were losing theirs and blaming it on you." (Apologies to Rudyard Kipling) Anyway Danner and I became friends and we covered each other's backs. Once at Jekyll Island, I was the teacher in charge of planning and daily announcements and another teacher who had joined the troop tried to take over, and Mel put her in her spot right quickly. Thanks Mel. Then near the end of my tenure as a teacher … around 2015 … Jekyll Island had just reopened after being closed for renovation for two years or so, and I was gathering support for our trip. We had a crop of young teachers on the team and Melissa decided she did not want to go to Jekyll that year and so she … well, let's just say she did not support my efforts. And of course the young teachers when confronted with the option of spending three days with their students almost continuously or just teaching in the classroom and going home at 4:30 or so, opted for the easy way … 4:30. And the whole wonderful Jekyll experience was denied to our fifth grade that year and following years. That was a tragedy. I will mention this again later as I am writing about closing out my teaching career, but that non-support from Mel hurt me. I thought we were closer than that.

Mount Bethel was one of the first schools to have a Foundation. This Foundation was dedicated to making sure Mt. Bethel children had the best opportunities. The Foundation would provide the teachers with a supply stipend each year above what the County offered. They would pay for a Drama teacher in the Specials rotation and a STEM teacher. They would make sure that if a teacher wanted to try a special program or something outside the box, the money would be available. The Foundation would raise money by having parents join and pay dues in the fall and then they would also have a silent auction in the fall to raise even more money. The silent auction had many offerings to bid on from student art work to each class parent having a project from the class to bid on to donations by parents like … only in East Cobb … a week at an Italian Villa! But in the living room under the front table opposite the grandfather clock is our class's offering for the 2005-2006 school year. It holds many sweet memories put in it by the students. It is covered in a hodgepodge of saying and clips from Maverick Mailgrams and pictures. It is beautiful. And a parent bought it, and then gave it to me. It is a very special keepsake that will undoubtedly be "black bagged" one day, but today, in my world, it means a lot. It means I was a good teacher and good at my craft and I was a positive influence on my children and my parents. Thank you parent who cared enough about me and what I was doing to buy the trunk and make it my gift forever. Also part of the silent auction, each teacher was urged to donate something to be bid on that evening. Teachers would donate a class party or a special art day or other things like that. But not Mr. Morris. One year my offering was A Day with Mr. M. for four students. We would begin the day being picked up at Mt. Bethel in Mr. Morris's two cars … I drove and Carolyn drove. We would go down to the High Museum of Art for a tour, then lunch at the Varsity downtown then the Atlanta History Center then return to the Morris home later in the day for a pizza party. Can you imagine actually seeing and being in the home of your fifth grade teacher? What a day it was! And we had a blast doing it. Several parents pooled their resources so their children would be the ones to go that day and it went for a record amount that evening. We had a great day. We even had Bryce along I believe.

A final remembrance of that year, I taught the son of Dirk and Barb, our next door neighbors down from us, to drive a stick shift. I had a stick shift Honda Civic at the time, and Dirk had noted this. And when his son wanted to learn, Dirk asked me if I would mind doing the honors. What could I say but, "Of course." And so I did. We started in the Kell parking lot and over the weeks graduated to the surface street and then the expressway. He was a natural and quick study. I talked to Dirk the other day, and he said that Stephen still had a stick shift car to this day and loves driving it … even with his wife and children!

2.

Oh my, my, my … 2007, epic. Hold on to your hats because this is going to take a while. This year has sadness, happiness, excitement, adventure, and of course, paying bills. We're going to start with January 7th. Virginia Shacklett Lyon, Nanny, passed away. I find myself struggling for the proper words surrounding this event. Nanny died at Kennestone Hospital with three of her four daughters around her. That was all. There were none of the daughter's husbands present. Carolyn can tell you better, but that is my recollection. Several days later we had her funeral. It was held at the funeral home, one up near the square in Marietta I think. Reverend Richard Lumpkin, a long time pastor at Powers Ferry United Methodist Church, officiated as now we come to the part I recall with clarity. Even though Reverend Lumpkin had known Virginia for years and was aided by notes from the daughters.

On a lighter note, James and Angela Dawn Swope decided to "tie the knot," and they set the date for May 27th. As you can imagine there are many short and tall tales surrounding this momentous event. I know Carolyn gave her a bridal shower or two, but I was a persona non grata at those secret affairs so I cannot speak to them. Again, ask Carolyn. But I was invited to one shower given by my very good friend from Mt. Bethel Church days, Carol Sumrell and her husband, Chris. It was a very sweet affair at Carol's home in the Highland subdivision (I think) off Wesley Chapel Road. I remember a lovely spring day and sitting on the deck at the Sumrell house. Jenna and Adam and The Boys were there, James and Angie, Angie's parents Mana and James, and Carolyn and me. There were others I think. I can't really recall others. It was very sweet of Carol Sumrell to do that for James. She and James had become good friends over the years since Mt. Bethel Church days.

But one of the biggest James getting married events I recall was *The Ultimate Two Boys Trip*. I cooked up that trip, and over Spring Break that year James and I would go on the ultimate trip. We had not done one for several years since he went off to college, and it was high time for a blowout. The plan was he and I would board a Royal Caribbean ship in New Orleans and heading out for seven days to the western Caribbean. The classic Cozumel, Roatán route that would take us all the way down to Roatán, Honduras and back. I have many memories of that trip, but I'll keep to some of the highlights. James and I drove down to NO and stayed the night at "some random hotel" (A phrase Caitlin would immortalize years later), and we strolled Jackson Square, ate some beignets and drank some coffee at the French Market. We found a parking deck near the ship, and I stowed the car, and we boarded the boat. We had a cabin with a window as I was not the balcony guy I became later in life. As we shoved off into the Mississippi and got situated to head south, James and I were hanging off the upper deck, James shooting pictures of everything and me shooting pictures of my boy, and we looked back over NO and saw a thunderstorm rolling in from the north. He and I scurried for a lower deck and some protection. I do not think others did the same because I recall a lot of squealing and people running when the deluge swept over us. It was a "frog strangler" … or to use another of my lovely colloquialisms – like a cow pissing off a flat rock! James and I just chuckled. But we were safely away and headed down the delta toward the great blue Caribbean. We got a table for just the two of us for our evening meals, and I recall one night on the ship it was lobster night. Now the way they did lobster night back then was that they would keep bringing you lobsters as long as you requested them and kept eating them. They stopped that around 2021, but "back in the day" you could have as many as you could eat. So, James and I decided we would put them out of business. I do not recall how many each of us ate that night but it had to be at least six lobster tails apiece. We were stuffed when we left that dining room! I do not think we impressed our waiter. He had probably seen college kids eat a whole lot more than James and I did that night, but we were very impressed with ourselves. Also, there was our run at roulette. We went to the table one afternoon as I recall. We were at sea and between ports, and I was the player, and James was the keeper of the cash. We played for several hours. There were a couple of other people who joined us at the table, but mostly it was just the Two Boys. And we did some damage! I would place bets and when we won, James would rake the chips to the side keeping my playing pile small. After a couple of hours, the wheel turned against me, and I depleted my pile of playing chips. I turned to James and asked for some of the chips he had been pulling to the side. He said, "No Dad. We're done here." And the Two Gambling Boys … think Wyatt Earp and Doc Holiday … retired with our winnings. We had come in with twenty dollars and walked out with over a hundred bucks. I know, I know … you wanted a huge pot, but we were pleased and we had "taken" Royal C that afternoon! We took our loot and went immediately and bought drinks and drank up all our winnings … right there, on the spot. So, I guess Royal Caribbean didn't really lose anything. They never do. But Two Boys had a great time and an awesome memory, and I think that is Royal C's business.

At one of our ports we traveled to some Mayan ruins other than Tulum, and I have distinct memories of James the photographer with cameras slung around his neck slogging around ancient pyramids in the heat and getting some awesome shots. But the four wheeler expedition we took had to be the ultimate. Now one year Carolyn and I had taken a family trip on Royal C one year with James and Angie and Jenna and Adam and Bryce and Bodie. One day James and Angie had gone off and taken a four wheeler trip around an island and had had an awesome adventure including a nude beach, and he wanted us to do something like that. I was all in … especially if there was to be a nude beach involved. There was not. Our excursion was a four wheeler expedition across dirty, dusty Mexican back county that almost killed me it was so rough. I <u>mean</u> almost killed me. When we got to this place they outfitted us with helmets, goggles and a kerchief to cover our mouths. That afternoon was the most brutal excursion I have ever been on. The course was miles and miles of scrub plains with pot holes the size of boulders. The reason they gave us the kerchiefs was the dust was unbelievable … clouds and clouds of brown dust. Well, I'll be honest with you, I had a hard time keeping up. At one point, one of the guides had to come back and tell me I was holding up the group, and I had to pick up the pace. That was embarrassing. I had never not kept up in my life … well, almost never. I have to remind you I had pictured this leisurely ride which included naked women, and here I was beating my kidneys to a pulp on this Bataan Death Ride. I mean it was so rough you did not sit down on the seat. You had to hold yourself up off the seat holding onto the throttle and other handle bar or you would die … literally die. Now, James had no problem keeping up with pack, so I doubled down and cranked the throttle, gritted my gritty teeth and prayed my kidneys would forgive me as we blasted across the filthy Mexican countryside. Mercifully it ended. James and I were caked with dirt from our hair to our feet. I mean our tennis shoes were destroyed. We had to ultimately throw them away they were so horrible. I remember as we were leaving, looking like third world rejects, there was this family walking up. There was a Mom and Dad a son and a daughter. They were all sparkly clean in white shorts and shirts. They looked and us. We looked at them. I do not recall us saying anything, but they got a good look at their future. All we could do was laugh to ourselves what this little family was going to look like in a few hours. When we got back to the boat, we were still covered in dirt and still looked like refugees, but with the proper identification R.C. reluctantly let us aboard. When I got a chance later on the ship at guest relations, I wrote a guest review of this excursion. I was not kind.

On another stop we made, James and I went snorkeling off a boat near some random island. We were tooling around having a gay old time when we swam over near the edge of the island's shelf. I do not know what else to call it. The island just sort of poked up out of the seabed, and we were swimming over near the edge where the island just sort of dropped off into oblivion.

We tootled over with our little masks and snorkel and fins and peered over the edge. It was disorienting and surreal. The bright, clear blue ocean dissolved into the blue black nothingness. It was like looking over a cliff down into night, and it was terrifying! I guess I have seen too many badly done Sci-Fi movies where the unsuspecting stupid tourists are gleefully unaware of the Megalodon shark swimming like a locomotive straight up … think *Jaws* poster or the movie *Meg*… toward them until it is too late, and they simply disappear in a fine red mist. Anyway, I gingerly backed away from the edge. I did not turn around and swim away, I backed away. If I was going to be eaten by a Caribbean monster shark, I wanted to see it coming rather than have it just sneak up on me and bite me in half. But, I did not get eaten, and James and survived our encounter with the Underwater Death Cliff of the Caribbean. I know you are glad to read that.

When the cruise was nearing the end, and we entered the mouth of the Mississippi Delta, it was evening. We would sail all night through the delta back to New Orleans. I loved the delta. It was like my marsh only on steroids. The wildlife was everywhere and the only civilization you would see was the very occasional run down fish camp. After dinner I was on the upper deck looking to the darkening east and the orange sun was setting on my back. I'm not sure where James was, but I was alone with my thoughts, and I thought back to a trip almost thirty years before with Eli Lugo on the Christobal. For the first of what were to be many times in my life as one ages, I had come full circle.

Disembarking the ship was a whole 'nother adventure. It seems when you travel with The James Man life just gets interesting. You see since we were in the islands, James decided he was going to buy a bunch of very well-priced liquor while we were down there. And I mean he loaded up. He bought more than he and I combined were allowed to bring back into the states. When we got on the boat, RC immediately takes stuff like that and holds it for you until you get to port and then delivers it back to you room for you to deal with the authorities about. Well, the morning of disembarkation came, and I was "all a twitter" about all this booze. And James, in his always cool demeanor, was not the least bit concerned. So we got the all clear, and it was time for us to leave the ship. I just knew we were going to be thrown under the New Orleans jailhouse. I could hear the immigration and customs people yelling, "Get on the grooound!" the moment we set foot on the dock, but being the dutiful father and bound and determined to stand by my son even if we both were going to Alcatraz or Lompoc Prison for a hundred years, I carried my share of the bootie. So, the two criminals walked toward the customs man who was already eying us both critically. Two guys with four hundred gallons of hooch being dragged across the floor probably looked like easy pickins that morning. But then, we just walked by him. He did not cuff us or anything! I thought to myself that they wanted us to get deep in the building where we couldn't just throw it all in water by the ship and plead innocence. They wanted us good and caught. Finally, in the building we got our luggage and got up to the little portal where they look at your declarations page and your passport and look you over … I knew we were dead men walkin'. The big, burly guy looked us over and waved us through. He didn't even look at our passports or anything! What kind of a country are we running here where two boys can just bring about a thousand gallons of illegal liquor into the United States and no one, not one soul, tried to stop us? I had to reassess my whole perspective on the United States Customs and Immigration Department, not to mention the whole Alcohol, Tobacco and Firearms branch of Justice. And James just shrugged.

James and Angela's wedding was to be held at City Hall in Atlanta thanks to Angela's daddy's contacts and working for the City. We had the rehearsal with Reverend Richard Lumpkin doing the honors. Afterward, Carolyn and I were in charge of the rehearsal dinner. We elected to have it at the Atlanta Marriott Northwest at 200 Interstate North Parkway near I-75 and I-285. As I noted earlier, this was the same place I had held the SAE Regional gathering back in 1989 and just down I-75 a little way from where we had our rehearsal dinner back in '73. Carolyn and I elected to have a buffet style evening and the one thing we did not want was rubber chicken. I think it was sort of Mexican faire evening, but I could have that all wrong. Ask Carolyn. It was a very nice evening as I recall and all the skeletons were there: The Colonel and Mom, Nelson and Toochie, Marybelle and all of Angela's side of the family who we did not know very well beyond Mana and James Swope, Angela's mom and dad. The dinner went well as I recall.

It was the day before the wedding, and it was time for the requisite Bachelor Party. Being the best man, I was allowed to arrange the evening. It was to be James, James's good college friend Ian, Adam and me. Somewhere along the way we added another of James's college buddies, but that was not until after dinner. The evening started with dinner at Ruth's Chris Steak House in Sandy Springs. Of course everyone had steaks all around with drinks, and it was all on Carolyn and me … well, me. I was to be the designated driver for the evening so I was alcohol free all night. After a delicious dinner we headed to The Pink Pony at 1837 Corporate Blvd. in Brookhaven and quite an evening it was. There were naked girls everywhere which was to be expected and enjoyed. James and Adam got their heads together and bought a lap dance for the alcohol free old man. It may surprise you that I do not remember the young lady's name. It wasn't to be a long term relationship so I did not bother with formal introductions or exchanging business cards or anything, but she was certainly energetic, and I was appreciative of her obvious charms. And James and Adam had great fun watching me be uncomfortable. But I was already cooking up my revenge of the evening. Late in the evening the headliner girl came out onto the stage. She was all naked and bouncing and actually did a cartwheel coming onto the raised stage. For some reason as I'm writing this I am seeing the color pink, but that may just be a trick of the mind. The main headlining lady comes cartwheeling out in just a G-string … interesting … I wonder why it is called a G-string … anyway, she comes out and as she is making her entrance down the stage about six feet in front of and a foot above us, I signaled for James and Adam to lean over. One was on each side of me. I think they were guarding me. And as they leaned over I said to them above the din of the music, "You know guys, this would be exciting if I didn't see Carolyn do this same routine every night!" Well, the reaction was immediate and worth every second. Both of them reeled back in their chairs away from me yelling for that vision to get out of their heads! Adam picturing his Mother-in-Law and worse James picturing his Mother cavorting around in six inch heels and a pink, rhinestone G-string. Ahhh, I absolutely loved it and reveled in <u>their</u> discomfort. I have also related this story many times and always get a massive eye-roll and a blush from Carolyn with each telling. The evening pounded on, and finally it was time to put a cork in the bottle so to speak and call it a night. And this is where I failed in my duties as a best man. James insisted on he and Ian going to his other friend's apartment for the night and not coming home with Adam and me. I was not happy with the arrangement, but was powerless to stop it short of being a horse's ass, so they did. I'm not sure about the rest of their night, but Adam and I got home around 2:30 safe and sound. Carolyn was not pleased, but I assured her it would all be fine. And the next morning, the 27th, true to my word, I was on the road down to some apartment complex in Atlanta somewhere and about 10:00 there was James, in his same clothes, standing outside the apartment. I scooped him up and took him home. I have no idea what happened to Ian. But as far as that bachelor evening, all's well that ends well I guess.

Saturday May 27th dawned clear and warm and after I corralled James and got him to the house things were better for Carolyn. She just knew James and I had screwed up and the whole day was going to fall apart, but Two Boys prevailed and we were in good shape. At least I was. James was still a little iffy based on the night before. James and I had gone down the day before and gotten our tuxes. And I changed. James elected to change once he was down there because I was going to have to return his tux so he needed clothes there at City Hall. The first problem came just hours before the ceremony when James pulled his tux out. All the tuxes for James and the groomsmen were to be the same except James was to have a white vest and tie and we all had red vests and ties to match the bridesmaids. James opened the tux bag and his vest was white but his tie was red. Crisis! Fortunately, Adam, bless him, jumped into action. We called an outlet of the tux place and explained the problem. There was a tie available at the outlet store on Peachtree and off Adam went. I mean we are talking only an hour or so until the wedding. It was tense, but Adam got back in time and whole wedding was saved because of Adam! And the wedding proceeded and everything was going great. Again Reverend Richard Lumpkin was there to preside for our family and he and James and I walked out. We stood in the center of the rotunda lined up with the other three groomsmen. Bryce and Bodie were the ring bearers and they dutifully walked out and joined the groomsmen. The bridesmaids came in resplendent in red. The maid of honor was April Swope, Angela's sister-in-law, and she came in with the flower girl, Clair Annette (yes, a musical family), who was Angela's niece. When we were all arrayed, Angela's father, James Swope, came down the stairs with Angela who was a vision. I may not have remembered much of my wedding or Bill's or Pete's or Rusty's or my sister's wedding, but like Jenna and Adam's wedding, I remembered this one. Angela was "given away" and stood with James. Vows were repeated, and then it was ring time. My only responsibility in the whole affair. Now James says he does not recall this, but I do – vividly. The ring on Bryce's pillow was a fake and sewn onto the pillow. I reached in my vest pocket and took out the ring. As I was handing it to Richard Lumpkin, I fumbled it, and it hit the podium. Fortunately, it did not bounce, and I leaned over and grabbed it. Up I came and put it securely in Reverend Lumpkin's hand. Whew. I had screwed up, but saved the entire wedding in one fell sleight of hand. You are welcome. Well, they got hitched and let the party begin. There was much family and much dancing and Bryce and Bodie, neither of whom thought much of the whole wearing tuxedo thing, looked like two ragamuffins pretty quickly. All the skeletons were there and many of James and Angela's family and friends. It was a good time. The party broke up late in the evening and the two newlyweds were off. I do not recall where they honeymooned. Check with James and Angela. It was another beautiful affair … Thank you God, Carolyn and I were "two for two" children raised. Two children graduated from college with no debt and two married and still happily married today.

This was a big transportation year for Carolyn and me. After Carolyn's mothers house finally sold (as is) there was a little money to distribute among the four daughters, and we took ours and bought a new Honda CR-V. It was white with tan interior and Carolyn absolutely loved that car! We bought it at Hennessey Honda on Georgia highway 92 near I-575 just beyond the Home Depot. We were pretty much sold on the car when we got there, so the only thing we needed a salesperson to do is to facilitate the paperwork. And they did and we did and the car did and we had her dream CR-V. But the real story is later that year when she and I were at dinner at a little place near the Walmart in Canton named Casey's. It is just the right of where I-575 intersects Riverstone Parkway. You turn right and then take the next right and it is down a little on the right. You could say Casey's is just right. Although Carolyn doesn't care to eat there anymore, I still like it. They have the best fried chicken and their country fare is very country. It is all a heart attack on a plate. Anyway, we are sitting there one evening and Carolyn says, "Why don't you look into getting a motorcycle?" I was floored! She knew I had ridden a little in college including when I worked in the Canal Zone, and I guess she knew I secretly harbored a love of cycles, but her suggestion caught me totally off guard. I was thrilled to say the least. The old joke I used a hundred times explaining why she wanted me to have a bike was that she figured at this point in our life and marriage I was worth more dead than alive! And I was! Anyway, we finished dinner and it just so happened down the Riverstone Parkway maybe a mile toward Canton was a motorcycle dealership called Power Motorsports of Canton. We drove down there. I was like a kid in a candy store! There were bikes and bikes and bikes. We looked around and priced a few and decided buying a bike was definitely something we could afford, but there was a major hitch. I did not have a license to ride one. So, we schemed and dreamed that evening, but first things first, I needed a license. I started researching how to get a motorcycle license. There were several ways from just getting a bike and going and taking a riding test at the DMV to taking a real course in learning how to ride. We opted for the real course which to this day I believe was the smartest thing you can do to learn how to ride well and safely. Being a Honda family I was drawn to the Honda Red Rider program administered at their facility off Ga400 at Haynes Bridge Road at Morrison Parkway, just south of Haynes Bridge Road. In the back, behind the American Honda Motor Company building is a training facility. The Red Rider course had both classroom and hands-on training. There were about five separate classes in the evenings over two or three weeks. We would arrive and go inside for the classroom portion. There we were taught by real motorcycle riding teachers who had been riding for years. We learned the rules of the road for motorcyclists which are the same as for automobile drivers except you have to be three times more careful. You want to ride where you can be seen and you want to be aware of "road gators." Usually road gators are preceded by "baby gators" so if you know what you are doing you can avoid them easily. Oh, I'm sorry … road gators are those random pieces of tire tread that come off of sixteen wheeler's retreaded tires and lay in wait on the highway for unsuspecting bikers to get bitten badly by them. Another is the technique of watching an automobile's hub caps to see if they are really stopped at a T-intersection or is the car actually rolling. The fact that if you are in a crash on a motorcycle it does not really matter if you are in the right or not, you are probably hurt badly if not killed. You weigh about 500 pounds. The car can weigh close to a ton or more. Mass plays a big part. Also how to dress if you're going to ride was a biggie. There was a ton of good information, and what to watch out for in the classroom portion. Probably the worst little platitude I heard one of the veteran teachers share was, "If you did not scrape one of the foot pegs, you did not ride." I can count on one gloved hand the number of times I scraped a foot peg! And so we headed outside each class for the hands on portion. We were on smaller Honda bikes. Our bikes were maybe 125cc bikes, but this did not matter because everything we did was slow motion. We never got out of second gear it seemed, because if you can control a bike at five miles per hour, you can control one at sixty-five miles per hour. We learned backing up and swerving between cones and stopping safely. I was in heaven. I was transported back to high school and my driver training course. Perfection was the name of the game, and I was going to be the star student. The most difficult part we had to master was The Box. On the ground was a rectangle marked off. It was about seven feet by five feet. There was a small unmarked opening on one side. Or challenge was to ride in and ride out of that small opening without ever putting out feet on the ground. It was a test of or slow speed bike maneuvering ability. It took some practice, but I got it. The rest of the course we had to accomplish was a piece of cake compared to that. At the end of the course we got a certificate and a piece of paper we could take to the DMV and they would give us a seal on our driver's license allowing us to ride motorcycles in Georgia. And I passed the course and was "bona fide." Now we got to buy the bike!

It was actually early in '08 when we got the bike, but we started the process late in '07. We went back to Power Motorsports of Canton, and I was jacked up! I could not wait. I was like a kid in a candy store. At first I looked at a smaller bike. I don't really remember what it was, but Carolyn said it looks too small for you. The salesperson agreed and said, "Look over here. This one is used. It has

eighty miles on it. The guy bought it and then found out two days later his wife was pregnant." I was smitten. It was love at first sight. She was a Honda Aero Shadow 2500cc in pearl white. She was pristine! I asked him if I could take her out for a test drive. He looked at my license and said sure, but he would have to drive a bike along with me. So, we did. We went back on the roads behind the dealership. She had five forward gears, one down and four up as we say in the motorcycle world. I was immediately taken as she had a shaft drive, no chain or belt, which made her quiet and shifting as smooth as glass. That evening we put a down payment down and started the paperwork to buy her. I bought two helmets and had them add a light bar with twin floods on it. I also added a blinking main light attachment so that in the day time when I was riding with my headlamp on (always) it would flash from high to low beams constantly. I wanted to be seen by everyone. I had researched this, and it was legal in Georgia and almost every state in the Union. I'm not sure exactly when I brought her home. I know it was cold and it was evening. Carolyn took me up to Canton. They had her decked out and washed and polished beautifully. We signed some papers and headed for the Falcon Wood. I distinctly remember pulling out onto 575 at Riverstone. I was terrified! I cranked her up and held on for dear life. Carolyn was my guardian angel following me. When I wanted to change lanes, she would pull over and block traffic and allow me space to pull out. It was nice to have an "angel on my shoulder." By the time we got home I was shaking like a leaf. It was both the cool of the evening and also the thrill of the drive down from Canton. I was a happy boy … the happiest of boys! In the following weeks I got a decal I put on her front fender that read *Rosinante*. This was her name. If you look up the name Rosinante relative

to Don Quixote de la Mancha, you will understand my choice of names. She and I sallied forth many, many times to search for a Dulcinea in distress we could save, or we simply went out to do battle with evil doers and dragons if we found any. She was a perfect machine for me. She was beautiful, fast and powerful. We were a team and had many wonderful exploits over the next fourteen years.

That year was the year Carolyn decided she was going to apply for a job at a construction firm called Brasfield and Gore. There was an opening in their Atlanta marketing department, and she was going to go for it. The morning came that she was going to go in for an interview. I happened to be on one of our fifth grade trips to Jekyll Island that morning. My Room Mom, Vonda Shoemaker, and I were talking as the bus rolled along, and she asked about Carolyn. I mentioned that, "Funny you should ask. Carolyn is on her way to an interview for a job with a construction firm in their marketing department at this moment." Vonda perked up and asked what firm. I told her it was Brasfield and Gorrie. Then she floored me when she said one of my students, Lucy Sanders, dad worked at Brasfield and Gorrie. I called Carolyn and she said she was going to meet with a Mr. Trey Sanders. I could not believe it. I called Trey immediately. I remember the call. He answered the phone and the first thing I said was that Lucy was fine! Then I told him that my wife Carolyn was about to interview for a job with his firm and if there was any help he could give us, it would be appreciated. Well, I do not know if Trey did anything or was swayed in the least, but Carolyn got the job! What a weirdly small world it was that morning. And there are pictures of us being "precious" as one of Carolyn's coworkers put it while we danced (I thought we were being kind of cool on the dance floor … I was giving it some of my best moves) at the B&G Christmas party that year.

Bryce and Bodie were six and four respectively that year. I remember that we got to have them over the summer, and we decided to take them to Six Flags one day. Now Jenna had warned us that Bodie was a little afraid of thunder, but I did not really think that would be a problem so I listened … kinda. And we were having a great day. We had done the Okefenokee River Boat ride and the Dahlonega Mine Train and ridden the sky buckets and been to the Crystal Pistol show and even had lunch near the Chevy Show and gotten The Boys funnel cakes. The day was just going gang busters! Then, wouldn't you know it, we had just put The Young Princes on a little swing merry-go-round thing, and they had just started whirling around when there was a clap of thunder and Bodie came apart! Fortunately, the ride guy shut the ride down immediately … not because of Bodie, but because of the thunder. And I rescued him immediately so all was good. And because discretion is the better part of valor, we decided to call it a day and head for the barn. This story reminds me of another time … it's amazing The Boys are not more messed up than they are what with being exposed to Pa and whatnot … but Carolyn and I had The Young Princes one day, and we were taking them to Dahlonega to pan for gold. We parked the car, and it was just spitting rain a little. Not hard enough to worry about. I knew we would make it the twenty yards from the parking lot to the gold panning place no sweat. We got The Boys all unbuckled got them out of the car, and we hadn't gone ten feet when the biggest blast of thunder I had ever heard … I mean double you over and scare you to death loud … boomed right above us! And once again, poor Bodie did the best he could but his Pa had failed him again. I snatched him up, and Carolyn had Bryce's hand and we high-tailed it to the safety of the building. Again I say, it is truly amazing The Boys turned out as good as they have. They are awesome, and children are resilient.

On the school front, I was back in my Mt. Bethel and things were going great. Robin was still my protector and friend and I had another good friend there also supporting me, Coach Chuck Jones. I mentioned him before talking about our Science Olympiad work. You see, gentle reader, I do not have many people whom I call friends. As they say, I have many acquaintances, but few friends. And that is by preference. I think it has to do with a bully you read about in my sixth grade year. And I count Chuck Jones as my friend. One fall day I had afternoon car pool duty. My part of car pool duty entailed going out and calling out the numbers displayed on the car's dashboards so the matching numbered children could be ready down the line to be picked up when the car pulled up to the gym door. Anyway as is the way of the fall in Georgia some days, the morning was warm and by the time came for my afternoon car pool duty the temperature had fallen to the low forties, and I had not left the house that morning prepared for this temperature plunge. So, I went to Coach's office and asked if he had a jacket I could use for car pool. I figured he had to be ready for all weather eventualities given the nature of his teaching job. He said that he absolutely had a jacket I could use and threw me one. I grabbed it in midair not wanting to embarrass myself in front of the coach … he was unimpressed, and I hustled out on my way to the front of the building. The jacket was a life saver. It was perfect. And I finished my duty good and warm, not to mention looking cool in the jacket with a Kent State University crest on it. And there was always a competition (at least in my mind there was competition) between car pool and bus duty. Bus duty was the challenge of getting all the children safely and accurately on the various buses lined up in the bus lanes. Bus duty was a monster job at the first of the year especially when the kindergarten children were loosed, and required a professional so Coach Jones had bus duty almost every day. By the time of this tale, things had settled into a relative routine so there was a competition who would finish their duty first, car pool or bus. And this afternoon my car pool had won. So, I headed over to the bus lanes to lord it over Coach. When I got there I was struck dumb. There Chuck stood getting the last of the babies on the busses in his gym shorts and tee shirt. He was frozen. He had loaned his ONLY jacket to me so I would be warm knowing he would suffer. Oh, if you listen to him he will tell you about how we have to protect our older adults … Chuck is probably twenty years my junior … but I know the real reason. Chuck Jones was/is my friend.

This is also the year I started a most wonderful educational experience, Federal History Grants. There were two of them, both multiyear experiences and overlapping time wise: Seeds of Democracy and Expanding Frontiers. Each had multiple parts and allowed me and about fifty other teachers to be exposed to various historical thinkers and writers and visit quite a few historical sites over the course of the five or six years of the grants. The grants were the hard work of several Henry County Teacher/Leaders and led by Ms. Robynn Holland. In the basement are four binders labeled Seeds and Frontiers that will allow you to see what we did and where we went, in depth if you are interested before the binders go into the black bags. And as part of the grants we assembled both binders of our experiences and what were known as Traveling Lesson Trunks. These were trunks of materials and a lesson plan(s) to support the materials that gave the children a hands on exposure to places and materials of points in and aspects of history. I made three trunks. James has them. The first was my Maps Trunk containing a real sextant and maps over time from the earliest maps of the New World and the world to more modern maps. The second was my Immigration Trunk centering around Ellis Island and immigration to the United States, and the third was my Surveying Trunk with a tripod and surveyors level and a lesson on how to develop a three- dimensional model of a piece of land and how to read a contour map.

The Seeds experience was amazing. The centerpieces were a winter trip down to Savannah and a summer trip to Williamsburg and Jamestown. The grant had a classroom portion where experts came and shared their historical perspectives and the field component. Our long weekend trip to Savannah was in February. We met early one morning at the school board in Henry County. I had come into town the night before so as not to have to make the trip down in the cold and dark. I stayed somewhere, not important, and went out to find dinner. I thought to myself of a time long ago when I was traveling to Panama from the states, and we stopped for the night at an Air force base in Puerto Rico. And no one knew where I was and how liberating it was. I had that same feeling that evening. I did not have to worry about anyone but myself for a few hours and it was liberating … and relaxing. I found a steak house place, more like Golden Corral than Longhorns … I am a simple man with simple tastes … and ate steak until I was full! The next morning, we got on a bus and headed to Savannah. A couple of things about the trip stick in my mind. Well, a lot of things stick in my mind, but I do not want to bore you to tears. One was, we were sitting in a conference room at the big, God-awful hotel there on River Street … you know the one … Cooper Carry designed it and they should be shot for it. Anyway, we were sitting in this conference room. We were facing a large bank of windows overlooking the Savannah River. There was a lady presenting information about Savannah's amazing history standing at a podium between us and the windows with her back to the windows. Can you see the layout? So, she is making her presentation and suddenly, behind her, the windows are filled with a huge cargo ship going up the river. Well, you know what everyone in the room was looking at, and where our attention was focused. The lady presenter was very astute. She paused, and without turning around to the windows said, "There is a large ship going by isn't there?" We all chuckled and she paused and we all watched in amazement as the leviathan quietly sailed by. We were all about listening then as she had "earned her stripes." You see there is NOTHING worse that presenting to a bunch of teachers. You better be really good and really be on your game to hold teacher's attentions. I guess being a teacher, we are always analyzing how we could make this presentation better and more interesting. At least the elementary teachers are doing this. We elementary teachers are always in the front row clapping and laughing. I think middle school teachers could care less as they are used to being ignored. They sit in the middle of the room and ask each other why they are here. And high school teachers just plain old do not care if you get it or not, and they sit in the back of the room with their chairs leaning back against the wall … sleeping. We elementary teachers are the more sensitive, and we want the students to WANT to learn and be excited about that learning and to remember that lesson. I think upper grade teachers do not care as much. At least that is my opinion. Anyway, the presenter earned her stripes with us that morning.

Later in the morning we got on a bus and headed down the coast to Fort King George in Darien, Georgia. Several years ago, Carolyn and I took The Boys and The Princess there one afternoon while we were staying on St. Simons. On the way the Grant bus stopped at Skipper's Fish Camp in Darien. Skipper's is a little restaurant just off the Altamaha River on one of its little tributaries. The restaurant kind of hangs off the land over the river. There are shrimp boats docked all along in front of Skipper's. You can still go there as of this writing. There are signs on I-95 where to get off. We arrived in the parking lot. Robynn Holland had called ahead because Skipper's folks were waiting for us. They had all the sweet tea you could hold and a buffet of coastal delectable faire. We had shrimp and crab cakes, shrimp and grits, boiled shrimp, steamed shrimp, cold shrimp with red dipping sauce, shrimp soufflé … I just realized I sound just like Bubba in the movie *Forrest Gump*. We went on to the fort in the town after that but Skipper's Fish Camp was the high point of my day! When we took Bryce and Bodie and Cait to the fort we also ate at Skippers but somehow, it just wasn't the same … go figure.

The summer part of the Seeds trip took place in the hottest part of the summer. I mean it was blistering. I was part of the second group to go, and we understood the temperature had broken a little for our part. We had flown from Atlanta to Richmond. When we gathered in the airport I was tickled looking at us. We were all going on a field trip, and we were just like children! The only thing we were missing was a little rope with knots in it that we could hold on to as we moved through the airport! Of course the middle and high school teachers had to act all cool, but we elementary types were excited and chattering like magpies. The flight was uneventful and once in Richmond we boarded a bus and headed to Williamsburg and then Jamestown. Again, there are a couple of events over that week that stood out. The first was the heat. The east coast was gripped in a heat wave with daily temperatures well above 95° F with humidity pushing 75%. The first week's group got the worst of it, but it was still pretty tough the second week.

When we arrived in Williamsburg we were oriented by a wonderful lady, Shelia Ward, who talked to us about our sleeping arrangements. She asked if we had any preferences. Being the elementary school teacher that I was and the Morris that I continued to be plagued with, I had done a little homework and determined that the one and only Thomas Jefferson had stayed at the Marks Street Tavern. I raised my hand and asked if it was possible for me to stay there … and it was and I did! In point of fact, I was able to stay in the very room where he had stayed. One of the other people from Cobb was JoAnn Wood. She was in the Central Office and was the Supervisor of Social Studies. Over the course of the History Grants we became close friends. JoAnn stayed in the Marks Street Tavern also. The next few days were filled with interviews with Thomas Jefferson and George Washington, fife and drum parades, wonderful talks about Parliament and the House of Burgesses and the courts system in early colonial America. The whole time I was pondering what my Traveling Trunk lesson would be about. One evening at dinner I hit upon the idea of maps. They were very important in the 16 and 1700's and often meant life or death. I talked to JoAnn Wood about it relative to the Cobb Social Studies Standards, and she agreed it would be an interesting choice. I had noticed quite a few maps and map related artifacts when we went through a museum gift shop earlier in the week. So, after dinner I hightailed it over there hoping to get there before it closed at 8:00. I remember it was a lovely, cloudless evening and the sun had just set. One could feel the day's heat just starting to ebb and the stars were just beginning to peek out. I remember the walkway from my tavern lodging to the museum was lit with colonial style lamp poles. It was a lovely evening. I got there in time to buy several maps and map books, a map CD, telescope and compass and the centerpiece I had my eye on ever since I had seen it, a sextant … yes, a real, live sextant. It was/is a beauty in its own velvet lined, cherry wood box all gleaming brass and flashing lenses. Check with James and find the trunk and you can see it for yourself. I trundled back to my room with all my booty.

We headed for Jamestown the next day. What stands out the most about that day were the ships the Susan B. Constant, the Discovery and Elizabeth. The Susan B. Constant was the largest, and it was only "twenty-six paces long." The size was startlingly small and each ship was an exact replica of the ones the Jamestown settlers had arrived in. I could not believe these brave people had sailed across the Atlantic in something that small. We learned where they stayed and what they ate, how they navigated and how they handled their "necessaries" … look it up, it's fascinating. We also learned about the guns they carried and the armor they wore. I got to try the armor on to the great delight of the team. The next day we headed out to the island where the actual settlement of Jamestown was located. We learned about the archeological efforts going on there and how the site is threatened by global warming and rising seas. We learned the famous, or rather infamous if you read his biography, John Smith arrived in the New World in chains. We learned about him and the famous Pocahontas, and how it was probably a fiction that she saved him at the last minute as his notes and letters have him being saved that way in his travels as a mercenary several times. Also a quick note that Pocahontas did not marry John Smith. She married John Rolfe. Anyway, it was a thrilling and informative day. Back to Williamsburg and a tour of the settlement home and plantation where we actually picked tobacco. Tobacco is a sticky, prickly, nasty plant that is backbreaking to harvest. We made bricks and slung a hammer at the blacksmith's forge. Life was hard in Colonial America. The dinner that last evening was delightful, and as we stood out front of Christiana Campbell's Tavern two of my good friends on the Mt. Bethel fifth grade team, Connie Perry and Eileen Jedlicka, decided to regale the others on the trip with us about the exploits of none other than my Barbie persona. It was all good natured fun, and I joined in adding little tidbits of behind the scenes attire and makeup for those aspiring to become transvestites. Many of my new Grant acquaintances who didn't really know me got to see a side of me that both shocked and entertained them. I believe my relationship with many of them going forward through several more History Grant adventures in the coming years warmed considerably after the story as they realized I was not quite as reserved as I appeared to be on the surface. And we flew home the next day with many wonderful memories and new friendships. Again, you can see and read more of my firsthand, hand written accounts of that trip in a white binder in the basement labeled Seed of Democracy 07-08.

3.

By all comparisons 2008 was a pretty quiet year. Carolyn was thriving at B&G, I was teaching with Robin Lattizori and life was good. We took a cruise that year with Jenna, Adam and The Boys up to Canada. It was an interesting cruise on Royal Caribbean, and we left out of Norfolk, Virginia. They have not left from there in a long time, and I am not sure why, but this cruise was up to Boston and Portland, Maine, Bar Harbor, St. John and up to Halifax, Nova Scotia, then returning. The adventure is rife with stories but several stand out. Our first stop was Boston. Of course old Mr. History wanted The Young Princes to see the USS Constitution as an absolute must. So, we shipped Jen and Adam off somewhere, and grabbed The Boys who were about five and seven years old. We hailed a taxi and headed off to a great adventure! When we got to the site of "Old Ironsides" we discovered that the ship was under a total refurbishment, and no one could go on board! We got close and peered over onto the ship and down into the hold and this huge blast of varnish smell enveloped The Boys and me, and we gagged and swooned and ran away! Well, what a piece of poop that was. So much for all the Old Ironsides history. But they had a fine museum and The Young Princes got to furl sails and touch cannons and lay in an actual ship's hammock. They ran around and had a gay old time oblivious to what could have been. Oh well. I should have taken that as an omen, but hope springs eternal in an optimist's heart! So, after that very minor disappointment of the centerpiece of the day, we caught the water taxi over to Boston's waterfront and some lunch. We wanted to really go to a restaurant The Boys would enjoy and not just some vendor on the street or, Lord forbid, Subway or McDonalds. In retrospect we should have opted for a Subway! We chose Legal Seafood instead. Wrong! Carolyn and I had a wonderful lunch of delicious seafood. The Boys … not so much. I'm not sure what Bryce ordered, but Bodie got chicken fingers … chicken fingers! So we ate our lunches in beautiful surroundings, black table cloths, waiters clad in black uniforms with handheld computers to take the orders, impeccable service and for Carolyn and I perfect food. And we're walking out of Legal Seafood and Mr. Bodie makes the pronouncement that Carolyn and I still laugh about today and have used ourselves on occasion, "Worst restaurant EVER!" That boy … anyway, I had visions of the Boston Tea Museum or Old North Church or Paul Revere's house on the Liberty Trail, but there, just down the street with a huge sign was … The Children's Museum. And The Children's Museum it was. It was the absolute best decision of the day. When we went in the first thing you see is a three story cargo net affair that children could climb in to their heart's content. Damn the safety regulations and who cares if they fall. It's a THREE STORY CARGO NET! The Young Princes were immediately enamored. You know, I do not remember much more about the place, but I do remember the net. I guess The Boys played on that thing and in the museum, for the whole afternoon. After the museum my intent was to grab a taxi to take us back to the ship. Well, we left the museum and started walking toward the dock which had to be, oh I don't know, several miles away thinking the whole time we'd get a taxi or some form of transportation would come by … not so. And it was hot. And we walked and we walked. We thought at one point we had found a small trolley/bus deal, but once we were on it in the blessed air conditioning, the driver said no he wasn't going that way. He was going home for the day. And as much as I tried there was no amount of money that would induce him to take these two small children and their elderly grandparents back to the ship. So we got off the stupid trolley/bus … that we didn't really like anyway … and kept on our "forced march." As we walked I remember there were some, shall we say, sketchy parts of town as we neared the docks. Anyway, we made it and the exhausted troupe staggered onto the ship with stories to tell and lies to propagate.

As the ship headed out from Boston toward Portland, Jenna and Adam had cooked up our next adventure. They had signed us up for a wine tasting. The next day The Boys were shipped off (no pun intended) to the Ocean Adventure Club and the four "adults," and I use the term loosely, headed for our 2:00 very sophisticated wine tasting. As groups came into the main dining room in couples and fours and sixes we all found tables and sat down. The room became full of quiet anticipatory conversations in hushed and reserved manners. In a few minutes, waiters started bringing to each table a carafe of wine. When we all had been served, the ship's sommelier began by telling us about the first wine. On the table we all had glasses and the waiters came around and poured about a third of a glass for each of us. The sommelier explained we would sniff the wine first to appreciate its bouquet and then sample the wine while he explained the tones and under tones and complexities of this particular wine he had selected. After we tasted the first wine the waiters brought out little plates of bread and apple to "clarify" out taste buds before the next sampling was brought out. Well, Jenna and Adam and Carolyn and I were seated facing each other across a table not too far from a large window overlooking the rushing ocean going by. This was to be a poor choice later. We quickly chose our teams. J&A were Team Red, and C and I were Team White. As the wines were brought out the red wines went to Jenna and Adam and the whites came to our side of the table. At about thirty-five minutes and four rounds of wine tasted, we were all getting into this whole wine tasting deal. By fifty minutes and six rounds the whole room was getting into it. The hushed conversations at the beginning were being discarded for cross table conversations, and a general raising of the level of hilarity. People were laughing and joking about the wines and the party was rolling along at the one hour and seven round mark. J&A were slurping their reds and Carolyn and I were handling all the whites. Rosés were shared and roundly and a little too loudly criticized. By the time the tasting ended we were all drunk as skunks along with the rest of the dining room. I am sure the very dignified sommelier had already decided this was a terrible idea, and that he would not want any part of doing this again! (In fact I have never seen this offered on R.C. since!) And the ocean rushed by. And the ship rocked ever so slightly. And there the four of us were … it was about 3:30 or so, and we were all "drunk as Lords." The sun outside was too bright. The noises on the ship were too loud and what in the world are we going to do now? Well, I'm not sure about Jenna and Adam. I know what Carolyn and I did. We headed for our cabin and took a long nap. I never knew, nor cared, what J&A did. Later, when we all met for dinner about 7:00 the four of us were a little better but still not over our afternoon's "excursion." I imagine The Boys wondered what in the world was wrong with us.

As I mentioned The Young Princes were involved with Ocean Adventures during the trip. It was a program for the little ones, and they were watched over and taken care of by young people with Royal C. Very often The Boys would elect to eat with the O.A. boys and girls and that happened one evening. The children had been working in O.A. on pirate costumes. Now this was back in the day on Royal C. when there was performance of some kind some nights, and this evening's performance was the Pirate Parade. After we had finished our dinner the lights were lowered and spot lights focused on the center main staircase that connected the upper and lower dining areas. Then O.A. staff lead all the children down the stairs complete with their paper hats, paper vests and makeup looking for all the world like darling little pirates, and there, in the center of the parade, were Bryce and Bodie. They looked so sweet, but the thing that plucked at my heartstrings was the sight of the two boys walking together, five-year-old Bodie holding fast to his big, seven-year-old, brother's hand. It was truly a moment for this Pa.

Back in '03, Carolyn and I had been invited by the family of Vangelis Zafiroulis, one of my students … known to Coach Jones and me in Science Olympiad as Vann-G … to go to the Atlanta Civic Center with them to see the Broadway play *The Lion King*. And this year Carolyn and I took the opportunity to take Bryce and Bodie to the Atlanta Civic Center Auditorium to see the play. We had picked up The Young Princes at Motorcycle McDonalds the day before, and they were spending the night with us on the bunk beds we had bought them. I'm sure there was pool time involved that week. The play was an afternoon performance as I recall and the seats were good but not as great as grandparents want for their grandchildren, but as I said, they were good seats. One of the highlights of the whole experience is when the characters, oversized, colorful and full of life, come down the aisles to mount the stage. It gives the children in the audience, both the young ones and the old ones, a chance to see the costumes and characters up close. We were not too far from an aisle and The Boys loved it. We had gotten popcorn and programs and goodies and the day was as perfect as a Nana and a Pa could make it. I'm not sure if I have commented on this, but I adopted the only grandfather name I ever wanted to carry when the Bryce was born. I wanted to be "Pa," named after my hero Pa, Dr. William E. Wofford. And Carolyn wanted to be "Nana," and so we are known to this day ... 6/15/2023 ... to our grandchildren ... and to Bryce's and Bodie's girlfriends and college friends.

An upsetting memory from this period was on June 9th, 2008, our anniversary, when Aunt Marybelle (Marybelle Morris Swift born 14 April 1924) passed away. This picture is a happy moment with her husband Don. I have spoken of Aunt Marybelle several times, and the fact that she became the template for Carolyn as to what an Aunt should be, just as Momma (my paternal grandmother Marie Louise Williams Morris – 10 Jan 1899 – 22 April 1997) was Carolyn's template as to what a grandmother should be.

My templates for being an uncle were Marybelle's husband Don (Donald C Swift 1920-1994) and Uncle Nelson (Nelson Kimball Rogers 1928-2013) and of course my Grandfather template was my Pa, my maternal grandfather, Dr. William Earl Wofford, MD (1889-1959). We learn from our parents and grandparents how to be and what to be like and how not to be and what not to be like. But back to my story ... Aunt Marybelle passed away. She had dementia in her last years, and it was very hard for her family. Carolyn went out to Dallas alone and served as a pallbearer. We loved Marybelle, and she saved Carolyn and me mentally and physically. She was a true heroine in all the senses of the work. God bless you Marybelle, Rest in Peace.

Carolyn's Sister Ginny, Virginia Lyon Grupe, remarried this year. She had been married to Paul Grupe for a number of years, but they got a divorce. Ginny remarried Tom Burling in 2008. There is not a lot of detail here as I am very light on information, and I apologize. I merely wanted to note that Ginny did remarry and it happened this year.

On the school front, 2008 was a good year. I met and became fast friends with Richard Mari that year. He had moved down here with his family from Long Island, New York, and took a fifth grade teaching position at Mt. Bethel. Robin let me adopt him and be his mentor that first year, and we became fast friends. He and his class went to Jekyll with all of the 5th grade and took his class to Charleston with me and mine, and worked on the Science Olympiad Team with coach Jones and me. It was rare that year not to see one of us without the other. He ended up only staying a couple of years at Mt. Bethel before he had to go find more lucrative work to feed his family. Although we had not really stayed in touch … he lives not three miles from me … I will always count him as a great friend and would love to see him again.

The big thrust education wise was the continuation of the Seeds of Democracy Federal History Grant I have already told you about. But there was a new Federal History Grant Brewing, Expanding Frontiers 1800-1889 and I definitely wanted to be part of that!

4.

2009, now there was a year! Barack Obama was inaugurated, James and I took The Colonel back to Fort Benning, there were Grandparent Days with Corn Mazes, Carolyn and I took a cruise, The Frontiers Grant started and we got a new principal and my trials began.

Carolyn and I had anticipated Barack winning the 2008 election, and I had made reservations in Arlington at a Hilton because we were planning to go to Washington for the Inauguration. Making the reservations early was one of the smartest things I have ever done because I got a really decent rate, but by December of 2008 the rooms were sky high. In fact, I had gotten a call from the Hilton in DC wanting to know if I wanted to cancel my reservation. A funny question to which I said no way! They were out of luck if they wanted to re-rent the room at a four or five times price. We scooted out of Marietta on Saturday, January 17th, headed for DC. We decided to not to try to make the whole ten-hour drive in one gulp, and we stopped in Richmond at "some random hotel" for the night. That way we could slip into Washington Sunday and see some stuff before the festivities began on Monday. I recall driving into northern Virginia and it was overcast as we drove by the Pentagon. Many memories flooded back of my time in Vienna and high school and what-not. We rode on into Alexandria and pulled into the parking lot of the N. Courthouse Road Hilton around lunch. It was a little early but they let us check in anyway. They were very accommodating. I had chosen this Hilton because of its proximity to the Court House Metro station on Clarendon Boulevard and the fact that the hotel had a shuttle over to the station even though it was only two blocks away. Once we got situated, the room was perfect, we grabbed the shuttle and hopped a train into the city. We caught the Blue train into DC and got off near the Mall and got lost in the site-seeing crowd. We headed over to where the new MLK Memorial was to be on the Tidal Basin and walked the mall until we were bushed and caught the train back to the hotel. Monday was going to be a big day! Monday dawned overcast and cold. Our plan was to get over to DC and attend, or get as close as we could, to the concert that was going to be the centerpiece of Monday's events. The train was full but not unreasonable, and we got a good spot to see the concert. We could not see Obama or Michelle, but we could see the performers and the music was our kind of music. It was nice to have a young president coming into the government. We ate at a restaurant in the new Museum of Native Americans on the Mall that day, and made our way to the Museum of American History. Carolyn sat out that museum on a comfortable stone bench in the thin, but welcome, January sunshine. I wandered around and saw some stuff, but I did not like her being out there alone, so I made it an abbreviated tour. But I did get to see some stuff as I said so don't feel badly that I was not enjoying myself. I usually do wherever I am. I think … I hope … people remember me and say, "He was a Happy Boy." After our day, we headed back to the hotel. I wish I could tell you we had tickets to some big soiree and got all dolled up and danced and stuff, but we did not. We just crashed and got ready for the big day. The Inauguration was to start at 12:00 on Tuesday the 20th, and I thought we could leave for the Metro about 10:00 and be fine. Well, my brilliant wife had other ideas and strongly suggested we should shoot for the 9:00 train, and we did. When we got to the open station platform at about 8:25 people were already gathering. We got a spot and more and more people were coming, and it began to get really crowded. By the time the train came, with a few passengers we filled it up. And I mean we filled it up! The term the Metro used was "crush capacity" and it was! There was no place to sit, and we stood for the ride into town. Somewhere under the Potomac River the car came to a stop … great … and we just sat there. Finally, an announcement came over the speaker that that the train was delayed because they were still clearing the station at the next stop. But you know what I remember? Nobody on the train was upset. No one complained at all. In fact, there were jokes being made about President Bush II screwing things up again and people were laughing. There was this happy, hopeful mood in that train car stuck under the river that morning. And finally we got moving only to face a bigger challenge. We passed up the Foggy Bottom station and headed for the Metro Center or Federal Triangle Station. I think we decided to try to get off at Metro Center and we found out why the trains were delayed. The system was set up that you had your ticket "punched" as you got off the train making that ticket a "used" ticket. At the Metro Center Station this happened at the up end of a long escalator and the problem was people could only pass through one at a time and it was taking forever. When we were finally able to get off the train onto the platform Carolyn and I were stuck there for probably twenty minutes as the crowd tried to get out of the hole in the ground. Finally, someone, a Metro cop I'm guessing, got the word to just open the gates and clear the station so the trains could get back on schedule. As soon as that happened, the crowd was able to move, and we saw daylight! And then we felt cool air! And then we burst out onto the street and the clear, beautiful January morning! Carolyn had been absolutely right … again. It was almost 11:00. If we had followed my advice, I have no idea how long it would have taken us! We hustled toward the Mall which was already packed. There are no official numbers, but it is counted as the largest event in DC history with an estimated 1.8 million people attending! We had not brought hats and it became obvious very quickly that we needed them, so we stopped at a vendor selling toboggans with the presidential seal and the names of Obama and Biden and 2009 on them. We bought two. They are in the closet in the den with coats. A real piece of history! Anyway, we jostled and walked and tried to find a good place to see the festivities. We ended up not far from the Washington Monument near 14th street and Madison Drive. There was a big television truck sitting there and it had generators running and warm air was coming off of it so we positioned ourselves on the Mall side of the truck and used it as a wind break. Seeing what was going on was not a problem because they had positioned Jumbo Tron television screens along the Mall every 100 yards or so, and you could see and hear everything. As we stood there it got more and more crowded as late comers started jostling for positions, and we had to stand our ground a couple of times. But for the most part, everyone was in a festive mood and nobody got upset with anyone. I wanted to photograph and document the occasion, but there was no way to capture Obama and what was going on a quarter of a mile away, so I concentrated on the faces of the people near us. We were a rainbow of colors and emotions and ages. Some were crying. Some were smiling. Some were laughing, and we all were cold! But we were being warmed by our first black president. When it was over, Carolyn and I headed for Pennsylvania Avenue to hopefully see Barack and Michelle walking to the White House, but it was not to be. We decided to try to head for the subway and lunch and check out, as we were leaving for home that day. We started to head to the Metro Center Station where we had arrived, but when we got there, "they" had closed the station! Whaaaaaat? Yep, for some reason the station was temporarily closed. This was a shock not only to us but also the several hundred others walking along with us. I think it was the McPherson Station that was open, and we caught a train back

to Alexandria. The ride back was not nearly as crowded, and we actually got a seat. There is a framed picture of us in the bedroom with a speech given by The Rt. Reverend Gene Robinson opening the Inauguration proceedings. The picture of us was a selfie on the train coming back from DC. On January 20th, 2009. If you find it, you can see we were all smiles and pink cheeks from the cold. An interesting factoid: that day

more people visited DC that any other day in its history, and there was not one single arrest by the DC police. Democrats celebrated peacefully with each other.

When Bryce started preschool and Jenna started teaching at Lakeview Academy in Gainesville, Carolyn and I had no idea the number of wonderful times that school would provide for us. I am sure we will talk more about the events, but I want to start with an annual tradition that Carolyn and I participated in for over ten years. It was Grandparent's Day at Lakeview. It was usually held on the first Friday in October. It was primarily to gin-up monetary support from grandparents for the school, but it was a heartwarming tradition that Carolyn and I looked forward to each year. In 2009 Bryce was eight and

Bodie was six, third and first grades I reckon. We would arrive and park either in the lot on the lower level or out in the field because the crowds were large for this cherished event. We would go to the school cafeteria where students would greet us, and we would be served cookies and punch and coffee. Then the children would trickle in with their teacher watching over them, and we would all que up for pictures. We had many taken over the years and you can watch The Boys grow and all the rest of us age. Some with just us with Young Princes and some with Adam's parents, Toby and Paula Blackwell, and us and The Boys. Toby and Paula have always been so gracious to us, and I believe there is a genuine friendship and appreciation of each other in that relationship. Paula is actually Adam's step-mother. Adam's biological mother, Sherry, is around but chooses to stay on the fringes of the family relationships. Sherry was married for a time to a man named Billy, but he passed away several years ago, around 2010 I'm guessing. Since then Sherry has cleaned up her life somewhat and now lives in Athens, Georgia. I do not think Sherry ever came to a Grandparent's Day.

Anyway after pictures, the students would go back to their rooms and the old folks would trundle down to the gym. Carolyn and I were always tickled because the invitations we would receive in the mail always asked to please let Lakeview know if you would require wheelchairs or oxygen while you were there. Fortunately, we never needed either one! Once we were in the gym, we would find our seats in the bleachers and settle in for a performance by each grade level with songs celebrating the fall season. It was all very wholesome Americana at its finest. As I am writing this my heart is warmed by the memories of watching my Jenna herd her class of fifth graders into the gym and get them all arranged on the floor over to left of the stage. Then the other classes would come in all the way down to the preschoolers who could barely walk in a line. God bless all teachers. Then the program would begin with the Pledge of Allegiance and a few words by the Headmaster and then song after song by the mostly enthusiastic classes. Each class having at least one child who was so thrilled to be there in front of his or her grandparents that they were about to burst with joy. After the program all the classes would return to their classrooms, and we would head up the walkway to find our boy's rooms and see their artwork and where they sit in class and meet their teacher and hear about all the wonderful things that our exceptional grandchildren are doing as they excelled in everything they did. Afterward we would corral The Boys and head over to the Media Center where the annual fund raising Book Fair was taking place. Carolyn and I (mostly Carolyn) made sure The Young Princes had whatever books they wanted and however many books they wanted. You see, Carolyn never met a book she did not love and want to own, so Bryce and Bodie always came out loaded with all kinds of literature. It was all for a good cause. We then took The Boys and checked in with Jenna in her classroom and oohed and aaahed as Jenna showed off for Mommy and Daddy, and we looked and learned about her classroom and her children. After that Bryce and Bodie were ours. We would take them to their house where we would meet Jenna and get everyone, including us, changed into outdoor clothes because we were off to ... as Momma, my Paternal Grandmother (Marie Louise Williams Morris) would say ... "open a keg of nails." This meant we were off to do whatever and find adventures and make memories. Lunch was always high on the list and usually involved a Subway sandwich for Bodie or a pizza and a sandwich at Schlotsky's there in Gainesville or lunch at Longstreet's Café or other exciting lunch spots across North Georgia. The lunch spots were across North Georgia because our "tradition" as Bodie would intone, was to find a corn maze somewhere and spend the usually hot and sweltering afternoon lost among the corn stalks at either Jaemor Farms or Uncle Bucks or any number of small pop-up mazes we would come across. Our adventures usually were a competition of some kind with the teams of Bryce and Carolyn versus Bodie and me, to see who could complete the course first. Usually we would head into the maze together and start testing Pa's old tried and true approach of the "Right Hand Discipline" (or Left Hand Discipline … you choose). This is the way you can solve any maze anywhere be it in a hedgerow, a corn maze or on paper. Simple keep one hand on one side of the maze and never let go. It may not take you on the shortest journey through the maze, but it will <u>always</u> take you through the maze to the exit. Of course there were cards we carried that had to get all their little symbols punched and we had a map of sorts that was always difficult to follow and no matter who won there were always accusations of cheating and malfeasance by the losing party and reasons why the losing party really won and the other party did not! Jaemor Farms at 5340 Cornelia Highway in Alto, Georgia, was one of our favorite haunts. They always had a hayride, a petting zoo, and long slide inside a tube that ended in a muddy ravine and a compressed air powered apple cannon or giant apple slingshot that The Boys HAD to do! All at an additional cost of course … no problem, we were out "opening kegs of nails" with Nana and Pa. Finally, we would make our way to the store and buy a pumpkin for each boy and ice cream and kettle corn. And as the sun was dropping in the west behind the pine trees, we took the exhausted and happily sweaty and dirty boys with full bellies and haul them back to Jenna and Adam. Another memory for the little boys to tell their grandchildren about some day in 2080 long after Carolyn and I are gone.

My mother (Mary Corinne Wofford Morris 4/21/1926-2/8/2013) told me that The Colonel wanted to go to the Infantry Museum at Fort Benning, Georgia, and asked me if I would take him. Of course I said yes. Dad would have been 85 on September 1st, 2009, and that trip would have been way too much for him at that point. Of course, as I write this in 12 short years I will be that age so it does not seem that old to me now, but back then … well, it was. So, I corralled my son James, and we picked a date and cleared it with The Colonel. James and I rode up to Cartersville and picked up Dad, and we headed down to Columbus, Georgia. It took about three hours, and we got there about 11:00. The first thing we did was go and find 166B Custer Terrace where I was two through five years old (1952-1955). Then we headed over to the museum which looked to be quite well done, a very impressive building. Once when I was teaching at Mountain View, the fifth grade had taken a field trip to The Little White house in Warm Springs and then we had come over to Fort Benning to a version of this museum in its infancy. That museum was nothing like what I was seeing that day. I was impressed. I asked a person out front to take a picture of the three of us. We walked into the museum and Dad was free to get in, and I paid for James and me. We then scouted out (note the Army terminology) a place to get some lunch. They had a little café off the lobby, and we got some chow (Army

Terminology). With our tummy's full … because an army travels on its stomach … we ventured into the museum proper. I do not recall much about the exhibits. Dad was fascinated and especially about the Korean War part. This was to be expected as he was a new Captain when he was sent there in 1950 and returned home in early 1952 and made Major … and ultimately met me. I do not recall much about the museum proper. I can tell you it does not hold a candle to the World War II Museum in New Orleans, but I do remember one thing in particular about that day. We got to the middle of the afternoon, and I guess we were maybe 3/4ths done with the museum, when Dad had to sit down. He just did not have the strength to walk around anymore. This was the first time I had ever seen him do that … to have to quit. It was startling to me and shook me a little. So, James continued, and I sat down with Dad. I wish I could tell you we shared a meaningful conversation about life, liberty and the pursuit of happiness, but we did not. We just sat there. When James came out of the last exhibit, we headed out. I had arranged a couple of hotel rooms nearby, one for Dad and James and I shared a room. We rested a minute and then headed out for dinner. I thought it would be fun to take Dad to Hooters, but when we got there and got a table the music was blasting so loud, amazingly loud, that the three of us left. We went to a nearby Applebee's or Ruby Tuesday's or something like that and had a very sedate meal which Dad paid for … as was appropriate I felt. Then we returned to the hotel and called it a night after arranging a time to meet for breakfast. We met in the dining area and ate a delicious Holiday Inn kind of white sausage gravy on slightly hard biscuits along with reconstituted eggs breakfast … yummy! Dad paid for the rooms, which again I felt was appropriate. I never knew with The Colonel what was going to happen with respect to things like that. Once, when the family attended a funeral in Marietta for the old African American maid that my Pa (Dr. William Earl Wofford) employed when I was little. You may recall, we called her Middy, and she was the one who went along with the family to Daytona Beach when Re and I were little to watch us. After the funeral, we all went to lunch at Shillings on the Square. It is gone now replaced by Mac's Chop House. It was on the north corner of Church Street and North Park Square. Anyway, when we all got done ordering my mother asked The Colonel if he intended to pay for the family. I'll never forget his response. He said, "Yes, but I didn't want to say anything until everyone had ordered. I didn't want them all ordering off the top of the menu." You learn from your parents … what to do and what to *never* do. Anyway, he paid for the rooms, and we were off. Before we left Columbus I wanted to visit the Confederate Naval Museum located on the banks of the Chattahoochee. And the three of us did. It was not very spectacular at all, and we were on the road by 11:00 in the morning that Sunday. We stopped near LaGrange at a little barbecue place I used to stop at with the honchos from C.P. Roberts back when I was a little working guy in the mid 70's, and we were coming back from the Darworth building site inspections. I cannot recall its name, but the C.P. Roberts big-wigs swore by it, and we stopped there to eat every time… so it must have been good! With full tummies, we headed home to Cartersville, getting there about 4:00 or so in the afternoon. I think Dad had a good time. I never really heard, but Mom seemed pleased so I did good I guess. You know, you never seem to outgrow your need for parental approval until after they die and by then it is too late. That is why I try to praise and compliment James and Angela and Jenna and Adam and Bryce and Bodie and Caitlin every chance I get. Children need your praise, compliments and approval all their lives, no matter how old they get. I mean, don't overdo it, but they do need to hear it. And they need you to mind what you say/text/email and how you say it … as The Colonel used to say, "It ain't what you say, it's the way what you say it." This was combined with another poorly followed axiom: "Don't do as I do; do as I say do." More "helpful hints for hopeful heroes" from my past.

An adventure the fifth grade team loved to undertake with the students was Immigration Day. It usually fell somewhere between Thanksgiving and the holidays at the end of the year. We chose this time frame so the students could talk to their families during TG about their family lineage and be ready to assume an identity on Immigration Day. In my classroom there was a huge lead up to the event. The children were given the assignment to trace their family tree back at least two generations before themselves, meaning their parents and grandparents. This was the minimum expectation. So you ask me, "What if a child was adopted?" Then the child could either use their biological family or their adopted family. "What if they wanted to go further back?" Absolutely! This was not only allowed it was encouraged. But my caveat was *to the extent this information is available*, meaning if you do not have the information, you do not have the information or cannot get it. No biggie. In my mind, as a fifth grade teacher, I wanted to promote cross generation discussions and family discussions. My reasoning was if a child came to a grandparent and asked about birth and death dates and who were my ancestors, any grandparent would, first of all, love being asked, and second, would be a treasure trove of family lore, and the child/grandparent/family would be richer for the experience. Perhaps that is why I am writing this book. But this would not be the way a few parents would see this in today's climate of criticizing every aspect of school and its requirements, but "back in the good old days" the students and parents reveled in the assignment. I had children bring in family trees that went back to the Pilgrims! Or the one with the student related to FDR. Or the one with the student related to Edison. The students were thrilled with their discoveries and could not wait to show off their new found family knowledge! I am sure there were some heartburn moments as family woodpiles were disturbed but by and large I truly felt this assignment was a healthy and positive one. My reputation as a teacher was that my classroom had a lot of large, long term assignments, that the curriculum was rigorous, and that a child was loved and ready for middle school when Mr. Morris was done with a fifth grader. As I mentioned earlier, when I looped a fourth grade class up to fifth grade, I only had one child choose to leave the class. I honestly felt in my twenty-five years of teaching, that most parents wanted their child in my room. I could be totally wrong … but I do not think so. But I digress.

In the days leading up to Immigration Day my children learned all about Ellis Island and the trials immigrants went through just to come to America. They also learned about the trials peoples still go through trying to come to this land of promise. I helped them learn about the immigration and naturalization test immigrants had to take and the test they would have to take on Immigration Day. There was a wonderful lady, Janet Astrom, who was a paraprofessional and worked in the Media Center. All the students knew her.

One day I would tell the students that we were going to have a real, live alien come to the classroom and talk to them about the whole immigration process and the test and everything about being an immigrant coming to the United States. I would really pump the class up about this. The day would finally arrive for our alien visitor to come to the class, all the students were holding their collective breaths waiting to see who would arrive, when in the door walks none other than Ms. Astrom. They were all shocked. You see Ms. Astrom was Canadian by birth! So, technically she had been an "alien." And she had gotten her American citizenship and so we spent the next little while asking her all kinds of questions about her experiences. There were a lot of smiles and even some good questions!

On the day of Immigration Day, the students arrived and went directly to the cafeteria. They could not go to their homerooms for anything as their rooms had been transformed into Ellis Island. The children were to arrive ready to participate as if they were arriving at Ellis Island in 1900. This meant they were to be dressed in the clothing of an immigrant of the time period. In class we had seen pictures of this period and read several books with pictures of what people wore. The child could bring a basket or suitcase or just a cloth bundle but they could not bring anything "modern" like a backpack. They also had to have their passport which was issued to them the day before. The passport was basically a booklet with pages dedicated to each station the immigrant had to visit and get signed off in order to be processed through the island and be allowed to arrive in America. If the student arrived without this passport, they went directly to Deportation. The second thing the child had to have was a card around their neck identifying their immigrant name and what country they were from and what was their skill. This card was made in class and then given to them the day before immigration Day to take home. If the student arrived without this card, they went directly to Deportation. It was requested that the student bring a food dish from their homeland to share. This was left in the cafeteria when they arrived in the morning. As I mentioned this was a volunteer intensive event. It required some sixty to seventy parent volunteers to make it run smoothly with all six fifth grade teachers on constant duty to make sure it all ran smoothly. The teachers were dressed as doctors (I became Dr. William E. Wofford) or guards in black coats and white shirts and black ties, and we even had a Statue of Liberty! The way the event worked was the cafeteria was set up in a long que line just like the immigrants had to stand in when they first arrived at the Island. While the children stood in lines like immigrants, guards wandered around questioning them and raising the level of anxiety: "Where are you from?", "How old are you?", for the girls "Is your husband here?", if not "Is someone meeting you?", "How are you going to support yourself if you get to America, what is your skill?", "Show me your passport." This was a nerve racking time as they stood in line not knowing what to expect. At the designated time, about 7:50, we opened the door from the cafeteria and let them begin to flow to the various clearance stations. The children would accumulate points as they flowed from one station to the next. The first station was Background. Did they have their passport? Did they have a card around their neck properly filled out? Station 2 was Character Check. Had they been jailed or convicted of a crime? Did they belong to a political party? Had they ever been exiled?

Points were tallied, the station was signed off and the immigrant sent to the Vocation Station. These questions were exactly what you would expect: schooling, skills, last job, ever been fired, any children. The points were tallied and student sent forward to the dreaded Health Station. This was a little tricky because if the student really had a handicap or a stutter or hearing problem the "doctors" had to be very careful. The doctors asked about Yellow Fever, Diphtheria, Whooping Cough, Typhoid, Tetanus and looked into their eyes with a flashlight and tested their strength by having them squeeze the doctor's fingers and things like that. If all went well, they were sent to another terrifying station, The Citizenship Test. Here the child took a real test covering questions that had been reviewed in class in the weeks prior to Immigration Day: the three branches of the government, name of the first ten amendments, three rights guaranteed in first amendment, who wrote the *Star Spangled Banner*, etc. All in all, pretty basic things we fifth grade teachers were required to teach. Prior to Immigration Day, I gave them a list of over one hundred real questions used on the real immigration test. Buried in there were the actual questions on the test. In fact, in my class this test was a real test grade in Social Studies! Their testes were graded on the spot and points logged in their passport. The next station was Clearance. Their points were grand totaled, and if they met the requisite total (I have to admit … it was pretty difficult not to meet the total even if you failed the Citizenship test) they were sent on to the Oath of Citizenship. If they had a problem with their total points, they were sent over to Appeals desk where they could plead their case. Generally, all problems were resolved and the immigrant was allowed to go to the Oath station. The goal of the day was to process immigrants through and have them experience Ellis Island not sit around. In the Oath Station, their passport was again reviewed, and if all was in order, the Oath of Citizenship was administered and the immigrant was welcomed to the United States by the Statue of Liberty, and they were then sent to the cafeteria to enjoy food from all over the world. I have never seen so many smiling faces as those children showing up in the cafeteria as American citizens. Now, what about the dreaded Deportation Station? It was a sad place. No passport or identification neck badge were the two most common reasons for ending up there. Another reason could be not accumulating enough total points. Teachers were instructed to swing by the Deportation Station periodically and solve the child's problem and send them back into the system. Again, the goal was for all children to experience Immigration Day and not be crushed by or left out of the experience. At the same time, they were to learn a little personal responsibility. After all, they were headed to middle school soon. It was quite an experience and quite a day for teachers, parent volunteers and especially the immigrants. In retrospect, I hope we were not too hard on the students. It was a day I hope they won't soon forget … as a highlight rather than a horror.

As a class we did Charleston again. This year was special as James joined me as a senior counselor making the whole event that much more heartwarming. And as a fifth grade, we all went to the Jekyll 4H again. I was able to talk our assistant principal to join us as a counselor that year. I do not recall his name, but he was a bagpiper. And one evening as the bell finished ringing for lights out, he took the field and played Amazing Grace. He positioned himself off, away from the U-shaped dorms so his music would echo off the buildings and so he would be barely visible in the darkness. The sound was almost ethereal and brought both children and counselors out onto the balcony walkways. A moment never to be repeated in history, and I was there to experience it.

The Federal History Grant *Expanding Frontiers 1800-1893* was starting up and it was going to be a doozy. We were going to east coast sites in the summer of 2010 and in 2011 we were going out West. The year 2009 was spent wrapping up the *Seeds of Democracy* the laying of the groundwork for Frontiers. I will share more about both of these in the 2010 and 2011 chapters.

I do want to get to the horror of 2009. Up until this point I had been blessed with fantastic principals. There was the one year at Mountain View after Oveby and Straka had left, that there was a weak principal (the one with the Bible on a stand), but I was able to escape to Mt. Bethel with Dr. Brown after just one year of her. After Dr. Brown came Robin Lattazori. She was my advocate and supporter and vice-versa for many years; who gave me hope when I was in Liberty County and who brought me back to Mt. Bethel from Cherokee County, and she was now going to move up to the Central Office. We were to get a new principal at "Mt. Special." Little did anyone of us – parents, teachers, Central Office personnel – suspect that this person's work at Mt. Special over the next four years would degrade this flagship elementary school. This school, where to get a position a teacher literally had to die to create a vacancy, was to be changed into a place where teachers and support staff were looking to escape from. Anyway, that fall of 2009 we were all blissfully unaware of the horror to come. In the spring of that 2009, Robin Lattazori had come to me and asked me to take over as the team leader of the fifth grade. With the solid backing of Danner, Perry, Scheer, Mari, Jones and Higginbotham, I took the job. I had held this position at Mountain View and was very successful there, so I figured, why not. In retrospect, I should have refused her request, but she had backed me and helped me return to Mt. Bethel, so I felt I sort of owed her this two-year commitment. I tried right off the bat to set a good tone by inviting the new principal, She Who Shall Not Be Named (SWSNBN), to lunch, and I felt it went pretty well. SWSNBN was coming to us from Shallowford Falls Elementary. SF is a school with a demographic about the same as Mt. Bethel. She had been an AP there for a period of time and had a strong endorsement from a fast rising Principal there. Coincidentally, I had actually taught with this "fast rising Principal" when she was a fifth grade teacher at Mountain View. Anyway, SWSNBN had only been in a second grade classroom for a couple of years, then gotten her Masters in Administration and those were her credentials to take over the 1000 students and 120 plus staff of Mt. Bethel. (i.e. She was in over her head.) I believe that any person who wants to be a principal of any school anywhere should have had to teach in a classroom for at least ten years before being considered for a principalship anywhere. Additionally, they should have to take management and leadership courses … actually more leadership than management because the principal's ONLY function in my opinion is to move obstacles from the classroom teacher's path to allow the classroom teacher to be more effective. The principal is NOT there to further their career or to receive any accolades. All accolades should be reflected onto and given to the teachers who are "… actually in the arena, whose face is marred by the dust and sweat and blood, who strives valiantly, who errs and comes up short again and again because there is no effort without error …" (from speech by President Teddy Roosevelt) So, several weeks later there was a big meeting of all the grade levels to establish the calendar for the new year. I'm going to be candid, during the meeting, I pressed the fifth grade's agenda and tried to get the best dates for our Immigration Day, the fifth grade holiday celebrations, the fifth grade end of year bash, the Jekyll trip and several other minor events. I guess I pressed too hard, although I do not think so, as hours later I was called to SWSNBN's office and was accused of insubordination. Well, I'll tell you gentle reader, as I hope you see by reading to this point in my life at fifty-nine, I am many things but insubordinate is NOT one of them. I do not recall the details of the conversation, but it was clear this was not the auspicious beginning I had hoped for. In my personal opinion the new Assistant Administrator was whispering in Ms. Johnson's ear and trying to cement her position. There was a lot of jockeying going on in the front office. Based on that meeting and being "called on the carpet" so to speak, I could see it was going to be a long two-year jaunt as the fifth grade team leader. SWSNBN and I butted heads again later that year as I recall, but I cannot remember what triviality that was about. What I do remember was that I submitted my resignation as Team Leader at the end of that year. I strongly believe, and am firmly convinced today, she felt threatened by this Cobb TOTY, and I knew I wanted to stay as far away from SWSNBN as possible.

I want to get all of this period in my career out right now, so I am going to tell you about the next significant run-in with what I am now convinced was an individual with significant mental problems. The third humiliating event with this principal was during a project I used to undertake called *Mavericks from History*. Now this had to be in the fourth and last year of SWSNBN's tenure (2012-2013) because she decided to change the way the fifth grade conducted classes. She wanted us all to change classes, like middle school. This had to have taken place her last year because this was the decision that "broke the camel's back" so to speak with Mt. Bethel's parents. And it was the stupidest idea ever. By then she had run off Ms. Jones, Ms. Sheer, Mr. Mari, and transferred Ms. Higginbotham to third grade. One of the several new fifth grade teacher replacements was one Mr. D. (I am purposely withholding his name). In my opinion he was not really interested in teaching fifth grade. He was angling for a PE slot, but fifth grade was all he could get. Anyway, come *Maverick from History* time. This was right before Halloween, and it was my way of allowing the children to dress up. The children would pick a character from history who was born between 1800 and 2011. They were to do a report on the person and come dressed as that person on History Day. The other piece of criteria was that the person had to be dead! So, in years past … and I had been doing this particular lesson for over fifteen years at this point … I let children be whomever they wished from Gandhi to Stalin, from Clara Barton to Mary Shelly, from FDR to Hitler, from the Wright Brothers to Mata Hari. I wanted the students to exercise their creativity. So, I had a student select Adolf Hitler (it was truly a more accepting time … or so I thought). In fact, when my son James had been in the fifth grade, in Ms. Sheer's class … Ms. Sheer was of the Jewish faith by the way … James had selected Hitler to do a report on and everything went well. Anyway, I had around 150 students and this young man's selection did not bother me at all. So, History day came and went and the next day Mr. D. and I were called into Ms. Johnson's office. Come to find out while this student who had selected Hitler was in Mr. D's homeroom, the student thought it would be cute to march around in his Hitler costume with the Nazi salute and yell, "Heil Hitler." Well, this offended a Jewish student who complained to Mom and Dad who complained to SWSNBN and so there we were in her office. I was in a quandary because I had no knowledge at all of this event, and Dietrich sat there like a bump letting me take the wrath of the Principal. After a few minutes of ranting and raving, she dismissed Mr. D. but kept me in there. I believe this was because she had hired Mr. D, but she had inherited me. With her door open so all the front office could hear, she continued the tongue lashing to which my only replies were calm and respectful "Yes, Ma'am." Long story short, I had to write a letter apologizing to a local Rabbi for my "poor choice" in allowing this student to select this person to learn about. I was, as I said, humiliated. But the whole front office heard the whole exchange, and they knew who the villain was. It is interesting to me that today, in 2023, we are fighting this very battle of the *truths from history* versus *what makes people feel badly* today. History is history. There is no right or wrong history. It is what it is, and we need to explore it and learn from it or as the saying goes "we are doomed to repeat it." *Political Statement: If we do not learn from four years of President (and I use the term president loosely) Donald Trump (2017-2021), we are a doomed nation, and this republic will be destined for the trash heap of history. Read my words and weep with me.* So, back to my story; I had three strikes with SWSNBN, and I am convinced the only thing that saved me and my teaching career from this psycho was my double edged armor of having been a Cobb County TOTY. On one edge, it was the reason that SWSNBN felt threatened, and on the other edge it was the thing that protected me the most. So, thank you Mountain View School. And thank you my loyal Mt. Bethel parents who stood with me and beside me. As an interesting aside, I met with Ms. Reba Bachrach, a personal friend of mine from Jenna and Adam's high school days, in 2023 at an event up at J&A's lake house. Reba's son, Marc, had been and still is a close friend of Jenna and Adam and had been in their wedding. In the wedding pictures, Marc is the one with the pony tail. Anyway Reba was an AP under the "woman who shall not be named" for two years, and Reba and I were talking at our lake meeting about our experiences and Reba confirmed to me that working in the front office under the SWSNBN was just as difficult as my experience. So a decade after my experiences, Reba vindicated me and confirmed what I suspected all along. It was not me. It was the SWSNBN. And again, to quote Forrest Gump, "That's all I have to say about that."

5.

There is only one way to start any stories about 2010, and that is to tell you a story that actually started on Thursday, December 31, 2009. It was during the morning of New Year's Eve Day when a very, very pregnant Angela Dawn Swope Morris, James Lyon Morris's wife, decided it was time to head over to Northside Hospital because Angela and James's child was about to arrive. James let Angela's family and Carolyn and I know, and

C and I were off to the Northside hospital near the intersection of Ga 400 and I-285. We let Jenna and Adam Blackwell know before we took off, and when we got there Angela was already admitted and was in labor. James was with her, so Carolyn and I did what grandparents have done for centuries, found two comfortable (?) chairs and settled in. In retrospect, it's funny, there is no place I would want to be except there with Carolyn waiting … supporting James and Angie. But when Carolyn was in labor with our children, The Colonel and my mother and Carolyn's mother were nowhere to be seen … interesting. Anyway, just an observation. Carolyn and I waited all afternoon and into New Year's Eve. It appeared Angela was going to go through the same thing Jenna had endured with her first child, a long, difficult and tiring labor. The afternoon stretched into evening, and we struggled to find some way to sit that was comfortable. Of course, our comfort was the least of the worries that night. James would come out periodically looking every bit the worried husband and give us an update. As the New Year approached Carolyn and I looked around for some dinner. The only thing available was a McDonald's there in the hospital, so McDonald's it was. A double cheeseburger for me and a Big Mac for Carolyn with fries and milkshakes; vanilla for me and chocolate for Carolyn. Yes sir, ring in that 2010 New Year! Angela's parents joined us at some point, but I'm not sure when. Of course I was pulling for the baby to come before midnight so they could get the 2009 tax deduction, but it was not to be. So, the night stretched on beyond midnight into the dark hours when you get that funny taste in your mouth and your body is screaming, "What the what?" That time when you have looked at all the magazines and you are now looking at Woman's Day hoping for some article that can hold your bleary-eyed attention for more than five minutes. I recall James coming out and being upset because he could not find a nurse or anyone to help at various points in time, but basically all I (we) could do is sit on our hands and be "interested bystanders." The clock crawled through the night. One dozed a little but never really slept. I could only imagine what was going on in the delivery room. Carolyn <u>knew</u> what was going on backstage. She did not rest well. Then at 6:39 AM after over twenty-four hours in labor Princess Caitlin Rose Morris made her debut in this world! All 6 pounds and 11 ounces and twenty-one inches of her had arrived and the world would never be the same. And the phone lines lit up all across North Georgia. Both Mother and baby were fine … ten fingers and ten toes … the Morris family was blessed and lucky again. Thank you God. It was a little while before we got to see her for the first time. There was cleaning up and weighing and a new Mommy to be attended to. Jenna, Adam, Bryce and Bodie arrived and joined the party. Finally, after an interminably long time we were allowed to view The Princess, and I have been smitten ever since. She was so beautiful, and as Carolyn says about all our grandchildren (but it's especially true about The Princess), "She is perfect in every way!" After seeing her and Angela and checking on James and feeling much like we did with our first grandson, Bryce, after his and Jenna lengthy birth ordeal, Carolyn and I headed for home to brush our teeth and crash. What a fantastic New Year's celebration it had been. Neither Carolyn nor I had had anything to drink, but we were definitely hung-over … and thankful. It is funny how all the trivialities of this world like war, famine, immigration, death, religion and politics take a backseat to really important things … like family.

302

Bryce was nine that year, and Bodie was seven and The Boys were into football and basketball. I remember Carolyn and I traveling to Gainesville so many times, to so many sports and family events that carry so many wonderful memories, that even today in 2023 when we head up there from Marietta a smile comes across our faces as we recall this football memory or that basketball event or this Krispy-Kreme or that Subway. The Young Princes were too young to play for Lakeview football as Lakeview did not have a team for "little" children so they played for the Gainesville Red Elephants. Yeah, I know …? But they did. Bryce was already becoming the "go to" for the position of center, and Bodie had the making of a running back even at seven years old. We laughed that if Bodie did not come out of the game with grass stains somewhere it had not been a game. Sometimes I believe he would just run and slide just to slide. Neither of the boys was afraid of physical contact and loved the team sports. Jenna and Adam supported both of them as much as two parents could and Carolyn and I and Toby and Paula Blackwell did the same. We were able to become very close to Toby and Paula over the years. They are good people. I recall one cold Saturday morning we were there in Gainesville where the Red Elephants played on Bobby Gruhn Field at City Park right where Glenwood Drive NE intersects Riverside Drive, not far from Longstreet's – my favorite southern buffet restaurant – and Bodie was involved in a collision on a play and broke his hand. There were a few tears but not many from this little warrior. Adam and Jenna carted him off to the North Georgia Medical Center, and he wore his cast like a badge of honor … as well he should have! You know, there is just no substitute for parental support. It makes all the difference in a child's life. One can argue about character traits relative to Nature versus Nurture, but constant, unwavering Parental Support in the form of positive feedback and loving discipline are the most critical parental gifts in a child's life.

Carolyn and I turned 60 that year. Well, I turned 60 and Carolyn turned 60 the next March, but we decided to take the family to Charleston over Thanksgiving, our treat. We booked a really nice hotel downtown, The Homewood Suites by the Historic District I think. It may have been something else but it was something like that. I remember when I turned 50 we had gone to Charleston and stayed at the Vendu Inn and taken Jenna and Adam but if you look back to 2000 you won't see anything about that because I remember very little about it. Oh, I do remember Carolyn gave me a Croquet Set! I remember that! It is hanging in the basement near the chain saw. It has been used once I think. And now that I think of it, in 2020 Jenna wanted to know if we were going to Charleston. (We didn't … Covid and whatnot.) But I get ahead of myself. Anyway, we all went to Charleston and there are several things I want to tell you about. First is we all were in the Market and just wandering along and Carolyn saw a plaster cast of an arch. It was a classic arch with two columns extending from each side. The Corinthian columns were cropped like they had been broken and it had a segment of the frieze and cornice of the entablature. The whole thing was about twelve inches by about eighteen inches, beautifully detailed in a cream color. It's hanging in the basement because I snuck back all by myself and bought it, and then gave it to her for a Christmas present that year. She is so hard to shop for, and she loved it so. I remember the first night there we ate at Hyman's Seafood, and we waited for a long time and finally got two separate, but close together tables. They do not take reservations, and there is always a line to get in. So, if you go to Charleston to try to retrace any of this story, you must eat there. I now recall back in 2000 in Charleston with Jenna and Adam we ate there, and it was at Hyman's that a five month along pregnant Jenna and Adam told us that their baby was going to be a boy. Well, Thanksgiving day arrived, and I had made no reservations for a Thanksgiving meal of any kind and everything was booked solid. We could not even get into Carolyn's and my favorite French restaurant La Mistral. (Don't try to find La Mistral though. It has long since closed.) So we were all wandering along down Church Street like a small procession of Thanksgivingless people; Bryce and Bodie and I were doing "old man walking" across every street to the embarrassment of the rest of the troupe (old man walking is what you see on the crossing light when it is time to cross – a bent over person with arms askew) when we came to Tommy Condon's Irish Pub just below South Market. And since there did not seem to be a huge demand for Irish food on thanksgiving (go figur') they were able to seat us all with no wait. It was the best T-G meal I had had all year! I do not recall what everyone had but I do remember it was a happy meal with lots of laughing. On the Friday or Saturday, I wanted everyone to go out to Sumter and to see the Yorktown. We knew that little Caitlin, who was now the ripe old age of eleven months, would not be a good sport about it (she was to be a good sport some ten or so years later) so Carolyn volunteered to stay with Cait at the hotel while we all went off adventuring. Carolyn's being a good Nana was going to be a real challenge the next day. Little did we know that while Jenna and Adam and Bryce and Bodie and James and Angela and I were trudging around Sumter, Carolyn was dealing with a sick little Princess. Caitlin had picked up something and had a spiking fever, which little ones do, and spitting up and diarrhea. Of course being a seasoned grandmother, Carolyn was more than a match for this little one's virus, and she took care of Cait's every need. However, when we got back to the hotel Carolyn was more than glad to turn her little charge over to Mommy Angela and Daddy James … well, more to Mommy than Daddy truth be told. And we found some dinner and everyone retired. The next day was leaving day. Caitlin had bounced back over night and was more than happy to greet the day. Angela looked a little worse for wear as I recall, but we all had breakfast and loaded up for the six-hour trip home. I understand that little Bryce had a touch of the Montezuma's Revenge on the way home, but I really do not know about that as Carolyn and I were dealing with a trip home that is now legend. As I recall we were barely outside Charleston proper when Carolyn first said that we needed to pull over to the side of the road. She indicated it was rather urgent and I did quickly. I had barely stopped when she flung open the door and vomited all over the ground. It wasn't a little choked off vomit it was a "full-throated, projectile, let's get rid of everything you ever thought of eating vomit." Fortunately, we had a bottle of water … water in bottles was just becoming a fad thing … and after she was done, she swished out her mouth and felt better. We got back on the road. We had gone another twenty or so miles, and we had to pull over again, and all the water came up. But once again, she felt better, and we headed on up the road. We were good for another two hours or so, and we got to just outside Columbia. The traffic was a mess as only traffic can be on the Sunday after Thanksgiving. And I had a sick wife in my car so I took the 178 cut over from

I-26 to I-20. Carolyn needed to stop again only this time when she vomited the diarrhea hit her. My poor, sweet darling was a mess. I mean a mess. Fortunately, we had pulled off the road in the middle of nowhere and there was no one around. We got her suitcase out and got her and the car cleaned up and got her in some new clothes. I hauled everything out of the backseat and made a pallet for her to lay down. She was now exhausted, dehydrated and just wanted to sleep. At least her system was quiet for now. As we neared I-20 she roused a little. We found a truck stop and got her to the bathroom again … in time this time. I bought her some ginger ales while she cleaned up and was able to restore a modicum of decorum. I believe we had gotten our hands on some Dramamine and some Pepto-Bismol by now and were combating the Caitlin Virus. I believe Carolyn was able to sleep the rest of the way home. And the nine-hour, six-hour trip was done. As in my food poisoning adventure of 1987, Carolyn's Caitlin Virus ordeal from Charleston to Marietta are the things you do for someone you love with every fiber of your being. And even today, we laugh about that weekend and Baby Cait and how she shared with her Nana.

In that year of 10/10/10 a number of events I want to mention are Carolyn joining the KSUCAC, the Kennesaw State University Community and Alumni Choir, and we took Bryce and Bodie to the airshow at Dobbin's Air Force Base. At that airshow I recall seeing a B-17 like Unca' Bill flew in WWII tucked under the wing of a B-52 bomber to keep it cooler in the bomber's shade. We also had The Boys for a long weekend and took them to Kennesaw Mountain Battlefield and then on to Huntsville where James had gone to Space Camp sixteen years earlier.

We headed over to the battlefield and took The Boys to the museum first where we watched the movie. Then we had to take some pictures at the cannons and The Boys, being boys, had to take some goofing around pictures that are precious. After some pictures we headed up to the mountain and all four of us trudged up the slope. Of course The Boys were hopping and skipping around every tree root and off of every rock and boulder much to their content while Carolyn and I sweated our way up. At the top The Young Princes dutifully looked at every cannon and sign with Pa and were good boys. We headed down and then we visited the holy of holies – the gift shop! And while I do not recall exactly what Bryce and Bodie purchased, I'm sure it was the coolest thing EVER! And now we were off to visit the Space Center in Huntsville, Alabama, but we are going go across country. We headed out through Dallas on 278 and then through Cedartown … by the way there are no cedar trees in Cedartown … just an FYI. After Cedartown we went up to Cave Spring … FYI, there is a cave and a cave spring here … to catch 411. As we were approaching Cave Spring, we were all getting hungry so we canvassed The Boys where they wanted to eat. Now this was Bodie's Subway period. All he wanted was Subway's white roll, mayonnaise, ham and cheese. That was it. Not some exotic sandwich that only Subway had, just the ham and cheese. I am sure Carolyn and Bryce and I said something like Chili's or Applebee's or something. But we said okay. Whatever restaurant we see first is the one we will stop at. Now it was getting on toward 1:00 and again "an army travels on its stomach," so we needed to find a place badly. As

we came into the "suburbs" of Cave Spring on 278 and came over a little rise and just pulled out of the pine forest into the blazing heat of an Alabama summer there, shimmering in the junction of an unused railroad track and "Bob's Road" was the only restaurant we had seen for miles — a Subway! And Subway has been in our family lore ever since. Whenever you are in some random place for no reason at all, you can count on finding one of Bodie's Subways sitting right there beckoning you to come in for a ham and cheese on white bread with mayo sandwich. After a hardy lunch and with full tummies, we sallied forth again in search of the elusive city on the hill, Huntsville. We traveled on 411 which became 411/68 and the 431 at Guntersville and finally into Huntsville in the late afternoon. We checked into our hotel, probably a Hilton of some ilk. I was into Hilton at that point. I recall it was pretty nice with a huge indoor pool that The Boys enjoyed immensely. For dinner that night we ate at Mellow Mushroom and were introduced to pizza crust pretzel bites which we HAD to order. They were good, and I rarely go to a Mellow Mushroom that I do not look for them on the menu and tell tall tales of The Boys. We got a good night's sleep and attacked the Space Center the next day full of vim and vigor. There were space ships of all sizes and shapes and we have several shots of Bryce and Bodie near the big old Space Shuttle mounted near the picnic area where we ate our lunch. There was only one ride The Boys were interested in … in fact there was really only one real ride there at all … and it was a centrifuge machine type thing where you stood in designated places along the walls of a circular drum room. You faced the center of the room and the drum started spinning, and as it gained speed you were pressed into your spot against the outside wall. The drum spun faster and faster and finally when you were pinned solidly to the wall, the floor fell away to the shrieks and delights of all the unfortunates who elected to ride this thing. Well, The Boys could not get enough of this thing so The Young Princes and I rode it over and over. Of course Carolyn, being the only intelligent adult in the group, wisely stood by and held our belongings. We refer to Carolyn not riding stuff at Six Flags and Huntsville and … well, anywhere else … as "riding the bench." Anyway, I was just not up to more than about three of the rides. My lunch was beginning to let know that it wanted to take a ride too! So we let The Boys ride it alone a couple of more times and then called it quits and gathered "the troops" and "headed for the barn" as The Colonel used to say. We used expressways as best we could coming home. Huntsville to Atlanta is kind of like Memphis to Atlanta. There ain't really any good way to make that drive. Of course you have to factor in we were dealing with Alabama. Anyway, on the way home all the spinning in Huntsville got the best of little Bryce, and we had to stop for his tummy, and the poor little guy puked all over the side of I-20. The perfect end to a perfect day in Alabama.

2010 was the year I took my biggest bike trip. Rosinante and I sallied forth to Savannah over Cobb County School's Spring Break. I know it was a Spring Break trip because at one point I had to stop and brush all the pine pollen off my jacket. My path was interstate down into Atlanta and then I-20 out toward Augusta. At the Madison exit I took 441 South which took me right by the Rock Eagle 4H Camp where I did the MCTM math Conference for years and years. That was now a thing of the past. I stopped doing it around 2005. My Kinesthetic Geometry shtick had gotten old. I followed 441 down through Milledgeville and on down to Dublin. In Dublin I stopped at a Kentucky Fried Chicken place and had a lunch as only KFC can provide a man when there is no woman around to tell him better. After lunch I got on I-16 for a spell. Interstate riding on a bike is some tough riding. At 75 miles per hour the wind is pounding you constantly and watching other drivers, making sure they see you, is a constant worry. You know if you go down or get tangled up with another driver, you are going to be the loser. No doubt. I gassed up at the Love's station at I-16 and 280 and went north for a mile or so to pick up 80 going east to get off the interstate. I then followed 80 and then 21 into Savannah. I recall I did stop once in Bloomingdale to get off the bike and stretch my legs and my back and get a drink. I slipped into Savannah late in the afternoon and headed for the Desoto Hilton. I got upgraded to a wonderful high up, corner room overlooking the city – not the waterfront. I threw the helmet on the bed and stripped out of my jacket, shirt and jeans. I was pooped! I called Carolyn and let her know I had arrived safely and lay down and before I knew it, it was about 7:30. Needing to smell the ocean and stretch my legs, I took the bike and rode out to Tybee Island. On the way I glanced over at Fort Pulaski in the evening light where James and I had gone years before … good memories. Night was falling and I cannot describe how wonderful my evening out there was. I was free … just my bike and me. I hadn't felt that free since college when I was coming home and was diverted to Puerto Rico and not a soul knew where I was. I ate in little dive called Sting Ray's Seafood and left the bike there under the lights and walked out to the beach, shucked off my boots and felt the sand between my toes. The moon was rising full, and I sat there in the sand and listened to the surf and loved … just me and my shadow. I love Tybee, and that night I really loved her. Except for the moon's glow, it was pitch dark when I made my way back across the causeway to the lights of Savannah, but Rosinante's twin floods glowed white and split the night wide open, and as I cruised, I felt the cool night air coming through the partially open faceplate of my helmet and down my half opened jacket caressing me. Rosinante hummed along never missing a beat, her motor vibrating between my legs, her heat warming my thighs. What a ride she was. As the song *The One I Loved Back Then* says: "… *She was hotter than a two-dollar pistol, she was the hottest thing around. Long and lean, every young man's dream, she turned every head in town. She was built and fun to handle, son …*" I got to the Hilton. I recall there was a light fog that night and the city lights were all wrapped in a halo. I slept soundly that night. In the morning I called Carolyn. I was originally planning to stay a couple of nights, but I missed her, and told her I was headed for home. In retrospect, I now wish I had stayed another day or two days or a week or a month, but it's waaaay too late for regrets. Blasting home, I did the whole thing on the interstate just to see if I could do it … if I could stand it … I could …

I-16 to gas in Dublin to I-75, a bite to eat in Macon, then I-75 to gas somewhere along the way and then Canton Road exit and safely home. Again, I was beaten up by the ride but a happy boy. If I ever have a headstone anywhere, I would want it to read: *He was a happy boy*. I loved that ride on Rosinante. It ended up being my longest and my hottest. She was a good, good bike, a faithful bike, and I love her still and miss her still and can still feel her throb in my thighs today. I wish I still had her in the basement. Not to ride, but to know I could if I wanted to. She never failed me and she warmed my boyish soul. I sold her in 2022. I felt I did not have the reaction time I used to have when I was younger, and I did not want to have her just one day too long. One day too long, and I might have hurt her. Ahhh memories, sweet memories.

But ever onward. I want to wrap all the Frontiers History Grant into a single story as all the trips are so intertwined. We took three major excursions over the years of 2008 through 2010. The first was going to take us up to Boston and New England. On the second we were going to NYC and then down through Pennsylvania and then a third trip would take us out west. It was an amazing time in my life. All likeminded history geeks traveling for nothing other than for historical education's sake. OMG! The first of the trips left late in the afternoon, and we arrived in Boston in the evening, boarded a bus and headed for Lowell just north of the city. Lowell was important as a mill town because of the 32 foot fall in the river as it circled the town on almost three sides. Canals were cut through the city from the upper waterway to the lower river. Mills used this natural fall to power water wheels. Water powered several mills and their looms, and it was all made possible by Eli Whitney and the Cotton Gin. As an aside Eli Whitney has a link to Cumberland Island on Georgia's coast. Check into it. There is a Cumberland Island book that Jenna gave me on the library shelf.

As the mills demanded more cotton, plantations expanded in the Antebellum South and the egregious practice of slavery expanded. So, the question is: were the northern mills just as culpable for slavery as the South? The Boott Mill building was saved and is a museum. I recall one part of the tour was to see an actual operating loom in action. Several of us were standing maybe five feet away as the operator started the loom weaving. The shuttle flew back and forth with such speed it was invisible and the noise was indescribable. It was literally ear shattering. One foot from the person beside me and you still, while yelling, could not hear what they were saying. And the young girls who operated these monsters had no ear protection, and there were maybe 250 to 300 looms on a floor. When the looms were all running, the massive brick building vibrated and shook with the forces being unleashed. After the museum and me actually weaving some cloth on a small loom, we rode on a boat in the rain and toured a part of the canal system. All and all I could have done without the rainy, humid boat ride but we actually got to go through a set of 19th Century locks which was kinda cool. From Lowell we went to New Bedford to look into the whaling industry and its practice of harvesting whales for their oil which was mainly used for lighting and lubrication. There is also a strong link between New Bedford and The Underground Railroad. The Massachusetts 54th was formed in New Bedford and William Carney was from New Bedford. Look him up. The Whaling Museum and the Whaler's Church were very interesting although some of our group's more uncouth and childish members did not treat the church with the reverence they should have by going up into the pulpit and pretending to be ministers. I thought that was a little immature for teachers. I was embarrassed for them. And Robyn Holland saw it all. We then traveled to John Adam's home, and I saw one of the most beautiful libraries in the world. When back in Boston we hiked the Freedom Trail (which I hope Carolyn and I will do someday). One of the coolest things … of which there were a number: Old North Church, Paul Revere's home and his statue … was seeing the Massachusetts 54th Memorial that was used in the closing credits of the movie *Glory*. I recall that at the site of the Boston Massacre, which was a street corner in front of a book store where luminaries of the time used to gather, it started to rain. Being the ever vigilant Boy Scout, I had an umbrella. It wasn't a large umbrella, but it was certainly better than no umbrella, which is the position one lady in our group found herself. And being the consummate Southern Gentleman, I offered her a space under mine as the rain turned from a drizzle into a steadier rain. She accepted. I anticipated her next to me shoulder to shoulder but she opted for the more familiar "I'll stand in front of you" position … which was fine … until the rain got heavier, and she backed up more and more under my little umbrella. Suffice to say it got more and more uncomfortable for me, and I did not hear a single thing about the Boston Massacre, and then the rain stopped. Interesting that I recall that so vividly. Then we flew home.

The next field trip we took was to New York and then down through Pennsylvania and Gettysburg ending in Philadelphia. This was the trip that I became sort of more or less linked to a woman in the group. She was kind of a strange bird. She was a thin, blond, kind of mousey, single mother with a complicated background, I could tell, although she never confided. I guess you would spot her as the last person chosen for the game you and everyone else were playing. I first noticed her a year before when there was a history grant presentation of some kind going on, and she got some disturbing news on her phone. And instead of quietly dealing with it, she started making noises and crying until she had interrupted everyone and Robynn had to quiet her down and help her deal with whatever it was. I never understood that. Anyway, on these trips we all had to choose a buddy. And this buddy was the person you would sit with on the interminable bus rides and make sure they were there for breakfast and on board the airplane and stuff like that. We always picked our buddies before the trips during meetings at the National Archives at Atlanta at 5780 Jonesboro Road on the south side of Atlanta where all our meetings were held. It is a beautiful building and right next door to the Georgia Archives. Both are worth a visit if you are a History Geek. Anyway, as we were getting ready for the New York excursion I noticed that while most people had already picked their partner. No one had picked this lady, and my heart went out to her. You know, being that last guy picked for anything in the sixth grade and being bullied has had a lifelong lasting effect on me. So I signed up next to her name. A chance to get to know a new person. So, the day arrived that we were flying out to Newark on Monday, June 8th, and Ms. G. arrives at the airport with a hurt foot, a crutch and pulling her suitcase. I immediately thought that this was going to be a long trip. I rushed over and helped her get checked in, and we were all off to the gate and Air Tran airlines. I don't think they even exist anymore. On our first day, we visited Ellis Island, and it had a profound effect on me. We had been doing our Immigration Day simulations at Mt. Bethel, but after my day at Ellis Island I vowed to make it even more realistic with real signage and extensive script note cards for parents to follow. The school dining room would feel even more like the gathering room at Ellis Island and the whole adventure would be even more harrowing. I purchased several books and DVDs to extend my classroom collection. I photographed many, many pictures of people focusing on their eyes … their haunting eyes … they were leaving everything they knew and heading literally into the unknown. The courage it took, how bad did the conditions have to be where you were living to make you take this perilous step? Would I have had that courage? I have a photograph taken through a dirty window and you can see the Statue of Liberty standing in the harbor so close, yet so far away. America, so close, yet so far away. How, by the Grace of God, was I so lucky as to be born in this country? And to be born white? And to be born to the upper middle class? And to have been given so many opportunities? I guess it was by the Grace of God. I have no other explanation. We had dinner that evening at Bella Casa in Little Italy in New York City and then our buss took us the two hours up the Hudson to West Point.

Now this adventure was surreal … the hallowed West Point. I had heard of this place ALL MY LIFE. It was the holy of holies … the center of the universe … the place from which all life springs. It, of course, was where my father, The Colonel, went to school. "Duty, Honor, Country" … "An Officer and a Gentleman" … We arrived at 9:00 in the evening after a very long day. The weather was proving to be iffy with a gentle rain falling when we were checked into the Thayer Hotel "on post." Before we left for this trip and we were all still prepping I had mentioned to Robyn Holland that both my father and my brother, Peter Charles – the "tail gunner," had attended West Point. She had taken this information and used it. During our orientation the next morning the gentleman who was to be our lecturer and guide called me out and presented me with yearbook copies of my father and my brother and included notations in his speech about both men. I was then asked to fill in a few of the gaps, and being as brief as possible because as a teacher I knew how boring all of this was to the total audience, I mentioned a very few of the highlights for both my father and my brother. It was very, very kind of Robynn to make this effort and again, she endeared herself to me. We toured the site and I saw the much family discussed Cadet Chapel where The Colonel sang. We saw where MacArthur's mother lived while her son attended The Point, and other legendary artifacts and locations. Momma (Marie Louise Williams Morris – Dad's mother) kept a scrap book of The Colonel's time at West Point, which I just looked at (2023). I have since found out that my father was a less than stellar student. He struggled. He struggled with most of his academics while at The Point and also when he was trying to get his Master's in Aerodynamic Engineering at the University of Michigan. He struggled with calculus, physics, Spanish and English. How I wish I had known this. I struggled as a student, especially with Calculus and French. It would have helped me to know of his struggles and how he overcame them rather than … well, it would have helped me, I think, to know these things when I was young. In the rain, we left West Point and rode north along the Hudson for Hyde Park, New York.

Hyde Park was a real "Enclave." I chuckle because the term is thrown around here in Cobb County … The Enclave at Shallowford, The Enclave at Paces Mill … like this is a gathering of the uber-rich. Around here in Cobb there are no enclaves like Hyde Park. Hyde Park was the enclave of the Vanderbilt's and the Roosevelts … the Bill Gates's and Jeff Bezos's and Mark Zuckerberg's of their times … the Robber Barons of the turn of the last century. The Frederick and Louise Vanderbilt family built a small, modest home overlooking the Hudson River with its own dock and three stories above ground. It was a classic situation seen around Cobb County all the time. People purchase a perfectly good home only to tear it down to build a mansion. This is exactly with the Vanderbilt's did. They tore down a Greek Revival mansion to build something "more tasteful" on the 600-acre estate. One of the coolest parts of being at the mansion was when a replica of Henry Hudson's ship the *Half Moon* sailed by the home going up the Hudson River celebrating the 400th anniversary of Henry Hudson's trip. And then we traveled to the home of one of my heroes.

Franklin Delano Roosevelt's home, Springwood, was modest as compared to the Vanderbilt estate, but it was still an overwhelmingly beautiful building, in both size and scope and architecture. This is the home where FDR grew up, and where he struggled to try to learn to walk again after being stricken with polio, the scourge of the first half of the 20th Century. I would like to interject an interesting family lore note here. My paternal grandfather Unca' Pete, Marion Wingfield Morris, absolutely loathed FDR according to my father, Col. James Wingfield Morris. The "why" is lost to history, but he disliked FDR so much that he would not take Social Security, and he did not allow his wife, my grandmother Momma, Marie Louise Williams Morris, to take it either. After Unca' Pete died in 1964, his three children, Col. James W. Morris, Marion Louise Morris Rogers and Marybelle Morris Swift, finally were able to supplement Momma's income with Social Security. I can partially understand his dislike of FDR as I have a similar unbridled dislike for a populist former president (2016-2020) Donald Trump. I saw the driveway where FDR struggled to learn to walk again, the crypts where he and his wife Eleanor are interred, his collection of ship paintings and models that he was so enamored with. I wish I had had more time to spend in his library. We moved on toward Gettysburg!

On the way to Gettysburg we traveled through Amish Country. We stopped at the Landis Valley Farm which was a recreation of a 1760's Pennsylvania farm. There were people recreating blacksmithing, spinning and weaving, but the most fascinating place was the one room school house with the outhouse privy in back. I could not wait to get back to my classroom and show my students what a REAL school should look like! Continuing our trip, we stopped, and I toured the Railroad Museum in Intercourse, Pennsylvania. I am not sure about these Pennsylvania folks. If you recall when I lived in Carlisle, Pennsylvania, a buddy and mine took our bikes to a town called Middlesex, and now here I was in Intercourse. What a state! There were several options that day of where to go. I'm not sure where the others went, but I was about the only one interested in railroads, so I had a ball touring on my own. Late that afternoon we left for the long trip to Gettysburg and to be honest, I think we got lost. We stopped for dinner in an Amish version of the Golden Corral. I dared a friend Tasha to eat a nasty looking pickled egg thing … she did. It cost me a buck. Then we headed out. We were to spend the night in Gettysburg, and it was already 8:00 or so, and I swear we got lost. The Pennsylvania Dutch country is nothing but square field after square field and we went left and right and left and right and never seemed to get anywhere. This was the early times of GPS and our cell phone reception was spotty at best so we relied on our driver. Well, it was close to midnight when we got to our hotel outside Gettysburg. I can tell you it was a scraggly bunch who got off that bus that night.

The next day dawned clear and hot, and I had one destination … Little Round Top. We started the day in the city itself and saw where Lincoln had stayed when he arrived to give his Gettysburg Address. We then saw the northern crossroads where John Reynolds directed his men from the cupola at the seminary. From there, we went by Lee's headquarters and down the western side of the battlefield and saw the Confederate positions looking up to the famous copse of trees. We went around the southern extremes of the Confederate lines and Devils Den came into view. The bus climbed Round Top and the across the saddle to Little Round Top. This is where on July 2nd a hero of mine, Joshua Lawrence Chamberlain and his Massachusetts 54th, made their stand and basically saved General Meade's Army of the Potomac from the Confederate Army turning his left flank that day. Chamberlain's 54th, repelled several attacks from the Confederates, and then out of ammunition and holding high ground on Little Round Top as the Rebels came up the slope as final time, the 54th made a dramatic bayonet charge down the hill forcing the Confederates back, halted the Confederate attempt to turn the Union flank and capturing over a 100 Confederate soldiers. I believe Chamberlain's charge was one of those pivotal moments in history upon which the whole of America's future turned. If Chamberlain had not saved the Union left, and Lee's forces had been successful in getting behind the Union lines, the road would have been open to Washington, DC. There would have been no disastrous July 3rd "Pickett's Charge" which gutted Lee's Army of Northern Virginia. Pressure would have been put on Lincoln's government in Washington to negotiate and possibly allow the Confederate States of America to remain separate from the United States of America thereby significantly weakening it. Fast forward to December 7th, 1941, and our joining World War II. Being two separate countries, we would not have had the industrial might to defeat Nazism and the Japanese Empire. The world could have been very different looking with Los Angeles being part of Japan. And I was standing where Major, soon to be General, Joshua Lawrence Chamberlain stood looking down the hill and into an uncertain future. My moment was somewhat dampened when the bus driver poo-pooed what Chamberlain did that day indicating it was not a big deal. I respectfully told him I did not think he had a full command of all the implications of the day, turned my back and continued thinking about how a hero acted. There is a video, *Gettysburg*, which came out in 1993. Jeff Daniels plays the part of Chamberlain. It is on my shelf. Watch the events of Day 2, and see history turning on a little hill in Pennsylvania.

From there we were off to our last stop, Philadelphia, and in all of that beautiful city there were two main places that fascinated me the most. Of course there was the State House, and the steps that Rocky Balboa ran up and shook his arms in victory, and there was a beautiful church and discussions of the city's very divided religious history, and the Fairmount Water Works and a Philly Cheese Steak I had for lunch, but the two things that impressed me the most were the Comcast Headquarters Building and the Eastern State Penitentiary. I know … a corporate office and jail.

The Comcast Headquarters building was an unremarkable edifice until you walked in the door into the lobby. There, the wall facing you, was a three story television wall. It was amazing! Perched about ten feet off the ground, allowing for doors to elevator lobbies and guard desks and whatnot, was a thirty to forty-foot-tall and easily eighty-foot-wide screen on which could project anything. I recall a huge moving solar system covering the whole screen that quickly dissolved into what appeared to be the side of an apartment building in the morning. And in each of the open or closed or curtained or un-curtained windows were people shaving, putting on make-up, eating breakfast, reading a paper. Just a normal morning and they might look out at you and wave or be insulted that you were a peeping-tom and shut their curtains … it was fascinating! Carolyn has to see it someday. I hope it is still there. Then there was the Eastern State Penitentiary. This where the Chicago mobster Al Capone captured by Elliot Ness and his untouchables was imprisoned. The penitentiary opened in 1829 and was used until 1971. The prison was actually used in the 2009 film *Law Abiding Citizen* with Gerard Butler. The building was revolutionary in concept, built like the spokes of a wheel radiating from a central core. Each cell had its own little yard and prisoners were "rehabilitated" in this prison. The concept was driven by the Pennsylvania Quaker morality and was a fascinating place for me to get lost in and get lost I did. I did see Capone's cell and Slick Willie Sutton's cell and as I said, I got lost and lost track of time. Meanwhile everyone was on the bus, and they were frantically trying to call me when I suddenly popped out of the prison and jumped on the bus. Everyone laughed at me, Mr. Goodie Two Shoes … Mr. Straight Arrow was finally human and late! It was a good moment, and I loved shucking off the image. Our last night's dinner was at the famous City Tavern dating back to the early 1700's. We flew home the next morning.

Summer of 2010 was our Frontier's Grant monster culmination trip. We were headed out West! This was to be a nine-day Wild West / Native American experience. We flew into Salt Lake City and caught a puddle jumper into Jackson Hole Airport. After a day in Jackson, we were off north into the Tetons and Yellowstone Park. Turned east to Cody and then on to Sheridan, north to the Bighorn Battlefield and then to Billings and home.

Flying to Salt Lake was reasonable, but flying into Jackson Hole Airport was a horse of a different color. It is called Jackson Hole because it sits in a hole. So you are flying along and then all of a sudden the plane nose dives into … well, a hole! It levels out at the last minute, and you slam into the runway with the engines immediately going into full reverse thruster mode, and you come to a screaming stop at the Jackson Hole Terminal. You know you are someplace else because when you walk into the terminal, you walk under a horseshoe shaped thing made of deer antlers … at least I guess they are deer antlers … maybe elk. I am such an eastern city boy. While we were getting our ground legs under us, the airport people wheeled out a little cart and started unloading our bags. We walked into the terminal which was very small. There was a ticket counter … <u>a</u> ticket counter. To the left was what looked like a baggage claim area, so we all kind of congregated there. Then a man said that our bags were being brought in the door around the corner to the right. We shuffled that direction and I commented that the bags were coming in at the north terminal baggage claim not the south terminal baggage claim. My attempt at humor. There were a few chuckles. We got our bags, loaded a bus and headed south toward Jackson for the night. This was June 8th, and there was **snow on the ground**! We settled into the Snow King Resort. I ended up bunking with four other guys. I got together with a group of mostly Cobb teachers, and we went out to find dinner. After some discussion, we ate at the Gun Barrel Steak and Game House. I ate buffalo … not impressed … too lean and stringy. The next day we were introduced to the Snake River Valley and personally to the Snake River via a boat trip in the cold spitting rain. Lunch was a classic at the Triple X Ranch where we met a waitress who basically could have doubled for the waitress in the movie *Hell or High Water* … the one who said, "What don't cha want?" She was classic. I'm not entirely sure what was in the stew we ate for lunch, but we all ate it with a smile on our faces.

Indians have been in the valley for 5 to 8,000 years, but now the uber-rich white men are here and making it fiscally impossible for Indians to live in this area. Our evening was spent at the Jackson Lake Lodge. The lodge is splendid and was built by the Rockefellers in the style of Frank Lloyd Wright. The lobby had a three story window opening onto the Grand Teton National Park and the Tetons are GRAND! They are baby mountains being first born only 30 million years ago and reaching maturity 10 million years ago. By comparison the Appalachian chain was born some 480 million years ago so the

Appalachians are hills compared to the peaks of the Tetons and Absarokas. I made some good friends that day. I met and befriended Jack Collins who was a former army Colonel except he had a sense of humor and was nice. Jack passed away from cancer some years later. It was a loss to the teaching world and the world in general. A second person was an attractive, petite, redhead named Tasha Van Nimwegen. She was a teacher from Tritt Elementary, and I ended up teaching her son in my fifth grade class about two years later. She eventually moved to Florida to teach. Anyway, we three had a good time together and hung out a lot. From the Tetons we rode north to Yellowstone National Park. It was a rush when the bus slowly moved along the Tetons and steadily climbed upward eventually stopping at an unremarkable roadside turnout where we all got off. The stop was unremarkable other than the fact that we were on the lip of the crater of a 30-mile by 40-mile caldera known as the Yellowstone volcano. And it is still active. And it last erupted a few minutes ago in geologic terms, 640,000 years ago. We all climbed back on board, and the bus then slid down into the caldera. It was a surreal landscape of bubbling strangely colored pools, geysers and wildlife. I have to be honest with you. The geyser Old Faithful was a letdown. It was a plume of hot water. Tadaaaaaa! Yellowstone's volcano is due to blow again any time now, and when it does we will experience four to five years of a volcanic worldwide winter. That is if we don't blow ourselves up first. We left Yellowstone late in the day and headed for Cody, Wyoming. It was a long, long ride, and we arrived on the steps of the Irma Hotel at almost midnight. As we were slowly pulling our suitcases along to the front of the double swinging, saloon type, old west doors a pair of men came tumbling out onto the dusty street fighting. It was almost as if it had been staged from an old western, but it was not. It was really two drunk guys fighting. We all stood around with our collective city mouths agape. The two guys stopped fighting and stood up shakily looking at their audience, and in a slightly embarrassed tone apologized to us, and then weaved off into the night. Welcome to Cody. The Irma hotel is circa 1902 and was established by Buffalo Bill Cody … a consummate showman in the ilk of P.T. Barnum and Donald Trump. "There is a sucker born every minute." My room had an old fashion pull chain toilet with the tank mounted high on the wall and a very comfortable bed. The next couple of days were spent at the Buffalo Bill Historical Center with members of the Crow Indian Tribe, Herman Viola – a Crow Indian expert and honorary Chief – and Jim Gary, our mentor and Wild West authority who had a thousand old west stories to share and did so in a soft Texas drawl. I am ashamed to say that with all I learned in Cody and the hours I spent in the museum, far and away my fondest memory was the evening of our last day in Cody. I was bumming around with three friends from Cobb County, getting dinner and browsing in shops while most of the rest of our group went to a rodeo, when we came upon a photographer's shop on the narrow dusty street that was the main drag. In the window they displayed their wares. The four of us decided this was for us! The photographer had a selection of outfits and backdrops. You have seen these places in all the tourist trap towns. The three ladies selected saloon girl outfits, and I was nominated to be the gun slinging gambler. We made several pictures. They were sweet to play along, and I loved

being the center of attention … as most males do. My friend Tasha is on the left of the picture. We had a good time, and at dinner that evening the lady on the right – whose name escapes me – and Tasha and I got Jack Collins going with a little too much to drink. Jack had been very reserved at all our meetings and on all our excursions to New England, but for some reason during this trip he loosened up and was actually fun to be with. As we all came to find out much later, Jack was having an affair with another teacher on the trip with us, but … because our group was so large, Robynn had split the group in two. One group followed our path and one group did the exact same things only in reverse. And Jack's paramour was in the other group, so for the first time we in our group were seeing Jack in his natural, jovial, unguarded state and he was delightful. On the last day before we were to leave to come home, the two large groups joined together for the flight home and as soon as the two groups came together, Jack became distant and cold to us. This coldness confused us and we suspected he was "involved." As I mentioned before, Jack passed away some years after this trip and the four of us from Cobb went to his funeral and that is when it all became clear to us. Jack had in fact gotten a divorce and married the teacher from the trip, and they were able to have a couple of years together. Jack was a good man and a friend.

Anyway … enough drama … we headed out of the Bighorn Mountain and spilled out onto the Great Plains headed for Sheridan, Wyoming, and Fort Phil Kearney and it was amazing. We went from huge steep mountains onto the flattest piece of earth I had ever seen. There were no trees, only flat earth, and you could see so far you could actually see the curve of the earth! Fort Phil Kearney has a deep history, and I am not going to bore you with the details. I am going to suggest you look it up or even go there and live the experience. We spent the night in Sheridan and then on our last full day "on the trail" we headed for the Little Bighorn Battlefield site. That morning we had learned about the massacre and the bravado and the man that was Custer. I recalled that my first recollections back in my ping-pong days was of living at Custer Terrace at Fort Benning. The massacre site is a hillside. It was beautiful with summer wildflowers growing over the graves. There were markers where each man fell and where the major groups gathered to defend themselves. Again I am not going to bore you with the minutia of a history lecture. I'm going to let you do your own research and possibly go West yourself and see what I have seen. I will say that Custer was an interesting and larger than life individual, and your research of him will not be wasted. That evening we went to a Crow Indian Reservation, and I was treated to the evening of my life. As I mentioned, Mr. Herman Viola was an honorary Crow Chief due to his work with and for the tribe and his tireless work for them in Washington and on the Museum for Native Americans of which he was a central figure. Our troupe was prepared for this evening with the generous Crows. We had gathered a great number of school supplies and books. This was our meager offering to the tribe in exchange for the dinner and entertainment they had planned for us. On my shelf are books written by Chief Medicine Crow and several other books about this period. There is a DVD called *The West*. All are worth your time. The evening with the Crow Indians humbled me. They offered us their food, cooked in their kitchen, in what looked like a cheaply made gathering hall. They are a poor but proud people. They fed us and danced for us and made me feel very awkward in that "there but for the grace of God go I" feeling. And I was struck again in that "to whom much is given, much is expected." I hope my life shows that I have at least tried to live up to what was expected of me given all the gifts and blessing I received. Only time and St. Peter will tell. And so let's move on from the Federal History Grants of 2007 through 2010.

6.

2011 was a quiet year according to my calendars. Carolyn and I went to Florida and saw a shuttle launch which was cool, but really not anything worth your time. She and I also discovered a little French Restaurant on the square in Marietta. It was located adjacent to the railroad tracks kind of behind a restaurant called Thaicoon. It closed several years ago, but Carolyn and I loved that place. You had better walk in with reservations, or you may not get a table, and you ate whatever the chef had on the menu. I recall a dinner one night sitting adjacent to a window facing the railroad tracks, and when a train passed by you had to pause your conversation. It was winter, and it started raining and sleeting, and we were warm and cozy in this very quaint, rustic restaurant eating the finest quiche and drinking the finest wine and the candles glowed and "God was in his heaven and all was right with the world." I recall we took Mary Lou Swift Beckmann and her husband Bob to this restaurant when they came into town for my brother Bill's daughter's wedding. Mary Lou was the elder daughter of The Colonel's youngest sister Marybelle Morris Swift. Mary Lou was about the same age as my sister Re - Mary Louise Morris Spicher Bramble. Back in the day in Cartersville in the late 50's and early 60's my sister Re and Mary Lou were as "thick as thieves." Anyway, Mary Lou and Bob had come all the way from California for the wedding which was to be held on October 29th … date sound familiar? In California Bob managed a restaurant, so Carolyn and I did not want them eating just anywhere. The day they arrived in Atlanta, we met them at Pappadeaux's Seafood Restaurant off Windy Hill Road and I-75. We figured being from Cali they might appreciate some N.O. food. Then the second night we took them to our French Restaurant on the Square. And since I mentioned the wedding, it was held in Cartersville at the First Presbyterian Church where The Colonel and his Lady had been married, and I have mentioned before. The reception was held at the Cartersville Country Club where I swam as a young lad. In fact, that night after the ceremony, and as we were going to the reception I took a detour by the pool. It looked very small compared to the monster pool of my childhood. Ah, *c'est la vie.* Given the date of the wedding, Bill and Janie were very kind to remember me and sing Happy Birthday to me with my very own cake.

That summer of 2011 was spent having Cait come and spend the night and going swimming in her little Sponge Bob swimsuit. She had started spending the night when she was still in a little bassinette and would sleep in our room. Then she graduated to sleeping in the bed with Carolyn, and I was relegated to the spare bedroom. Don't get me wrong. This was my choice. I did not want her waking up in the middle of the night in a strange room with no one around. So, she slept in my place until 2020 when she came to live with us during Covid and I helped teach her in fifth grade. Along about this time Jenna and Adam purchased a condominium in St. Simons, Georgia, at the Salt Air Villas. It was a beautiful set-up with two adjoining condos. The purchase of the condos was a gift Adam and Jenna shared with the whole family, and we had many awesome family gatherings there at Thanksgiving and other times. The time I am thinking about in particular, and I may be off on the year by a year or two, we were all on the beach: Adam, Jenna, Bryce, Bodie, Carolyn, Angela, James, Caitlin and me. A movie had come out called *Frozen,* and one of its central songs, *Let it Go,* was hugely popular. I was clueless, but apparently Caitlin Rose, by now Cait to all who knew her – as in "Kate" as in Katherine Hepburn … one of the strongest women I know and admire, had heard the song many times and had, even at less than four years old, memorized it and all of the motions that went with it. Well, the song came on the radio Jenna had brought and Cait took off singing and running around the beach mimicking every movement that Elsa from the movie made. It was darling and a moment never to be recreated but forever fondly remembered.

That summer I got a wild notion that the pitiful front porch of our house needed to be redone, and it was going to be magnificent! Kind of like when I saw Journey to Bethlehem in my mind and it had arrived fully formed and clearly detailed … the same thing happened with the new porch design. I did make one change for the better from my original design, but other than that, I saw it in my mind "as clear as day." The original design is in a file right behind my desk – fully drawn and detailed and estimated. And the whole porch went together as seamlessly as it could. I started by tearing off the old wood porch and steps which were on a concrete wall foundation. I then rebuilt the platform of the porch and made my first minor boo-boo. I did not get the platform exactly level and if you look closely at the brick work that overlays the platform you can see a slight rise just about where the storm door opens to its widest point. Anyway, the four columns arrived along with the two half round columns. The assembly went easily in the July heat, but I was fast approaching a deadline of school starting. Carolyn looked at the build as it was progressing and suggested rather than a messy internal gutter design, I go to a shed roof, and then suggested a barrel vault on the underside. They were two excellent ideas and incorporating them made the whole design better. That is why she is the design architect, and I am the project manager. The most painful part of the project was grouting between the brick faces I had installed and it tore my fingers to pieces. To save time I reinstalled the old steps which was a time saver but meant that in 2019 I would have to tear them off and install stone steps. I also modified the roof in about 2007 or 2008 and reworked some of the interior that had sustained water damage. But, all in all, the project came out well and enhanced the value of the house well beyond the $2500 I spent.

School wise it was a calm year. I struggled to keep my head down and stay out of SWSNBN's way, but in the fall of 2011 a most wonderful thing happened. I got a new co-teacher. I was still doing an inclusion classroom, and I was introduced to Ms. Chrissi Mauldin … soon to be Denman. Chrissi and I were a perfect match. She was easy going, very intelligent, child centered, not too hard to look at meaning she was very slim … she

would say "I have to keep my boyish figure." She had dark hair, was quite a lovely, gentle person and she was very, very kind to me and accepting of me. Not easy to do with a Morris, I know. We were together for five years. One of my favorite pictures of us was at a class holiday party. She is wearing a wolf hat Carolyn and I got her as a gift. She and I had our first adventure late in the summer of 2011 right after we met when she went with me on a day trip to Augusta to look at its suitability for fifth grade field trips. I was looking for an experience for our fifth grade that would approximate Lowell, Massachusetts. We agreed that it was a good fit, and the whole of fifth grade made the trip but only once. I found out she was a motorcyclist and owned a flat black, chopped Harley. It was a beast, but she handled it with grace. We went on several rides together, including one to both the upper level and lower level of the Altoona Dam near Cartersville. Her on black, me on white. We were also asked to lead the Mt. Bethel Fun Run a couple of times. Usually they got a Cobb policeman, but that became problematic, and so the two of us were asked, and we were more than happy to oblige. Some of those Fun Run mornings were very cold, but Chrissi and I "got 'er done." Chrissi went to Jekyll with me several times, and we even had to mimic the game "alligator dodge" on one outing. She made me laugh. She walked in the marsh, did marsh mud, sweated and loved the children. We went to Charleston at least once together … just us and thirty of our closest companions! And while all this was going on, she handled hundreds of IEP meetings and helped tailor my lessons and grading for our inclusion children. She was the best thing that ever happened to me in my career. Yep, the best five years of my teaching career – hands down. I love/loved Chrissi. I wish we had never parted. I think after five years she had had enough of me. I do not blame her. If we had not parted, I might still be teaching today. She was amazing.

7.

If last year was quiet, 2012 was quieter. Carolyn continued at B&G and loving her KSUCAC. I was asked to present for one of the Federal History Grant leaders, Dr. Kathy Geiss. The car I was driving, a black Chevrolet Monte Carlo coughed up its transmission on a trip to Statesboro, Georgia, forcing me to buy a new Honda Civic, but the big event was changing classes at Mt. Bethel.

The 2012-2013 school year was SWSNBN's fourth and last year although nobody knew that yet, and she decided, without consulting any fifth grade teacher, that what we needed to do was change classes like middle schools so the students would get used to it. It sucked. I mean it really sucked, and the Mt. Bethel parents finally yelled loud enough to get her canned. Looking at it from a purely time level – 180 days of school x 5 class changes per day x 3 wasted minutes x 150 children equaled a waste of 405,000 child/minutes that year …or 6750 child/hours … or 281 child/days of instruction lost due to this person's stupid unilateral and unproductive and unneeded decision. This was also the school year of the Hitler incident. The only upside to the whole thing was that I insisted on teaching Social Studies for the whole year, so all the fifth grade was exposed to some of the best 1800 to 2012 history I could muster. Ms. Denman unfortunately had to follow the inclusion children class around, and that year was somewhat lost to us. Not to mention an online gradebook system that did not really accommodate what we were doing and children having to carry their books everywhere … this was before laptops. Generally, it was an example of management run amuck. But as I said, this school year was to be her last, so we endured, as all teachers have to do when confronted with an untrained and ill-equipped principal. In to every life a little rain must fall. But let's move on to 2013.

8.

2013 was a much more event heavy year. The year started with the death of my mother, Mary Corrine Wofford Morris (1926-2013). Carolyn and I cruised the Eastern Mediterranean. My favorite uncle, Nelson Kimball Rogers, died that year also. My sister Re retired from nursing. I was given a new award and some other stuff happened, so let's get into the year that was 2013.

In February, my mother who would have been 87 in April of 2013, passed away. Mom had fallen the year before and hurt her shin. She was getting off of a beauty shop chair and somehow caught her leg and cut it on the shin as I understand it. At this point in her life she was also suffering from Scoliosis, the curvature of the spine. If you see pictures of her late in her life you will see her bent over. At any rate, these two maladies were causing her pain, and she was taking some pretty heavy duty painkillers apparently. And painkillers tend to slow one's body metabolism and digestion down. Well, as I understand it, she got a bowel blockage and during the resulting surgery there was sepsis and an infection and on February 8th, 2013, she passed away at the Cartersville Medical Center. I was there. Re was there. The Colonel was there. I recall calling Carolyn from the Intensive Care waiting room. As soon as she picked up the phone, I started crying. It was a scenario I would repeat in the future. I think it was more the stress of the moment rather than the sense of loss that caused my tears. Carolyn knew immediately what had happened. I did not even need to tell her. She was on the road to Cartersville before I had ended the call. Such is my wife Carolyn. My brothers Brian Meroney Morris, William Cranston Morris and Peter Charles Morris were not there, although they came in for the funeral on the 12th. The funeral was held at First Presbyterian Church there on the corner of Main Street and North Bartow Street where Mom and Dad were married in 1948. They had been married 65 years. I did not speak at the church service, but I spoke at the graveside in Oak Hill Cemetery where there is a marker for her in the Wofford plot. She rests with her father, my Pa, William Earl Wofford, her mother, Mary Louise Meroney Wofford, her brother, Unca' Bill the WWII pilot, William Earl Wofford, Jr and his wife Aunt Dar, Doris Virginia Whitfield Wofford.

While we are on the topic of death, my Unca' Nelson, Nelson Kimball Rogers – husband of my father's youngest sister, Aunt Toochie, Marian Louise Morris Rogers – passed away from cancer on September 15th. He had been a lifelong and unrepentant smoker. He was 88. He and Toochie had lived at 9 Ridgeview Drive in Cartersville since the early 60's and raised their children there. Unca' Nelson was always a bigger than life man in my life, and as far as I was concerned, a real father to me. Unca' Nelson loved my Carolyn where as my mother and father always held her at arm's length … for what reason I will never understand. As you have read, it was Unca' Nelson who suggested I go to Southern Tech which changed my life and put me where I am today. He was a professor of some note in the Industrial Engineering College at Georgia Tech and was the Professor of the Year the same year I was a TOTY. He backed me when I had the idea of getting a car in college which my father nixed. He insured me on his cars so I could drive them when I came to Cartersville. Unca' Nelson was a graduate of the Naval Academy and had served on a minesweeper during the Korean Conflict. I already told you the story of me being there at his wedding when I was just "knee high to a grasshopper."

Nelson was a good man. He traveled the world representing Coca Cola and speaking at seminars. I thought I ran into him at the Atlanta Airport once, but it was his doppelganger. I was asked by his daughter, Kimball Amanda Rogers, to speak at his funeral, and I did so proudly and mentioned that it was rare for a man to have to have two fathers, but I did. I helped bury him too in the Oak Hill Cemetery in Cartersville. He is interred in a plot under the Morris/Rogers marker. I have to admit to you, gentle reader, that I have a regret. My Unca' Nelson spent the last year of his life in a nursing home not one mile from my house, yet I never once visited him. NEVER ONCE. And that pains me to this day. It is said that when you are dying, you will not regret the things you did. You will regret the things you did not do. I will regret this all my life. In my pitiful defense, I just could not face seeing this hero in my life wasted away by Cancer. But again, that was about me. I wish I had thought about my Unca' Nelson's feelings. But, then again, he might not have wanted me to see him dying. I will never know, but I will live with my regret forever.

On to happier recollections: Carolyn and I took our first cruise to the Eastern Mediterranean that year. Our trip took us into Rome first. We landed on a beautiful June morning at about 6:00 in the morning Rome time. Of course to our body clocks it was the middle of the night, around 2 or 3:00. I had prearranged with our hotel to have a car waiting. It was awesome. We cleared customs and headed to the transportation area and there, standing in a black suit, white shirt and black tie was a gentleman with a sign reading "Morris." I know Carolyn was impressed. This was the first time I had been able to do this for her, and I was so pleased it worked. The gentleman took Carolyn's suitcase, and we walked into the beautiful Rome summer sun. The man led us to a black, polished Mercedes and helped us load everything. From the airport, our chauffer, toured us all the way from the airport, which is on the coast and adjacent to the cruise port, to our hotel in downtown Rome. We had chosen a little B&B named The Lancelot. It was within view of the Coliseum just down the street and was perfect. We checked in and even though it was about 10:00 and breakfast was technically over, we were invited into the dining room and were served. Our room was made ready even though it was way before check in time. Basically, we were treated like royalty. After breakfast we sacked out for about five hours and awoke, freshened up and walked into the Rome late afternoon feeling right on the local time. We had learned this trick back in the 80's when we went to Paris. We could not wait to see the coliseum and made a beeline down the street. We ate at a little café called The Gladiator and then made our way to another of the holy of holies. I wanted a picture of Carolyn's hand with her wedding ring over my hand with my ring touching a column of the Coliseum. Then we bummed around a little and were tired again and headed for The Lancelot. Our first full day started by meeting our *Rome Walks* guide near the Coliseum. It was Carolyn and me and another three-person family. We first toured the ruins in the Roman Forum seeing where Caesar was murdered on the Ides of March, and then headed up and into the Coliseum itself. I felt our time inside the great building was a little limited but adequate. That afternoon we took one of my great "forced marches" to see the Pantheon, and from there we walked to the Tivoli Fountains which were so crowded we had to fight for a position to throw our coins in. It is said if you turn your back and throw your coins over your shoulder into the fountain, you will return to

Rome. So, we did, and we did again four years later. And I will go again if I can! By the end of that day we were bushed and headed for The Lancelot. After some rest and freshening up we went out to find dinner. We found a beautiful little restaurant. I do not recall the name, but Carolyn order scallops I think and I ordered exploding lobster! Yeah, being the slob that I am the lobster I was wrestling with cracked

at the wrong time and red lobster juice and melted butter splashed all over my nice crisp white shirt. Of course, Carolyn was nonplussed. When we got back to our hotel she produced a Tide Stick from thin air and proceeded to make my shirt as good as new. Full Day Two in Rome was another *Rome Walks* tour of the Vatican, and it was the day I was a typical sloppy American tourist. We left the hotel for our 12:30 tour appointment a little early so we would have time to grab a bite to eat. And being stupid, I had my phone attached to my belt in my little holster in plain view of God and everybody even though I had been warned about the pickpockets. And, yep … we got out of the taxi about six feet from the curb and by the time I had walked ten steps I realized my cell phone was gone. Panic! We looked on the ground and all around. Well, it was gone. I had been pickpocketed. Dumbass haughty American. So we went to a little café and explained our plight. We (I) were (was) visibly upset (for no real reason). The café people were SOOOOO nice to us and pointed out where we could find an internet café to contact Adam and Jenna so they could contact Verizon and disable the phone. We ventured forth and found the internet café down some very suspicious stairs in the basement of a cheesy shop with a bunch of men hunched over old computers. Somehow we communicated what we wanted and the man pointed us to a computer and somehow we got on line and somehow left an email for Jen and Adam. Then, with our time paid for and still smarting from my stupidity (which Carolyn now takes in stride … these things never seem to happen to her) we headed for our Vatican rendezvous. And it was the longest, most involved tour of my life. I was probably a little distracted by what had happened earlier, in fact I know I was, but the whole tour was kind of wasted on me. We saw statue after statue and tapestry after tapestry after statue which would normally have thrilled me to the core, but I was just walking through it. When we got to the Sistine Chapel which I envisioned being a silent and reverent space from which to gaze up at Michelangelo's masterpiece, it was crowded with shoulder to shoulder people … picture our Tivoli Fountain experience inside a room! And there were people talking and babies crying and children who could have cared less chattering away. But, I saw it. Then we went on to Saint Peter's Basilica. I had settled down a little, and it was better, but we went way too fast past some divinely inspired masterpieces. I vowed to return … and as I mentioned, we did. The next day was bumming around day, and I remember ending our last day going out and getting Carolyn some delicious gelato, and as I was walking along in the neighborhood near our B&B, I was propositioned by a young lady of the evening. That had never happened to me before! In faltering Italian/English I politely refused trying to indicate that all I wanted was some ice cream. The next morning, we had a young man in a black Mercedes take us to the cruise port, Civitavecchia, and we boarded our Royal Caribbean ship for our week in the eastern Med.

We sailed out of Rome and down the coast toward Sicily, through the strait of Messina. I think we were to port in Messina, but Carolyn and I stayed on the boat. We headed out into the Ionian Sea and its deep blue sailing toward Piraeus harbor, the port for Athens, Greece. We had one objective in Athens, The Acropolis. You have to have guessed that, two architects loose in the Med. There was only one place for us to go. We climbed the steps up through the Propylaea in the heat, but somehow it did not matter. At the top we got our first up close look at the Parthenon, a temple to the Goddess Athena. It is magnificent in spite of the explosion in a war in the 1600's that decimated many of the buildings. Who stores dynamite in a building like the Parthenon? A couple of my favorite facts about this building are that when it was being built, the builders understood to increase the height of base of the temple at the center just a few inches along the long side so the building would not appear to sag in the middle. They also employed entasis, which is a slight convex curvature at the center of the columns as the column rises. This is done because as the white columns play against the dark shadows between columns they appear straight. Without entasis the columns would appear to narrow at their centers. And they did all these things working with ancient tools and working in marble … just amazing. Another of my favorites on the Acropolis is the Erechtheion, a temple to Poseidon and specifically its south porch, the Porch of the Maidens, so named because of the six caryatids. Statues of women serving as the columns supporting the porch. The six figures there now are reproductions as they have moved the actual figures to the Acropolis Museum. They were disintegrating in the polluted Athenian air. Unknown at the time,

Carolyn and I would be returning to the Acropolis in a few years. From Athens we cruised to Turkey to the port of Kuşadasi in Turkey. This was the Royal Caribbean port that would link us to Ephesus where The Library is. We caught our bus and guide and were off. On the way to Ephesus, we stopped in a little village and visited a modest little house where it is said that The Virgin Mary lived her final days. It was  religiously touching and moving to think that the mother of Christ actually lived here. When we arrived in Ephesus it was a mob scene. Apparently almost everyone in the world had decided that this would be a good day to visit The Library with us. It was magnificent in spite of the crowds. From The Library we followed a path that led to an amphitheater built into a hillside. The guide told us that the Apostle Paul had preached here and written his letter to the Church at Ephesus while here.

From the magnificence of Ephesus, we headed to Crete and docked at what could only be described as a Russian missile silo complex. I have no idea why that port was the only cruise port on the island, but it was apparently. Being undeterred, we grabbed a bus and went on an excursion to the major city market. It was miles and miles and miles away, but we got there. I recall plucked raw chickens hanging up by their necks, butchered hogs hanging in the same market. It was gruesome. But eventually we discovered the tamer areas, and I actually bought two belts. We scurried back to the boat! The cruise was about seven days, and we headed back to Civitavecchia. From there we took a taxi to the airport and a Hilton attached to it to spend the night and fly out in the morning. It was there I had my first initiation to the European way of making a bed. There is a bottom sheet and no top sheet, just a duvet cover. I did not know this. Apparently it is very common in Europe, and we colonials are always baffled by it. So, being a baffled colonial I called the front desk assuming someone made a mistake and requesting the bed be fixed. No one came. I called again. No one came. I went to the front desk and complained. They listened and were sympathetic … but still no one came. I was upset, but not too upset and vowed to write a "sternly worded letter" to Hilton when I got home. Needless to say when I got home, I did a little research and found out what a colonial fool I had been. I did not write a letter and make an even bigger fool out of myself. And now I know, and I am a suave, debonair James Bondy kind of guy. Yeah, right. Anyway, we got home safe and sound. And I got a new phone and vowed to take pickpocket warnings seriously from now on and to not worry about top sheets!

That summer Erin Sumrell, the elder daughter of my friend Carol Sumrell from the church, got married in Washington, Georgia. This was interesting as that was the town that Momma, Marie Louise Williams Morris, was born in. Carolyn and I were there for just an overnight stay and I did not get a chance to do any real research. I would love to go there, and see the house Momma grew up in if possible. Perhaps someday soon I can make that happen. (I did in 2024.)

Also that summer my friend from Mt. Bethel, Coach Chuck Jones, took me sailing on Lake Lanier. Chuck had grown up around boats and sailing all his life and sailing was something I sort of dreamed of learning how to do and perhaps buying a sailboat someday and saying "the heck with it all" and just sailing away. On the bookshelves are even a couple of books about sailing. Well, one afternoon on the lake taught me there was a whole lot more to it than that, and it was not nearly as much fun as I thought it was. So, that dream was immediately trashed. And that was okay. Better to learn now.

Probably the biggest and greatest event of 2013 happened that fall at the beginning of school. SWSNBN was ousted as principal from Mt. Bethel. This was fortunate, but the damage to the school's reputation, its staff, its faculty and to me had been done. I did not know it yet, but I was on my way out of the teaching profession. There was to be no return to Mt. Bethel's glory years … only a steady slide downward. But the upside, or so I thought at the time, was that Ms. Jessica Appleyard would be principal. You may recall that name from over a decade earlier when I first came to Mt. Bethel in 2001. Well, Ms.

Appleyard had been steadily working her way up the ladder and was now assigned by the Board of Education to be coming back to Mt. Bethel where she started as a part time Paraprofessional teaching Spanish from a rolling cart to be our new principal. Hallelujah … or so everyone thought. Anything was better than SWSNBN. So, in the fall of 2013 Ms. Jessica Appleyard took the now shaky reins of Mt. Bethel amongst much fanfare and delight and everyone wearing Ruby Slippers (red spray painted tennis shoes) at the Holiday party as we mimicked Dorothy coming back to Kansas from Oz after killing the Wicked Witch of the West. At that moment in time, we were all happy to be saved from Hell.

9.

2014 started with a bang! Or rather a quiet snowfall. In January a little before lunchtime a gentle snowfall started. By lunch, it was starting to come down and Cobb County was making arrangements to get children home early. There is a law that says all children have to have a lunch period so we sped up lunch and classes were eating in their rooms. By 12:30 the snow was coming down in big, heavy, wet flakes, and we were piling children in cars and buses. Elementary were always the first to start in the mornings, and the first to be let go from school followed by high school and lastly middle school. We got all the children away and teachers were scrambling to bail out. I was last leaving because I had volunteered to stay overnight if there were children who could not get home. Anyway, about 1:30 I finally gathered my stuff and headed for my car. There had to be four or five inches of snow piled on it. I brushed it all away so I could see and climbed in. The car was the 2012 Honda Civic I had bought when the Monte Carlo died, and it was still very new, so I knew I had great tires and a solid vehicle. I pulled out of the school parking lot and slowly made my way up the slight incline to Johnsons Ferry Road and saw my first obstacle. Traffic was bumper to bumper going north on JFR. I made my way to the front of the line and someone begrudgingly let me into the line. Working my way northward through the Roswell Road light, everyone was being pretty civilized even though the snow was really falling now. When I got to the top of a rise at Lassiter Road I could see the intersection of JFR and Shallowford Road was a mess. If you go there and look at the convergence of the roads and the slopes and envision slick conditions you will see why. So I turned left onto Lassiter Road, a little side street cut through. Now, while Lassiter Road has dips and inclines there was almost no traffic on it, so I made it to its intersection with Shallowford Road pretty easily and there I ran into an interesting problem. There was so much snow on the road and my car was so small that the light at the intersection did not register my car was there, and the light was not on a timer at that time of day. So, I sat there waiting … and waiting … and waiting … watching the line of traffic on Shallowford crawl by. Finally, I saw a gap and I took my chance. Without the light in my favor I pulled out turning left and snuggled into the west bound lane and began a long slow crawl toward Sandy Plains Road. After an hour or so I got to the car clogged northbound SPR. As I made my way north I was thinking of the SPR intersection with Wigley Road, a mostly T intersection in a scooped out bowl and could smell trouble before I ever saw it. As I topped the hill and saw the mess that was the intersection, I opted for a side street into a subdivision, Pete Shaw Road. I followed Pete Shaw with very little trouble even though it was hilly. Pete Shaw intersected Steinhauer flowing northward. I was flowing with the path of least resistance and using my knowledge of the roads and their intersections to set my path. I opted for a turn to the right on Jims Road and encountered my first real problem. Jims Road went right by Mabry Middle School and by now, three hours into my journey, they were trying to get buses out of the school parking lot. The snow was still coming down and sticking to everything. With some artful dodging and careful hill climbing I got past Mabry and to the intersection with Wigley Road. From there it was pretty easy sailing. The intersection with Trickum was a little nasty but I was on the flat stretch so I mainly just plowed ahead. All in all, it took almost four hours to make a twenty-five drive. That night there were children sleeping in middle and high schools because they could not get home. At my school, we got everyone home. Carolyn was already at home and was waiting for me. I had called her during my travels and kept her abreast of the trip, so she was not overly concerned. She was also monitoring the news and was able to tell me where the significant messes were. And that was just the start to 2014! There were trips to Jekyll, a TG at St. Simons and a meeting with a Civil Rights icon.

I believe it was that summer that I built Cait a swing set in the "hine yard." It is still there as I write this … unused as my Cait is now going into the eighth grade and much too old for such childish things. Someday she will return and remember, but that summer I had a project! I planned it all out so it would last a lifetime. Four by four verticals sunk into concrete, a two by ten cross member with through bolted stainless steel eye bolts to support the swings. I had to lay out the verticals on the driveway to get the angle of the cut notches for the two by ten right. I did not have a blade big enough for the notch cuts so I had to use my chainsaw. I hauled the verticals to the back yard and approximated the distances of where the feet would land and started digging. This was tricky because the top two by ten had to be level. I finally got the holes right and had the verticals in place without concrete yet. Somehow I had to lift the massive two by ten into place about nine feet in the air, then place it in the notches without having the verticals secured. I will be honest with you, gentle reader, I am not quite sure how I did it. I know it took me several tries and a lot of frustrated grunting, but finally the whole rickety structure was in place. Now I could start securing the structure. First I had to bore through the notches and the two by ten cross member and through bolt them. With that done, I could level the top piece and make sure the verticals were in fact vertical and tighten the bolts on the structure for its final time. The pouring of concrete was the easiest of the whole production. My princess's swing was ready. And we have had many sessions of "One for the money …" on it. I can hear her now in her little high pitched giggly voice as she anticipated the tummy flipping excitement to come, "Pa, do one for the money!" One for the money involved pulling the swing back and saying, "One for the money." And then pulling it back a second time and saying. "Two for the show." Then a third pull back, "Three to get ready." And finally as you push your little Princess high in the air and run under her yelling, "Four to go!" Many memories and much laughter tinged with terror ensued.

That summer we took a trip down to St. Simons with Bryce, Bodie, Cait, Carolyn, Jenna and me. We planned to stay at Jenna and Adam's condo and visit Jekyll Island and Cumberland Island. At Jekyll we visited the new turtle complex and looked at several old mansions which bored the children tremendously. I do remember taking them to Boneyard Beach. If you ever go to Jekyll, you have to go to the north end and see the beach area. The north end of Jekyll is slowly eroding and the south end is slowly silting up. This is causing the north end trees to die and fall over and that, combined with the salt spray, causes the trees to become weirdly shaped ghosts of their former glory, and the beach looks to be strewn with bones, hence Boneyard Beach. Another high point was when I took them out into the marsh. I absolutely love the marsh. I love its wildlife, its flora, its smell and the way it looks. To me, it is fascinating. To the girls, particularly Carolyn and Caitlin, not so much. So, we parked at the designated turn out off the Jekyll Causeway and headed into the beautiful marsh. It was midday and the sun was high … and hot. We wound around to a hummock and on the way, Carolyn and Cait saw a herd of little crabs scurrying out of their way. Now I have to admit, when I see hundreds of little crabs, or really hundreds of any little animals, even I get creeped out, but C and C did not like these little guys at all! And they let me know about it quickly and with much enthusiasm! But, they forged ahead anyway. We crossed the hummock pushing aside branches and undergrowth and came out onto the broad flat area that is the marsh. It was low tide so the tidal plane was dry and sandy. And the sun was beating down. And it was hot. And that is when there was a mutiny. I can see the scene now in my mind's eye. Carolyn and Cait stood there under a little umbrella. Cait standing next to Carolyn's right and reaching up to hold Nana's hand. "We are going back to the car. We are going to turn on the air conditioner." There was no discussion. It was obvious there was to be no disagreement. This was mutiny pure and simple, and that was all there was to it. With that, the two ladies turned on their heels and walked away from the marsh. Jenna and Bryce and Bodie and I sallied forth and with liberal applications of marsh mud on Bodie and Pa's faces, everyone tolerated Pa's discourse on the beauty and importance of this miracle of nature. There are three pictures in a frame on the dining wall called Adventures with Pa made by Jenna documenting Bodie and Pa's marsh mud, Boneyard Beach and our Cumberland Island adventure. We left Jekyll, and I am not sure if it was that day or another day that we traveled down to St. Mary's and caught the ferry to Cumberland Island. At any rate, it was another hot day and the children and grandchildren put up with me well. You know, now that I think about it was later that year … probably Thanksgiving because Angela and James were with us that day. Yep, Thanksgiving because the whole family came down to Adam and Jenna's condo and Carolyn and I took a room over at the King and Prince in one of their out buildings. Anyway, we saw the requisite Dungeness ruins and walked all over the island while C and C complained about the heat. But there was no car to mutiny to, so they were stuck and could only whine. The

absolute best part of it was the third picture in the dining room set. It is Bryce and his Pa kneeling by a big pile of horse manure. I was always into kneeling pictures. When James and I would travel I would have him make pictures of me kneeling everywhere … the White House, On the Border, Cape Canaveral, The Yorktown, The Hunley Submarine, The Alabama, Fort Sumter … everywhere. So, this picture of me and my grandson kneeling by a steaming pile of horse crap is a memory evoking favorite.

JoAnn Wood of History Grant lore asked me to fill out the paperwork for possibly being the Civic Educator of the Year in the 3rd through 5th Grades. This was an award sponsored by the Georgia Center for Civic Engagement. I did, highlighting my History Grant travels and our Ellis Island Immigration Day as my center piece. And was informed I was selected as a finalist, and could I attend the gathering in September of 2014? The Awards gathering was to be in the fall of 2014 in the Classic Center in Athens, and the speaker was to be a Civil Rights Icon, Representative John Lewis. Needless to say, Carolyn and I were there! We were to hear Representative Lewis at 11:00 after the awards ceremony. We left early and were in Athens about 9:00. We wandered around and found the table for the Georgia Center for Civic Engagement. All who were there at the table were very solicitous of Carolyn and me. At the time for the awards ceremony we all found our seats. To my surprise Robynn Holland and JoAnn Wood were there along with several people from the History Grant. I introduced them to Carolyn. I have to admit, at this point I was getting a little excited. We all took our seats and listened to the main person talk about their organization and the importance of civics. As he droned on, I was looking at the awards on the table behind him, and one caught my eye. It was an eagle alighting on a rock with its wings spread. Secretly, just between you and me … I wanted THAT award. Finally, the names were read and I was the Georgia Civic Educator of the Year, and that eagle trophy was for me. I accepted it, and said a short thank you to all of those whose shoulders I stood on, like Robynn and JoAnn and Carolyn, and all the unsung teachers in Georgia, like my son and my daughter. I kept my speech short, because I had learned that nobody really cares. The award is on the book shelf in my office above pictures of my grandsons. We wrapped up, and I was congratulated, and we got ready for Representative Lewis. We then got the word he had been delayed and would not speak until 2:00, so Carolyn and I headed out to find some lunch. We found a little hole in the wall place and got some of the most delicious fried chicken I've ever had and it came with a little surprise. The restaurant did not take credit cards! And they didn't take checks! Fortunately, C and I did scrape together the cash we needed and didn't have to wash dishes. I looked around as we left and there were no warnings about credit cards or checks … I guess you just had to know … college town stuff. We hustled back up to the Center and got a seat. Representative Lewis and his publicist were there. What struck me was how frail he looked. I had only seen him

as a robust, young accomplice of MLK and as a powerful speaker on the floor of the House. Today he looked tired, but he held forth on the virtues of public life and the necessity for vigilance. Afterward we all stood in line for a picture with him. I had brought my graphic novels he and the publicist had written (on the Billy book shelf – nonfiction side) and got him to sign them and had our picture made with him. It too is hanging in my office. It is a prize of mine. Rep. Lewis passed away in 2020 and that was a huge loss to the United States and all of us who knew and loved him. He really was … an icon.

10.

Ah yes, 2015, a year of Kindergarten, babies, swamps, mountains, the loss of a friend, and eyes. It was quite a year!

Some quick hits are My Princess, Caitlin Rose Morris, started Kindergarten. She is growing up too quickly. We also went to the very weird Babyland General Hospital in Cleveland, Georgia. My only advice about that place is do not take a child there if they at all understand the *facts of life*. Children do not come from cabbages or out of trees or whatever else is going on there! Caitlin actually got to name a baby that day. She named it Sparkle Three Moon or something equally imaginative. That almost sounds like an Indian name. Anyway, we visited there and also spent some time at Chucky Cheese … another very strange place.

It was about this time also that we took The Boys (Bryce and Bodie) to another corn maze and this one had a haunted house. Bryce wanted to go into the house and so I volunteered to go with him. In the beginning it was your standard creepy country people with chainsaws, but once we got inside it got really creepy. There was a box like thing you went into that was supposed to be an elevator. Bryce and I went in right behind a mother with a small child. They closed the door and the lights went out and the box shook like you were going down, down, down. Then the child with the lady started screaming, and they had to let him and Mom out. Well, Bryce and I were pretty creeped out already, too (okay, it was mostly <u>me</u> who was creeped out – Bryce was cool – let's just be honest here) and so when the Mom and kid bailed … Bryce and I were right behind them! I'm a

real chicken about that stuff. I know it's all fake but I still get frightened. So, we just did the tried and true corn maze and called it a day with ice cream. Oh, around this time, maybe a few years earlier, we took the boys to Helen, Georgia, and convinced them to get all dressed up in cowboy duds and had pictures of them, and Pa, playing cards and drinking in a saloon. One of the pictures is framed and in the grandson's collection in my office. That was the same year Bodie and I climbed Kennesaw Mountain. Why we were the only two I do not know, but we were together, and we did. It was during that climb that I knew something was not right with me. Bodie bounded up the hill no problem, I actually had to rest on a bench halfway up. You know you don't really know if it is just aging or a real problem. You have never been this age before and you don't know if this is how you are supposed to feel or what. Anyway … as it turned out it was very much a precursor of things to come.

I also got it in my head to take the boys to the Okefenokee Swamp. We must have been down at St. Simons, probably Thanksgiving or something. I could not convince anyone else to come and so just the boys and I went to the swamp. Now, I have done some great things, but this was not my best one. It had not rained a lot that year and the swamp was down and everything was brown. We got a boat ride with another older couple and our docent (HA!) guide was a genuine redneck idiot. He kept cracking all these redneck jokes and talking real southern and generally just acting like a fool. When we were all done, quiet Bodie summed it all up when he said, "You know Pa, when we were driving back from the Keys with my mom and dad, and we went through the Everglades, there were alligators everywhere. Even just along the side of the road! What did we see today, maybe one little one? Pitiful." That Bodie can certainly sum it up for you. Anyway, we ate a late lunch and headed home for St. Simons. Speaking of Thanksgiving, we ended up having several TG's at St. Simons over the years. C and I would bring paper plates that always looked like they had someone's heart on them. I think it was supposed to be grapes or something but it was a running joke. We would all gather around their big table, and it was a feast. I always love TG with my little family.

On the school scene Carolyn's younger sister Ginny won the Cobb County Elementary Teacher of the Year Award that year. They started giving awards at each level of school which was different than the way they did it when I was TOTY. After selecting the grade level TOTY's, they then select the overall TOTY from those three. We were all very proud of her hard work. The 2014/2015 school year was my last year with Chrissi Denman. We just had to separate, and I will be brutally honest. Leaving Chrissi was the biggest mistake in my teaching career, and I believe ultimately led to my retirement. I recall our last field trip to the Center for Civil and Human Rights. She gave permission for one of our children to go all the way across the field to a coke machine. Now admittedly this child was not one of my most reliable students, so I immediately assumed he had just wandered off, and I got really upset. And when she told me she had okayed it I was doubly upset. I felt she should have known better. Anyone could have snatched him which would have been okay with me, but his parents would probably not have seen it that way … or maybe they would have. Anyway, I was tired of school, tired of that boy and just plain, old tired, and I did not do well with it. I decided that Chrissi and I needed to part. As it turned out she felt the same way and so at the end of the 14/15 school year we parted. I've regretted it ever since. We were one hell of a team! And I was an idiot … a tired idiot.

For the 15/16 school year I continued my inclusion class and requested Richard Williamson be my co-teacher. I was thinking he was a good man, we had done Science Olympiad several years together, and we'd make a good co-teaching team, but there was just no replacing Chrissi. But Richard and I made a good go of it. We started the year off at Meet and Greet as the Blues Brothers, not that any of the children had the slightest idea who Jake and Elwood Blues were. Some of the parents got it, but it went over the heads of most. I think this 15/16 school year was the first year I started to feel I was a caricature of myself. I was doing all the things I did, but there was no excitement. There was no Charleston trip. There was no Jekyll trip. The other teachers felt it was too much of a liability. This thinking was led by my "friend" Danner and it succeeded in scrubbing the whole Jekyll excursion. This was a big deal as Jekyll had been closed for two years as the whole camp got a makeover and was turned from a 1950's motel into a really first class destination. I went to Appleyard and pled my case. There were enough fourth grade teachers who would gladly go and let the fifth grade teachers who did not want to go take their classes, but Appleyard was now firmly drinking the administrative, central office Kool-Aid (for this reference look up the 1978 Jonestown Massacre). Ms. Appleyard had asked what the teachers thought about the school getting a new paint job. I had firmly said please save the art work. For the past twenty years each class had paid to have an artist paint beautiful murals all over the school with names of classes that had graduated and remembrances of children who had passed away. I pleaded that none of this history be lost. Ms. Applewood had it all painted over. I cannot believe that the teachers voted to allow this. I believe it was a sham vote and like the birds that were painted over in Mountain View, the school's soul was torn out. Anyway, Appleyard said that either the whole fifth grade was behind going to Jekyll or there would be no trip. And the children lost again. The heart of my teaching was being destroyed. To this day I will tell you that I did not leave teaching. Teaching left me. And so I "endeavored to persevere" (*Outlaw Josey Wales*) and Richard and I made the best of 15/16 … but I started thinking about retiring. I went to an information session up at Georgia Highlands College in Cartersville put on by the Teacher's Retirement System of Georgia and started gathering information. I contacted the Social Security Administration to find out what that would yield. I was turning 65 in the fall of 2015 and Carolyn and I attended a seminar at Dalton State College. My mind was evidently setting a course out of teaching.

My Carolyn got cataract surgery that year, and it made quite a difference in her outlook … pun intended. I recall after she had the first eye done, and we went in for the removal of the eyepatch. When she saw the doctor's coat for the first time she exclaimed how white it was! And all the way home all she could do is talk about the colors and how vivid they were. We got the second one done soon thereafter and now she is my critic on all things color.

11.

This was the year that initiated my final year of teaching and a preview of medical problems to come. With that earth shaking intro, 2016 really was a relatively quiet year actually other than electing a buffoon for a president.

Two exciting events on the family side were a trip with Bodie and Cait and a trip with four boys to New Orleans. Why Carolyn and I were blessed with a Bodie/Cait trip is lost to time. It would not be unusual to have a Caitlin trip, but to be able to have Bodie, now thirteen, and Cait, a precocious six, together was pretty cool actually. Carolyn and I decided a trip to Chattanooga's aquariums, a trip we had not made in years, and some cave fun would excite both age groups, and so we planned a getaway. We headed to Chattanooga and spent the day in both the freshwater and the salt water aquariums. As a side note here, if you decide to try Charleston's aquarium sometime, save your money. It does not "hold a candle" to Chattanooga or Atlanta. Anyway, the combination of a cool thirteen-year-old and a somewhat smitten to be with a thirteen-year-old good looking cousin, active, slightly ADHD six-year-old is a fascinating combination. Cait would want to rip through the aquariums one minute and then want to hang back with her cousin the next. Carolyn and I watched with fascination as the two interacted for the first time over an extended period. Cait was a sprite. Bodie exuded confident cool as only a seventh grader can. That night we stayed at a Hampton Suites on the north side of the city and our two charges played in the pool even through the evening was a little cool. Cait anxious to show off to Bodie her abilities acquired from hours at our subdivision pool, and Bodie more interested in the slide and the other boys (and lone girl) at the pool. The next day we headed for Raccoon Caverns just outside the city. I had not been to these caverns since I was a new teacher at Mountain View, and we took the fifth grade to the aquarium (there was only one), the downtown Children's Museum and the caverns on a long day field trip. I think both children enjoyed the caverns. I know they enjoyed them more than when we took the boys on one trip and Cait on another and saw the world famous Ruby Falls … a well-worn and tired cave experience closer in the city. I recall Cait wanting to help the docent as we toured Raccoon, and at one point in particular the docent stopped our small group … us and one other family of four … and pointed out a stalactite formation on the roof of the cave. She asked if anyone could guess what they called it? Cait immediately piped up, "An iguana!" The leader was both surprised and impressed that a first grader would guess this and asked why Cait thought this. That was the absolute wrong thing to do as it opened up Cait to give a lengthy explanation saying "I have been to St. Simons Island many times and my absolute favorite restaurant on the island is a restaurant called *Iguanas,* and they have free ice cream." She further explained that, "I usually got fried shrimp and French Fries or mac and cheeze, but usually I do not have to eat all my dinner when I am with Nana and Pa [pointing at us]. They let me get ice cream no matter what. You can get your ice cream in a cup or on a cone. I usually get mine in a cup because I can get more, and then there is a choice of toppings. I always get the hot chocolate topping and sprinkles, and sometimes put on a few gummy worms, but the ice cream makes the gummy worms hard, and that was not good. And Pa always got the caramel topping. He does not get the sprinkles, although he does like gummy worms … just not on his ice cream." The other family just stood by and smiled. After the caving experience, we had to do some gemstone panning and Bodie, while mildly embarrassed, pitched in and was his usual good sport. And of course, traveling up and back we had to play the license plate game of which Pa is famous. Bodie threw in some new rules like the game started over at the top of each hour and trucks did not count which made the game more challenging and, I have to admit, more fun. Cait was kind of "whatever" about the whole game as she was barely able to see above the window sills of the car and was just learning to read the names of states. Although this does bring to mind an event recently when Cait and I were in the car and we were on Roswell Road (Why? Don't know.) and she says to me, "Pa, what does I O W A spell?" I told her Iowa to which she replied, "Iowa, I win." To which I gave the standard Cait reply, "Not playing." You see Cait, and Carolyn, do not ever play the license plate game … unless they do.

Another big event that year was a Four Boys Trip to New Orleans over Thanksgiving. Jenna and Adam allowed Bryce, now fifteen, and Bodie to skip school on Monday and Tuesday of TG week in order to go with James and me to New Orleans to go to the WWII Museum. When James and I had gone to NO years ago back in '99 and had our world famous Bourbon Street epiphany, the museum was just getting started. Now it had grown up and was totally worthwhile. So on Monday the four of us drove down stopping for lunch at Hooters. This became a must  do if for no other reason than we always got the skinniest and the flattest waitress in the place, and it became a running joke. We stayed at another Hampton Inn (free breakfast!) and on Tuesday we met up with Angela's very, very cool and somewhat eccentric cousin, Nigel Campbell, who lives in New Orleans with his spouse. Anyway, we went to the two museums. There is one for the European Theater of World War II and one for the Pacific. We spent the whole day there, and <u>I</u> had a ball. A proud father and grandfather with his boys.

I was now beginning to realize that these kinds of events … Four Boys, and even Two Boys … were rapidly becoming once in a lifetime events, and I was running out of lifetime. So, I reveled in every minute of our time. I recall the boys at the end of the tours goofing around in the gift shop. They were now old enough that the cheap stuff did not really interest them. Angela's cousin took us to a real NO restaurant and helped us order some real NO food which the boys mostly turned their noses up at. I know they wanted more Hooter's fare. ☺ After lunch we headed to Jackson Square and Bourbon Street just to say we had been and stopped at the French Market at Café Du Monde and had some beignets and coffee. In an *it's small world* incident, James ran into some of his students from Atlanta while we were there. We all headed for the barn to sleep because we were headed for St. Simons the next day. On Wednesday, we got an early start and headed for the coast. What I had not thought about, stupid head, was that the distance from the Mississippi River to the east coast is a tolerable distance … over 600 miles … about a third of the USA … and when you factor in meals and potty breaks it become almost a twelve-hour ordeal. So we got on the road about 8:00 and James and I tag teamed the driving (stopping at Hooter's for lunch) along I-10 and got to the condo in the dark about 8:00 at night. Whew. Anyway, Four Boys made it, and I appreciated and loved every minute of the trip I got to spend with my James, my Bryce and my Bodie … never to be repeated again.

I finished my 15-16 school year with Richard Williamson and decided I did not want another inclusion class. I wanted a "normal" fifth grade class, whatever that was, and so I went to Jessica Appleyard and requested to be released and turn over the inclusion class reins to someone else. I had been doing inclusion basically since Mountain View and wanted a change. Ms. Appleyard agreed. And while we were talking I told her that the 16-17 school year was to be my last year in the harness, but I asked her to keep that to herself. She did. In making the decision to retire, Carolyn and I had an interesting "small world" event. As part of the whole retirement thing we went to a meeting in Dalton at the Dalton High School to meet with TRS (Teacher Retirement System) people. It was like a Wednesday, and we got there and had a good meeting discussing the various ways TRS could distribute funds and in what amounts. After the meeting, we were headed out to our car and James called. He asked, "What are y'all doing in Dalton at the high school?" This was a strange question. Did he have a tracker on our car or was our phone being tracked or just what the heck was going on? As it turned out, James who was now teaching in Gordon County, of which Dalton is part, was at a meeting at the high school that morning and saw what he thought was our white CR-V. He confirmed it was our car by looking at the tires. Long story short – James had left teaching for a period and sold tires and then gotten an engineering degree and worked as a CADD draftsman and then returned to teaching in STEAM in Gordon County – ask James for the full story. Anyway, he confirmed it was us by our tires. I told him we were just discussing TRS options. He wanted to know if I was retiring. I said I wasn't sure. He said, "Dad, you are. If you are so serious you took time off from school to come to Dalton to talk to TRS then your mind is made up." When had my boy become so intuitive? We then laughed about the coincidence of it all, and then Carolyn and I went to downtown Dalton, found some lunch and headed home. And James was right. 16-17 was my last year.

I believe it was that fall of 2016 or possibly spring of 2017 that my first sign of things to come presented itself. I went to the doc in a box one day after school thinking I had a sinus infection or was coming down with something and was hoping that he would prescribe an antibiotic or something. The doctor did not, but he did say I needed to go see a urologist because I had trace amounts of blood in my urine. Humph. Okay, sometime soon I will do that.

Meanwhile my last year teaching was proceeding. Appleyard had moved me to the third grade hall a year before. Why? Not sure, but she had. So I was separated from all the new teachers that had filled in positions on the fifth grade team. Danner was gone and teaching Target. All the others of the old guard were long gone, driven off by SWSNBN and time to retire, and "I've got to do something else." So, I was up on the third grade hall, alone. You know all the signs of why I retired were there for me to see now. People ask me, "Why did you leave teaching?" and I reply, "I did not leave teaching. Teaching left me." As I have said before, I was trained in the "hands on" approach to teaching. That the only way a child really learns and retains anything is to experience it. I did this by Glusabi Pot Ceremonies, Sam Scalene – Agent 003, searching for gold, making string telephones, tie dying tee shirts, 50's Day, 60's Day, learning songs about sinking the Bismarck and the Battle of New Orleans and Snoopy and the Red Barron and the Ring of Fire, Captain

Grid, field trips to Charleston, to Jekyll 4H, to The Atlanta History Museum, to The Center for Civil and Human Rights, by learning to measure perimeter by measuring the perimeter of the school by walking around the outside walls, by separating hydrogen and oxygen and lighting the hydrogen when discussing the Hindenburg, Civil War Bowls and World War II Bowls requiring children to dig information out of books rather than using the internet so they were exposed to what I call "collateral information," by having them learn to write by writing, by having them read both out loud and silently and learning to pull out information, by having them make a family tree even though the information was sometimes uncomfortable, by becoming a Maverick from History in order to walk in someone else's shoes (even though it backfired on me once), becoming an Immigrant even though it was uncomfortable, having a room that looked more like a museum than a classroom and by trying to meet each child where they were and making them want to come to school just to see what old Mr. Morris had up his sleeve for that day. Yes, I was a teacher who believed in learning by experiencing learning and it was fun. By '16-'17 everything was teaching the test, using the computer labs to force feed fast, shallow research and learning reading and writing through the biggest boon-doggle of all time – the Lucy Caulkins reading program. Yes, teaching left me. And in retrospect, I was a sick man physically and did not know it.

I have to close 2016 year with a sad comment. There were two people running to follow Barack Obama as president: Hillary Clinton and P.T. Barnham … I mean Donald Trump. I cannot tell you how much I loathe that man. He is the consummate grifting con artist, and anyone who would vote for him is … well, as P.T. Barnham put it: *There is a sucker born every minute.* And I am sure … I am praying, that by the time you are reading this, history has judged him and the truth has won out. At least I hope so. If not, we are living in a fascist state, and Carolyn and I are living in Canada having renounced our citizenship.

12.

I'm going to lead 2017 with the earth shattering story that I retired from teaching. I asked Jessica Appleyard to keep it quiet, and she did. The end of year approached and everyone got ready for the announcements and plans were made to roast/honor retirees and no word was leaked. And the day came for the honors, and there I was, as part of the committee that put on these affairs (I blessedly have forgotten the actual name of the committee – I ought to remember, I wrote the by-laws governing the damn thing), in the back cutting and serving cake like nothing was happening. So, why, you ask? Well, I guess if my old cohort of Jedlicka and Jones and Scheer and Cooper and Duvall and Fleming and Perry had been there, I would have. I respected them, and they respected me. But most of them had already retired, and I had no use for the fifth grade team that was left. Those left were a bunch of clickety-clacks (teachers who wear high heels that make a clicking noise when they walk down the hall) and think they are all that, who did not want to extend one bit of effort beyond the classroom for the children. Oh, I know Coach Jones would have had a ball roasting me and Richard Williamson would have played along too, but … well, I did not want to be the center of attention from a bunch of people who did not really know me or mean what they would say. So, I just stood down. I hope I do not sound bitter because I am not. I outlined all the reasons I felt teaching left me, and I was/still am good with the decision. In the seven years since I left and the writing of this book, I have not once regretted my decision although my brief quasi-return in 20/21 was a labor of love more than anything.

On the family front, Kimball Amanda Rogers the daughter of Unca' Nelson and Toochie (Marian Louise Morris Rogers) passed away this year. Carolyn and I felt the need to attend the funeral in Nashville representing the Morris family. My father, Col. James Wingfield Morris, who was now 88 and one of the two of his generation of Morrises was just not up to the task of attending. Kimball's mother, Toochie, was also not able to attend as she was now in the Fite Street Nursing Home in Cartersville. So, Carolyn and I represented. Kimball had had many physical problems in her life and her passing was almost a blessing ending her pain. While we were in Nashville, Tennessee, for the funeral, Carolyn and I took the opportunity to visit Carolyn's grandmother Shacklett's old home place. Carolyn's mother, Mildred Virginia Shacklett Lyon, was born and raised in Nashville and her mother, Carolyn's grandmother and grandfather, Orlena and John Shacklett, lived there along with Carolyn's mother's three other sisters and three brothers. I particularly enjoyed this trip down memory lane as I had heard of these places in Carolyn's family tales, but had never seen them. And another fun part of the visit to these "historic" landmarks was that the closer we got to them, the more Carolyn's polished façade slipped. Her accent became more country and her recollections of sleeping on a porch and driving all night to get to Nashville from Marietta and the train trips from the Marietta Station, and Carolyn and her sister Kathy walking to a little grocery store to get Cokes became more vivid and full of details. It was very endearing and revealing even though we had been married forty-four years in 2017. The next day, after the funeral and the visit to Nolensville Road, we made a pilgrimage to The Parthenon. Yep. In Nashville there is a full scale recreation of The Parthenon in Greece. The only difference is this one was not blown up so one can see all the fenestration and beauty that was the original. The one thing I never knew about the Parthenon, that I learned from visiting the one in Nashville, is that there is a gift shop in the basement! Who knew! Carolyn and I went there because we were getting ready to travel again to the Eastern Mediterranean!

That fall we headed out again to the Med. Lordy, I love that part of the world, and I fervently hope to make one more trip there, perhaps with Caitlin, before it is too late. There is no way I can share the experience of our October 1st to October 19th Barcelona Med trip. There is just no way. There is a Christmas present I gave Carolyn hanging in the bedroom titled *Mediterranean 2017* and it chronicles every single day in cryptic notes only Carolyn and I can decipher. It would mean nothing to anyone else, but let me excerpt it and give you a taste our trip. We flew into Barcelona into the middle of a Catalonian strike for independence. When we arrived we were met by a car and driver (very continental – I love doing that). The driver had a black Mercedes van, and we headed off to our "boutique hotel." The driver had directions and everything, but there was only one little problem. The directions took him down this very long alleyway that got narrower and narrower until we reached a point that he had to make a turn and couldn't. Another man came up to him and they "hablaed" in Catalonian for a few minutes and then the driver proceeded to back the van up for about 300 yards in this alley … never touching a mirror or anyone in the alley … before turning on another street. Finally, we got to an intersection of a street and a pedestrian walkway and through hand motions and broken English he let us know the hotel was about 100 yards "that way." I hoped he was right and we got out in the middle of Barcelona's Gothic District and started pulling our luggage along. We saw a lot of this while we were there. Apparently this driver was very busy dropping folks off almost at their destinations! But we found our hotel, Musik … it was in fact "that way." Musik was not quite ready for us when we arrived at about 9:30 AM Spain time so we left our luggage with the Musik and headed off to find breakfast. Right down the street we found a little café and walked inside to a giant television talking about the Las Vegas shootings. We pretended to be from Canada. We were so embarrassed to be from a "shithole country." About 10 we came back to the hotel and they still did not have a room for us. Carolyn found a little back room and napped and I sat down in the lobby and promptly fell asleep. The room was ready about 12:00. In the three days we were in Barcelona, we were immersed in the Catalonian strike for independence as The Market and many shops were closed and as we got tangled up in the peaceful demonstrations all over the city. It was righteous! While exploring we actually found "La Biblioteca" of every Spanish class's lore (¿Dondé esta la Biblioteca?). And we found the Barcelona Disney Store. The black rat is everywhere! We secured for Master Bodie (Bodie Lang Blackwell) a Lionel Messi shirt as Bodie was fourteen and into his soccer phase at Lakeview Academy. And after three wonderful days. we boarded the Brilliance of the Seas and headed off to Cannes followed by Florence and Michelangelo's The David … absolutely breathtaking. In Rome we took the world's slowest express train, think Thomas the Train, from the port to Rome with one destination in mind … St. Peter's Basilica. I (we) felt we had not really seen the cathedral when we were in Rome before what with me being pickpocketed and wanted to invest our time only there. Another opportunity in your life not to be missed is to climb the over 300 steps to the top of the dome of St. Peter's and view Rome. The law is that no building in Rome can exceed the height of the basilica's dome. We stopped in Athens again and adored the Acropolis again. From Athens we were off to Mykonos – my favorite of the Greek Isles we have visited. While on Mykonos I found out two earth shattering facts: 1. The Greeks do not eat lamb on their Gyros and 2. The Mediterranean is COLD! I wanted to swim in the Med, and so I wore my swim suit that day under my pants. When I had an opportunity, I crossed the very pebbly and uncomfortable beach barefooted to the blue Aegean Sea only to find out it was too cold to do any more than wade into your waist and then scamper out! I was expecting a bath water temperature swim in this gorgeous azure water – not! From there we were off to Santorini where we discovered an archeological gem, Akrotiri, another must visit site! It was home to the ancient Minoan civilization that was all but wiped from the face of the earth in 3,200 BC by the volcanic explosion that blew Santorini apart and left the caldera rim one sees today. Our next stop was Malta, and we took a carriage ride around the city of Valetta with Jason and his horse Legend. It was totally worth it. Back "home" in Barcelona at the Musik Hotel, room 55 again, we went exploring again and this is when we saw the Sagrada Familia. Truly it was a high point. Gaudi's creation, the Sagrada Familia Catholic Cathedral, is indescribable. Please, if you do nothing else in your life, go see this wonder of the world. From the blues and greens that wash the church in the morning to the reds, yellows and oranges in the afternoon, your breath will be taken away when you see one of human being's finest creations. We also discovered fantastic underground, Roman ruins that Barcelona rose from. Our last night in beautiful Barcelona, two lovers walked from a favorite restaurant near the Basilica de Santa Maria de la Mar as a cool, light rain blew in and the city cried for our having to leave. We landed in Atlanta at 3:10 PM, got our car and ate at the Cracker Barrel. What a come down. But as MacArthur said, "[We] shall return!"

Another exciting event in 2017 besides the snow and ice storm in early January was Carolyn and Angela and me going down to Atlanta on January 20th to protest Donald Trump as President elect. Our protest walk in Atlanta was in sympathy with The Women's March in Washington, DC. Protests took place in every major city in the United States and on six continents. It seemed strange to me that just eight years before, Carolyn and I were in Washington celebrating Barack Obama, and now we were protesting against the low-life who apparently had been elected thanks to people like The Colonel. C and I could clearly see the coming darkness this man portended, and it was a terrifying vision of a dystopian future that did, in fact, unfold in many ways as we had foreseen. [*Coincidentally, literally as I am writing this section, the DOJ's attorney Jack Smith just unveiled four counts of conspiracy concerning the events of January 6th, 2020, and Trump's efforts to inflame a march on the capital and overturn the election results that elected Joseph Biden.*] Anyway, Carolyn and I got the ball rolling by letting Angela and James know we were going to protest, and we all met down near the Center for Civil and Human Rights. There were signs and bullhorns and flags. Congressman John Lewis came and addressed the crowd. And then we all walked several blocks up to the state capital to protest. It all felt very 1960's and it … felt … GOOD. Little did we know at the time all of the things Donald Trump was going to try to do and would do to stay in power in 2020. And as I write this, Trump is again running for the Republican nomination to be the president and oppose Joe Biden again in 2024. And he is leading the pack of Republican idiots! Unbelievable.

Carolyn and I checked off another of our bucket-list items in August of that year. We

saw a total eclipse of the sun! The path of totality was from northwest to southeast on Monday, August 21st, and it was going to cut its swath of totality just north of Chattanooga, and Carolyn and I decided we were going to be right in its path! The period of greatest duration was going to be just a little north of where we were going to be. We left on Sunday and headed to Chattanooga so we would be right on the doorstep of totality. Our target was to be in place by 11:00 with the beginning of the eclipse starting to be seen about 12:00 somewhere up I-

75 toward Knoxville a few miles above the Georgia line. We got up early after staying at a hotel in Chattanooga. Instead of trying to go back down I-24 to the junction with I-75 and then heading northward, we cut across town to the east in order to join I-75 around the 153 interchange. And we were surprised at the volume of traffic going north like we were for the very same reason we were! It was bumper to bumper, but we had time. I had no idea where we were going except north. We drove and just above the Tennessee Route 39 exit I saw a rest area, but the northbound side of the rest area was already filling up. The southbound side was almost empty. So we blasted up to the Route 30 interchange and turned around. All along I-75 were lighted moveable signs telling drivers to not stop on the interstate to view the eclipse. We headed back south and pulled off at the rest area called Rest Area Athens. We unloaded our cooler with drinks and lunch stuff we had bought and our very important eclipse viewing glasses! By now the first effects of the eclipse were beginning to be seen. It was like a light overcast color seemed to be creeping, very Stephen King-like across the landscape. The overall twilight colors I was seeing were very reminiscent of the movie of King's book *The Langoliers*. It was very eerie. As the eclipse progressed, it became more and more surreal. The day turned to twilight and then evening at noon. The landscape seemed to glow with an otherworldly light. Then the full solar eclipse was upon us. It was like night, but because the edges of the sun were still visible, off in the distance it got lighter. So, night but not quite. It was everything I had hoped it would be and the experience was totally worthwhile. If you get a chance to experience a total solar eclipse, make the effort. The heavens are amazing, and you will not regret a minute of it. And remember, you read it here.

13.

Now, you want to talk about a year, 2018 had it all. I laughed, I cried, I almost died. It was so full I do not really know where to start. I think I'm going to save the scariest parts for the last of this chapter, so you will have something to look forward to. Around March Carolyn got a call from Reverend Alice Rogers. The same Alice Rogers who married Jenna and Adam. Alice had been (and still is) our minister through the years. We followed her as she left Mt. Bethel UMC and was posted at Jackson UMC in Jackson, Georgia. Then she went to a church in Atlanta, and then posted to Emory as a professor. By 2018 she was a PhD, and Alice was tapped to become the District Superintendent in the Gainesville area, and she needed a high powered assistant that "had her back." She called and asked Carolyn if she would fill that role, and Carolyn said yes. We looked into where Carolyn would live in Gainesville because commuting was just too unreasonable. We looked at leases and apartments, but Jenna (Jenna Morris Blackwell) would not hear of it. Carolyn would stay in the downstairs bedroom suite in her home and that was all there was to that. So, Carolyn started working for the United Methodist Church … again. "The more things change, the more they stay the same." Her office was a scary little house at 344 Northside Drive. It is Acuna's Cake shop now. It was the District Super's office, and it was a mess. The lady who had been the "Carolyn" before had been there for years and years and eons and had never cleaned anything … or thrown anything out! Security was nonexistent and the whole place was a little ramshackle … think 1950's funeral home in décor and smell. But that never stopped Carolyn and Jim! We immediately jumped into the challenge. I would come up every so often and replaced all the locks and hardware, repainted the entrance door, rebuilt the mailbox and secured it and "black bagged" tons of out of date "who gives a sh_t" records and useless papers. And don't even get me started on the half basement/crawl space. I know there were bodies buried down there … you know … old preachers the church did not know what to do with and various other stuff. Then there was the weeks long battle with AT&T who provided the phone/internet connection. The connection was spotty at best and AT&T would promise to have someone come out, and so I would go up, and then no one would come and it was a nightmare. It never fully resolved except that to this day I would have two tin cans and string before I would have AT&T 's Death Star associated with our house. There are no strong feelings here … and it has been what … five years? Anyway, Carolyn worked for Dr. Rogers for almost all of 2018, and personally I think she did that just to avoid being at the house for the remodeling.

Carolyn and I decided it was time to spend a little of our money and upgrade the old homestead. We planned on a new kitchen with new appliances, new floors, and new paint throughout. The first piece and the piece that almost killed me was new paint. I'm going to use the first person for all of this because Carolyn was up in Gainesville, and I was point man. So, I contracted with a firm who put on a good front. They were the worst. I got a second tier crew who were not interested in doing the work. I should have fired them the first day. Granted we were doing a lot of work. We were painting over dark stained trim and doors with gloss white, every wall was going to be painted and even the spindles on the stairs were to be worked over. But one evening I came down to the basement, and the idiots had cleaned a brush in the garage, and there was paint all over the floor! Long story short it was a two-week long battle with a four-page punch list. Finally, I just told them to get out. When they wanted a recommendation I told them I would not give them a favorable review, and likewise I would not write a negative review. Just get out of my house. And that was just the paint! The next and slightly overlapping event was the new kitchen. Now THAT was a pleasure. We used Frugal Kitchens and it was the greatest experience from the first meeting with John (the design assistant) to the install. I would recommend this firm to any and every one. Carolyn's design insights of a refrigerator depth cabinet wall with new oven and microwave replacing the crappy counter POS we had to the black subway tile backsplash to the stove top and its vent that actually vented to the outside (!!!) to the granite countertops, the whole experience was as smooth as silk. During one of the final design sessions, we were in the Frugal Kitchen offices with John Gettys looking at finishes on granite. To me, it seems everyone gets polished granite, but it so happened John had a table top in the office, and it was finished what is called "leathered." I loved it, and asked if we could have that finish. He said, "Absolutely." The we particularly enjoyed our day picking out the marble. We went to several places recommended and used by Frugal and found the perfect Brazilian (who knew) gray granite up on I-85. Then we got to go down to de Beer Granite in Tyrone, Georgia one very hot Saturday and inspect our granite right before it was cut and honed. We had new sinks I had picked out and ordered. They are an acrylic/granite combination in black. I picked out and ordered the fixtures for the sink also. I do have to give credit where credit is due, and that goes to Carolyn. I was looking for a super deal on appliances, and Lowe's was having a sale. Well, I had priced everything all over the place, and Lowe's definitely had the best deal going. So, I went and picked out everything I wanted. Now by this time Carolyn had started up in Gainesville so she wasn't here. When she came home over the weekend, we went over to Lowe's, and I showed her everything. She said that she thought we should select everything from the same manufacturer. That had never occurred to me. And, in fact, with my selections all the stainless steels were just a little bit different. So, we changed to Carolyn's much better idea. And, as I said, everything, including the install, was a breeze. Every subcontractor, electrical, HVAC, plumbing, were on time and knew exactly what they had to do and there was no finger pointing or "well, I didn't include that" going on. It was awesome. The flooring contractor was similarly professional. New hardwood floors on the ground floor. New carpet everywhere else. The biggest challenge with the floors – and the painting – was the book shelves. All the books had to be removed and boxed so the shelves could be moved. That was a lot of work, but it got done and the house was now much more modern. It was a solid investment. And considering we'll be here forever, we're pleased.

Throughout all of this – including Caitlin (Caitlin Rose Morris) getting to help place some of the kitchen wall tile – Cait would come, and we would go swimming and she would spend the night and swing and generally just have summertime at Nana and Pa's house. Cait and I adventured one day up to the Etowah Indian Mounds after we had stopped by for the requisite visit with The Colonel. I remember it was a very, very hot day, but that called to my mind all the very hot Cartersville summers I had enjoyed and my visits to the Mounds with my grandfather (Unca' Pete – Marion Wingfield Morris). We went to the museum and saw the skeletons, and then ran out to the mounds and climbed all three starting with the tallest one. When you are up there you can see for miles. Or so it seemed when I was seven like my Cait was that day. After the mounds, we were back to the gift shop for the sacred ceremony of selecting just the right souvenir for the day. You recall when I was little, I selected three styrofoam totem poles I could paint all in a neat little kit. Never mind that the Etowah Indians no more had totem poles than they had automobiles. Those things did not matter back in 1957. Carolyn and I also took Cait to the condo on St. Simons that summer and took her on a Jekyll Island boat ride where she got to sort various sea creatures hauled in with a net. She was not too fond of that particular adventure and enthusiastically reminded Nana and me that, "She wanted to be an ornithologist, <u>not</u> a marine biologist!"

Jumping ahead a little in the year to October, the 22nd to be exact, Aunt Toochie (Marian Louise Morris Rogers) passed away. She was the Mother I never had and loved me and Carolyn like one of her own. Her son Edward Morris Rogers asked me if I would arrange pall bearers for the funeral. Of course I said yes. I included myself, Edward's son and son-in-laws, my son James Lyon Morris. The funeral was held at the First United Methodist Church of Cartersville where Toochie and Nelson had been married and where she had attended church all her life. She is buried in the Morris/Rogers plot in Oakhill Cemetery in Cartersville with her husband Nelson Kimball Rogers. That left my father, The Colonel, as the last of his generation. He was lonely and unknown to us, he would pass away in only two years.

That fall our son James and his wife Angela invited Carolyn and me to join them over Thanksgiving to go with them to Savannah for the holiday. As I recall we had our, what was then normal, TG at the St. Simons condo, and then we went up to Savannah on Friday and Saturday to come home on Sunday. We all stayed at the Hampton Inn down on Bay Street. I think this was the raining Thanksgiving and it had rained so much that the causeway out to Tybee was flooded. But James being James, we just waited a little while and the waters parted for him! We went out and headed for the north end of the island. Cait and Angie and I climbed the lighthouse and memories of Bryce plaintively whining in his little high pitched voice, "Lighthouse Pa," a hundred years before echoed in my ears. Carolyn and James investigated the "fort" that is there adjacent to the lighthouse. After a short walk on the beach and some snacks at the little stand involving sticky cotton candy for The Princess (Caitlin Rose), we all headed back to Savannah. That evening was the event Carolyn and I had been brought to be part of. We took the little ferry boat out to Hutcheson Island where memories of James racing his Honda there maybe eight years or so before still echoed. On the island at the hotel there was a gingerbread house competition and Santa! We took the ferry back and found a place to watch the Boat Parade which is another *must do* if you are in Savannah around TG. All kinds of boats don Christmas lights and all kinds of regalia and compete for prizes as they parade up and down the Savannah River for all of us on the docks. I would caution you to get there early and get a good front row seat. As we were waiting we managed to scramble and get some gyros and the mandatory praline or two as well as popcorn for The Princess. As the boat parade petered out we headed back to the Hampton and got some good seats up on the roof top pool deck to await the fireworks which did not disappoint. Saturday was a day for cruising the shops in the city and just bumming around. That afternoon Carolyn and I took Cait so James and Angela could have a little time to themselves, and we could have our Princess to just us. We had a plan to go to the Juliet Gordon Lowe house. Cait was interested in the Girl Scouts, and this seemed like a perfect time. As we were touring the house with gaggle of little girls we stopped in one room and the lady asked if anyone knew the name Sir Robert Baden-Powell? Everyone looked around and Caitlin's hand immediately went up. The lady seemed surprised and called on her. Cait then addressed the gathered multitude and told everyone, including all the chatty little girls, that he was the founder of the Boy Scouts and had met with Juliette Gordon Lowe and that is where she got the idea to form the Girl Scouts. The lady was floored as were Carolyn and me. Later we asked Cait where she heard that? "In a book I read once." We were impressed. Cait was and continues to be a prolific reader much to Carolyn's pleasure and admiration. We then met James and Angela at a little pub place where they had managed to wrangle

a table. It was a good, good time. And James and Angela were so sweet to include us. We have been back several times but it was never as cool as that first time. Maybe a little scarier, but that is a story for a later time.

So, let's get to the "heart" of the year that was 2018. As I mentioned earlier I had gone to a Doc in a Box and there was blood in my urine. I had visited a urologist and done a second test and it came back clear so I put it out of my mind. Then one day early in the year I had gone to see my father. He had a tool shed kind of building at his home at 17 Forest Hill Drive in Cartersville and the way it was sited it was slowly tilting and sinking into the hole it was built in. Dumb. Anyway he wanted me to "fix it, Jimbo." I went out and looked it over and tried to move a block to make it sit straighter, and a pain hit me in my lower left side. I stopped what I was doing and told Dad it was no use, and that we would have to get some real help for the shed, and then I headed home. When I got home I went to use the restroom. Now I do not want to get too graphic here, but when I peed, it was blood red, and even I knew that was bad. It was time to act. I made another appointment at another urologist and was assigned to a very competent man. We got CT scans and x-rays and ultrasounds, and the verdict was that I had at least one very large stone in my left kidney, and it had to come out … surgically. It was as big as my little finger nail - about a centimeter - which is huge for a stone. On March 16th I went in to Fulton Wellstar in Alpharetta. The first thing they had to do was open a port into my kidney through which the doctor would work. And they did. They had to let the port settle down. So I had a tube sticking out of my back. I slept in the chair downstairs, and nurse Carolyn took care of me. A few days later I went back into the hospital, and he removed the stone … er … rock. Everything went well except he could not get the second stone. The port had to stay open and I had a bag strapped to my leg so the kidney could drain. Excellent. While all this is going on Jenna (Mary Virginia Jenna Morris Blackwell) was awarded 2018 Master in Teaching Award from Featherbone Communiversity for her work in Gainesville and at Lakeview. And while I was a little distracted, I was not going to miss this award's ceremony. Carolyn drove us up to Gainesville, and I was there for my baby girl. So, when you look at pictures with us at the award presentation, and I look a little rumpled, I was. On the 28th the doctor went in again after the second stone and closed the port. Twenty-five years of teaching school and therefore not drinking enough water because you don't want to have to go to the bathroom every five minutes took its toll. And I "paid the piper."

That was Phase One of my 2018 medical misadventures. It seems I saved everything up for one spectacular year. What follows is a note I wrote to the family after my second medical adventure of 2018. This was a 2018/2019 excursion. I have modified the letter a little from its original form to include a little more detail just for this book. You will read the additions for the most part as non-italicized text.

Dear Every Loving Sister and Brothers and Father and Cousins and Nephews and in-laws and caring friends,

I wanted to write you all this brief recap of Carolyn's and my closing escapades of 2018 and initial foray into 2019 relative to me scaring the hell out of everyone. It is not meant as a cautionary tale, but you all have been so kind to heed my wishes and be satisfied with getting your updates as Carolyn and I were able to feed them to you through and with the help of our excellent nurse sister. Thank you Re.

Enough preamble … on Sunday, December 30, at about 1:00 after a very normal morning, I felt a burning sensation in the front of my throat. This did not surprise me. In retrospect, I had been feeling this for the last several months as I worked out at the Planet Fitness on the treadmill. What surprised me was I was not on the treadmill! At Planet Fitness, a pause and drink of water were able to assuage the feeling, so I had a drink, but the expected results did not come. Another sign I now recognize is that several months before I had been cutting the grass in the back yard. Carolyn was in Gainesville working and was not there. Suddenly I had an overwhelming need to lay down and rest. I thought I had fallen asleep right there on the lawn, but now I realize I must have fainted. *Then my chest started contracting like someone had a grip on it … another classic sign. I took two 325 aspirin and hoped. It did not back off. Now the pain was heading up to the top of my left shoulder. Next was nausea although I did not throw up. Carolyn was upstairs working, and I decided it was time to ruin her day. No sense in it just being a bad day for only me!* When I got to the bedroom I was cold sweating and my left hand was on my chest. I told her I thought we needed to go to the emergency room. *Carolyn "knew" exactly what was going on and immediately called 911. She was fantastic. We went down to the living room. I could still walk, and we had a firetruck and EMS at the door in ten minutes. Five minutes later an ambulance arrived. My living room was full of "Chippendale" firefighter boys who were monitoring and giving me nitroglycerine and they were as cool as ice. My good, good neighbor Richard Novotney from across the street was here immediately to lend support and take care of Carolyn.*

After I was stabilized, one of the Chippendales commented, *"Some people will do anything to not have to take down their Christmas tree!"* I was loaded in an ambulance and taken to Kennestone Hospital. I did not even get a siren which to this day I feel gypped about. I think I got a flashing light, but I am not sure about that either. What a crap deal. Anyway *by about 2:30 I was at Kennestone Hospital, and they had me "under control."* The ER Doctor on duty, Dr. Ahuja, who ultimately became my cardiologist, attended me. *The initial scenario presented was we would have a stress test, cardiac catheter me and maybe a stent. But by 5:30 we had determined through* some tests and *a cardiac catheterization procedure that* I had in fact had a heart attack, and that *I had 3 and possibly 4 of my main cardiac arteries 95% blocked, and we were headed to triple or possibly quadruple open heart bypass surgery.* There was to be no easy fix for this boy. It's that old saying I heard from The Colonel all my life: "Any job worth doing is worth doing well" and "Polish the heel as well as the toe. (The Colonel was a big Saturday night shoe polisher.) *So, I was admitted to the hospital and was attended to by a staff of doctors with most of the heavy lifting being done by the nurses of Blue Five* — the floor and wing of Kennestone — especially my mostest favoritest nurse, Nurse Brittany McAllister. I convinced Carolyn to not to try to spend the night with me … that was a first — I had been trying to get her to spend the night with me for over forty-five years! … but to go home and try to rest. She eventually agreed over strong objection. But each morning she was right back at my side by 7:00 AM. *I was put on the surgical rotation, and we thought that we would have surgery on Wednesday, January 2nd.* No surgeries were to be done on New Year's Day (thank goodness). I recall watching the New Year's fireworks celebrations coming up from the Square in Marietta from my window. My room had a beautiful view of Kennesaw Mountain and several times my mind drifted to children and grandchildren and climbing that hill. The January 2nd surgery fell through. The *doctors had an "emergency" come into the hospital, and I was bumped to Thursday (1 / 3).* I was told that being bumped was a good thing as I was stable enough to be able to wait. *At about 11:00 on Thursday I was taken back to surgery and for about 5 hours a team led by the diminutive Dr. Luu worked on me. I was back in the Cardiac ICU with reports of everything going great ... very minimal time on the heart lung machine,* no donor blood needed, *and 4 bypasses successfully in place with no permanent damage to my heart.* If you want to know about those five hours of surgery and term in the Cardiac ICU afterward, you will need to talk to Carolyn. I got nothin'. But I do recall one event just before I was released from Cardiac ICU. My nurse attendant, Nurse Tim Cable, was standing by my side as was Carolyn when the doctor on duty came by with a gaggle of Interns and Residents. She asked how I was and I said I was fine giving credit to Nurse Tim Cable. Then she asked if I needed anything. Being a smartass I said, "Yes, could all of you do Doctor poses for me?" This is from a commercial on the television. She, the lead Doctor, looked confused, the Interns and Residents got it right away, then it dawned on the Doctor. She smirked, smiled and off they went. I was obviously feeling better. Late *on Friday, January 4th,* I was back in my room. Getting my pain meds balanced was a trick, and I had a couple of terrifying dreams while they got everything where it should be. The worst was the first night. I tried to sleep in the chair sitting up which was most comfortable for me, but in the middle of the night I saw haunting faces coming out of the walls and swirling around me like in the Indiana Jones movie when they opened the Arc of the Covenant. We determined I was allergic to Oxycodone.

And running up my chest is a scar where they glued me back together ... no stiches for me. *They had me up and walking and by Sunday, January 6th, we were taking chest tubes out and discussing possible hospital release on Monday. Sunday afternoon I was walking 4 to 6 laps around the cardiac wing.* On one lap, a pair of nurses were following Carolyn and me ... me in my little open back gown ... as we made our rounds and one of them commented on my beautiful calves. Of course this led to a whole Barbie dress-up explanation. *Late Monday I came home. My son James drove Carolyn and me.* There would be no driving for me for about six weeks. During that time, I was to attend rehabilitation classes which were mostly walking on treadmills. By the end of January, I was setting the pace in the class and wanting to quit. Dr. Ahuja checked me out and gave me a green light to leave that program. Dr. Ahuja said because I was in such good shape coming into this experience, my recovery time was going really quickly. Today, in 2023, I am still walking four to five miles a day, sometimes more, almost every day. I never want Carolyn to go through anything like that again.

In retrospect the precursors of this coming problem were there, I just could not see the forest for trees. I was slowing down, naps during the day that were uncharacteristic, the throat burning, and I wasn't eating as I should. The doctors all told me, "You can eat right, not be diabetic, keep your weight reasonable, exercise and keep your stress down, but all of those go out the window when it comes to genetics. Genes can overrule all of the other factors." Given my father's heart problems and my paternal grandfather (Unca' Pete – Marion Wingfield Morris) and his heart problems and eventual death from congestive heart failure, I was doomed from the day I was born. It just took sixty-eight years to catch up with me. So, that was the gist of the letter and my New Year's celebration welcoming in of 2019 … which was a much better year, but now you know why Carolyn's hair is a beautiful silver gray.

14.

As I look over my notes for 2019, it seems that other than Carolyn's and my trip to Alaska, everything is children and grandchildren. We took the year easy, as I got back on my feet. We took Catlin to Fernbank one day. I recall it was pouring down rain that day. I mean buckets and buckets, but we had a good day. Another adventure was of my cooking up, we took Cait to Birmingham for a couple of days, and it ended up being an adventure and a half! When we arrived in B-ham we headed to check in at the Embassy Suites. Now normally this chain is exceptional. We had stayed at Embassy Suites before numerous times before cruises and had great breakfasts that were made to order! So, what could go wrong? Well, everything. First check in was a mess. As we stood in the long, slow line … which gave us time to look around and see the uncleaned dishes from lunch still on tables, we ran into a friend from Lakeview Academy, Rena Millwood, which was cool. After checking in, we headed to the room. Caitlin wanted nothing more than to go to the indoor pool. So, we headed there and Carolyn unpacked in the cool. Well, the room being cool was the only thing nice about the room. There were unidentified stains on the bed linen, something on the wall, and the floor was also stained with something that looked like chocolate. Meanwhile, Cait and I were at the beautiful, luxurious indoor pool. The water was a sickly green and cloudy. The room stank of chlorine as if someone had tried to shock the pool into clarity. I was literally afraid Caitlin's hair would either come out white from the chemicals or her hair would just come out! The pool was crowded with all kinds of out of control children and parents who could care less. So, we went back up to the room pretty quickly where we ran into a very distraught Carolyn. And we made the decision immediately to get out of there. As C and C packed up what little stuff Carolyn had unpacked, I headed down to do battle with the front desk. Which ended up being no battle at all. They apparently knew what a dump they had on their hands and refunded all our money on the spot. I handed over keys, and the three of us were homeless in Birmingham. After some internet browsing, we ended up somewhere down near the University of Birmingham. I think we stayed at a branch of Hilton for some reason. It was a new place and the only place to eat nearby was a Chili's. There was an IHOP but when we walked in the place was a mess and the teenagers working there were all sitting around not even trying. We left there too. Our first target was the McWane Science Museum. You know what? We may have even gone there before we tried to check in at the Embassy Suites … oh well, it doesn't matter. The museum was awesome! When you first walk in there was the bed of nails. Cait wanted no part of it, but after C and I laid down she was

all about it. There was the electricity exhibit with the giant Van de Graff machine to make your hair stand up. Cait loved the shark and ray touch tank, the chaotic pendulum, giant levers, and the tightrope traveling cart. The bubble room and the dinosaurs were quick hits as, "The bubbles were 'baby stuff,'" and "We have seen all these dinosaurs before," intoned the well-traveled Princess. The same was true with the itty bitty magic city. "All baby stuff." The science on a sphere fascinated her, but her mostest favoritest was being an on-air weather person. She stood in front of a green screen and watched herself on camera trying to point to the right place at the right time. The ocean journey and river journey were also, "Boring … the ones in Chattanooga is so much better." Of course we had to stop at the cool stuff store, but I have no recollection of what The Princess selected. It must have been very cool though! The next day, after dinner at the Chili's again, was the Birmingham Zoo, and what I remember the most about it was it was "hot as Billy blue blazes" (another quaint Southern saying that I don't know what it means but has been around the Morris family since forever). And we saw all the requisite zoo animals, but Caitlin riding a camel stands out in my mind above all. And again we saw every animal you would expect and a few that we were supposed to see but were hiding from the heat somewhere in the cool of their enclosures. The gift shop was an important stop near the end, but neither Carolyn nor I can recall exactly what she chose, but I do recall it was a bargain. Seriously, it was like a big red fox or something, but it was on sale at a ridiculously good price, and we were able to snag it much to The Princess's glee. I do not remember what she named it. Probably something like "Foxy Three Moon." I do remember being with Bodie once, probably at the Chattanooga Aquarium, and be bought a stuffed otter and named it "Ottie." My grandchildren are brilliant. The next morning, Sunday morning, I wanted Cait to have her liberal dose of history while we were there. Right before we had left to go to Birmingham I made sure she had learned about the four little girls who were killed in the 15th Street Baptist Church bombing in 1963, and the Civil Rights marches and the terror that Theophilus Eugene "Bull" Connor inflicted on the blacks in the 1960's including the May 2nd and 3rd, 1963, fire hosing and using attack dogs on children during the Children's Campaign. This incident was centered in a park diagonally across from the church. I wanted Cait to see the church and the park and visit the museum that is there. Well, the museum was closed that weekend, and we had to settle for seeing the church and where the bomb was placed and walking around the park and seeing the art and memorials to that infamous day. And then, C and C had both had enough of me … of history … of Birmingham, and we headed for home … with Foxy.

Carolyn and I visited Blue Ridge, Georgia, one Saturday to see an art show they were having downtown. We rolled in looking for a place to eat and discovered the Circle J Restaurant. Yes, I know … unfortunate name, but it was a good place to eat. It was a walk in and order your stuff and then they bring it out to you. We both got steaks and they were tasty but of the quality you would expect in a converted Sizzlin' Steak House

The thing that tickled Carolyn and me was the cake lady. A lady came around and asked us what kind of cake we wanted. Desert was included in the price. And apparently she cooks all the cakes, so she told us what the choices were, we decided and she scurried off and magically, our choices appeared. After a delicious lunch we went downtown and scoped out the art. Let's just say it was interesting. And while downtown we looked into the Scenic Blue Ridge Railroad which leaves Blue Ridge and goes up to Copperhill, TN/McCaysville, GA, stays a little while and then returns. Its four hours or so all together. So, we cook up a plan to take The Princess on this once in a lifetime excursion. We buy the tickets and everything. It occurs to us that McCaysville is the town that Caitlin's other grandparents, Angela's mom and dad, Mana and James Swope, have their cabin. The plot now thickens! Over the next several weeks, we get in touch with them and find out that the day we are planning to take the train, they are going to be in McCaysville! So, the day comes to take Cait, and we head up to Blue Ridge. And, of course, it is hotter than … well, it is hot and of course Pa, me, decided the best experience would NOT be to be cooped-up in the air conditioned train car! Of course not! We (me) opted for the open, fresh air experience as we railroaded through the Blue Ridge Mountains following the Toccoa River. So there we were, sitting in the heat waiting for the train to start and the ladies start whining. And the only thing that will placate them is a cold lemonade which Pa gets off the train to get. Anyway, after much too long (according to the women) the train finally starts to move and the air is a blessing … as is the silence.

We chugged along enjoying the trees and lush vegetation. Quite by accident we had chosen the side of the train that looked over the landscape and not the side that looked into the hillside. It was a kind of neat ride. You see, I have never really taken a real train ride, and it is on my bucket list, so any train ride is kind of cool to me. Finally, after about an hour we pull into beautiful McCaysville right on the Georgia Tennessee border. In fact, the border line goes right through McCaysville which is kind of interesting … where do you pay taxes? What about police and fire? Anyway, we get off the train and head toward town, all the while Cait suspects nothing. There was still a little bit of ping pong ball in her, and if for whatever reason Nana and Pa wanted to end up here, it was okay with her. She was sure there is ice cream here somewhere, and then, out of nowhere her other grandparents appear as if by magic! It was kind of a cool moment. Cait does a good job of balancing her affection between the two sets of grandparents, and we both dote on her embarrassingly. Carolyn and I are growing to love Mana and James. They did, after all, take Caitlin to Disney World and saved us from having to do it, so they are pretty special in our book. So, the big surprise was pulled off! We all went to a little Mexican place the Swope's knew, and then we got to see the famous cabin which really is beautiful. It overhangs a flowing creek … well, really it is bigger than a creek, but I wouldn't call it a river. But it was pretty cool anyway. Mana had gotten a cheesecake, but we had a train to catch, and so we all headed back to the station. We said our thanks and goodbyes and rumbled south toward Blue Ridge. The ride back was a little buggy as we had to ride on the uphill side of the train, but The Princess discovered the train car with the candy bars and whatnot so she was a pretty chill camper. I stood at the back of our train car where the air was flowing a little more. Carolyn held onto Cait for dear life. We rolled into town right on schedule, and then we trundled home with a tuckered but happy Princess and two pleased grandparents.

That summer we also took Cait to St. Simons again. She was getting to be a real beach bunny. We had started a ritual with her second or third visit to the beach in that we would buy a big Jug 'O Cheese Balls and take them out for the sea gulls. And every single time since then we had done that. It does not matter if it is Tybee or St. Simons or where, the Jug 'O Cheese Balls was mandatory. Princess Caitlin would become the Queen of the Gulls. She would toss handfuls into the air and the gulls would swoop and grab them in midair to Cait's delight, or chase the orange nuggets down the beach as the wind blew them along. After a few minutes the birds would rush down to the surf to "cleanse their delicate palates" and then rush back into the fray to Cait's immense delight. Cait would become quite concerned if there was a little gull or other beach bird that the bigger birds would chase away, and she would try to make sure the little ones got their share too. Of greatest concern was "One Leg." Through an accident or birth defect, a one legged gull would show up. This concerned the future ornithologist Cait tremendously, although it did not seem to concern the bird in the slightest. One Leg would hop around chasing the Cheetos with the best of them occasionally knocking the

other gulls out of the way with its little crutch. We never saw any gulls with canes. And we never saw any with walkers or wheelchairs. I guess their health insurance does not cover any of that. At any rate, for years Cait fancied her lifetime calling was to be an Ornithologist. One Halloween she was even a Red Tailed Hawk, and another Halloween she was a Snowy Barn Owl (or something like that). Her mommy, Angela Dawn Swope Morris, is an amazing costume designer as you will soon read about. I will be fascinated to see if Caitlin Rose Morris does in fact become an ornithologist!

While we are on the subject of St. Simons, Caitlin's favorite restaurant, hands-down, without a doubt, no question, would eat there every single day – in fact, when she and I took our trip all by ourselves, we did eat lunch and dinner there every day – was *Iguanas*. I have mentioned this place before when Cait was in a cave, and if you ever find yourself headed out to the St. Simons pier on Mallery Street, and you find yourself at the corner of Mallery and Lord Avenue. Stop in at *Iguanas*. Their food is average, but their FREE ice cream bar is a Caitlin reason for living! Carolyn and I even bought her an *Iguanas'* hoodie for Christmas which she still wears. As I mentioned before, The Princess used to choke down a mandatory minimum amount of lunch, usually heavy on the French fries or mac and cheese, in order to be allowed to hit the ice cream bar. I guess it was just the thought of all the ice cream just flowing out of the machine into cones or cups, as much as you could eat, with piles and piles of sprinkles is all that really matters to when selecting a gourmet dining establishment. I will have to remember that the next time Carolyn and I are in Paris.

2019 was the year Bryce graduated from Lakeview Academy High School, and what a graduation it was! The mega event started with us meeting his Anna. She was graduating with him. Oh, we had seen Anna Grace Wylie before in prom pictures and at a party at Toby and Paula Blackwell's home, but this evening was the first time we really got to know her, and what a lovely lady she is. She is poised, well-spoken, accomplished and just a beautiful young lady. (And let me add that Bryce and Anna will be getting engaged to be married in just a few weeks on September 1st, 2023. Carolyn and I wish them love and happiness all the days of their lives.) But, back to Bryce's awards. Bryce got the *Golden Lion Award* for playing three sports and maintaining outstanding academic status, the *Crumley Cup*, and *The Senior Award* recognizing his athletic achievements over four years, then on another occasion there were the academic awards which he garnered. The actual graduation day was a classic Southern affair. The gentlemen in white tie and tails and the ladies all in virginal white. Lordy mercy, what an amazing grandson!

The Colonel had his 95th birthday that year. It was to be his next to the last birthday. How fortunate we are that we cannot see into the future. Rusty (Brian Meroney Morris), Re (Mary Louise Morris Spicher Bramble), Bill (William Cranston Morris) Carolyn and I were there. A friend of Rusty's, Jan, came also. Jan was Rusty's first wife's (Jill's) sister. I am sure my gift was a bottle of Chivas Regal Scotch Whiskey, my father's gasoline of choice. That stuff was the most expensive liquor I have ever bought and never drunk any of. It tastes like … well, gasoline. My brother Rusty had moved back to Cartersville from Dallas, Texas, a year or so before and moved in with Dad. Rusty would work in the day and come home and cook Dad's dinner and watch over him at night. I cannot compliment Rusty enough for doing this. Near the end, Rusty would actually bathe Dad and perform other necessary cleanliness duties – God Bless you, Rusty. During the day, Dad had Malcolm Cooley, the grown son of Glenda Cooley, Dad's housekeeper, come every day and stay with him during the day. Malcolm would prepare his lunch and chauffer Dad around town to pay bills, get haircuts, grocery shop and go to the dry cleaners.

It was around this time that Re and I decided it was time to take my father's car keys away. He had had a couple of run-ins with the Cartersville police about his driving and bunged his car up a little, and we just got worried and decided it was time. One Saturday, we both met at Dad's house at 17 Forest Hill Drive, SW, and sat down with Dad. I have to say he took it remarkably well. I believe it was almost a relief to him even though one of his loves in his life was automobiles. That may be where I get it and my son, James Lyon Morris, gets it. So, with Malcolm and Rusty around, Dad's loss of keys was no real hardship. It was also around this time that I took over Dad's finances. He had made a few check book errors and overdrawn his account, and Dad and Re and I decided it was time for Dad to let that day to day money management chore go. I can tell you that forensic accounting someone else's finances is difficult … my father had not balanced his check book in a couple of years … this is what led to the overdraw. In the end things just work out the way they are supposed to I guess, because no matter how big a pain it was at the time, I was very glad I was familiar with Dad's finances a year later. My father's world was shrinking almost daily. I would visit him every couple of weeks to pay bills, and he and I would drive around Cartersville and up to Oak Hill Cemetery. I would trim the family plot edges with clippers where my mother, Mary Corinne Wofford Morris, my "Pa," Dr. William Earl Wofford, his wife known as "Mom," Mary Louise Meroney Wofford, my Uncle Bill, William Earl Wofford Jr., and Uncle Bill's Wife, Doris Virginia Whitfield Wofford, are all buried, and then I would walk with him as he would use his walker to slowly walk up and down the paved areas. In cold weather he would wear his brown bomber jacket and Army baseball cap. I can see him now struggling up the slight incline in his Velcro strapped "running" shoes with his walker clicking along. Me at his elbow ready to help if he stumbled, but not wanting to be so close he would feel like a … well, feel like an old man. It was a male pride thing I was sensitive to. I have his bomber jacket in the living room closet now. I wear it occasionally. It is the only article of clothing of his I have to remember him by. As he and I walked, we would talk about this and that. After the cemetery we would go to the Scott's Walk Up Bar-B-Que place at 206 North Tennessee Street in Cartersville. We would each get the chili dog special, two chili dogs, chips and an iced tea. He would get his chili dogs with raw, chopped onions on his dogs, and as long as he was eating that, I knew he was alright. We would eat there very occasionally … Dad did not like the ambient noise due to his hearing aids … so mostly we would bring the hot dogs back to his house and sit at his little round breakfast table where he had probably eaten thousands of breakfasts, lunches and dinners with his wife. Where for seven years Dad had bought a new red rose every few days and put it in a bud vase to remember her, and we would sit and eat our dogs and talk … sitting amongst his memories. I kind of even got a taste for cold chili dogs. But finally, in the cemetery and there at the table, I want to think the two of us were actually talking to each other and not just talking at each other. I would like to believe that in those final years; some kind of a tiny bond was developed although neither of us could admit it. Dad would ask me questions like if all the moving around he made the family do with his career in the Army had hurt us children? I lied and told him no. He was too old for me to confront him with my truth. I went on and said I thought the moving had made us more adaptable and worldly. It had actually. That much was true. And I can tell you I would not be the man I am today if my life had been any different … but still, that sword cuts two ways. And you know what? Right now … tonight … writing and recalling … I sort of miss my father

... perhaps after so many pages of writing there is emotional progress ... perhaps too little ... definitely too late ... but progress none the less.

Carolyn and I took our mandatory old age trip to Alaska, and really, it was pretty neat. For our trip we started when we flew to Seattle. We stayed at a place named, of all things, The Mediterranean Inn which was complete with paintings in the lobby of the Italian countryside! That first evening we found we needed a hair dryer. "Didn't you pack it?"

"No, I thought you packed it."

"Well, I didn't, and I remember telling you I did not have room and could you please pack it and you said you would."

"I do not remember that at all, and I did not pack it."

☺ So, we walked up the street to a CVS and bought one ... and some beard balm for my now luxurious moustache and beard. Then, for lack of a better choice, we cozied into a little burger place and got a hamburger even though our tummies said it was time for sleep, not burgers. That night we slept with the window open – unheard of in August in Atlanta – letting in the cool maritime air and listened to the gulls arguing and the noises from the ships in the sound.

The next day was our adventuring day. For breakfast I found a cool little hole in the wall coffee and pastry place, and then we did the whole tourist thing. We walked over to the Space Needle through a beautiful, lush park and went to the very top of the iconic 1960's structure. It was built for the 1962 World's Fair named "The Age of Space." And along with the needle they built a really cool monorail to take you downtown. So, after a ride to the top and many selfies of us, we jumped on the train and headed to the must see tourist destination that is the Pike Place Market. Picture Walmart on steroids. After wandering aimlessly through racks and racks of everything from snow globes to snow cones, from tee shirts to golf shirts we found our way out of the maze and down several flights of stairs to the Puget Sound water front. There, we were looking for one restaurant in particular recommended by Jenna and Adam Blackwell (daughter and husband) ... Ivars. A renowned local eatery serving fish. It was a little early for lunch, but we were still adjusting to west coast time, so we opened the place. We ordered from the overpriced menu and ate a delicious filling lunch of so-so food. I think Ivars, like Captain Anderson's in Panama City, is resting on its laurels and is known now for its nautical ambience and reputation rather than its food. Anyway, with tummies full we perused the water front and saw the Ferris Wheel and the boats and young adults whose lives were being wasted on drugs. That was so sad, but every place has its lost people. Running out of steam, we finally scrambled up some very steep stairs and through the market and made our way back into the city, found the monorail again and were whisked back north toward our hotel. After a nap, we were hungry. I found a pizza place nearby and got us a pizza, and we headed up to the roof top patio on the hotel. There we ate pizza and drank beer ... well, I had a beer and Carolyn had a sugar free ginger ale ...and we watched the sun set into the mountains on the other side of Puget Sound. The hotel had a shuttle to take us over to the Royal Caribbean docks and our ship, The Ovation of the Seas. With all our paperwork in order, we were sitting in the Windjammer (the "Jammer") buffet with our carry-ons and with plates and plates of food in no time. Around 2:00 our balcony room was ready and we headed off. All of our luggage arrived except one piece. We asked the cabin attendant, and he said we had to go down to the hold and see the security people! Oh Lord, what have we done wrong? We took the elevator to Deck 1. Nobody goes to Deck 1 unless you are disembarking or going to the brig! We got off the elevator and had to cross over "Broadway," the main artery running the length of the ship where all the real backstage action takes place. We walked into a cavernous room full, and I mean full of luggage. A serious security man asked us to pick out our bag. We located it, and he informed us that the hair straightening iron was **not** allowed. They would hold it, and we could come get it when we disembarked. We said, "Yes sir. Sorry sir. Thank you, sir!"

We grabbed our bag and ran for the elevator! Actually, we walked slowly and confidently so as to not garner too much attention and get shot, or have someone yell, "Get on the ground!"

When we got back up to our cabin, we tried to look casual and nonchalant so no one would say, "Eeeeeew, y'all are criminals!"

After that, somehow the captain managed to undock the boat and get us headed out of Puget Sound without Carolyn's or my help, and we were on our way to the famed, not-to-be-missed Alaska, but Carolyn and I were on a secret mission. We had a day at sea as we headed for the first destination. When you do a not-to-be-missed Alaska cruise you never really get "out to sea." One kind of stays in an intercoastal waterway ... at least our cruise did. On each of our cruises I get up one morning and catch a sunrise or two. There is something magical, certainly Zen and religious to me about watching the earth's movement allowing our closest star to rise as if by some divine intercession out of the sea on the horizon and explode its streams of light into the early morning clouds and warm this tiny, blue, insignificant ball of confusion. In my hundreds of pictures of this event, I have witnessed this celestial display with a bunch of my beautiful fifth graders gathered on a Jekyll Island beach, in the Caribbean at various times including the winter solstice and the summer solstice and on New Year's day, in the Mediterranean twice, the Outer Banks of North Carolina, soon over Paris and London, and that morning an Alaska sunrise as it peaked over the mountains of Canada and spilled onto our little Ovation or as the maître d' in the Jammer called it, "The O'ation." Some of my best captures are on the wall in the bedroom. I realize all of them are destined for "the black bag" but for right now, they give me peace and solace.

The next morning, we docked in Juneau. The capital of the great state of Alaska. It kind of sits next to the water in the V of two mountain ranges, and it looked very late 1800's to me. To be brutally honest, I was not really that impressed. Sort of like when we cruised into the port in Crete with the Russian missile silos ... just not that breathtaking. But, I am always game for a new place, and we got off the ship and headed into town on our secret mission. Looking around as we walked down the main street into this almost "cowboyesk" town, I could almost feel transported to a bygone era if it were not for all the shorts-wearing, white-legged tourists wandering aimlessly around. We knew it had to be here somewhere. We just had to find it, so out onto main street we ventured, and it wasn't long before we spotted it ... a marijuana shop! Yep, our mission in Alaska was to try marijuana. Neither of us had ever done this before. In college, as I have said, to be caught would mean no license and no future. Later it would mean no teaching credential for me, but now we had nothing holding us back, so we ventured up to the shop front. A person behind a pass through window wanted to see our driver's licenses before he could "buzz us in." Once inside we were strangers in a strange land. There were pipes and bowls and shirts and hats and every imaginable thing you could use with pot. While I looked around in amazement, Carolyn seemed right at home. A young man sensing two old people who were lost offered to help, and I immediately confessed we had no idea what we were doing. He smiled the knowing smile of a person who has heard this refrain over and over. We explained we wanted edibles and that was all we knew. So he started explaining about sativa and indica and blah, blah, blah … then he suggested a small package of five, five milligram key lime gummies. And we said, "Okay." The price seemed too high (pardon the pun) for what we were getting, but I had no idea what it would cost. Today we are much more discerning pot buyers.

I get out my credit card and am immediately informed this is a cash only transaction. And Carolyn, somehow already understanding this, was prepared and whipped out the required bills. The man also explained we had to be at least fifty yards away from the shop before imbibing. He also told us that it would take about thirty minutes for us to feel anything so don't rush and eat them all too fast. As we walked out into the bright light of that Alaska morning, I had the same feeling I did in college when a bunch of us Southern Tech guys would stumble out of an X-rated theater in Atlanta … yeah, that too had happened. Anyway, you just knew everyone was eyeballing you and judging you and saying to themselves, "Yep, I knew it. Pot-heads." We made our way to a little park and ripped open the package and each took one of the little gummies. We stood there … nothing. We had tickets to ride the incline railroad car (just like Lookout Mountain in Chattanooga) up to a museum and theater, so we started making our way in that direction … feeling nothing. After the requisite thirty minutes we were still just standing there feeling ripped off. So … we each took another "hit" and kept wandering toward the incline rail car place. We got there and went in with our tickets in hand stood in line. As we stood there reading the posters and various warnings and information I started feeling funny. I started feeling like I had just had four quick glasses of wine. I turned to Carolyn, and when she looked at me, her pupils were as big as dimes! I got close to her and said, "We're wasted!" She giggled and said back, "We're wasted!" Then the effect really started to roll over each of us. We really were "wasted"! Well, then the trick became not to look "wasted." You know, how to not look drunk when you are drunk, and you are out in public. That was what we were trying to do, all the while laughing and giggling at everything. We got on the car for the ride up and stood near the window holding onto the rail for dear life. Now, mind you this was not some open air contraption. It was totally enclosed and safe as could be, but we were "wasted" so none of that mattered. We finally got to the top and still trying to look normal, we made our way into the little room that counted for the museum. Attached to it was a much, much larger room that was the gift shop … naturally. Anyway, there was a theater that promised to tell the story of the indigenous peoples of the area, and we both thought (as best we could) a short movie in a darkened theater was just the right thing for us, so in we went. We got seats on the second row and settled in ready for a calm, interesting National Geographic-like movie of the history of the natives of Alaska. What we got instead was a live performance of a Native Americans singing and chanting and … God forbid … banging drums … banging drums over and over and over … continuously for what seemed like hours. The only break I can remember is when Carolyn looked at me, and we started giggling like two little school girls. Really the show was only about thirty minutes, but it really did seem much longer! When they were finally finished, C and I looked at each other and started laughing again. We had to get out of here. We headed off to the tram car to get a ride down the hill. When we were in the far too long line, we both needed some water or something, so I reversed course and made a beeline to the concession stand still trying not to appear stoned. Naturally there was a family man in front of me ordering like seven drinks, and three sandwiches, five bags of chips and two ice cream cones which the single little girl running the stand had to make by hand, and I don't know what-all else, but it was taking far too long. I looked up the corridor toward the tram and saw Carolyn getting closer and closer, and then the time was up! I ran up the hall toward her just as she was ready to board the car. I jumped in and we broke up laughing as the tram slowly inched down the mountainside. At the bottom, we almost literally tumbled out of the building onto the central patio area in front of the tram building, and Carolyn came face to face with a huge, white wolf! Yep, I kid you not … a giant, as tall as she was, white, arctic wolf (she calls it a rabbit – she was stoned) … standing there on two legs! She almost literally fell into the animal's arms, and I got several pictures to prove it. And there we

were, two grown up adults laughing like children as the wolf mugged for the camera with my beautiful wife. When I was done shooting, Mr. Wolf (I'm guessing it was a male person inside the beautiful costume … based on the way the wolf was pawing Carolyn) got a healthy tip in his little box. It was probably way too big a tip, but neither Carolyn nor I were entirely sure the wolf was even there, so the tip may or may not have been real either! After all of that, we decided it was time to call it a day and make our way back to the O'ation. As we boarded the ship and had to pass by all the security personnel, we were sure one would yell, "Get on the grooound!" but they didn't, and we did manage to escape back to our cabin and fall into bed. It was good nap. We were still a little messed up at dinner, but we managed to giggle our way through something delicious, and then we crashed for the night.

Our next big adventure came in Skagway. We decided to take a train up to, well, I'm not sure where, White Pass I think … but we went. My second train ride was an old timey train, and it chugged and puffed its way up the route that miners used to have to take on their way to the Klondike gold fields. It was an interesting ride that seemed to take forever to get up to the top, and then we turned around and headed back down on a hang-onto-your-hats rail ride that had the countryside literally whizzing by our coach. Then we were back. I keep trying to have a meaningful train ride, and they all seem to be a kind of a disappointment. Back at the ship, we strolled into town and browsed around, but could not find a single thing we could not live without except a wolf hat for Caitlin (Caitlin Rose Morris).

We were kind of jazzed because we had two new and novel experiences coming up, and we were really looking forward to them. The next day we were to see a real, live glacier! I think it must have been Glacier Bay National Park and Preserve. We were to see it in the morning with the sunlight glinting off of this spectacular event of nature. We started sailing up what I will call a fjord like bay. As we were sailing toward the glacier we started seeing icebergs that had calved off the glacier. Actually they were baby-bergs, but that was exciting enough for me! I wanted to put on my life jacket and run up to the main deck a' la Titanic, but Carolyn drew the line there. She wanted no part of me being that big of a fool, so I relented. But we were very excited to see our first glacier, and we scrambled up to the top deck to view this magnificent natural phenomenon. We got there, slightly out of breath due to our anticipation, and there it was. The walls of the canyon on each side of us converging in the near distance. A real sense of perspective as the walls came together and disappeared into a fog bank! A dense, white, billowy cloud spread before us completely hiding the glacier. Awesome! Check that one off our bucket list! The captain did everything he could do. He rotated the ship 360 degrees and lingered as long as he could all to no avail. And we had to finally had to leave as another ship was ready to head into the inlet. But we still had one more adventure ahead of us the next day. The O'ation was equipped with a sphere called the North Star that was on a long boom, and it would life up into the air above the ship, and one could view Alaska's magnificence from over a hundred feet above the ship and over three hundred feet above the water. Carolyn and I had scheduled our assent for the final day at sea so as to capture one last exciting event to cap off our cruise. We were all a titter as we arrived at the sphere station and boarded. The twenty-foot diameter clear globe rose majestically from its cradle, and we ascended into the air and then directly into … you guessed it … another fog bank! Check off that item also from our bucket list. Our final port was beautiful Vancouver, British Columbia. Carolyn and I headed inland on another of Jim's famous forced marches to the city. We found a little café for a couple of chai tea lattes and some scones. Fully refreshed, we headed for a church in the heart of Vancouver known for its stained glass and beautiful gothic interior. We found it and were treated to an interesting historical surprise. After his humiliation in World War I and before his rise to be the greatest Prime Minister in British history, Churchill resided for a period in Vancouver and worked as a brick mason. Who knew? But we found a brick in the wall of this magnificent cathedral with his name on it. Pretty neat. After a long hike back, we boarded our boat and then our airplane to return to reality. It had been so beautifully cool in Washington State and Canada and Alaska. We landed in Atlanta and got our bags and headed for the car. It was about 8:30 at night, but to us it was still early afternoon. The airport doors whooshed open, and we were literally slammed with late fall 90° heat of our hometown, Hotlanta. Now this was late in 2019 and poor Carolyn was very, very sick with congestion and fever for several weeks after we arrived back home. We went to the Doc-in-a-Box and they were clueless saying it must be pneumonia or something.

No one was sure. Carolyn and I have decided she had to have contracted a little known virus that the world was to become very familiar with in 2020 – Covid-19.

That Thanksgiving our dear sweet James and Angela and Cait invited Carolyn and me to Savannah again to spend some time with them. Angela decided we would stay out at Tybee Island in a little condo she found, and as a surprise the first night, they brought everything we would need for Pa (me) to make Low Country Boil. I struggled a little with the stove, but finally we got some dinner well after dark. The next day, Friday, was centered around the island and then that evening's boat parade on the Savannah River. It was a beautiful affair as always with Santa bringing up the last float. Saturday we went to the Oatland Island Wildlife Center just off the Islands Expressway. Originally a plantation, it was used for a retirement center for railroad conductors in the 1920's. It was held briefly by the CDC and used as a communicable disease center in the late 40's. Today it is a sprawling open marsh (awesome) and wetlands sanctuary. We spent a beautiful November afternoon traipsing around and seeing up close some of the Center's guests including owls and hawks who were rescued and are recovering. Saturday evening, we had scheduled a ghost tour. I had never been on one of these, and I was really excited to see what it was all about. At the designated 8:30 or so, we all gathered at Madison Square, I believe. We were met by a little, blond haired, cutie-pie SCAD student girl who made up for her youth by being **very** much into the whole ghost tour thing … which was excellent! We started making are rounds of the various sites of note in Savannah as darkness fell around our intrepid little band. Cait (Caitlin Rose Morris – the most beautiful granddaughter in the whole world) was right there in the thick of it soaking up every word. The evening was going along peacefully until we came upon a particular house. I do not recall the story behind it, but a person had been murdered there. We were all standing across the street looking at the house. There were various street lamps on between us and the house so the façade was plainly visible. As I was looking at the house a lady in front of me opened up her camera to take a picture. I glanced over her shoulder and saw something. I looked at the house and then looked at the camera's picture. There was a difference. Now I would not be relating this tale if this was not something that truly disturbed me so bear with me. In the camera's picture, on the right side of the balcony there was a blue glow near the ceiling. I looked up again with my naked eye and saw no such glow. As I was pulling my camera out, I looked at the lady's picture again, and there was definitely a blue orb in the picture that was not visible without the camera. I finally got my camera open and snapped away. I captured it. I showed it to James and Angela and Carolyn and Caitlin, and they were all looking for ways to discredit it … but they knew they couldn't really. It was real. I think the adults were trying to play it down so as to not creep-out Caitlin, but they were not convincing. If you can get ahold of Caitlin, ask her about it. We have discussed it many, many times and she really does not want to believe it, but she does. At the end of the whole ghost walk, the little SCAD girl took from her bag a bundle of sage called a smudge stick. She explained that she would light it and then with her hand draw the smoke around her, and as the smoke drifted into the night it would carry any negative energy with it. She said many people including many native Americans strongly believe in this ritual. She said she

was not that sure about it, but one cannot be too careful, and as long as she has been doing this tour, and she has been ending her tours with the smoke ritual, she has not had any problems. So anyone who would like to come forward, she would help cleanse them. As people looked at each other, I immediately stepped forward. She waved the smoke around me, and I stepped back. I hadn't noticed, but right behind me was my faithful sidekick, Caitlin. The little SCAD girl waved the sage smoke around Cait. I guess Caitlin had seen enough tonight that "better safe than sorry" and "if it is good enough for Pa, it is good enough for me" was a good approach to wrap up her evening.

15.

"It was the best of times, it was the worst of times …" *A Tale of Two Cities*, Charles Dickens. Man, you want to talk about a couple of years with ups and downs. That would be 2020 and 2021. I can tell you they were packed with awesome fun events and things that happened that will crush you. I have said it before; it is good we cannot see into the future. If we could see the future, I think I would have just sat out these two years, but enough preamble, let's dive in.

For those of you reading this who were alive in 2020, you will recall this is the year that the Covid-19 pandemic gripped the world. As of this writing in August of 2023 the WHO puts global deaths at 770 million and United States deaths at 104 million. To put those numbers in perspective, the city of Atlanta's population is about 500,000 … so in the United States about 200 times the population of Atlanta died in the last three years from Covid-19 and its variants. I am not going to pontificate or lay blame, I am just setting the stage … the backdrop if you will, for everything in '20 and '21.

In the early part of 2020 no one was sure what was happening. As I mentioned, when Carolyn and I came home from Alaska via Seattle, Carolyn was sick with something the doctors could not quite diagnose and that we now believe it was Covid. But all the doctors could say was what it was not. As it turned out, once the epidemiologists at the CDC had identified what they thought was going on, i.e. Covid-19, they identified that one of the first major outbreak areas was Seattle, Washington, where Carolyn and I had traveled from late in 2019. Hmmmmmm. Anyway, it was the spring of 2020 before people were told to start wearing masks and to start separating from each other. Then things started shutting down and people started getting scared. Nursing homes were overrun with deaths from Covid. Refrigerated tractor trailers were brought to hospitals to deal with the overflow of deaths. Emergency rooms were swamped. There were not enough oxygen tanks and respiratory machinery for all who needed them. People stopped traveling, going to grocery stores, out to eat, schools started shutting down, and President Trump was useless … or at least more useless than he had been up to this point in his presidency. There were officials in his cabinet who tried to tell the truth and help, but by and large the federal government, beyond the CDC, was paralyzed. The government basically stopped working. Okay, enough, you get the idea.

That spring I got into a battle with Allstate over whether our home needed a new roof due to hail damage. I had three different contractors identify the hail damage and one which stuck by my side and had to meet with Allstate representatives three or four times before Allstate finally relented. I was not happy and seriously contemplated leaving Allstate who I had been with since 1972. As I said, they ultimately agreed the roof had been damaged, but it was a long and hard fought fight and left a bad taste in my mouth concerning Allstate. I have stayed with them mostly because of the close family tie with them. Jenna's husband, Adam Blackwell is our Allstate representative. We have our house and cars with Allstate. So, not rocking the family boat is always foremost in my mind. I guess if I had it to do over again, I would not mix family and business … a word to the wise. But as I said, it all worked out and we ultimately got a new roof partially paid for by our homeowner's policy … I can be a "dog with bone" once I "get my back up." Ah, you gotta love southern colloquialisms.

Bryce had graduated and was off to the University of Georgia in the fall of '19, but we still had Master Bodie Lang Blackwell at Lakeview Academy, and he was heavily involved in sports. Like Bryce, Bodie was a triple athletic threat – Bodie's passions were football, basketball and soccer. Carolyn and I realized quickly that this very brief period of young grandsons was going to come to a close quickly, and so we redoubled our efforts to be at every sporting event Bodie was involved in. In the winter of 2020 it was basketball which rapidly evolved into soccer, and then in the fall was football. We loved basketball. Carolyn had played in high school and was rabid about the game. I got into it and all the great players who were Bodie's family at Lakeview. Carolyn and I worked hard at learning soccer and a few of the phrases: "Good thought!" and "Backdoor!" This was used when a player attempted a goal but failed. It did not matter if it was a good try or not, "Good thought!" rang up from the crowd with enthusiasm regardless. We never really figured out "Backdoor" but loved yelling it. Football was far and away our favorite. Carolyn and I sat on rain and cold and heat and wind in some of the oddest places in Sandy Springs or Clayton or Tallulah Falls or Hiawassee or Toccoa to name a few. While at a game in Toccoa, we visited the museum of Easy Company of the 506th regiment of the 101st Airborne known as the Band of Brothers from the television special of the same name. We visited Toccoa Falls that day and generally made an adventure out of the whole event. I recall us meeting Jenna and Adam in many small town cafes and restaurants before out-of-town football or basketball games. We have driven to Gainesville so many times Carolyn and I laugh that the cars could probably drive themselves to Gainesville from Marietta if we just told them that was where we were going!

Far and away my mostest favoritest place to eat would have to be Longstreet's Café at 1043 Riverside Terrace in Gainesville. We have met Jenna and Adam and Bryce and Bodie there many, many times. Carolyn and I have eaten there with just the two of us, and even bought a couple of bird houses from the old gentleman who plies his wares when you walk in the door. Their fried chicken is "to die for" and their butter beans, when mixed with their rice and maybe a little of their brown gravy … mmmmm. But I stray from my topic. Bryce and Bodie have no idea how many great memories they have afforded their grandparents. And let me say that right beside us at most of these sporting events were Bryce and Bodie's other grandparents, Toby and Paula Blackwell, two very fine people as I have said before. So, thank you Boys for all the memories. No matter what you do with your lives, Carolyn and I are so proud to be your grandparents. Nothing you can do will change that.

As the pandemic deepened Carolyn and I would do sidewalk art with Caitlin, now a precocious ten-year-old, via Zoom over our phones. Angela (Angela Dawn Swope Morris) would arrange game night with us over the computers, and we would all laugh as "the grandparents" struggled with all this "new-fangled technology"! Angela is an angel. Then, one evening in August, James and Angela called with a serious question. They said that due to Covid Caitlin's fifth grade school year was going to be done remotely, and since I taught fifth grade, could Caitlin come on Sunday evening and stay at our house through Friday and then come home Friday afternoon. During the day she would do remote school, and I could be there to help with homework and fill in the gaps if there was anything she did not understand. Wednesdays were off days from school, and we could catch up on those days. Well, I hope you can imagine what Carolyn and I said … ABSOLUTELY! And so began the greatest and coolest time Carolyn and I could ever imagine. Having our beautiful granddaughter actually living here, with us, everyday! In August we started this wonderful, once-in-a-lifetime event … actually having Caitlin live with us! She had her very own bedroom with a queen size bed upstairs in the front. Now remember, up until now, I had been unceremoniously dumped out of my half of Carolyn's and my bed whenever The Princess came over, so she could sleep with "Nana." Cait had been sleeping in our bedroom since she would come and sleep in a baby crib. So sleeping in our bed was "a tradition" that sadly had to come to an end. But, in her new room, The Princess would be awakened with breakfast in bed, usually consisting of a heaping bowl of her favorite … Frosted Flakes … and the television in her bedroom immediately lit up with what would become a family favorite show, *Sponge Bob*. We set up an antique fold out desk in the corner of the dining room near the washer/dryer room. She had her supplies and computer set up and it was a central enough location that I could help when she needed it. Lunch was a quick affair involving cheese and grapes and ham … which was her "go to" meal since she was tiny and would come over. Afternoons were study halls and

Tuesday was tennis day. I would take her over to Hot Shotz tennis in the Howell Farms Subdivision off Hickory Grove Road, NW. She would practice tennis for two hours, and I would walk around the subdivision getting my "steps" in. I walked for miles in that little

subdivision, and still have a warm place in my heart every time we go there for one of her tennis matches. As of this writing she is still playing tennis and has become quite good at it. Her team played in the State Finals in '22 and '23. More about that later. Cait was an excellent house guest and brought life and laughter into our home. Dinners were lively affairs centering around me cooking whatever she wanted. We ate spaghetti with meat sauce, Caesar salads and her mostest favoritest – cheeseburgers and French fries a lot. While eating dinner, we would watch another of her favorite shows named *Nailed It*. In it, people with very little cooking skill would try to duplicate a very fancy cake or dessert of some kind. They usually failed with hilarious results. Occasionally a person would copy it reasonably well, and it was said that they "Nailed It." Mostly people didn't though.

We took Wednesdays as a field trip day, and Cait and I, and many times Carolyn, would go on fifth grade related content field trips. One trip was to the Southern Museum of Civil War and Locomotive History in downtown Kennesaw where Caitlin got a thorough dose of local Civil War history relative to the Great Locomotive Chase. Another trip was to the Atlanta History Center where she learned about Atlanta and got to see the newly relocated Cyclorama painting of the Battle of Atlanta. One trip was to the Tellus Science Museum in Cartersville. Carolyn and I took her downtown to Fernbank another time (it rained … again). We went to the ruins of the Roswell Mill one day, and then for a nature field trip to the Chattahoochee Nature Center and walked along the Chattahoochee River one beautiful afternoon after a delicious BBQ lunch in Roswell. Another trip was to Rope Mill Park above Woodstock for a good exercise workout walking and watching the leaves change color. I recall another very cold trip to the Leita Thompson Memorial Park on Highway 92 near Hardscrabble Road too. We almost froze! But we had great times and hopefully Caitlin will remember her fifth grade year with Nana and Pa. Talk about "It was the best of times …."

It is funny how God can balance things in your life. During all this wonderfulness of having Caitlin with us, my father, Colonel James W. Morris, passed away on Wednesday, September 30th, 2020. It was not Covid. It was his heart. It just quit. I will recall the day as long as I live. I was there. Caitlin had gone home that week as it was Cobb County School's Fall Break to be with "her mommy and daddy." Angela and James missed Caitlin tremendously that school year as they generously shared her with us, and so Caitlin was not at our house. And I randomly decided to use that day to go up and see Dad and pay bills and whatnot. Dad had been declining little by little over the weeks that September. He had just turned 96 on the first of that month and seemed more tired than usual at the birthday party, but he and I had gone to the cemetery the Saturday before that Wednesday, and he had walked a little but not much. Re (Mary Louise Morris Bramble) had thought it a good idea to contact hospice, and put them on notice. As a retired nurse, she was that concerned as she watched Dad's decline through September. She had also ordered a hospital bed through hospice. It was to be delivered that Wednesday. Malcolm Cooley was there helping Dad. Rusty (Brian Meroney Morris) was at work at Kroger. Re was there. I came a little after lunch. Dad ate his usual lunch sitting in "his" chair. There was a matching one my mother used to sit in adjacent to his where she would knit and they would talk watching the fire in the fireplace and maybe the television. Malcom had helped the man who came to set up Dad's new bed back down the hall in his bedroom that morning.

Dad seemed tired and Re suggested he go back and try out his new bed and lay down. Re and Malcom helped him back to the bedroom. I was sitting at the little round table in the kitchen eating area where my father and I had eaten many chili dogs, working on the check book and bills under the watchful eye of a new red rose in the bud vase. Around 2:00 Re had Malcom come get me to come back to the bedroom. Somehow … I knew why and hurried back. Dad was in the bed with a sheet covering his arms. Re was kneeling on his right side, and I came to stand by his left. He looked up at me and then seemed to look beyond me. Re said, "Dad? Dad? What do you see Dad?" but he said nothing. At that moment, he passed away from us. Out of my life forever. This man who had loved me as best he could. Who had guided me as best he could by the light he had been given. Who took care of our family through all the storms that life threw at him and Mom … quietly left me. Re started weeping. Malcom started crying. I left the room … crying quietly … and called Carolyn. She somehow knew when she answered the phone what had happened. I guess it was my pause trying to gather myself before I spoke. It was the first time in my life I had ever seen a person die. I wish I had not seen it. Selfish I know. But when it comes to sickness and death, I am a very private person.

I called my brothers: Rusty (Brian Meroney Morris), Pete (Peter Charles Morris) and Bill (William Cranston Morris) and talked to them about the events. Re (Mary Louise Morris Bramble) called the Hospice people and told them. They were to send a Hospice nurse over to officially make the declarations necessary and sign the death certificate. My sister's call also set in motion a group of volunteer veterans who came to officially, and with great dignity and solemnity, transport the body to Owen Funeral Home in Cartersville. The men who transported him were with the In Their Honor Transports. And then … "Not with a bang, but a whimper" (T.S. Eliot – *The Hollow Men*) the house was quiet. I stood with Carolyn, Re and Malcom. Later in the day, after work, Rusty came home. Rusty would continue to live in the house and take care of everything. I gathered up the 3-ring binder that supposedly contained everything I needed to know. Dad had tried very hard to get me to go through it with him, and I looked through it several times, but as I have said to my siblings, I did not really get into it until I had to. Now I had to, and by the end of that "day of days," I had to. The weight of being the executor of my father's estate settled on my shoulders.

I met with a lawyer on Friday and then all of the siblings, except Pete (Peter Charles Morris), gathered at Dad's house on Saturday, the 10th of October. I reviewed with them a list of the assets I was aware of. We included Pete via *Zoom*. Then we went to the bank, and the siblings all signed off that they consented that I was to be the Executor, and finally we went to the funeral home and reviewed the arrangements. The basic decision was made that, since Covid shutdowns had made conducting the funeral as Dad wished at the Georgia National Cemetery at 1080 Scott Hudgens Drive in Canton impossible, Owen

Funeral home would hold Dad's and Mom's cremains at their secure facility until we were ready for a funeral. I had asked Dad several times didn't he want half of his cremains to be buried with Mom at the cemetery in Cartersville, and he was insistent that he wanted all of his cremains to be at the Georgia National Cemetery. "So let it be written, so let it be done." We returned to the house and had a bite of lunch, and then we looked through the house tagging various items that each child wanted. I filed the appropriate papers with the court in Bartow County to be named the official executor on October 22nd. For the next six months I worked to clear up insurance policies and to get the house ready for sale. I will not bore you with all the trivialities involved with that. Everyone pitched in to help, and we had the house on the market in the spring of the next year. Once we had the right realtor (thank you Edward Kimball Rogers) and the right price, his home sold relatively quickly. And so I began to close that chapter of my life, although I find that losing your parents sometimes takes years to come to grips with. "… it was the

worst of times …" Around the time all of this was happening, one of our two very loving kittens, Delmar, woke up with a problem. The kittens, Jenna (pictured left) and Delmar, slept in their basement apartment at night, and every morning they would be at the door to the basement pawing on their little cat door wanting to be let

up. Except this morning they were not doing that. I went downstairs to see what was going on. Delmar was sitting on the carpet and Jenna was right next to her. When I called to them, Jenna came forward, but Delmar hesitated. When little Delmar (pictured right) started toward my voice, she bumped into one of the legs of the futon. I knelt down and petted her and said let's go upstairs. Jenna hesitated and waited for her younger sister to move. Delmar came forward and bumped into the steps. Delmar was blind. Later that day after discussions with the veterinarian, I had her put to sleep. I cried like a baby that afternoon. It was like the tears I could not shed for my father came welling up, and I came apart right there in the vet's office. At least we still had her sister, Jenna, but for Jenna the next few months would be difficult. She had never been without her sister, and now she was all alone. The pain and confusion in her little kitten brain must have been indescribable. Carolyn and I loved her as much as we could. We even let her sleep upstairs, but Jenna preferred to sleep in her apartment for about four months until she, too, passed away.

Along in November the United States held a presidential election and Donald Trump was thrown out of office, thank the Lord. Joe Biden was elected. But that was only the beginning of the "unprecedented" electoral struggle that ensued. To this day some three years later Trump is still spreading venomous lies that the election was stolen. In fact, as I write this he was just indicted on nineteen counts under the RICO Statute in Georgia for trying to overturn the election in this state. I wish I could live long enough to see how history treats this aberration of American politics, but I am afraid I will not live to see the

full toll of accounting historians will access. I will speak more about this in the next chapter about 2021.

I want to close 2020 on a high note. The musical Hamilton was a huge hit during this period. Jenna and Adam Blackwell even took all of us to the Fox Theater to see the production and Miss Caitlin Rose was enthralled. She was especially taken with the King George segment which was one of the funniest comic relief acts in the whole show. In fact, she could even sing most of his soliloquy song … and do a credible job of it. So, what did my Princess want to be on All Hallow's Eve? Yep, King George, and "her mommy," Angela Swope Morris, made her the most amazing costume EVER! We "trick-or-treated" here in the Falcon Wood subdivision, and she was a hit at every house we went to. It was awesome, and she and I trick-or-treated until late into the night. Caitlin Rose Morris is one amazing human being.

While thinking about James and Angela and Caitlin, we all went to Panama City Beach for our TG trip and Angela found us a perfect condo. And it was in the Edgewater Beach Resort complex! The same place that Carolyn and I had taken the children in 1987 and '88 when James was only six and Jenna was maybe fifteen! Ah, the memories. We had a great time even though Covid was raging, and we mostly cooked in the condo kitchen, and it was really too rainy for the beach. Just being with family was a treat for Carolyn and me. And for a whole family gathering, we all decided we would do a single Thanks-mas on the fifth of December up at Jenna and Adam's new property on Lake Lanier. Everyone was there including Bryce Blackwell's Anna and Bodie Blackwell's Margot. The house we gathered in sadly is no more. As Adam and Jenna got more and more into the house that came on the property they bought, they decided it was not suited to their needs, so they had the old house torn down and a new one built that they just moved into about a year ago.

Finally, closing on a musical note (sorry), Carolyn and I wanted to support Caitlin in a special way as she headed into 2021 and ended her elementary years. Carolyn had it in her mind to get Caitlin a keyboard and help her take some music lessons while she was with us for the second half of fifth grade. What we ended up getting her was a full size electronic upright piano for Christmas. Being able to give her that was a personal high for Carolyn and for me. You see, I am woefully ignorant when it comes to music, but Carolyn grew up around the piano and the French horn. So, when I see Caitlin playing piano and Carolyn singing and the two of them reading music, it is somewhat akin to alchemy to me. A fascinating process I cannot understand, but am amazed by none-the-less. The piano is inscribed with a plate dedicating the piano to Caitlin Rose Morris from Nana and Pa, Christmas 2020.

16.

2021 started with a bang … literally. The ex-president, Donald Trump, had one last card to play to try to overturn the 2020 election. He had failed on multiple fronts to prove election fraud and corruption, and he had one last desperate move to make. To send hundreds of his armed acolytes and minions into the Capitol and disrupt the final count of electors from the state's elections and to stop congress from putting their formal seal on Joe Biden as President. So, on January 6th, 2021, he stood before a massed crowd of armed morons and idiots and sent them down the mall from the Lincoln Memorial to "hang Mike Pence," his own Vice President, and the man constitutionally charged with overseeing the elector count. I challenge you to conjure up the video of that day when Capitol policemen died and hundreds were injured and not be ashamed of Donald Trump as he tried to overthrow the government and have himself installed as … well, basically a dictator. The parallels, as I have mentioned before, between the maniac Trump and Adolf Hitler are terrifyingly real. I fear for our country as Donald Trump makes another run for the White House in 2024, and am amazed every day at the number of people who are still taken in by this swindler, this charlatan, con-artist and grifter. But a quote attributed to the infamous P.T. Barnum rings so true: "There is a sucker born every minute." I am not going to belabor this. You can look up the history and see for yourself and decide for yourself.

January was also marred by the death of our second kitten, Jenna. As I mentioned in 2020, she and her sister Delmar had been our loving companions for seventeen years and never were there two sweeter cats. Jenna had cancer. There was a sore on her back that the vet could not heal. When I took her in for the last time on January 29th, I knew she was not coming home ever again. Dr. Barnwell and I made the terrible decision. Jenna was given a sedative to calm her. I was petting her. After a few minutes, Dr. Barnwell gave her a shot that put her to sleep. She lay there, and I hovered over her stroking her soft fur … weeping like a baby as she, too, left me. I truly had entered the part of my life where God has stopped giving and started taking away. As I write this part of my story my eyes are full of tears, and I can hardly see the keyboard to type. I am going to stop for today … it is too late and there is too much heartache with this subject.

A happier topic: Carolyn and I had several cool adventures over the year involving just the two of us in St. Louis, the Outer Banks and the Caribbean. All the trips were fraught with masks and separation from people, and all the Covid hand sanitizing and everything, but things were starting to look a little better than in 2020. A vaccine had been developed, and Carolyn and I were right there in line to get ours. We had no fears about the government injecting tracking devices into us … yes, that was a real thing … stupid, I know, right? And we got all kinds of in home Covid tests from President Biden that we used to insure our safety. Our trip to St. Louis involved staying in a little town in Ohio named Marion. The reason will be more clear in a minute. We loved the drive up. It was about an eight or nine hour drive up through Chattanooga and Nashville and Paducah and over the mighty Ohio, that border river that so many slaves prayed to be able to cross into freedom. The Ohio featured prominently in the book *Uncle Tom's Cabin* by Harriet

Beecher Stowe. Anyway, we loved the ride up. The day we went it was raining of course, and we dodged it with our umbrellas as best we could. We found a great little BBQ spot in the city called Sugarfire Smoke House. It is at 605 Washington Avenue, and it was totally worth it! We saw the Wainwright Building which was a classic we all studied in school and of course The Arch and the City Hall building near The Arch. A lot of stuff was closed due to Covid, but the two of us had fun splashing around and seeing stuff.

We made a trip up to North Carolina to visit Pete (Peter Charles Morris) and his wife Elizabeth (Frances Elizabeth Allen Morris) later in the year. The reason was that Elizabeth's father, Bona Allen had passed away the year before, the same year as Dad, and due to the same Covid restrictions the family were finally having a remembrance service for him. You may remember me mentioning the fine gentleman Mr. Bona Allen. In 1999 when Carolyn and I stayed at the Brasstown Valley Resort, Bona was the one who came over to our table and greeted us. Carolyn and I drove up from Atlanta and the drive up I-85, especially in South Carolina, was brutal. They were "working" on the interstate, and it was a three-ring-circus of cones and stops and starts and traffic back-ups. Anyway, we arrived, and we gathered at Pete and Elizabeth's house in Clemmons, North Carolina, one cool evening. Pete and Liz's daughters were there as were their beaus. My brother Rusty and my sister Mary Louise came up from Atlanta also. We met several of the neighbors and friends. Elizabeth's mom, Jane King Allen, arrived. She is such a refined lady. The gathering was the next day. The sun was shining, and it was a beautiful service. After the service there was a get together at Jane's senior adult community where she lived. It was a lovely day remembering her husband, Bona. The next day Carolyn and I headed for the Outer Banks. We had not been there since 2012 when Caitlin was just a little one just learning to walk. We stayed at a little hotel on the waterfront with a view of the Atlantic. I caught a beautiful sunrise one morning. Our stay was nothing special,

just a little get-away. But I do have to tell you. If you decide to go to OBX, the drive to and from Atlanta is brutal!

At the end of the year Carolyn and I took a seven-day jaunt on Royal Caribbean out of Fort Lauderdale. We decided to make the run to Lauderdale in one day's drive … that too is a long haul. We stopped for the first time in our lives at a Buc-ees just south of Macon on the way down I-75. Now there is a must go to place if ever there was one. Any Buc-ees will do. They are all the same. The world's largest gas stations, and if you can't find it at Buc-ees, it ain't made! So, we were heading down we stopped to eat several times and get gas and whatnot and then the "goocher" (a weird event or strange chance occurrence) of all "goochers" happened. We're blasting down I-75 somewhere in mid-Florida, and a car pulls up and looks to pass us, but then it doesn't. It slows down and a little behind us, then pulls up next to us. The window rolls down, and it is Chuck Chapeau and Toby Blackwell! Chuck Chapeau is a Georgia State Patrolman married to Adam Blackwell's sister Angela, and of course Toby is Adam's dad. They were headed down to Miami to a UGA vs. Florida football game and came across us in the middle of nowhere Florida! Cool! What were the chances? Anyway, we each went our separate ways, and Carolyn and I got to our hotel after dark. We had started the day in line very early at the Wellstar Hospital on Roswell Road to get an "official" Covid test to prove we were negative, so we could board the boat. These were things we had to do during the pandemic. We were assured if we got to the hospital early, we would have our results that evening. Well, we didn't … have the results … naturally. And the next morning, we still did not have the results. Ahhh, "The best laid plans of mice and men often go awry." (Robert Burns, 1785). But Royal Caribbean had us covered, and for a mere $99.00 each we could get an "instant" test right there at the dock. So, we wheeled our luggage all over the dock area, finally found the makeshift clinic, were proved negative for the virus, got our papers and boarded the ship. It was an interesting sailing. We were supposed to go deep into the leeward islands, but Covid had shut down many of the ports we were to visit. This we found out after we sailed. So, C and I joked that we may be spending seven days at the RC private island and then coming home. But this did not happen. We did get to go to a couple of ports, St. Maarten and St. Kitts & Nevis, but mostly we just sailed around the beautiful Caribbean. Believe me … I've got no complaints. It was truly a "First World Problem." One of my series of four shot collections on the bedroom wall is of Carolyn riding in what I will call an open air cheeva bus. It is dated January 2022. Her silver hair is blowing in the breeze as she had just lost her hat off the back of the bus. (It was an ugly hat and no big loss. I bought her a much more attractive one later that evening.) And she is wearing the ultimate in fashion that year in the pictures … a KN95 protective mask against Covid. I did capture a 180° full rainbow in port one day which I had never in my life seen before. It was very cool. We befriended a very, very, nice man from the Philippines on the ship. His first name was Jake and we met him in the Windjammer of the ship we were on, the Allure. We could not handle his last name, so he just told us he was "Jake … from State Farm." After we got home we have continued to keep up with him and hopefully, one day we will meet him again.

Probably the highlight of the whole cruise was our day excursion to Kim-Sha Beach. We were anticipating it being like another trip's excursion when we were in Roatán, Honduras. At Roatán we were almost all alone with the beautiful Caribbean spread before us. This was not like that. First the ride to the beach was about an hour on a school bus situation, and when we got there the "guide" (and I use the term loosely) just sort of walked off. We found our designated area. We were in the blue umbrella area and we were like three rows back from the beach. Our view was a dangerously overweight woman in a two-piece swim suit in front of us (I just threw-up in my throat at the memory) and then some guy in a Speedo in front of her. It was ridiculous. The upside was a drink and lunch were included. I walked off to find our delicious rum punch "included drink" soon after we had arrived. I finally found some teenage girls with a bottle of rum, plastic cups and some Hawaiian punch looking stuff in a jug. They tossed two ice cubes in a cup, and without measuring or anything they poured in some rum and then added the warm punch. It was nasty. So, finally it was time for lunch. Well, the only place we had seen serving food was a two-story bohío kind of place as we trudged in. So, we went there to eat. As it turns out, they fed us but it was the wrong place. Our place was somewhere on down the beach which we would have known if our "guide" had been anywhere to be found. And the lunch was about as you would expect given the tone of the day. But one of the best parts was the large, local lady who wanted to give you a massage. Not on your life! Or the other large, local lady who wanted to braid your hair. Or the other large, local lady who wanted to sell you her wares which were woven leather things and various trinkets. All in all, it was a glorious day! I left RC a "sternly worded" assessment of the excursion. I am positive it made absolutely no difference! But I must say of all the things that day, the random rooster strutting around on the dock absolutely took the day. Oh, oh, we did go shopping in St. Maarten and Carolyn bought the most beautiful Moo-moo kind of lounge house dress sort of thing. It is various shades of gorgeous blue like the Caribbean. She looks striking in it with her silver hair. So, that was our end of 2021 beginning of 2022 trip. Ho-hum.

Continuing our Caitlin fifth grade field trips that year we went down to the Aquarium and the Center for Civil and Human Rights. Actually we did the Civil Rights place first and held out the Aquarium as a tantalizing tid-bit for the afternoon. The Princess was as good as she could be that day at the Center for Civil and human Rights and soaked up everything from the memorial to the four little girls killed in Birmingham and made the connection to our previous trip to Birmingham immediately. Afterward we went to the Aquarium and The Princess was immediately drawn to the special shark display in the aquarium. Somehow we squeezed in a trip to St. Simons, and an Intracoastal boat ride. During the ride, Cait got to be up close and personal with many aquatic specimens. Caitlin was not impressed. There was one time, I don't know if it was this trip or an earlier trip, but Caitlin had picked up a beautiful little conch type shell at the beach. She kept it in her bucket for a day or so. It really was lovely. As we were leaving the island and rolling along the F.J. Torras Causeway on our way home suddenly there was a squeal from the back seat and then Carolyn, who always rides in the back seat with Caitlin (Carolyn says, "I'm going to ride back here with her as long as she will have me.") shrieks and throws something up to the front seat where I am driving! I manage to finally pull over on the crushed shell shoulder and pick it up. The girls are still hysterically yelling, "There is something in there!" And sure enough, after hiding for a day or so, a little hermit crab had decided to make his presence known. I took the shell with its little guest and threw it down from the road into my beautiful marsh. It took the ladies hours to settle down. And not to let Caitlin's fifth grade education be incomplete and to not let her escape without another field trip, Caitlin, her mom and dad and Carolyn and I took the mandatory trip to Charleston to see the Yorktown Aircraft Carrier, Fort Sumter and The Hunley. Again, this trip was very nostalgic for James and me as we had made this trip when he was young, and we made a Two Boys Trip, and when he was older, and he accompanied me as a senior chaperone with my fifth grade class a couple of times. Now here he was with his daughter. As a Grandfather it was life coming full circle. One of my favorite pictures of Caitlin was when it was just her and me out on the lawn of Fort Sumter. I am looking at the picture this minute on my desk. She walked over to the low wire with the sign that reads: DO NOT CROSS. And she puts her foot over the wire and looks at me and says, "Look at me Pa. I'm a bad girl just like Nana [Carolyn]." I knew when I told Carolyn what she said, Carolyn would beam with pride. My two "Bad Girls." The ladies, Carolyn and Angie, chose to forgo the carrier and Fort Sumter that day to go shopping. Boooring! They missed all the fun! Our last stop of the trip was just Carolyn and Cait and me. James and Angela headed back to Atlanta letting Carolyn and me bring the Princess back with us. The three of us went to The C.S.S. Hunley Museum. I had showed Cait the movie about the submarine and filled her in with background stories about Queenie and the silver dollar that saved the leg of the Hunley's Captain, Lt. George Dixon. How the submarine had successfully sunk the U.S.S. Housatonic, and then disappeared under the waves until being rediscovered by Clive Cussler and his NUMA organization in 2000. As a sidebar, if you want to read some exciting, fun books read some Clive Cussler novels. I suggest you start with one of my mostest favoritest books, *Valhalla Rising*. You will not be disappointed. Anyway, Caitlin looked into the tank of water and saw the submarine. She understood its place in history. And she got a cool souvenir, but I cannot tell you what she finally chose. This was her final fifth grade field trip. The Capstone of her fifth grade year with

Nana and Pa, and it was a time I will cherish forever. I wish every Grandfather and Grandmother could have Grandchildren like Bryce, Bodie and Caitlin and could have children like Jenna and Adam and James and Angela willing to trust and share their beautiful, precious angels with you.

Speaking of amazing grandchildren, young Master Bodie Lang Blackwell graduated from Lakeview Academy that year. And if when Bryce Blackwell graduated two years

before he took every Lakeview award, Master Bodie took every award and then one more! Bodie began his walk that year at the annual May Day celebration when, instead of taking his girlfriend to walk the honor walk of seniors, he took the same young lady who he had walked with in fifth grade. Needless to say, that act touched this Grandfather's heart. Next came the sports awards. It was a sunny Sunday, May 2nd, around 2:00 when we all gathered at the roof top area at Carroll Daniel Construction. Jenna and Adam were there. Toby and Paula were there. Carolyn and I would not have missed it for the world. We just turned on the CR-V and told it we wanted to go to Gainesville, and it took over almost driving itself to 400 and off at Keith Bridge Road Exit 17. Follow Keith Bridge Road (over the Keith Bridge), and then to Highway 53 and into Gainesville. That beautiful late spring afternoon Bodie was awarded the Defensive Player of the Year award and the Pride of the Lion Award. On May 6th, Toby and Paula had a reception for Bodie at their home on the lake in Gainesville at 3159 Dockside Drive. Again a beautiful Georgia day and all of Bodie's close friends were there, and we got to

formally meet Bodie's girlfriend Margot Marie Murphy for the first time. Bryce and his (now very soon to be fiancée!) Anna Grace Wylie were there as were relatives from all over including Chuck Chapeau and his wife, Adam's only sister, Angela and their boys. Carolyn's and my contribution to the affair was to bring Bodie's fifth grade diorama project and paper on The Battle of Atlanta. Of course his historian grandfather, me, was especially proud of his work and everyone including Bodie loved the throw back!

The next award stop was at Lakeview on May 12th. That evening, with Margot there and all his family to watch, like Bryce before him, Bodie received the *Golden Lion Award* for playing three sports while maintaining his Honor Roll status, and the *Senior Award* in recognition of playing five different sports representing Lakeview. And to cap it all off only he and a single young lady each received the *Senior Athletic Most Valuable Player Award for 2020-2021*. But the most amazing accomplishment was yet to be revealed. In the days following Bodie was singled out and awarded the *H. Ferrell Singleton Cup* which was given to the best all-round student in the class. Following all of this was the baccalaureate/graduation service where he received his diploma. Again, like Bryce before him, the gentlemen were in white tie and tails and the ladies in various white gowns. After the service was the "big reveal." The gentlemen lined up and opened their shirts to reveal their college of choice. Bodie

would be attending UGA following in his now Sophomore brother Bryce's footsteps. Grandparents could not be more proud than we were at that moment. In the picture, from the left, are Anna Grace Wylie, Bryce Harper Blackwell, Timothy Adam Blackwell, Jenna Morris Blackwell, Bodie Lang Blackwell and Margot Marie Murphy. With Bodie's graduation, Jenna decided she had had all the fun at Lakeview Academy she wanted and decided it was time for a change. So she left and took a position with Hilliard Wilbanks Middle School in Habersham County teaching her first love, Social Studies.

There was a second graduation that year. Miss Caitlin Rose Morris graduated from fifth grade and Chalker Elementary School. She would be attending Palmer Middle School in the fall. And while she loved her piano and had learned how to play quite well, she dreamed of being a percussionist! She spent the summer that year practicing and when the fall came, she won herself one of the coveted percussionist slots on the Palmer Band … our "Little Drummer girl."

That October, only a year and a week after my father, Col. James Wingfield Morris, had passed, we held his funeral at the Georgia National Cemetery. All the family gathered including Edward Rogers and his wife Jeanette, Bill Boswell and his wife Mary (a related branch of the family on my father's side) and Malcolm Cooley and his mom and dad were there. Dad was the last of his generation of the Wofford/Morris line to die. And his children, grandchildren and great grandchildren all gathered that day. It was a beautiful service at the Georgia National Cemetery. Re had my father's old preacher come and say a few words and had a bag piper play Amazing Grace. If you wish to visit where my dad and mom (half of Mom's ashes are in the Cartersville cemetery and half are with buried with Dad) his grave marker is in section 16 and the number is 16-1816. Pick a beautiful day in the spring or fall and visit. The cemetery is an awesome sight. After the interment ceremony we all returned for refreshments at the fellowship hall at the First Presbyterian Church of Cartersville. The same one that had been diagonal from my Pa's original house location, and the same one Mom and Dad had been married in on January 19th, 1948, before they spent the night at the Biltmore Hotel in Atlanta and then left for a honeymoon in Charleston where they stayed at the Francis Marion Hotel. Dad's house finally sold late in 2021, and I was able to distribute the last of the estate funds and close my executorship.

On the home front that year, Carolyn and I invested in a new car. It seems we only get cars when a car dies or someone in the family dies. We got a beautiful Pearl Gray 2021 Hybrid Cr-V with leather interior … the hybrid was my choice; all other choices were Carolyn's. I also undertook to renovate our pitiful back deck. The old deck had reasonably good bones but it looked like crap. The top deck had been painted gray and was pealing and rotten and the bottom deck was stained red and rotting also. So, that summer I stripped both decks down to their foundation structure, secured the deck to the house properly, re-flashed it and made sure rain would not get into the little storage area under the deck, re-clad the vertical surfaces and completely replaced the decking and stairs and rails. Not to pat myself on the back, but I must admit it only looks about a 1000% better when I had finished and stained the whole thing. It will not be allowed to fall apart again under my watch.

17.

Now we are really getting into recent history as far as my autobiography is concerned. I mentioned to Carolyn the other day that my writing has stopped being foggy recollections of happy past days and turned into more of a recitation of events and details. Gentle reader, for this I apologize, but I think it is the nature of the beast. I am no longer a ping-pong ball, but the fully mature seventy-two-year-old senior male of this branch of the Morris clan. Wow, to say I'm mature even at this age is a stretch even for me! But I guess I have earned the stripes and have the scars to at least say it. As I write this, it is now August of 2023. 2022 was just last year and it is still vivid in my memory, so let us sally forth.

I have to lead this year with two sad events. Two of Carolyn's three sisters lost their husbands. Virginia "Ginny" Lyon Grupe Burling lost her husband, Tom Burling in April of 2022, and Carolyn's older sister Kathleen "Kathy" Lyon Snelgrove lost her husband

Cary Jack Snelgrove in December of 2021 Yes, Jack is the same Jack from many years ago when Carolyn and I were first married and the same Jack who lost a truck in the Altoona Lake. I am not going to belabor these two gentlemen's deaths. They were good men, and they are missed. I counted Jack as friend, and of those, I have few. Jack is also buried in the Georgia National Cemetery coincidentally in the same Section 16 as my father. His marker is numbered 16-2328.

Around Falcon Wood Drive, Carolyn and I finally bought new windows for the old homestead. We had quite a few companies come in and give us the hard sell. It was an interesting and motley group of salesmen. In the end we went with a very low pressure salesman named Sean Pinto with Window World. We had actually met him almost a year before at a home show at The Galleria. He was in the Window World area, and we had chatted. Carolyn and I told him we did not want any tint to our windows, and he said that was not a problem. We had decided we absolutely hated colored green glass in the homes we looked at. It just looked weird, and we did not want it. All the other salesmen thought this was a sacrilege and hemmed and hawed about how they did not know if it was even possible to get glass with no tint, but old Pinto Bean just said, "Okay." We went with Window World. We went with them not only because of the glass question, but they had none of this "buy two get one free" or "buy three and get 50% off the next" or "this week only 10% off everything but you have to sign up this second" stuff. Sean was just, "Here's the price and it is good for six months. Also we will finance you purchase for eighteen months no interest." And it was the absolute best price far and away. About three months later their crew came and installed the windows and did a superb job. So, not to sound like a commercial, but if you need new glass in your house, give Window World a shot. Because "they not only stand behind their windows, they stand on them!" Also, running on my great looking deck high, I finally put handrails on the stone porch steps. My mother had been after me to do this long before she passed away, and so I finally did it. It ended up a bigger project than I first imagined, but they came together well, and I think they complement the house.

Carolyn had a wild thought in the spring that she wanted to go find some Georgia waterfalls. I guess she was really turned on by the Toccoa Falls we had visited, and so we adventured one day off to somewhere in North Georgia, and we found a really beautiful set of falls somewhere in the back side of nowhere. I cannot even begin to tell you where they were, but we found them thanks to GPS and "flying the wire." That is when we don't have any idea where we are going and we just follow whatever the GPS lady's voice says. We also adventured on a trip to Chicago. Both of us had flown through The Windy City; Carolyn flew through Midway, and I had flown through O'Hare, but neither of us had ever seen the city. And after I had read *The Devil*

in the White City, by Erik Larson, I had to go see Chicago. On the way up we stopped over in our favorite little town of Marion. The next day as we cruised through Kankakee, Illinois, I thought of Willie Nelson and his rendition of *The City of New Orleans*, one of my favorites We stayed right downtown on the river at a Hilton or something and we had to park our car down the street under a building in an underground garage … cool. On the way into town we stopped at the Chicago Metropolitan Art Museum, and I located a painting by one of my current favorite artists, Fredric Edwin Church, named *The Cordilleras, Sunrise*. Actually I really like all The Hudson School painters. They paint the way I try to get my photographs to look. Anyway, after that we went to the hotel. We had a corner room with a view of the river. Dinner was at a restaurant not far away, and we shared lobster rolls. While there we took an evening river cruise on the Chicago River that is another bucket list thing you gotta do. As night fell over the city, it was a site to behold. The next day was cathedral and Frank Lloyd Wright adventuring. We dug the car out of the underground garage and took off and discovered several gems. We ranged as far north as O'Hare where we found lunch in a wonderful little middle eastern diner. The owner was so pleased to introduce us to some of his country's favorite foods. On the way back south and east we located a couple of FLW homes. The Robie House we toured together and in the gift shop bought the two pillows with a prairie styled stained glass motif on them … very "Frank Lloyd Wrightian." We also found Hemmingway's boyhood home. (Read *The Old Man and the Sea*) Our last day in town we took an architectural walking tour: Historic Treasures of Chicago. It was basically the last 150 plus years of significant architecture in Chicago. Why 150 years? Well, supposedly Ms. Catherine O'Leary was milking a cow, and it kicked over a lantern in 1871, and over the next two October days basically the whole city burned to the ground. So, they do not have a whole lot of downtown that is over 150 years old! On the way out of town the next day, we went by the University of Chicago where one Barack Obama once taught and discovered a beautiful church built by the Rockefellers in the 1920's.

Princess Caitlin boomed into 6th grade and was taking Palmer Middle School by storm. Not only was she taking all advanced courses … no doubt from her magnificent year of fifth grade at The Lyon Morris Center for Exceptional Grandchildren … she was loving percussion and was in the sixth grade chorus. On top of all of that she was a mainstay on the Hot Shotz Tennis Team and their team was invited to the State Tournament in Macon that July. Needless to say we ALL wanted to go and Angela found us a great, slightly in need of exterior repair, but equipped with an awesome new A/C system four bed, two bath house where we all stayed. Now, ladies and gentlemen, there is no real heat like Macon in July heat. It is everywhere, all around and as steamy as you could ever imagine. But armed with thirty-five battery operated fans and a wagon load of cold water and knowing all we had to do was sit in the shade while Cait was out on the burning hot black or blue tennis court … we "endeavored to persevere." And The Hot Shotz came in third overall out of seven teams. And Caitlin never flagged or quit or even gave a hint she was tiring. She is my beautiful, special, amazing granddaughter.

We also took a short cruise with James and Angela and Caitlin which was just a little three-day jaunt mainly to Royal Caribbean's private island CocoCay. Carolyn and I had actually visited there on our cruise the year before, but we had not paid for the part of the island that cost money to get in. We had saved that experience for our trip with Caitlin. It was a beautiful early morning when we pulled up to dock. The sun was just on the horizon and CocoCay was already lit up like a carnival. Caitlin and I were interested in the next little island over. It was apparently the Norwegian Cruise Lines private island. It was all dark except for one small lighthouse. I guess they had to have that so ships would not bump into it while they were all looking a CocoCay. This poor little island had no dock or anything, and Cait and I felt sorry for it and we named it Dismal Cay. I have read about it since then, and apparently one of the big deal things to do is swim with the pigs. Yech. I have heard of swimming with dolphins but swimming with pigs? And that is your BIG draw? Wow. Anyway, after a hearty breakfast of over-light fried eggs and corned beef hash (Bodie's favorite), we all headed to the Cay. We grabbed a couple of great seats near the wave pool, and then James and I got Cait and headed for the Western Hemisphere's tallest water slide … I kid you not! It was unbelievable! With the line it took almost two hours to ascend and then about forty-five seconds to descend, but it was worth every second of the 120 minutes and forty-five seconds! Would I do it again? … Yeah, with Caitlin and James and enough goading I would. After the Cay we went to our only other stop in Nassau where we took Caitlin shopping and gave James and Angela a day. We bought her a hoodie, and as we were walking along, The Princess suddenly stopped and pulled out her little purse. She rummaged in it for a second and then pulled out some of "her" money. She then walked over to a little old man working hard at playing a guitar and put her dollars in his cup. Carolyn's and my hearts soared. She was truly a Child of the Universe. We are talking about taking her to the Mediterranean when she is sixteen in about three years or so. We'll see what fate has in store.

2022 was also Jenna and Adam's family's big trip to the Med. They were also taking Anna Wylie and Margot Murphy with them. It was to be a huge deal: Rome, Naples, Ephesus, Santorini and Mykonos. Truly a cruise of a lifetime. Well, Rome went fine. They had decided to stay in the same hotel we stayed in, The Lancelot. Their experience was a little less than perfect as Adam and Jenna's room had A/C problems. The children were fine. Then they boarded the ship and the problems began. Adam had a little cough and scratchy throat so he decided to go to the on-ship clinic … big mistake! He was diagnosed with the dreaded Covid-19! He was separated from the family and isolated in a cabin. Then, yep, they tested Jenna, and she went down. A separate cabin but no more cruise for either of them. All meals were brought to the cabin and they were stuck. Meanwhile Bryce and Anna and Bodie and Margot HAD A BALL! Young and loose in the Mediterranean. They visited Naples and Pompeii (on my bucket list) and all the other stops on the cruise, ate dinners and went to shows and played in the pool and all without "Mom and Dad." What a deal!

But 2022 was not all boo-hoo's for Jenna and Adam. Their new house was finally finished about the time Jenna had to head back to school. She was going to be teaching Seventh Grade Social Studies, and that was a good thing! And their house was/is magnificent! We actually had

our first family Thanksgiving there that year, and christened the house with love and family. In the picture you can see the house up on the hill, and starting on the left and working clockwise we see James Lyon, Bodie, Bryce, James W. Carolyn, Adam, Angela, Caitlin and Jenna.

We did the Thanksgiving on a Wednesday and then James and Angela and Caitlin and Carolyn and I headed for Savannah again. This time Angie let me do the honors of picking our place to stay and I found a really cool little house on East 37th Street just west of Broad Street. It was perfect with three bedrooms and one and a half baths. But it did have one small draw back … there was a railroad nearby. I did not even notice it when I was looking at it online. And of course the renters did not mention it. But, every morning at 6:30 a train would slowly rumble into town and because there were no railroad crossing lights or arms, he/she would blow his/her horn to warn everyone. And every time the train rolled in, it caused great glee and excitement around the house that Pa (me) had picked out! Of all the houses in Savannah, I chose this one! I don't think Angela will let me choose again. We went down on Friday and saw the boat parade although some of "the bloom was off the rose" for some reason. Can't really say why. But the big surprise was waiting for the next day. Caitlin had always wanted to go on the big paddlewheel boat The Georgia Queen, and little did she know that Nana and Pa (Carolyn and me) had arranged that very thing. We all arrived in our finery Saturday evening, and she was still clueless. Then we got in line, and she started to suspect something. And when the line started the moving, and we boarded the boat she was alight with anticipation. When I booked the cruise I had splurged for a window table. CAUTION: If you do this dinner cruise do NOT pay for a window table. Anyway, they led us to our table and it was not a window table. I told them this was unacceptable. The table was nice, but it was not a window table. The people explained that they were booked solid, and there were no more tables for a group our size. Well, Carolyn had had all she was going to have of this and explained in no uncertain terms this was not going to cut it. A deal was finally struck in that we would agree to the table we had been assigned, and the premium we had been paid for the window seat, not a small sum, would be refunded. Acceptable, although some of the specialness of the night had been lost due to the need for a confrontation. But the buffet was good, and my Princess Caitlin was able to ride on her Georgia Queen on a lovely Savannah evening on the river.

While in Savannah that year I was on a mission. I had been reading The Atlanta Historical Bulletin volumes that my grandmother "Momma" had given me. In particular, I had been reading the War Diary of Captain Cornelius R. Hanleiter which is in the volumes of December 1969, and spring, summer and fall of 1970. They are now in Jenna Blackwell's house. Captain Hanleiter is my Great, Great, Great Grandfather on my father's side. In the December 1969 volume on page 95 it denotes on June 2nd, 1862, the burial of a young soldier. In pages previous Captain Hanleiter notes the slow health decline of Private Benjamin J. Johnson. This young man under his command had touched Captain Hanleiter in some way as the Captain took a special interest in him. The private's burial was to be in Laurel Grove Cemetery, North. It was only meant to be a temporary burial until his brother, who attended the funeral, could arrange to

Grave marker of Benjamin J Johnson in North Laurel Cemetery, Savannah GA – a soldier in C. R. Hanleiter's artillery company

get the body home to north Georgia. For some reason, he was never moved, and I wanted to see his grave. I wanted to stand where my 3 Greats Grandfather had stood. So, Saturday morning I announced I was going to walk over to the cemetery and asked if anyone wanted to go with me? It was a lovely morning, and the walk was only about a mile and a half or so to the cemetery. And to my joy, my Caitlin wanted to go with me. I cannot tell you how good that made me feel, and so the two intrepid adventurers launched off into the clear fall morning. We located the proper cemetery, but we had no idea where on the grounds he might be. A little walking around located the Confederate burial area separated from the rest of the graves by a neat fence. The headstones were all neatly laid out just as my father's cemetery is. So, Caitlin and I started walking row by row looking for Pvt. Benjamin J. Johnson. After about thirty minutes we located him. I had the diary with me, and standing over the grave I read to My Princess words written over a century ago about this young man, taken too soon. She respectfully listened. We then each said a tiny quiet prayer and walked away. As we walked, I talked to her about the Latin phrase Carpé Diem. After a minute or so, I told her we had to locate another grave. She did not look excited until I told her the grave was that of Juliette Gordon Lowe who was buried in this same cemetery. So, we adventured off again and finally located the family plot of the Lowe family and there, amongst all kinds of Girl Scout rememberings, was her grave. Cait was moved. And then I sensed it was time to call it quits and be done with all this somberness. Two buddies headed for our little railroad shaken house doing "special walking" at all the crosswalks, and making sure we punched the button for the crosswalks where we had to stop several times just, so we could hear the electronic voice say, "Wait" "Wait" "Wait" over and over and over and giggled at our special joke.

That year was also the year I came to the conclusion that it was time for Rosinante (my motorcycle) and me to part ways. Taking her out was getting to be a chore rather than a pleasure. Oh, once I got her out of the city and into the hills of North Georgia she and I bonded. But getting to Fort Mountain, one of my favorites, or even just getting up around

Tate, Georgia, was getting to be a chore, and I was not a spring chicken any more. My rides were exhilarating. Why, in the fall of 2021 I had ventured off to Augusta and left a little too late in the evening. The sun set on my back and the temperature dropped, and by the time I got to Augusta I was so cold I could literally hardly get off my bike. I also knew my reaction times were not what they had been fifteen years earlier, and the last thing I wanted to do, as I have said, was to have the bike just one day too long. I also knew my rides were making Carolyn nervous. And while I was still, maybe even a little more so, worth more dead than alive, she was not keen on the idea of me dying or worse yet, paralyzed. You see on a bike, if you are in an altercation with even a tiny car, you are going to lose. There is just no way around it. So, I made up my mind to sell my beautiful baby. But what was going to take her place? What Carolyn did not know was I had been looking on the "World Wide Web" for a sports car. I had in mind another MG, but I knew they were pieces of crap, and something like a Jag E-type was out of the financial question. Besides, if I thought the Thunderbird I owned was a "pain in the a_ _," a Jag would be that on a whole other level of pain! So, I started reading and looking and looking and reading and kind of started focusing on the Mazda MX-5 Miata. I looked on all the Mazda dealership lots and private sellers and looked all over the southeast. Then I hit pay dirt in Chattanooga. A red, 2008, Mazda MX-5 Miata Touring with 104,000 miles in good condition with a six speed gearbox. I contacted the person, and he said it was still for sale. I shared my plan with Carolyn. I would sell my Honda Civic to CarMax if the price was right and sell my bike and buy this MX-5. She was totally onboard. Anything that got rid of the bike and made me happy in the exchange would work for her. I went over to CarMax that evening to get a price. The CarMax guys really wanted my car and offered me more than I expected. Then Saturday, I corralled my car guru son James Lyon Morris to go with me to see the car. On a Saturday morning, we blasted off and met the car and the guy in a Walmart parking lot. The car was as perfect as a car with 104,000 miles could be, and I knew it checked out on the Carfax website. It was a beauty. I asked the guy to not sell to anyone else, I would be back. Well, badda-bing, I sold the Honda and bought the MX-5. Next all I had to do was sell my bike. I had looked at sites saying they would buy bikes but they were all offering a pittance. Carolyn suggested putting it on the Next Door website. I had nothing to lose so I did. My

sweet, faithful Rosinante was gone in twenty-four hours for full price. And that is where my hot, red convertible came from, and she too is *"hotter than a two-dollar pistol, she [is] the hottest thing around. Long and lean, every young man's dream, she [turns] every head in town."* But I will always love you, Rosinante.

18.

Over the years since I retired I have kept my hand in one beloved activity from my teaching days, and that was Science Olympiad. Everyone always considered me a math nerd or a science geek, but honestly my true love has always been history. In literature I have always loved the antihero who finds himself in impossible circumstances: Captain Ahab, Julius Caesar, Michelangelo, John Wick, Raylan Givens, Boyd Crowder, Jack Reacher, Dirk Pitt, Augustus McCrea. But the area I have kept working in is Cobb County's Elementary Science Olympiad and most particularly the Water Rocket Event. Since my retirement seven years ago, I have kept my hand in by making sure that the children of Georgia get to have this challenging event each year. The event basically is to make a two-liter Coke bottle into a large water rocket propelled by water and compressed air and held aloft by a parachute. To win one needs to keep the rocket in the air the longest. Over the years, I have loaded up Cobb County's launching gear and traveled all over the metro area talking to classes about how to build a rocket and then, when they are ready, launching them, so they can test their rocket before the big events of which there are three. We have the Cobb Title I Event in which only Title I schools may compete. We have the Cobb Regional Event which is primarily for Cobb County Schools. And there is the State Science Olympiad held at Kennesaw State University where all the schools that qualified from their regional events compete. My friends Coach Chuck Jones and Richard Williamson originally worked the event with me, but they have since lost interest. Although I know if I needed them, they would come to assist me. But today the event is managed by my son, James Lyon Morris and me. But this event really takes three people to run it effectively, and at the 2023 State event this past May we did have an invaluable helper, The Princess, Caitlin Rose Morris, now thirteen years old. I am looking forward to this fall when schools start getting their teams together, and I get to be with children again.

I have to comment on a family event that took place this year, but I can only fill in the edges of the details. On March 15th, 2023, Paula Blackwell, Adam Blackwell's step mother and Toby Blackwell's wife, left her house one morning to go to her bible study. As she turned south onto I-985 at YMCA Drive (formerly "Howard the Duck" Road – ask Carolyn) in her CR-V, she did not realize that a road rage incident was unfolding down the road from her. Two men were being idiots, and one had driven his car quickly up 985 to the intersection that Paula was turning south at and had stopped. He was waiting for the second man who was also traveling south to catch up. When the second man caught up, the first man who had already stopped, stepped out of his car and started firing his pistol at the second man. The second man drove through the light, and the first man with the gun tracked the moving car firing the gun. As the man with the gun swept his hand south shooting, Paula's car came into his line of fire. A bullet struck the tailgate of Paula's car, passed through the tailgate, through the back seat, through the driver's seat, through Paula and finally struck the firewall of the CR-V. Somehow Paula made it to the emergency room at Northwest Georgia Medical Center, thank the Lord. What began was a long and arduous recovery process with many touch and go moments as the doctors worked to first save Paula's life, and then get her on the long road to recovery. I am happy to tell you that she is doing well and will live, what we all pray, will be a long and healthy life. But this event has taken its toll on Paula and her husband Toby. And has reminded us all how sacred life and how fleeting life can be. Carpé Diem.

On a lighter note, Bryce Harper Blackwell graduated from the University of Georgia with a degree from The Terry College of Business and has his eyes firmly set on going into the medical field. We are all so proud of him. The graduation was in two parts. On Wednesday, May 10th, there was the degree conferring ceremony from the Terry College of Business. This was held in the overflowing biggest room I have been in in a long time at the Classic Center on North Thomas Street. There had to be at least a hundred million people in there … at least! And we all watched the children march across the stage and

culminate four years of hard work. After that event, we all went to dinner at a little hole in the wall restaurant in a strip center in Athens. But the food was good and the company even better. In the picture, from left, are Jenna, Carolyn, Anna, Bryce, Adam and me. After dinner Carolyn and I headed home. We were to return on Friday. Now, apparently people make these reservations years in advance. That reminds me, I better get started on reservations for Bodie's graduation in 2025 today! When we returned on Friday we checked in to a kind of sketchy hotel. The room was passable and the breakfast pitiful but later that day was Bryce's whole class graduation in the UGA stadium, and there were a hundred million people going to be there too … actually only about 50,000 by my calculations. But before we went to the stadium, we all met at Bryce's apartment and Adam and Jenna and the parents of Bryce's roommates all chipped in, and we ate BBQ. Then, around four o'clock, Anna Grace Wylie and two other of Bryce's roommates got in the car with Carolyn and me, and we drove over to a parking deck where Bodie's girlfriend, Margot Marie Murphy, had secured a parking spot for Carolyn and me. What a sweetie. As we drove to the deck, we saw Bryce and friends making their way to wherever graduates were supposed to go, and we all hung out of the car and yelled, "We love you Bryce! We're proud of you!" Now this may seem strange, but this day was one gigantic party as only the children at the University of Georgia can do it! After parking, we made our way to just outside the bookstore where we met up with Jenna and Adam, and then all of us headed into the stadium. We found some seats in the upper level facing the setting sun at one end of the stadium. Somewhere down on that field was Bryce sitting with his college. The degrees were conferred by college … thankfully. In other words, the whole college stood up at one time, and they were "blessed" all at one time rather than each student, I'm guessing 6,000 of them, crossing the stage one at a time. If they had done that, we would still be there and it's 2024! When everyone had gotten their blessing and thrown their mortar boards in the air, it was every person for themselves. Carolyn and got lost trying to get back to our car, but a helpful security guard pointed us in the right direction, and we "headed for the barn." Congratulations Bryce Harper Blackwell. We are so proud of you and cannot wait to see what you and Anna do with your lives together. May God bless you both.

379

Last month The Princess, Caitlin Rose Morris, and her Hot Shotz tennis team took us all to Macon again for the State Championships and like last July it was Hell's doorstep in Macon. But again, all us old guys … Carolyn and me and James and Mana Swope … again "endeavored to persevere," keeping in mind the whole time that it was Caitlin who was really suffering out on the tennis court. We were just watching the suffering. Kind of like the people who went to the Coliseum in Rome to watch the gladiators. We ate dinner both nights downtown at a place called The Rookery. The first night it was with Mana and James Swope, Angela and Caitlin as James had a school event to attend and would not get to Macon until Friday. Friday night just Mana and James Swope and Carolyn and I ate at the same restaurant … just up the street from the Dozier Law Firm (an inside joke – ask Carolyn). It was a delightful evening and the first time just the four of us were able to sit down together and really get to know each other, and that was a very good thing. James was late coming down because he is making a huge leap this school year. He has been teaching STEAM (Science, Technology, Engineering, Art and Math) in Gordon County for the last six years and this school year he is moving to Cherokee County to do the same thing. This is a good and positive step for him, and I know until he has a year or so under his belt, he will not feel comfortable. But he is an extremely competent teacher, father, and man and I know it will go well for him. Saturday morning Carolyn and I had a few extra minutes before Cait had a match, and we stole away to look at what had to be the most beautiful Cathedral in Macon. The St. Joseph Catholic Church has some of the most magnificent stained glass in the Southeast, and if you ever get a chance to see this church it will be a blessing. We finished the day and Caitlin's team came in third again out of seven teams, and she was pleased with herself … exhausted but pleased … as she should be.

Caitlin is now an Eighth Grader at Palmer Middle School. She is in all AP courses and is even taking some high school credit courses this year. She is headed to North Cobb High School next year where her cousin Claire Annette Swope is a senior this year. Caitlin is still loving her chorus and has become the backbone of the percussion section of the band at Palmer. Again, watching her grow up thrills Carolyn and me, and I am so thankful that my Carolyn had the insight to follow the lead from my paternal grandmother, "Momma" Marie Louise Williams Morris, who showed us that grandchildren do not NEED grandparents. Grandchildren have, for the most part, a Mommy and a Daddy and they do not NEED us. So it is your job as grandparents to insert yourself into their lives and if you do that, hopefully, you will become an indispensable part of their lives, and there is nothing grander than that.

Carolyn and I spent three weeks in New York City, and took a Norwegian Cruise through the Canadian Atlantic Maritime Provinces, and the stories from our adventure are just too delicious not to include. We left Atlanta on a Wednesday, August 31st, 2023, on a Delta flight to New York City (NYC), and I must say the city was on its best behavior for us. The plans for the city and the cruise had been painstakingly planned and massaged and reworked by me until I could recite them in my sleep. You know by now in your reading that if Morrises are anything, they are obsessive. I think you can easily see that about me by now. Carolyn and I were like two little children with Christmas morning looming that night before. We had packed everything including our newest technological devices, Apple Air Tags. Yep, we were crawling, kicking and screaming into the 21ˢᵗ Century … but why not? They seemed prudent. Now, being a Wednesday morning in Atlanta and knowing that traveling anywhere in around Atlanta can either take about forty minutes or it can take you the rest of your life, we decided to leave about 7:00 for our 10:30 flight. You know, two hours ahead of the flight and all that. And we were armed with our new TSA super-duper we're really honest and won't blow anyone up secret code numbers so we wouldn't have to strip down to our underwear when we made our way out through security. The plan was to use the Park Ride and Relax remote parking which only serves the International Terminal because we would be coming back from the INTERNATIONAL city of Montreal, and therefore would be arriving back in the ATL on the international side. But this morning we were would be flying out to a "domestic" destination, LaGuardia, so once at the airport we would take the "blue shuttle bus" from the international side to the domestic side to leave … as you see, I had overthought the whole program. Anyway, we got down to the airport in record time and were standing with about a million other early morning people at the Delta ticket counters by 8:00. I love it when a plan comes together! Now, C and I have not flown anywhere since about this time in 2019 … four years ago … so we were a little rusty. Well, a cute young thing took pity on the old folks and helped us get our bags all tagged and of course the weight was perfect … note to world from old guys, buy one of those bag weighing things … they too are worth their weight in gold. So, we finally got the two 6,000 pound suitcases safely into Delta's hands, and we were off to our gate, T-14. The T's are right there at the terminal so it was piece of cake to get there. "Man, this is going well I thought to myself. And there is a Spanish Padre flying with us so I KNOW we are going to be fine." We got there and were all perky and excited. I decided, being the world traveler that I am, to check my Delta App (on my phone – I am so 21ˢᵗ century) and discovered that in the time it took to get from the ticket taking bag person to our T gate, Delta made a little doo-doo and forgot where they put our plane so they said, "Sorry all you people waiting, we thought the plane was at T-14 but it is really at A-3 … our bad." No problem for C and me, and off we trundle to A concourse. 'Course this meant down into the tunnel and hopping the train from T to A, piece of cake, and we were there in record time and settled into our not that comfortable seats. Well again, being the world traveler and manic, type-A personality who sweats every detail until I have the runs, I casually wandered over to the big board and checked our flight departure gate … again. Well, in the time it had taken us to get from T-14 to A-3, Delta had found their plane and it was in fact exactly where they originally thought it was … at T-14, so they had not really lost it … they just didn't believe it was sitting at T-14 when it really was. A perfectly normal mistake anyone could have made when it comes to a 127,520 pound 757 airliner. So, they really did not make a mistake after all. They just thought they had, but they hadn't really, so no harm, no foul. And with smiles on our faces and enthusiasm in our hearts, back to the original gate we went, and the plane was there … I think the padre helped too … so, that was a plus. We, C, me and the Padre all boarded the plane right on schedule. C and I were in Delta Comfort + seating because we are all that, but the Padre had to ride in the back. I had picked our seats and C and I were sitting on the "Oh MY God we're gonna crash, let's get out of this plane row," so the stewardess was giving us the hairy eyeball to make sure we could operate everything, and she must have been sort-of satisfied because she did not make us move … but she did sit in a special little seat next to us … honestly, I don't think she trusted us. She was probably correct in that belief.

So, we got to LaGuardia airport on time with minimal snacks being eaten. It was around lunch time now, and we were getting hungry, but we decided to push on to baggage claim before eating. Well, even though LaGuardia has really cleaned up their act since I had flown in there over twenty-five years before, once you step outside the "secure TSA area" to get your bags, there are no restaurants anywhere. But C had made sure we were ready for just that eventuality, and we had our own snacks! Which we snarfed! Now! We were ready to attack the Big Apple, and my plan was to grab a taxi, and we'd be off quickly and economically, but as we were dragging our bags along the concrete walkway under the street somewhere, an aggressive UBER Black driver named Gio jumped out from behind a column and tackled me and lured us into his UBER Black car with wild promises of cheap, clean transportation. So begrudging again, Carolyn and I were dragged screaming and kicking into the 21st Century, and that is how we were hood-winked into taking our <u>first</u> UBER ride. Once safely in his UBER Black car, I told him we wanted to take a little side trip to an address in Jackson Heights so Carolyn could see the apartment where she had come when she was a little girl and her family had come up to NYC to visit the legendary Granny and Grandpa Koch. Gio immediately lit up! "Of course! Grandpa Koch! He was a legend. I actually met him when I was a child! He came up to me as I was about six and riding by and said, 'Hey Kid, what'd you pay for that dump of a bike?' I was honored he had talked to me!" No, really we just drove by the apartments, and I took a couple of pictures, and Carolyn relived a few childhood memories of being with her father and walking around the neighborhood and shopping for bagels and riding the subway with him. Reliving childhood memories is a very personal thing, and I was honored to be allowed to be part of that reliving with her. And eventually Gio got us to The Pearl, our 49th Street hotel just a half a block off Broadway … literally. C loved The Pearl from the moment we arrived and were greeted by Keagan, who could have been our Edward Jones money manager Ryan Walker's long lost twin brother (and that was a good thing). Yep, when it came to the hotel, old Jimbo had, with luck, come out smelling like a rose. With the help of Booking.com, I had picked out the perfect hotel in a perfect location in the theater district of NYC.

Our first day in the city was to be our 9/11 Memorial visit. The day was to be as heart-rending as one could imagine. The day was sunny, bright and cool, and we took the 1 train to downtown. There was a metro station at each end of our block … lucky Jim. We found the two waterfalls, Reflecting Absence is the title of the pools, and they are stirring. Of course they "reflect" where the two buildings sat on that 9/11 morning. We found a name, Lynne Irene Morris. There is no relation except for the surname. I took a picture of it. The structures around where the towers stood are magnificent and stand in mute tribute to that horrific morning. Our time came, and we went into the museum. I'll be honest. Visiting here was not my first priority. I had lived through that day back in 2001 as you know from reading, and I was not a fan of revisiting that day, but I was wrong. We went into the museum and traveled into the foundations. As one might expect, for two architects it was fascinating to see the way the towers were built. Carolyn was very sensitive to me that morning. I think she knew I harbored unresolved feelings. There is a section of the museum that has pictures of each of the almost 3,000 people who died that day. Carolyn was not sure if I was going to go in the room. I said I wanted to go in, so into hell we went. I wanted to see the picture of Lynne Irene Morris … and we did. She was so very young. She was maybe twenty-five. I started to choke-up but pushed my emotions down like I can do … except when kittens die. The next stop on the museum tour was a video area where they warned you that some of the images were graphic. I could imagine people choosing to leap to their death rather than being incinerated. C and I were walking hand in hand, and I stopped. She looked at me. I told her I just could not go in there, and I started crying. I started sobbing like a baby. She took me in her arms, and all my unresolved feelings from that morning came streaming out. I had taken care of my fourth graders that day. I had taken care of my wife and children, but I had not taken care of me, and it all came spilling out. Carolyn took me in her arms, and I let everything out right there in the middle of the museum … and I left everything there.

We left, and we were starving. We happened on a perfect little second floor NYC pizza place. In fact, the entire rest of the time in NYC we did not have any pizza that would compare. From there looked into St. Paul's Chapel right across the street, and then we wandered down to Trinity Church and found Alexander Hamilton's grave and his wife's grave. We decided to scrap the Staten Island Ferry and head for the barn, because we had tickets to see the Broadway production of *Wicked* that evening. Go Jimbo!

Wicked was fantastic! We were three rows back from the stage and to the left. We were so close that when the smoke rolled, it rolled all over us, and I took two things away from the evening … well, three actually. One, the play *Wicked* was WICKED! It was awesome. I sort of knew the basic concept of the play, but not all the nuances, and I was swept away into the story. The play was written to wrap up all the details left over from the original *Wizard of Oz* story. Two, I will never look at Glenda (Galinda) the Good Witch the same again. She was a whiney, self-centered, self-serving, little bitch. And Three, the flying monkeys are STILL terrifying. They were costumed perfectly, climbed around the scenery like … well, monkeys … and basically were … well, terrifying.

That evening, Friday, September 1st, while Carolyn and I were watching *Wicked* a momentous event took place in the life of our family. Bryce Harper Blackwell got engaged to Anna Grace Wylie. It took place on the dock on the lake at Jenna and Adam's new home on Lake Lanier at 4345 McEachern Drive in Lula, Georgia. Their plans are to get married on October 19th, 2024. They had to choose this date because the University of Georgia is not playing a football game that day! I know, but that is the reason. We were not able to talk to them until Saturday, because we were in the play Friday night. Carolyn was just about to burst with excitement! Saturday was our day to see St. Patrick's Cathedral, Grand Central Station and the Guggenheim. All were great except for the Guggenheim. Going there was kind of a pilgrimage for two architects as it was designed by Frank Lloyd Wright and blah, blah, blah. It looked just like the pictures and the inside was a mirror of the outside except there did not seem to be any real art inside. Oh there was a single Picasso and a Gauguin and a Renoir and an exhibit by some lady who loved Erector Sets because all her art looked like it came from one of their boxes. I am almost embarrassed to say we were in there for all of fifteen minutes. I think old F.L.W. would be pissed, except he is dead so who cares? Anyway, before our Grand Central Station tour … which was excellent – we had a guide who loved his station … C and I sat down for an $80.00 lunch of a pair of lobster rolls. Little did I know, that would be the closest I would come to lobster the entire trip. I'm basically a penny-pincher … a trait the Scottish arm of the Morris family are famous for, and paying hundreds of dollars for

lobster is not a thing for me. At 12:00 that Saturday we were basically able to Face Time Anna and Bryce. Carolyn was quite literally beside herself. I was too, but it seems different for women. That is not a sexist statement. It is just emotionally different for them. We had a wonderful call. We saw the ring, which is exquisite, and heard all about the evening with wine and the dock lit up with lights and … well, it was beautiful. Apparently even Bryce's brother Bodie made time in his schedule from UGA and Margot to be there at the house. It was supposed to be a surprise, but based on the manicure Anna had gotten earlier that day and her overall emotional astuteness, I'm guessing she had the whole evening scoped out long before Bryce even knew it was happening.

Sunday morning started with an interesting text from Norwegian. Apparently this particular cruise line cannot anticipate where hurricanes are or are anticipated to track, and the ship we were to board on Monday was trapped in Hamilton, Bermuda, by Hurricane Idalia. Yeah, again, I know. The Norwegian Joy would not arrive in NYC until Tuesday cutting our cruise one day short and extending our NYC stay by one day. So, I immediately got in touch with The Pearl's front desk and they said sure you can stay. You can even keep your same room … for a price. So, we did. And we took a rest day and just sort of strolled around. On Monday we went up to the "Upper West Side" The cooler weather we had experienced was abating and the temp was pushing the upper 80's and humidity was coming back. We saw Grant's Tomb (Don't waste your time). You lean over a marble rail in a huge gothic structure and look down on two giant marble caskets. Ta – Daaaaa! Also the first cathedral we went up to see, Riverside Church, even though it was all about welcome and join our service and come see us … was closed.

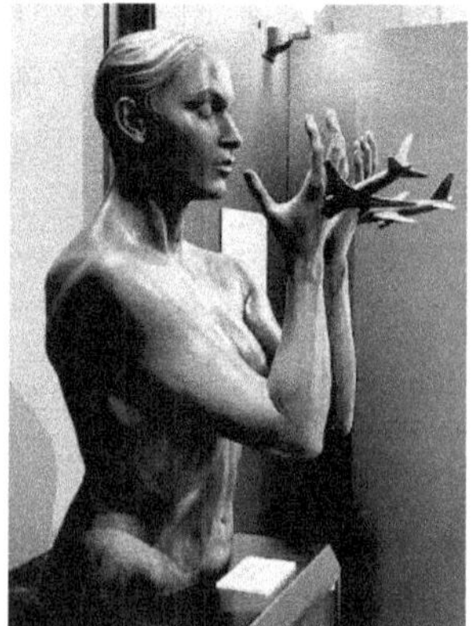

But the second cathedral, St. John the Devine, MORE than made up for it. It was truly magnificent, and a 9/11 sculpture inside was beautifully conceived and executed.

On Tuesday the Joy finally made port. She was a little salt sprayed, and I'll bet the people were glad to get off, but she had made port. After a short taxi ride we accomplished the labyrinth that is getting on a ship and were sitting in the Garden Café (we called it the "Not the Windjammer") ready to chow down. This was our first realization that this really was going to be an old person's cruise. We had never seen so many canes, walkers and scooters. Scooters have replaced wheelchairs in the 21st Century. We finally scored our room, 13290, and almost all our luggage had arrived by 9 that night. So, I went on a quest. Norwegian's Lost Luggage folks and Guest Relations people are worthless. This was to be my first realization that Norwegian is not Royal Caribbean, but their food is good. Finally, my bag did miraculously reappear about 10 that night, so I had underwear. That was a good thing. Now because the ship had been delayed a day, Norwegian cut out two ports, Boston and Portland and replaced Portland with a Sea Day. This was a good thing as C did not have to endure one of Jimbo's famous forced history marches around Boston, and we had already been to Portland with the Blackwell's on another cruise. Portland has crummy lighthouses anyway. But dropping those two ports meant Norwegian could keep the other four ports … the other four of the most worthless ports ever conceived by a cruise line. Well, Halifax was not too bad and they do have a great fort (which we had also visited with the Blackwells on that previous cruise). We walked into town, bought Stephen King's new book *Holly*, and then walked back to the ship. But the other three ports: Sydney and Charlottetown and Corner Brook were nothing. And I mean nothing. We did decide the Corner Brook was where all the fog in the world was generated … their major town factory is a paper factory and it puts out tons of smoke. But I must say the Corner Brookians seemed very glad to see us. They even hauled out an old school bus to help shuttle us old folks the quarter mile to their little town where one of the high points was a lake … we never saw it. We are considering recommending Corner Brook to Bryce and Anna for a destination wedding … NOT. But I have to admit that Corner Brook has now found a special place in a corner of my heart. The town was just so dog-gone sincere.

Finally, we did make it to Quebec. I am skipping the parts where we saw the play *Footloose* on the boat undertaken by some hard working and talented young people who undoubtedly see themselves on Broadway soon, the myriad of old people who would be walking along in the "not-the-Windjammer" restaurant and just stop in front of you for a Mitch McConnell moment (look it up in 2023 history) causing you to bob and weave around them, and a hundred other little mundane events that would make you want to stab yourself in the eye with a fork if I detailed all of them here. Interestingly, we had two days in Quebec. The first we actually slept on the boat that night. Then we disembarked the second day. This was the day the parking lot gate arm came down on Carolyn's head as we were dragging our luggage from the boat to The Priori Hotel. One minute she was following me as I made my way out of the parking lot through the open gate, and the next moment the gate had come down and whacked her on the head and face giving her a real shiner. Fortunately, she was not hurt badly, but I felt terrible for letting her get hurt. The Priori was a perfect little hotel in Old Quebec. That second day in Quebec we went on a Viator excursion to the Cathedral St. Anne de Beaupré which was stunningly magnificent.

The next morning, we were off to the Gare du Palais and caught the train to Montreal. The Gare du Palais is another beautiful piece of architecture on its own. The four plus hour train ride was the longest train ride I had ever taken (just a quirk of my life). For Carolyn it paled in comparison to her childhood all night train rides from Marietta to Nashville. I found the ride to be quite ho-hum. Perhaps I was just exhausted. We finally got to Montreal and went one stop further to the Dorval Station where we almost did not get off. The people in charge of making the announcements forgot to call that stop! But we made it, a night in the Fairfield Inn, and we were off to the Montréal-Pierre Elliot Trudeau International Airport which was beautiful and our flight to the big ATL. Our flight was perfect. And in spite of leaving a little late, we landed a half hour early. Now, a couple of things affected our return. As you recall we were coming in from the international city of Montreal, so I had put our car where we could grab the shuttle from the International Terminal and zip right to the car. Well, for some reason we cleared Customs in Montreal as we were taxiing the jet pulled up to a domestic gate of some number at D Terminal … not the International Terminal! Then we were told our bags were on Carousel 2. I do not remember if they said Domestic or not, but it was logical if we were at D, the bags would be in Domestic. So, C and I headed into the transportation tunnel and were met with absolute pandemonium … ABSOLUTE PANDEMONIUM! In the two plus weeks we had been gone they had started a construction project in the tunnel and all the return train cars were shut down. I cannot adequately explain the disaster that was going on in the tunnel. The shuttles that were working would go D out to International and then reverse. Another set went C to A and then reverse. A final set would go T to Baggage Claim and reverse. So you walked between D and C, and then A to T. The tunnel was crammed with lost people, people late for flights who were running, people pushing others in wheelchairs. It was a disaster. We finally made it all the way from D to domestic baggage. The little sign said our flight's bags were on Carousel 2. I parked Carolyn with our carry-ons and waded through to the carousel. No bags appeared. Finally, I got my phone and punched the "Find My" app. God bless Apple Air Tags. The app said we had two of our bags … which we did. And the other two bags were … wait for it … at the International Terminal Baggage Claim! By now Carolyn and I were both exhausted and fed up. It was truly a Comedy of Errors. Long story short, we finally walked all the way to the other end of the terminal, caught the "blue shuttle bus" back to International which took the scenic route back through East Point and stopped at the Varsity for some chili dogs and finally arrived at the International Terminal. "Find My" indicated the bags were literally just feet away, and there on Carousel 7 were our two bags doing what bags do … just going around and around. We then caught the shuttle, got our car, headed home, ate at the Waffle House on Canton Road just south of Jamerson Road, got home and crashed. The next day I cancelled the Paris/London trip which we were due to leave in three weeks. We were done … until April of 2024!

The rest of 2023 finished quietly. Carolyn and I took a little weekend trip to St. Simons and bought the greatest bird houses to be used as White Elephant gifts at the family Christmas do. In December, Carolyn's youngest sister, Roberta (Bobbie) Miller, and her husband Gregg threw a great wedding party out at a farm in Roopville, Georgia, for their son Jordon who got married. We were fearful the weather was not going to cooperate, but the sun came out at just the right time and all was good. The funny part of the evening was that Adam and Jenna (Blackwell) wanted to whoop it up, and so they were staying overnight in Roopville, but they needed a way to get back and forth from their hotel to the wedding. They called upon that famous chauffer service now known as Puber (Pa Uber). Yes, Carolyn and I were their chauffeurs that evening. We did it up right of course with waters and magazines and extremely deferential treatment … lots of bowing and scraping and obsequious "yes ma'ams" and "no sirs." It was fun, and we all had a good time especially since my Princess, Caitlin Rose Morris, was there with "her daddy," James Lyon Morris.

During the fall of 2023, I spent a lot of time traveling to schools and tutoring Science Olympian hopefuls on the best way to make water rockets. I mentioned this activity earlier, and I continued with my water rockets into the late fall. This has sort of become my thing I do. Cobb County Schools pays me, and I travel around to schools in Cobb, and even a Cherokee school this season, and help school children learn the intricacies of using a two-liter coke bottle to make a powerful water rocket. I enjoy it and they seem to enjoy it and it helps the ESO coaches … so it is a win, win, win.

The year closed with a great Christmas and celebrations. Carolyn and I won the "White Elephant" gift giving in my opinion. We had two bird houses we bought while on the weekend jaunt to St. Simons. They were really cute with license plates for roofs. One plate was a University of Georgia plate, and one was Georgia Southern. Jenna and Adam snagged them both and they are proudly attached to trees at their lake house … at least today (5/28/24) they are.

19.

For me, 2024, began with even more traveling to schools and rocket launchings. The Title I Elementary Science Olympiad (ESO) was to be on February 10th, and so coaches and schools started getting ready early. Title I ESO is an event peculiar to Cobb County. This special event is just for Title I schools who do not always have a parental and monetary support other schools in Cobb have. It was started by a forward looking teacher named Lisa Green probably fifteen years ago. It gives these Olympians a chance to compete and win medals and ribbons in events they might be shut out in when they compete with better funded teams from other parts of the county. In March we had the Cobb Regional ESO. James and Caitlin and I were asked if we could run the water rocket event for Cherokee County the week following and of course we did. All this was in preparation for the big State Science Olympiad in May at KSU.

In March our beautiful daughter Jenna Morris Blackwell asked for one thing for her 50th birthday. She wanted to come down to our house at 1920 Falcon Wood Drive NE, Marietta, GA 30066, and then spend the day driving around to all her old "haunts" while she was growing up. So, once again, Puber was called into action. Carolyn and I devised this whole birthday program. We plotted the entire route that you have read about in this book and visited all the places C and I have lived together starting with our apartment block at

Bordeaux West Apartments on "The 41 Highway" adding for the groan factor, "This is where you were conceived!" Carolyn put together a whole book with pictures and commentary for Jenna's trip down memory lane. It was a great day of memories and laughter when we would come across a place, where Carolyn and I were married for instance, and find nothing but a dirt patch because the building had been razed. Or the Hazelwood house lot where an auto shop now sits. Or East Cobb Middle School on Holt road which had been wiped from the face of the earth and a brand new, very modern elementary school erected in its place. There were moments though when she saw the Sherwood Drive house and teared up, and then she and Adam walked across the street to her old Powers Ferry Elementary School together. So much for memories … but there are two things I will always recall from that day: the sound of my beautiful daughter's laughter as we happened upon one of her memories that day, and the old adage "the only thing that is constant is change." Adam capped the whole 50th birthday experience by treating Jenna to a surprise birthday party at their favorite restaurant Bones. The surprise part was the entire family … Toby and Paula Blackwell, Bryce Blackwell, Bryce's fiancé Anna Wylie, Bodie Blackwell, Carolyn and me, were there waiting for her. Now THAT is an evening! Way to go Adam!

The highlight of 2024 has to be Carolyn's and my long waited 50th Anniversary trip to Paris and London. It started off a little shaky thanks to Delta Airlines as you will read, but all turned out well. The writing format is going to change a little as a day-by-day accounting is the best way to explain our adventure.

Wednesday April 10th to Thursday April 11th, 2024

When I booked the flight on Delta, I booked it as Delta Comfort+. This meant you could pick your own seats, and so C and I were together. Me on the aisle her by the window. At this time the plane was a 2-3-2 seating arrangement. Then Delta changed the aircraft to a 2-5-2 plane. Apparently when D does this, a computer reseats everyone. When the computer reseated us, it split us up! We were on the same row but both on aisle seats. S S - S S S S Me - C S. So, C was going to sit next to who knows who. So, I started emailing Delta all the way up to the CEO and no one could help me. The way Delta deals with it meant if a family was flying the child could be split up from the Mom and Dad. And that is exactly what happened! Long story short a great gate agent named Clara solved the problem and C and I were happy and the family were happy to have their child back. I am not done with Delta on this issue yet, I assure you. Anyway … we got to the FastPark&Relax place at 12:00ish for a flight at 4:55. (park, ride, bags, lunch, gate … 12:00 is not as early as it sounds when they want you there 3 hours early) And everything went as smooth as silk. We ate at a Chinese place out on the International Terminal on the mezzanine overlooking everything. We found our gate … like F8 or something and settled in. This is when our savior, Clara, ended our seating problem. Bless her. And she confessed that Delta's way of reassigning seats is messed up. We ended up in 31 H and J … with my C by the window. All that worry for nothing. Or maybe it was for something … rather than just rolling over and whining, "I can't do anything." One needs to fight the problem. And so we flew into the night and morning of Thursday, 4/11, landing in Paris at Charles de Gaulle a little ahead of schedule at 8:00A. And the fun begins.

So, here you are at 8 something in AM and your body says it is 2AM something and you have this funny taste in your mouth and everyone is "jibber-jabbing" in French and you are just trying to *Sortie* the CDG. Then you are confronted with your first hurdle of the morning in France … Customs and Border Control. The line was backed up FOREVER! There had to be at least 800 people in the line … perhaps even more than that! I tell you these Frenchies are going to play hell in a couple of months when about a billion people descend on this place for the Olympics! I had planned for a little French dude in a beret to be waiting on the other side of customs for us, holding a little *Morris* sign and be ready to whisk us off in a limousine to the Hotel du College de France … then my first call in Paris! "Where are you, Mr. Morris?"

"I am standing in the world's longest Customs line."

"How much longer?"

"Well, I don't know. At least 15 minutes, and then we have to get our bags…"

"I can only wait 10 more minutes. I have other people to pick up, and the agreement was I was wait 45 minutes, and then I have to go."

"Well, I do not know what to tell you. I cannot get through this line any faster than I am."

And he was gone. And when we finally got our bags there was no little French Dude in a beret. (Expletive deleted) But, never fear, we got our bags and after a circuitous route we found the taxis, and it only cost about 3 Euros more than the little beret guy. Booking.com will hear about this too!

The ride to our hotel was uneventful and took about an hour. Traffic was just as pitiful as Atlanta. We were greeted at Hôtel du College de France by a sweet young lady named Yana who offered us some breakfast and a place to sit until the room was ready. When we finally crashed in the room, we went to sleep immediately, and then we were up at 5P or so and off to see *Gay Paree* … and find some dinner. Dinner ended up at the little café on a corner a little way down from the hotel on St. George Street named the Café Metro as it was near the St. George Metro Station. It was quite good, and we were "on Paris time," and could actually converse in French and get food! Of course there was a lot of menu pointing and "merci" and "merci beaucoup," but we got some food. After dinner and a little stroll down to the Isle de Cité we saw the icon … Notre Dame de Paris. She is beautiful. The scaffolding is still there and they are working furiously around the clock to have her ready for the Olympics, but they have raised the new spire in place. Considering it has only been five years, France is working a miracle. On the way home we stopped at a little church on Rue Saint Séverin and lit a candle for our children and grandchildren. If you look carefully at my picture and blow it up you can see the church architect's one twisted column right behind the altar beyond the cross. Walking away I caught a picture of the setting sun catching the spire of this beautiful church tucked away in Paris … and its gargoyles. I love gargoyles!

Friday, April 12th, 2024

Rallying after a good night's sleep … the "douvillier" (duvet) was a little heavy, and so I asked if we could just get an extra sheet which our wonderful young people, Eric and Neils, running the desk were more than happy to provide. And C and I agreed after negotiation that 22°C (71.2°F) was the right number for the room A/C. And we were off! Our first stop that morning was up the hill above our hotel to the Pantheon where some of France's most distinguished lay. We saw the crypts of Rousseau and Voltaire, but the most surprising and interesting was in the basement where we found a temporary exhibit of the life and early death at the hands of the Nazis of the World War II Parisian Underground hero Missak Manouchian. Manouchian led a group of partisans who harassed and wrecked German efforts to maintain control of Paris and its surroundings. He and several of his group were executed after a sham trial on February 21, 1944. Our plan was to visit St. Chapelle, but we quickly found out one needed timed entry tickets, so we abandoned that venue and just struck out across Paris. We found a very helpful man in the Cluny La Sorbonne Metro station who helped us purchase a Metro Navigo card … I promptly lost mine and had to get another … Dork … and we were set to go. (AH HA! Jumping ahead to when we got home to Marietta, I found my lost Metro card stuck in my check book … I did not lose it, and I was not a dork after all! Or at least not as big a dork.)

Let me mention that the temperature which was promised in the 60's was touching 80°, and we were both a little ranked out as we had packed turtle necks and jackets and gloves and scarves. But all this was to turn around soon, so not to worry. The day was scheduled to be an easy day. The Pantheon, St. Chappelle Church and Montmartre. As I mentioned, when we got to St. Chapelle we discovered that getting in without a timed entry pass was going to be very time consuming. Rick Steves warned me, but I did not believe him. So, we abandoned that idea, and later in the day I got timed tickets for Sunday at 1:00. I am really glad I brought my lap top. Even though it was heavy, I was able to do things much more easily than I could have on my phone. We headed off for a bite to eat and a little rest before our excursion to Montmartre. This time it was a little café on a corner, and we actually had some Kir with our lunches. Everyone in Paris has wine with lunch and dinner, and we just joined in! It was deliciously awesome.

Around 3:00 we headed off on the Metro to our reservation at Montmartre that afternoon at 4:30P (10:30A in Atlanta … still thinking that way) for a visit to the Montmartre Museum and Sacré-Cœur and wine tasting. I love the Metro in Paris. It is so easy to use and navigate and the trains are clean and on time. The hardest part for me when you come up out of a station is getting your bearings as to which way is which unless you have a massive landmark like Notre Dame to help you. Being honest, this led the world famous Barcelona saying "I know exactly where we are." We successfully arrived at the Barbès Rochechouart station and then made our way up the Boulevard de Rochechouart to the Anvers station where we were to meet our guide. At a little before 4, right on time, a young man, Johnny, introduced himself and we were off with two other ladies for our tour. Our first stop after taking the Funicular (think glass elevator car moving like an escalator) was to take in the sweeping views of Paris at our feet. The picture I took was from the same place that in the movie *John Wick 4* the duel at sunrise was fought. We were able to go in Sacré-Cœur (means sacred heart) as the line moved quickly. This beautiful bone white church's exterior is a travertine limestone called Chateau-Landon and washes itself clean by exuding calcite each time it rains. I will not bore you with its complicated history, but it is only about a hundred years old and beautiful. Carolyn's phone has all the pictures.

There is a short story by Marcel Aymé named *Le passe-muraille* (*The passer-through-walls*) about a man who could suddenly walk through walls and the shenanigans and downside to an ability like that could and would present. Anyway, there is a representation of this book in the form of a man coming out of a wall there on Montmartre, and we took several cute photographs there before going into the art museum. The wine tasting part of the experience took place in a little vineyard behind the museum. We were greeted by an attractive lady who not only helped tend the vineyard, but also gave tours and recounted the history. There are several pictures of us with her and Johnny as well as the vineyard. The wine tasting was a delightful Rosé … not too tart and not too sweet. And the cool thing was we got to keep the glasses. One of which we almost immediately broke on the way home … dork. After the wine tasting we headed for our B&B as Versailles was on the docket for "the morrow." Instead of taking the Funicular I wanted to walk down the *John Wick 4* steps. If you watch *JW4* you will see him trying to reach Sacré-Cœur before dawn, and the bad guys try to stop him on the 222 steps leading up the hill. I took several pictures! It was when we were walking down the street after that, and we were getting ready for the Metro that I discovered I was missing my Navigo card. We paused by the side of the street, and I searched high and low for my card … no could find. The nice vineyard lady on her way home even saw us and stopped to ask if there was a problem. There was not really … and Carolyn calmed me down, and I vowed from then on that she would carry all the critical stuff in her pocketbook rather than me being responsible with my over the shoulder backpack thing. It's hell being irresponsible! But please recall that I did not *actually* "lose" my Navigo card per se.

Getting to Versailles on Saturday required a special train ticket that was above and beyond the regular Metro pass, so on the way home from Sacré-Cœur we stopped at a Metro station agent booth and (got me a new Navigo Card) bought tickets for the "C" line to Versailles. This is where our wine tasting glass met its fate as glass and tile floors do not mix well. But we got our passes and were squared away for Saturday.

Saturday, April 13th, 2024

Versailles Day! Hoping for cooler weather we were the first down to breakfast at 7:15 so we could get a train at 8:15 to 8:30 to be at Versailles for our rendezvous with our guide at 10:15. I had everything timed and thought through. *I will be honest here … I did not find this vacation relaxing. There were many deadlines and many times I had to count on other people to do their part and many times I had to rely on the internet, and all of that always gets my blood pressure up. But I have to say, looking back, it all went well. And while I am confessing, there was one thing I could always count on … my Carolyn. She was always ready for the next adventure and (as my father would say) "a real soldier."* And so we ate, and caught the correct train at the Cluny-Sorbonne Station and were in the town of Versailles at 9:00. We were to meet our guide at the equestrian statue of Louis XIV except it was all boxed up and covered, so we had to guess we were in the right place. A young lady walked up and told us we were in the right place except we were about an hour early … that was okay with me. Carolyn and I headed to the town to find a coffee or something. We did not find coffee, but we found the morning market on the square and the Cathedral Saint Louis. It was a simple unadorned church with lovely light. As we made our way back toward Versailles the temperature started to climb. It was going to be another "not in the 60's" day. We met our guide, Marion, near the boxed up man on a horse at the appointed hour, and for the next three hours (after a rest room break) we saw gardens … many were naturally being rehabilitated so they were more like acres of dirt … and fountains and miles of paths and room after room of luxurious tapestries and paintings and splendor and people and crowds and people. I really cannot describe the opulence, but one could grasp a profound understanding why there was a French Revolution with people losing their heads. An interesting fact Marion shared was that Louis XIV, "The Sun King," built Versailles, Louis XV enjoyed Versailles and Louis XVI (the husband of Marie-Antoinette) paid for Versailles … with his/their life/lives. There was also disgusting information about the nobility relieving themselves anywhere in the gardens or in the halls of Versailles wherever they could. There were stories of ostrich feathers on bed posts and the bed bugs and lice would climb up and get caught in the feathers and the maids would the take the feathers outside and dispense with the critters. Marion was so full of information it was almost impossible to keep up. The only part of Versailles I was really interested in was the Hall of Mirrors, and like the Sistine Chapel in Rome, it was so crowded one could not appreciate the beauty, majesty or history of the huge space. The room faced west so the beauty of the sunset would stream in the windows and be caught in the opposite mirrored wall for "The Sun King." When we finished the tour, we were both pretty much done and hungry. We went back into the town to find some lunch and ended up in an Asian café. It was interesting, the mamma-san who waited on us spoke zero English, and we spoke very little French but between the mamma-san poking her finger at the menu repeatedly like a machine gun and our tiredness and acceptance of any food they wanted to give us, we ate lunch. After that, we world travelers slogged our way back to the train station and boarded a too crowded train back to Paris. We ate dinner at a little café off St. Michel Street. We got two Quiche Loraine and fizzy water and an apricot tart, ate them and headed for the B&B calling it a day.

Sunday, April 14ᵗʰ, 2024

This day we did not have anything planned for the morning. We did have our timed tickets to St. Chapelle at 1:00 and the Louvre at 2:30, but our morning was free … so we had a leisurely breakfast and then chilled out and tried to recover our "powers." We grabbed lunch somewhere and were on our way to the Île de Cité by 12:30. It was a beautiful day, and the temperature had finally started to turn. The high was to be in the 60's. I have multiple lovely pictures of Carolyn in her white jacket.

St. Chappelle is known for its stained glass, and it did not disappoint! I have photos and video of the interior that were breathtaking, but as is with so much of what we saw, pictures and videos cannot capture the amazing and awesome beauty and majesty of these places. One MUST go see them in person. This magnificent "chapel" was built in the 1200's by King Louis IX, who was to become Saint Louis, as a place to keep the "most prestigious relic of the Passion of Christ: The Crown of Thorns." This relic stayed there until the French Revolution when it was moved to Notre Dame Cathedral for safety. The church was constructed in a record time of just seven years which was unreal for the time. I will never forget just sitting and quietly admiring the majesty of the glass and the space. Truly awe inspiring.

We left St. Chappelle and took a stroll along the north side of the Île de Cité along the Seine, over the Pont de Neuf Bridge (me making jokes about the man who built the bridge was also famous for nerf balls … sorry) and to the Louvre. We passed through the portals on the Eastern end and after weaving around some gates there was I.M. Pei's pyramid solution to the entry at the large open plaza. It was flanked by two smaller pyramids, and goofy tourists were all trying to get photos of themselves "touching" the tops of the pyramids … like people do when they are "holding up" the leaning tower in Pisa. Some people think the pyramid was an brilliant solution. And some people think it a grandiose display of architecture for the sake of architecture and an homage to one architect's name that he could foist this chunk of glass off on a committee whose taste was all in their collective mouths. Anyway, our timed tickets allowed us to whoosh right in which was good because the 60's had given way to the 70's, but the bright cloudless sky was always welcome. The first thing I want to say is that The Louvre is HUGE! Much more than can be taken in in one day or two days or even a week. But I had a target that afternoon and it wasn't Mona or Venus. The most original part of the Louvre was a castle built by Philip II in 1190 at the eastern end of the complex and one can tour the foundations of this original castle. The upper northern and eastern part of the castle are gone and southern and western parts have been incorporated into the present buildings, so if you do not know what you are looking for you will never see it. Knowing we had Chartres the next day and everything else we had done so far, Carolyn and I "sortied" the Louvre. But "sortieing" the Louvre proved to be a task reserved for the not faint of heart … and we did see Venus on the way out. When we FINALLY emerged above ground, we were on the Champs-Élysées, hungry and ready to shop for Caitlyn! Shopping was a bust as everything was very high end and not suited to our needs, but we found dinner at a restaurant on the Champs and drank Kir and watched people. I think I had a lobster roll and Carolyn had a salad and bread! After dinner we walked in the Jardin du Tuileries and up toward the Arc de Triumph and stopped at the Place de Concord where the Egyptian obelisk is and where the guillotine was located during La Revolution. From there we grabbed the Metro for home because we had a monster big day planned for Monday, Chartres!

Monday, April 15th, 2024

Today began bright and early and finally the heat had broken. During the night a front had come through, and the wind was up, and it was in the 50's, and we had a train to catch! We were headed out on a 10:09 train out of Montparnasse Station. Since there were no Metro trains directly there, and I did not feel like jumping through several station's hoops that early in the morning, we just took a 9:15 taxi which our darling front desk children at our hotel were glad to arrange for us. Thanks to Rick Steve's book, I sort of knew what I was doing and where I was going which was a good thing because the station was a confusing place. After paying one Euro each to use the potty, we found our train on track 23 and got good seats and settled in for the ninety-minute ride. We had two main targets: Chartres Cathedral and The International Stained Glass Museum, and when we stepped off the train at a very unassuming little station and walked out the front door, there she was … standing proudly and watching over the town … Chartres Cathedral with her two dissimilar spires. After walking up a little avenue, we arrived at the very windy and very cold (much to Carolyn's glee) town square which was dominated by a bold six-foot high individual lettered sign reading C H A R T R E S. Corner Brook, NS, would have been proud. My first order of business was to get some food, so we took a couple of touristy selfies and found what looked like one of the only open cafes right at the … I think … west facade of the church, Le Café Serpente … Café of the Snake? Don't know. And so straining our French to its limit and the waiter straining his English to its limit, we kind of ordered something we thought we wanted, and the waiter then told us they were out of something, but he could substitute something, and so I kind of got a chacuterie board thing and Carolyn got some kind of salad thing. The coolest part of the chacuterie board was it had a cylindrical blob of what HAD to be Spam and another loaf thing that if it wasn't corned beef hash from a can I would eat my napkin! Maybe it was snake, who knows. Of course Carolyn was grossed out, but I woofed it all down. Bodie would have had to move to a different table (inside joke … ask Bodie Blackwell). After lunch we headed out into the wind and the cathedral. Technically Our Lady of Chartres Cathedral (Notre Dame de Chartres) was partially built in 1145 and then reconstructed over a 26-year period after a fire in 1194. It is considered a high point of French Gothic Architecture. One notable feature that strikes most visitors is the contrasting spires. The plain spire was from the original construction in 1060 and was left standing after the fire. The second very flamboyant spire was constructed in the early 1500's during a completely different architectural style's popularity. Ah, architects, one has to love their vanity. But the interior and its almost mythic stained glass does not disappoint. Again, there are no pictures that do it justice so you just have to go there and stand where Carolyn and I and literally hundreds of thousands of pilgrims have stood and admire the craftsmanship and inspiration and dedication it took to build these masterpieces. I did take a couple of pictures of Carolyn sitting on the base of a column. These pictures are significant because pilgrims rested their weary bones on this very spot for over a thousand years. This majesty and beauty could not be duplicated today even if we wanted to. The skills are lost. So, go … look … see … please.

Our second destination of the day was The International Stained Glass Museum … *Centre International du Vitrail de Chartres* to be more precise … not two hundred feet and one block over from the church. Carolyn was in heaven and I learned more that day about her passion than I ever knew. The art form has not changed in a thousand years. Everything Carolyn is doing is basically the same as the artisans and craftsmen have done to build Chartres, St. Chappelle, Paris's Notre Dame and a thousand - thousand other churches. So cool. Let me just add one kind of stupid epiphany … there is "clear glass" and there is glass that is colored or painted on. We call that second type of glass "stained glass"! DUH! And the processes of staining and painting are very, very complicated and go back centuries. Carolyn says she is fascinated by this craft because it combines the artistry of design and inspiration and the meticulous precision we both used to employ in our architectural drawings … which is a lost art as no one really physically "draws" architectural drawing any longer. It is all computerized. I want to add that the building all this was housed in had to be several hundred if not a thousand years old itself. The ladies at the front desk of the museum had no idea how old he building was or its history. The construction was post and beam with pegs and roughhewn wood. The lower area where the art of Kim En Joong, a Korean Dominican Priest, was displayed was rough stone block and beautifully complimented his amazing glass work which is displayed and used all over the world.

The day was getting late. We found a little brasserie, Le Week End, and shared an apple tart and some hot chocolates and were off to the train station. On the way to the station the weather turned, and we made our way in a beginning windy rain. After we got to the station it started to pour in buckets, and we found ourselves at 5:00 wet and sitting on a cold, six-inch, hard tile stoop on the floor of the train station backed up to a glass rail eating some stale French bread I had wrapped in a napkin and absconded from lunch in my jacket pocket and our little packets of nuts and cranberries and drinking from our water bottles as undoubtedly Academy des Beaux-Arts students returning to Paris after a mandatory trip to Chartres stood around us and jibber-jabbered. I am such a classy guy. And the train sped us home. When we got back to the Gare du Montparnasse, we were starving and found a great little place in the station and ate. We also found a gift shop with a very helpful young lady and got Cait some more "treasures." As the day was getting late, we grabbed another taxi because we were both too tired to mess with the Metro, got home to Hotel du College, and we crashed.

Tuesday, April 16th, 2024

This rainy morning, after breakfast, I let Carolyn sleep in. I can tell you that two weeks in Europe is exhausting. It is a physical and mental experience so if you are going, get yourself ready. While Carolyn was hanging out and getting her "powers" back for whatever experience Jim had next in line, I walked down the street to the Musée de Cluny – Musée National du Moyen Âge, the National Museum of the Middle Ages. This was not on my original list, but as with all things Paris, one finds unexpected beauty around EVERY corner. The display centered around the art of France and Charles VII – 1422-1464. Again, the building was breathtakingly old, a thousand years at least, and I had to finally stop photographing the building and concentrate on the art, although I did take time out for the most magnificent modern spiral stair I had ever seen. The alter carvings from 1515 to 1520 were spectacular in their detail and craftsmanship. Again, there is no artisan today who could duplicate this masterpiece … and there was not just one, there were fifteen or twenty from all over Europe. I made a stop at the gift shop and bought my Princess, Caitlin Rose Morris, a special book mark and then made my way out. The rainy morning gave way to sun and much cooler weather by the time I left.

Carolyn was up when I got back, and she was ready for our next adventure! After several stops and train changes we arrived at the Musée Rodin, the Rodin Museum, which sits adjacent to the Hotel des Invalides which is neither a hotel nor a place for invalids. It was a hospital for wounded soldiers once upon a time but it is now where Napoleon is interred. In the Rodin Museum, which was his former residence, I was interested in just one specific creation of his, the intensely erotic (to me at least) 1886 sculpture titled *The Kiss*. All the rest of his art was interesting including learning about the "lost wax process" of sculpturing bronze, but seeing the original *The Kiss* was my Mona Lisa moment. I say the original as he made several duplicates over his lifetime. It must have been one of his favorites too, but this was an original. And as you look at his other work, old Rodin had an eye for sculpting women and the erotic.

Across the street and down just a little from Rodin is the Hotel des Invalides. And the first thing that strikes you is the magnificent building constructed by the French people to house one thing, Napoleon's remains. It is the most amazing cathedral looking edifice built for a single purpose I think I have ever seen, and it echoes the love the French people have for this, their former leader and emperor. Carolyn and I were tickled as we walked in and peered down to the magnificent crypt that holds his body. It seemed like very much like the day we went to Grant's Tomb in NYC and peered over a knee wall and looked down. Only there was NO competition when it came to the building. If there is one thing the French can do is build a building! I wanted specifically to visit this site for several reasons, architectural, emotional, historical … as I have a photograph of Adolf Hitler visiting this very place on June 23rd, 1940, and standing where I stood. I know it seems weird but once I had seen the tomb, like seeing *The Kiss*, I was done. Flanking and behind the building we were in, was the entire Army Museum. In my heart I just could not make Carolyn endure several hours of tanks and guns and uniforms and French military history. Although she would have done it. There is no doubt in my mind. She is the absolute best!

A quick stop up the Metro brought us to the FDR station and we were back at the Champs-Élysées. Our thoughts were to go to the Arc de Triomphe but that proved to be a "bridge too far" so I just stepped into the bike lane and snapped a photo and headed home. We were running out of gas.

Wednesday, April 27th, 2024 … our last day in Gay Paree

The day dawned cool, windy and partly cloudy and by 10:00 we were on the move. Our target 'o the day: The Eiffel Tower! Jumping on the Metro after a hardy breakfast, we headed for the Place du Trocadero adjacent to the tower. Again, I had two secret missions on my mind. One: get some pictures of us at the landmark, and again, stand where Hitler stood in 1940 on his one-day touring Paris. This particular spot was also prominent in *John Wick 4*, and Two: take Carolyn to the Cité de l'architecture et du Patrimoin … the City's architectural heritage museum.

Standing on the open courtyard overlooking the tower it was very, very cold. The wind was whipping and the sky was blue and as clear as a bell. It was beautiful! You can see from the pictures of Carolyn how cold it was. We grabbed two chocolate chaud(es), and then I took her to the architecture museum and she was in heaven! It was more than I could have ever hoped for. We watched an in-depth video about the restoration efforts at Notre Dame, and then loved room after room of models of cathedrals and stained glass windows and gargoyles and sculptures and paintings and got closer to a model of the Arc de Triomphe and saw more of it than we could have ever seen from the ground. Watching Carolyn totally immersed in her love, architecture, made my heart sing. A favorite of mine, among many, was the gargoyle display. There were priests and monsters there was even what looked to be a peasant emptying a water cask. The skill and craftsmanship in these … well, downspouts, was amazing. I am hoping to actually see one doing its spouting thing on this trip. When we were done, we only did the first floor as Rick Steves said to not waste time on the second floor, we headed out for home to pack, but I had one more stop to make.

After lunch on the way home, I packed and was done with time for one more adventure. Carolyn's packing was a little more involved and so she opted not to go out in the damp Quebec-like misting rain. I headed down to The Archaeological Crypt of the Île de la Cité. This area in the plaza of Norte Dame was unearthed between 1965 and 1970 as a construction firm was excavating for an underground car park. What they discovered were Roman ruins of a military outpost city built here around 308 AD. The city was named Lutetia. It was on the border of two Roman provinces, Celtica and Belgica. Later these provinces were joined and were to be known as Gaul. This area was inhabited by "barbarians." The peoples were called this as they were not Roman, they had a different culture and language … ergo … barbarians. The entire 1,800 square meter area strongly reminded me of the ruins Carolyn and I saw under my beautiful Barcelona. There were orphanages, hospitals, baths, a market area and signs of a thriving dock. It was a hub of commerce. The archeologists even discovered evidence of a visit by wandering nomadic Neanderthals dating some 70,000 years ago. I was fascinated.

Thursday, April 18th, 2024

Our travel day to London on the Eurostar dawned bright and partly cloudy. We were headed to the Gare du Nord train station, and once again Rick Steves and the internet prepared me (I want to say well?) for the day. Our train was to depart at 1:12. And being a belt and suspenders guy when I arrange travel, I wanted to be at the station at 11:30 at the latest. Our taxi arrived at 11:00. We bid a sad good bye to our Yana who had greeted us the day we had arrived one week earlier and tumbled our suitcases into the trunk.

Gare du Nord is Paris's newest flagship station and home to the Eurostar which not only travels to London but also Amsterdam and other points east. Being an architect I must tell you, the layout is one of the dumbest and most inconvenient from a traveler standpoint I have ever seen. If you are ever lucky enough to experience it, be warned. Basically you arrive with luggage in tow. Carolyn and I had two almost 50 pound big suitcases and two smaller cases weighing about 20 plus pound each. All were four-wheel roller cases … highly recommended. When you arrive, you immediately have to ride an escalator (there is an elevator) up to a mezzanine. On this mezzanine overlooking the Eurostar tracks is border control and customs for both leaving France and entering Great Britain and it is a mess! Like we experienced coming into France at Charles de Gaul (Charles of Gaul … France) airport the lines were huge, slow moving and confusing. I thought being there by 11:30 (actually 11:15) would give us beaucoup time. It did not. As it ended up, we could not have arrived one minute later. Anyway, we made it through the complicated pylon arrangement. The people manning the area were as concerned as we were at the confusion and length of time. Carolyn and I again believe France desperately needs to get it together before the Olympics this summer or it is going to be a three-ring-circus … I have a feeling it is going to be anyway. But I could see another problem still looming. How to get from the mezzanine back down to the level where the trains were. The overall signage indicating where to board was weak, but Carolyn and I managed to join the biggest line and fortified with some water and a giant croissant we made our way to the door to the platform overlooking the train. Ah! There was … an elevator. So that was the trick. As we got nearer there was an attendant allowing some people to use the elevator … older people, people in wheelchairs, people with strollers, and two very blond obviously entitled young ladies … but when Carolyn and I got there, we were refused! I could not believe it! Instead, she pointed back several hundred feet, back the way we had come after standing in line for over thirty minutes to an escalator. Well, by now we were ten to fifteen minutes before the train was about to leave, so what did we do? Carolyn looked at me, and I looked at Carolyn, then Carolyn hefted the two smaller bags, and I hefted the two monsters and down the stairs we went. So, when I say traveling is a physical experience … it is. Later, comparing notes, both of us could see ourselves going head over heels down the staircase, but we made it. We were to be in Coach 15. At the bottom of the stairs we were about halfway down the train at Coach 12. So, I chose to go right. And as with any 50/50 choice I'm given, it was wrong. So we backtracked and found our coach. And there was no room for our luggage in the rack. I eventually found space in the number 14 coach and we settled in. Whew.

The ride was amazing! We actually hit one hundred plus miles per hour at one point, and the ride was as smooth as glass. Lunch was served and we had some wine with our quiche and salad and for desert we had a delicious brownie that if it had been any richer, would have been fudge. I was tracking us on my GPS because I wanted to see when we were in the Channel Tunnel (not the Chunnel anymore – too gauche). Along the way we saw little French villages and town churches and wind farms and acres and acres of beautiful farm land. We were approaching the tunnel! I was stoked! And then we were in it! It was pitch, black dark. I could not see anything! I was hoping to see the inside of the completed tunnel like when we pulled into a Metro station, but nooooooo. Just pitch, black dark. Bummer. Then we popped out into beautiful English sunshine, and in about twenty minutes we were pulling into St. Pancras International Train Station, London, England. After grabbing our bags off the train (one does ALL one's own baggage handling) we headed to "sortie" the place, and there I snapped one of the best pictures of Carolyn I had taken the whole trip. She is standing by a down stair looking back over her shoulder manhandling her suitcases and smiling beautifully. In the background is a clock reading 2:50 and a pink neon sign below it reading "*I want my time with you.*" It is a perfect picture. It will be on my desk soon. I had not scheduled anyone to meet us, and I probably will never schedule anyone again after our Charles De Gaul experience. We found the underground taxi stand, and after a little shuffling of taxis, we were in a world famous "Black Cab" and on our way southeast to the neighborhood of Westminster and our hotel, The Sanctuary House.

We got settled in and went touring. It was much cooler in London, and we were ready with coats and whatnot. We wandered down and saw Buckingham Palace and quickly found out that London was getting ready for the running of a marathon on Sunday so there were barricades going up and "Bobbies" everywhere. And you know you hear about the Bobbies not carrying guns … that's a lie. Kevlar and long guns were everywhere! We wandered around St. James Park, saw Big Ben, Parliament and Westminster Abbey. All sights to behold, but both of us were running out of energy, so we made our way back to the hotel ("I know exactly where we are"). We ate at a corner pub attached to our hotel. It is where we would eat breakfast each morning … my helpful hint: always get breakfast included with your room – it just makes mornings so much more pleasant.

Friday, April 19th, 2024

Carolyn's first remark upon wandering around London was how absolutely brutal much of their architecture is, and I agree. Massive hulking concrete monsters are everywhere. Don't get me wrong, there are beautiful middle ages buildings, but much of their skyline is either glass and steel or crouching concrete bunkers. I suspect this is due to the influence of the architect Le Corbusier in the mid twentieth century. London was bombed heavily in World War II and possibly the influence of this cubist, concrete happy architect's movement's influence was felt in the rebuilding of London. Paris was declared an "open city" by the French so that Hitler would not destroy it, hence the lovely architecture survives today. London did not submit, so they have a very eclectic mix of old and new especially in the East End which received the heaviest punishment from the Nazis.

Friday evening was our tickets to see *The Book of Mormon* so I did not want to exhaust us running all over London. We spent the day just walking here and there through St James's Park and up to Piccadilly Circus. We were searching for the perfect touristy store to buy The Princess some perfect London/Great Britain goodies, but we struck out … that morning. But that evening, when we went to the Prince of Wales Theater by cab we hit the jackpot! The play was spectacular! I mean a hilarious combination of irreverence, slapstick and innuendo that only could really be appreciated by those who see *organized* religion for what it is … as Marx put it: "an opium of the masses." Before the play, Carolyn was excited because I actually was able to get her a ginger ale with ice! She is so easy. Once inside the theater proper, our seats were second row, center orchestra, and like our NYC play experience with *Wicked*, we were in the play! We agreed one of our favorite characters was the man who was the head Mormon in the Africa mission. He was fighting his natural impulses to be gay, and he played the part perfectly. Of course the whole play was that much more hilarious to me because of me dating a Mormon, Leslie A. in Panama, when I was in college. Anyway, the play was awesome and afterward we strode out into the lights and glitter of the nighttime Piccadilly Circus. Now this was exactly what we had been searching for earlier! There were tourist shops on each corner, and we hit the jackpot with treasures for The Princess. Hats and shirts and hoodies and all kinds of what-not. When we were suitably exhausted I hailed a black cab, and we were home at The Sanctuary House in no time.

Saturday, April 20th, 2024

Today was a big day. Our targets were Westminster Abbey and St. Paul's Cathedral. It was blustery and cold and Quebec raining so I had to start the day with what else but a traditional English breakfast! Hear Carolyn still groaning. There were two fried eggs, two hash browns, two awesome pieces of barely cooked lean bacon, a little half cup deal of baked beans, a big fat sausage and something called black pudding. I think you get all the first parts, but the blood pudding was something else. It looked like a hash brown patty and had that consistency, but that is where the similarity ended. It was a mix of barley oats and pigs blood. (See Bodie move to another table … again) And it tasted exactly like you think it would taste. And I ate every bit of everything … I was a good boy and cleaned my plate! See Carolyn still groaning. Then we were off to Westminster Abbey. The original Abbey was built before 1066, almost a thousand years ago, and held it first coronation in 1066. The church we see today was built by Henry III in 1245, almost 800 years ago. It is the resting place of seventeen monarchs, and forty have been crowned here, and it is where Prince William and Kate Middleton were married. We took many pictures, but I implore you to go there yourself because no picture can capture the Abbey's majesty and delicate gothic beauty. We were particularly enamored when we climbed the brand new, and very well done, steps up to the "attic." Called the triforium, it is an area closed to the public for hundreds of years and just recently opened to display jewels and gowns and armor and trinkets from the Abbey's illustrious past. Carolyn and I were particularly fascinated because when we were going up the stairs we were literally inches away from historic stained glass and flying buttresses that have stood the test of almost a thousand years. If the stairs had not been enclosed, we could have reached out and touched history. But we were able to get some pictures as we ascended, and that had to do because there was no photography allowed once in the triforium proper. From the upper reaches of the cathedral we were able to look down on the entire Westminster layout. It was stunning.

When we left, it was raining. We made our way back toward the hotel. We grabbed some lunch and a taxi, and then we were off to St. Paul's. Again it is impossible to describe the overwhelming majesty and beauty of Sir Christopher Wren's church. Again, I shot a many pictures and even some video, but one must see St. Paul's to believe it. The original church was founded on this site in AD 604. The present church was completed in 1710. The style is considered English Baroque. Its reconstruction took place after the Great Fire of London which raged for four days in 1666. With its dome at 365 feet, it was the tallest building in London until 1963. Funerals for and the internment of many took place there … Admiral Lord Nelson, the Duke of Wellington, and Sir Christopher Wren himself. The cathedral is not a popular place for royal weddings though as we found out from the cabbie of the Black Cab who brought us to the cathedral. Prince Charles and Lady Diana Spencer were married in St. Paul's rather than Westminster, and their marriage ended in divorce. Again, I could overwhelm you with the architectural history of this amazing place, but I will give you a break. It was an iconic image during the Blitz standing tall amid the ruin of the Nazi onslaught. It was struck by as many as 28 bombs, but survived and was a symbol of the British people and Winston Churchill's resolve during World War II.

While we were there the clergy held a Holy Eucharist and the church was filled with chanting and music and light and was beautiful. I was fascinated by a video artwork by Bill Viola. It was titled *Martyrs (Earth, Wind, Fire and Water)* and was composed in 2014. I have a picture and video if it. Haunting. And so ended our Saturday. We were both very tired, and so we headed home to The Sanctuary House. We had one day left in London.

Sunday, April 21st, 2024

The day dawned partly cloudy, but as we discovered (and is legendary) London's weather can turn on a dime. We struck out for nowhere in particular other than my secret plan. This was the day of the London Marathon, so streets were blocked every which way, and there were crowds all over the place. I guided us along a path away from crowds, down along a street where we found, of course, a Subway restaurant (again talk to Bodie Blackwell). Then a walk along the famous Thames River, and we arrived at an art museum named The Tate. This is not to be confused with the Tate Modern on the south Bank. This is the Tate Britain and was known from 1897 to 1932 as the National Gallery of British Art. The building was built in 1893 and is a work of art unto itself. We started with a special exhibit of the works of J.M.W. Turner and were fascinated by this artist neither of us had heard of. As an aside, when we bought some coco later we noticed it was Mr. Turner's image on the British pound note we used! We made our way to the art of the 1500's to 1700's section and were rewarded with some of the most beautiful paintings we had seen anywhere. To us, the quiet intimacy of this rambling old building made this art museum far surpass The Louvre. After the Tate, we decided it was time to head home and pack, so we strolled along the Thames again and grabbed some selfies of ourselves when we went by Big Ben and caught The London Eye in the background of the picture, Parliament and Westminster one last time. As the clouds gathered and crowds were dispersing from the marathon, we grabbed a late lunch at our favorite corner pub and got busy packing.

Monday, April 22nd, 2024

We had the cab pick us up at 7:30ish. Our flight from Heathrow was at 11:40A and they wanted us there three hours before (8:40A) flight time. With a ride to the airport timed at 40 minutes Old Belt and Suspenders felt pretty good. The morning traffic was typical of all big cities, and we walked into Delta Terminal 3 at about 8:15. The ladies helped us find our lines and get us some paper (!) boarding passes … I love paper boarding passes. London was trying out a new program where you schedule your appointment time with customs. I had set our time as 9:15 plus or minus 15 minutes. We got to the entry point a little early, but the custom's officers let us zip through anyway. As we went through, you want to talk about strict! We had to open everything and put it in clear baggies, and then a guy looked through all our stuff and decided he needed some toothpaste, so he said my toothpaste tube was too big and he absconded it. Cool … I didn't like that kind anyway. Then we put our clothes back on ☺ and poof … we had made it through Heathrow customs! It was time for some breakfast. We found a place, and I had pancakes, and Carolyn had some eggs and toast. They had a "Full English Breakfast" on the menu, but I let it pass. Baked beans and me and a nine-hour flight … no thanks! Carolyn chuckled. Our gate was something like Gate 28, and it was at the end of long, long corridor. Interestingly, and looking at it with an architect's eye, Heathrow is laid out like there was no overall plan ever even considered! And we boarded. Seats 31A and 31B, no Delta shenanigans this time. Carolyn had a window, and I had the aisle, and we blasted off exactly at 8:40 to cross the pond. We were to land in Atlanta at 4:15P Atlanta time.

The flight was uneventful. I love to be able to write that in this day and time of crazies and weird events like doors coming off Boeing planes and wheels falling off … look it up. We watched movies and ate whatever they put in front of us. Again, we were flying Delta Comfort+, and we won't fly any other way from now on if I can help it. Landing in Atlanta was a breeze and the outdoor temp was about 75°… quite pleasant. We let the children know we were "on the ground." Customs on our end was a quick and efficient. I was expecting a European repeat, but it was not to be. I love the International Terminal. At baggage claim, our bags popped up, and we caught the Easy Park and Relax shuttle and bingo we were on the road home. We got home about 6:15. We let the children know we were home SAS, and so ended our one year put off 50th Anniversary Extravaganza.

At the end of May, I launched off in Zoomer (my Miata) with the top down toward Atlanta and East Georgia on a mission to try to find some more graves. My first target was Rock Spring Presbyterian Church on Piedmont Avenue at Montgomery Ferry Drive, NE, to try to find William Foster Wofford's grave. W. F. Wofford was my Pa's father's grave, my grandfather's father's grave. So he would be my great-grandfather. Well, as it turns out that church is no longer there. The church sold out to a school, Heritage Preparatory School Lower School, however the cemetery is still there and is maintained.

A very nice lady helped me access the fenced off and lock gated grounds, and after a little searching I found his marker, William Foster Wofford 1863-1918. Along with him there were a number of Woffords I have just researched … Howard Walker Wofford 1896-1899 (three years old) … William Forster Wofford's son! Alfred Greenberry Wofford 1899-1967 … another son! I also located a grave for Mary Clark Hensolt 1825-1910, the mother of Florence May Hensolt, William Foster Wofford's wife. Another grave was one for Florence H. Wofford 1866-1959. This was William Foster Wofford's wife, Florence May Hensolt Wofford – with her grave marker dropping her maiden middle name (May) and substituting the H (Hensolt) in its place! As a note, William Foster Wofford and Florence May Hensolt had not only William Earl Wofford (my grandfather "Pa"), but they also had a daughter Mary Corinne Wofford 1894-? This is who my mother Mary Corinne Wofford Morris is named after. Look in the appendix of this book for the Mary Corinne Wofford Pedigree Chart, and you will see many of these names.

After my Rock Spring successes, I headed off pursuing the Morris - Williams lineage (see the James Wingfield Morris Pedigree Chart). I was chasing the Captain Cornelius Redding Hanleiter grave marker. You will recall reading about my adventures with Captain Hanleiter back in 2022 when I went chasing the grave of a soldier mentioned in Hanleiter's diary who had died under his command during the Civil War when he was stationed in Savannah. I knew my Great-Great-Great Grandfather on my father's side was buried at the Oakland Cemetery in Atlanta, but I did not know where on the 48 acres among the over 70,000 graves he was. But that did not deter this optimist. All I knew was he was buried in Section 8, Lot 171. I arrived downtown and parked adjacent to the cemetery. I did not realize you could actually drive in and drive around. I walked onto the grounds and following the assumption he would be buried in the Confederate Section headed there. Upon arriving at that part of the cemetery and realizing there were no section numbers or lot numbers anywhere, the magnitude of my task appeared overwhelming. So, I headed to the main office at the Bell Tower. Inside there was a delightful young lady who upon listening to my plight, called a guy. Rather, she called The Guy. He never introduced himself, but he was Mr. Oakland Cemetery! After some explaining and a false start we retreated to his office which was exactly what you would expect the office of a guy who knew more about these 48 acres and its 70,000 residents than anyone would look like. It was in the basement of the Bell Tower building. It had no windows and was a jumbled mess of papers and filing cabinets and detritus of years of work. He went to his beat-up old gray filing cabinet and from the top drawer, he pulled a manila file folder. "Ah yes! Here we are," he said gleefully, "Captain Cornelius Redding Hanleiter, lot 171." Then he pulled a raggedy old map of the whole cemetery that had been affixed to a piece of foam core board years ago and proceeded to point out exactly where the grave was. It was not in the Confederate Section, and I had walked within forty feet of it on my way into the cemetery. The grave is located in what is called the "Original Six Acres." So, you walk into Oakland at the main entrance off Oakland Avenue. About sixty yards in on your left is an old, brick guard building. On the right side and just down the road maybe five feet from the guard's building are two brick walkways extending perpendicular to the road and to the right. The second one has a label set in the brick.

The label reads Jas. G. Woodward Drive even though it is only three feet wide. Down this walkway maybe fifty feet on the left side shaded by two lovely is a small plot with four markers. The center upright headstone is Captain Cornelius Redding Hanleiter's marker. Next to him on the right is his son, George Hanleiter. An interesting aside … in the cabinet behind me where I am writing this is a picture my son James Lyon Morris and I had made while on one of our infamous Two Boys Trips. We are dressed as Civil War soldiers, and I messed with my fifth graders for years telling them this was Cornelius Hanleiter and his son George. I don't think the children ever really believed me, but as one student put it years ago, "Just humor him." But this day, I had found the graves and honored my relatives. Now I was off to Washington, Georgia, trying to track down one more place.

Washington, Georgia is where my Paternal Grandmother, Marie Louise Williams, was born. I wanted to find her house. I headed to the Washington-Wilkes (County) Historical Society at 308 E. Robert Toombs Avenue. There, in the basement of the old house that served as an office and fascinating museum I found a wonderfully helpful lady who was all about my quest. After researching for about a half hour the best we could do is state unequivocally that the house she had lived in was one block away on Water Street. We could not establish exactly which house, but we knew it was along this short street. I thanked her, paid nine dollars to tour the museum, enjoyed that and then drove the short block to Water Street. I parked and walked along the street. The sun was shining brightly on this beautiful late May day, and I could almost envision a little four-year-old Marie Louise Williams over a hundred years ago in 1903 chasing up and down this street with her little friends. Undoubtedly the street was not paved back then, but many of the houses looked as if they were from the period. This was as close as I was going to get to my wonderful Momma's childhood home. I spent the night and then headed back home with the top down in my little red Mazda.

Caitlin Rose Morris is headed to North Cobb High School this coming fall of 2024. Bryce Harper Blackwell and Anna Grace Wylie will wed on October 19th, 2024. Bodie Lang Blackwell will graduate from UGA in May of 2025. Carolyn and I have a lot to look forward to, but let me close this effort. This has been a four-year endeavor, and I have both laughed, agonized and at times cried over these recollections. I hope you have gained some insight into my life. At the very least, I hope you have found a few interesting revelations about me and a few laughs at my life to date. As Carolyn says, "He is a happy boy." I am including my father's ancestral research in the Appendix. I would hate for all of my father's detailed work that he spent the last twenty years of his life painstakingly gathering not to be handed down. I am going to include some family pictures in addition to the ones in the text of this book. May God bless you Mom and Dad for all you gave me. I know you made the best decisions for me that you could, given the light, and the son, you had been given. You did good. My Sibs … Re, Bill, Rusty and Pete — thank you for your love even when I did not deserve it. And thank you Carolyn Ethel Lyon Morris in advance for your constant love, your companionship, being my friend and my wife for over fifty years and helping me edit and proofread this mess. But mostly, thank you Carolyn, for helping grow me into the man I am today. Date: July 23rd, 2024.

Appendix

Ancestral Research
Done by Col. James W. Morris (1924-2020)

His research will be presented in the following order:
PATERNAL
Morris
Williams/Gullatt
Hangleiter/Hanleiter
Walford/Wofford
Meroney
Nelson
MATERNAL
Lyon
Shacklett

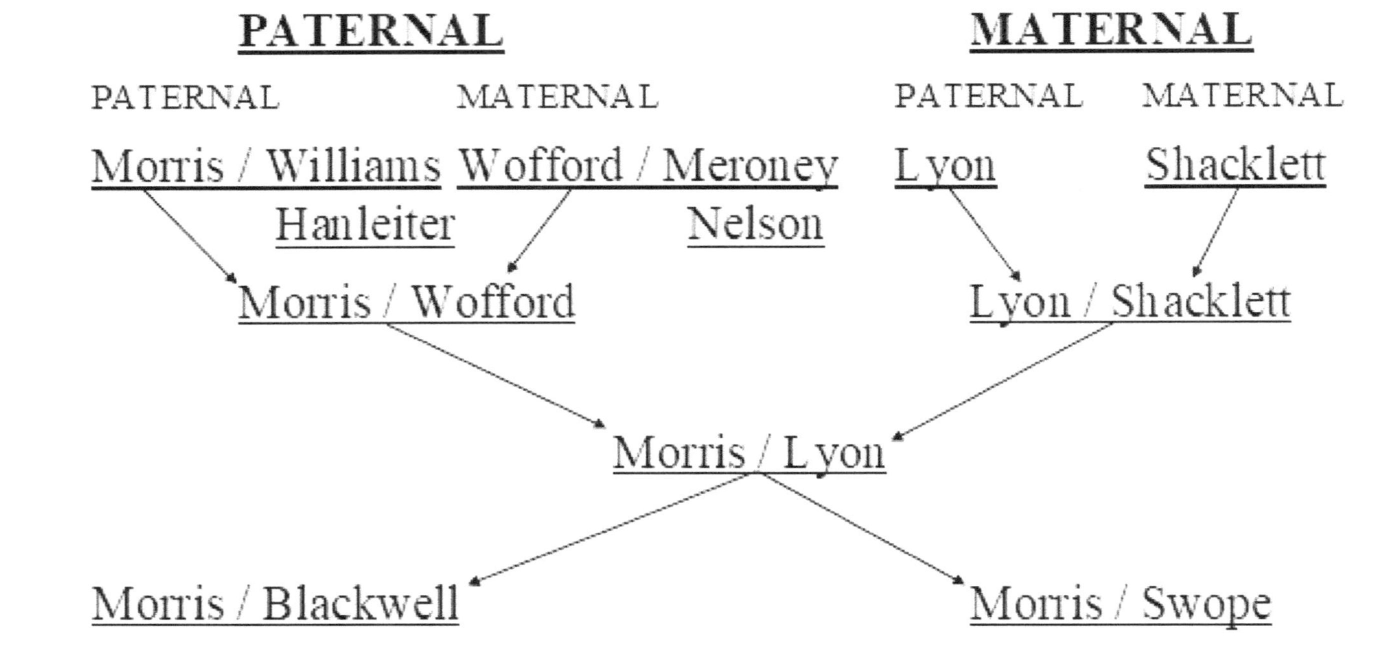

Overview of Family Tree Information

PATERNAL FIVE GENERATIONS

407

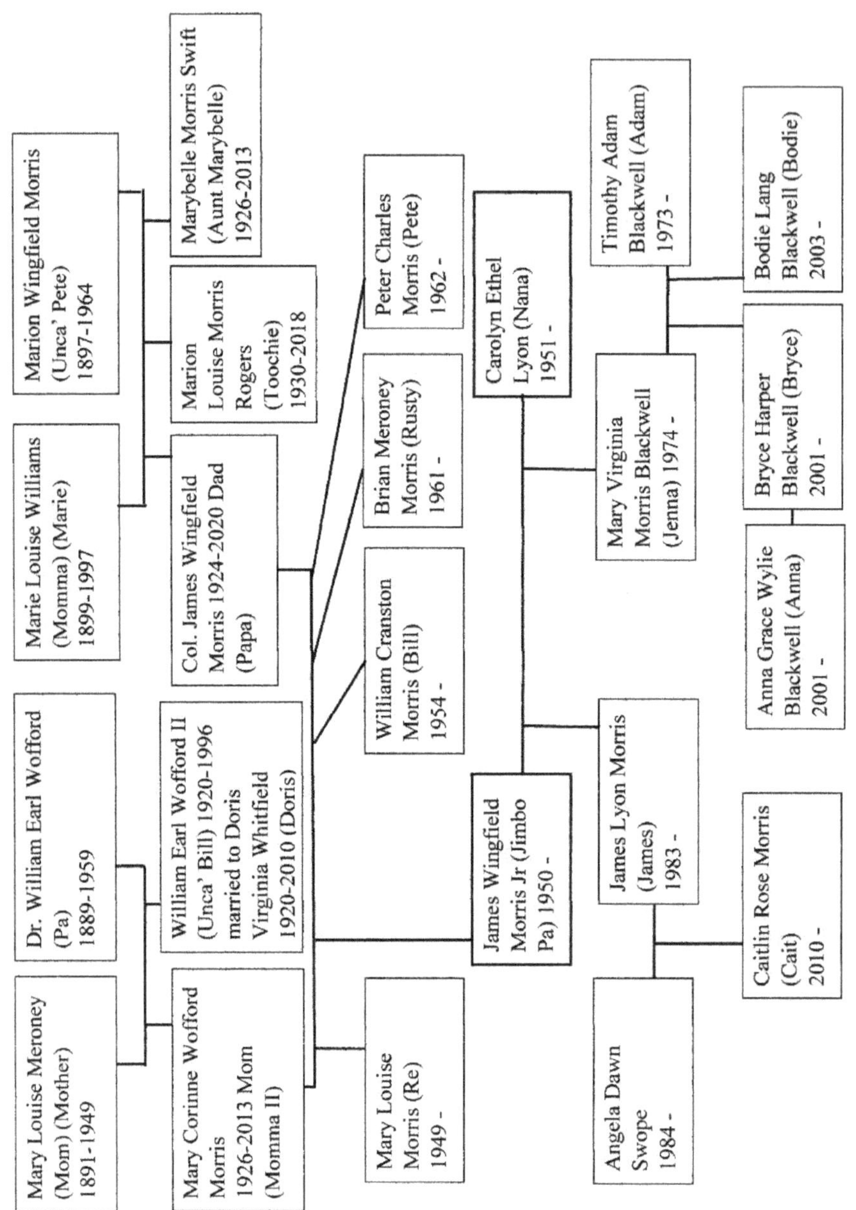

Mary Louise Meroney (Mom) (Mother) 1891-1949
Dr. William Earl Wofford (Pa) 1889-1959
Marion Wingfield Morris (Unca' Pete) 1897-1964
Marie Louise Williams (Momma) (Marie) 1899-1997
Marybelle Morris Swift (Aunt Marybelle) 1926-2013
Marion Louise Morris Rogers (Toochie) 1930-2018
William Earl Wofford II (Unca' Bill) 1920-1996 married to Doris Virginia Whitfield 1920-2010 (Doris)
Mary Corinne Wofford Morris 1926-2013 Mom (Momma II)
Col. James Wingfield Morris 1924-2020 Dad (Papa)
Peter Charles Morris (Pete) 1962 -
Brian Meroney Morris (Rusty) 1961 -
William Cranston Morris (Bill) 1954 -
Carolyn Ethel Lyon (Nana) 1951 -
James Wingfield Morris Jr (Jimbo Pa) 1950 -
Mary Louise Morris (Re) 1949 -
Mary Virginia Morris Blackwell (Jenna) 1974 -
James Lyon Morris (James) 1983 -
Angela Dawn Swope 1984 -
Timothy Adam Blackwell (Adam) 1973 -
Bodie Lang Blackwell (Bodie) 2003 -
Bryce Harper Blackwell (Bryce) 2001 -
Anna Grace Wylie Blackwell (Anna) 2001 -
Caitlin Rose Morris (Cait) 2010 -

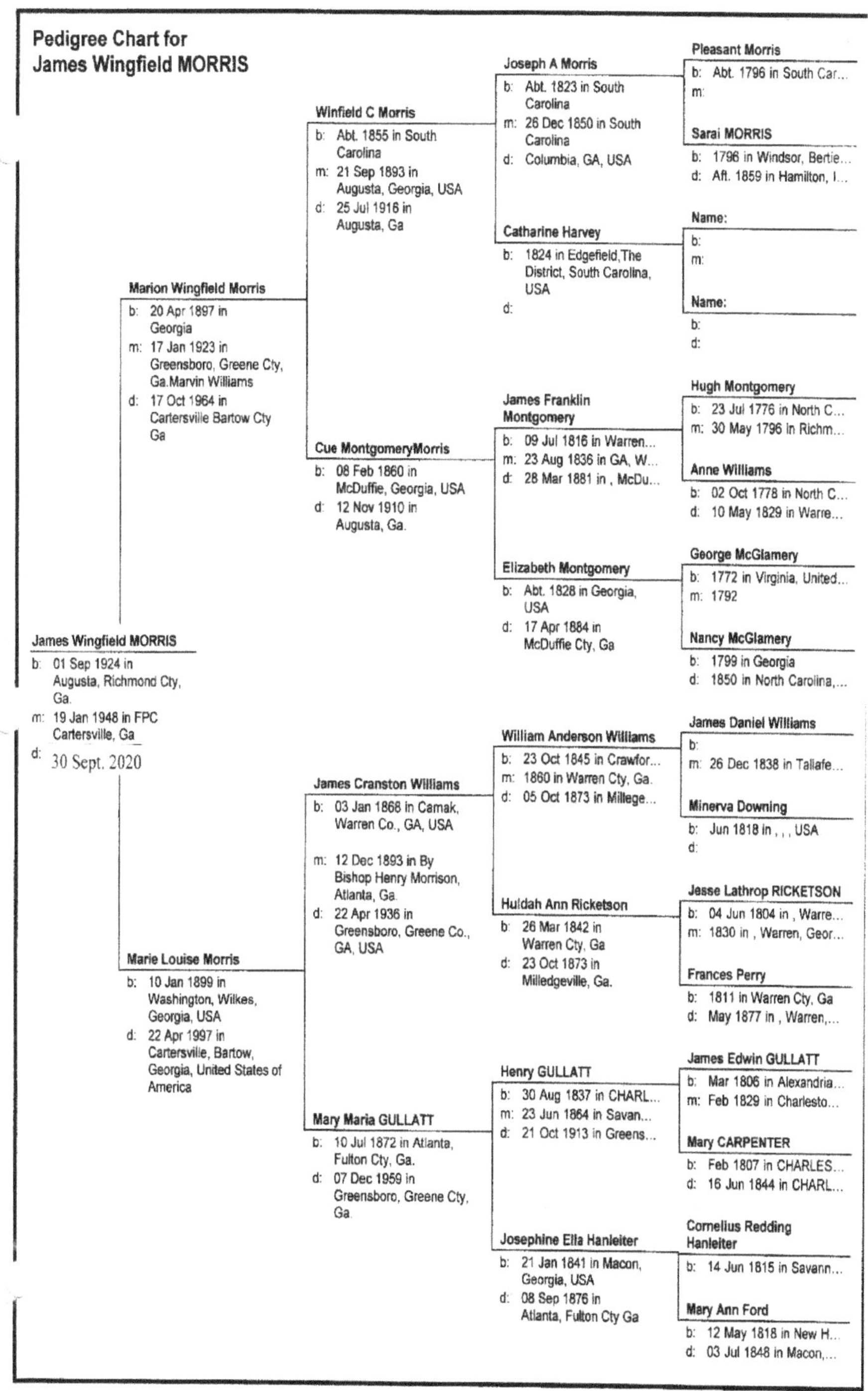

Pedigree Chart for
James Wingfield MORRIS

James Wingfield MORRIS
b: 01 Sep 1924 in Augusta, Richmond Cty, Ga.
m: 19 Jan 1948 in FPC Cartersville, Ga
d: 30 Sept. 2020

Marion Wingfield Morris
b: 20 Apr 1897 in Georgia
m: 17 Jan 1923 in Greensboro, Greene Cty, Ga.Marvin Williams
d: 17 Oct 1964 in Cartersville Bartow Cty Ga

Marie Louise Morris
b: 10 Jan 1899 in Washington, Wilkes, Georgia, USA
d: 22 Apr 1997 in Cartersville, Bartow, Georgia, United States of America

Winfield C Morris
b: Abt. 1855 in South Carolina
m: 21 Sep 1893 in Augusta, Georgia, USA
d: 25 Jul 1916 in Augusta, Ga

Cue MontgomeryMorris
b: 08 Feb 1860 in McDuffie, Georgia, USA
d: 12 Nov 1910 in Augusta, Ga.

James Cranston Williams
b: 03 Jan 1868 in Camak, Warren Co., GA, USA
m: 12 Dec 1893 in By Bishop Henry Morrison, Atlanta, Ga.
d: 22 Apr 1936 in Greensboro, Greene Co., GA, USA

Mary Maria GULLATT
b: 10 Jul 1872 in Atlanta, Fulton Cty, Ga.
d: 07 Dec 1959 in Greensboro, Greene Cty, Ga

Joseph A Morris
b: Abt. 1823 in South Carolina
m: 26 Dec 1850 in South Carolina
d: Columbia, GA, USA

Catharine Harvey
b: 1824 in Edgefield,The District, South Carolina, USA
d:

James Franklin Montgomery
b: 09 Jul 1816 in Warren...
m: 23 Aug 1836 in GA, W...
d: 28 Mar 1881 in , McDu...

Elizabeth Montgomery
b: Abt. 1828 in Georgia, USA
d: 17 Apr 1884 in McDuffie Cty, Ga

William Anderson Williams
b: 23 Oct 1845 in Crawfor...
m: 1860 in Warren Cty, Ga.
d: 05 Oct 1873 in Millege...

Huldah Ann Ricketson
b: 26 Mar 1842 in Warren Cty, Ga
d: 23 Oct 1873 in Milledgeville, Ga.

Henry GULLATT
b: 30 Aug 1837 in CHARL...
m: 23 Jun 1864 in Savan...
d: 21 Oct 1913 in Greens...

Josephine Ella Hanleiter
b: 21 Jan 1841 in Macon, Georgia, USA
d: 08 Sep 1876 in Atlanta, Fulton Cty Ga

Pleasant Morris
b: Abt. 1796 in South Car...
m:

Sarai MORRIS
b: 1796 in Windsor, Bertie...
d: Aft. 1859 in Hamilton, I...

Name:
b:
m:

Name:
b:
d:

Hugh Montgomery
b: 23 Jul 1776 in North C...
m: 30 May 1796 in Richm...

Anne Williams
b: 02 Oct 1778 in North C...
d: 10 May 1829 in Warre...

George McGlamery
b: 1772 in Virginia, United...
m: 1792

Nancy McGlamery
b: 1799 in Georgia
d: 1850 in North Carolina,...

James Daniel Williams
b:
m: 26 Dec 1838 in Tallafe...

Minerva Downing
b: Jun 1818 in , , , USA
d:

Jesse Lathrop RICKETSON
b: 04 Jun 1804 in , Warre...
m: 1830 in , Warren, Geor...

Frances Perry
b: 1811 in Warren Cty, Ga
d: May 1877 in , Warren,...

James Edwin GULLATT
b: Mar 1806 in Alexandria...
m: Feb 1829 in Charlesto...

Mary CARPENTER
b: Feb 1807 in CHARLES...
d: 16 Jun 1844 in CHARL...

Cornelius Redding Hanleiter
b: 14 Jun 1815 in Savann...

Mary Ann Ford
b: 12 May 1818 in New H...
d: 03 Jul 1848 in Macon,...

Descendants of John Morris

Generation 1

1. JOHN[1] MORRIS was born on 03 Mar 1652 in Boston, Suffolk, Massachusetts, United States. He died on 30 Jun 1680 in Pasquotank, North Carolina, United States. He married Damaris Page, daughter of Isaac Page and Demaris Shattuck, in 1678. She was born in Jun 1659 in Salem, Essex, Massachusetts, United States. She died on 12 Sep 1722 in Pasquotank, North Carolina, United States (Age: 63).

   John Morris and Damaris Page had the following children:

   i. MARY[2] MORRIS was born in 1674 in Boston, Middlesex, Massachusetts, USA. She died in 1720 in Dudley, Worcester, Massachusetts, USA.

   ii. SARAH MORRIS was born in 1679 in Perquimans, North Carolina, United States. She died in 1750 in Henrico, Virginia, United States.

   iii. ELIZABETH MORRIS was born in 1680 in Isle, Virginia, United States. She died in 1750 in Henrico, Virginia, United States.

   2. iv. JOHN MORRIS III was born on 31 Mar 1680 in Pasquotank Co., NC. He died on 20 Sep 1739 in Elizabeth City, Pasquotank, NC (Age: 59). He married Mary Symons, daughter of Thomas Symons and Rebacah Symons, on 04 Sep 1703 in Pasquotank Co, NC. She was born on 04 Dec 1687 in Elizabeth City, Pasquotank, North Carolina, USA. She died on 14 Oct 1745 in Pasquotank, North Carolina (Death Age: 58).

Generation 2

2. JOHN[2] MORRIS III (John[1]) was born on 31 Mar 1680 in Pasquotank Co., NC. He died on 20 Sep 1739 in Elizabeth City, Pasquotank, NC (Age: 59). He married Mary Symons, daughter of Thomas Symons and Rebacah Symons, on 04 Sep 1703 in Pasquotank Co, NC. She was born on 04 Dec 1687 in Elizabeth City, Pasquotank, North Carolina, USA. She died on 14 Oct 1745 in Pasquotank, North Carolina (Death Age: 58).

   John Morris III and Mary Symons had the following child:

   3. i. AARON[3] MORRIS was born on 14 Jul 1704 in Pasquotank, North Carolina, United States. He died on 10 Sep 1770 in Pasquotank, North Carolina, United States. He married Mary Morris, daughter of Benjamin Pritchard and Sarah Culpepper, on 20 Jun 1724 in Pasquotank Co., NC. She was born on 28 Jul 1707 in Pasquotank, North Carolina, United States. She died on 10 Dec 1791 in Pasquotank, North Carolina, United States.

Generation 3

3. AARON[3] MORRIS (John[2] III, John[1]) was born on 14 Jul 1704 in Pasquotank, North Carolina, United States. He died on 10 Sep 1770 in Pasquotank, North Carolina, United States. He married Mary Morris, daughter of Benjamin Pritchard and Sarah Culpepper, on 20 Jun 1724 in Pasquotank Co., NC. She was born on 28 Jul 1707 in Pasquotank, North Carolina, United States. She died on 10 Dec 1791 in Pasquotank, North Carolina, United States.

   Aaron Morris and Mary Morris had the following children:

   i. JOSHUA[4] MORRIS was born on 06 Apr 1726 in Pasquotank, North Carolina, United States. He died on 14 Feb 1777 in Perquimans, North Carolina, United States.

   ii. BENJAMIN MOORE MORRIS was born on 20 Aug 1728 in Pasquotank, North Carolina, United States. He died on 31 Jan 1762 in Pasquotank, North Carolina, United States.

   4. iii. JOSEPH MORRIS was born on 01 Feb 1731 in Symons Creek, Pasquotank, Colonial North Carolina. He died on 24 Nov 1798 in Pasquotank, North Carolina (Death Age: 60). He married (1) ELIZABETH PARKER in 1769 in Pasquotank, North Carolina, United States. She was born in 1741 in Pasquotank, North Carolina, United States. She died in 1800. He married (2) MARY NEWBY in 1755 in Pasquotank, North Carolina, United States. She was born on 28 Jul 1732 in Pasquotank, North Carolina, United States. She died on 05 Sep 1763 in Pasquotank, North Carolina, United States.

1

iv. JOSEPH MORRIS was born on 01 Feb 1731 in Pasquotank, North Carolina, United States. He died on 24 Nov 1798 in Pasquotank, North Carolina, United States.

v. JOHN ALLEN MORRIS was born in 1733. He died in 1830 in probably, Page, Virginia, United States.

vi. MIRIAM MORRIS was born on 14 Mar 1733 in Pasquotank, North Carolina, United States. She died on 13 Dec 1789 in Narrows, Pasquotank, North Carolina, United States.

vii. SUSANNAH MORRIS was born on 06 Jul 1735 in Pasquotank, North Carolina, United States. She died in 1758 in Pasquotank, North Carolina, United States.

viii. JOHN MORRIS was born on 11 Dec 1737 in MO, Pasquotank, North Carolina, United States. He died on 11 Oct 1776 in Pasquotank, North Carolina, United States.

ix. MARY MORRIS was born on 08 Jan 1739 in Pasquotank, North Carolina, United States. She died in 1760 in North Carolina, United States.

x. SARAH MORRIS was born on 05 Jan 1743 in Pasquotank, North Carolina, United States. She died on 26 Sep 1743 in Pasquotank, North Carolina, United States.

xi. AARON MORRIS SR was born on 05 Sep 1744 in Pasquotank, North Carolina, United States. He died on 08 Dec 1796 (Age: 52). He married Lydia Symons in 1782 in NC. She was born in 1757 in NC.

xii. ELIZABETH MORRIS was born on 22 Apr 1747 in Pasquotank, North Carolina, United States. She died on 27 Oct 1832 in Washington, Wayne, Indiana, United States.

Generation 4

4. JOSEPH[4] MORRIS (Aaron[3], John[2] III, John[1]) was born on 01 Feb 1731 in Symons Creek, Pasquotank, Colonial North Carolina. He died on 24 Nov 1798 in Pasquotank, North Carolina (Death Age: 60). He married (1) ELIZABETH PARKER in 1769 in Pasquotank, North Carolina, United States. She was born in 1741 in Pasquotank, North Carolina, United States. She died in 1800. He married (2) MARY NEWBY in 1755 in Pasquotank, North Carolina, United States. She was born on 28 Jul 1732 in Pasquotank, North Carolina, United States. She died on 05 Sep 1763 in Pasquotank, North Carolina, United States.

Joseph Morris and Elizabeth PARKER had the following child:

5. i. JAMES R[5] MORRIS was born on 21 May 1769 in Rutherford, North Carolina, USA. He died on 24 Sep 1849 in Edgefield, Edgefield, South Carolina, USA. He married Elizabeth Brooks on 14 Jun 1842 in Craven Cty,South Carolina. She was born between 1775-1776 in South Carolina, USA. She died before 1860 in Edgefield, South Carolina, USA.

Generation 5

5. JAMES R[5] MORRIS (Joseph[4], Aaron[3], John[2] III, John[1]) was born on 21 May 1769 in Rutherford, North Carolina, USA. He died on 24 Sep 1849 in Edgefield, Edgefield, South Carolina, USA. He married Elizabeth Brooks on 14 Jun 1842 in Craven Cty,South Carolina. She was born between 1775-1776 in South Carolina, USA. She died before 1860 in Edgefield, South Carolina, USA.

James R Morris and Elizabeth Brooks had the following children:

i. PLEASANT[6] MORRIS was born in Jun 1790 in Edgefield, South Carolina, USA. He died before 1860 in Edgefield, South Carolina, USA.

6. ii. REV JOSEPH MORRIS was born in 1794 in Edgefield, South Carolina, USA. He died on 29 Aug 1849 in Edgefield, South Carolina, USA. He married SARAI MORRIS. She was born in 1798 in Edgefield Co., South Carolina, USA. She died on 02 Jul 1860 in Edgefield Co., South Carolina, USA.

iii. WILLIAM M MORRIS was born about 1795 in South Carolina, United States. He died after 1860 in Talladega, Alabama, United States.

iv. MARY C 'MARTHA' MORRIS was born on 15 Aug 1795 in Edgefield, South Carolina, United States. She died on 03 Dec 1872 in McNeil, Columbia, Arkansas, United States.

2

v. MARY MORRIS was born about 1800 in Edgefield, South Carolina, USA. She died in 1875 in Warrior, Jefferson, Alabama, USA.

vi. NANCY MORRIS was born about 1802 in Edgefield, South Carolina, USA. She died in 1870 in Stoddard, Missouri, USA.

vii. ELIZABETH MORRIS was born in Jun 1804 in South Carolina, USA. She died about 1861 in Montery, Butler, Alabama.

viii. WILLIAM H. MORRIS was born on 19 Jul 1804 in South Carolina. He died on 08 Mar 1876 in Johnson County, Arkansas.

ix. WILLIAM L MORRISS was born about 1805 in Edgefield, South Carolina, USA. He died in 1870 in Desoto, Mississippi, USA.

x. BARBARA (BORBERRY) MORRIS was born on 15 Feb 1807 in Edgefield, Edgefield, South Carolina, USA. She died on 05 Aug 1867 in Fayette, Georgia, USA.

xi. JEREMIAH MORRIS was born about 1810 in South Carolina, USA. He died before 1848 in South Carolina, USA (He was des'd in father's will dated 10 Feb 1848).

xii. PARMELIA (AMELIA) MORRIS was born about 1813 in Edgefield, South Carolina, USA. She died before 1880 in Talladega, Alabama, United States.

xiii. SARAH MORRIS was born in 1815 in South Carolina, USA. She died between 1843-1848 in Edgefield County, South Carolina, USA (Her youngest child, Joseph S, was born in 1843 per the 1850 US Census and she was listed as Des'd in her father's will dated 10 Feb 1848).

Generation 6

6. REV JOSEPH[6] MORRIS (James R[5], Joseph[4], Aaron[3], John[2] III, John[1]) was born in 1794 in Edgefield, South Carolina, USA. He died on 29 Aug 1849 in Edgefield, South Carolina, USA. He married SARAI MORRIS. She was born in 1798 in Edgefield Co., South Carolina, USA. She died on 02 Jul 1860 in Edgefield Co., South Carolina, USA.

Rev Joseph Morris and Sarai MORRIS had the following children:

i. MALCHIGA[7] MORRIS was born about 1815 in Edgefield, South Carolina, USA.

ii. ADELINE MORRIS was born on 06 Mar 1817 in Edgefield County, South Carolina, USA. She died on 19 Feb 1885 in Russell Co., Alabama.

iii. REV EDMUND MORRIS was born on 11 Aug 1818 in Edgefield County, South Carolina, USA. He died on 20 Jul 1893 in Blythe, Richmond County, Georgia, USA.

7. iv. JOSEPH A MORRIS was born in 1821 in Edgefield District, SC. He died in Columbia Cty,GA. He married (1) CATHARINE HARVEY on 26 Dec 1850 in South Carolina. She was born in 1824 in Edgefield,The District, South Carolina, USA. He married (2) MARY ANDERSON. She was born in 1822 in Edgefield District, SC.

v. ANN J MORRIS was born about 1829 in Edgefield, South Carolina, USA.

vi. SARAH H (MORRIS) was born about 1834 in Edgefield, South Carolina, USA.

vii. GEORGE J. MORRIS. He died on 10 Dec 1857.

Generation 7

7. JOSEPH A[7] MORRIS (Rev Joseph[6], James R[5], Joseph[4], Aaron[3], John[2] III, John[1]) was born in 1821 in Edgefield District, SC. He died in Columbia Cty,GA. He married (1) CATHARINE HARVEY on 26 Dec 1850 in South Carolina. She was born in 1824 in Edgefield,The District, South Carolina, USA. He married (2) MARY ANDERSON. She was born in 1822 in Edgefield District, SC.

Joseph A Morris and Catharine Harvey had the following children:

i. JOSEPH A[8] MORRIS JR was born in 1851 in Edgefield,TheDistrict, South Carolina, USA.

8. ii. ORIN E MORRIS was born in 1853 in Edgefield,TheDistrict, South Carolina, USA. He married (1) SUSAN A MORRISS. She was born in 1847 in South Carolina. He married (2) AMANDA. She was born in 1850 in Georgia.

9. iii. WINFIELD C MORRIS was born in 1854 in South Carolina (The District Edgefield). He

3

died on 25 Jul 1916 in Augusta, Richmond County, Georgia, USA (Age: 62). He married Cue MontgomeryMorris, daughter of James Franklin Montgomery and Mrs Elizabeth Montgomery, on 22 Sep 1893 in Richmond, Georgia, USA. She was born on 08 Feb 1860 in McDuffie, Georgia, USA. She died on 12 Nov 1910 in Augusta, Ga..

    iv.   GOODWIN N MORRIS was born in 1856 in Edgefield,TheDistrict, South Carolina, USA.

    v.   GEORGE W MORRIS was born in 1858 in Edgefield,TheDistrict, South Carolina, USA.

Notes for Mary Anderson:
HIST: 1880 Census; age 60, Columbia Cty, Ga.

Joseph A Morris and Mary Anderson had the following children:

    vi.   SUSAN ANDERSON was born in 1851.

    vii.   SARA ANDERSON was born in 1857.

    viii.   RACHEL M ANDERSON was born in 1858.

    ix.   JONES A ANDERSON was born in 1861.

Generation 8

8.   ORIN E[8] MORRIS (Joseph A[7], Rev Joseph[6], James R[5], Joseph[4], Aaron[3], John[2] III, John[1]) was born in 1853 in Edgefield,TheDistrict, South Carolina, USA. He married (1) SUSAN A MORRISS. She was born in 1847 in South Carolina. He married (2) AMANDA. She was born in 1850 in Georgia.

Orin E Morris and Susan A Morriss had the following child:

10.   i.   FANNIE E[9] MORRIS was born in Sep 1881 in Georgia. She married James Morris in 1899. He was born in May 1876 in Georgia.

Orin E Morris and Amanda had the following children:

    ii.   FRANCES C. MORRIS was born in 1880 in Georgia.

    iii.   ALBERT MORRIS was born in 1854.

9.   WINFIELD C[8] MORRIS (Joseph A[7], Rev Joseph[6], James R[5], Joseph[4], Aaron[3], John[2] III, John[1]) was born in 1854 in South Carolina (The District Edgefield). He died on 25 Jul 1916 in Augusta, Richmond County, Georgia, USA (Age: 62). He married Cue MontgomeryMorris, daughter of James Franklin Montgomery and Mrs Elizabeth Montgomery, on 22 Sep 1893 in Richmond, Georgia, USA. She was born on 08 Feb 1860 in McDuffie, Georgia, USA. She died on 12 Nov 1910 in Augusta, Ga..

Notes for Winfield C Morris:
HIST: 1880 Census; age19, laborer,Columbia Cty,Ga.
HIST: 1910 Census; age 55, watchman.Plantation Oil Co,Augusta Ga.
HIST: 21Sept 1893 Marriage, Augusta,Ga.(Family Bible)
HIST: 25 July 1916:Death,Augusta,Ga.(Family Bible)

Notes for Cue MontgomeryMorris:
Montgomery Family Cemetery is on Quail Farm Road,north of Big Briar Creek. On private property, approx 1/2 miles east of Quail Farn Road.
HIST: 1880 Census:age 19,Mcduffie Cty, Ga.(Quetin)
HIST: 1910 Census: age 50,Richmond Cty,Ga.
HIST: Augusta Chronical, Sunday, 13 Nov 1910:Funeral   Announcement.

Winfield C Morris and Cue MontgomeryMorris had the following children:

11.   i.   CLARABELLE[9] FAUCETT was born on 22 Oct 1882 in South Carolina. She died on 08 Sep 1964 in Fredericksburg, Gillespie, Texas, USA (Age: 81). She married Francis Marion DesCombes, son of Charles E Descombes and Mary E Descombes, in 1905. He was born on 13 Aug 1884 in South Carolina. He died on 26 Jan 1959 in Fulton, Georgia (Age: 74 Years).

    ii.   OTIS FAUCETT was born about 1885 in Georgia. He died on 19 Oct 1931 in Atlanta, Ga.. He married CARRIE L FRANCETTE. She was born in 1893 in Georgia.

Notes for Otis Faucett:
Died of a brain tumor

12.   iii.   MARION WINGFIELD MORRIS was born on 20 Apr 1897 in Georgia
(Augusta,Richmond Cty, Ga). He died on 17 Oct 1964 in Cartersville Bartow Cty Ga
(Oak Hill Cemetery). He married Marie Louise Williams, daughter of James
Cranston Williams and Mary Maria GULLATT, on 17 Jan 1923 in Greensboro,
Greene Cty, Ga.Marvin Williams (Williams Home). She was born on 10 Jan 1899 in
Washington, Wilkes, Georgia, USA. She died on 22 Apr 1997 in Cartersville,
Bartow, Georgia, United States of America.

Generation 9

10.   FANNIE E[9] MORRIS (Orin E[8], Joseph A[7], Rev Joseph[6], James R[5], Joseph[4], Aaron[3], John[2] III,
John[1]) was born in Sep 1881 in Georgia. She married James Morris in 1899. He was born in May
1876 in Georgia.

James Morris and Fannie E Morris had the following children:

13.   i.   BENJ F[10] MORRIS was born in Sep 1899 in Georgia. He married MARGIE L MORRIS.
She was born about 1897 in Georgia.

ii.   MAGGIE H MORRIS was born about 1902 in Georgia.

11.   CLARABELLE[9] FAUCETT (Winfield C[8] Morris, Joseph A[7] Morris, Rev Joseph[6] Morris, James R[5]
Morris, Joseph[4] Morris, Aaron[3] Morris, John[2] Morris III, John[1] Morris) was born on 22 Oct 1882 in
South Carolina. She died on 08 Sep 1964 in Fredericksburg, Gillespie, Texas, USA (Age: 81). She
married Francis Marion DesCombes, son of Charles E Descombes and Mary E Descombes, in
1905. He was born on 13 Aug 1884 in South Carolina. He died on 26 Jan 1959 in Fulton, Georgia
(Age: 74 Years).

Francis Marion DesCombes and Clarabelle Faucett had the following child:

14.   i.   VIVIAN[10] DESCOMB was born on 27 Jan 1907 in Augusta Rich, Georgia. She died on
30 Jun 1997 in Collin, Texas. She married (1) BERNARD L MATHEWS. He was born
on 23 Feb 1916. He died in Feb 1965. She married (2) ROOP DORSETT. He was
born on 30 Jul 1906 in Carroll, Georgia, USA. He died on 15 Dec 1974 in Duval,
Florida, United States (Age: 68).

12.   MARION WINGFIELD[9] MORRIS (Winfield C[8], Joseph A[7], Rev Joseph[6], James R[5], Joseph[4], Aaron[3],
John[2] III, John[1]) was born on 20 Apr 1897 in Georgia (Augusta,Richmond Cty, Ga). He died on 17
Oct 1964 in Cartersville Bartow Cty Ga (Oak Hill Cemetery). He married Marie Louise Williams,
daughter of James Cranston Williams and Mary Maria GULLATT, on 17 Jan 1923 in Greensboro,
Greene Cty, Ga.Marvin Williams (Williams Home). She was born on 10 Jan 1899 in Washington,
Wilkes, Georgia, USA. She died on 22 Apr 1997 in Cartersville, Bartow, Georgia, United States of
America.

Notes for Marion Wingfield Morris:
SSN:253 10 7100
Served USMarine Corps--9 Aug1918-6 Sep1919
ReHonsymoonPix:Restored7/2014-originsl:early1923Jax,Fl

Notes for Marie Louise Williams:
SSN; 255 70 2116
Re:Honeymoonpix:seeMWMmediafile

Marion Wingfield Morris and Marie Louise Williams had the following children:

15.   i.   JAMES WINGFIELD[10] MORRIS was born on 01 Sep 1924 in Augusta, Richmond Cty,
Ga.. He married Mary Corinne WOFFORD, daughter of William Earl WOFFORD
and Mary Louise Meroney, on 19 Jan 1948 in FPC Cartersville, Ga. She was born
on 21 Apr 1926 in Cartersville, Bartow, Georgia, USA. She died on 08 Feb 2013 in
Cartersville Bartow Cty Ga.

16.   ii.   MARYBELLE MORRIS was born on 14 Apr 1926 in Atlanta City, Fulton, Georgia. She
died on 09 Jun 2008 in Fountain Valley, Orange, California. She married (1)
DONALD CHARLES SWIFT, son of George S SWIFT and Florence Harriet Jager, on 29

Mar 1946 in Cartersville Bartow Cty Ga. He was born on 13 Feb 1920 in Northampton MA. He died on 26 Dec 1994 in Laguna Hills, Orange, California, USA. She married (2) ALEX THOMAS DENT, son of Fredrick William "Fritz" Dent and Ida Pearl Dodd, on 23 Sep 1997 in Euharlee, Bartow, Cty, Ga. He was born on 22 Feb 1920 in Euharlee, Bartow Cty, Georgia. He died on 14 Nov 2002 in Cartersville, Bartow, Georgia, United States of America.

17. iii. MARIAN LOUISE MORRIS was born on 29 Nov 1930 in Atlanta, Fulton Cty, Ga. She married Nelson Kimball ROGERS, son of Lewis Edward ROGERS and Marion Ruth NELSON, on 20 Jun 1953 in Cartersville, Bartow, Georgia, USA. He was born on 17 May 1928 in New York, NY. He died on 15 Sep 2013 in Cartersville Bartow Cty Ga.

Generation 10

13. BENJ F[10] MORRIS (Fannie E[9], Orin E[8], Joseph A[7], Rev Joseph[6], James R[5], Joseph[4], Aaron[3], John[2] III, John[1]) was born in Sep 1899 in Georgia. He married MARGIE L MORRIS. She was born about 1897 in Georgia.

Benj F Morris and Margie L Morris had the following child:

 i. CECIL J[11] MORRIS was born about 1920 in Georgia.

14. VIVIAN[10] DESCOMB (Clarabelle[9] Faucett, Winfield C[8] Morris, Joseph A[7] Morris, Rev Joseph[6] Morris, James R[5] Morris, Joseph[4] Morris, Aaron[3] Morris, John[2] Morris III, John[1] Morris) was born on 27 Jan 1907 in Augusta Rich, Georgia. She died on 30 Jun 1997 in Collin, Texas. She married (1) BERNARD L MATHEWS. He was born on 23 Feb 1916. He died in Feb 1965. She married (2) ROOP DORSETT. He was born on 30 Jul 1906 in Carroll, Georgia, USA. He died on 15 Dec 1974 in Duval, Florida, United States (Age: 68).

Roop DORSETT and Vivian Descomb had the following children:

 i. TOMMY M[11] DORCETT was born about 1932 in Georgia.

 ii. MARY CLAIRE DORSETT was born about 1935 in Georgia. She married CHARLES DUNN.

15. JAMES WINGFIELD[10] MORRIS (Marion Wingfield[9], Winfield C[8], Joseph A[7], Rev Joseph[6], James R[5], Joseph[4], Aaron[3], John[2] III, John[1]) was born on 01 Sep 1924 in Augusta, Richmond Cty, Ga.. He married Mary Corinne WOFFORD, daughter of William Earl WOFFORD and Mary Louise Meroney, on 19 Jan 1948 in FPC Cartersville, Ga. She was born on 21 Apr 1926 in Cartersville, Bartow, Georgia, USA. She died on 08 Feb 2013 in Cartersville Bartow Cty Ga.

Notes for James Wingfield MORRIS:
Graduate,USMA,1945:BS Aeronautical Engineering, Univ Michigan 1959: MA,International Affairs, George Washington Univ, 1964

Notes for Mary Corinne WOFFORD:
Graduated Vanderbilt School of Nursing, Nashville, Tn 1948

James Wingfield MORRIS and Mary Corinne WOFFORD had the following children:

18. i. MARY LOUISE[11] MORRIS was born on 03 May 1949 in Cartersville, Bartow, Georgia, USA. She married (1) SHELDON G. SPICHER III, son of Samuel S. Spicher and Edith Marie Morgan, on 20 Dec 1970 in Charlottesville Va. He was born on 19 Jul 1948. She married (2) TIMOTHY CARR BRAMBLE, son of Roy H Bramble and Lois Jean Bennett, on 01 Feb 1985 in Dunwoody, Ga... He was born on 13 Mar 1952 in Detroit, Mich.

19. ii. JAMES WINGFIELD MORRIS JR was born on 29 Oct 1950 in Cartersville, Bartow, Georgia, USA. He married Carolyn Ethel LYON, daughter of Robert Fredrick LYON and Mildred Virginia Shacklett, on 09 Jun 1973 in Marietta, Ga.. She was born on 14 Mar 1951 in Nashville, Davidson Cty, Tn.

20. iii. WILLIAM CRANSTON MORRIS was born on 02 Mar 1954 in Cartersville, Bartow, Georgia, USA. He married Beverly Jane TIPTON, daughter of James Darrell{J.D.} TIPTON and Barbara Jean HAVENS, on 10 Jul 1976 in Maryville, Tennessee. She was born on 06 Feb 1954 in Maryville, Blount Cty, Tn.

6

21. iv. BRIAN MERONEY MORRIS was born on 28 Jan 1961 in Washington D.C.. He married (1) JILL HAROLYN KING, daughter of Harold Vernell King and Daisy Jewell Waits, on 20 Aug 1983 in Cartersville, Ga.. She was born on 10 Aug 1959 in Rome, Floyd Cty, Ga.. He married (2) MICHELE ALLEN EWEN on 10 Jun 2000 in Dallas, Texas. She was born on 11 Jun 1967 in Denver, Co.

22. v. PETER CHARLES MORRIS was born on 22 Jun 1962 in Arlington, Virginia, USA. He married Frances Elizabeth ALLEN, daughter of Bona ALLEN IV and Jane King, on 15 Jun 1985 in Dunwoody, Ga.. She was born on 26 Feb 1963.

16. MARYBELLE[10] MORRIS (Marion Wingfield[9], Winfield C[8], Joseph A[7], Rev Joseph[6], James R[5], Joseph[4], Aaron[3], John[2] III, John[1]) was born on 14 Apr 1926 in Atlanta City, Fulton, Georgia. She died on 09 Jun 2008 in Fountain Valley, Orange, California. She married (1) DONALD CHARLES SWIFT, son of George S SWIFT and Florence Harriet Jager, on 29 Mar 1946 in Cartersville Bartow Cty Ga. He was born on 13 Feb 1920 in Northampton MA. He died on 26 Dec 1994 in Laguna Hills, Orange, California, USA. She married (2) ALEX THOMAS DENT, son of Fredrick William "Fritz" Dent and Ida Pearl Dodd, on 23 Sep 1997 in Euharlee, Bartow, Cty, Ga. He was born on 22 Feb 1920 in Euharlee, Bartow Cty, Georgia. He died on 14 Nov 2002 in Cartersville, Bartow, Georgia, United States of America.

Donald Charles Swift and Marybelle MORRIS had the following children:

23. i. MARY LOUISE[11] SWIFT was born on 10 Jan 1950 in Cartersville Bartow Cty, Ga. She married Robert H Beckmann on 12 Jun 1971 in Dalas Texas. He was born in 1943.

24. ii. ANNE ELIZABETH SWIFT was born on 29 May 1954 in Dallas Tx. She married (1) TOM FRANKLIN. She married (2) JAMES T PARKER on 03 Feb 1973 in Dallas Tx (WalnutHills,MethodistChurch).

17. MARIAN LOUISE[10] MORRIS (Marion Wingfield[9], Winfield C[8], Joseph A[7], Rev Joseph[6], James R[5], Joseph[4], Aaron[3], John[2] III, John[1]) was born on 29 Nov 1930 in Atlanta, Fulton Cty, Ga. She married Nelson Kimball ROGERS, son of Lewis Edward ROGERS and Marion Ruth NELSON, on 20 Jun 1953 in Cartersville, Bartow, Georgia, USA. He was born on 17 May 1928 in New York, NY. He died on 15 Sep 2013 in Cartersville Bartow Cty Ga.

Notes for Marian Louise MORRIS:
Graduate Wesleyan College, Macon, Ga..1951.BA,English Major(CumLaude)

Notes for Nelson Kimball ROGERS:
Graduate,USNA, Annapolis, Md 1950. MS.Georgia Tech:IndustrialTechnology,1956

Nelson Kimball ROGERS and Marian Louise MORRIS had the following children:

25. i. EDWARD MORRIS[11] ROGERS was born on 09 May 1960 in Summit, NJ. He married Jeanette Lynn RAINES, daughter of Dennis Wayne RAINES and Janice Rollins, on 08 Oct 1983 in Germantown, Tn. She was born on 16 Mar 1960 in Jackson, Tn.

ii. KIMBALL AMANDA ROGERS was born on 23 Feb 1962 in Summit, NJ.

Notes for Kimball Amanda ROGERS:
Shorter College: BS.Sociology, B.A.English.1983

iii. JAMES MADISON ROGERS was born on 11 Jun 1963 in Summit, NJ.

Notes for James Madison ROGERS:
Graduate Furman,Univ,SC,1985,BA Religion

iv. CAREY SUSAN ROGERS was born on 31 Oct 1965 in Cartersville Bartow Cty Ga. She died on 31 Oct 1965 in Cartersville Bartow Cty Ga (OakHillCemetery).

Generation 11

18. MARY LOUISE[11] MORRIS (James Wingfield[10], Marion Wingfield[9], Winfield C[8], Joseph A[7], Rev Joseph[6], James R[5], Joseph[4], Aaron[3], John[2] III, John[1]) was born on 03 May 1949 in Cartersville, Bartow, Georgia, USA. She married (1) SHELDON G. SPICHER III, son of Samuel S. Spicher and Edith Marie Morgan, on 20 Dec 1970 in Charlottesville Va. He was born on 19 Jul 1948. She married (2) TIMOTHY CARR BRAMBLE, son of Roy H Bramble and Lois Jean Bennett, on 01 Feb 1985 in Dunwoody, Ga... He was born on 13 Mar 1952 in Detroit, Mich.

7

Notes for Mary Louise MORRIS:
Education:Mary Washington College/ BSN Univ Virginia School Nursing1970

Sheldon G. Spicher III and Mary Louise MORRIS had the following children:

26.   i.   AMY LYNNE[12] SPICHER was born on 11 May 1973 in Medford Or. She married (1) CHARLES ANDREW SHROPSHIRE on 15 May 1999 in Cartersville, Ga.. He was born on 30 Oct 1969 in Atlanta, Fulton Cty, Ga.. She married (2) PAUL WILLIAM ETHERIDGE, son of Philip F Etheridge and Brenda Williams, on 07 Jun 2014 in Atlanta, Fulton, Georgia. He was born on 20 May 1970 in Atlanta City, Fulton, Georgia.

27.   ii.   SHANNON ELIZABETH SPICHER was born on 24 Oct 1975 in Atlanta, Fulton Cty Ga. She married Corey Wayne TOWE on 28 Apr 2001 in Cartersvile, Ga.. He was born on 09 Aug 1976.

28.   iii.   PHILLIP MATTHEW SPICHER was born on 07 Apr 1978 in Atlanta, Fulton Cty, Ga. He married Kelly Christine Wittorff, daughter of Jon Whitoff and Karen Whitokk, on 11 Jul 2009 in San Diego, California, USA. She was born on 17 Oct 1976 in Indianapolis, Hamilton, Indiana, USA.

Timothy Carr BRAMBLE and Mary Louise MORRIS had the following child:

i.   REBECCA KATHLEEN[12] BRAMBLE was born on 02 Aug 1986 in Atlanta, Fulton Cty Ga.

19.   JAMES WINGFIELD[11] MORRIS JR (James Wingfield[10], Marion Wingfield[9], Winfield C[8], Joseph A[7], Rev Joseph[6], James R[5], Joseph[4], Aaron[3], John[2] III, John[1]) was born on 29 Oct 1950 in Cartersville, Bartow, Georgia, USA. He married Carolyn Ethel LYON, daughter of Robert Fredrick LYON and Mldred Virginia Shacklett, on 09 Jun 1973 in Marietta, Ga.. She was born on 14 Mar 1951 in Nashville, Davidson Cty, Tn.

Notes for James Wingfield MORRIS Jr:
Education: BSArchitectural Technology,SouthernTechnical Institute 1972/Registered Arctitect 1982,BA,Education Kennesaw State Univ, 1995

Notes for Carolyn Ethel LYON:
Education: BS, Architectural Technology,Southern Technical Institute,1973 Registered architect,22September 1988.

James Wingfield MORRIS Jr and Carolyn Ethel LYON had the following children:

29.   i.   MARY VIRGINIA[12] MORRIS was born on 18 Mar 1974 in Marietta, Cobb Cty, Ga.. She married Timothy Adam BLACKWELL, son of Toby Long BLACKWELL and Sherrill McGARITY, on 16 Dec 1995 in Marietta, Ga.. He was born on 20 Feb 1973 in Atlanta, Fulton Cty, Ga.

30.   ii.   JAMES LYON MORRIS was born on 11 Jan 1983 in Marietta, Cobb Cty, Ga. He married Angela Swope, daughter of James Leonard Swope and Mana Sue Campbell, on 27 May 2007 in Atlanta, Fulton Cty, Ga.Atlanta City Hall. She was born on 07 Mar 1984 in Friendship, Harris, Texas.

20.   WILLIAM CRANSTON[11] MORRIS (James Wingfield[10], Marion Wingfield[9], Winfield C[8], Joseph A[7], Rev Joseph[6], James R[5], Joseph[4], Aaron[3], John[2] III, John[1]) was born on 02 Mar 1954 in Cartersville, Bartow, Georgia, USA. He married Beverly Jane TIPTON, daughter of James Darrell{J.D.} TIPTON and Barbara Jean HAVENS, on 10 Jul 1976 in Maryville, Tennessee. She was born on 06 Feb 1954 in Maryville, Blount Cty, Tn.

Notes for William Cranston MORRIS:
Education:BS,Civil engineering,USAFA, 1976: MS,AF Institute of Technology,WrightPatterson AFBase, 1985

Notes for Beverly Jane TIPTON:
Education: BS,Home Economics, Univ of Tennessee, 1976: Teacher Certification Program, Univ of Texas, San Antonio, 1994.   NOTE:For Havens Family Story see John Lee Havens, media file.

William Cranston MORRIS and Beverly Jane TIPTON had the following children:

31.   i.   KEVIN JAMES[12] MORRIS was born on 11 Nov 1980 in Laughlin AFB, Val Verde, Texas, USA (Del Rio Tx). He married Jessica Lynn Dayton, daughter of George Francis Dayton and Wendy Joy Whitehead, on 17 Dec 2011 in Denver, Colorado,

8

417

USA (Wellshire Presbyterian Church). She was born on 01 May 1982 in Wheat Ridge Colorado.

32.   ii.   EMILY SARAH MORRIS was born on 09 Aug 1985 in Wright Patterson AFB (Dayton OH). She married Christopher John Matheis, son of Nicolas Aloyasius Matheis and Lisa A Matheis, on 29 Oct 2011 in Cartersville, Bartow, Georgia, USA (First Presbyterian Church). He was born on 27 Apr 1982 in Jasper Indiana (Memorial Hospital).

21.   BRIAN MERONEY[11] MORRIS (James Wingfield[10], Marion Wingfield[9], Winfield C[8], Joseph A[7], Rev Joseph[6], James R[5], Joseph[4], Aaron[3], John[2] III, John[1]) was born on 28 Jan 1961 in Washington D.C.. He married (1) JILL HAROLYN KING, daughter of Harold Vernell King and Daisy Jewell Waits, on 20 Aug 1983 in Cartersville, Ga.. She was born on 10 Aug 1959 in Rome, Floyd Cty, Ga.. He married (2) MICHELE ALLEN EWEN on 10 Jun 2000 in Dallas, Texas. She was born on 11 Jun 1967 in Denver, Co.

Notes for Brian Meroney MORRIS:
Graduate: BBA,North Georgia College, 1983

Notes for Jill Harolyn King:
Graduated North Georgia College 1982

Brian Meroney MORRIS and Jill Harolyn King had the following child:

    i.   DAVID BRIAN[12] MORRIS was born on 05 Nov 1988 in Winfield, DuPage County, Illinois, USA.

        Notes for David Brian MORRIS:
        Cartersville High School, Graduated May 27, 2007
        Certified Nursing Assistant, Graduated August 29, 2014
        Phlebotomist, Patient Care Technician, EKG Technician, Graduated 14 Sept 2016

22.   PETER CHARLES[11] MORRIS (James Wingfield[10], Marion Wingfield[9], Winfield C[8], Joseph A[7], Rev Joseph[6], James R[5], Joseph[4], Aaron[3], John[2] III, John[1]) was born on 22 Jun 1962 in Arlington, Virginia, USA. He married Frances Elizabeth ALLEN, daughter of Bona ALLEN IV and Jane King, on 15 Jun 1985 in Dunwoody, Ga.. She was born on 26 Feb 1963.

Notes for Peter Charles MORRIS:
Graduate, USMA 1984, BS Aeronautics

Notes for Frances Elizabeth ALLEN:
Graduate Birmingham Southern,BA,1985,childhood education: TroyStateUniv, Ala, MA, Education.1990

Peter Charles MORRIS and Frances Elizabeth ALLEN had the following children:

    i.   KATELYN ELIZABETH[12] MORRIS was born on 21 Apr 1992 in Atlanta, Fulton Cty, Ga.

        Notes for Katelyn Elizabeth MORRIS:
        Graduate;UNC-Chapel hill BS'Psycology,minorReligiousStudies/Music
    ii.   SARA CAROLINE MORRIS was born on 17 Feb 1995 in Marietta, Cobb Cty, Ga..

23.   MARY LOUISE[11] SWIFT (Marybelle[10] MORRIS, Marion Wingfield[9] Morris, Winfield C[8] Morris, Joseph A[7] Morris, Rev Joseph[6] Morris, James R[5] Morris, Joseph[4] Morris, Aaron[3] Morris, John[2] Morris III, John[1] Morris) was born on 10 Jan 1950 in Cartersville Bartow Cty, Ga. She married Robert H Beckmann on 12 Jun 1971 in Dalas Texas. He was born in 1943.

Robert H Beckmann and Mary Louise SWIFT had the following children:

33.   i.   MATTTHEW NOLAN[12] BECKMANN was born on 19 Aug 1975 in Garden Grove, Ca.. He married Kenya Marie Mayfield on 15 Jul 2000 in Ann Arbor, Mi.. She was born on 16 Apr 1974.

    ii.   BENJAMIN SCOTT BECKMANN was born on 06 Nov 1977 in Santa Ana, Ca..

24.   ANNE ELIZABETH[11] SWIFT (Marybelle[10] MORRIS, Marion Wingfield[9] Morris, Winfield C[8] Morris, Joseph A[7] Morris, Rev Joseph[6] Morris, James R[5] Morris, Joseph[4] Morris, Aaron[3] Morris, John[2] Morris III, John[1] Morris) was born on 29 May 1954 in Dallas Tx. She married (1) TOM FRANKLIN.

9

She married (2) JAMES T PARKER on 03 Feb 1973 in Dallas Tx (WalnutHills,MethodistChurch).
James T PARKER and Anne Elizabeth SWIFT had the following child:

34. i. MICHAEL CHARLES[12] PARKER was born on 07 Aug 1975 in Dallas, Tx.. He married JODY UNKNOWN.

25. EDWARD MORRIS[11] ROGERS (Marian Louise[10] MORRIS, Marion Wingfield[9] Morris, Winfield C[8] Morris, Joseph A[7] Morris, Rev Joseph[6] Morris, James R[5] Morris, Joseph[4] Morris, Aaron[3] Morris, John[2] Morris III, John[1] Morris) was born on 09 May 1960 in Summit, NJ. He married Jeanette Lynn RAINES, daughter of Dennis Wayne RAINES and Janice Rollins, on 08 Oct 1983 in Germantown, Tn. She was born on 16 Mar 1960 in Jackson, Tn.

Notes for Edward Morris ROGERS:
BIE, Bachelor of Industrial Engineering, GA Institute of Technology, 1982:Master of Science Engineering Managment,Univ of Dayton, 1993:MS,International Logistics, Georgia Tech, 2002

Notes for Jeanette Lynn RAINES:
BChE, Chemical Engineering Georgia Institute of Technology, 1983

Edward Morris ROGERS and Jeanette Lynn RAINES had the following children:

 i. KYLA LOUISE[12] ROGERS was born on 05 Apr 1987 in Dayton, OH. She married William Edward Mantzel II, son of William Edward Mantzel and Sara Lee Morrow, on 13 Sep 2014 in Roswell, Fulton, Georgia, USA (Northbrook UMC). He was born on 16 Jul 1980 in Harris, Texas.

  Notes for Kyla Louise ROGERS:
  Graduate, Georgia Institute of Technology,2009,BS Economics annd International Affairs

 ii. MATLOCK NELSON ROGERS was born on 16 Aug 1989 in Dayton, OH.

  Notes for Matlock Nelson ROGERS:
  Graduate,Georgia Institute of Technology,2011.BS,IndustrialEngineering

 iii. KIRBY LEE ROGERS was born on 06 Aug 1991 in Lawrenceville, Ga..

  Notes for Kirby Lee ROGERS:
  Graduate Agnes ScottCollege,Atlanta,2013,BA,Mathematics.Graduate Belmont Univ.Nashville, TN.2014,MA in Teaching

Generation 12

26. AMY LYNNE[12] SPICHER (Mary Louise[11] MORRIS, James Wingfield[10] MORRIS, Marion Wingfield[9] Morris, Winfield C[8] Morris, Joseph A[7] Morris, Rev Joseph[6] Morris, James R[5] Morris, Joseph[4] Morris, Aaron[3] Morris, John[2] Morris III, John[1] Morris) was born on 11 May 1973 in Medford Or. She married (1) CHARLES ANDREW SHROPSHIRE on 15 May 1999 in Cartersville, Ga.. He was born on 30 Oct 1969 in Atlanta, Fulton Cty, Ga.. She married (2) PAUL WILLIAM ETHERIDGE, son of Philip F Etheridge and Brenda Williams, on 07 Jun 2014 in Atlanta, Fulton, Georgia. He was born on 20 May 1970 in Atlanta City, Fulton, Georgia.

Charles Andrew SHROPSHIRE and AMY Lynne SPICHER had the following children:

 i. CHARLES ANDREW[13] SHROPSHIRE JR was born on 27 Oct 2001 in Atlanta, Fulton Cty, Ga..

 ii. WOFFORD HILL SHROPSHIRE was born on 17 May 2005 in Atlanta, Fulton Cty, Ga..

 iii. JAMES WHITFIELD SHROPSHIRE was born on 02 Mar 2007 in Atlanta, Fulton Cty, Ga..

 iv. MARY EVELYN SHROPSHIRE was born on 10 Feb 2009 in Atlanta, Fulton Cty, Ga.

27. SHANNON ELIZABETH[12] SPICHER (Mary Louise[11] MORRIS, James Wingfield[10] MORRIS, Marion Wingfield[9] Morris, Winfield C[8] Morris, Joseph A[7] Morris, Rev Joseph[6] Morris, James R[5] Morris, Joseph[4] Morris, Aaron[3] Morris, John[2] Morris III, John[1] Morris) was born on 24 Oct 1975 in Atlanta, Fulton Cty Ga. She married Corey Wayne TOWE on 28 Apr 2001 in Cartersvile, Ga.. He was born on 09 Aug 1976.

Corey Wayne TOWE and Shannon Elizabeth SPICHER had the following children:

10

    i.   JOSHUA ELLIOT[13] TOWE was born on 09 Feb 2005 in CHARLESTON, S.C..

    ii.   JACOB OWEN TOWE was born on 17 Jul 2007 in Atlanta, Fulton Cty, Ga..

    iii. ANNISTON KATHRYN TOWE was born on 18 Oct 2010 in Alphretta,Forsyth Cty, Ga.

28.   **PHILLIP MATTHEW**[12] **SPICHER** (Mary Louise[11] MORRIS, James Wingfield[10] MORRIS, Marion Wingfield[9] Morris, Winfield C[8] Morris, Joseph A[7] Morris, Rev Joseph[6] Morris, James R[5] Morris, Joseph[4] Morris, Aaron[3] Morris, John[2] Morris III, John[1] Morris) was born on 07 Apr 1978 in Atlanta, Fulton Cty, Ga. He married Kelly Christine Wittorff, daughter of Jon Whitoff and Karen Whitokk, on 11 Jul 2009 in San Diego, California, USA. She was born on 17 Oct 1976 in Indianapolis, Hamilton, Indiana, USA.

Notes for Kelly Christine Wittorff:
Education:Political ScienceandJournaism,Univof Indiana,Law degree.Univ of Florida.
Passed Bar in California and Florida.Specialty,Corporate Law

Phillip Matthew SPICHER and Kelly Christine Wittorff had the following children:

    i.   SAMUEL BEAR[13] SPICHER was born on 20 Oct 2010 in San Diego, California, USA.

    ii.   ETHAN CHASE SPICHER was born on 15 Nov 2012 in San Diego,CA.

    iii. LEVI MATTHEW SPICHER was born on 16 Sep 2015 in San Diego, California, USA.

29.   **MARY VIRGINIA**[12] **MORRIS** (James Wingfield[11] Jr, James Wingfield[10], Marion Wingfield[9], Winfield C[8], Joseph A[7], Rev Joseph[6], James R[5], Joseph[4], Aaron[3], John[2] III, John[1]) was born on 18 Mar 1974 in Marietta, Cobb Cty, Ga.. She married Timothy Adam BLACKWELL, son of Toby Long BLACKWELL and Sherrill McGARITY, on 16 Dec 1995 in Marietta, Ga.. He was born on 20 Feb 1973 in Atlanta, Fulton Cty, Ga.

Notes for Mary Virginia MORRIS:
Education: BS,Middle Grades Education, Georgia Southern Univ.1995: MS, Education,GSU,1997.

Timothy Adam BLACKWELL and Mary Virginia MORRIS had the following children:

    i.   BRYCE HARPER[13] BLACKWELL was born on 07 Feb 2001 in Gainesville, Ga..

    ii.   BODIE LANG BLACKWELL was born on 14 Feb 2003 in Gainesville, Ga..

30.   **JAMES LYON**[12] **MORRIS** (James Wingfield[11] Jr, James Wingfield[10], Marion Wingfield[9], Winfield C[8], Joseph A[7], Rev Joseph[6], James R[5], Joseph[4], Aaron[3], John[2] III, John[1]) was born on 11 Jan 1983 in Marietta, Cobb Cty, Ga. He married Angela Swope, daughter of James Leonard Swope and Mana Sue Campbell, on 27 May 2007 in Atlanta, Fulton Cty, Ga.Atlanta City Hall. She was born on 07 Mar 1984 in Friendship, Harris, Texas.

Notes for James Lyon MORRIS:
Education:BS, Middle Grades Education, Georgia Southern Univ, 2005

James Lyon MORRIS and Angela Swope had the following child:

    i.   CAITLIAN ROSE[13] MORRIS was born on 01 Jan 2010 in Atlanta, Fulton Cty Ga.

31.   **KEVIN JAMES**[12] **MORRIS** (William Cranston[11], James Wingfield[10], Marion Wingfield[9], Winfield C[8], Joseph A[7], Rev Joseph[6], James R[5], Joseph[4], Aaron[3], John[2] III, John[1]) was born on 11 Nov 1980 in Laughlin AFB, Val Verde, Texas, USA (Del Rio Tx). He married Jessica Lynn Dayton, daughter of George Francis Dayton and Wendy Joy Whitehead, on 17 Dec 2011 in Denver, Colorado, USA (Wellshire Presbyterian Church). She was born on 01 May 1982 in Wheat Ridge Colorado.

Notes for Kevin James MORRIS:
Education: BS,Computer Science, Ga Tech,2003; MS, Computer Science, Ga Tech(GA Instotute of Technology), 2005.

Kevin James MORRIS and Jessica Lynn Dayton had the following child:

    i.   OLIVER DAYTON[13] MORRIS was born on 20 Aug 2016 in Denver, Colorado, USA.

32.   **EMILY SARAH**[12] **MORRIS** (William Cranston[11], James Wingfield[10], Marion Wingfield[9], Winfield C[8], Joseph A[7], Rev Joseph[6], James R[5], Joseph[4], Aaron[3], John[2] III, John[1]) was born on 09 Aug 1985 in Wright Patterson AFB (Dayton OH). She married Christopher John Matheis, son of Nicolas

//

Aloyasius Matheis and Lisa A Matheis, on 29 Oct 2011 in Cartersville, Bartow, Georgia, USA (First Presbyterian Church). He was born on 27 Apr 1982 in Jasper Indiana (Memorial Hospital).

Notes for Emily Sarah MORRIS:
Education: BA, Liberal Arts, Colorado State Univ,2007

Notes for Christopher John Matheis:
Education:Pittsburg State Univ, Pittsburg,KS, BS(Automotive Technology)2004

Christopher John Matheis and Emily Sarah MORRIS had the following children:

  i. PIERCE MORRIS[13] MATHEIS was born on 06 Jan 2016 in Franciiscan St Francis Hosp, Indianapolis,ID (Older of Twins).

  ii. CLAIRE SARAH MATHEIS was born on 06 Jan 2016 in Franciscan St.Francis Hosp,Indianapolis, ID (2nd of tins).

33. MATTTHEW NOLAN[12] BECKMANN (Mary Louise[11] SWIFT, Marybelle[10] MORRIS, Marion Wingfield[9] Morris, Winfield C[8] Morris, Joseph A[7] Morris, Rev Joseph[6] Morris, James R[5] Morris, Joseph[4] Morris, Aaron[3] Morris, John[2] Morris III, John[1] Morris) was born on 19 Aug 1975 in Garden Grove, Ca.. He married Kenya Marie Mayfield on 15 Jul 2000 in Ann Arbor, Mi.. She was born on 16 Apr 1974.

Mattthew Nolan BECKMANN and Kenya Marie Mayfield had the following children:

  i. BROOKS PORTER[13] BECKMANN was born on 12 Aug 2006.

  ii. WESTON DEAN BECKMANN was born on 09 Oct 2002 in Ann Arbor, Mi..

  iii. CHARLOTTE SWIFT BECKMANN was born on 04 Feb 2008 in Irvine, Orange, California, USA.

34. MICHAEL CHARLES[12] PARKER (Anne Elizabeth[11] SWIFT, Marybelle[10] MORRIS, Marion Wingfield[9] Morris, Winfield C[8] Morris, Joseph A[7] Morris, Rev Joseph[6] Morris, James R[5] Morris, Joseph[4] Morris, Aaron[3] Morris, John[2] Morris III, John[1] Morris) was born on 07 Aug 1975 in Dallas, Tx.. He married JODY UNKNOWN.

Michael Charles PARKER and Jody UNKNOWN had the following children:

  i. ALLISON[13] PARKER.

  ii. SARAH PARKER.

12

Descendants of Lewis Williams

Generation 1

1.   **LEWIS[1] WILLIAMS** was born in 1625 in Wales. He died in 1699 in Surry, Virginia, USA. He married (1) **ANN MOSS**. She was born in 1634 in Isle, , Virginia, USA. She died on 13 Feb 1670 in Isle, , Virginia, USA.

Lewis Williams and Ann Moss had the following child:

2.   i.   WILLIAM[2] WILLIAMS (son of Lewis Williams and Ann Moss) was born in 1667 in Surry, Virginia, USA. He died in 1692 in Bertie, North Carolina, USA. He married (1) ANN WILLIAMS. She was born in 1671 in Surry, Virginia, USA. He married (2) ANN WHITLEY in 1637. She was born in 1620 in Isle, , Virginia, USA. She died in Isle, , Virginia, USA.

Generation 2

2.   **WILLIAM[2] WILLIAMS** (Lewis[1]) was born in 1667 in Surry, Virginia, USA. He died in 1692 in Bertie, North Carolina, USA. He married (1) **ANN WILLIAMS**. She was born in 1671 in Surry, Virginia, USA. He married (2) **ANN WHITLEY** in 1637. She was born in 1620 in Isle, , Virginia, USA. She died in Isle, , Virginia, USA.

William Williams and Ann Williams had the following child:

3.   i.   JOHN[3] WILLIAMS (son of William Williams and Ann Williams) was born on 26 Jan 1679 in Surry, Virginia, USA. He died in 1741 in Bertie, North Carolina, USA. He married Mary Keeling in Granville, North Carolina, USA. She was born on 26 Sep 1684 in Hanover, Virginia, USA. She died in 1705 in York, Virginia, USA.

William Williams and Ann Whitley had the following children:

3.   i.   JOHN[3] WILLIAMS (son of William Williams and Ann Williams) was born on 26 Jan 1679 in Surry, Virginia, USA. He died in 1741 in Bertie, North Carolina, USA. He married Mary Keeling in Granville, North Carolina, USA. She was born on 26 Sep 1684 in Hanover, Virginia, USA. She died in 1705 in York, Virginia, USA.

    iii.   THEOPHILUS WILLIAMS (son of William Williams and Ann Whitley) was born on 09 Mar 1690 in Isle, , Virginia, USA.

Generation 3

3.   **JOHN[3] WILLIAMS** (William[2], Lewis[1]) was born on 26 Jan 1679 in Surry, Virginia, USA. He died in 1741 in Bertie, North Carolina, USA. He married Mary Keeling in Granville, North Carolina, USA. She was born on 26 Sep 1684 in Hanover, Virginia, USA. She died in 1705 in York, Virginia, USA.

John Williams and Mary Keeling had the following children:

4.   i.   JOSEPH[4] WILLIAMS (son of John Williams and Mary Keeling) was born on 01 Jan 1721 in Henrico, Virginia, USA. He died in Sep 1791 in Duplin, North Carolina, USA. He married (1) PHOEBE LITTLE in 1755 in North Carolina, USA. She was born in 1735 in North Carolina, USA. She died in 1779 in , Duplin, North Carolina, USA. He married (2) MARY PHOEBE LITTLE. She was born in 1735 in , Duplin, North Carolina, USA. She died in 1779 in , Duplin, North Carolina, USA.

    ii.   MARIA WILLIAMS (daughter of John Williams and Mary Keeling) was born on 26 Jul 1723 in Virginia, USA. She died in 1802.

Generation 4

4.   **JOSEPH[4] WILLIAMS** (John[3], William[2], Lewis[1]) was born on 01 Jan 1721 in Henrico, Virginia, USA. He died in Sep 1791 in Duplin, North Carolina, USA. He married (1) **PHOEBE LITTLE** in 1755 in North Carolina, USA. She was born in 1735 in North Carolina, USA. She died in 1779 in , Duplin, North Carolina, USA. He married (2) **MARY PHOEBE LITTLE**. She was born in 1735 in , Duplin, North Carolina, USA. She died in 1779 in , Duplin, North Carolina, USA.

Joseph Williams and Phoebe Little had the following children:

5.   i.   JOSEPH[5] WILLIAMS (son of Joseph Williams and Phoebe Little) was born on 29 Dec 1759 in Duplin, North Carolina, USA. He died on 28 Dec 1850 in Telfair, Georgia, USA. He married (1) MEALY BEVIN in 1780 in , Duplin, North Carolina, USA. She was born in 1759 in Duplin, North Carolina, USA. She died in Duplin, North

/

Carolina, USA. He married (2) MARY EVANS in 1777 in Duplin, North Carolina, USA. She was born in 1762 in , , North Carolina, USA. She died in 1821 in Philadelphia, Philadelphia, Pennsylvania, USA. He married (3) NANCY NANNIE EVANS in 1780 in , Duplin, North Carolina, USA. She was born in 1759 in , , North Carolina, USA. She died in , Telfair, Georgia, USA.

    ii.   BYRD WILLIAMS (son of Joseph Williams and Phoebe Little) was born in 1765 in North Carolina, USA. He died in Jul 1821 in Duplin, North Carolina, USA.

Joseph Williams and Mary Phoebe Little had the following children:

    iii.   STEPHEN WILLIAMS (son of Joseph Williams and Mary Phoebe Little) was born in 1764 in Duplin, North Carolina, USA. He died on 19 Jan 1841 in Duplin, North Carolina, USA.

6.   iv.   DAVID WILLIAMS (son of Joseph Williams and Mary Phoebe Little) was born on 27 Jan 1765 in Duplin, North Carolina, USA. He died in 1830. He married Elizabeth Anderson in 1790 in , , North Carolina, USA. She was born in 1770 in , , North Carolina, USA. She died in 1791.

    v.   JOHN WILLIAMS (son of Joseph Williams and Mary Phoebe Little) was born on 17 Jun 1768 in Duplin, North Carolina, USA. He died on 27 Jul 1830 in Bethel, Posey, Indiana, USA.

    vi.   PHEBE WILLIAMS (daughter of Joseph Williams and Mary Phoebe Little) was born in 1770 in New Hanover, North Carolina, USA. She died on 23 Dec 1803 in New Hanover, North Carolina, USA.

Generation 5

5.   JOSEPH[5] WILLIAMS (Joseph[4], John[3], William[2], Lewis[1]) was born on 29 Dec 1759 in Duplin, North Carolina, USA. He died on 28 Dec 1850 in Telfair, Georgia, USA. He married (1) MEALY BEVIN in 1780 in , Duplin, North Carolina, USA. She was born in 1759 in Duplin, North Carolina, USA. She died in Duplin, North Carolina, USA. He married (2) MARY EVANS in 1777 in Duplin, North Carolina, USA. She was born in 1762 in , , North Carolina, USA. She died in 1821 in Philadelphia, Philadelphia, Pennsylvania, USA. He married (3) NANCY NANNIE EVANS in 1780 in , Duplin, North Carolina, USA. She was born in 1759 in , , North Carolina, USA. She died in , Telfair, Georgia, USA.

Joseph Williams and Mealy Bevin had the following children:

    i.   ELIZABETH[6] WILLIAMS (daughter of Joseph Williams and Mealy Bevin) was born in 1799 in Duplin, North Carolina, USA. She died in 1860 in Telfair, Georgia, USA.

    ii.   SUSAN WINNIFORD WILLIAMS (daughter of Joseph Williams and Mealy Bevin) was born on 18 Oct 1826 in , Telfair, Georgia, USA. She died on 15 Oct 1868 in , Dodge, Georgia, USA.

Joseph Williams and Mary Evans had the following children:

7.   iii.   JOSEPH WILLIAMS (son of Joseph Williams and Mary Evans) was born on 20 Dec 1760 in Duplin, N.C.. He died in 1850 in Telfair Ga.. He married (1) MARY EVANS. She was born in 1762.

    iv.   MARY WILLIAMS (daughter of Joseph Williams and Mary Evans) was born in 1781 in Duplin, North Carolina, USA. She died in Jan 1859 in Telfair, Georgia, USA.

    v.   REBECCA WILLIAMS (daughter of Joseph Williams and Mary Evans) was born on 05 Mar 1783 in Duplin, North Carolina, USA. She died in 1870 in Telfair, Georgia, USA.

    vi.   PHOEBE WILLIAMS (daughter of Joseph Williams and Mary Evans) was born in 1785 in Duplin, North Carolina, USA. She died on 29 Apr 1857 in Telfair, Georgia, USA.

8.   vii.   DANIEL WILLIAMS (son of Joseph Williams and Mary Evans) was born in 1786 in Telfair Ga.. He died on 04 Jun 1860 in Telfair, Georgia, USA. He married Rebecca Watson on 23 Dec 1813 in Wilkes Cty, Ga..

    viii.   NANCY WILLIAMS (daughter of Joseph Williams and Mary Evans) was born in 1787 in Duplin, North Carolina, USA. She died in 1860 in Washington, Indiana, USA.

i. ELIZABETH[6] WILLIAMS (daughter of Joseph Williams and Mealy Bevin) was born in 1799 in Duplin, North Carolina, USA. She died in 1860 in Telfair, Georgia, USA.

x. WILLIAM H WILLIAMS (son of Joseph Williams and Mary Evans) was born in 1802 in Duplin, North Carolina, USA. He died in 1850.

Joseph Williams and Nancy Nannie Evans had the following children:

iv. MARY WILLIAMS (daughter of Joseph Williams and Mary Evans) was born in 1781 in Duplin, North Carolina, USA. She died in Jan 1859 in Telfair, Georgia, USA.

vi. PHOEBE WILLIAMS (daughter of Joseph Williams and Mary Evans) was born in 1785 in Duplin, North Carolina, USA. She died on 29 Apr 1857 in Telfair, Georgia, USA.

8. vii. DANIEL WILLIAMS (son of Joseph Williams and Mary Evans) was born in 1786 in Telfair Ga.. He died on 04 Jun 1860 in Telfair, Georgia, USA. He married Rebecca Watson on 23 Dec 1813 in Wilkes Cty, Ga..

6. DAVID[5] WILLIAMS (Joseph[4], John[3], William[2], Lewis[1]) was born on 27 Jan 1765 in Duplin, North Carolina, USA. He died in 1830. He married Elizabeth Anderson in 1790 in , , North Carolina, USA. She was born in 1770 in , , North Carolina, USA. She died in 1791.

David Williams and Elizabeth Anderson had the following child:

i. STEPHEN[6] WILLIAMS (son of David Williams and Elizabeth Anderson) was born on 31 May 1791 in , Duplin, North Carolina, USA.

Generation 6

7. JOSEPH[6] WILLIAMS (Joseph[5], Joseph[4], John[3], William[2], Lewis[1]) was born on 20 Dec 1760 in Duplin, N.C.. He died in 1850 in Telfair Ga.. He married (1) MARY EVANS. She was born in 1762.

Joseph WILLIAMS and Mary Evans had the following children:

8. i. DANIEL[6] WILLIAMS (son of Joseph Williams and Mary Evans) was born in 1786 in Telfair Ga.. He died on 04 Jun 1860 in Telfair, Georgia, USA. He married Rebecca Watson on 23 Dec 1813 in Wilkes Cty, Ga..

ii. ELIZABETH WILLIAMS (daughter of Joseph Williams and Mealy Bevin) was born in 1799 in Duplin, North Carolina, USA. She died in 1860 in Telfair, Georgia, USA.

iii. JOSEPH WILLIAMS (son of Joseph WILLIAMS and Mary Evans).

iv. MARY WILLIAMS (daughter of Joseph Williams and Mary Evans) was born in 1781 in Duplin, North Carolina, USA. She died in Jan 1859 in Telfair, Georgia, USA.

v. REBECCA WILLIAMS (daughter of Joseph Williams and Mary Evans) was born on 05 Mar 1783 in Duplin, North Carolina, USA. She died in 1870 in Telfair, Georgia, USA.

vi. PHOEBE WILLIAMS (daughter of Joseph Williams and Mary Evans) was born in 1785 in Duplin, North Carolina, USA. She died on 29 Apr 1857 in Telfair, Georgia, USA.

vii. NANCY WILLIAMS (daughter of Joseph Williams and Mary Evans) was born in 1787 in Duplin, North Carolina, USA. She died in 1860 in Washington, Indiana, USA.

viii. WILLIAM H WILLIAMS (son of Joseph Williams and Mary Evans) was born in 1802 in Duplin, North Carolina, USA. He died in 1850.

8. DANIEL[6] WILLIAMS (Joseph[5], Joseph[4], John[3], William[2], Lewis[1]) was born in 1786 in Telfair Ga.. He died on 04 Jun 1860 in Telfair, Georgia, USA. He married Rebecca Watson on 23 Dec 1813 in Wilkes Cty, Ga..

Daniel Williams and Rebecca Watson had the following child:

9. i. JAMES DANIEL[7] WILLIAMS (son of Daniel Williams and Rebecca Watson). He died in 1881 in , , , USA. He married (1) MINERVA DOWNING (daughter of George Downing) on 26 Dec 1838 in Taliaferro Cty, Ga by T.T Town, Justice of the Peace. She was born in Jun 1818 in , , , USA. He married (2) MALINDA EDGE (daughter of Nehemiah Edge and Elizabeth Doster) on 23 Dec 1836 in Taliaferro, Ga.. She was born in 1814 in Wilkes, Georgia, USA. She died in 1869 in Elba, Alabama, USA.

Generation 7

2a

9. JAMES DANIEL[7] WILLIAMS (Daniel[6], Joseph[5], Joseph[4], John[3], William[2], Lewis[1]). He died in 1881 in ,
    , , USA. He married (1) **MINERVA DOWNING** (daughter of George Downing) on 26 Dec 1838 in
    Taliaferro Cty, Ga by T.T Town, Justice of the Peace. She was born in Jun 1818 in , , , USA. He
    married (2) **MALINDA EDGE** (daughter of Nehemiah Edge and Elizabeth Doster) on 23 Dec 1836 in
    Taliaferro, Ga.. She was born in 1814 in Wilkes, Georgia, USA. She died in 1869 in Elba, Alabama,
    USA.

Notes for James Daniel Williams:
!. Pvt, Creek War Service. Capt Sanford Co 1, Reg Porters of Ga Inf (3 months 1836) enrolled 4
Jun 1836. Columbus muster; outroll Columbus 12 Jul 1836. CWJr1992

James Daniel Williams and Minerva Downing had the following child:

> 10. i. WILLIAM ANDERSON[8] WILLIAMS (son of James Daniel Williams and Minerva Downing)
> was born on 23 Oct 1845 in Crawfordville, GA, USA. He died on 05 Oct 1873 in
> Millegeville, Georgia, USA. He married Huldah Ann Ricketson (daughter of Jesse
> Lathrop RICKETSON and Frances Perry) in 1860 in Warren Cty, Ga.. She was born
> on 26 Mar 1842 in Warren Cty, Ga. She died on 23 Oct 1873 in Milledgeville, Ga..

10. WILLIAM ANDERSON[8] WILLIAMS (James Daniel[7], Daniel[6], Joseph[5], Joseph[4], John[3], William[2], Lewis[1])
     was born on 23 Oct 1845 in Crawfordville, GA, USA. He died on 05 Oct 1873 in Millegeville,
     Georgia, USA. He married Huldah Ann Ricketson (daughter of Jesse Lathrop RICKETSON and
     Frances Perry) in 1860 in Warren Cty, Ga.. She was born on 26 Mar 1842 in Warren Cty, Ga. She
     died on 23 Oct 1873 in Milledgeville, Ga..

Notes for Huldah Ann Ricketson:
!. Death Date by CWJr. Family Collection:12 Aug 1873

William Anderson Williams and Huldah Ann Ricketson had the following children:

> 11. i. MAMIE[9] WILLIAMS (daughter of William Anderson Williams and Huldah Ann
> Ricketson) was born on 27 Jul 1863 in Camak, Georgia, USA. She married (1)
> STEPHEN JOSEPH LYNON. She married (2) STEPHENS JOSEPH LYONS. She married (3)
> WILLIAM GLENN TILLER JR (son of Wiliam Glenn Tiller and Henrietta Ritter Pass) on
> 25 Dec 1883. He was born on 20 May 1825 in Oglethorpe, Georgia, USA. He died
> on 16 Jan 1892 in Athens, Ga..

> 12. ii. JAMES CRANSTON WILLIAMS (son of William Anderson Williams and Huldah Ann
> Ricketson) was born on 03 Jan 1868 in Camak, Warren Co., GA, USA. He died on
> 22 Apr 1936 in Greensboro, Greene Co., GA, USA. He married Mary Maria
>  GULLATT (daughter of Henry GULLATT and Josephine Ella Hanleiter) on 12 Dec
> 1893 in By Bishop Henry Morrison, Atlanta, Ga.. She was born on 10 Jul 1872 in
> Atlanta, Fulton Cty, Ga.. She died on 07 Dec 1959 in Greensboro, Greene Cty, Ga..
>
> Notes for James Cranston Williams:
> 1. Aftre the death of both parents in Oct 1873 (his age 5) he was sent to live with a
> minister Downing who was cruel to him, whipping him. James ran away. M Carey
> Jones took him in and raised him. CWJr Family info.
> 2. Family moved to Greensboro in 1906 from Crawfordville, Ga. Gullatt Family
> Bible.

> 13. iii. JOHN HENRY WILLIAMS (son of William Anderson Williams and Huldah Ann
> Ricketson) was born on 17 Nov 1871 in Camak, Georgia, USA. He died on 06 Dec
> 1937 in Hattiesburg Mississippi. He married Mary Frances SMITH on 22 Dec 1893
> in Selma, Alabama, USA. She was born in 1874.

> iv. NETTIE WALTON WILLIAMS (daughter of William Anderson Williams and Huldah Ann
> Ricketson) was born on 12 Oct 1873. She died on 21 Nov 1909 in Columbia,
> Richland, SC.

Descendants of James Cranston Williams

Generation 1

1. **JAMES CRANSTON**[1] **WILLIAMS** was born on 03 Jan 1868 in Camak, Warren Co., GA, USA. He died on 22 Apr 1936 in Greensboro, Greene Co., GA, USA. He married Mary Maria GULLATT, daughter of Henry GULLATT and Josephine Ella Hanleiter, on 12 Dec 1893 in By Bishop Henry Morrison, Atlanta, Ga.. She was born on 10 Jul 1872 in Atlanta, Fulton Cty, Ga.. She died on 07 Dec 1959 in Greensboro, Greene Cty, Ga..

   Notes for James Cranston Williams:
   1. Aftre the death of both parents in Oct 1873 (his age 5) he was sent to live with a minister Downing who was cruel to him, whipping him. James ran away. M Carey Jones took him in and raised him. CWJr Family info.
   2. Family moved to Greensboro in 1906 from Crawfordville, Ga. Gullatt Family Bible.

   James Cranston Williams and Mary Maria GULLATT had the following children:

   2. i. CRANSTON GULLATT[2] WILLIAMS was born on 28 Jul 1895 in Augusta, Ga.. He died on 08 Jan 1989 in Lynchburg, Va.. He married Caroline HUTTER, daughter of Christian Sextus Hutter and Ernestine Hutter, on 10 Jan 1925 in Lynchburg, Virginia, USA. She was born on 03 Aug 1900 in Lynchburg, Campbell, Virginia, USA. She died on 23 Apr 1995 in Rivermont, Lynchburg, Virginia, USA.

   3. ii. HULDAH GULLATT WILLIAMS was born on 28 Jul 1897 in Augusta, Ga.. She died on 26 Mar 1983 in Geensboro, Greene cty, Ga.. She married (1) CHARLES ROSCOE CALDWELL SENIOR, son of Baley H Caldwell and Erma V Caldwell, on 06 Oct 1923 in Jackson, Missouri. He was born on 21 Jul 1890 in Tyler Smith Texas. He died on 09 Jan 1981 in Dallas, Dallas, Texas, United States of America. She married (2) IKE HOLDEN.

   iii. HULDA W CALDWELL was born about 1897 in Georgia.

   iv. ~~HULDA W HOLDER was born about 1898 in Georgia~~

   4. v. MARIE LOUISE MORRIS was born on 10 Jan 1899 in Washington, Wilkes, Georgia, USA. She died on 22 Apr 1997 in Cartersville, Bartow, Georgia, United States of America. She married Marion Wingfield Morris, son of Winfield C Morris and Cue MontgomeryMorris, on 17 Jan 1923 in Greensboro, Greene Cty, Ga.Marvin Williams (Williams Home). He was born on 20 Apr 1897 in Georgia (Augusta,Richmond Cty, Ga). He died on 17 Oct 1964 in Cartersville Bartow Cty Ga (Oak Hill Cemetery).

   5. vi. CARY JONES WILLIAMS was born on 06 Apr 1901 in Washington, Wilkes Cty, Ga.. He died on 03 Jul 1991 in Greensboro, Greene Cty, Ga.. He married Sara Celeste COPELAN on 02 Jul 1935 in Greensboro, Greene Cty , ga. She was born on 30 Nov 1903. She died on 05 Aug 1991 in Greensboro Greene Cty, Ga..

   vii. MARY JOYCE WILLIAMS was born on 20 Jan 1904 in Crawfordville, Ga.. She died on 27 Jul 1904 in Greene Cty.

   viii. JOSEPHINE HANLEITER WILLIAMS was born on 06 Apr 1905 in Crawfordville, Ga.. She died on 27 Aug 1928 in Greensboro, Ga..

   ix. JAMES CRANSTON WILLIAMS JR was born on 12 Mar 1910 in Greensboro, Ga.. He died on 14 Mar 1910 in Greensboro,Greene Cty, Ga..

   6. x. MARY JIM WILLIAMS was born on 12 Nov 1914 in Greensboro, Ga.. She died on 09 Apr 2014 in Watkinsville, Oconee, Georgia (Burial.Penfield, GA). She married William Reid Boswell, son of Edgar Reid Boswell and Edna Mae Callaway, on 02 Nov 1938 in Cartersville, Bartow Cty , Ga.. He was born on 03 Nov 1912 in Penfield, Ga. He died on 26 Mar 1995 in Atlanta, Fulton, Georgia.

Generation 2

2. **CRANSTON GULLATT**[2] **WILLIAMS** (James Cranston[1]) was born on 28 Jul 1895 in Augusta, Ga.. He died on 08 Jan 1989 in Lynchburg, Va.. He married Caroline HUTTER, daughter of Christian Sextus Hutter and Ernestine Hutter, on 10 Jan 1925 in Lynchburg, Virginia, USA. She was born on 03 Aug 1900 in Lynchburg, Campbell, Virginia, USA. She died on 23 Apr 1995 in Rivermont, Lynchburg, Virginia, USA.

4

Cranston Gullatt WILLIAMS and Caroline HUTTER had the following children:

7. i. CRANSTON GULLATT[3] WILLIAMS JR was born on 12 Aug 1926 in Chattanooga, Hamilton Cty, Tn. He married Marilyn Virginia Johnson, daughter of Harry Graves Johnson and Sallie Kathleen Nance, on 01 Oct 1960 in Roanoke, Va. She was born on 11 Aug 1923 in Vinton, Va.

    ii. HUTTER WILLIAMS was born on 18 Aug 1932 in Chattanooga, Hamilton Cty, Tn. He died on 26 Mar 1975 in Lynchburg, Va.. He married Mary Rutledge Clement on 10 Jun 1966 in Chatham,Va..

3. **HULDAH GULLATT[2] WILLIAMS** (James Cranston[1]) was born on 28 Jul 1897 in Augusta, Ga.. She died on 26 Mar 1983 in Geensboro, Greene cty, Ga.. She married (1) **CHARLES ROSCOE CALDWELL SENIOR**, son of Baley H Caldwell and Erma V Caldwell, on 06 Oct 1923 in Jackson, Missouri. He was born on 21 Jul 1890 in Tyler Smith Texas. He died on 09 Jan 1981 in Dallas, Dallas, Texas, United States of America. She married (2) **IKE HOLDEN**.

Charles Roscoe Caldwell Senior and Huldah Gullatt WILLIAMS had the following child:

8. i. CHARLES ROSCOE[3] CALDWELL JR. was born on 04 Sep 1925 in Atlanta, Fulton Cty, Ga.. He died on 09 Mar 2005 in Atlanta, Fulton Cty Ga. He married (1) ELIZABETH JUNE BOSWELL. She was born on 21 Jun 1931 in Wrightsville, Johnson Cty, Ga.. She died on 25 Dec 2013 in Bogart, GA (Mary'sHospiceHouse). He married (2) RACHEL FREEMAN.

4. **MARIE LOUISE[2] MORRIS** (James Cranston[1] Williams) was born on 10 Jan 1899 in Washington, Wilkes, Georgia, USA. She died on 22 Apr 1997 in Cartersville, Bartow, Georgia, United States of America. She married Marion Wingfield Morris, son of Winfield C Morris and Cue MontgomeryMorris, on 17 Jan 1923 in Greensboro, Greene Cty, Ga.Marvin Williams (Williams Home). He was born on 20 Apr 1897 in Georgia (Augusta,Richmond Cty, Ga). He died on 17 Oct 1964 in Cartersville Bartow Cty Ga (Oak Hill Cemetery).

Notes for Marie Louise Morris:
SSN; ~~XXXXXXXXX~~

Notes for Marion Wingfield Morris:
SSN~~XXXXXXXXX~~
Served USMarine Corps--9 Aug1918-6 Sep1919

Marion Wingfield Morris and Marie Louise Morris had the following children:

9. i. JAMES WINGFIELD[3] MORRIS was born on 01 Sep 1924 In Augusta, Richmond Cty, Ga.. He married Mary Corinne WOFFORD, daughter of William Earl WOFFORD and Mary Louise Meroney, on 19 Jan 1948 in FPC Cartersville, Ga. She was born on 21 Apr 1926 in Cartersville, Bartow, Georgia, USA. She died on 08 Feb 2013 in Cartersville Bartow Cty Ga.

10. ii. MARYBELLE MORRIS was born on 14 Apr 1926. She died on 09 Jun 2008 in Fountain Valley, Orange, California. She married (1) ALEX THOMAS DENT, son of Fredrick William "Fritz" Dent and Ida Pearl Dodd, on 23 Sep 1997 in Euharlee, Bartow, Cty, Ga. He was born on 22 Feb 1920 in Euharlee, Bartow Cty, Georgia. He died on 14 Nov 2002 in Cartersville, Bartow, Georgia, United States of America. She married (2) DONALD C SWIFT, son of George S SWIFT and Florence Harriet Jager, on 29 Mar 1946 in Cartersville Bartow Cty Ga. He was born on 13 Feb 1920. He died on 26 Dec 1994 in Orange Cty, CA.

11. iii. MARIAN LOUISE MORRIS was born on 29 Nov 1930 in Atlanta, Fulton Cty, Ga. She married Nelson Kimball ROGERS, son of Lewis Edward ROGERS and Marion Ruth NELSON, on 20 Jun 1953 in Cartersville, Bartow, Georgia, USA. He was born on 17 May 1928 in New York, NY. He died on 15 Sep 2013 in Cartersville Bartow Cty Ga.

5. **CARY JONES[2] WILLIAMS** (James Cranston[1]) was born on 06 Apr 1901 in Washington, Wilkes Cty, Ga.. He died on 03 Jul 1991 in Greensboro, Greene Cty, Ga.. He married Sara Celeste COPELAN on 02 Jul 1935 in Greensboro, Greene Cty , ga. She was born on 30 Nov 1903. She died on 05

Aug 1991 in Greensboro Greene Cty, Ga..

Cary Jones WILLIAMS and Sara Celeste COPELAN had the following children:

12.   i.   CAREY JONES[3] WILLIAMS JR was born on 29 Dec 1938 in Emory Univ Hosp, Decalb Cty, Ga.. He married (1) MARJORIE SHELTON MERITT.

13.   ii.   SARA ANNE WILLIAMS was born on 05 Dec 1943 in Emory Univ Hosp, dekalb Cty , ga.. She died on 05 Jun 2008 in Athens Ga.. She married Thomas Wade Stephens, son of Victor Wade Stephens and Martha Louise Dial, on 12 Aug 1967 in Greensboro Greene Cty, Ga.. He was born on 18 Jan 1943 in Athens Clarke Cty, Ga. (St Mary's Hospital). He died on 30 Mar 2001 in Athens Ga.

6.   MARY JIM[2] WILLIAMS (James Cranston[1]) was born on 12 Nov 1914 in Greensboro, Ga.. She died on 09 Apr 2014 in Watkinsville, Oconee, Georgia (Burial.Penfield, GA). She married William Reid Boswell, son of Edgar Reid Boswell and Edna Mae Callaway, on 02 Nov 1938 in Cartersville, Bartow Cty , Ga.. He was born on 03 Nov 1912 in Penfield, Ga. He died on 26 Mar 1995 in Atlanta, Fulton, Georgia.

Notes for William Reid Boswell:
Buried:28 Mar 1995, Penfield, Ga
Married at home of Sister, Marie Louise Morris, in Cartersville, Ga

William Reid Boswell and Mary Jim WILLIAMS had the following children:

i.   WILLIAM R[3] BOSWELL JR was born on 11 Jun 1940 in Atlanta, Fulton Cty, Ga. (Emory Univ Hospital). He married Mary Evelyn Parham, daughter of Joseph Connell Parham and Evelyn Lyle, on 18 Jun 1983 in Athens, Clarke, Georgia, USA. She was born on 23 Jul 1949 in Atlanta, Fulton Cty Ga.

14.   ii.   MARY JO BOSWELL was born on 31 May 1945 in Atlanta, Fulton, Georgia, United States (Emory Univ Hospital). She married (1) BERNARD HERRING III. She married (2) HILTON ECHOLS HIGHTOWER on 23 Apr 1983 in Blakely, Ga..

iii.   EDNA ELIZABETH BOSWELL was born on 09 Jan 1952 in Atlanta, Fulton Cty, Ga. She married (1) ALBERT WILSON RHODES JR, son of Albert Wilson Rhodes and Gladys Loeona Yearwood, on 31 Dec 1980. He was born on 01 Feb 1955 in Greene County Ga. He died on 02 Sep 2005 in Athens Clarke Cty, Ga.. She married (2) RONNALD EUGENE TRUBY on 23 Jul 1973.

Generation 3

7.   CRANSTON GULLATT[3] WILLIAMS JR (Cranston Gullatt[2], James Cranston[1]) was born on 12 Aug 1926 in Chattanooga, Hamilton Cty, Tn. He married Marilyn Virginia Johnson, daughter of Harry Graves Johnson and Sallie Kathleen Nance, on 01 Oct 1960 in Roanoke, Va. She was born on 11 Aug 1923 in Vinton, Va.

Notes for Cranston Gullatt WILLIAMS Jr:
1. Married :Virginia Heights Babtist Church, Roanoke, Va.

Notes for Marilyn Virginia Johnson:
1. Married :Virginia Heights Babtist Church, Roanoke, Va.

Cranston Gullatt WILLIAMS Jr and Marilyn Virginia Johnson had the following children:

i.   CRANSTON READE[4] WILLIAMS was born on 14 Sep 1963 in Roanoke, Va..

ii.   SALLY WARNER WILLIAMS was born on 26 Feb 1966 in Roanoke, Va..

8.   CHARLES ROSCOE[3] CALDWELL JR. (Huldah Gullatt[2] WILLIAMS, James Cranston[1] Williams) was born on 04 Sep 1925 in Atlanta, Fulton Cty, Ga.. He died on 09 Mar 2005 in Atlanta, Fulton Cty Ga. He married (1) ELIZABETH JUNE BOSWELL. She was born on 21 Jun 1931 in Wrightsville, Johnson Cty, Ga.. She died on 25 Dec 2013 in Bogart, GA (Mary'sHospiceHouse). He married (2) RACHEL FREEMAN.

Notes for Charles Roscoe Caldwell Jr.:   *6*

Divorced: Elizabeth June Boswell,August, 1972
(Cremated)- Buried, Greensboro, Ga.

Charles Roscoe Caldwell Jr. and Elizabeth June Boswell had the following children:

       i.   SUSAN[4] GULLATT was born on 13 Nov 1951 in DeKalb Cty, Ga..

15.   ii.   CHARLES ROSCOE CALDWELL III was born on 05 Dec 1953 in Atlanta, Fulton Cty Ga (Georgia Baptist Hospital). He died on 02 Oct 2001 in Atlanta, Fulton Cty Ga.. He married (1) PATRICIA MONIQUE GOODMAN. He married (2) CHERYL STEVENS.

9.   **JAMES WINGFIELD**[3] **MORRIS** (Marie Louise[2], James Cranston[1] Williams) was born on 01 Sep 1924 in Augusta, Richmond Cty, Ga.. He married Mary Corinne WOFFORD, daughter of William Earl WOFFORD and Mary Louise Meroney, on 19 Jan 1948 in FPC Cartersville, Ga. She was born on 21 Apr 1926 in Cartersville, Bartow, Georgia, USA. She died on 08 Feb 2013 in Cartersville Bartow Cty Ga.

Notes for James Wingfield MORRIS:
Graduate,USMA,1945:BS Aeronautical Engineering, Univ Michigan 1959: MA,International Affairs, George Washington Univ, 1964

Notes for Mary Corinne WOFFORD:
Graduated Vanderbilt School of Nursing, Nashville, Tn 1948

James Wingfield MORRIS and Mary Corinne WOFFORD had the following children:

16.   i.   MARY LOUISE[4] MORRIS was born on 03 May 1949 in Cartersville, Bartow, Georgia, USA. She married (1) SHELDON G. SPICHER III on 20 Dec 1970 in Charlottesville Va. He was born on 19 Jul 1948. She married (2) TIMOTHY CARR BRAMBLE, son of Roy H Bramble and Lois Jean Bennett, on 01 Feb 1985 in Dunwoody, Ga... He was born on 13 Mar 1952 in Detroit, Mich.

17.   ii.   JAMES WINGFIELD MORRIS JR was born on 29 Oct 1950 in Cartersville, Bartow, Georgia, USA. He married Carolyn Ethel LYON, daughter of Robert Fredrick LYON and Mldred Virginia Shacklett, on 09 Jun 1973 in Marietta, Ga.. She was born on 14 Mar 1951 in Nashville, Davidson Cty, Tn.

18.   iii.   WILLIAM CRANSTON MORRIS was born on 02 Mar 1954 in Cartersville, Bartow, Georgia, USA. He married Beverly Jane TIPTON, daughter of James Darrell{J.D.} TIPTON and Barbara Jean HAVENS, on 10 Jul 1976 in Maryville, Tennessee. She was born on 06 Feb 1954 in Maryville, Blount Cty, Tn.

19.   iv.   BRIAN MERONEY MORRIS was born on 28 Jan 1961 in Washington D.C.. He married (1) JILL HAROLINE KING on 20 Aug 1983 in Cartersville, Ga.. She was born on 10 Aug 1959 in Rome, Floyd Cty, Ga.. He married (2) MICHELE ALLEN EWEN on 10 Jun 2000 in Dallas, Texas. She was born on 11 Jun 1967 in Denver, Co.

20.   v.   PETER CHARLES MORRIS was born on 22 Jun 1962 in Arlington, Va. He married Frances Elizabeth ALLEN, daughter of Bona ALLEN IV and Jane KING, on 15 Jun 1985 in Dunwoody, Ga.. She was born on 26 Feb 1963.

10.   **MARYBELLE**[3] **MORRIS** (Marie Louise[2], James Cranston[1] Williams) was born on 14 Apr 1926. She died on 09 Jun 2008 in Fountain Valley, Orange, California. She married (1) **ALEX THOMAS DENT**, son of Fredrick William "Fritz" Dent and Ida Pearl Dodd, on 23 Sep 1997 in Euharlee, Bartow, Cty, Ga. He was born on 22 Feb 1920 in Euharlee, Bartow Cty, Georgia. He died on 14 Nov 2002 in Cartersville, Bartow, Georgia, United States of America. She married (2) **DONALD C SWIFT**, son of George S SWIFT and Florence Harriet Jager, on 29 Mar 1946 in Cartersville Bartow Cty Ga. He was born on 13 Feb 1920. He died on 26 Dec 1994 in Orange Cty, CA.

Donald C Swift and Marybelle MORRIS had the following children:

21.   i.   MARY LOUISE[4] SWIFT was born on 10 Jan 1950 in Cartersville Bartow Cty, Ga. She married Robert H Beckmann on 12 Jun 1971. He was born in 1943.

22.   ii.   ANNE ELIZABETH SWIFT was born on 29 May 1954 in Dallas Tx. She married (1) TOM FRANKLIN. She married (2) JAMES T PARKER on 08 Feb 1973.

11.   **MARIAN LOUISE**[3] **MORRIS** (Marie Louise[2], James Cranston[1] Williams) was born on 29 Nov 1930 in Atlanta, Fulton Cty, Ga. She married Nelson Kimball ROGERS, son of Lewis Edward ROGERS and Marion Ruth NELSON, on 20 Jun 1953 in Cartersville, Bartow, Georgia, USA. He was born on

7

17 May 1928 in New York, NY. He died on 15 Sep 2013 in Cartersville Bartow Cty Ga.

Notes for Marian Louise MORRIS:
Graduate Wesleyan College, Macon, Ga..1951.BA,English Major(CumLaude)

Notes for Nelson Kimball ROGERS:
Graduate,USNA, Annapolis, Md 1950. MS.Georgia Tech:IndustrialTechnology,1956

Nelson Kimball ROGERS and Marian Louise MORRIS had the following children:

23.   i.   EDWARD MORRIS[4] ROGERS was born on 09 May 1960 in Summit, NJ. He married Jeanette Lynn RAINES, daughter of Dennis Wayne RAINES and Janice Rollins, on 08 Oct 1983 in Germantown, Tn. She was born on 16 Mar 1960 in Jackson, Tn.

         ii.   KIMBALL AMANDA ROGERS was born on 23 Feb 1962 in Summit, NJ.

            Notes for Kimball Amanda ROGERS:
            Shorter College: BS.Sociology, B.A.English.1983

         iii.   JAMES MADISON ROGERS was born on 11 Jun 1963 in Summit, NJ.

            Notes for James Madison ROGERS:
            Graduate Furman,Univ,SC,1985,BA Religion

         iv.   CAREY SUSAN ROGERS was born on 31 Oct 1965 in Cartersville Bartow Cty Ga. She died on 31 Oct 1965 in Cartersville Bartow Cty Ga (OakHillCemetery).

12.   CAREY JONES[3] WILLIAMS JR (Cary Jones[2], James Cranston[1]) was born on 29 Dec 1938 in Emory Univ Hosp, Decalb Cty, Ga.. He married (1) **MARJORIE SHELTON MERITT**.

Carey Jones WILLIAMS Jr and Marjorie Shelton MERITT had the following children:

         i.   KAREN MICHELLE[4] WILLIAMS was born on 12 Mar 1967 in Athens Clarke Cty, Ga.. She married (1) BLANK WAGES.

         ii.   STANLEY TIMOTHY WILLIAMS was born on 03 Dec 1968 in Morgan Cty, Ga.. He died on 02 Aug 2008 in Corpus Christi, Texas.

13.   SARA ANNE[3] WILLIAMS (Cary Jones[2], James Cranston[1]) was born on 05 Dec 1943 in Emory Univ Hosp, dekalb Cty , ga.. She died on 05 Jun 2008 in Athens Ga.. She married Thomas Wade Stephens, son of Victor Wade Stephens and Martha Louise Dial, on 12 Aug 1967 in Greensboro Greene Cty, Ga.. He was born on 18 Jan 1943 in Athens Clarke Cty, Ga. (St Mary's Hospital). He died on 30 Mar 2001 in Athens Ga.

Thomas Wade Stephens and Sara Anne WILLIAMS had the following children:

24.   i.   WADE WILLIAMS[4] STEPHENS was born on 18 Dec 1969 in Athens Clarke Cty, Ga.. He married Ami Taylor Pitts, daughter of William Carl Pitts Jr and Diane Johnson Pitts, on 15 Jul 2000 in Decatur,DeKalb Cty, Ga.. She was born on 16 Jul 1974 in Decatur,Dekalb Cty, Ga.

25.   ii.   CAREY THOMAS STEPHENS was born on 11 Sep 1973 in Athens Clarke Cty, Ga.. He married Stacey Lynn Hall on 23 Feb 2002 in Valdosta, Lowndes, Georgia, First United Methodist ChurchUSA. She was born on 18 Jun 1970 in Valdosta, Lowndes, Georgia, First United Methodist ChurchUSA.

14.   MARY JO[3] BOSWELL (Mary Jim[2] WILLIAMS, James Cranston[1] Williams) was born on 31 May 1945 in Atlanta, Fulton, Georgia, United States (Emory Univ Hospital). She married (1) **BERNARD HERRING III**. She married (2) **HILTON ECHOLS HIGHTOWER** on 23 Apr 1983 in Blakely, Ga..

Notes for Bernard Herring III:
Divorced :June 1981

Bernard Herring III and Mary Jo Boswell had the following child:

26.   i.   KIMBERLY AMANDA[4] HERRING was born on 24 Sep 1968 in Athens Clarke Cty, Ga.. She married (1) BENJAMIN HAYDEN COOK JR.

Generation 4

B

15.   CHARLES ROSCOE[4] CALDWELL III (Charles Roscoe[3] Jr., Huldah Gullatt[2] WILLIAMS, James Cranston[1] Williams) was born on 05 Dec 1953 in Atlanta, Fulton Cty Ga (Georgia Baptist Hospital). He died on 02 Oct 2001 in Atlanta, Fulton Cty Ga.. He married (1) PATRICIA MONIQUE GOODMAN. He married (2) CHERYL STEVENS.

Charles Roscoe Caldwell III and Patricia Monique Goodman had the following child:

    i.   HEATHER MONIQUE[5] CALDWELL was born on 07 Sep 1976 in Atlanta, Fulton Cty Ga (G. Baptist Hospital).

Charles Roscoe Caldwell III and Cheryl Stevens had the following child:

    ii.   JAMES KYLE CALDWELL was born on 13 Aug 1983 in Atlanta, Fulton Cty Ga (Georgia. Baptist hospital).

16.   MARY LOUISE[4] MORRIS (James Wingfield[3], Marie Louise[2], James Cranston[1] Williams) was born on 03 May 1949 in Cartersville, Bartow, Georgia, USA. She married (1) SHELDON G. SPICHER III on 20 Dec 1970 in Charlottesville Va. He was born on 19 Jul 1948. She married (2) TIMOTHY CARR BRAMBLE, son of Roy H Bramble and Lois Jean Bennett, on 01 Feb 1985 in Dunwoody, Ga... He was born on 13 Mar 1952 in Detroit, Mich.

Notes for Mary Louise MORRIS:
Education:Mary Washington College/ BSN Univ Virginia School Nursing1970

Sheldon G. Spicher III and Mary Louise MORRIS had the following children:

    i.   AMY LYNNE[5] SPICHER was born on 11 May 1973 in Medford Or. She married Charles Andrew SHROPSHIRE on 15 May 1999 in Cartersville, Ga.. He was born on 30 Oct 1969 in Atlanta, Fulton Cty, Ga..

    ii.   SHANNON ELIZABETH SPICHER was born on 24 Oct 1975 in Atlanta, Fulton Cty Ga. She married Corey Wayne TOWE on 28 Apr 2001 in Cartersvile, Ga.. He was born on 09 Aug 1976.

    iii.   PHILLIP MATTHEW SPICHER was born on 07 Apr 1978 in Atlanta, Fulton Cty, Ga. He married Kelly Christine Wittorff on 11 Jul 2009 in San Diego, California, USA.

Timothy Carr BRAMBLE and Mary Louise MORRIS had the following child:

    i.   REBECCA KATHLEEN[5] BRAMBLE was born on 02 Aug 1986 in Atlanta, Fulton Cty Ga.

17.   JAMES WINGFIELD[4] MORRIS JR (James Wingfield[3], Marie Louise[2], James Cranston[1] Williams) was born on 29 Oct 1950 in Cartersville, Bartow, Georgia, USA. He married Carolyn Ethel LYON, daughter of Robert Fredrick LYON and Mldred Virginia Shacklett, on 09 Jun 1973 in Marietta, Ga.. She was born on 14 Mar 1951 in Nashville, Davidson Cty, Tn.

Notes for James Wingfield MORRIS Jr:
Education: BSArchitectural Technology,SouthernTechnical Institute 1972/Registered Arctitect 1982,BA,Education Kennesaw State Univ, 1995

Notes for Carolyn Ethel LYON:
Education: BS, Architectural Technology,Southern Technical Institute,1973 Registered architect,22September 1988.

James Wingfield MORRIS Jr and Carolyn Ethel LYON had the following children:

    i.   MARY VIRGINIA[5] MORRIS was born on 18 Mar 1974 in Marietta, Cobb Cty, Ga.. She married Timothy Adam BLACKWELL, son of Toby Long BLACKWELL and Sherrill McGARITY, on 16 Dec 1995 in Marietta, Ga.. He was born on 20 Feb 1973 in Atlanta, Fulton Cty, Ga.

         Notes for Mary Virginia MORRIS:
         Education: BS,Middle Grades Education, Georgia Southern Univ.1995: MS, Education,GSU,1997.

9

ii. JAMES LYON MORRIS was born on 11 Jan 1983 in Marietta, Cobb Cty, Ga. He married Angela Swope, daughter of James Leonard Swope and Mana Sue Campbell, on 27 May 2007 in Atlanta, Fulton Cty, Ga.Atlanta City Hall. She was born on 07 Mar 1984 in Friendship, Harris, Texas.

Notes for James Lyon MORRIS:
Education:BS, Middle Grades Education, Georgia Southern Univ, 2005

18. WILLIAM CRANSTON[4] MORRIS (James Wingfield[3], Marie Louise[2], James Cranston[1] Williams) was born on 02 Mar 1954 in Cartersville, Bartow, Georgia, USA. He married Beverly Jane TIPTON, daughter of James Darrell{J.D.} TIPTON and Barbara Jean HAVENS, on 10 Jul 1976 in Maryville, Tennessee. She was born on 06 Feb 1954 in Maryville, Blount Cty, Tn.

Notes for William Cranston MORRIS:
Education:BS,Civil engineering,USAFA, 1976: MS,AF Institute of Technology,WrightPatterson AFBase, 1985

Notes for Beverly Jane TIPTON:
Education: BS,Home Economics, Univ of Tennessee, 1976: Teacher Certification Program, Univ of Texas, San Antonio, 1994.   NOTE:For Havens Family Story see John Lee Havens, media file.

William Cranston MORRIS and Beverly Jane TIPTON had the following children:

i. KEVIN JAMES[5] MORRIS was born on 11 Nov 1980 in Laughlin AFB (Del Rio Tx). He married Jess Lynn Dayton, daughter of George Francis Dayton and Wendy Joy Whitehead, on 17 Dec 2011 in Denver, Colorado, USA (Wellshire Presbyterian Church). She was born on 01 May 1982 in Wheat Ridge Colorado.

Notes for Kevin James MORRIS:
Education: BS,Computer Science, Ga Tech,2003; MS, Computer Science, Ga Tech(GA Instotute of Technology), 2005.

ii. EMILY SARAH MORRIS was born on 09 Aug 1985 in Wright Patterson AFB (Dayton OH). She married Christopher John Matheis, son of Nicolas Aloyasius Matheis and Lisa A Matheis, on 29 Oct 2011 in Cartersville, Bartow, Georgia, USA (First Presbyterian Church). He was born on 27 Apr 1982 in Jasper Indiana (Memorial Hospital).

Notes for Emily Sarah MORRIS:
Education: BA, Liberal Arts, Colorado State Univ,2007

Notes for Christopher John Matheis:
Education:Pittsburg State Univ, Pittsburg,KS, BS(Automotive Technology)2004

19. BRIAN MERONEY[4] MORRIS (James Wingfield[3], Marie Louise[2], James Cranston[1] Williams) was born on 28 Jan 1961 in Washington D.C.. He married (1) JILL HAROLINE KING on 20 Aug 1983 in Cartersville, Ga.. She was born on 10 Aug 1959 in Rome, Floyd Cty, Ga.. He married (2) MICHELE ALLEN EWEN on 10 Jun 2000 in Dallas, Texas. She was born on 11 Jun 1967 in Denver, Co.

Notes for Brian Meroney MORRIS:
Graduate: BBA,North Georgia College, 1983

Brian Meroney MORRIS and Jill Haroline KING had the following child:

i. DAVID BRIAN[5] MORRIS was born on 05 Nov 1988 in Chicago, DuPage Cty, Ill.

Brian Meroney MORRIS and Michele Allen EWEN had the following children:

ii. JULIA GABRIELLE EWEN was born on 26 Aug 1993 in Dallas, Texas.

iii. PATRICK GATE EWEN was born in Apr 1995 in Dallas, Texas.

20. PETER CHARLES[4] MORRIS (James Wingfield[3], Marie Louise[2], James Cranston[1] Williams) was born on 22 Jun 1962 in Arlington, Va. He married Frances Elizabeth ALLEN, daughter of Bona ALLEN IV and Jane KING, on 15 Jun 1985 in Dunwoody, Ga.. She was born on 26 Feb 1963.

Notes for Peter Charles MORRIS:
Graduate, USMA 1984, BS Aeronautics

10

Notes for Frances Elizabeth ALLEN:
Graduate Birmingham Southern,BA,1985,childhood education: TroyStateUniv, Ala, MA, Education.1990

Peter Charles MORRIS and Frances Elizabeth ALLEN had the following children:

    i.   KATELYN ELIZABETH[5] MORRIS was born on 21 Apr 1992 in Atlanta, Fulton Cty, Ga.

    ii.   SARA CAROLINE MORRIS was born on 17 Feb 1995 in Marietta, Cobb Cty, Ga..

21.   **MARY LOUISE[4] SWIFT** (Marybelle[3] MORRIS, Marie Louise[2] Morris, James Cranston[1] Williams) was born on 10 Jan 1950 in Cartersville Bartow Cty, Ga. She married Robert H Beckmann on 12 Jun 1971. He was born in 1943.

Robert H Beckmann and Mary Louise SWIFT had the following children:

    i.   MATTTHEW NOLAN[6] BECKMANN was born on 19 Aug 1975 in Garden Grove, Ca.. He married Kenya Marie Mayfield on 15 Jul 2000 in Ann Arbor, Mi.. She was born on 16 Apr 1974.

    ii.   BENJAMIN SCOTT BECKMANN was born on 06 Nov 1977 in Santa Ana, Ca..

22.   **ANNE ELIZABETH[4] SWIFT** (Marybelle[3] MORRIS, Marie Louise[2] Morris, James Cranston[1] Williams) was born on 29 May 1954 in Dallas Tx. She married (1) **TOM FRANKLIN**. She married (2) **JAMES T PARKER** on 08 Feb 1973.

James T PARKER and Anne Elizabeth SWIFT had the following child:

    i.   MICHAEL CHARLES[5] PARKER was born on 07 Aug 1975 in Dallas, Tx.. He married (1) JODY UNKNOWN.

23.   **EDWARD MORRIS[4] ROGERS** (Marian Louise[3] MORRIS, Marie Louise[2] Morris, James Cranston[1] Williams) was born on 09 May 1960 in Summit, NJ. He married Jeanette Lynn RAINES, daughter of Dennis Wayne RAINES and Janice Rollins, on 08 Oct 1983 in Germantown, Tn. She was born on 16 Mar 1960 in Jackson, Tn.

Notes for Edward Morris ROGERS:
BIE, Bachelor of Industrial Engineering, GA Institute of Technology, 1982:Master of Science Engineering Managment,Univ of Dayton, 1993:MS,International Logistics, Georgia Tech, 2002

Notes for Jeanette Lynn RAINES:
BChE, Chemical Engineering Georgia Institute of Technology, 1983

Edward Morris ROGERS and Jeanette Lynn RAINES had the following children:

    i.   KYLA LOUISE[5] ROGERS was born on 05 Apr 1987 in Dayton, OH.

        Notes for Kyla Louise ROGERS:
        Graduate, Georgia Institute of Technology,2009,BS Economics annd International Affairs

    ii.   MATLOCK NELSON ROGERS was born on 16 Aug 1989 in Dayton, OH.

        Notes for Matlock Nelson ROGERS:
        Graduate,Georgia Institute of Technology,2011.BS,IndustrialEngineering

    iii.   KIRBY LEE ROGERS was born on 06 Aug 1991 in Lawrenceville, Ga..

        Notes for Kirby Lee ROGERS:
        Graduate Agnes ScottCollege,Atlanta,2013,BA,Mathematics

24.   **WADE WILLIAMS[4] STEPHENS** (Sara Anne[3] WILLIAMS, Cary Jones[2] WILLIAMS, James Cranston[1] Williams) was born on 18 Dec 1969 in Athens Clarke Cty, Ga.. He married Ami Taylor Pitts, daughter of William Carl Pitts Jr and Diane Johnson Pitts, on 15 Jul 2000 in Decatur,DeKalb Cty, Ga.. She was born on 16 Jul 1974 in Decatur,Dekalb Cty, Ga.

Wade Williams Stephens and Ami Taylor Pitts had the following children:

II

    i.   WADE WILLIAMS[5] STEPHENS JR was born on 18 Apr 2003 in Fulton Cty, Ga..

    ii.   TAYLOR HOWARD STEPHENS was born on 13 Dec 2005 in Marietta, Cobb Cty, Ga.

25.   CAREY THOMAS[4] STEPHENS (Sara Anne[3] WILLIAMS, Cary Jones[2] WILLIAMS, James Cranston[1] Williams) was born on 11 Sep 1973 in Athens Clarke Cty, Ga.. He married Stacey Lynn Hall on 23 Feb 2002 in Valdosta, Lowndes, Georgia, First United Methodist ChurchUSA. She was born on 18 Jun 1970 in Valdosta, Lowndes, Georgia, First United Methodist ChurchUSA.

Carey Thomas Stephens and Stacey Lynn Hall had the following children:

    i.   CAREY THOMAS[5] STEPHENS JR was born on 25 Oct 2005 in Atlanta, Fulton Cty Ga.

    ii.   HENRY HALL STEPHENS was born on 15 Feb 2007.

26.   KIMBERLY AMANDA[4] HERRING (Mary Jo[3] Boswell, Mary Jim[2] WILLIAMS, James Cranston[1] Williams) was born on 24 Sep 1968 in Athens Clarke Cty, Ga.. She married (1) BENJAMIN HAYDEN COOK JR.

Benjamin Hayden Cook Jr and Kimberly Amanda Herring had the following children:

    i.   HERRIN BOSWELL[5] COOK was born on 04 Jul 2005 in Atlanta, Fulton Cty Ga..

    ii.   BENJAMIN HAYDEN COOK LLL was born on 18 Mar 2008 in Atlanta, Fulton Cty Ga (Piedmont Hospital).

Prepared By:

Preparer: *JAMES W MORRIS*	Address	James W Morris
Phone:		17 Forest Hill Dr SW
Email: *5/14/14*		Cartersville GA 30120

12

Descendants of Veit Hangleiter

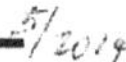

Generation 1

1. **VEIT[1] HANGLEITER** was born in 1600 in Langschlag, Austria. He died in 1654. He married (1) **SUZANE**. He married (2) **SUZANNE** about 1623 in Langschlag, Austria.

    Veit Hangleiter and Suzane had the following child:

    2.   i. ADAM[2] HANGLEITER (son of Veit Hangleiter and Suzane) was born in 1633 in Langschlag, Austria (Master Hammersmith). He died on 15 Apr 1693 in Mergelstetten, Gwrmany. He married Anna Lindenmayer about 1660. She was born in 1640. She died on 02 Aug 1710 in Mergelstetten, Gwrmany.

    Veit Hangleiter and Suzanne had the following child:

    2.   i. ADAM[2] HANGLEITER (son of Veit Hangleiter and Suzane) was born in 1633 in Langschlag, Austria (Master Hammersmith). He died on 15 Apr 1693 in Mergelstetten, Gwrmany. He married Anna Lindenmayer about 1660. She was born in 1640. She died on 02 Aug 1710 in Mergelstetten, Gwrmany.

Generation 2

2. **ADAM[2] HANGLEITER** (Veit[1]) was born in 1633 in Langschlag, Austria (Master Hammersmith). He died on 15 Apr 1693 in Mergelstetten, Gwrmany. He married Anna Lindenmayer about 1660. She was born in 1640. She died on 02 Aug 1710 in Mergelstetten, Gwrmany.

    Notes for Adam Hangleiter:
    A master Hammersmith

    Adam Hangleiter and Anna Lindenmayer had the following child:

    3.   i. HANNS JACOB[3] HANGLIETER (son of Adam Hangleiter and Anna Lindenmayer) was born on 14 Mar 1661 in Mergelstetten, Gwrmany. He died on 16 May 1731 in Niederstotzingen Germany. He married (1) ANNA MARIA MAHLER in 1680. He married (2) URSULA ZIEGLER. She was born on 22 Dec 1662 in Neiderstotzingen. She died on 13 Feb 1728.

Generation 3

3. **HANNS JACOB[3] HANGLIETER** (Adam[2] Hangleiter, Veit[1] Hangleiter) was born on 14 Mar 1661 in Mergelstetten, Gwrmany. He died on 16 May 1731 in Niederstotzingen Germany. He married (1) **ANNA MARIA MAHLER** in 1680. He married (2) **URSULA ZIEGLER**. She was born on 22 Dec 1662 in Neiderstotzingen. She died on 13 Feb 1728.

    Notes for Hanns Jacob Hanglieter:
    A Saddlemaker and Judge

    Hanns Jacob Hanglieter and Anna Maria Mahler had the following child:

    4.   i. HANNS ADAM[4] HANGLEITER (son of Hanns Jacob Hanglieter and Anna Maria Mahler) was born on 10 Mar 1690 in Niederstotzingen Germany. He died on 01 Jul 1735 in Niederstotzingen Germany. He married (1) ANGELICA HITZLER on 28 Apr 1734. He married (2) CATHARINA KASTLER (daughter of Michael Kastler) on 18 Nov 1721. She was born in 1697 in Asselfingen, Alb-Donau-Kreis, Baden-Württemberg, Germany. She died on 07 Dec 1733 in Niederstotzingen Germany.

Generation 4

4. **HANNS ADAM[4] HANGLEITER** (Hanns Jacob[3] Hanglieter, Adam[2], Veit[1]) was born on 10 Mar 1690 in Niederstotzingen Germany. He died on 01 Jul 1735 in Niederstotzingen Germany. He married (1) **ANGELICA HITZLER** on 28 Apr 1734. He married (2) **CATHARINA KASTLER** (daughter of Michael Kastler) on 18 Nov 1721. She was born in 1697 in Asselfingen, Alb-Donau-Kreis, Baden-Württemberg, Germany. She died on 07 Dec 1733 in Niederstotzingen Germany.

    Notes for Hanns Adam Hangleiter:
    A Saddlemaker

    Hanns Adam Hangleiter and Catharina Kastler had the following child:

    5.   i. JOHANN[5] HANGLIETER (son of Hanns Adam Hangleiter and Catharina Kastler) was

born on 17 Feb 1732 in Niederstotzingen Germany. He died on 07 Jun 1786 in Ebnenzer, Ga. He married (1) MARIA MAGDALENNA in 1774. She was born in 1758. He married (2) URSALA in 1750. She was born in 1729. She died on 06 Dec 1773 in Ebenezer Effingham Cty Ga..

Generation 5

5. JOHANN[5] HANGLIETER (Hanns Adam[4] Hangleiter, Hanns Jacob[3], Adam[2] Hangleiter, Veit[1] Hangleiter) was born on 17 Feb 1732 in Niederstotzingen Germany. He died on 07 Jun 1786 in Ebnenzer, Ga. He married (1) **MARIA MAGDALENNA** in 1774. She was born in 1758. He married (2) **URSALA** in 1750. She was born in 1729. She died on 06 Dec 1773 in Ebenezer Effingham Cty Ga..

Johann Hanglieter and Maria Magdalenna had the following child:

    i.   CHRISTIAN[6] HANGLIETER (son of Johann Hanglieter and Maria Magdalenna) was born on 10 Oct 1777 in Ebenezer, Georgia, USA.

Johann Hanglieter and Ursala had the following children:

6.   ii.   JOHN JACOB HANDLEIGHTER (son of Johann Hanglieter and Ursala) was born on 12 May 1762 in Ebenezer, Georgia, USA. He died in 1796 in Effingham Cty, Georgia, USA. He married (1) CATHARINE WEIDMAN.

    iii.   AGATHA HANGLIETER (daughter of Johann Hanglieter and Ursala) was born on 23 Sep 1765 in Ebenezer, Georgia, USA.

7.   iv.   ANNA CATHARINA HANGLIETER (daughter of Johann Hanglieter and Ursala) was born in Georgia, USA. She died in Georgia, USA. She married (1) CHRISTOPH KRAEMER (son of Christopher Kraemer) on 01 Mar 1774. He was born in Georgia, USA. He died in 1793 in Georgia, USA. She married (2) DANIEL WEIDMANN on 08 Jul 1794.

    v.   MARIA MAGDALENA HANGLIETER (daughter of Johann Hanglieter and Ursala) was born on 02 Jan 1758 in Ebenezer, Georgia, USA.

    vi.   HANNA ELISABETH HANGLIETER (daughter of Johann Hanglieter and Ursala) was born on 05 Oct 1759 in Ebenezer, Georgia, USA. She died on 05 Feb 1779. She married John Chris Buntz on 13 Mar 1778.

    vii.   JOHANNA HANGLIETER (daughter of Johann Hanglieter and Ursala) was born on 08 Jun 1769 in Ebenezer, Georgia, USA. She died on 23 Nov 1773.

Generation 6

6. JOHN JACOB[6] HANDLEIGHTER (Johann[5] Hanglieter, Hanns Adam[4] Hangleiter, Hanns Jacob[3] Hanglieter, Adam[2] Hangleiter, Veit[1] Hangleiter) was born on 12 May 1762 in Ebenezer, Georgia, USA. He died in 1796 in Effingham Cty, Georgia, USA. He married (1) **CATHARINE WEIDMAN**.

John Jacob Handleighter and Catharine Weidman had the following children:

    i.   WILLIAM R[7] HANDLEIGHTER (son of John Jacob Handleighter and Catharine Weidman).

8.   ii.   JOHN JACOB HANLEITER (son of John Jacob Handleighter and Catharine Weidman) was born in 1791 in Ebenezer, Georgia, USA. He died on 13 Mar 1815 in Savannah, Georgia, USA. He married Elizabeth McFARLANE (daughter of William McFARLANE and Living Shields) on 11 May 1812. She was born on 13 Mar 1786. She died about 1823 in Savannah, Ga..

7. ANNA CATHARINA[6] HANGLIETER (Johann[5], Hanns Adam[4] Hangleiter, Hanns Jacob[3], Adam[2] Hangleiter, Veit[1] Hangleiter) was born in Georgia, USA. She died in Georgia, USA. She married (1) **CHRISTOPH KRAEMER** (son of Christopher Kraemer) on 01 Mar 1774. He was born in Georgia, USA. He died in 1793 in Georgia, USA. She married (2) **DANIEL WEIDMANN** on 08 Jul 1794.

Christoph Kraemer and Anna Catharina Hanglieter had the following children:

    i.   JOHN CHRISTOPHER[7] CRAMER (son of Christoph Kraemer and Anna Catharina Hanglieter) was born on 21 Dec 1774 in Georgia, USA.

    ii.   SOLOMON CRAMER (son of Christoph Kraemer and Anna Catharina Hanglieter) was born on 27 Aug 1777 in Ebenezer, Georgia, USA. He died on 18 Feb 1839 in Ebenezer, Effingham, Georgia, USA.

    iii. AGATHA CRAMER (daughter of Christoph Kraemer and Anna Catharina Hanglieter) was born on 21 Aug 1781 in Georgia, USA. She died on 02 Aug 1846 in Georgia, USA.

    iv. CHRISTOPHER III (4) CRAMER (son of Christoph Kraemer and Anna Catharina Hanglieter) was born on 15 Sep 1781 in Georgia, USA. He died on 30 Oct 1819 in Georgia, USA.

    v. ANN CATHERINE CRAMER (daughter of Christoph Kraemer and Anna Catharina Hanglieter) was born in 1791 in Georgia, USA. She died on 03 Sep 1866 in Georgia, USA.

Generation 7

8.   JOHN JACOB[7] HANLEITER (John Jacob[6] Handleighter, Johann[5] Hanglieter, Hanns Adam[4] Hangleiter, Hanns Jacob[3] Hanglieter, Adam[2] Hangleiter, Veit[1] Hangleiter) was born in 1791 in Ebenezer, Georgia, USA. He died on 13 Mar 1815 in Savannah, Georgia, USA. He married Elizabeth McFARLANE (daughter of William McFARLANE and Living Shields) on 11 May 1812. She was born on 13 Mar 1786. She died about 1823 in Savannah, Ga..

Notes for John Jacob Hanleiter:
also John Jacob Hanleiter Junior

John Jacob Hanleiter and Elizabeth McFARLANE had the following children:

    i. ALEXANDER[8] HANLEITER (son of John Jacob Hanleiter and Elizabeth McFARLANE). He died in Savannah Cemeterty.

    ii. CATHERINE CHRISTINA HANLEITER (daughter of John Jacob Hanleiter and Elizabeth McFARLANE). She died before 1899. She married (1) J.E. WELLS. He was born in Macon, Ga..

9.   iii. CORNELIUS REDDING HANLEITER (son of John Jacob Hanleiter and Elizabeth McFARLANE) was born on 14 Jun 1815 in Savannah, Georgia, USA. He died on 24 Apr 1897 in Atlanta, Georgia, USA. He married (1) MARY ANN FORD on 22 Feb 1837 in Macon, Georgia, USA. She was born on 12 May 1818 in New Haven, Connecticut, USA. She died on 03 Jul 1848 in Macon, Ga.. He married (2) ANN ELIZABETH SHAW (daughter of George Shaw and Louisa Trout) on 07 Nov 1849 in Dekalb Cty, Ga. She was born on 16 Nov 1830 in Jefferson, Jackson Cty, Ga.. She died on 10 Dec 1876 in Atlanta, Fulton Cty Ga. He married (3) ANN ELIZABETH SHAW in Sep 1850. She died in 1876 in Atlanta, Fulton, Georgia.

    iv. JANE ELIZABETH HANLEITER (daughter of John Jacob Hanleiter and Elizabeth McFARLANE). She married (1) SOLFNER.

Generation 8

9.   CORNELIUS REDDING[8] HANLEITER (John Jacob[7], John Jacob[6] Handleighter, Johann[5] Hanglieter, Hanns Adam[4] Hangleiter, Hanns Jacob[3] Hanglieter, Adam[2] Hangleiter, Veit[1] Hangleiter) was born on 14 Jun 1815 in Savannah, Georgia, USA. He died on 24 Apr 1897 in Atlanta, Georgia, USA. He married (1) MARY ANN FORD on 22 Feb 1837 in Macon, Georgia, USA. She was born on 12 May 1818 in New Haven, Connecticut, USA. She died on 03 Jul 1848 in Macon, Ga.. He married (2) ANN ELIZABETH SHAW (daughter of George Shaw and Louisa Trout) on 07 Nov 1849 in Dekalb Cty, Ga. She was born on 16 Nov 1830 in Jefferson, Jackson Cty, Ga.. She died on 10 Dec 1876 in Atlanta, Fulton Cty Ga. He married (3) ANN ELIZABETH SHAW in Sep 1850. She died in 1876 in Atlanta, Fulton, Georgia.

Notes for Cornelius Redding Hanleiter:
Cornelius R Hanleiter (June14, 1815-April 24,1897) was probably born in Savannah: at least he lived there at one time.He also lived in Madison, Ga.,from which place he moved (along with

'Southern Miscellany', a newspaper of which he was editor) to Atlanta, Ga. onJuly 2,1847. In 1849 Hanleiter sold the type and press and took over Atlanta's first telegraph office. In 1857 he reentered the Atlanta newspaper field by taking over the outfit of the defunct' Weekly Republican and Disicpline' and established the 'National American' which changed its name at the outbreak of the Civil War to the' Gate City Guardian', and subsequently to the 'Southern Confederacy'.On September 26, 1861 Hanlieter was mustered into the Confederate army. His experiences are the subject of his diary. In his diary he refers frequently to his famly - his wfe, his son William who was married and the father of a small child: a much younger son, named George: daughters , Josephine, Ida,Bertha, Louise, Catherine and Mary, a child who died shortly after he entered the service. William Hanleiter was publisher of the Atlanta Directories of 1870,1871,1872.
Data relating to the Cornalius R .Hanleiter Diary,Emory University Library,Special Collection (Copied from Edie Dougherty, Family Collection, 1998)

Cornelius Redding Hanleiter and Mary Ann Ford had the following children:

      i.   WILLIAM ROBERTSON[9] HANLEITER (son of Cornelius Redding Hanleiter and Mary Ann Ford) was born on 09 Apr 1838 in Macon. Ga. He married Mattie Brewer on 21 Aug 1859.

10.   ii.   JOSEPHINE ELLA HANLEITER (daughter of Cornelius Redding Hanleiter and Mary Ann Ford) was born on 21 Jan 1841 in Macon, Georgia, USA. She died on 08 Sep 1876 in Atlanta, Fulton Cty Ga. She married Henry GULLATT (son of James Edwin GULLATT and Mary CARPENTER) on 23 Jun 1864 in Savannah, Chatham, Georgia, USA. He was born on 30 Aug 1837 in CHARLESTON, S.C.. He died on 21 Oct 1913 in Greensboro, Greene Cty, Ga..

      iii.   IDA MAY HANLEITER (daughter of Cornelius Redding Hanleiter and Mary Ann Ford) was born on 04 Mar 1843 in Madison, Ga.

      iv.   CATHERINE ANNA HANLEITER (daughter of Cornelius Redding Hanleiter and Mary Ann Ford) was born on 12 Feb 1845 in Madison, Ga. She died in Jun 1937. She married Josiah Peterson on 25 Apr 1889.

      v.   SARA JANE HANLEITER (daughter of Cornelius Redding Hanleiter and Mary Ann Ford) was born on 25 Jun 1848 in Macon. Ga. She died on 07 Aug 1848 in Macon. Ga.

Cornelius Redding Hanleiter and Ann Elizabeth SHAW had the following children:

      vi.   BERTHA CALDERWOOD HANLEITER (daughter of Cornelius Redding Hanleiter and Ann Elizabeth Shaw) was born on 30 Sep 1850 in Atlanta, Fulton Cty, Ga.. She died in Apr 1905 in Atlanta, Fulton Cty, Ga. She married Issac Lester in Dec 1895.

      vii.   AMANDA LOUISA HANLEITER (daughter of Cornelius Redding Hanleiter and Ann Elizabeth SHAW) was born on 05 Sep 1853 in Atlanta, Fulton Cty, Ga. She died on 26 Sep 1872 in Atlanta, Fulton Cty, Ga.

      viii.   CORNELIUS REDDING HANLEITERJR (son of Cornelius Redding Hanleiter and Ann Elizabeth SHAW) was born on 27 Jul 1855. He died on 14 Jul 1856.

      ix.   GEORGE SHAW HANLEITER (son of Cornelius Redding Hanleiter and Ann Elizabeth Shaw) was born on 14 Feb 1857.

      x.   CLARA ANN HANLEITER (daughter of Cornelius Redding Hanleiter and Ann Elizabeth SHAW) was born on 28 Mar 1859. She died on 23 Jul 1860 in Atlanta, Fulton Cty, Ga.

      xi.   MARY CLELAND HANLEITER (daughter of Cornelius Redding Hanleiter and Ann Elizabeth SHAW) was born on 12 Jul 1861 in Atlanta, Fulton Cty, Ga. She died on 25 Nov 1861 in Atlanta, Fulton Cty, Ga.

      xii.   VICTORINE JORDAN HANLEITER (daughter of Cornelius Redding Hanleiter and Ann Elizabeth Shaw) was born on 20 Feb 1863 in LaGrange, Ga. She died in 1956 in

Atlanta, Ga.. She married Lewis H Stowers on 21 Jun 1882.

xiii. CORA EMELINE HANLEITER (daughter of Cornelius Redding Hanleiter and Ann Elizabeth Shaw) was born on 31 Jan 1866 in LaGrange, Ga. She married Walter Batchings on 18 Jun 1891.

xiv. JAMES MCPHERSON HANLEITER (son of Cornelius Redding Hanleiter and Ann Elizabeth Shaw) was born on 30 Oct 1868 in Augusta, Ga.. He died on 04 Apr 1907 in Atlanta, Fulton Cty, Ga.

xv. ELIZABETH MACFARLANE HANLEITER (daughter of Cornelius Redding Hanleiter and Ann Elizabeth Shaw) was born on 16 Mar 1875 in Cottage Hill Ga.. She died on 14 Oct 1956 in Atlanta, Fulton Cty, Ga. She married Samuel W McCallie (son of Andrew Jackson McCallie and Harriet Theodoshia A. Cunnyngham) on 25 Dec 1899. He was born on 02 Aug 1856 in Knoxville, Tn.. He died on 26 Oct 1933 in Atlanta, Fulton Cty, Ga.

Cornelius Redding Hanleiter and Ann Elizabeth Shaw had the following children:

vi. BERTHA CALDERWOOD HANLEITER (daughter of Cornelius Redding Hanleiter and Ann Elizabeth Shaw) was born on 30 Sep 1850 in Atlanta, Fulton Cty, Ga.. She died in Apr 1905 in Atlanta, Fulton Cty, Ga. She married Issac Lester in Dec 1895.

ix. GEORGE SHAW HANLEITER (son of Cornelius Redding Hanleiter and Ann Elizabeth Shaw) was born on 14 Feb 1857.

xii. VICTORINE JORDAN HANLEITER (daughter of Cornelius Redding Hanleiter and Ann Elizabeth Shaw) was born on 20 Feb 1863 in LaGrange, Ga. She died in 1956 in Atlanta, Ga.. She married Lewis H Stowers on 21 Jun 1882.

xiii. CORA EMELINE HANLEITER (daughter of Cornelius Redding Hanleiter and Ann Elizabeth Shaw) was born on 31 Jan 1866 in LaGrange, Ga. She married Walter Batchings on 18 Jun 1891.

xiv. JAMES MCPHERSON HANLEITER (son of Cornelius Redding Hanleiter and Ann Elizabeth Shaw) was born on 30 Oct 1868 in Augusta, Ga.. He died on 04 Apr 1907 in Atlanta, Fulton Cty, Ga.

xv. ELIZABETH MACFARLANE HANLEITER (daughter of Cornelius Redding Hanleiter and Ann Elizabeth Shaw) was born on 16 Mar 1875 in Cottage Hill Ga.. She died on 14 Oct 1956 in Atlanta, Fulton Cty, Ga. She married Samuel W McCallie (son of Andrew Jackson McCallie and Harriet Theodoshia A. Cunnyngham) on 25 Dec 1899. He was born on 02 Aug 1856 in Knoxville, Tn.. He died on 26 Oct 1933 in Atlanta, Fulton Cty, Ga.

Generation 9

10. JOSEPHINE ELLA[9] HANLEITER (Cornelius Redding[8], John Jacob[7], John Jacob[6] Handleighter, Johann[5] Hanglieter, Hanns Adam[4] Hangleiter, Hanns Jacob[3] Hanglieter, Adam[2] Hangleiter, Veit[1] Hangleiter) was born on 21 Jan 1841 in Macon, Georgia, USA. She died on 08 Sep 1876 in Atlanta, Fulton Cty Ga. She married Henry GULLATT (son of James Edwin GULLATT and Mary CARPENTER) on 23 Jun 1864 in Savannah, Chatham, Georgia, USA. He was born on 30 Aug 1837 in CHARLESTON, S.C.. He died on 21 Oct 1913 in Greensboro, Greene Cty, Ga..

Notes for Josephine Ella Hanleiter:
1. Marriage place, Beulieu Battery, Savannah, Ga by Rev. C.F. McRae

Notes for Henry GULLATT:
1. Marriage place, Beulieu Battery, Savannah, Ga by Rev. C.F. McRae

Henry GULLATT and Josephine Ella Hanleiter had the following children:

   i.   WILLIAM CORNELIUS[10] GULLATT (son of Henry GULLATT and Josephine Ella Hanleiter) was born on 24 Apr 1865 in Winsborough S.c.. He married Mamie Reid on 22 Nov 1893. She was born in South Carolina.

   ii. HARRY ELLIS GULLATT (son of Henry GULLATT and Josephine Ella Hanleiter) was born on 04 Dec 1868 in Atlanta, Fulton, Georgia, USA.

   iii. CLIFFORD GULLATT (son of Henry GULLATT and Josephine Ella Hanleiter) was born on 06 Jan 1870 in Atlanta, Fulyon Cty, Georgia, USA.

   iv. MARY MARIA GULLATT (daughter of Henry GULLATT and Josephine Ella Hanleiter) was born on 10 Jul 1872 in Atlanta, Fulton Cty, Ga.. She died on 07 Dec 1959 in Greensboro, Greene Cty, Ga.. She married James Cranston Williams (son of William Anderson Williams and Huldah Ann Ricketson) on 12 Dec 1893 in By Bishop Henry Morrison, Atlanta, Ga.. He was born on 03 Jan 1868 in Camak, Warren Co., GA, USA. He died on 22 Apr 1936 in Greensboro, Greene Co., GA, USA.

   Notes for James Cranston Williams:
   1. Aftre the death of both parents in Oct 1873 (his age 5) he was sent to live with a minister Downing who was cruel to him, whipping him. James ran away. M Carey Jones took him in and raised him. CWJr Family info.
   2. Family moved to Greensboro in 1906 from Crawfordville, Ga. Gullatt Family Bible.

   v.   JULIA FORD GULLATT (daughter of Henry GULLATT and Josephine Ella Hanleiter) was born on 20 Aug 1874 in Atlanta, Fulton Cty, Ga..

   vi. JOSEPH LYMAN GULLATT (son of Henry GULLATT and Josephine Ella Hanleiter) was born on 25 Aug 1876 in Atlanta, Fulton Cty, Ga..

   vii. WILLIAM JOSEPH GULLATT (son of Henry GULLATT and Josephine Ella Hanleiter) was born in Sep 1890 in Augusta, Columbia, Georgia, United States.

   viii. MARY STEWART GULLATT (daughter of Henry GULLATT and Josephine Ella Hanleiter) was born on 06 Jan 1892 in Augusta, Columbia, Georgia, United States.

Pedigree Chart for
Mary Corinne WOFFORD

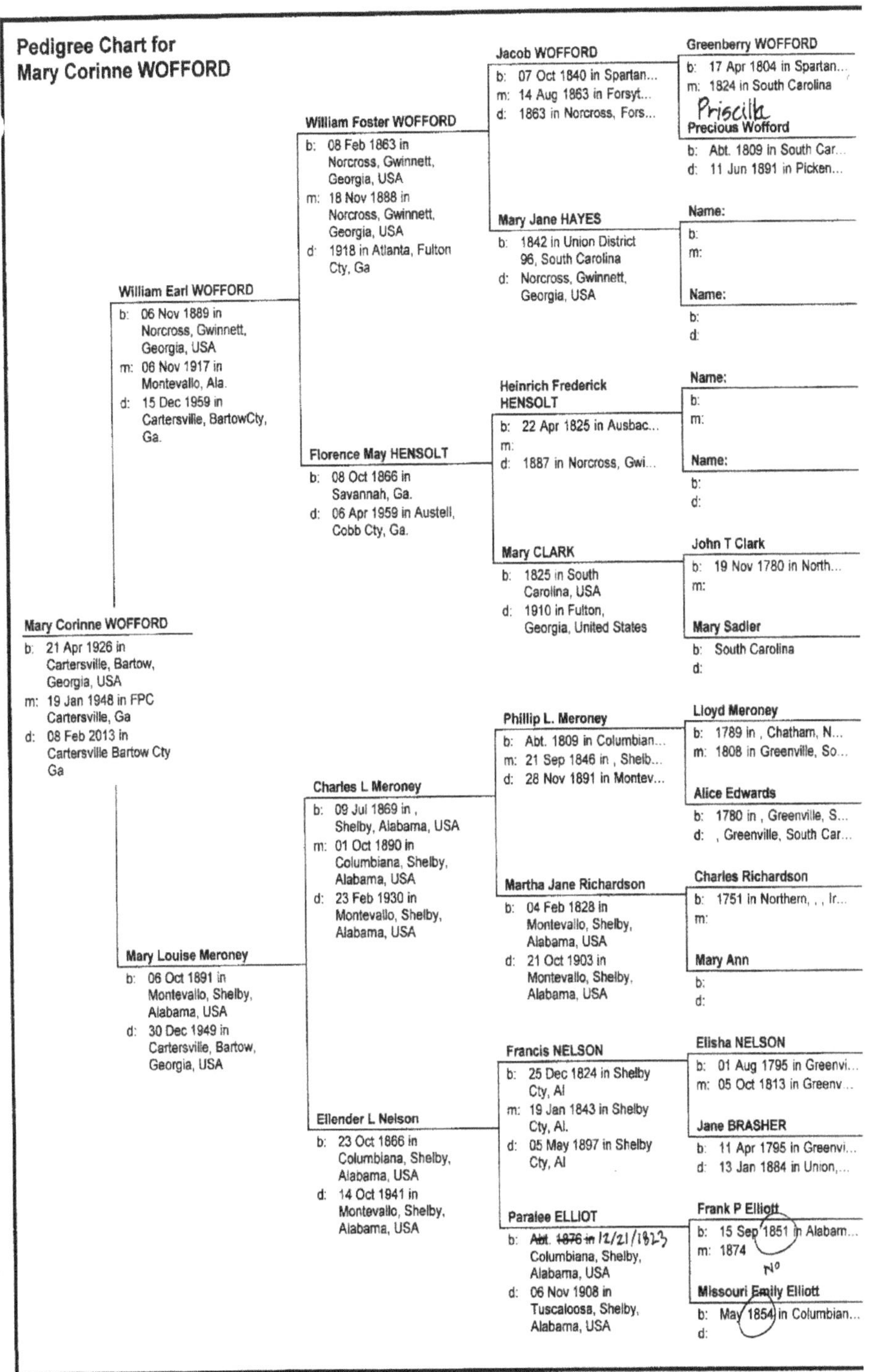

Mary Corinne WOFFORD
- b: 21 Apr 1926 in Cartersville, Bartow, Georgia, USA
- m: 19 Jan 1948 in FPC Cartersville, Ga
- d: 08 Feb 2013 in Cartersville Bartow Cty Ga

William Earl WOFFORD
- b: 06 Nov 1889 in Norcross, Gwinnett, Georgia, USA
- m: 06 Nov 1917 in Montevallo, Ala.
- d: 15 Dec 1959 in Cartersville, BartowCty, Ga.

William Foster WOFFORD
- b: 08 Feb 1863 in Norcross, Gwinnett, Georgia, USA
- m: 18 Nov 1888 in Norcross, Gwinnett, Georgia, USA
- d: 1918 in Atlanta, Fulton Cty, Ga

Florence May HENSOLT
- b: 08 Oct 1866 in Savannah, Ga.
- d: 06 Apr 1959 in Austell, Cobb Cty, Ga.

Mary Louise Meroney
- b: 06 Oct 1891 in Montevallo, Shelby, Alabama, USA
- d: 30 Dec 1949 in Cartersville, Bartow, Georgia, USA

Charles L Meroney
- b: 09 Jul 1869 in , Shelby, Alabama, USA
- m: 01 Oct 1890 in Columbiana, Shelby, Alabama, USA
- d: 23 Feb 1930 in Montevallo, Shelby, Alabama, USA

Ellender L Nelson
- b: 23 Oct 1866 in Columbiana, Shelby, Alabama, USA
- d: 14 Oct 1941 in Montevallo, Shelby, Alabama, USA

Jacob WOFFORD
- b: 07 Oct 1840 in Spartan...
- m: 14 Aug 1863 in Forsyt...
- d: 1863 in Norcross, Fors...

Mary Jane HAYES
- b: 1842 in Union District 96, South Carolina
- d: Norcross, Gwinnett, Georgia, USA

Heinrich Frederick HENSOLT
- b: 22 Apr 1825 in Ausbac...
- m:
- d: 1887 in Norcross, Gwi...

Mary CLARK
- b: 1825 in South Carolina, USA
- d: 1910 in Fulton, Georgia, United States

Phillip L. Meroney
- b: Abt. 1809 in Columbian...
- m: 21 Sep 1846 in , Shelb...
- d: 28 Nov 1891 in Montev...

Martha Jane Richardson
- b: 04 Feb 1828 in Montevallo, Shelby, Alabama, USA
- d: 21 Oct 1903 in Montevallo, Shelby, Alabama, USA

Francis NELSON
- b: 25 Dec 1824 in Shelby Cty, Al
- m: 19 Jan 1843 in Shelby Cty, Al.
- d: 05 May 1897 in Shelby Cty, Al

Paralee ELLIOT
- b: Abt. 1876 in 12/21/1873 Columbiana, Shelby, Alabama, USA
- d: 06 Nov 1908 in Tuscaloosa, Shelby, Alabama, USA

Greenberry WOFFORD
- b: 17 Apr 1804 in Spartan...
- m: 1824 in South Carolina

Priscilla
Precious Wofford
- b: Abt. 1809 in South Car...
- d: 11 Jun 1891 in Picken...

Name:
- b:
- m:

Name:
- b:
- d:

Name:
- b:
- m:

Name:
- b:
- d:

John T Clark
- b: 19 Nov 1780 in North...
- m:

Mary Sadler
- b: South Carolina
- d:

Lloyd Meroney
- b: 1789 in , Chatham, N...
- m: 1808 in Greenville, So...

Alice Edwards
- b: 1780 in , Greenville, S...
- d: , Greenville, South Car...

Charles Richardson
- b: 1751 in Northern, , , Ir...
- m:

Mary Ann
- b:
- d:

Elisha NELSON
- b: 01 Aug 1795 in Greenvi...
- m: 05 Oct 1813 in Greenv...

Jane BRASHER
- b: 11 Apr 1795 in Greenvi...
- d: 13 Jan 1884 in Union,...

Frank P Elliott
- b: 15 Sep 1851 in Alabam...
- m: 1874
- N⁰

Missouri Emily Elliott
- b: May 1854 in Columbian...
- d:

Descendants of William Walford

Generation 1

1. **WILLIAM[1] WALFORD** .

   William Walford had the following child:

   2.   i.   WILLIAM[2] WALFORD was born in 1537 in Pattingtam, Staffordshire, England. He died in 1578 in Pattingtam, Staffordshire, England. He married Alice Walford in 1562 in Pattingham, Staffordshire, England. She was born in 1541 in Pattingham, Staffordshire, England.

Generation 2

2. **WILLIAM[2] WALFORD** (William[1]) was born in 1537 in Pattingtam, Staffordshire, England. He died in 1578 in Pattingtam, Staffordshire, England. He married Alice Walford in 1562 in Pattingham, Staffordshire, England. She was born in 1541 in Pattingham, Staffordshire, England.

   William Walford and Alice Walford had the following child:

   3.   i.   RICHARD[3] WALFORD was born in 1563 in Pattingham, Staffordshire, England. He died in 1624 in Pattingham, Staffordshire, England. He married Alice Walford in 1588 in Pattingham, Staffordshire, England. She was born in 1567 in Pattingham, Staffordshire, England.

Generation 3

3. **RICHARD[3] WALFORD** (William[2], William[1]) was born in 1563 in Pattingham, Staffordshire, England. He died in 1624 in Pattingham, Staffordshire, England. He married Alice Walford in 1588 in Pattingham, Staffordshire, England. She was born in 1567 in Pattingham, Staffordshire, England.

   Richard Walford and Alice Walford had the following child:

   4.   i.   WILLIAM WALFORD[4] WOFFORD was born on 16 Sep 1589 in Pattingtam, Staffordshire, England. He died in 1655 in Pattingtam, Staffordshire, England. He married Joane Blakemore on 27 Jul 1618 in Pattingham, Staffordshire, England.

Generation 4

4. **WILLIAM WALFORD[4] WOFFORD** (Richard[3] Walford, William[2] Walford, William[1] Walford) was born on 16 Sep 1589 in Pattingtam, Staffordshire, England. He died in 1655 in Pattingtam, Staffordshire, England. He married Joane Blakemore on 27 Jul 1618 in Pattingham, Staffordshire, England.

   William Walford Wofford and Joane Blakemore had the following children:

      i.   JOHN[5] WALFORD was born in Pattingtam, Staffordshire, England.

      ii.   MARGERY WALFORD.

   5.   iii.   WILLIAM WOFFORD was born in 1620 in Cumberlandshire, England. He died in 1655 in St Mary's Cty Md.. He married Mary Willoughby in 1647. She was born in 1626 in Scotland.

      iv.   RICHARD WALFORD was born on 21 Feb 1621 in Pattingtam, Staffordshire, England. He died on 26 Oct 1678 in Pattingham, Staffordshire, England.

Generation 5

5. **WILLIAM[5] WOFFORD** (William Walford[4], Richard[3] Walford, William[2] Walford, William[1] Walford) was born in 1620 in Cumberlandshire, England. He died in 1655 in St Mary's Cty Md.. He married Mary Willoughby in 1647. She was born in 1626 in Scotland.

   William Wofford and Mary Willoughby had the following child:

   6.   i.   WILLIAM[6] WOFFORD was born in 1648 in St Mary's Cty Md.. He died in 1680 in Saint Marys, Maryland, USA. He married Elizabeth Wofford in 1673 in MD. She was born in 1648 in Maryland, USA. She died in Saint Marys, Maryland, USA.

Generation 6

6. **WILLIAM[6] WOFFORD** (William[5], William Walford[4], Richard[3] Walford, William[2] Walford, William[1] Walford) was born in 1648 in St Mary's Cty Md.. He died in 1680 in Saint Marys, Maryland, USA. He married Elizabeth Wofford in 1673 in MD. She was born in 1648 in Maryland, USA. She died in

l

Saint Marys, Maryland, USA.

William Wofford and Elizabeth Wofford had the following children:

7.   i.   WILLIAM[7] WOFFORD was born in 1674 in St. Mary's Cty Md. He died in 1746 in Prince George's Cty , Md. He married Mary in 1696. She was born in 1679 in Prince Georges, Maryland, USA. She died in 1737 in Prince Georges, Maryland, USA.

    ii.   JOHN WOFFORD was born in 1678 in Saint Marys, Maryland, USA. He died in 1756 in Frederick, Maryland, USA.

Generation 7

7.   WILLIAM[7] WOFFORD (William[6], William[5], William Walford[4], Richard[3] Walford, William[2] Walford, William[1] Walford) was born in 1674 in St. Mary's Cty Md. He died in 1746 in Prince George's Cty , Md. He married Mary in 1696. She was born in 1679 in Prince Georges, Maryland, USA. She died in 1737 in Prince Georges, Maryland, USA.

William Wofford and Mary had the following children:

    i.   WILLIAM[8] WOFFORD was born in 1701 in Prince George's Cty , Md. He died in 1788 in 96 District S.C.. He married (1) HANNAH CROSS in 1739 in Maryland, USA. She was born in 1725 in Prince Georges, Montgomery, Maryland, USA. She died in 1772 in Union, South Carolina, USA. He married (2) ABIGAIL TERRELL in 1773 in Prince Georges, Montgomery, Maryland, USA. She was born in 1701 in Prince Georges, Montgomery, Maryland, USA. She died in 1788.

8.   ii.   ABASALOM WOFFORD was born in 1703 in Prince George's Cty, Md. He died in 1755 in Rock Creek, Fredrick Cty, Md. He married Sarah Bell Holsey, daughter of John Hosey, in 1727 in Prince George's Cty, Md. She was born in 1710 in Prince Georges, Maryland, USA. She died in 1754 in Rock Creek, Montgomery, Maryland, USA.

    iii.   ELIZABETH WOFFORD was born in 1705 in Prince Georges, Maryland, USA. She died on 14 Aug 1727 in Prince Georges, Maryland, USA.

    iv.   JANE WOFFORD was born in 1705 in Caroline, Virginia, USA. She died on 09 Dec 1737 in Virginia, USA.

    v.   SARAH WOFFORD was born in 1707 in Prince Georges, Maryland, USA.

    vi.   JOB WOFFORD was born in 1709 in Prince Georges, Maryland, USA.

    vii.   JAMES WOFFORD was born in 1711 in Prince Georges, Maryland, USA.

    viii.   JOHN WOFFORD was born in 1713 in Prince Georges, Maryland, USA.

    ix.   BENJAMIN WOFFORD was born in 1715 in Prince Georges, Maryland, USA.

Generation 8

8.   ABASALOM[8] WOFFORD (William[7], William[6], William[5], William Walford[4], Richard[3] Walford, William[2] Walford, William[1] Walford) was born in 1703 in Prince George's Cty, Md. He died in 1755 in Rock Creek, Fredrick Cty, Md. He married Sarah Bell Holsey, daughter of John Hosey, in 1727 in Prince George's Cty, Md. She was born in 1710 in Prince Georges, Maryland, USA. She died in 1754 in Rock Creek, Montgomery, Maryland, USA.

Abasalom Wofford and Sarah Bell Holsey had the following children:

9.   i.   WILLIAM[9] WOFFORD was born on 25 Oct 1728 in Rock Creek, Montgomery, Maryland, USA. He died in 1823 in Toccoa, Stephens, Georgia, USA. He married Sarah Cameron in 1748 in Rock Creek, Montgomery, Maryland, USA. She was born on 04 Apr 1732 in Virginia, USA. She died in 1772 in Spartanburg, South Carolina, USA.

10.   ii.   JOHN WOFFORD was born in 1730 in Rock Creek, FredrickCty, Md.. He died in 1812 in Spartanburg Dist, S.C.. He married Elenor BUSHROD in 1760 in Maryland. She was born on 10 Jan 1748 in South Carolina, USA. She died in 1805 in Spartansburg Dist, Charleston, South Carolina, USA.

2

iii.   SARAH WOFFORD was born in 1738 in Rock Creek, Prince Georges, MD. She died in 1815.

11.   iv.   JOSEPH WOFFORD was born in 1742 in Rock Creek, Prince Georges, Maryland, USA. He died on 06 Feb 1856 in Spartanburg, South Carolina, USA. He married (1) MARTHA LLEWELLYN. She was born in 1752 in Lancaster, Pennsylvania, USA. She died on 24 Mar 1826 in Spartanburg, South Carolina, USA.

v.   JAMES WOFFORD was born on 03 Sep 1743 in Rock Creek, Fredrick Cty, Md. He died on 14 Jul 1815 in Spartanburg, S.C.. He married (1) ANNA KATHERINE HOUPOUGH. She was born on 10 Jan 1748 in Fairfax Cty VA. She died on 17 Jan 1826 in Spartanburg, South Carolina, USA.

vi.   BENJAMIN WOFFORD was born in 1745 in Rock Creek, Frederick, MD. He died in Mar 1815 in Huntsville, Madison, AL. He married Mary Llewellyn, daughter of Hugh Llewellyn, in 1765 in Union, Ninety Sixth District, SC. She was born in 1749 in Lancaster, Pennsylvania, USA. She died in 1816 in Huntsville, Madison, Alabama, USA.

vii.   REBECCA WOFFORD was born in 1750 in Rock Creek, Fredrick Cty, Md. She died in 1824 in York Cty, S.C.. She married William Camp in 1770.

viii.   HANNAH WOFFORD was born in 1751. She died in 1820 in Jackson, Georgia, USA.

ix.   JEREMIAH WOFFORD was born in 1752. He died in South Carolina, USA.

x.   ABSALOM WOFFORD was born in 1754. He died in Habersham, Georgia, USA.

Generation 9

9.   WILLIAM[9] WOFFORD (Abasalom[8], William[7], William[6], William[5], William Walford[4], Richard[3] Walford, William[2] Walford, William[1] Walford) was born on 25 Oct 1728 in Rock Creek, Montgomery, Maryland, USA. He died in 1823 in Toccoa, Stephens, Georgia, USA. He married Sarah Cameron in 1748 in Rock Creek, Montgomery, Maryland, USA. She was born on 04 Apr 1732 in Virginia, USA. She died in 1772 in Spartanburg, South Carolina, USA.

William WOFFORD and Sarah Cameron had the following children:

i.   CHARLOTTE[10] WOFFORD.

ii.   ELIZABETH WOFFORD.

iii.   JAMES WOFFORD.

iv.   JOSEPH WOFFORD was born in 1737 in Rock Creek, Prince Georges, Maryland, USA. He died on 14 May 1828 in Spartanburg, South Carolina, USA.

v.   WILLIAM WOFFORD was born in 1749 in Frederick, Maryland, USA. He died in 1795 in Franklin, Georgia, USA.

vi.   JEREMIAH WOFFORD was born in 1751 in Rock Creek, Prince Georges, Maryland, USA.

vii.   ABASALOM WOFFORD was born in 1753 in Rock Creek, Prince Georges, Maryland, USA.

12.   viii.   BENJAMIN J WOFFORD was born in 1758 in Frederick, Maryland, USA. He died on 02 Mar 1836 in Bartow, Georgia, USA. He married (1) MARY HOLLINGSWORTH.

ix.   ANN WOFFORD was born in 1769 in Frederick, Maryland, USA.

x.   JOHN WOFFORD.

xi.   NATHANIEL WOFFORD was born in 1766 in Montgomery, Frederick, Maryland, USA. He died in Feb 1846 in Arkansas, USA.

xii.   MARY WOFFORD was born in 1770 in Frederick, Maryland, USA.

xiii.   SARAH WOFFORD was born in 1775 in Frederick, Maryland, USA. She died in 1869 in Mcdowell, North Carolina, USA.

10.   **JOHN⁹ WOFFORD** (Abasalom⁸, William⁷, William⁶, William⁵, William Walford⁴, Richard³ Walford, William² Walford, William¹ Walford) was born in 1730 in Rock Creek, FredrickCty, Md.. He died in 1812 in Spartanburg Dist, S.C.. He married Elenor BUSHROD in 1760 in Maryland. She was born on 10 Jan 1748 in South Carolina, USA. She died in 1805 in Spartansburg Dist, Charleston, South Carolina, USA.

John WOFFORD and Elenor BUSHROD had the following children:

13.   i.   JOSEPH¹⁰ WOFFORD was born in 1741. He died in 1826.

14.   ii.   JOHN WOFFORD was born in 1761 in Fredrick Cty, Md.. He died in 1790 in , Forsyth, Georgia, USA. He married Mary Lee in 1790. She was born in 1721 in Seneca Creek, Prince Georges, Maryland, USA. She died in 1760 in Frederick, Maryland, USA.

iii.   JESSE WOFFORD was born in 1766 in Ninety Six Dist, South Carolina, USA.

iv.   DORCAS WOFFORD was born on 09 Dec 1766 in Rock Creek, Frederick, Maryland, USA. He died in 1811 in Spartenburg, South Carolina, USA.

v.   JAMES WOFFORD was born in 1768 in Ninety Six Dist, South Carolina, USA.

vi.   BENJAMIN WOFFORD was born in 1772 in Spartanburg Dist, South Carolina, USA. He died in 1858 in Tippah, Mississippi, USA.

vii.   DANIEL WOFFORD was born on 22 Nov 1774 in Spartanburg, South Carolina, USA. He died on 19 Jun 1846 in Liberty, Texas, USA.

viii.   NATHANIEL WOFFORD was born in 1776 in Ninety Six Dist, South Carolina, USA.

ix.   HIRAM WOFFORD was born in 1778 in South Carolina, USA.

x.   ELEANOR WOFFORD was born in 1780.

xi.   CLARA WOFFORD was born in 1784 in Holly Spring, Marshall, Mississippi, USA.

xii.   CYNTHIA WOFFORD was born in 1788 in Holly Spring, Marshall, Mississippi, USA.

xiii.   ISSAC WOFFORD. He died in 1848 in Spartanburg, South Carolina, USA.

xiv.   PRISCILLA WOFFORD was born in 1786 in Holly Spring, Marshall, Mississippi, USA.

xv.   SARAH WOFFORD was born in 1790 in Holly Spring, Marshall, Mississippi, USA. She died in Holly Springs, Marshall, Mississippi, USA.

xvi.   WILLIOAM BUSHROD WOFFORD.

11.   **JOSEPH⁹ WOFFORD** (Abasalom⁸, William⁷, William⁶, William⁵, William Walford⁴, Richard³ Walford, William² Walford, William¹ Walford) was born in 1742 in Rock Creek, Prince Georges, Maryland, USA. He died on 06 Feb 1856 in Spartanburg, South Carolina, USA. He married (1) **MARTHA LLEWELLYN**. She was born in 1752 in Lancaster, Pennsylvania, USA. She died on 24 Mar 1826 in Spartanburg, South Carolina, USA.

Joseph WOFFORD and Martha Llewellyn had the following children:

15.   i.   BENJAMIN¹⁰ WOFFORD was born on 19 Oct 1780 in Spartanburg Cty, S.C.. He died in 1850 in Spartanburg Cty, S.C.. He married (2) MARIA SEVIER BARRON on 06 Sep 1836. He married (3) ANNA TODD on 30 Jul 1807.

ii.   JOSEPH LLEWELLYN WOFFORD. He died in 1858. He married (1) JANE HUCKABEE.

Generation 10

12.   **BENJAMIN J¹⁰ WOFFORD** (William⁹, Abasalom⁸, William⁷, William⁶, William⁵, William Walford⁴, Richard³ Walford, William² Walford, William¹ Walford) was born in 1758 in Frederick, Maryland, USA. He died on 02 Mar 1836 in Bartow, Georgia, USA. He married (1) **MARY HOLLINGSWORTH**.

Benjamin J WOFFORD and Mary Hollingsworth had the following child:

16.   i.   WILIAM HOLLINGSWORTH¹¹ WOFFORD. He married (1) NANCY TATUM.

4

13. **JOSEPH[10] WOFFORD** (John[9], Abasalom[8], William[7], William[6], William[5], William Walford[4], Richard[3] Walford, William[2] Walford, William[1] Walford) was born in 1741. He died in 1826.

Joseph WOFFORD had the following child:

15. i. BENJAMIN[10] WOFFORD was born on 19 Oct 1780 in Spartanburg Cty, S.C.. He died in 1850 in Spartanburg Cty, S.C.. He married (2) **MARIA SEVIER BARRON** on 06 Sep 1836. He married (3) **ANNA TODD** on 30 Jul 1807.

14. **JOHN[10] WOFFORD** (John[9], Abasalom[8], William[7], William[6], William[5], William Walford[4], Richard[3] Walford, William[2] Walford, William[1] Walford) was born in 1761 in Fredrick Cty, Md.. He died in 1790 in , Forsyth, Georgia, USA. He married Mary Lee in 1790. She was born in 1721 in Seneca Creek, Prince Georges, Maryland, USA. She died in 1760 in Frederick, Maryland, USA.

John WOFFORD and Mary Lee had the following children:

i. BENJAMIN[11] WOFFORD was born in Spartanburg Dist, South Carolina, USA.

ii. ELANOR WOFFORD was born in Spartanburg Dist, South Carolina, USA.

17. iii. GEORGE WOFFORD was born on 16 Oct 1793 in Spartanburg Cty, S.C.. He died on 07 Mar 1857 in Forsyth Cty, Ga.. He married Mary Foster, daughter of William Foster, on 18 Apr 1816 in Spartanburg Cty, S.C.. She was born on 07 Sep 1794 in Spartanburg, South Carolina, USA. She died on 04 Feb 1879 in Forsyth, Georgia, USA.

18. iv. GREENBERRY WOFFORD was born on 17 Apr 1804 in Spartanburg Dist, S.C.. He died on 26 Apr 1864 in Jasper, Pickens Cty, Ga.. He married Precious Wofford, daughter of George West and Edith Colista McHanie, in 1824 in South Carolina. She was born about 1809 in South Carolina. She died on 11 Jun 1891 in Pickens, Georgia, USA.

v. JOHN WOFFORD was born in Spartanburg Dist, South Carolina, USA.

vi. MARY WOFFORD was born in Spartanburg Dist, South Carolina, USA.

vii. PRECIOUS WOFFORD was born in 1805 in Frederick, MD, USA.

viii. SARAH WOFFORD was born in Spartanburg Dist, South Carolina, USA.

ix. WILLIAM WOFFORD.

15. **BENJAMIN[10] WOFFORD** (Joseph[9], Abasalom[8], William[7], William[6], William[5], William Walford[4], Richard[3] Walford, William[2] Walford, William[1] Walford) was born on 19 Oct 1780 in Spartanburg Cty, S.C.. He died in 1850 in Spartanburg Cty, S.C.. He married (2) **MARIA SEVIER BARRON** on 06 Sep 1836. He married (3) **ANNA TODD** on 30 Jul 1807.

Benjamin WOFFORD had the following child:

i. DANIEL[11] WOFFORD was born on 22 Nov 1774.

Generation 11

16. **WILIAM HOLLINGSWORTH[11] WOFFORD** (Benjamin J[10], William[9], Abasalom[8], William[7], William[6], William[5], William Walford[4], Richard[3] Walford, William[2] Walford, William[1] Walford). He married (1) **NANCY TATUM**.

Wiliam Hollingsworth WOFFORD and Nancy Tatum had the following child:

i. WILLIAM TATUM[12] WOFFORD was born on 24 Jun 1823 in Habersham Cty, Ga. He died on 22 May 1884 in Bartow Cty, Ga.. He married (1) **JULIA A DWIGHT** on 16 Aug 1859 in Hopedale, Murray Cty, Ga. He married (2) **MARGARET LANGTON** on 02 Oct 1880 in Atlanta, Fulton Cty, Ga..

17. **GEORGE[11] WOFFORD** (John[10], John[9], Abasalom[8], William[7], William[6], William[6], William Walford[4], Richard[3] Walford, William[2] Walford, William[1] Walford) was born on 16 Oct 1793 in Spartanburg Cty, S.C.. He died on 07 Mar 1857 in Forsyth Cty, Ga.. He married Mary Foster, daughter of William Foster, on 18 Apr 1816 in Spartanburg Cty, S.C.. She was born on 07 Sep 1794 in Spartanburg, South Carolina, USA. She died on 04 Feb 1879 in Forsyth, Georgia, USA.

5

George WOFFORD and Mary Foster had the following children:

19.   i.   JOHN FOSTER[12] WOFFORD was born on 14 Feb 1817 in South Carolina, USA. He died on 03 Mar 1884 in Gibson, Tennessee, USA. He married (2) MARY CUNNINGHAM on 23 Apr 1840 in Union, Georgia, USA. She was born on 24 Sep 1818. She died on 08 Apr 1856 in Forsyth, Georgia, USA.

       ii.   SALLEY WOFFORD was born on 29 Dec 1817.

       iii.   MARY WOFFORD was born on 24 Sep 1818 in South Carolina, USA. She died on 08 Apr 1856.

       iv.   MOSES WOFFORD was born on 11 Jul 1824 in South Carolina, USA. He died on 10 Oct 1844 in South Carolina, USA.

       v.   MARIANNE WOFFORD was born on 19 May 1826 in South Carolina, USA.

20.   vi.   AMANDA MELVINA WOFFORD was born on 29 Sep 1827 in South Carolina, USA. She died on 28 Dec 1909. She married (1) HENRY WILLIAM SHERRILL. He was born on 29 Dec 1823 in North Carolina, USA. He died in 1863 in Delaware, USA.

       vii.   ELIHU WOFFORD was born on 25 Apr 1829 in Glen Springs, S.C.. He died in 1885. He married (1) PACIFIC BUFORD in 1853. He married (2) ELIZA in 1875.

       viii.   BENJAMIN WOFFORD was born on 10 Sep 1833.

       ix.   WILLIAM FOSTER WOFFORD was born on 13 Nov 1834 in South Carolina, USA. He died on 19 Jun 1908. He married F R Blanton on 22 Dec 1870. She was born on 07 Jan 1849. She died on 20 Jul 1888.

18.   **GREENBERRY[11] WOFFORD** (John[10], John[9], Abasalom[8], William[7], William[6], William[5], William Walford[4], Richard[3] Walford, William[2] Walford, William[1] Walford) was born on 17 Apr 1804 in Spartanburg Dist, S.C.. He died on 26 Apr 1864 in Jasper, Pickens Cty, Ga.. He married Precious Wofford, daughter of George West and Edith Colista McHanie, in 1824 in South Carolina. She was born about 1809 in South Carolina. She died on 11 Jun 1891 in Pickens, Georgia, USA.

Greenberry WOFFORD and Precious Wofford had the following children:

21.   i.   JOHN P[12] WOFFORD was born on 30 Oct 1825 in Spartanburg Dist, S.C.. He died on 03 Jan 1889 in Smyrna, Cobb Cty Ga.. He married (1) MARTHA UNKNOWN.

       ii.   BERRYMAN WOFFORD was born in 1829 in Spartanburg, Spartanburg, South Carolina, USA. He died in 1872 in Ft Smith Sebastian, Arkansas, USA.

       iii.   JANE WOFFORD was born in 1829 in , , South Carolina, USA. She died in 1925 in , Gordon, Georgia, USA.

       iv.   UNKNOWN WOFFORD was born in 1830 in , Spartanburg, South Carolina, USA. She died in 1840 in , Spartanburg, South Carolina, USA.

       v.   ELIZABETH JANE WOFFORD was born on 30 Jan 1830 in Spartanburg, South Carolina, USA. She died in 1925 in , Gordon, Georgia, USA.

       vi.   JOSEPH WOFFORD was born in 1834 in Spartanburg, South Carolina, USA. He died on 01 Jan 1864 in Atlanta, Georgia, USA.

       vii.   JOSEPH WOFFORD was born on 22 Nov 1834 in Spartanburg, Spartanburg, South Carolina, USA. He died on 13 Mar 1879 in Talking Rock, Pickens, Georgia, USA.

       viii.   BENJAMIN J WOFFORD was born on 30 Oct 1836 in Spartanburg Cty, S.C.. He died on 13 Jan 1913 in Blue Ridge, Fannin Cty, Ga.. He married (1) MALISSAA FERGUSON.

22.   ix.   JACOB WOFFORD was born on 07 Oct 1840 in Spartanburg County, South Carolina, USA. He died in 1863 in Norcross, Forsyth, Georgia, USA. He married Mary Jane HAYES on 14 Aug 1863 in Forsyth Cty, Ga.. She was born in 1842 in Union District 96, South Carolina. She died in Norcross, Gwinnett, Georgia, USA.

x.   EBER WOFFORD was born on 04 Apr 1844 in Spartanburg Dist, South Carolina, USA. He died on 04 Dec 1916 in Pickens Cty, Ga.. He married (1) SUDIE UNKNOWN.

xi.   MARY ANN WOFFORD was born on 27 Jan 1847 in Georgia, USA. She died on 04 May 1926 in Jasper, Pickens, Georgia, USA.

xii.   BENJAMIN WOFFORD was born about 1830 in SOUTH CAROLINA,USA. He died on 03 Jan 1889 in Smyrna, Cobb, Georgia, USA.

Generation 12

19.   JOHN FOSTER[12] WOFFORD (George[11], John[10], John[9], Abasalom[8], William[7], William[6], William[5], William Walford[4], Richard[3] Walford, William[2] Walford, William[1] Walford) was born on 14 Feb 1817 in South Carolina, USA. He died on 03 Mar 1884 in Gibson, Tennessee, USA. He married (2) MARY CUNNINGHAM on 23 Apr 1840 in Union, Georgia, USA. She was born on 24 Sep 1818. She died on 08 Apr 1856 in Forsyth, Georgia, USA.

John Foster WOFFORD had the following children:

i.   JOHN W[13] WOFFORD was born in 1838 in Georgia, USA. He died on 09 Oct 1862 in Bean Station, Tennessee, USA.

ii.   J ALBERT WOFFORD was born in Jan 1864 in Georgia, USA.

John Foster WOFFORD and Mary Cunningham had the following children:

iii.   FRANCES WOFFORD was born in 1841 in Forsyth, Georgia, USA.

iv.   FRANCES WOFFORD.

v.   GEORGE WOFFORD was born on 07 Apr 1843 in Forsyth, Georgia, USA. He died on 04 Sep 1908 in Gibson, Tennessee, USA.

vi.   HESTER WOFFORD.

vii.   MOSES WOFFORD was born on 20 Apr 1850 in Forsyth, Georgia, USA. He died on 09 Sep 1915 in Malden, Dunklin, Missouri, USA.

viii.   HESTER ANN WOFFORD was born in May 1850 in Forsyth, Georgia, USA.

ix.   JOHN WOFFORD was born in 1862 in Forsyth, Georgia, USA.

x.   MARY WOFFORD was born in Forsyth, Georgia, USA.

xi.   WILLIAM WOFFORD was born in Forsyth, Georgia, USA.

20.   AMANDA MELVINA[12] WOFFORD (George[11], John[10], John[9], Abasalom[8], William[7], William[6], William[5], William Walford[4], Richard[3] Walford, William[2] Walford, William[1] Walford) was born on 29 Sep 1827 in South Carolina, USA. She died on 28 Dec 1909. She married (1) HENRY WILLIAM SHERRILL. He was born on 29 Dec 1823 in North Carolina, USA. He died in 1863 in Delaware, USA.

Henry William Sherrill and Amanda Melvina WOFFORD had the following children:

i.   JOSEPH P[13] SHERRILL was born on 25 Dec 1850. He died on 21 Jan 1902 in Coweta, Georgia, USA.

ii.   MARY E SHERRILL was born on 24 Oct 1852.

iii.   RUTHA C SHERRILL was born on 03 Sep 1854.

iv.   MARTHA JANE SHERRILL was born on 24 Jul 1857.

v.   ELI STANHOPE SHERRILL was born on 07 Oct 1859 in Georgia, USA. He died on 11 Jan 1925 in Concord Forsyth, Georgia, USA.

vi.   SAROWE AMANDA SHERRILL was born on 01 Oct 1861.

21.   JOHN P[12] WOFFORD (Greenberry[11], John[10], John[9], Abasalom[8], William[7], William[6], William[5], William Walford[4], Richard[3] Walford, William[2] Walford, William[1] Walford) was born on 30 Oct 1825 in Spartanburg Dist, S.C.. He died on 03 Jan 1889 in Smyrna, Cobb Cty Ga.. He married (1) MARTHA UNKNOWN.

John P WOFFORD and Martha UNKNOWN had the following child:

7

    i.   BERRYMAN[13] WOFFORD was born in 1829.

22.   JACOB[12] WOFFORD (Greenberry[11], John[10], John[9], Abasalom[8], William[7], William[6], William[5], William Walford[4], Richard[3] Walford, William[2] Walford, William[1] Walford) was born on 07 Oct 1840 in Spartanburg County, South Carolina, USA. He died in 1863 in Norcross, Forsyth, Georgia, USA. He married Mary Jane HAYES on 14 Aug 1863 in Forsyth Cty, Ga.. She was born in 1842 in Union District 96, South Carolina. She died in Norcross, Gwinnett, Georgia, USA.

Jacob WOFFORD and Mary Jane HAYES had the following children:

23.   i.   ALFRED GREENBERRY[13] WOFFORD was born on 24 Mar 1867 in Norcross, Gwinnett Cty, Ga. He died on 08 Dec 1930 (Age: 63). He married Minnie Greer, daughter of Robert Simeon Greer and Emalyn, in 1888. She was born in Mar 1871 in Georgia. She died on 10 Jul 1957 in Fulton, Georgia (Age: 86 Years).

    ii.   RUBY WOFFORD. She died in Infancy.

24.   iii.   WILLIAM FOSTER WOFFORD was born on 08 Feb 1863 in Norcross, Gwinnett, Georgia, USA. He died in 1918 in Atlanta, Fulton Cty, Ga. He married Florence May HENSOLT, daughter of Heinrich Frederick HENSOLT and Mary CLARK, on 18 Nov 1888 in Norcross, Gwinnett, Georgia, USA. She was born on 08 Oct 1866 in Savannah, Ga.. She died on 06 Apr 1959 in Austell, Cobb Cty, Ga..

Generation 13

23.   ALFRED GREENBERRY[13] WOFFORD (Jacob[12], Greenberry[11], John[10], John[9], Abasalom[8], William[7], William[6], William[5], William Walford[4], Richard[3] Walford, William[2] Walford, William[1] Walford) was born on 24 Mar 1867 in Norcross, Gwinnett Cty, Ga. He died on 08 Dec 1930 (Age: 63). He married Minnie Greer, daughter of Robert Simeon Greer and Emalyn, in 1888. She was born in Mar 1871 in Georgia. She died on 10 Jul 1957 in Fulton, Georgia (Age: 86 Years).

Alfred Greenberry WOFFORD and Minnie Greer had the following children:

    i.   EMMA MAY[14] WOFFORD was born on 01 Sep 1888. She died on 26 Jul 1914. She married (1) J.R.SMITH.

25.   ii.   LOURY GREENBERRY WOFFORD was born on 23 Dec 1890 in Norcross, Georgia, USA. He died in May 1966 in Suwanee, Gwinnett, Georgia, USA (Age at Death: 75). He married (1) EDITH B WOFFORD. She was born about 1900 in Virginia.

    iii.   RUTH WOFFORD. She married (1) MCADAMS.

    iv.   MINNIE A WOFFORD was born about 1893 in Georgia.

24.   WILLIAM FOSTER[13] WOFFORD (Jacob[12], Greenberry[11], John[10], John[9], Abasalom[8], William[7], William[6], William[5], William Walford[4], Richard[3] Walford, William[2] Walford, William[1] Walford) was born on 08 Feb 1863 in Norcross, Gwinnett, Georgia, USA. He died in 1918 in Atlanta, Fulton Cty, Ga. He married Florence May HENSOLT, daughter of Heinrich Frederick HENSOLT and Mary CLARK, on 18 Nov 1888 in Norcross, Gwinnett, Georgia, USA. She was born on 08 Oct 1866 in Savannah, Ga.. She died on 06 Apr 1959 in Austell, Cobb Cty, Ga..

Notes for Florence May HENSOLT:
Fredrick Hensolt, father of Florie May Hensolt,was owner of a tanning factory near Savannah , Georgia,where he manufactured fine leather goods. The factory was burned during "Sherman's March through Georgia" in the War between the States. "Grammy", as Florie May was known, said she was born in a Negro slaves cabin after the "Big house" had been burned. (Family papers of W.E. Wofford Jr.)

William Foster WOFFORD and Florence May HENSOLT had the following children:

26.   i.   WILLIAM EARL[14] WOFFORD was born on 06 Nov 1889 in Norcross, Gwinnett, Georgia, USA. He died on 15 Dec 1959 in Cartersville, BartowCty, Ga. (Age: 70). He married Mary Louise Meroney, daughter of Charles L Meroney and Ellender L Nelson, on 06 Nov 1917 in Montevallo, Ala.. She was born on 06 Oct 1891 in Montevallo, Shelby, Alabama, USA. She died on 30 Dec 1949 in Cartersville,

B

Bartow, Georgia, USA.

27. ii. MARY CORRINE WOFFORD was born on 02 Jun 1894 in Fulton Cty Georgia, USA. She married Clifford Plaster HOPE on 17 Nov 1912 in Atlanta, Fulton Cty, Ga.. He was born on 29 Sep 1892.

iii. HOWARD WALKER WOFFORD was born in 1896. He died in 1899.

iv. ALFRED GREENBERRY WOFFORD was born on 26 Aug 1899 in Norcross, Gwinnett Cty, Ga.. He died in Mar 1967 in Nashville Tn, 37205. He married Mary Katherine IVEY in ?.

Generation 14

25. LOURY GREENBERRY[14] WOFFORD (Alfred Greenberry[13], Jacob[12], Greenberry[11], John[10], John[9], Abasalom[8], William[7], William[6], William[5], William Walford[4], Richard[3] Walford, William[2] Walford, William[1] Walford) was born on 23 Dec 1890 in Norcross, Georgia, USA. He died in May 1966 in Suwanee, Gwinnett, Georgia, USA (Age at Death: 75). He married (1) EDITH B WOFFORD. She was born about 1900 in Virginia.

Loury Greenberry WOFFORD and Edith B Wofford had the following children:

I. EDITH R[15] WOFFORD was born about 1924 in Virginia.

ii. JOHN G WOFFORD was born about 1926 in Virginia.

26. WILLIAM EARL[14] WOFFORD (William Foster[13], Jacob[12], Greenberry[11], John[10], John[9], Abasalom[8], William[7], William[6], William[5], William Walford[4], Richard[3] Walford, William[2] Walford, William[1] Walford) was born on 06 Nov 1889 in Norcross, Gwinnett, Georgia, USA. He died on 15 Dec 1959 in Cartersville, BartowCty, Ga. (Age: 70). He married Mary Louise Meroney, daughter of Charles L Meroney and Ellender L Nelson, on 06 Nov 1917 in Montevallo, Ala.. She was born on 06 Oct 1891 in Montevallo, Shelby, Alabama, USA. She died on 30 Dec 1949 in Cartersville, Bartow, Georgia, USA.

Notes for William Earl WOFFORD:
For William E Wofford Sr:
"Dr W.E.Wofford, president of the Bartow County Medical Society an local practicing physicians, was born in Norcross, Nov 6 , 1889, and was educated in Atlanta schools and at Emory University, from which he was graduated in1913 with the degree of MD.
After graduation Dr Wofford spent two years in hospital work in the New York Nursery and Child's hospital.
In March, 1925 ,the doctor moved to Cartersville to start his practice. He was named a member of the draft board in 1917-18 and served in that capacity until he enlisted in the United States Army in February, 1918. In July of that year he was called to service as a first lieutenant attached to the Medical Corps.After one month in training at Camp Greeleaf, Fort Oglethorpe, he was sent to Fort Myer, Va. In September he sailed for France landing at St.Nazaire and being sent to Tours. For ten months he was in service at the Central Prisoner of War Enclosure No. 1 where prisoners captured by American troops were sent.
......June 1929 Tribune News, Cartersville, Ga.(see complete text attached)

William Earl WOFFORD and Mary Louise Meroney had the following children:

28. i. WILLIAM EARL[15] WOFFORD JR was born on 02 Dec 1920 in Cartersville, Bartow Cty, Ga. He died on 07 Feb 1996 in Cartersville, Bartow Cty, Ga. He married Doris Virginia WHITFIELD, daughter of Western WHITFIELD and Stella M Campbell, on 02 Apr 1944 in Blue Ridge, Fannin, Georgia, USA. She was born on 22 Jun 1920 in Ducktown, Polk, Tennessee, USA. She died on 14 Dec 2010 in Cartersville, Bartow, Georgia, USA.

29. ii. MARY CORINNE WOFFORD was born on 21 Apr 1926 in Cartersville, Bartow, Georgia, USA. She died on 08 Feb 2013 in Cartersville Bartow Cty Ga. She married James Wingfield MORRIS, son of Marion Wingfield Morris and Marie Louise Morris, on 1ᵉ Jan 1948 in FPC Cartersville, Ga. He was born on 01 Sep 1924 in Augusta, Richmond Cty, Ga..

9

27. **MARY CORRINE**[14] **WOFFORD** (William Foster[13], Jacob[12], Greenberry[11], John[10], John[9], Abasalom[8], William[7], William[6], William[5], William Walford[4], Richard[3] Walford, William[2] Walford, William[1] Walford) was born on 02 Jun 1894 in Fulton Cty Georgia, USA. She married Clifford Plaster HOPE on 17 Nov 1912 in Atlanta, Fulton Cty, Ga.. He was born on 29 Sep 1892.

Clifford Plaster HOPE and Mary Corrine WOFFORD had the following child:

    30.   i.   MARION WILLENE[15] HOPE was born on 05 Sep 1913 in Fulton Cty, Ga.. She died in Apr 1981. She married (1) JOHN HOWARD BULLARD in ?. She married (2) ROLAND ROWELOFS on 11 May 1930 in ?.

Generation 15

28. **WILLIAM EARL**[15] **WOFFORD JR** (William Earl[14], William Foster[13], Jacob[12], Greenberry[11], John[10], John[9], Abasalom[8], William[7], William[6], William[5], William Walford[4], Richard[3] Walford, William[2] Walford, William[1] Walford) was born on 02 Dec 1920 in Cartersville, Bartow Cty, Ga. He died on 07 Feb 1996 in Cartersville, Bartow Cty, Ga. He married Doris Virginia WHITFIELD, daughter of Western WHITFIELD and Stella M Campbell, on 02 Apr 1944 in Blue Ridge, Fannin, Georgia, USA. She was born on 22 Jun 1920 in Ducktown, Polk, Tennessee, USA. She died on 14 Dec 2010 in Cartersville, Bartow, Georgia, USA.

William Earl WOFFORD Jr and Doris Virginia WHITFIELD had the following child:

    31.   i.   WILLIAM EARL[16] WOFFORD III was born on 20 Mar 1945 in Cartersville, Bartow Cty, Ga. He married (1) KERI ANNE CONNORS on 10 Jun 1994 in Brewster, Barnstable Cty, Massachusetts. He married (2) DONNA MARIE GRIPPO in ?. He married (3) LYNNE ELIZABETH LOONEY in ?.

29. **MARY CORINNE**[15] **WOFFORD** (William Earl[14], William Foster[13], Jacob[12], Greenberry[11], John[10], John[9], Abasalom[8], William[7], William[6], William[5], William Walford[4], Richard[3] Walford, William[2] Walford, William[1] Walford) was born on 21 Apr 1926 in Cartersville, Bartow, Georgia, USA. She died on 08 Feb 2013 in Cartersville Bartow Cty Ga. She married James Wingfield MORRIS, son of Marion Wingfield Morris and Marie Louise Morris, on 19 Jan 1948 in FPC Cartersville, Ga. He was born on 01 Sep 1924 in Augusta, Richmond Cty, Ga..

Notes for Mary Corinne WOFFORD:
Graduated Vanderbilt School of Nursing, Nashville, Tn 1948

Notes for James Wingfield MORRIS:
Graduate,USMA,1945:BS Aeronautical Engineering, Univ Michigan 1959: MA,International Affairs, George Washington Univ, 1964

James Wingfield MORRIS and Mary Corinne WOFFORD had the following children:

    32.   i.   MARY LOUISE[16] MORRIS was born on 03 May 1949 in Cartersville, Bartow, Georgia, USA. She married (1) SHELDON G. SPICHER III on 20 Dec 1970 in Charlottesville Va. He was born on 19 Jul 1948. She married (2) TIMOTHY CARR BRAMBLE, son of Roy H Bramble and Lois Jean Bennett, on 01 Feb 1985 in Dunwoody, Ga... He was born on 13 Mar 1952 in Detroit, Mich.

    33.   ii.   JAMES WINGFIELD MORRIS JR was born on 29 Oct 1950 in Cartersville, Bartow, Georgia, USA. He married Carolyn Ethel LYON, daughter of Robert Fredrick LYON and Mldred Virginia Shacklett, on 09 Jun 1973 in Marietta, Ga.. She was born on 14 Mar 1951 in Nashville, Davidson Cty, Tn.

    34.   iii.   WILLIAM CRANSTON MORRIS was born on 02 Mar 1954 in Cartersville, Bartow, Georgia, USA. He married Beverly Jane TIPTON, daughter of James Darrell{J.D.} TIPTON and Barbara Jean HAVENS, on 10 Jul 1976 in Maryville, Tennessee. She was born on 06 Feb 1954 in Maryville, Blount Cty, Tn.

    35.   iv.   BRIAN MERONEY MORRIS was born on 28 Jan 1961 in Washington D.C.. He married (1) JILL HAROLINE KING on 20 Aug 1983 in Cartersville, Ga.. She was born on 10 Aug 1959 in Rome, Floyd Cty, Ga.. He married (2) MICHELE ALLEN EWEN on 10 Jun 2000 in Dallas, Texas. She was born on 11 Jun 1967 in Denver, Co.

    36.   v.   PETER CHARLES MORRIS was born on 22 Jun 1962 in Arlington, Va. He married Frances Elizabeth ALLEN, daughter of Bona ALLEN IV and Jane KING, on 15 Jun 1985 in Dunwoody, Ga.. She was born on 26 Feb 1963.

10

30. **MARION WILLENE**[15] HOPE (Mary Corrine[14] WOFFORD, William Foster[13] WOFFORD, Jacob[12]
WOFFORD, Greenberry[11] WOFFORD, John[10] WOFFORD, John[9] WOFFORD, Abasalom[8]
Wofford, William[7] Wofford, William[6] Wofford, William[5] Wofford, William Walford[4] Wofford, Richard[3]
Walford, William[2] Walford, William[1] Walford) was born on 05 Sep 1913 in Fulton Cty, Ga.. She died
in Apr 1981. She married (1) **JOHN HOWARD BULLARD** in ?. She married (2) **ROLAND ROWELOFS** on
11 May 1930 in ?.

Roland ROWELOFS and Marion Willene HOPE had the following child:

      i.   HOPE[16] ROWELOFS was born in ?.

31. **WILLIAM EARL**[16] **WOFFORD III** (William Earl[15] Jr, William Earl[14], William Foster[13], Jacob[12],
Greenberry[11], John[10], John[9], Abasalom[8], William[7], William[6], William[5], William Walford[4], Richard[3]
Walford, William[2] Walford, William[1] Walford) was born on 20 Mar 1945 in Cartersville, Bartow Cty,
Ga. He married (1) **KERI ANNE CONNORS** on 10 Jun 1994 in Brewster, Barnstable Cty,
Massachusetts. He married (2) **DONNA MARIE GRIPPO** in ?. He married (3) **LYNNE ELIZABETH
LOONEY** in ?.

William Earl WOFFORD III and Keri Anne CONNORS had the following children:

      i.   WILLIAM EARL[17] WOFFORD IV was born on 23 Apr 1996 in Santa Monica, Los
           Angeles Cty, CA.

      ii.   JAMES FOSTER WOFFORD was born on 22 Dec 1998 in Sant Monica, Los Angeles
           Cty, CA.

32. **MARY LOUISE**[16] **MORRIS** (Mary Corinne[15] WOFFORD, William Earl[14] WOFFORD, William Foster[13]
WOFFORD, Jacob[12] WOFFORD, Greenberry[11] WOFFORD, John[10] WOFFORD, John[9]
WOFFORD, Abasalom[8] Wofford, William[7] Wofford, William[6] Wofford, William[5] Wofford, William
Walford[4] Wofford, Richard[3] Walford, William[2] Walford, William[1] Walford) was born on 03 May 1949
in Cartersville, Bartow, Georgia, USA. She married (1) **SHELDON G. SPICHER III** on 20 Dec 1970 in
Charlottesville Va. He was born on 19 Jul 1948. She married (2) **TIMOTHY CARR BRAMBLE**, son of
Roy H Bramble and Lois Jean Bennett, on 01 Feb 1985 in Dunwoody, Ga... He was born on 13
Mar 1952 in Detroit, Mich.

Notes for Mary Louise MORRIS:
Education:Mary Washington College/ BSN Univ Virginia School Nursing1970

Sheldon G. Spicher III and Mary Louise MORRIS had the following children:

      i.   AMY LYNNE[17] SPICHER was born on 11 May 1973 in Medford Or. She married
           Charles Andrew SHROPSHIRE on 15 May 1999 in Cartersville, Ga.. He was born
           on 30 Oct 1969 in Atlanta, Fulton Cty, Ga..

      ii.   SHANNON ELIZABETH SPICHER was born on 24 Oct 1975 in Atlanta, Fulton Cty Ga.
           She married Corey Wayne TOWE on 28 Apr 2001 in Cartersvile, Ga.. He was born
           on 09 Aug 1976.

      iii. PHILLIP MATTHEW SPICHER was born on 07 Apr 1978 in Atlanta, Fulton Cty, Ga. He
           married Kelly Christine Wittorff on 11 Jul 2009 in San Diego, California, USA.

Timothy Carr BRAMBLE and Mary Louise MORRIS had the following child:

      i.   REBECCA KATHLEEN[17] BRAMBLE was born on 02 Aug 1986 in Atlanta, Fulton Cty Ga.

33. **JAMES WINGFIELD**[16] **MORRIS JR** (Mary Corinne[15] WOFFORD, William Earl[14] WOFFORD, William
Foster[13] WOFFORD, Jacob[12] WOFFORD, Greenberry[11] WOFFORD, John[10] WOFFORD, John[9]
WOFFORD, Abasalom[8] Wofford, William[7] Wofford, William[6] Wofford, William[5] Wofford, William
Walford[4] Wofford, Richard[3] Walford, William[2] Walford, William[1] Walford) was born on 29 Oct 1950
in Cartersville, Bartow, Georgia, USA. He married Carolyn Ethel LYON, daughter of Robert
Fredrick LYON and Mldred Virginia Shacklett, on 09 Jun 1973 in Marietta, Ga.. She was born on

//

14 Mar 1951 in Nashville, Davidson Cty, Tn.

Notes for James Wingfield MORRIS Jr:
Education: BSArchitectural Technology,SouthernTechnical Institute 1972/Registered Arctitect
1982,BA,Education Kennesaw State Univ, 1995

Notes for Carolyn Ethel LYON:
Education: BS, Architectural Technology,Southern Technical Institute,1973 Registered
architect,22September 1988.

James Wingfield MORRIS Jr and Carolyn Ethel LYON had the following children:

     i.   MARY VIRGINIA[17] MORRIS was born on 18 Mar 1974 in Marietta, Cobb Cty, Ga.. She
married Timothy Adam BLACKWELL, son of Toby Long BLACKWELL and Sherrill
McGARITY, on 16 Dec 1995 in Marietta, Ga.. He was born on 20 Feb 1973 in
Atlanta, Fulton Cty, Ga.

        Notes for Mary Virginia MORRIS:
Education: BS,Middle Grades Education, Georgia Southern Univ.1995: MS,
Education,GSU,1997.

     ii.   JAMES LYON MORRIS was born on 11 Jan 1983 in Marietta, Cobb Cty, Ga. He
married Angela Swope, daughter of James Leonard Swope and Mana Sue
Campbell, on 27 May 2007 in Atlanta, Fulton Cty, Ga.Atlanta City Hall. She was
born on 07 Mar 1984 in Friendship, Harris, Texas.

        Notes for James Lyon MORRIS:
Education:BS, Middle Grades Education, Georgia Southern Univ, 2005

34.   **WILLIAM CRANSTON**[16] **Morris** (Mary Corinne[15] WOFFORD, William Earl[14] WOFFORD, William
Foster[13] WOFFORD, Jacob[12] WOFFORD, Greenberry[11] WOFFORD, John[10] WOFFORD, John[9]
WOFFORD, Abasalom[8] Wofford, William[7] Wofford, William[6] Wofford, William[5] Wofford, William
Walford[4] Wofford, Richard[3] Walford, William[2] Walford, William[1] Walford) was born on 02 Mar 1954
in Cartersville, Bartow, Georgia, USA. He married Beverly Jane TIPTON, daughter of James
Darrell{J.D.} TIPTON and Barbara Jean HAVENS, on 10 Jul 1976 in Maryville, Tennessee. She
was born on 06 Feb 1954 in Maryville, Blount Cty, Tn.

Notes for William Cranston MORRIS:
Education:BS,Civil engineering,USAFA, 1976: MS,AF Institute of Technology,WrightPatterson
AFBase, 1985

Notes for Beverly Jane TIPTON:
Education: BS,Home Economics, Univ of Tennessee, 1976: Teacher Certification Program, Univ of
Texas, San Antonio, 1994.　 NOTE:For Havens Family Story see John Lee Havens, media file.

William Cranston MORRIS and Beverly Jane TIPTON had the following children:

     i.   KEVIN JAMES[17] MORRIS was born on 11 Nov 1980 in Laughlin AFB (Del Rio Tx). He
married Jess Lynn Dayton, daughter of George Francis Dayton and Wendy Joy
Whitehead, on 17 Dec 2011 in Denver, Colorado, USA (Wellshire Presbyterian
Church). She was born on 01 May 1982 in Wheat Ridge Colorado.

        Notes for Kevin James MORRIS:
Education: BS,Computer Science,　Ga Tech,2003; MS, Computer Science, Ga
Tech(GA Instotute of Technology), 2005.

     ii.   EMILY SARAH MORRIS was born on 09 Aug 1985 in Wright Patterson AFB (Dayton
OH). She married Christopher John Matheis, son of Nicolas Aloyasius Matheis and
Lisa A Matheis, on 29 Oct 2011 in Cartersville, Bartow, Georgia, USA (First
Presbyterian Church). He was born on 27 Apr 1982 in Jasper Indiana (Memorial
Hospital).

        Notes for Emily Sarah MORRIS:
Education: BA, Liberal Arts, Colorado State Univ,2007

        Notes for Christopher John Matheis:

12

453

Education:Pittsburg State Univ, Pittsburg,KS, BS(Automotive Technology)2004

35.   **BRIAN MERONEY**[16] **MORRIS** (Mary Corinne[15] WOFFORD, William Earl[14] WOFFORD, William Foster[13] WOFFORD, Jacob[12] WOFFORD, Greenberry[11] WOFFORD, John[10] WOFFORD, John[9] WOFFORD, Abasalom[8] Wofford, William[7] Wofford, William[6] Wofford, William[5] Wofford, William Walford[4] Wofford, Richard[3] Walford, William[2] Walford, William[1] Walford) was born on 28 Jan 1961 in Washington D.C.. He married (1) **JILL HAROLINE KING** on 20 Aug 1983 in Cartersville, Ga.. She was born on 10 Aug 1959 in Rome, Floyd Cty, Ga.. He married (2) **MICHELE ALLEN EWEN** on 10 Jun 2000 in Dallas, Texas. She was born on 11 Jun 1967 in Denver, Co.

Notes for Brian Meroney MORRIS:
Graduate: BBA,North Georgia College, 1983

Brian Meroney MORRIS and Jill Haroline KING had the following child:

      i.   DAVID BRIAN[17] MORRIS was born on 05 Nov 1988 in Chicago, DuPage Cty, Ill.

Brian Meroney MORRIS and Michele Allen EWEN had the following children:

      ii.   JULIA GABRIELLE EWEN was born on 26 Aug 1993 in Dallas, Texas.

      iii.   PATRICK GATE EWEN was born in Apr 1995 in Dallas, Texas.

36.   **PETER CHARLES**[16] **MORRIS** (Mary Corinne[15] WOFFORD, William Earl[14] WOFFORD, William Foster[13] WOFFORD, Jacob[12] WOFFORD, Greenberry[11] WOFFORD, John[10] WOFFORD, John[9] WOFFORD, Abasalom[8] Wofford, William[7] Wofford, William[6] Wofford, William[5] Wofford, William Walford[4] Wofford, Richard[3] Walford, William[2] Walford, William[1] Walford) was born on 22 Jun 1962 in Arlington, Va. He married Frances Elizabeth ALLEN, daughter of Bona ALLEN IV and Jane KING, on 15 Jun 1985 in Dunwoody, Ga.. She was born on 26 Feb 1963.

Notes for Peter Charles MORRIS:
Graduate, USMA 1984, BS Aeronautics

Notes for Frances Elizabeth ALLEN:
Graduate Birmingham Southern,BA,1985,childhood education: TroyStateUniv, Ala, MA, Education.1990

Peter Charles MORRIS and Frances Elizabeth ALLEN had the following children:

      i.   KATELYN ELIZABETH[17] MORRIS was born on 21 Apr 1992 in Atlanta, Fulton Cty, Ga.

      ii.   SARA CAROLINE MORRIS was born on 17 Feb 1995 in Marietta, Cobb Cty, Ga..

Descendants of James Meroney

Generation 1

1. JAMES[1] MERONEY was born in 1650 in Clare, Ireland. He died in 1708 in Prince George's, Maryland, United States. He married (1) DELANCEY. She was born in 1705 in , , Clare, Ireland.

    James Meroney and DeLancey had the following child:

    2. i. JAMES[2] MERONEY was born in 1681 in , , Clare, Ireland. He died in Prince George's, Maryland, United States.

Generation 2

2. JAMES[2] MERONEY (James[1]) was born in 1681 in , , Clare, Ireland. He died in Prince George's, Maryland, United States.

    James Meroney had the following child:

    3. i. HENRY[3] MARONEY was born in 1700 in , Prince George's, Maryland, USA. He died in 1783 in Valentines, Frederick, Maryland, USA. He married Rachel Duvall, daughter of John DUVALL and Hester IJAMS, in 1749 in Anne Arundel, Maryland, United States. She was born on 14 Mar 1704 in All Hallowes, Anne Arundel, MD, USA. She died on 12 Jun 1783 in , Frederick, Maryland, USA.

Generation 3

3. HENRY[3] MARONEY (James[2] Meroney, James[1] Meroney) was born in 1700 in , Prince George's, Maryland, USA. He died in 1783 in Valentines, Frederick, Maryland, USA. He married Rachel Duvall, daughter of John DUVALL and Hester IJAMS, in 1749 in Anne Arundel, Maryland, United States. She was born on 14 Mar 1704 in All Hallowes, Anne Arundel, MD, USA. She died on 12 Jun 1783 in , Frederick, Maryland, USA.

    Henry MARONEY and Rachel Duvall had the following children:

    4. i. PHILIP DELANCY MERONEY was born in 1734 in Frederick, Frederick, Maryland, United States. He died on 03 Dec 1830 in Travelers Rest, Greenville, South Carolina, USA. He married (1) MARTHA SEMMES MASSEY on 03 Jan 1785 in Edenton, N.C.. She was born in 1757 in , Franklin, North Carolina, USA. She died on 10 Aug 1858 in Marshall, Buckingham, Virginia, USA. He married (2) SARAH NELSON in 1768 in Baltimore, Maryland, USA. She was born in 1738 in Maryland, USA. She died in 1777 in Frederick, Maryland, USA.

        ii. HANRY MARONEY was born in 1747 in , Gates, North Carolina, USA. He died in 1810 in , Gates, North Carolina, USA.

        iii. MARY MARONEY was born in , , Maryland, USA. She died in New Orleans, Orleans, Louisiana, USA.

Generation 4

4. PHILIP DELANCY MERONEY (Henry[3] MARONEY, James[2], James[1]) was born in 1734 in Frederick, Frederick, Maryland, United States. He died on 03 Dec 1830 in Travelers Rest, Greenville, South Carolina, USA. He married (1) MARTHA SEMMES MASSEY on 03 Jan 1785 in Edenton, N.C.. She was born in 1757 in , Franklin, North Carolina, USA. She died on 10 Aug 1858 in Marshall, Buckingham, Virginia, USA. He married (2) SARAH NELSON in 1768 in Baltimore, Maryland, USA. She was born in 1738 in Maryland, USA. She died in 1777 in Frederick, Maryland, USA.

    Philip Delancy Meroney and Martha Semmes Massey had the following children:

        i. WILLIAM BRITTON MERONEY was born on 19 Oct 1769 in Annapolis, Anne Arundel, Maryland, USA. He died on 01 Aug 1816 in , Person, North Carolina, USA.

        ii. PHILLIP D MERONEY was born in 1770 in Annapolis, Anne Arundel, Maryland, USA. He died in 1869 in Ducktown, Polk, Tennessee, USA.

        iii. SARAH MERONEY was born in 1771 in Annapolis, Anne Arundel, Maryland, USA. She died in 1827 in , Morgan, Georgia, USA.

        iv. HENRY MERONEY was born in 1786 in Travelers Rest, Greenville, South Carolina, USA. He died in 1862 in Medon, Madison, Tennessee, USA.

    5. v. LLOYD MERONEY was born in 1789 in , Chatham, North Carolina, USA. He married

I

Alice Edwards in 1808 in Greenville, South Carolina, USA. She was born in 1780 in , Greenville, South Carolina, USA. She died in , Greenville, South Carolina, USA.

vi. RACHEL MERONEY was born on 20 Sep 1791 in , Chatham, North Carolina, USA. She died on 27 Aug 1858 in , Bradley, Tennessee, USA.

vii. ELIZABETH MERONEY was born in 1797 in , Chatham, North Carolina, USA. She died in 1860.

viii. GEORGE WASHINGTON MERONEY was born in 1802 in , Laurens, South Carolina, USA. He died in 1845 in , Bradley, Tennessee, USA.

ix. DELIA MERONEY was born in 1816 in , Laurens, South Carolina, USA. She died on 14 Mar 1880 in Birmingham, Jefferson, Alabama, USA.

x. SALLIE MERONEY.

xi. LLOYD MERONEY was born in 1789 in , Chatham, North Carolina, USA.

xii. SALLY MERONEY.

Philip Delancy Meroney and Sarah NELSON had the following children:

xiii. WILLIAM BRITTON MERONEY was born in 1733 in Annapolis, Anne Arundel, Maryland, USA. He died on 01 Aug 1816 in , Person, North Carolina, USA.

iii. SARAH MERONEY was born in 1771 in Annapolis, Anne Arundel, Maryland, USA. She died in 1827 in , Morgan, Georgia, USA.

6. xv. PHILLIP DELANCEY MERONEY II was born in 1775 in Anapolis, Maryland, USA. He died in 1864 in Ducktown, Polk, Tennessee, USA (Age: 91). He married (1) MARTHA DAVIS. She was born in 1776. She died in 1853 (Age: 77). He married (3) MARTHA DAVIS in 1799. She was born in 1781 in South Carolina, USA. She died in 1853 in Hamblen, Tennessee, USA.

xvi. RACHEL SEMMS MERONEY was born in 1776. She died in 1818 in , Marshall, Mississippi, USA.

Generation 5

5. LLOYD MERONEY (Philip Delancy, Henry^3 MARONEY, James^2, James^1) was born in 1789 in , Chatham, North Carolina, USA. He married Alice Edwards in 1808 in Greenville, South Carolina, USA. She was born in 1780 in , Greenville, South Carolina, USA. She died in , Greenville, South Carolina, USA.

Notes for Lloyd Meroney:
1.Marrige:South Carolina in 1808 did not issue marrige licenses and accordingly kept no official records off marriges.Family Bible was usedto establishdate of Lloyd Meroney's Marriage in 1808 to Alice Edwards. WEWIII

Notes for Alice Edwards:
1.Marrige:South Carolina in 1808 did not issue marrige licenses and accordingly kept no official records off marriges.Family Bible was usedto establishdate of Lloyd Meroney's Marriage in 1808 to Alice Edwards. WEWIII

Lloyd Meroney and Alice Edwards had the following children:

7. i. PHILLIP L. MERONEY was born about 1809 in Columbiana, Shelby, Alabama, USA. He died on 28 Nov 1891 in Montevallo, Shelby, Alabama, USA. He married Martha Jane Richardson, daughter of Charles Richardson and Mary Ann, on 21 Sep 1846 in , Shelby, Alabama, USA. She was born on 04 Feb 1828 in Montevallo, Shelby, Alabama, USA. She died on 21 Oct 1903 in Montevallo, Shelby, Alabama, USA.

ii. THOMAS E MERONEY was born in 1812 in Tennessee, USA. He died in 1897 in Bibb, Alabama, USA.

iii. NOLAN I MERONEY was born on 22 Jan 1813 in Greenville, South Carolina, USA. He died on 24 Jun 1867 in Nacogdoches, Texas, USA.

8. iv. MARY G MERONEY was born on 13 Dec 1813 in Greenville, South Carolina, USA. She died on 08 Nov 1892 in Helena, Shelby, Mississippi, USA. She married Peter Harris in 1830. He was born in 1804 in Tennessee, USA. He died in 1870.

2

6. PHILLIP DELANCEY MERONEY II (Philip Delancy, Henry[3] MARONEY, James[2], James[1]) was born in 1775 in Anapolis, Maryland, USA. He died in 1864 in Ducktown, Polk, Tennessee, USA (Age: 91). He married (1) MARTHA DAVIS. She was born in 1776. She died in 1853 (Age: 77). He married (3) MARTHA DAVIS in 1799. She was born in 1781 in South Carolina, USA. She died in 1853 in Hamblen, Tennessee, USA.

Phillip Delancey MERONEY II had the following children:

10.   i.   PHILIP NELSON MERONEY was born on 30 Oct 1800 in Piedmont, South Carolina, USA. He died on 15 Feb 1872 in Sumner, Tennessee, USA (Age: 71). He married Elizabeth Reagan on 18 Jan 1820 in Blount, Tennessee, USA. She was born in 1799. She died in 1858 (Age: 59).

       ii.   WILLIAM HYDE MERONEY was born in 1802 in South Carolina, USA. He died in 1888 in Murphy, Cherokee, North Carolina, USA.

       iii.   AUGUSTUS DUVALL MERONEY was born on 06 Mar 1806 in Greene, Tennessee, USA. He died on 02 Jul 1885 in Coryell, Texas, USA.

       iv.   WALTER K MERONEY was born in 1810. He died in 1861 in Chatanooga, Hamilton, Tennessee, USA.

       v.   BENJAMIN DAVIS MERONEY was born on 10 May 1810 in Chatham, North Carolina, USA. He died on 23 Sep 1902 in Jacksonville, Calhoun, Alabama, USA.

       vi.   SARA NELSON MERONEY was born on 13 Feb 1814 in Pendleton, South Carolina, USA. She died on 10 Oct 1843 in Greene, Tennessee, USA.

Phillip Delancey MERONEY II and Martha Davis had the following child:

10.   i.   PHILIP NELSON MERONEY was born on 30 Oct 1800 in Piedmont, South Carolina, USA. He died on 15 Feb 1872 in Sumner, Tennessee, USA (Age: 71). He married Elizabeth Reagan on 18 Jan 1820 in Blount, Tennessee, USA. She was born in 1799. She died in 1858 (Age: 59).

Generation 6

7. PHILLIP L. MERONEY (Lloyd, Philip Delancy, Henry[3] MARONEY, James[2], James[1]) was born about 1809 in Columbiana, Shelby, Alabama, USA. He died on 28 Nov 1891 in Montevallo, Shelby, Alabama, USA. He married Martha Jane Richardson, daughter of Charles Richardson and Mary Ann, on 21 Sep 1846 in , Shelby, Alabama, USA. She was born on 04 Feb 1828 in Montevallo, Shelby, Alabama, USA. She died on 21 Oct 1903 in Montevallo, Shelby, Alabama, USA.

3

Phillip L. Meroney and Martha Jane Richardson had the following children:

11.   i.   MARY ANNA MERONEY was born on 09 Jan 1848 in Shelby, Alabama, USA. She died on 26 May 1924 in Shelby, Alabama, USA. She married (1) GEORGE WASHINGTON SHRINER in 1880. He was born on 15 Mar 1844. He died on 01 Apr 1905. She married (2) CHARLES VANPATTEN in 1862 in Alabama, USA. He died in 1862 in Civil War.

    ii.   DRUCILLA BOWDEN MERONEY was born on 13 Nov 1849 in Shelby, Alabama, USA. She died on 22 Aug 1932 in Montevallo, Shelby, Alabama, USA.

    iii.   EMMA MERONEY was born in 1855 in Shelby, Alabama, USA. She died in 1886 in Shelby, Alabama, USA.

12.   iv.   WALTER STORRS MERONEY was born on 13 Nov 1859 in , Shelby, Alabama, USA. He died on 15 Mar 1923. He married Mary Nelson on 05 Dec 1878 in Shelby, Alabama, USA.

13.   v.   CHARLES L MERONEY was born on 09 Jul 1869 in , Shelby, Alabama, USA. He died on 23 Feb 1930 in Montevallo, Shelby, Alabama, USA. He married Ellender L Nelson, daughter of Francis NELSON and Paralee ELLIOT, on 01 Oct 1890 in Columbiana, Shelby, Alabama, USA. She was born on 23 Oct 1866 in Columbiana, Shelby, Alabama, USA. She died on 14 Oct 1941 in Montevallo, Shelby, Alabama, USA.

8.   **MARY G MERONEY** (Lloyd, Philip Delancy, Henry[3] MARONEY, James[2], James[1]) was born on 13 Dec 1813 in Greenville, South Carolina, USA. She died on 08 Nov 1892 in Helena, Shelby, Mississippi, USA. She married Peter Harris in 1830. He was born in 1804 in Tennessee, USA. He died in 1870.

Peter Harris and Mary G MERONEY had the following children:

    i.   MARTHA J HARRIS was born in 1834 in Tennessee, USA.

    ii.   ELIZA HARRIS was born in 1838 in Tennessee, USA.

    iii.   PHILIP HARRIS was born in 1840 in Tennessee, USA.

    iv.   ROBERT DOUGLAS HARRIS was born in 1842 in Tennessee, USA.

    v.   ORLENA HARRIS was born in 1846 in Shelby, Tennessee, USA.

    vi.   MARY C HARRIS was born on 15 Aug 1846 in Montevallo, Shelby, Alabama, USA. She died on 30 Mar 1931 in Anniston, Calhoun, Alabama, USA.

    vii.   PETER HARRIS was born in 1848 in Tennessee, USA. He died in 1870 in Shelby, Tennessee, USA.

    viii.   NANCY HARRIS was born in Jul 1849 in Tennessee, USA.

    ix.   BUNCH E HARRIS was born in 1856 in Tennessee, USA.

    x.   THOMAS HARRIS was born in 1857 in Tennessee, USA.

    xi.   NEWTON HARRIS was born in May 1860 in Tennessee, USA.

9.   **MARY LOUISE MERONEY** (Lloyd, Philip Delancy, Henry[3] MARONEY, James[2], James[1]) was born on 06 Oct 1891 in Montevallo, Shelby, Alabama, USA. She died on 30 Dec 1949 in Cartersville, Bartow, Georgia, USA. She married William Earl WOFFORD, son of William Foster WOFFORD and Florence May HENSOLT, on 06 Nov 1917 in Montevallo, Ala.. He was born on 06 Nov 1889 in Norcross, Gwinnett, Georgia, USA. He died on 15 Dec 1959 in Cartersville, BartowCty, Ga. (Age: 70).

Notes for William Earl WOFFORD:
For William E Wofford Sr:
"Dr W.E.Wofford, president of the Bartow County Medical Society an local practicing physicians, was born in Norcross, Nov 6 , 1889, and was educated in Atlanta schools and at Emory University, from which he was graduated in1913 with the degree of MD.
After graduation Dr Wofford spent two years in hospital work in the New York Nursery and Child's hospital.
In March, 1925 ,the doctor moved to Cartersville to start his practice. He was named a member of

4

the draft board in 1917-18 and served in that capacity until he enlisted in the United States Army in February, 1918. In July of that year he was called to service as a first lieutenant attached to the Medical Corps.After one month in training at Camp Greeleaf, Fort Oglethorpe, he was sent to Fort Myer, Va. In September he sailed for France landing at St.Nazaire and being sent to Tours. For ten months he was in service at the Central Prisoner of War Enclosure No. 1 where prisoners captured by American troops were sent.
......June 1929 Tribune News, Cartersville, Ga.(see complete text attached)

William Earl WOFFORD and Mary Louise Meroney had the following children:

14.   WILLIAM EARL WOFFORD JR was born on 02 Dec 1920 in Cartersville, Bartow Cty, Ga. He died on 07 Feb 1996 in Cartersville, Bartow Cty, Ga. He married Doris Virginia WHITFIELD, daughter of Western WHITFIELD and Stella M Campbell, on 02 Apr 1944 in Blue Ridge, Fannin, Georgia, USA. She was born on 22 Jun 1920 in Ducktown, Polk, Tennessee, USA. She died on 14 Dec 2010 in Cartersville, Bartow, Georgia, USA.

15.   MARY CORINNE WOFFORD was born on 21 Apr 1926 in Cartersville, Bartow, Georgia, USA. She died on 08 Feb 2013 in Cartersville Bartow Cty Ga. She married James Wingfield MORRIS, son of Marion Wingfield Morris and Marie Louise Morris, on 19 Jan 1948 in FPC Cartersville, Ga. He was born on 01 Sep 1924 in Augusta, Richmond Cty, Ga..

10. **PHILIP NELSON MERONEY** (Phillip Delancey II, Philip Delancy, Henry[3] MARONEY, James[2], James[1]) was born on 30 Oct 1800 in Piedmont, South Carolina, USA. He died on 15 Feb 1872 in Sumner, Tennessee, USA (Age: 71). He married Elizabeth Reagan on 18 Jan 1820 in Blount, Tennessee, USA. She was born in 1799. She died in 1858 (Age: 59).

Philip Nelson Meroney and Elizabeth Reagan had the following child:

     i.   WILLIAM D MERONEY was born in 1823. He died in 1882 (Age: 59).

Generation 7

11. **MARY ANNA MERONEY** (Phillip L., Lloyd, Philip Delancy, Henry[3] MARONEY, James[2], James[1]) was born on 09 Jan 1848 in Shelby, Alabama, USA. She died on 26 May 1924 in Shelby, Alabama, USA. She married (1) **GEORGE WASHINGTON SHRINER** in 1880. He was born on 15 Mar 1844. He died on 01 Apr 1905. She married (2) **CHARLES VANPATTEN** in 1862 in Alabama, USA. He died in 1862 in Civil War.

George Washington Shriner and Mary Anna MERONEY had the following children:

     i.   ALMA SHRINER was born on 27 Jun 1882 in East St Louis, Missouri, USA.

     ii.   NELLE SHRINER was born in 1885 in East St Louis, Missouri, USA. She died in 1885 in East St Louis, Missouri, USA.

     iii.   PHILLIP LLOYD SHRINER was born on 27 Jun 1887 in East St Louis, Missouri, USA.

12. **WALTER STORRS MERONEY** (Phillip L., Lloyd, Philip Delancy, Henry[3] MARONEY, James[2], James[1]) was born on 13 Nov 1859 in , Shelby, Alabama, USA. He died on 15 Mar 1923. He married Mary Nelson on 05 Dec 1878 in Shelby, Alabama, USA.

Walter Storrs MERONEY and Mary Nelson had the following children:

     i.   LUCILLE MERONEY.

     ii.   LULAN MERONEY.

     iii.   CHARLES NERONEY.

13. **CHARLES L MERONEY** (Phillip L., Lloyd, Philip Delancy, Henry[3] MARONEY, James[2], James[1]) was born on 09 Jul 1869 in , Shelby, Alabama, USA. He died on 23 Feb 1930 in Montevallo, Shelby, Alabama, USA. He married Ellender L Nelson, daughter of Francis NELSON and Paralee ELLIOT, on 01 Oct 1890 in Columbiana, Shelby, Alabama, USA. She was born on 23 Oct 1866 in Columbiana, Shelby, Alabama, USA. She died on 14 Oct 1941 in Montevallo, Shelby, Alabama, USA.

Charles L Meroney and Ellender L Nelson had the following children:

5

9. i. <u>MARY LOUISE MERONEY</u> was born on 06 Oct 1891 in Montevallo, Shelby, Alabama, USA. She died on 30 Dec 1949 in Cartersville, Bartow, Georgia, USA. She married William Earl WOFFORD, son of William Foster WOFFORD and Florence May HENSOLT, on 06 Nov 1917 in Montevallo, Ala.. He was born on 06 Nov 1889 in Norcross, Gwinnett, Georgia, USA. He died on 15 Dec 1959 in Cartersville, BartowCty, Ga. (Age: 70).

Notes for William Earl WOFFORD:
For William E Wofford Sr:
"Dr W.E.Wofford, president of the Bartow County Medical Society an local practicing physicians, was born in Norcross, Nov 6 , 1889, and was educated in Atlanta schools and at Emory University, from which he was graduated in1913 with the degree of MD.
After graduation Dr Wofford spent two years in hospital work in the New York Nursery and Child's hospital.
In March, 1925 ,the doctor moved to Cartersville to start his practice. He was named a member of the draft board in 1917-18 and served in that capacity until he enlisted in the United States Army in February, 1918. In July of that year he was called to service as a first lieutenant attached to the Medical Corps.After one month in training at Camp Greeleaf, Fort Oglethorpe, he was sent to Fort Myer, Va. In September he sailed for France landing at St.Nazaire and being sent to Tours. For ten months he was in service at the Central Prisoner of War Enclosure No. 1 where prisoners captured by American troops were sent.
......June 1929 Tribune News, Cartersville, Ga.(see complete text attached)

ii. MILDRED NELSON MERONEY was born on 29 Apr 1893 in Montevallo, Shelby Cty, Al. She died on 19 Sep 1965 in Montevallo, Shelby, Alabama, USA.

iii. ETHEL GERTRUDE MERONEY was born on 09 Jul 1895 in Montevallo, Shelby, Alabama, USA. She died on 26 Feb 1985 in Aliceville, Pickens, Alabama, USA. She married William Battle Peebles, son of Frank Darrow Peebles, on 02 Sep 1920 in Montevallo, Shelby, Alabama, USA. He was born on 13 Jul 1887 in Vienna, Pickens, Alabama, USA. He died on 01 Oct 1963 in Montevallo, Shelby, Alabama, USA.

iv. ELOISE W MERONEY was born on 04 Apr 1898 in Montevallo, Shelby Cty, AL.. She died on 04 Nov 1996 in Birmingham, Al..

v. SON MERONEY was born on 31 Mar 1902 in Montevallo, Shelby, Alabama, USA. He died on 31 Mar 1902 in Montevallo, Shelby, Alabama, USA.

14. **WILLIAM EARL WOFFORD JR** (Mary Louise Meroney, Lloyd Meroney, Philip Delancy Meroney, Henry[3] MARONEY, James[2] Meroney, James[1] Meroney) was born on 02 Dec 1920 in Cartersville, Bartow Cty, Ga. He died on 07 Feb 1996 in Cartersville, Bartow Cty, Ga. He married Doris Virginia WHITFIELD, daughter of Western WHITFIELD and Stella M Campbell, on 02 Apr 1944 in Blue Ridge, Fannin, Georgia, USA. She was born on 22 Jun 1920 in Ducktown, Polk, Tennessee, USA. She died on 14 Dec 2010 in Cartersville, Bartow, Georgia, USA.

William Earl WOFFORD Jr and Doris Virginia WHITFIELD had the following child:

i. WILLIAM EARL WOFFORD III was born on 20 Mar 1945 in Cartersville, Bartow Cty, Ga. He married (1) KERI ANNE CONNORS on 10 Jun 1994 in Brewster, Barnstable Cty, Massachusetts. He married (2) DONNA MARIE GRIPPO in ?. He married (3) LYNNE ELIZABETH LOONEY in ?.

15. **MARY CORINNE WOFFORD** (Mary Louise Meroney, Lloyd Meroney, Philip Delancy Meroney, Henry[3] MARONEY, James[2] Meroney, James[1] Meroney) was born on 21 Apr 1926 in Cartersville, Bartow, Georgia, USA. She died on 08 Feb 2013 in Cartersville Bartow Cty Ga. She married James Wingfield MORRIS, son of Marion Wingfield Morris and Marie Louise Morris, on 19 Jan 1948 in FPC Cartersville, Ga. He was born on 01 Sep 1924 in Augusta, Richmond Cty, Ga..

Notes for Mary Corinne WOFFORD:
Graduated Vanderbilt School of Nursing, Nashville, Tn 1948

Notes for James Wingfield MORRIS:
Graduate,USMA,1945:BS Aeronautical Engineering, Univ Michigan 1959: MA,International Affairs, George Washington Univ, 1964

James Wingfield MORRIS and Mary Corinne WOFFORD had the following children:

 i. MARY LOUISE MORRIS was born on 03 May 1949 in Cartersville, Bartow, Georgia, USA. She married (1) SHELDON G. SPICHER III on 20 Dec 1970 in Charlottesville Va. He was born on 19 Jul 1948. She married (2) TIMOTHY CARR BRAMBLE, son of Roy H Bramble and Lois Jean Bennett, on 01 Feb 1985 in Dunwoody, Ga... He was born on 13 Mar 1952 in Detroit, Mich.

  Notes for Mary Louise MORRIS:
  Education:Mary Washington College/ BSN Univ Virginia School Nursing1970

 ii. JAMES WINGFIELD MORRIS JR was born on 29 Oct 1950 in Cartersville, Bartow, Georgia, USA. He married Carolyn Ethel LYON, daughter of Robert Fredrick LYON and Mldred Virginia Shacklett, on 09 Jun 1973 in Marietta, Ga.. She was born on 14 Mar 1951 in Nashville, Davidson Cty, Tn.

  Notes for James Wingfield MORRIS Jr:
  Education: BSArchitectural Technology,SouthernTechnical Institute 1972/Registered Arctitect 1982,BA,Education Kennesaw State Univ, 1995

  Notes for Carolyn Ethel LYON:
  Education: BS, Architectural Technology,Southern Technical Institute,1973 Registered architect,22September 1988.

 iii. WILLIAM CRANSTON MORRIS was born on 02 Mar 1954 in Cartersville, Bartow, Georgia, USA. He married Beverly Jane TIPTON, daughter of James Darrell{J.D.} TIPTON and Barbara Jean HAVENS, on 10 Jul 1976 in Maryville, Tennessee. She was born on 06 Feb 1954 in Maryville, Blount Cty, Tn.

  Notes for William Cranston MORRIS:
  Education:BS,Civil engineering,USAFA, 1976: MS,AF Institute of Technology,WrightPatterson AFBase, 1985

  Notes for Beverly Jane TIPTON:
  Education: BS,Home Economics, Univ of Tennessee, 1976: Teacher Certification Program, Univ of Texas, San Antonio, 1994. NOTE:For Havens Family Story see John Lee Havens, media file.

 iv. BRIAN MERONEY MORRIS was born on 28 Jan 1961 in Washington D.C.. He married (1) JILL HAROLINE KING on 20 Aug 1983 in Cartersville, Ga.. She was born on 10 Aug 1959 in Rome, Floyd Cty, Ga.. He married (2) MICHELE ALLEN EWEN on 10 Jun 2000 in Dallas, Texas. She was born on 11 Jun 1967 in Denver, Co.

  Notes for Brian Meroney MORRIS:
  Graduate: BBA,North Georgia College, 1983

 v. PETER CHARLES MORRIS was born on 22 Jun 1962 in Arlington, Va. He married Frances Elizabeth ALLEN, daughter of Bona ALLEN IV and Jane KING, on 15 Jun 1985 in Dunwoody, Ga.. She was born on 26 Feb 1963.

  Notes for Peter Charles MORRIS:
  Graduate, USMA 1984, BS Aeronautics

  Notes for Frances Elizabeth ALLEN:
  Graduate Birmingham Southern,BA,1985,childhood education: TroyStateUniv, Ala, MA, Education.1990

7

Generation 1

1. **ELISHA[1] NELSON** was born in 1755 in Greenville, North Carolina, USA. He died in 1829 in Greenville, South Carolina, USA. He married (1) **ELIZABETH ROGERS**. She was born in 1793 in Williamsburg, South Carolina, USA. She died in 1845 in Covington, Mississippi, USA.

   Elisha NELSON and Elizabeth Rogers had the following children:

       i.   DANIEL[2] NELSON. He died in Autauga, Alabama, USA.

2.   ii.   ELISHA NELSON was born on 01 Aug 1795 in Greenville, S.C.. He died on 30 Nov 1865 in Union Cty, AK. He married Jane BRASHER on 05 Oct 1813 in Greenville Dist S.C.. She was born on 11 Apr 1795 in Greenville, South Carolina, USA. She died on 13 Jan 1884 in Union, Arkansas, USA.

       iii.   ELIZABETH NELSON. She married (1) TILMAN DAVIS.

       iv.   HARDY NELSON was born in 1827. He died in 1901 in Miles Sw Shreveport, Louisiana, USA.

       v.   JANE NELSON. She married (1) WILLIAM AUSTIN.

       vi.   LAVICY NELSON. She married (1) THOMAS DACEY.

       vii.   MARY NELSON. She married (1) JEDEKIAH COOK.

       viii.   WILLIAM NELSON.

Generation 2

2. **ELISHA[2] NELSON** (Elisha[1]) was born on 01 Aug 1795 in Greenville, S.C.. He died on 30 Nov 1865 in Union Cty, AK. He married Jane BRASHER on 05 Oct 1813 in Greenville Dist S.C.. She was born on 11 Apr 1795 in Greenville, South Carolina, USA. She died on 13 Jan 1884 in Union, Arkansas, USA.

   Elisha NELSON and Jane BRASHER had the following children:

       i.   THORISA[3] NELSON was born on 15 Jul 1815. She died on 11 Jul 1905 in Union, Arkansas, USA.

       ii.   ELIZABETH NELSON was born on 16 Feb 1818. She died on 15 Nov 1890 in Collinsville, Texas, USA.

       iii.   SILVENES NELSON was born on 29 Jun 1820. He died on 30 Aug 1820 in Shelby, Alabama, USA.

       iv.   SIMPSON NELSON was born on 19 Jun 1822 in Shelby Cty, Al.. He died on 16 Sep 1889 in Union Parish, La.. He married Nancy ELLIOT on 06 Jul 1843 in Shelby Cty, Al..

3.   v.   FRANCIS NELSON was born on 25 Dec 1824 in Shelby Cty, Al. He died on 05 May 1897 in Shelby Cty, Al. He married Paralee ELLIOT, daughter of Frank P Elliott and Missouri Emily Elliott, on 19 Jan 1843 in Shelby Cty, Al.. She was born about 1876 in Columbiana, Shelby, Alabama, USA. She died on 06 Nov 1908 in Tuscaloosa, Shelby, Alabama, USA.

       vi.   HARDY NELSON was born on 13 Nov 1827 in Shelby Cty, Al.. He died on 28 Jun 1901 in Shelby, Alabama, USA.

       vii.   HENRY NELSON was born on 05 May 1830 in Shelby Cty, Al.. He died in 1863 in in Seige.

       viii.   WILLIAM DANIEL NELSON was born on 16 Mar 1833. He died on 22 Aug 1867 in

Union, Arkansas, USA.

    ix.   ELLENDER PARALEE NELSON was born on 13 Apr 1835. She died on 18 Jan 1918 in Dallas, Dallas, Texas, USA.

    x.   MARY JANE NELSON was born on 19 Jun 1839. She died on 19 Jun 1839 in Ashley, Arkansas, USA.

    xi.   ELISHA NELSON was born on 14 Jan 1884. He died in 1840 in Life.

Generation 3

3.   FRANCIS[3] NELSON (Elisha[2], Elisha[1]) was born on 25 Dec 1824 in Shelby Cty, Al. He died on 05 May 1897 in Shelby Cty, Al. He married Paralee ELLIOT, daughter of Frank P Elliott and Missouri Emily Elliott, on 19 Jan 1843 in Shelby Cty, Al.. She was born about 1876 in Columbiana, Shelby, Alabama, USA. She died on 06 Nov 1908 in Tuscaloosa, Shelby, Alabama, USA.

Francis NELSON and Paralee ELLIOT had the following children:

    i.   LOU QUINCY[4] NELSON was born in 1843 in , Shelby, Alabama, USA.

    ii.   LOU QUINCY NELSON was born in 1843 in , Shelby, Alabama, USA. She died in Nov 1914 in New Orleans, Jefferson, Louisiana, USA.

    iii.   JOHN NELSON was born in 1845. He died in 1935.

    iv.   ANNIE NELSON was born on 05 Feb 1847 in , , Alabama, USA. She died on 05 Nov 1876.

    v.   AMOS NELSON was born on 22 Jan 1849 in , , Alabama, USA. He died on 31 Mar 1913 in Shelby, Alabama, USA.

    vi.   MARY ELIZABETH NELSON was born on 20 Mar 1855. She died on 20 Jun 1929.

    vii.   SHELBY WALKER NELSON was born on 30 Jan 1858 in , , Alabama, USA. He died on 04 Jul 1928.

    viii.   WYLIE SANDERS NELSON was born on 12 Apr 1859 in , , Alabama, USA. He died on 03 Aug 1914 in , , Alabama, USA.

    ix.   WILL NELSON NELSON was born in 1860 in , , Alabama, USA. He died in 1897.

4.   x.   ELLENDER L NELSON was born on 23 Oct 1866 in Columbiana, Shelby, Alabama, USA. She died on 14 Oct 1941 in Montevallo, Shelby, Alabama, USA. She married Charles L Meroney, son of Phillip L. Meroney and Martha Jane Richardson, on 01 Oct 1890 in Columbiana, Shelby, Alabama, USA. He was born on 09 Jul 1869 in , Shelby, Alabama, USA. He died on 23 Feb 1930 in Montevallo, Shelby, Alabama, USA.

Generation 4

4.   ELLENDER L[4] NELSON (Francis[3], Elisha[2], Elisha[1]) was born on 23 Oct 1866 in Columbiana, Shelby, Alabama, USA. She died on 14 Oct 1941 in Montevallo, Shelby, Alabama, USA. She married Charles L Meroney, son of Phillip L. Meroney and Martha Jane Richardson, on 01 Oct 1890 in Columbiana, Shelby, Alabama, USA. He was born on 09 Jul 1869 in , Shelby, Alabama, USA. He died on 23 Feb 1930 in Montevallo, Shelby, Alabama, USA.

Charles L Meroney and Ellender L Nelson had the following children:

5.   i.   MARY LOUISE[5] MERONEY was born on 06 Oct 1891 in Montevallo, Shelby, Alabama, USA. She died on 30 Dec 1949 in Cartersville, Bartow, Georgia, USA. She married William Earl WOFFORD, son of William Foster WOFFORD and Florence May HENSOLT, on 06 Nov 1917 in Montevallo, Ala.. He was born on 06 Nov 1889 in Norcross, Gwinnett, Georgia, USA. He died on 15 Dec 1959 in Cartersville, BartowCty, Ga. (Age: 70).

    ii.   MILDRED NELSON MERONEY was born on 29 Apr 1893 in Montevallo, Shelby Cty, Al. She died on 19 Sep 1965 in Montevallo, Shelby, Alabama, USA.

6.   iii.   ETHEL GERTRUDE MERONEY was born on 09 Jul 1895 in Montevallo, Shelby, Alabama, USA. She died on 26 Feb 1985 in Aliceville, Pickens, Alabama, USA. She married William Battle Peebles, son of Frank Darrow Peebles, on 02 Sep 1920 in

2

Montevallo, Shelby, Alabama, USA. He was born on 13 Jul 1887 in Vienna, Pickens, Alabama, USA. He died on 01 Oct 1963 in Montevallo, Shelby, Alabama, USA.

 iv. ELOISE W MERONEY was born on 04 Apr 1898 in Montevallo, Shelby Cty, AL.. She died on 04 Nov 1996 in Birmingham, Al..

 v. SON MERONEY was born on 31 Mar 1902 in Montevallo, Shelby, Alabama, USA. He died on 31 Mar 1902 in Montevallo, Shelby, Alabama, USA.

Generation 5

5. MARY LOUISE[5] MERONEY (Ellender L[4] Nelson, Francis[3] NELSON, Elisha[2] NELSON, Elisha[1] NELSON) was born on 06 Oct 1891 in Montevallo, Shelby, Alabama, USA. She died on 30 Dec 1949 in Cartersville, Bartow, Georgia, USA. She married William Earl WOFFORD, son of William Foster WOFFORD and Florence May HENSOLT, on 06 Nov 1917 in Montevallo, Ala.. He was born on 06 Nov 1889 in Norcross, Gwinnett, Georgia, USA. He died on 15 Dec 1959 in Cartersville, BartowCty, Ga. (Age: 70).

Notes for William Earl WOFFORD:
For William E Wofford Sr:
"Dr W.E.Wofford, president of the Bartow County Medical Society an local practicing physicians, was born in Norcross, Nov 6 , 1889, and was educated in Atlanta schools and at Emory University, from which he was graduated in1913 with the degree of MD.
After graduation Dr Wofford spent two years in hospital work in the New York Nursery and Child's hospital.
In March, 1925 ,the doctor moved to Cartersville to start his practice. He was named a member of the draft board in 1917-18 and served in that capacity until he enlisted in the United States Army in February, 1918. In July of that year he was called to service as a first lieutenant attached to the Medical Corps.After one month in training at Camp Greeleaf, Fort Oglethorpe, he was sent to Fort Myer, Va. In September he sailed for France landing at St.Nazaire and being sent to Tours. For ten months he was in service at the Central Prisoner of War Enclosure No. 1 where prisoners captured by American troops were sent.
......June 1929 Tribune News, Cartersville, Ga.(see complete text attached)

William Earl WOFFORD and Mary Louise Meroney had the following children:

 7. i. WILLIAM EARL[6] WOFFORD JR was born on 02 Dec 1920 in Cartersville, Bartow Cty, Ga. He died on 07 Feb 1996 in Cartersville, Bartow Cty, Ga. He married Doris Virginia WHITFIELD, daughter of Western WHITFIELD and Stella M Campbell, on 02 Apr 1944 in Blue Ridge, Fannin, Georgia, USA. She was born on 22 Jun 1920 in Ducktown, Polk, Tennessee, USA. She died on 14 Dec 2010 in Cartersville, Bartow, Georgia, USA.

 8. ii. MARY CORINNE WOFFORD was born on 21 Apr 1926 in Cartersville, Bartow, Georgia, USA. She died on 08 Feb 2013 in Cartersville Bartow Cty Ga. She married James Wingfield MORRIS, son of Marion Wingfield Morris and Marie Louise Morris, on 19 Jan 1948 in FPC Cartersville, Ga. He was born on 01 Sep 1924 in Augusta, Richmond Cty, Ga..

6. ETHEL GERTRUDE[5] MERONEY (Ellender L[4] Nelson, Francis[3] NELSON, Elisha[2] NELSON, Elisha[1] NELSON) was born on 09 Jul 1895 in Montevallo, Shelby, Alabama, USA. She died on 26 Feb 1985 in Aliceville, Pickens, Alabama, USA. She married William Battle Peebles, son of Frank Darrow Peebles, on 02 Sep 1920 in Montevallo, Shelby, Alabama, USA. He was born on 13 Jul 1887 in Vienna, Pickens, Alabama, USA. He died on 01 Oct 1963 in Montevallo, Shelby, Alabama, USA.

William Battle Peebles and Ethel Gertrude Meroney had the following children:

 9. i. BETTY ELLEN PEEBLES.[6] KING was born on 17 Oct 1921 in Aliceville, AL (Pickens Cty). She died on 22 Aug 2008 in Birmingham, Al.. She married Harris Newton King, son of John Parrish King and Nannie Nabors ward, on 20 Jan 1945 in Aliceville, Pickens Co, AL. He was born on 10 Jul 1914 in Columbiana, Shelby, Alabama, USA. He died on 11 Apr 1995 in Anniston, Calhoun, Alabama, United States of America.

10.   ii.   WILLIAM BATTLE PEBBLES JR was born on 07 Dec 1923 in Aliceville, Pickens, Alabama. He died on 28 May 2010 in Aliceville, Pickens, Alabama. He married Sara Wood, daughter of Allen Simpson Wood and Ida Elma Burkhalter, on 29 Dec 1963 in Pickens, Alabama, USA. She was born on 27 Dec 1935 in Pickens Co, AL.

Generation 6

7.   WILLIAM EARL[6] WOFFORD JR (Mary Louise[5] Meroney, Ellender L[4] Nelson, Francis[3] NELSON, Elisha[2] NELSON, Elisha[1] NELSON) was born on 02 Dec 1920 in Cartersville, Bartow Cty, Ga. He died on 07 Feb 1996 in Cartersville, Bartow Cty, Ga. He married Doris Virginia WHITFIELD, daughter of Western WHITFIELD and Stella M Campbell, on 02 Apr 1944 in Blue Ridge, Fannin, Georgia, USA. She was born on 22 Jun 1920 in Ducktown, Polk, Tennessee, USA. She died on 14 Dec 2010 in Cartersville, Bartow, Georgia, USA.

William Earl WOFFORD Jr and Doris Virginia WHITFIELD had the following child:

11.   i.   WILLIAM EARL[7] WOFFORD III was born on 20 Mar 1945 in Cartersville, Bartow Cty, Ga. He married (1) KERI ANNE CONNORS on 10 Jun 1994 in Brewster, Barnstable Cty, Massachusetts. He married (2) DONNA MARIE GRIPPO in ?. He married (3) LYNNE ELIZABETH LOONEY in ?.

8.   MARY CORINNE[6] WOFFORD (Mary Louise[5] Meroney, Ellender L[4] Nelson, Francis[3] NELSON, Elisha[2] NELSON, Elisha[1] NELSON) was born on 21 Apr 1926 in Cartersville, Bartow, Georgia, USA. She died on 08 Feb 2013 in Cartersville Bartow Cty Ga. She married James Wingfield MORRIS, son of Marion Wingfield Morris and Marie Louise Morris, on 19 Jan 1948 in FPC Cartersville, Ga. He was born on 01 Sep 1924 in Augusta, Richmond Cty, Ga..

Notes for Mary Corinne WOFFORD:
Graduated Vanderbilt School of Nursing, Nashville, Tn 1948

Notes for James Wingfield MORRIS:
Graduate,USMA,1945:BS Aeronautical Engineering, Univ Michigan 1959: MA,International Affairs, George Washington Univ, 1964

James Wingfield MORRIS and Mary Corinne WOFFORD had the following children:

12.   i.   MARY LOUISE[7] MORRIS was born on 03 May 1949 in Cartersville, Bartow, Georgia, USA. She married (1) SHELDON G. SPICHER III on 20 Dec 1970 in Charlottesville Va. He was born on 19 Jul 1948. She married (2) TIMOTHY CARR BRAMBLE, son of Roy H Bramble and Lois Jean Bennett, on 01 Feb 1985 in Dunwoody, Ga... He was born on 13 Mar 1952 in Detroit, Mich.

13.   ii.   JAMES WINGFIELD MORRIS JR was born on 29 Oct 1950 in Cartersville, Bartow, Georgia, USA. He married Carolyn Ethel LYON, daughter of Robert Fredrick LYON and Mldred Virginia Shacklett, on 09 Jun 1973 in Marietta, Ga.. She was born on 14 Mar 1951 in Nashville, Davidson Cty, Tn.

14.   iii.   WILLIAM CRANSTON MORRIS was born on 02 Mar 1954 in Cartersville, Bartow, Georgia, USA. He married Beverly Jane TIPTON, daughter of James Darrell{J.D.} TIPTON and Barbara Jean HAVENS, on 10 Jul 1976 in Maryville, Tennessee. She was born on 06 Feb 1954 in Maryville, Blount Cty, Tn.

15.   iv.   BRIAN MERONEY MORRIS was born on 28 Jan 1961 in Washington D.C.. He married (1) JILL HAROLINE KING on 20 Aug 1983 in Cartersville, Ga.. She was born on 10 Aug 1959 in Rome, Floyd Cty, Ga.. He married (2) MICHELE ALLEN EWEN on 10 Jun 2000 in Dallas, Texas. She was born on 11 Jun 1967 in Denver, Co.

16.   v.   PETER CHARLES MORRIS was born on 22 Jun 1962 in Arlington, Va. He married Frances Elizabeth ALLEN, daughter of Bona ALLEN IV and Jane KING, on 15 Jun 1985 in Dunwoody, Ga.. She was born on 26 Feb 1963.

9.   BETTY ELLEN PEEBLES.[6] KING (Ethel Gertrude[5] Meroney, Ellender L[4] Nelson, Francis[3] NELSON, Elisha[2] NELSON, Elisha[1] NELSON) was born on 17 Oct 1921 in Aliceville, AL (Pickens Cty). She died on 22 Aug 2008 in Birmingham, Al.. She married Harris Newton King, son of John Parrish King and Nannie Nabors ward, on 20 Jan 1945 in Aliceville, Pickens Co, AL. He was born on 10 Jul 1914 in Columbiana, Shelby, Alabama, USA. He died on 11 Apr 1995 in Anniston, Calhoun, Alabama, United States of America.

Harris Newton King and Betty Ellen Peebles. King had the following child:

<ul>
<li>17.   i.   BETTY ELLEN[7] KING was born on 06 Oct 1945 in Childersburg, Talladega, Alabama, USA. She died on 01 Feb 2009 in Danville, Danville City, Virginia. She married (1) JR LUTHER HERSCHEL HAMRICK. She married (2) BILLY JOE HODNETT, son of George Houston Hodnett and Janie Gaylor, on 03 Feb 1968 in Anniston, Calhoun, Alabama. He was born on 15 Sep 1936 in Fairfax, Chambers, Alabama, USA. He died on 28 May 1977 in Birmingham, Jefferson, Alabama, USA. She married (3) JACK NILES WILKERSON.</li>
</ul>

10.   WILLIAM BATTLE[6] PEBBLES JR (Ethel Gertrude[5] Meroney, Ellender L[4] Nelson, Francis[3] NELSON, Elisha[2] NELSON, Elisha[1] NELSON) was born on 07 Dec 1923 in Aliceville, Pickens, Alabama. He died on 28 May 2010 in Aliceville, Pickens, Alabama. He married Sara Wood, daughter of Allen Simpson Wood and Ida Elma Burkhalter, on 29 Dec 1963 in Pickens, Alabama, USA. She was born on 27 Dec 1935 in Pickens Co, AL.

Notes for William Battle Pebbles Jr:
Religion: United Methodist. Burial: Oak Grove -Franconia Cemetery, Aliceville, Pickens Cty, Alabama. Marriage : near Gordo, Pickens Cty , Ala.(home of Elma B Wood).Occpation:Farmer, Salesman,CocaCola Bottling Co.Aliceville, Ala

William Battle Pebbles Jr and Sara Wood had the following children:

<ul>
<li>18.   i.   SARA ELIZABETH[7] PEBBLES was born on 26 Jan 1967 in Tuscaloosa ALA. She married Richard Lowery Johnson, son of John Henry Johnson and Etta Oree Cullum, on 11 Jul 1987 in Aliceville, Pickens Co, AL. He was born on 22 Jan 1952 in Meridian Lauderdale, Mississippi, USA.</li>
<li>19.   ii.   JULIE CELESTE PEBBLES was born on 18 Dec 1968 in Tuscaloosa ALA. She married Kenneth Grey Hankins, son of James Earl Hankins and Betty Irene Eads, on 12 Aug 1989 in Aliceville, Pickens Co, AL. He was born on 08 Jun 1962 in Alamorgordo, Otero, New Mexico, USA.</li>
<li>20.   iii.   VIRGINIA ELOISE PEBBLES was born on 10 Nov 1970 in Tuscaloosa ALA. She married Michael Dwain Latham, son of Richard Gerald Latham and Shelby Bridges, on 13 Jun 1992 in Aliceville, Pickens Co, AL. He was born on 23 Jul 1962 in Tuscaloosa ALA.</li>
</ul>

Generation 7

11.   WILLIAM EARL[7] WOFFORD III (William Earl[6] Jr, Mary Louise[5] Meroney, Ellender L[4] Nelson, Francis[3] NELSON, Elisha[2] NELSON, Elisha[1] NELSON) was born on 20 Mar 1945 in Cartersville, Bartow Cty, Ga. He married (1) KERI ANNE CONNORS on 10 Jun 1994 in Brewster, Barnstable Cty, Massachusetts. He married (2) DONNA MARIE GRIPPO in ?. He married (3) LYNNE ELIZABETH LOONEY in ?.

William Earl WOFFORD III and Keri Anne CONNORS had the following children:

<ul>
<li>i.   WILLIAM EARL[8] WOFFORD IV was born on 23 Apr 1996 in Santa Monica, Los Angeles Cty, CA.</li>
<li>ii.   JAMES FOSTER WOFFORD was born on 22 Dec 1998 in Sant Monica, Los Angeles Cty, CA.</li>
</ul>

12.   MARY LOUISE[7] MORRIS (Mary Corinne[6] WOFFORD, Mary Louise[5] Meroney, Ellender L[4] Nelson, Francis[3] NELSON, Elisha[2] NELSON, Elisha[1] NELSON) was born on 03 May 1949 in Cartersville, Bartow, Georgia, USA. She married (1) SHELDON G. SPICHER III on 20 Dec 1970 in Charlottesville Va. He was born on 19 Jul 1948. She married (2) TIMOTHY CARR BRAMBLE, son of Roy H Bramble and Lois Jean Bennett, on 01 Feb 1985 in Dunwoody, Ga... He was born on 13 Mar 1952 in Detroit, Mich.

Notes for Mary Louise MORRIS:
Education:Mary Washington College/ BSN Univ Virginia School Nursing1970

Sheldon G. Spicher III and Mary Louise MORRIS had the following children:

<ul>
<li>i.   AMY LYNNE[8] SPICHER was born on 11 May 1973 in Medford Or. She married Charles Andrew SHROPSHIRE on 15 May 1999 in Cartersville, Ga.. He was born on 30 Oct</li>
</ul>

1969 in Atlanta, Fulton Cty, Ga..

    ii.   SHANNON ELIZABETH SPICHER was born on 24 Oct 1975 in Atlanta, Fulton Cty Ga. She married Corey Wayne TOWE on 28 Apr 2001 in Cartersvile, Ga.. He was born on 09 Aug 1976.

    iii.   PHILLIP MATTHEW SPICHER was born on 07 Apr 1978 in Atlanta, Fulton Cty, Ga. He married Kelly Christine Wittorff on 11 Jul 2009 in San Diego, California, USA.

Timothy Carr BRAMBLE and Mary Louise MORRIS had the following child:

    i.   REBECCA KATHLEEN[8] BRAMBLE was born on 02 Aug 1986 in Atlanta, Fulton Cty Ga.

13.   **JAMES WINGFIELD[7] MORRIS JR** (Mary Corinne[6] WOFFORD, Mary Louise[5] Meroney, Ellender L[4] Nelson, Francis[3] NELSON, Elisha[2] NELSON, Elisha[1] NELSON) was born on 29 Oct 1950 in Cartersville, Bartow, Georgia, USA. He married Carolyn Ethel LYON, daughter of Robert Fredrick LYON and Mldred Virginia Shacklett, on 09 Jun 1973 in Marietta, Ga.. She was born on 14 Mar 1951 in Nashville, Davidson Cty, Tn.

Notes for James Wingfield MORRIS Jr:
Education: BSArchitectural Technology,SouthernTechnical Institute 1972/Registered Arctitect 1982,BA,Education Kennesaw State Univ, 1995

Notes for Carolyn Ethel LYON:
Education: BS, Architectural Technology,Southern Technical Institute,1973 Registered architect,22September 1988.

James Wingfield MORRIS Jr and Carolyn Ethel LYON had the following children:

    i.   MARY VIRGINIA[8] MORRIS was born on 18 Mar 1974 in Marietta, Cobb Cty, Ga.. She married Timothy Adam BLACKWELL, son of Toby Long BLACKWELL and Sherrill McGARITY, on 16 Dec 1995 in Marietta, Ga.. He was born on 20 Feb 1973 in Atlanta, Fulton Cty, Ga.

    Notes for Mary Virginia MORRIS:
    Education: BS,Middle Grades Education, Georgia Southern Univ.1995: MS, Education,GSU,1997.

    ii.   JAMES LYON MORRIS was born on 11 Jan 1983 in Marietta, Cobb Cty, Ga. He married Angela Swope, daughter of James Leonard Swope and Mana Sue Campbell, on 27 May 2007 in Atlanta, Fulton Cty, Ga.Atlanta City Hall. She was born on 07 Mar 1984 in Friendship, Harris, Texas.

    Notes for James Lyon MORRIS:
    Education:BS, Middle Grades Education, Georgia Southern Univ, 2005

14.   **WILLIAM CRANSTON[7] MORRIS** (Mary Corinne[6] WOFFORD, Mary Louise[5] Meroney, Ellender L[4] Nelson, Francis[3] NELSON, Elisha[2] NELSON, Elisha[1] NELSON) was born on 02 Mar 1954 in Cartersville, Bartow, Georgia, USA. He married Beverly Jane TIPTON, daughter of James Darrell{J.D.} TIPTON and Barbara Jean HAVENS, on 10 Jul 1976 in Maryville, Tennessee. She was born on 06 Feb 1954 in Maryville, Blount Cty, Tn.

Notes for William Cranston MORRIS:
Education:BS,Civil engineering,USAFA, 1976: MS,AF Institute of Technology,WrightPatterson AFBase, 1985

Notes for Beverly Jane TIPTON:
Education: BS,Home Economics, Univ of Tennessee, 1976: Teacher Certification Program, Univ of Texas, San Antonio, 1994.   NOTE:For Havens Family Story see John Lee Havens, media file.

William Cranston MORRIS and Beverly Jane TIPTON had the following children:

    i.   KEVIN JAMES[8] MORRIS was born on 11 Nov 1980 in Laughlin AFB (Del Rio Tx). He

married Jess Lynn Dayton, daughter of George Francis Dayton and Wendy Joy Whitehead, on 17 Dec 2011 in Denver, Colorado, USA (Wellshire Presbyterian Church). She was born on 01 May 1982 in Wheat Ridge Colorado.

Notes for Kevin James MORRIS:
Education: BS,Computer Science, Ga Tech,2003; MS, Computer Science, Ga Tech(GA Instotute of Technology), 2005.

ii.   EMILY SARAH MORRIS was born on 09 Aug 1985 in Wright Patterson AFB (Dayton OH). She married Christopher John Matheis, son of Nicolas Aloyasius Matheis and Lisa A Matheis, on 29 Oct 2011 in Cartersville, Bartow, Georgia, USA (First Presbyterian Church). He was born on 27 Apr 1982 in Jasper Indiana (Memorial Hospital).

Notes for Emily Sarah MORRIS:
Education: BA, Liberal Arts, Colorado State Univ,2007

Notes for Christopher John Matheis:
Education:Pittsburg State Univ, Pittsburg,KS, BS(Automotive Technology)2004

15.   BRIAN MERONEY[7] MORRIS (Mary Corinne[6] WOFFORD, Mary Louise[5] Meroney, Ellender L[4] Nelson, Francis[3] NELSON, Elisha[2] NELSON, Elisha[1] NELSON) was born on 28 Jan 1961 in Washington D.C.. He married (1) JILL HAROLINE KING on 20 Aug 1983 in Cartersville, Ga.. She was born on 10 Aug 1959 in Rome, Floyd Cty, Ga.. He married (2) MICHELE ALLEN EWEN on 10 Jun 2000 in Dallas, Texas. She was born on 11 Jun 1967 in Denver, Co.

Notes for Brian Meroney MORRIS:
Graduate: BBA,North Georgia College, 1983

Brian Meroney MORRIS and Jill Haroline KING had the following child:

i.   DAVID BRIAN[8] MORRIS was born on 05 Nov 1988 in Chicago, DuPage Cty, Ill.

Brian Meroney MORRIS and Michele Allen EWEN had the following children:

ii.   JULIA GABRIELLE EWEN was born on 26 Aug 1993 in Dallas, Texas.

iii.   PATRICK GATE EWEN was born in Apr 1995 in Dallas, Texas.

16.   PETER CHARLES[7] MORRIS (Mary Corinne[6] WOFFORD, Mary Louise[5] Meroney, Ellender L[4] Nelson, Francis[3] NELSON, Elisha[2] NELSON, Elisha[1] NELSON) was born on 22 Jun 1962 in Arlington, Va. He married Frances Elizabeth ALLEN, daughter of Bona ALLEN IV and Jane KING, on 15 Jun 1985 in Dunwoody, Ga.. She was born on 26 Feb 1963.

Notes for Peter Charles MORRIS:
Graduate, USMA 1984, BS Aeronautics

Notes for Frances Elizabeth ALLEN:
Graduate Birmingham Southern,BA,1985,childhood education: TroyStateUniv, Ala, MA, Education.1990

Peter Charles MORRIS and Frances Elizabeth ALLEN had the following children:

i.   KATELYN ELIZABETH[8] MORRIS was born on 21 Apr 1992 in Atlanta, Fulton Cty, Ga.

ii.   SARA CAROLINE MORRIS was born on 17 Feb 1995 in Marietta, Cobb Cty, Ga..

17.   BETTY ELLEN[7] KING (Betty Ellen Peebles.[6], Ethel Gertrude[5] Meroney, Ellender L[4] Nelson, Francis[3] NELSON, Elisha[2] NELSON, Elisha[1] NELSON) was born on 06 Oct 1945 in Childersburg, Talladega, Alabama, USA. She died on 01 Feb 2009 in Danville, Danville City, Virginia. She married (1) JR LUTHER HERSCHEL HAMRICK. She married (2) BILLY JOE HODNETT, son of George Houston Hodnett and Janie Gaylor, on 03 Feb 1968 in Anniston, Calhoun, Alabama. He was born on 15 Sep 1936 in Fairfax, Chambers, Alabama, USA. He died on 28 May 1977 in Birmingham, Jefferson, Alabama, USA. She married (3) JACK NILES WILKERSON.

Billy Joe Hodnett and Betty Ellen King had the following children:

i.   AIMEE WYNETTE[8] HODNETT was born on 02 Aug 1972 in Anniston, Calhoun, Alabama. She married Charles Eugene Buchfield, son of James Clinton Birchfield

7

and Alice Faye Smith, on 27 Mar 1993 in Oxford, Calhoun Cty Ala. He was born on 28 Sep 1972 in Ashland Clay Cty Ala.

ii. DAVID WAYNE HODNETT was born on 18 Nov 1968 in Anniston, Calhoun County, Alabama.

18. SARA ELIZABETH[7] PEBBLES (William Battle[6] Jr, Ethel Gertrude[5] Meroney, Ellender L[4] Nelson, Francis[3] NELSON, Elisha[2] NELSON, Elisha[1] NELSON) was born on 26 Jan 1967 in Tuscaloosa ALA. She married Richard Lowery Johnson, son of John Henry Johnson and Etta Oree Cullum, on 11 Jul 1987 in Aliceville, Pickens Co, AL. He was born on 22 Jan 1952 in Meridian Lauderdale, Mississippi, USA.

Richard Lowery Johnson and Sara Elizabeth Pebbles had the following children:

i. SARAH LAREN[8] JOHNSON was born on 10 Jan 1989 in Aliceville, Pickens Co, AL.

ii. RICHARD BATTLE JOHNSON was born on 06 Jun 1991 (Tuscalooa, Al). He died on 17 Jan 2006 in Aliceville, Pickens Co, AL.

   Notes for Richard Battle Johnson:
   Burial: Oak Grove -Franconia Cemetry, Aliceville. Ala

iii. CATHERINE ELISABETH JOHNSON was born on 18 May 1992 in Tuscaloosa ALA.

19. JULIE CELESTE[7] PEBBLES (William Battle[6] Jr, Ethel Gertrude[5] Meroney, Ellender L[4] Nelson, Francis[3] NELSON, Elisha[2] NELSON, Elisha[1] NELSON) was born on 18 Dec 1968 in Tuscaloosa ALA. She married Kenneth Grey Hankins, son of James Earl Hankins and Betty Irene Eads, on 12 Aug 1989 in Aliceville, Pickens Co, AL. He was born on 08 Jun 1962 in Alamorgordo, Otero, New Mexico, USA.

Notes for Julie Celeste Pebbles:
Education:Unv of Alabama and University of West Ala:Qccupation:Teacher,Elementary School,Aliceville,ALA.:Religion:United Methodist

Kenneth Grey Hankins and Julie Celeste Pebbles had the following children:

i. KENNETH GREY[8] HANKINS JR was born on 30 Jun 1992 in Tuscaloosa ALA.

ii. ELISABETH CELEST HANKINS was born on 10 Mar 1995 in Tuscaloosa ALA.

20. VIRGINIA ELOISE[7] PEBBLES (William Battle[6] Jr, Ethel Gertrude[5] Meroney, Ellender L[4] Nelson, Francis[3] NELSON, Elisha[2] NELSON, Elisha[1] NELSON) was born on 10 Nov 1970 in Tuscaloosa ALA. She married Michael Dwain Latham, son of Richard Gerald Latham and Shelby Bridges, on 13 Jun 1992 in Aliceville, Pickens Co, AL. He was born on 23 Jul 1962 in Tuscaloosa ALA.

Michael Dwain Latham and Virginia Eloise Pebbles had the following children:

i. ALLISON VIRGINIA[8] LATHAM was born on 05 Jan 2000 in Tuscaloosa ALA.

ii. JESSI MICHAELA LATHAM was born on 15 Nov 2001 in Tuscaloosa ALA.

Prepared By:
Preparer:	Address:
Phone:	
Email:	

8

Lyon / Shacklett Family Tree

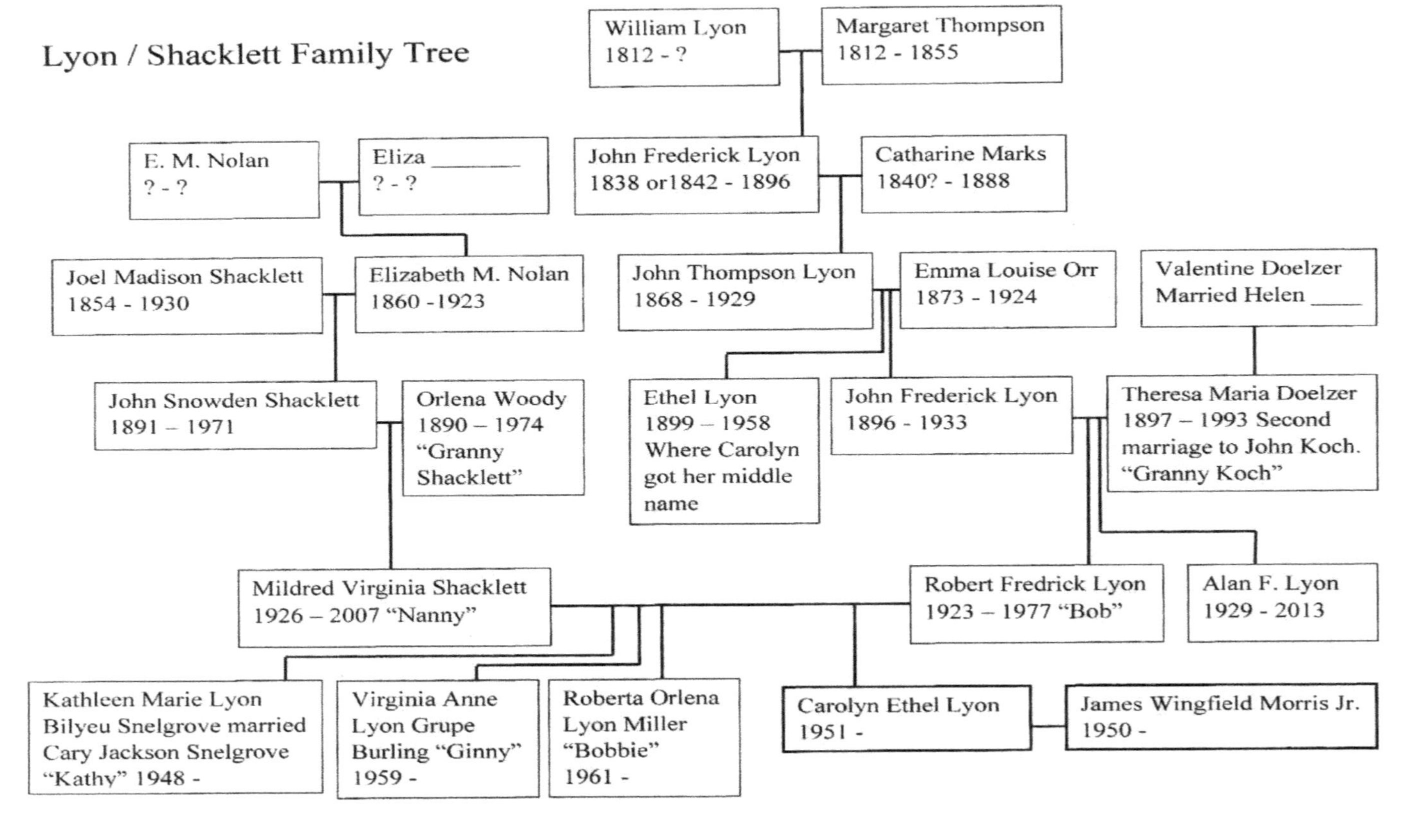

Descendants of William Lyon

Generation 1

1. WILLIAM[1] LYON was born in 1812 in New York, New York. He married MARGARETT LYON (THOMPSON). She was born about 1812 in New York. She died on 26 Jun 1855.

    William Lyon and Margarett Lyon (Thompson) had the following children:

    i.   EMILY FRANCIS[2] LYON was born in Nov 1835 in New York. She died on 11 Dec 1918 in Kings County, NY.

2.   ii.   JOHN F LYON was born between 1838-1842 in NY. He died on 02 Nov 1896 in Brooklyn, Kings, NY. He married Catharine MARKS about 1861. She was born about 1840 in Massachusetts. She died on 16 Mar 1888 in Brooklyn, Kings, NY.

    iii.   MARY LOUISA LYON was born about 1843 in New York.

    iv.   OSCAR W LYON was born in Aug 1847 in New York. He died on 06 Mar 1850 in Brooklyn, Kings, New York.

    v.   WILLIAM W LYON was born in Aug 1851 in New York.

Generation 2

2. JOHN F[2] LYON (William[1]) was born between 1838-1842 in NY. He died on 02 Nov 1896 in Brooklyn, Kings, NY. He married Catharine MARKS about 1861. She was born about 1840 in Massachusetts. She died on 16 Mar 1888 in Brooklyn, Kings, NY.

    John F LYON and Catharine MARKS had the following children:

    i.   WILLIAM WORTH[3] LYON was born in Sep 1862 in New York.

3.   ii.   JOHN THOMPSON LYON JR was born on 26 Dec 1868 in Brooklyn, Kings County (Brooklyn), New York, USA. He died on 23 May 1929 in Bronx, Bronx County, New York, USA. He married Emma Louisa ORR on 24 Jun 1894 in New York, New York, NY. She was born on 05 Sep 1873 in New York, New York, NY. She died on 12 Feb 1924 in Bronx, Bronx, NY.

Generation 3

3. JOHN THOMPSON[3] LYON JR (John F[2], William[1]) was born on 26 Dec 1868 in Brooklyn, Kings County (Brooklyn), New York, USA. He died on 23 May 1929 in Bronx, Bronx County, New York, USA. He married Emma Louisa ORR on 24 Jun 1894 in New York, New York, NY. She was born on 05 Sep 1873 in New York, New York, NY. She died on 12 Feb 1924 in Bronx, Bronx, NY.

    John Thompson Lyon Jr and Emma Louisa ORR had the following children:

4.   i.   JOHN FREDRICK[4] LYON was born on 03 Jan 1896 in Westchester, New York. He died on 03 Nov 1933 in Kings County (Brooklyn), New York, USA. He married Therese Maria Doelzer, daughter of Valentine Doelger and Helen Doelger, on 03 Sep 1921 in Manhattan County, NY. She was born on 11 Nov 1897 in Manhattan, New York, NY. She died on 24 Feb 1993 in Scarsdale, Westchester, New York, USA (Age at Death: 95).

    ii.   ETHEL LYON was born about 1899 in United States. She died on 28 Dec 1958 in NY.

    iii.   CHESTER W LYON was born about 1903 in United States. He died on 05 Sep 1971 in Elmhurst, Queens, NY.

Generation 4

4. JOHN FREDRICK[4] LYON (John Thompson[3] Jr, John F[2], William[1]) was born on 03 Jan 1896 in Westchester, New York. He died on 03 Nov 1933 in Kings County (Brooklyn), New York, USA. He married Therese Maria Doelzer, daughter of Valentine Doelger and Helen Doelger, on 03 Sep 1921 in Manhattan County, NY. She was born on 11 Nov 1897 in Manhattan, New York, NY. She died on 24 Feb 1993 in Scarsdale, Westchester, New York, USA (Age at Death: 95).

    John Fredrick Lyon and Therese Maria Doelzer had the following children:

5.   i.   ROBERT FREDRICK[5] LYON was born on 16 Dec 1923 in New York City, New York. He died on 23 Oct 1977 in Nashville, Davidson, Tennessee, USA. He married MIdred Virginia Shacklett, daughter of John Snowden Shacklett Sr and Orlena Shacklett,

/

on 10 Jan 1946 in Davidson, Tennessee, United States. She was born on 25 Apr 1926 in Nashville, Davidson Cty, Tn. She died on 07 Jan 2007 in Marietta, Cobb Cty, Ga. (Heart attack).

6.   ii.   ALAN F LYON was born on 21 Sep 1929 in Queens New York, New York. He died on 22 Sep 2013 in Scarsdale, Westchester, New York, USA (Our Lady of Fatima Church). He married Anne Rosemary CIRILLO, daughter of Giuseppi CIRILLO and Santa LAMAGNA, in 1956. She was born on 09 Sep 1931 in New York. She died on 17 Oct 2002 in Scarsdale, Westchester, New York, USA (Age at Death: 71).

Generation 5

5.   ROBERT FREDRICK[5] LYON (John Fredrick[4], John Thompson[3] Jr, John F[2], William[1]) was born on 16 Dec 1923 in New York City, New York. He died on 23 Oct 1977 in Nashville, Davidson, Tennessee, USA. He married Mldred Virginia Shacklett, daughter of John Snowden Shacklett Sr and Orlena Shacklett, on 10 Jan 1946 in Davidson, Tennessee, United States. She was born on 25 Apr 1926 in Nashville, Davidson Cty, Tn. She died on 07 Jan 2007 in Marietta, Cobb Cty, Ga. (Heart attack).

Robert Fredrick LYON and Mldred Virginia Shacklett had the following children:

    i.   CAROLYN ETHEL[6] LYON was born on 14 Mar 1951 in Nashville, Davidson Cty, Tn. She married James Wingfield MORRIS Jr, son of James Wingfield MORRIS and Mary Corinne WOFFORD, on 09 Jun 1973 in Marietta, Ga.. He was born on 29 Oct 1950 in Cartersville, Bartow, Georgia, USA.

       Notes for Carolyn Ethel LYON:
       Education: BS, Architectural Technology,Southern Technical Institute,1973
       Registered architect,22September 1988.

       Notes for James Wingfield MORRIS Jr:
       Education: BSArchitectural Technology,SouthernTechnical Institute
       1972/Registered Arctitect 1982,BA,Education Kennesaw State Univ, 1995

    ii.   PRIVATE.

6.   ALAN F[5] LYON (John Fredrick[4], John Thompson[3] Jr, John F[2], William[1]) was born on 21 Sep 1929 in Queens New York, New York. He died on 22 Sep 2013 in Scarsdale, Westchester, New York, USA (Our Lady of Fatima Church). He married Anne Rosemary CIRILLO, daughter of Giuseppi CIRILLO and Santa LAMAGNA, in 1956. She was born on 09 Sep 1931 in New York. She died on 17 Oct 2002 in Scarsdale, Westchester, New York, USA (Age at Death: 71).

Alan F Lyon and Anne Rosemary CIRILLO had the following children:

    i.   MARIANNE[6] LYON. She married JOSEPH HICKMAN.

    ii.   ELIZABETH LYON. She married MARK MILANI.

    iii.   PATRICIA LYON.

    iv.   MATTHEW LYON.

    v.   DOUGLAS LYON. He married CARMEN.

2

Geneological background – Robert Frederick and Alan Franklin Lyon

Patricia Lyon has become interested in geneology and has gathered new information in addition to what I already knew.

Our father John Frederick Lyon was born in the Bronx in the nineties.He went to public school there and went to St Anne's Episcopal Sunday School. I don't know if he went to high school. He served in the Coast Guard in WW1, and contracted rheumatic fever while on active duty, which led to rheumatic heart disease, which in turn made it impossible for him to overcome the pneumonia which killed him in 1933.

Our mother was born Therese Marie Doelzer in Manhattan in 1897 and died of multi-infarct dementia in 1993. She went to St. Josephs grammar school on 87th street in Manhattan. She told me that the nuns came to their apartment to try to convince her parents to let her go to high school but they refused and she was apprenticed to a dressmaker. Their marriage was shortly after the war. There are no pictures because it was an elopement; both families disapproved because of the religious difference. Their first son, Charles was born in 1921 but died a few hours later.

Therese moved with her two sons into her parents' apartment in Astoria until she remarried in 1944 and moved to Jackson Heights. Bob was already in service and never lived there.

We know less about the German side of the family. Therese' father was Valentine Doelzer. He migrated to the US about 1894 from a town called Alteburg in Bavaria. We know that his mother's maiden name was Becker and that his sister Katie also came to the US and lived her life till she died in about 1936 in Queens. She was married to Herman Zeh. I also knew a variety of cousins who also migrated to the New York area. Interestingly, my grandfather told me that his father was a younger brother whose older brother inherited the farm. Therefore Val's father migrated to the US and started a mill in Arkansas. Then his older brother died and he returned to Germany to take over the farm probably before the civil war started, so Val was born in Germany.

Our maternal grandmother's maiden name was Helene Schwindt. She was born I village called Weckbach a few miles from a lovely cathedral town on the Main River called Miltenberg-am-Main. She was four years older than Val and came to New York in 1885. Her parents went to Miltenberg and had a picture taken that she could bring with her. I still have it. She met a man from a different part fo Germany on the ship and later in New York they were married. His name was Michael Steuer. They had two sons and she was pregnant with a third when he died of pneumonia. A year or so later Val Doelzer married the widow with three sons. Together they had a daughter, Therese, a son, Otto, and another daughter, Lillian.

Helene's brother Willi, stayed in Bavaria and became the mayor of someplace. He had a son Eugen, who was killed in a bike accident when he was thirteen or fourteen and Helene was sent a picture of his tombstone, which Therese was very aware of and which resulted in neither Bob nor I ever being allowed to ride a bike.

As a result of papers that Aunt Ethel had and things that Pat has found out we know more about our paternal side. Pat and I recently went to my father's grave in Orange New Jersey, and found not only his grave but those of his parents and one set of his grandparents. His father was John Thompson Lyon Jr. who was born in Brooklyn in

1a

the 1860's.He married Emma Orr and they had three children , John Frederick. Ethel and Chester. Ethel married Tom Smith , had no children and are buried in the same plot in Orange New Jersey. Chester and his wife Frances, had two daughters. Virginia and Barbara, both of whom married and had children. Virginia died about three years ago. I have lost track of my cousin Barbara. John Thompson Lyon Sr is listed in the bible as having been born in 1842, but I don't know where. He married Kate Marx but I don't know if they had any other children other that John Thompson Lyon Jr. This is a dead end that Pat is trying to clarify. According to Aunt Ethel the Lyon family roots are in Connecticut; she claimed that Lyon House, a state historical site buit in 1640 is from our family, but I don't know if this is true.

Emma Orr Lyon, our paternal grandmother, was the daughter of John Orr and Mary Emma Rapp. John Orr, who was born and grew up on Orr's Island , Maine. off the shore near Bath and Bruswick. His ancestors came from Scotland to Boston in 1708 and bought Orr's Island in 1730, over generations they were shipbuilders and sea captains. John Orr was a sea captain who came to New York and married Mary Emma Rapp . She was from Orange New Jersey. They settled in New York and had three children including Emma before he died, I think at sea. I have an Orr family document obtained from my father's first cousin Lillian Orr Schneider, in which all the Orr births. deaths and marriages going back to Scotland in the 1690's are listed

Mary Emma Rapp was the daughter of Alexander Rapp and Charlotte Munn. both of whom were born and raised in Orange New Jersey. We don't know much about Alexander. but Pat has found out that his brother and his brothers two sons moved to Carbondale Illinois and that to Chicago and became a major architectural firm that designed 400 movie theaters including the New York Paramount. the La Fonda Hotel and the New Mexico State capital in Santa Fe.

Charlotte Munn left us the Munn Family Bible which Pat has now. The bible was printed in 1846 but many of the prior family births and deaths were entered by Charlotte.Incidentally one of the streets leading to the cemetery in Orange is Munn Street. Charlottes mother was a Harrison and her mother an Ogden. Pat has found that one of the Ogdens was a Revolutionary war general.

That brings you up to date. As we discover more. will let you know.

2a

Dear Kathy and Jack,

It's Monday afternoon and I took down Christmas this morning, so it's time to answer your E-mail questions.

As you must know your father served in the army air corps in WW2, and served as an engineer calculating the load distribution on cargo planes, in Homestead, Florida and Nashville. After his discharge he was assigned to the reserves. He followed the aircraft industry from Grumman on Long Island to Chance-Vought near Nashville, and then to Convair in Fort Worth. He was doing well there and involved in a classified design project. I got to see him two or three times in 1949 and early 1950 when he would fly into New York with classified plans for a subcontractor in New Jersey taped to his leg. When the Korean war started he was informed by the military that he was being called to active duty even though he was doing classified work for the Air Force at Convair. He expected to be assigned to a project using his skills as an aeronautical engineer. He was very surprised to be told that he was to be assigned to a military intelligence facility in Washington, DC. He was told that his testing had shown a very good language aptitude, and that he would be taught a central Asian language and spend his military duty translating and interpreting spy reports.

I visited you at your home in nearby Virginia during an Easter vacation from medical school. Every morning he drove into Washington to his workplace, which was an unmarked building in the city proper. I would leave him there, spend the day sightseeing and join him for the ride home. As closemouthed as he was I never expected him to tell anything more about it and he never did. He always went to work in uniform and had regular hours.

That is all I know and all that I spoke about at the wedding in that regard. As for your other genealogical questions, that will be the subject of another letter.

Love,
Uncle Alan

Undated letter from
Alan F. Lyon to Kathleen
Snelgrove (Carolyn Lyon
Morris's older sister)
And Kathleen's husband
Cary Jack Snelgrove

Forgive the typos. I haven't learned how to go back + fix them if I don't spot them right away

3a

Descendants of Joel Madison Shacklett

Generation 1

1. JOEL MADISON[1] SHACKLETT was born on 08 Apr 1854 in Davidson County, Tennessee, USA. He died on 28 Dec 1930 in Nashville, Davidson, Tennessee (Age: 76). He married (1) ELIZABETH M NOLEN, daughter of E M Nolan and Eliza Nolan, in 1879. She was born on 16 Sep 1860 in Tennessee. She died on 05 Jun 1923 in Nashville, Davidson, Tennessee (Age: 62).

Joel Madison Shacklett had the following child:

     i.   CLAUDE K[2] SHACKLETT was born about 1898 in Tennessee.

Joel Madison Shacklett and Elizabeth M Nolen had the following children:

     ii.   LEONA SHACKLETT was born in Dec 1879 in Davidson County, Tennessee, USA. She died on 13 Nov 1961 in Nashville, Davidson County, Tennessee, USA.

     iii.   CLARENCE SHACKLETT was born on 16 Jan 1885 in Davidson County, Tennessee, USA. He died on 03 Feb 1927 in Nashville, Davidson County, Tennessee, USA.

     iv.   WILLIAM EDWARD SHACKLETT was born on 20 Dec 1886 in Davidson County, Tennessee, USA. He died on 08 Sep 1953 in Detroit, Wayne County, Michigan, USA.

     v.   CLEO SHACKLETT was born in Mar 1889 in Tennessee.

2.   vi.   JOHN SNOWDEN SHACKLETT SR was born on 07 Dec 1891 in Davidson, Tennessee, USA. He died on 21 Aug 1971 in Nashville, Davidson, Tennessee. He married ORLENA SHACKLETT. She was born on 24 Jun 1890 in Tennessee, USA. She died on 04 Oct 1974 (Age at Death: 84).

     vii.   JOEL A SHACKLETT was born on 29 Feb 1896 in Davidson County, Tennessee, USA. He died on 03 Feb 1961 in Nashville, Davidson County, Tennessee, USA.

     viii.   CLAUDE SHACKLETT was born in Mar 1898 in Tennessee.

Generation 2

2. JOHN SNOWDEN[2] SHACKLETT SR (Joel Madison[1]) was born on 07 Dec 1891 in Davidson, Tennessee, USA. He died on 21 Aug 1971 in Nashville, Davidson, Tennessee. He married ORLENA SHACKLETT. She was born on 24 Jun 1890 in Tennessee, USA. She died on 04 Oct 1974 (Age at Death: 84).

John Snowden Shacklett Sr and Orlena Shacklett had the following children:

     i.   BETTY LOUISE[3] SHACKLETT was born about 1911 in Tennessee.

     ii.   MAMMIE O SHACKLETT was born about 1914 in Tennessee.

     iii.   CHRISTINE SHACKLETT was born about 1916 in Tennessee.

     iv.   EARL C SHACKLETT was born about 1920 in Tennessee.

3.   v.   MLDRED VIRGINIA SHACKLETT was born on 25 Apr 1926 in Nashville, Davidson Cty, Tn. She died on 07 Jan 2007 in Marietta, Cobb Cty, Ga. (Heart attack). She married Robert Fredrick LYON, son of John Fredrick Lyon and Therese Maria Doelzer, on 10 Jan 1946 in Davidson, Tennessee, United States. He was born on 16 Dec 1923 in New York City, New York. He died on 23 Oct 1977 in Nashville, Davidson, Tennessee, USA.

Generation 3

3. MLDRED VIRGINIA[3] SHACKLETT (John Snowden[2] Sr, Joel Madison[1]) was born on 25 Apr 1926 in Nashville, Davidson Cty, Tn. She died on 07 Jan 2007 in Marietta, Cobb Cty, Ga. (Heart attack). She married Robert Fredrick LYON, son of John Fredrick Lyon and Therese Maria Doelzer, on 10 Jan 1946 in Davidson, Tennessee, United States. He was born on 16 Dec 1923 in New York City, New York. He died on 23 Oct 1977 in Nashville, Davidson, Tennessee, USA.

Robert Fredrick LYON and Mldred Virginia Shacklett had the following children:

4.   i.   CAROLYN ETHEL[4] LYON was born on 14 Mar 1951 in Nashville, Davidson Cty, Tn. She married James Wingfield MORRIS Jr, son of James Wingfield MORRIS and Mary Corinne WOFFORD, on 09 Jun 1973 in Marietta, Ga.. He was born on 29 Oct

1950 in Cartersville, Bartow, Georgia, USA.

    ii.   PRIVATE.

Generation 4

4.   CAROLYN ETHEL[4] LYON (MIdred Virginia[3] Shacklett, John Snowden[2] Shacklett Sr, Joel Madison[1] Shacklett) was born on 14 Mar 1951 in Nashville, Davidson Cty, Tn. She married James Wingfield MORRIS Jr, son of James Wingfield MORRIS and Mary Corinne WOFFORD, on 09 Jun 1973 in Marietta, Ga.. He was born on 29 Oct 1950 in Cartersville, Bartow, Georgia, USA.

Notes for Carolyn Ethel LYON:
Education: BS, Architectural Technology,Southern Technical Institute,1973 Registered architect,22September 1988.

Notes for James Wingfield MORRIS Jr:
Education: BSArchitectural Technology,SouthernTechnical Institute 1972/Registered Arctitect 1982,BA,Education Kennesaw State Univ, 1995

James Wingfield MORRIS Jr and Carolyn Ethel LYON had the following children:

5.   i.   MARY VIRGINIA[5] MORRIS was born on 18 Mar 1974 in Marietta, Cobb Cty, Ga.. She married Timothy Adam BLACKWELL, son of Toby Long BLACKWELL and Sherrill McGARITY, on 16 Dec 1995 in Marietta, Ga.. He was born on 20 Feb 1973 in Atlanta, Fulton Cty, Ga.

6.   ii.   JAMES LYON MORRIS was born on 11 Jan 1983 in Marietta, Cobb Cty, Ga. He married Angela Swope, daughter of James Leonard Swope and Mana Sue Campbell, on 27 May 2007 in Atlanta, Fulton Cty, Ga.Atlanta City Hall. She was born on 07 Mar 1984 in Friendship, Harris, Texas.

Generation 5

5.   MARY VIRGINIA[5] MORRIS (Carolyn Ethel[4] LYON, MIdred Virginia[3] Shacklett, John Snowden[2] Shacklett Sr, Joel Madison[1] Shacklett) was born on 18 Mar 1974 in Marietta, Cobb Cty, Ga.. She married Timothy Adam BLACKWELL, son of Toby Long BLACKWELL and Sherrill McGARITY, on 16 Dec 1995 in Marietta, Ga.. He was born on 20 Feb 1973 in Atlanta, Fulton Cty, Ga.

Notes for Mary Virginia MORRIS:
Education: BS,Middle Grades Education, Georgia Southern Univ.1995: MS, Education,GSU,1997.

Timothy Adam BLACKWELL and Mary Virginia MORRIS had the following children:

    i.   BRYCE HARPER[6] BLACKWELL was born on 07 Feb 2001 in Gainesville, Ga..

    ii.   BODIE LANG BLACKWELL was born on 14 Feb 2003 in Gainesville, Ga..

6.   JAMES LYON[5] MORRIS (Carolyn Ethel[4] LYON, MIdred Virginia[3] Shacklett, John Snowden[2] Shacklett Sr, Joel Madison[1] Shacklett) was born on 11 Jan 1983 in Marietta, Cobb Cty, Ga. He married Angela Swope, daughter of James Leonard Swope and Mana Sue Campbell, on 27 May 2007 in Atlanta, Fulton Cty, Ga.Atlanta City Hall. She was born on 07 Mar 1984 in Friendship, Harris, Texas.

Notes for James Lyon MORRIS:
Education:BS, Middle Grades Education, Georgia Southern Univ, 2005

James Lyon MORRIS and Angela Swope had the following child:

    i.   CATLIN ROSE[6] MORRIS was born on 01 Jan 2010 in Atlanta, Fulton Cty Ga.

2

Photographs

Carolyn Ethel Lyon Morris Circa 1985

James Wingfield Morris Jr
Circa 1985

Carolyn Ethel Lyon Morris
and James W. Morris Jr
Circa 1997

James Wingfield Morris Jr
Circa: 2012

James W. Morris Jr and Carolyn Ethel Lyon Morris Circa 2020

Carolyn Ethel Lyon Morris and James Wingfield Morris Jr Wedding June 9, 1973

Dad and Mom, Colonel James Wingfield Morris (1924-2020) and Mary Corinne Wofford Morris (1926-2013) C: 2010

Carolyn Ethel Lyon Morris and James W.
Morris Jr wedding with Robert Fredrick Lyon
and Mildred Virginia Shacklett Lyon
June 1973

Dad and Mom … Col. James Wingfield
Morris and Mary Corinne Wofford Morris
Circa 1989

Angela Dawn Swope Morris and
James Lyon Morris C:2007

Mary Virginia "Jenna" Morris
Blackwell and Timothy Adam
Blackwell circa 1985

Carolyn and Jim Wedding 1973 From left: John Koch, Therese Maria Doelzer Lyon Koch, Orlena Woody Shacklett, Carolyn Ethel Lyon Morris, James W. Morris Jr, Marie Louise Williams Morris

Carolyn Ethel Lyon Morris and son, James Lyon Morris C:2007

Jenna/Adam Wedding Dec. 1995 from left: James W. Morris Jr, Carolyn Ethel Lyon Morris, Mary Virginia "Jenna" Morris Blackwell, Timothy Adam Blackwell, James Lyon Morris

From left: James Wingfield Morris, Jr.
Col. James Wingfield Morris Caitlin Rose Morris
Circa 2019

Great Grandmother Marie
Louise Williams Morris and
Mary Virginia "Jenna" Morris
Blackwell C: 1978

September 16, 1964 – Morris family clockwise from lower left: Col James Wingfield Morris with Peter Charles Morris in lap, Mary Louise Morris Bramble, James Wingfield Morris Jr, William Cranston Morris, Mary Corinne Wofford Morris (Mom) with Brian Meroney Morris in lap

October 2, 1954 A Family Gathering - Clockwise from front: Mary Louise Morris Bramble, James W. Morris Jr, James W. Morris, Mary Corinne Wofford Morris, Marian Louise Morris Rogers (Aunt Toochie), Nelson Kimball Rogers (Unca' Nelson), Dr. William Earl Wofford (Pa), Marie Louise Williams (Momma)

Carolyn Ethel Lyon Morris brings James Lyon Morris to meet
Great Grandmother Marie Louise Williams Morris
C: 1983

Marion Wingfield Morris making whipped cream and James
Wingfield Morris Jr recreates that moment 80 years later
C: 1943/2023

Col. James W. Morris and Mary W. Morris 50th Anniversary
Gathering – January 31, 1998

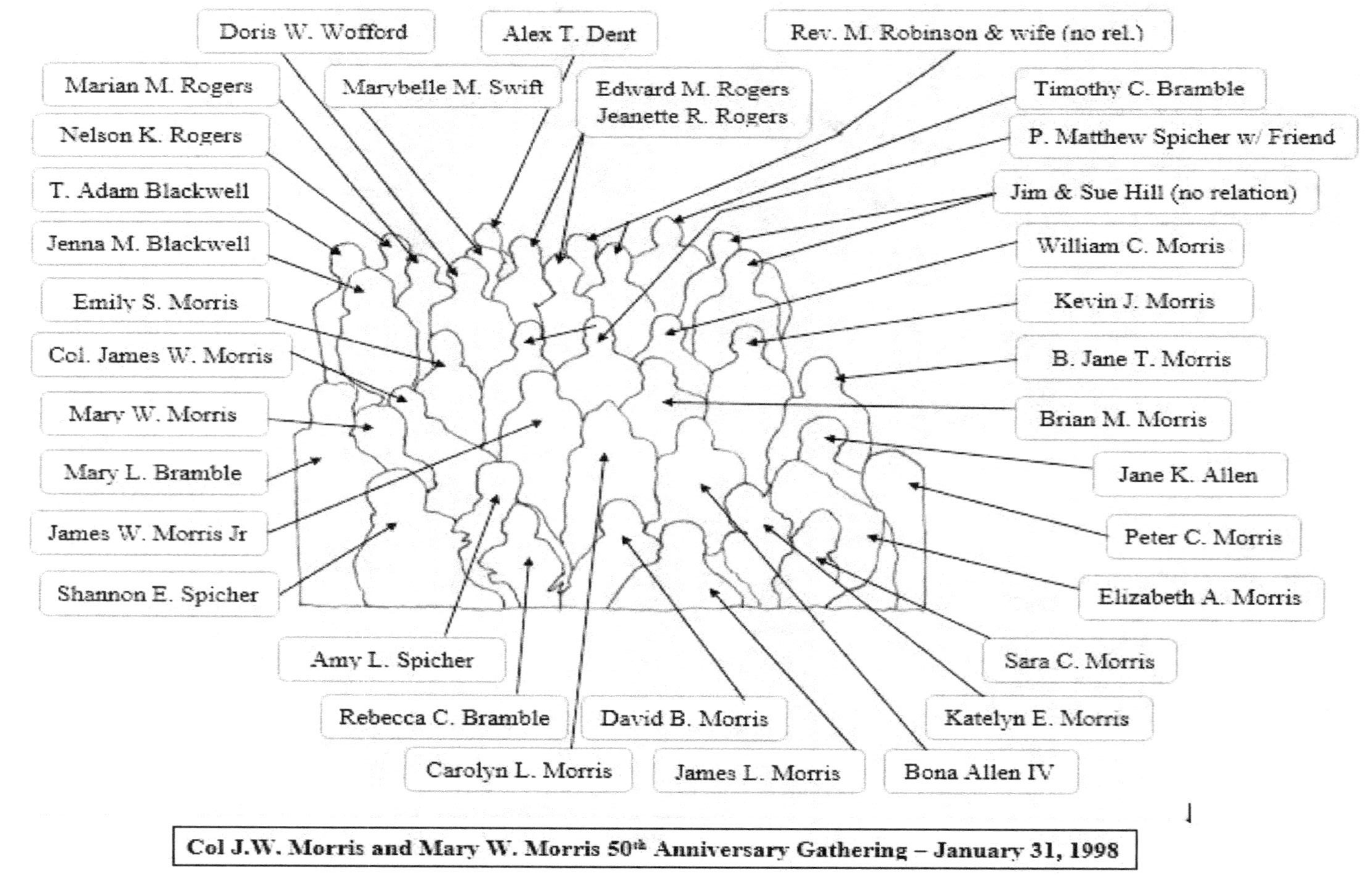

Col J.W. Morris and Mary W. Morris 50th Anniversary Gathering – January 31, 1998

September 1, 2014, Col. James Wingfield Morris – 90th birthday family gathering

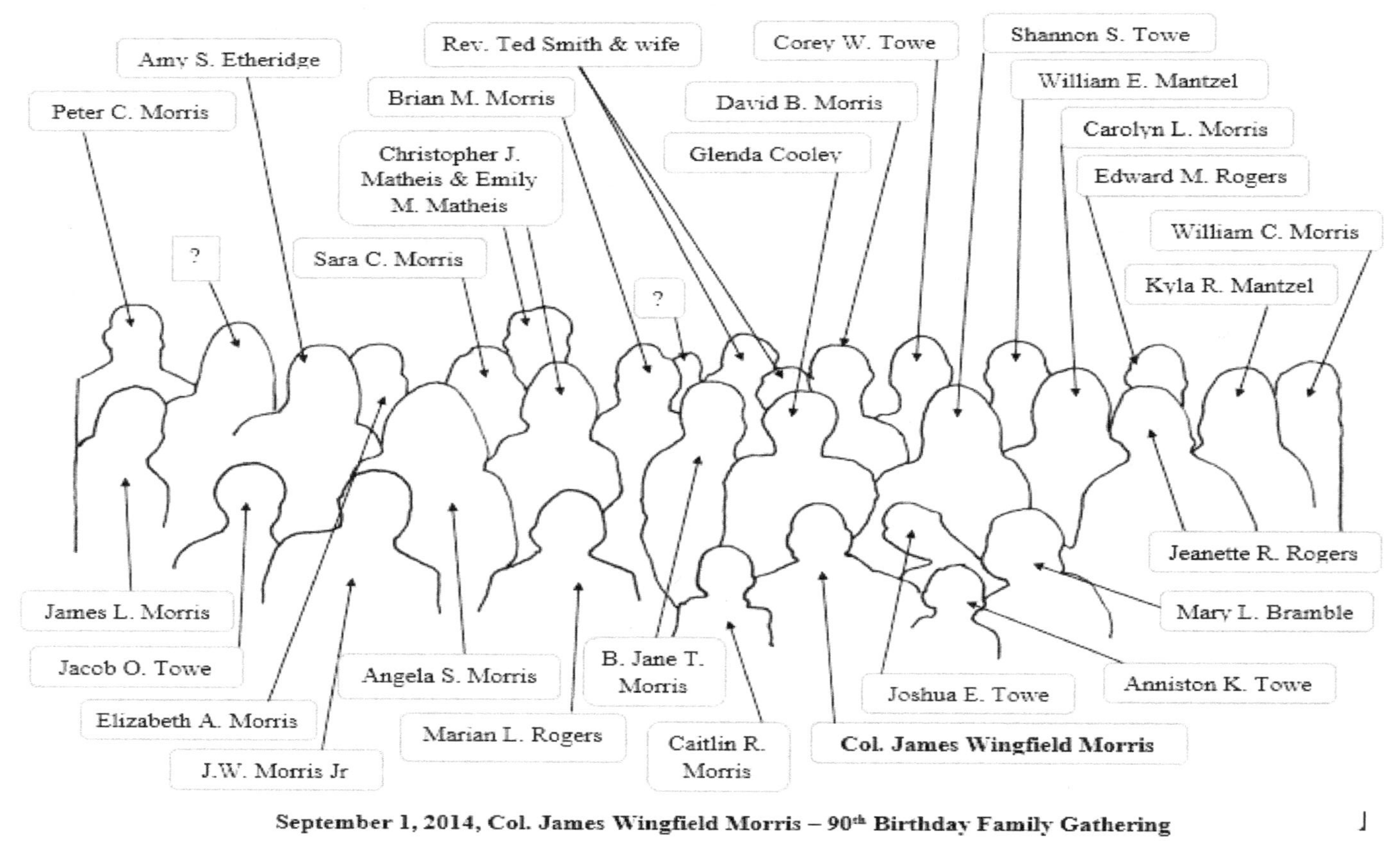

September 1, 2014, Col. James Wingfield Morris – 90th Birthday Family Gathering

488

Newly wed hands on the Panama City Florida tower – Carolyn and Jim Morris C: June, 1973

1954 from left: James W. Morris Jr., Unca'Pete -- Marion Wingfield Morris, (behind) Momma - Marie Louise Williams Morris, (front) Mary Lou Swift Beckman, Mary Louise Morris Bramble

Wedding from left: James W Morris Jr, Carolyn Ethel Lyon Morris, James Lyon Morris, Angela Dawn Swope Morris, Mana Sue Campbell Swope, and James Leonard Swope C:2007

Angela Dawn Swope Morris and James Lyon Morris w/ Col. James W. Morris in background and Sara Caroline Morris to right C:2007

Caitlin Rose Morris at Pa's handprints on the Square in Marietta C:2023

The Big Three 2023 from left: Bryce Harper Blackwell, Caitlin Rose Morris, Bodie Lang Blackwell

Caitlin Rose Morris in costume with Nana, Carolyn Ethel
Lyon Morris, and Pa, James Wingfield Morris Jr. C: 2023

Carolyn Ethel Lyon Morris and
James W Morris Jr in Europe C:2023

Capt. Cornelius
Redding Hanleiter
1815-1897

Quiter Montgomery Faucett Morris
"Que" 1860-1910

Mary Maria Gullatt
Williams (Granny)
1872-1959

James Cranston Williams
1868-1936

Earliest Picture of Marie Louise Williams Morris
(Momma) with family: From left – Marie Louise
Williams Morris, Cranston Gullatt Williams,
Josephine Hanleiter Williams, Huldah Gullatt
Williams, Cary Jones Williams (front) C:1914

Mary Maria Gullatt Williams and
Mary Louise Morris Spicher
Bramble C:1950

Marie Louise Williams
Morris C: 1939

Jan. 1923 Marion Wingfield Morris "Unca' Pete" 26 y/o and Marie Louise Williams Morris "Momma" 24 y/o on their honeymoon

Seated from left: Marian Louise Morris Rogers, Marie Louise Williams Morris, Marybelle Morris Swift, standing Col. James W. Morris C:1978

1940 High School graduation James Wingfield Morris – to left, Marie Louise Williams Morris (Momma) – to right, Mary Maria Gullatt Williams (Grannie)

April 1, 1941 James Wingfield Morris 17 y/o and father Marion Wingfield Morris (Unca' Pete) 51 y/o

494

From left: Marie Louise Williams Morris (Momma), James W. Morris (Dad), Marian Louise Morris Rogers (Toochie), kneeling Marybelle Morris Swift
Circa 1944

From left: James W. Morris, Jr., Unca' Pete – Marion Wingfield Morris, Mary Lou Swift Beckman, Mary Louise Morris Bramble, Momma (behind) –Marie Louise Williams Morris C: 1954

Marybelle Morris Swift Dent and Donald Charles Swift C: 1985

Marybelle Morris Swift & Donald Charles Swift "Aunt Marybelle and Unca' Donnie" circa 1945

Nelson K. Rogers & Marian L. Morris
Rogers (Toochie) circa 2010

Marian Louise Morris Rogers
(Toochie) 1930-2018

Nelson K. Rogers
1928-2013

"The Fab Five" from left: Peter Charles Morris, William Cranston Morris, Mary Louise Morris Spicher Bramble, James Wingfield Morris Jr, Brian Meroney Morris C: 2007

Charles L. Meroney & Ellender L. Nelson Meroney
1869-1930   Circa 1900   1866-1941

Charles L. Meroney
1869-1930

Greenberry (G.B.) Wofford
1804 - 1864

Priscilla (Precious) West
Wofford (wife of G.B.
Wofford) 1809 ± - 1891

Greenberry Wofford
1804 - 1864

Earliest picture of William
Earl Wofford (±21y.o.)
C:1910

Dr. W. E. Wofford (lower left)
with 3 others circa 1914

1915 Mary Louise Meroney Wofford "Mom"
24 y/o

Dr. William Earl Wofford (Pa)
Circa 1940   1889-1959

499

Mary Louise Meroney Wofford
1891-1949

1941 Dr. William Earl Wofford 52 y/o and wife Mrs. Mary
Louise Meroney Wofford 50 y/o

Dr. William Earl Wofford and
Mary Corinne Wofford Morris
at Vanderbilt Graduation
C: 1948

Mary Corinne Wofford Morris
(L) and mother Mary Louise
Meroney Wofford C:1942

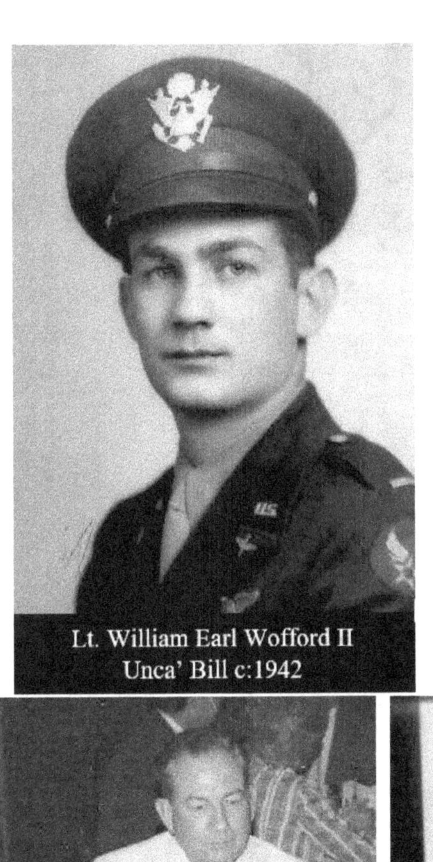

Lt. William Earl Wofford II
Unca' Bill c:1942

Lt. William Earl Wofford II
Unca' Bill in B-17 Flight Gear
c:1942

"Unca' Bill"
William Earl Wofford II C: 1973

Doris Virginia Whitfield Wofford
(Aunt Dar) C:1975

Mary Louise Meroney
Wofford and Mary Louise
Morris Spicher Bramble
C: 1949

John Snowden Shacklett (back 2nd fm left) and
Father Joel Madison Shacklett (center front)
and brothers   C: 2011

Theresa Maria Doelzer
Lyon Koch C: 1912

Theresa Maria Doelzer Lyon Koch (white arrow) Lillian Doelzer (red Arrow) John Fredrick Lyon (Robert Lyon's biological father – earliest picture) driving C: 1915

Theresa Maria Doelzer Lyon Koch and friend C: 1915

Robert Fredrick Lyon and father John Fredrick C: 1927

John Fredrick Lyon (Robert Lyon's biological father) Theresa Maria Doelzer Lyon Koch C: 1920

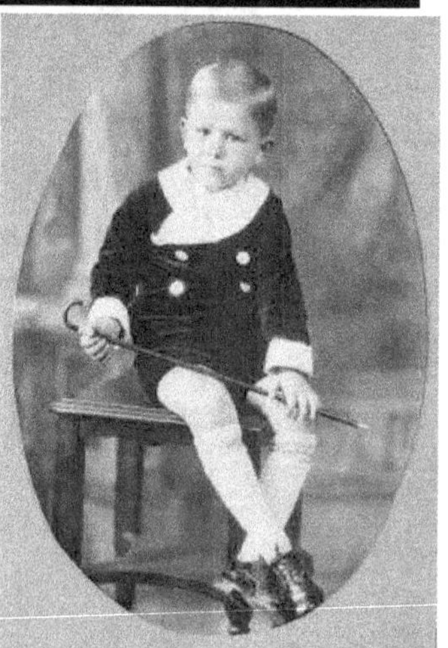

Robert Fredrick Lyon C: 1927

Theresa Maria Doelzer Lyon Koch Robert Fredrick Lyon Alan F Lyon (front) C: 1933

Robert Fredrick Lyon and Alan F Lyon C: 1935

Tom Smith, Ethel Lyon Smith (Aunt Ethel is where Carolyn Ethel Lyon Morris got her middle name), Robert Fredrick Lyon C: 1943

Theresa Maria Doelzer Lyon Koch Alan F Lyon (left) Robert Fredrick Lyon C: 1942

Mildred Virginia Shacklett Lyon   C:1945

Orlena Woody Shacklett – Granny Shacklett (L) and John Snowden Shacklett C: 1925

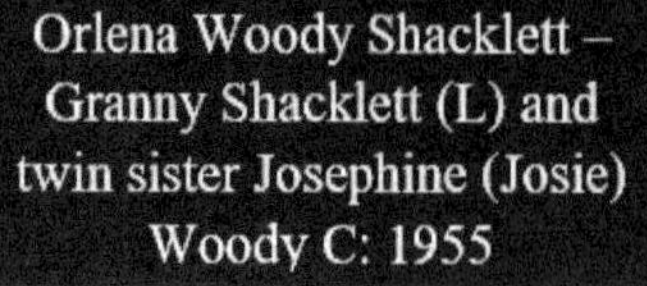

Orlena Woody Shacklett – Granny Shacklett (L) and twin sister Josephine (Josie) Woody C: 1955

Orlena Woody Shacklett – Granny Shacklett (L) and John Snowden Shacklett C: 1950

Mildred Virginia Shacklett
Robert Fredrick Lyon C: 1946

From left: Carolyn Ethel Lyon Morris, Virginia Anne Lyon Grupe Burling, Kathleen Marie Lyon Bilyeu Snelgrove, Roberta Orlena Lyon Miller C: 1966

From left: Robert Fredrick Lyon, Kathleen Marie Lyon Bilyeu Snelgrove, Mildred Virginia Shacklett, Carolyn Ethel Lyon Morris C: 1957

From left: Virginia Anne Lyon Grupe Burling, Robert Orlena Lyon Miller, Carolyn Ethel Lyon Morris, Mildred Virginia Shacklett Lyon, Kathleen Marie Lyon Bilyeu Snelgrove C: 2011

From left: Virginia (Ginny) Anne Lyon Grupe Burling, Carolyn Ethel Lyon Morris, Roberta (Bobbi) Orlena Lyon Miller, Kathleen (Kathy) Marie Lyon Bilyeu Snelgrove C:2023